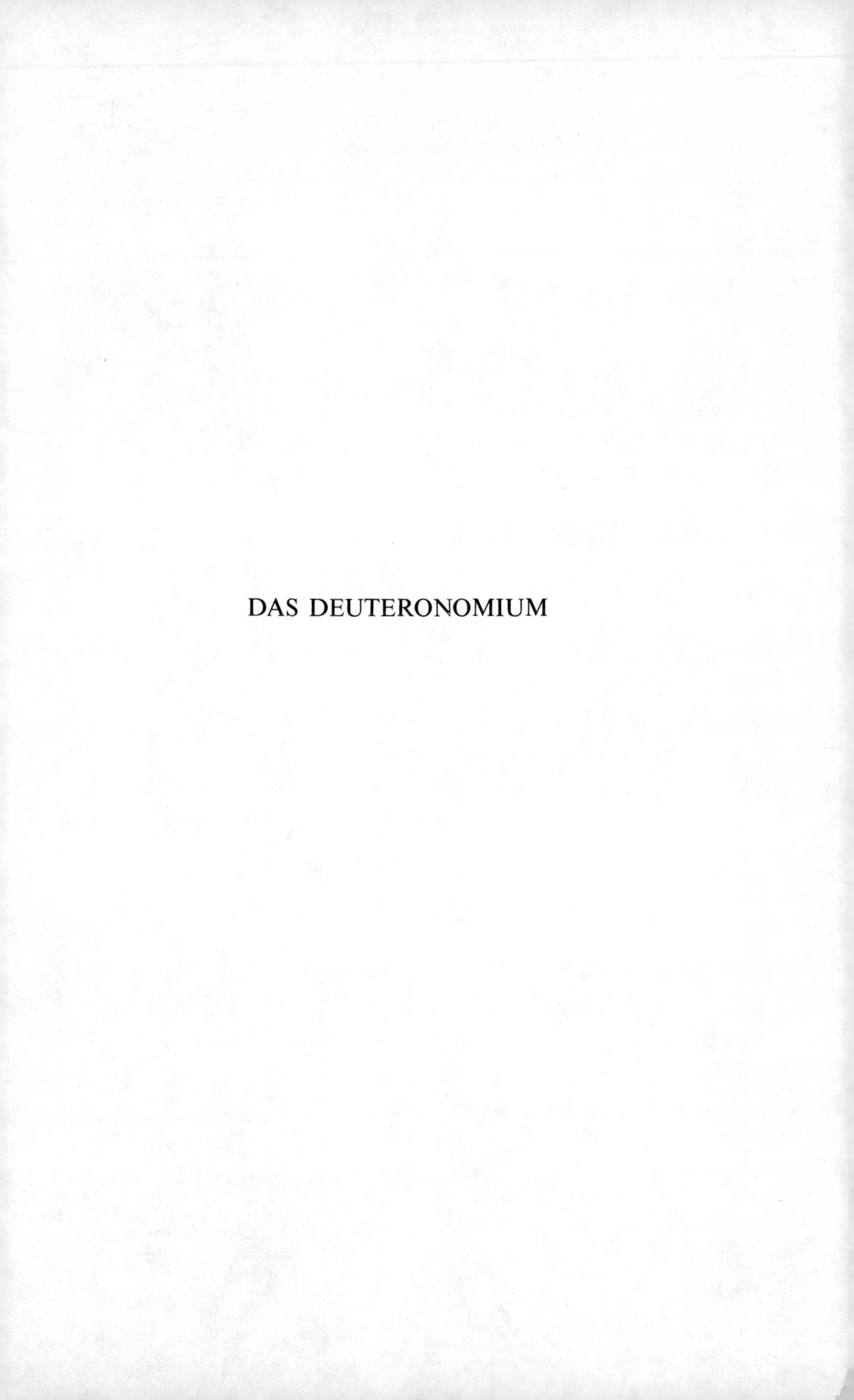

DAS DEUTERONOMIUM

BIBLIOTHECA EPHEMERIDUM THEOLOGICARUM
LOVANIENSIUM

LXVIII

DAS DEUTERONOMIUM

ENTSTEHUNG, GESTALT UND BOTSCHAFT

HERAUSGEGEBEN VON

DEUTERONOMY
ORIGIN, FORM AND MESSAGE
EDITED BY

NORBERT LOHFINK

S. AMSLER — M. ANBAR — C.T. BEGG — P.-M. BOGAERT — G. BRAULIK
C. BREKELMANS — H. CAZELLES — D.L. CHRISTENSEN — H.-J. FABRY
F. GARCÍA LÓPEZ — J. HALBE — W.L. HOLLADAY — L.J. HOPPE
S.A. KAUFMAN — L. LABERGE — C.J. LABUSCHAGNE — C. LOCHER
J. LUST — J. LUYTEN — A.D.H. MAYES — M.J. PAUL — L. PERLITT
A. ROFÉ — J. VAN GOUDOEVER — G. VANONI — J. VERMEYLEN — M. WEINFELD

LEUVEN
UNIVERSITY PRESS

UITGEVERIJ PEETERS
LEUVEN

1985

C.I.P. KONINKLIJKE BIBLIOTHEEK ALBERT I

Deuteronomium

Deuteronomium: Entstehung, Gestalt und Botschaft: origin, form and message / herausgegeben von Norbert Lohfink; edited by Norbert Lohfink. – Leuven: Leuven University Press: Peeters, 1985. – 400 p.; 24 cm. – (Bibliotheca Ephemeridum Theologicarum Lovaniensium; 68).

ISBN 90-6186-171-3.
SISO 226.4 UDC 222.1
Onderwerpen: Bijbel. O.T. Deuteronomium – Congressen

D/1984/1869/17

Universitaire Pers Leuven
Krakenstraat 3, B-3000 Leuven-Louvain (Belgium)

Uitgeverij Peeters, Bondgenotenlaan 153, B-3000 Leuven (Belgium)

VORWORT

Das 33. *Colloquium Biblicum Lovaniense* fand vom 17.-19. August 1983 statt. Sein Thema war das Buch Deuteronomium und die damit zusammenhängenden Fragen. Es kamen etwa 140 Kolleginnen und Kollegen zusammen. Unter ihnen waren viele, die über das Deuteronomium gearbeitet hatten oder darüber zur Zeit arbeiten. Vor allem waren auch mehrere Verfasser von Deuteronomiumskommentaren anwesend.

Dieser Band enthält alle Hauptreferate, dann die aus den Seminaren erwachsenen Beiträge der Seminarleiter, einen Teil der zahlreichen Kurzreferate und einen von J. Lust dem Kongreß aus Anlaß des 50. Todestages von A. Van Hoonacker schriftlich vorgelegten Aufsatz. Es ist leider nicht möglich, die beiden abendlichen Diskussionen zu dokumentieren, in denen noch einmal über alle Hauptveranstaltungen des jeweiligen Tages gemeinsam gesprochen wurde.

Die in diesen Band aufgenommenen Beiträge sind zum Teil die ursprünglichen Vortragsmanuskripte, zum Teil aufgrund der Diskussionen und privater Gespräche erweiterte und überarbeitete Fassungen. Die Entscheidung lag bei den Verfassern. Ich danke allen für die bereitwillige, gründliche und schnelle Mitarbeit. Ich habe mich bei der Redaktionsarbeit möglichst zurückgehalten und selbst Unterschiede in der Verweistechnik in Kauf genommen. Auch Aussagen, die sich mit Aussagen anderer Beiträge vielleicht nicht ohne weiteres zusammenreimen, habe ich stehen lassen. Der Leser kann sich dann selbst sein Urteil bilden.

Das *Colloquium* war eine angenehme und fruchtbare Begegnung vieler Kollegen und Interessenten. Die Löwener Gastgeber haben ihr Bestes dazu beigetragen. Man kann sich bei ihnen und bei der *Leuven University Press* und *Uitgeverij Peeters* nur immer wieder für diese regelmäßig wiederkehrende Möglichkeit wissenschaftlich-menschlicher Begegnungen und gelehrter Publikation bedanken. Auch das *Nationaal Fonds voor Wetenschappelijk Onderzoek*, ohne dessen Unterstützung dies alles nicht möglich wäre, verdient unseren Dank. Mein ganz besonderen Dank gilt C. Brekelmans, der mir immer wieder zur Seite stand.

Rom, 24. November 1983 NORBERT LOHFINK

INHALTSVERZEICHNIS

N. Lohfink (Frankfurt am Main), *Einführung* 1-5

ERSTER TEIL

FORSCHUNGSGESCHICHTE

M.J. Paul (Leiden), *Hilkiah and the Law (2 Kings 22) in the 17th and 18th Centuries: Some Influences on W.M.L. de Wette* 9-12

J. Lust (Leuven), *A. Van Hoonacker and Deuteronomy* . . 13-23

N. Lohfink (Frankfurt am Main), *Zur neueren Diskussion über 2 Kön 22-23* 24-48

ZWEITER TEIL

DAS DEUTERONOMISCHE PHÄNOMEN UND DAS BUCH ALS GANZES

S. Amsler (Lausanne), *Loi orale et loi écrite dans le Deutéronome* 51-54

J. Halbe (Preetz), *«Gemeinschaft, die Welt unterbricht»: Grundfragen und -inhalte deuteronomischer Theologie und Überlieferungsbildung im Lichte der Ursprungsbedingungen alttestamentlichen Rechts* 55-75

M. Weinfeld (Jerusalem), *The Emergence of the Deuteronomic Movement: The Historical Antecedents* 76-98

H. Cazelles (Paris), *Droit public dans le Deutéronome* . . . 99-106

L.J. Hoppe (Chicago), *Jerusalem in the Deuteronomistic History* 107-110

C.J. Labuschagne (Groningen), *Divine Speech in Deuteronomy* 111-126

DRITTER TEIL

TEXTE UND EINZELPROBLEME IM DEUTERONOMIUM

L. Laberge (Ottawa), *La Septante de Dt 1-11: Pour une étude du «texte»* 129-134

D. L. CHRISTENSEN (Berkeley), *Form and Structure in Deuteronomy 1-11* 135-144

J. VAN GOUDOEVER (Amsterdam), *The Liturgical Significance of the Date in Dt 1,3* 145-148

L. PERLITT (Göttingen), *Deuteronomium 1-3 im Streit der exegetischen Methoden* 149-163

C. BREKELMANS (Leuven), *Deuteronomy 5: Its Place and Function* 164-173

J. VERMEYLEN (Bruxelles), *Les sections narratives de Deut 5-11 et leur relation à Ex 19-34* 174-207

C. T. BEGG (Washington D.C.), *The Destruction of the Calf (Exod 32,20/Deut 9,21)* 208-251

G. BRAULIK (Wien), *Die Abfolge der Gesetze in Deuteronomium 12-26 und der Dekalog* 252-272

S. A. KAUFMAN (Cincinnati), *Deuteronomy 15 and Recent Research on the Dating of P* 273-276

F. GARCÍA LÓPEZ (Salamanca), *Le roi d'Israël: Dt 17,14-20* . 277-297

C. LOCHER (Zürich), *Deuteronomium 22,13-21: Vom Prozeßprotokoll zum kasuistischen Gesetz* 298-303

M. ANBAR (Tel-Aviv), *The Story about the Building of an Altar on Mount Ebal: The History of Its Composition and the Question of the Centralization of the Cult* 304-309

A. ROFÉ (Jerusalem), *The Covenant in the Land of Moab (Dt 28,69-30,20): Historico-literary, Comparative, and Formcritical Considerations* 310-320

A. D. H. MAYES (Dublin), *Deuteronomy 29, Joshua 9, and the Place of the Gibeonites in Israel* 321-325

W. L. HOLLADAY (Newton Centre), *A Proposal for Reflections in the Book of Jeremiah of the Seven-Year Recitation of the Law in Deuteronomy (Deut 31,10-13)* 326-328

P.-M. BOGAERT (Louvain-la-Neuve), *Les trois rédactions conservées et la forme originale de l'envoi du Cantique de Moïse (Dt 32,43)* 329-340

J. LUYTEN (Leuven), *Primeval and Eschatological Overtones in the Song of Moses (Dt 32,1-43)* 341-347

VIERTER TEIL
DEUTERONOMISTISCHES GESCHICHTSWERK

H.-J. FABRY (Bonn), *Spuren des Pentateuchredaktors in Jos 4,21ff.: Anmerkungen zur Deuteronomismus-Rezeption* . 351-356

G. VANONI (Wien-Mödling), *Beobachtungen zur deuteronomistischen Terminologie in 2 Kön 23,25-25,30* 357-362

Appendix: A. Van Hoonacker Bibliography 363-368

Verzeichnis der Autoren 369-375

Verzeichnis der Bibelstellen 376-382

EINFÜHRUNG

Als es im vorigen Jahrhundert um die Datierung der Pentateuchquellen ging, war das feste Datum des Deuteronomiums der Hebelpunkt. Doch kann man nicht behaupten, daß damals über das Deuteronomium mehr als über andere Bücher des Alten Testaments nachgedacht worden wäre. Bei Gerhard von Rad und den Alttestamentlern, die man um ihn herum gruppieren muß, war das deuteronomische Phänomen die geheime Mitte der alttestamentlichen Traditionsgeschichte und Theologie. Umso erstaunlicher ist es, wie viele etwa noch im „Kampf um das Deuteronomium" heiß umstrittene Fragen damals fast vergessen wurden. In der neuesten Phase der alttestamentlichen Forschung hat das Deuteronomium und die deuteronomische Literatur kaum noch eine offene oder geheime Sonderstellung in der Sicht des ganzen. Trotzdem ist vielleicht noch nie so viel über diesen Bereich gearbeitet worden. Die Forschung geht auch immer mehr ins Detail. Ebenso gilt jedoch, daß die vorgelegten Hypothesen und die oft beanspruchten «Ergebnisse» immer weiter auseinanderlaufen.

So war von dem Löwener *Colloquium* über das Deuteronomium von Anfang an nicht zu erwarten, daß ein großes und einheitliches Gesamtbild entstünde oder daß an einem voraussetzbaren vorhandenen und sicheren Gesamtbild nur einzelne Detailretuschen angebracht würden. Eher war zu hoffen, daß man den Wurzeln mancher Divergenzen auf die Spur käme und manche Scheindivergenzen sich vielleicht auch auflösen würden. Die eingeladenen Redner kamen aus verschiedenen Richtungen. Die zahlreichen spontan angemeldeten Kurzreferate haben die Buntheit des Bildes noch erhöht.

Die *Forschungsgeschichte* wurde, von forschungsgeschichtlichen Einführungen vieler Einzelreferate abgesehen, vor allem in drei Beiträgen berührt. M.J. Paul (Leiden) zeigte, daß de Wette nicht ganz so monumental am Anfang der Deuteronomiumsforschung steht, wie es oft den Anschein hat. Mit der Identifizierung des unter Joschija aufgefundenen Gesetzes mit dem Deuteronomium und mit der Annahme, es sei erst damals verfaßt worden, griff er einen Topos auf, der in aufgeklärten Kreisen des 18. Jahrhunderts schon gang und gäbe war. J. Lust (Leuven) gab einen Einblick in die Entwicklung der Auffassungen zum Deuteronomium im Werk des großen Löwener Gelehrten A. Van Hoonacker. Ich selbst habe in meinem Einführungsvortrag zum *Colloquium* nach einem kurzen Rückblick auf den «Kampf um das Deuteronomium» in den zwanziger Jahren und das Desinteresse an dessen Streitthemen in den folgenden Jahrzehnten die etwa seit 1960 wieder sehr lebhafte Beschäftigung mit den Joschija-Kapiteln der Königsbücher besprochen.

Alle drei Beiträge bezogen sich eigentlich mehr auf die historischen Fragen, die an 2 Kön 22-23 anknüpfen, als auf die Geschichte der Auslegung des Buches Deuteronomium selbst.

Mein Einführungsvortrag ging auch ausdrücklich auf die heute virulenten *methodologischen Fragen* ein. Ich vertrat das Nebeneinander und die Gleichberechtigung der bisher vor allem gepflegten diachronen und der neuerdings sich stärker meldenden synchronen Fragestellungen und der ihnen jeweils zugeordneten Methoden. L. Perlitt (Göttingen) verteidigte im ersten, methodologischen Teil seines Referats die älteren Methoden, vor allem die Literarkritik, gegen von ihm gesehene Absolutheitsansprüche der neueren synchronen Betrachtung. Er warnte davor, die ernsthafte wissenschaftliche Arbeit durch «Methodenlyrik» zu ersetzen. Die hier hervorgetretenen, nach meiner Meinung eher atmosphärischen als grundsätzlichen Gegensätze füllten dann auch noch einmal einen Teil eines der beiden Abendgespräche, an denen der ganze Kongreß teilnahm.

Im übrigen konnte der Kongreß den verschiedensten Methoden im praktischen Vollzug begegnen. Um nur Extreme aus dem Spannungsfeld Diachronie-Synchronie zu benennen: J. Vermeylen (Brüssel) trieb subtilste, viele Schichten voneinander abhebende Literarkritik, ebenso F. García López (Salamanca). Einzig an der Analyse des masoretischen Textes interessiert waren C. Labuschagne (Groningen) und D. Christensen (Berkeley).

Eine vergleichbar große Spannweite zeigte sich beim *historischen Ansatz des deuteronomischen Phänomens*. J. Halbe (Preetz) arbeitete zunächst als Typikum des deuteronomischen Rechts heraus, daß es eine Gemeinschaft konstituiert, die «Welt unterbricht». Dann zeigte er durch eine Analyse von Ex 23,1-9, daß diese Funktion des Rechts schon in vorstaatlicher Zeit ihren Anfang genommen hatte. A. Rofé (Jerusalem) rekonstruierte aus Texten von Dtn 29-30 einen Text aus einer Bundesliturgie, die schon im 8. Jahrhundert obsolet gewesen sein müßte. M. Weinfeld (Jerusalem) stellte alte und neue Argumente für die Herkunft des Deuteronomiums aus dem Nordreich zusammen. H. Cazelles (Paris) legte dem französischen Seminar die These vor, das im Deuteronomium entworfene öffentliche Recht sei ein Versuch, die Jerusalemer Priesterschaft in die maßgebende Position zu bringen. G. Braulik (Wien) analysierte im deutschen Seminar die Gesetzesdisposition in Dtn 12-26. Dabei kam er zu der Hypothese, daß der größere Teil des Textes von Dtn 19-25 erst in spät- oder nachexilischer Zeit in das Gesetzeskorpus eingebracht worden sein könnte. L.J. Hoppe (Chicago) schließlich verlagerte selbst das Kernstück des Deuteronomiums, die Kultzentralisation, in die Zeit nach 586 und war so auf dem *Colloquium* der Vertreter der exilisch-nachexilischen Datierungen von Deuteronomium und Deuteronomistik.

Zur *Textkritik* gab es zwei Beiträge. L. Laberge (Ottawa) glaubt, daß, wenn auch in viel geringerem Ausmaß, im Deuteronomium eine ähnliche Situation vorliegt wie im Jeremiabuch: zwischen der Septuagintavorlage und dem Masoretischen Text herrscht nicht einsinnige Abhängigkeit, sondern beide haben schon voneinander unabhängige Textentwicklungen hinter sich. Er brachte dafür Einzelbeispiele aus Dtn 1-11. P.-M. Bogaert (Louvain-la-Neuve) legte eine neue Hypothese über die Urform von Dtn 32,43 vor und zeigte vor allem, daß die verschiedenen Gestalten dieses Verses verschiedene theologische Gesamtauffassungen des Moseliedes bezeugen.

Nimmt man die Stoffdisposition des Deuteronomiums einmal zum Leitfaden, so läßt sich sagen, daß natürlich nicht der gesamte Text besprochen wurde, doch eine *repräsentative und sich über das ganze Buch verteilende Auswahl.* J. Van Goudoever (Amsterdam und Duisburg) sprach über den liturgischen Hintergrund der Datumsformel in Dtn 1,3. L. Perlitt (Göttingen) gab in der zweiten Hälte seines Referats Vorblicke auf die Positionen, die er in seinem Kommentar zu Dtn 1-3 vertreten möchte (Biblischer Kommentar). Im niederländischen Seminar wurde unter Leitung von C. Brekelmans (Leuven) über die Einordnung des Dekalogs und des ganzen Kapitels 5 in die relative Schichtenabfolge des Deuteronomiums diskutiert. Während J. Vermeylen (Brüssel) Schichtenidentitäten zwischen Dtn 5-11 einerseits und der älteren Sinaiperikope andererseits herstellte und die einzelnen Schichten dann, beginnend mit dem Fall Jerusalems 586, datierte, konzentrierte sich im gleichen Bereich C. Begg (Washington) auf einen einzigen Vers (Dtn 9,21) und dessen Parallelen in Ex 32, in der altorientalischen Literatur und in 2 Kön 23. S. A. Kaufman (Cincinnati) verglich Dtn 15 mit Texten aus dem Heiligkeitsgesetz und zog daraus Schlußfolgerungen für den Zeitansatz der Priesterschrift. C. U. Manus (Ife) lehnte eine Abhängigkeit des Gesetzes über die Sklavenfreilassung in Dtn 15,12-18 von der Parallele im Bundesbuch ab. F. García López (Salamanca) analysierte das Königsgesetz Dtn 17,14-20 auf seine Schichten und Zusammenhänge hin. Er rechnet, ebenso wie in seinen früheren Arbeiten für Dtn 5-11, mit einem Grundtext aus dem Nordreich vor dem Fall Samarias. C. Locher (Zürich und Chur) stellte unter Beiziehung sumerischer und akkadischer Rechtstexte die These auf, daß Dtn 22,13-21 ein Gesetz sei, das literarisch aus einem Prozeßprotokoll heraus entwickelt wurde. Das erkläre verschiedene Spannungen, die deshalb nicht literarkritisch interpretiert werden dürften. M. Anbar (Tel-Aviv) untersuchte die gegenseitigen Beziehungen der beiden Texte über den Bau eines Altars auf dem Ebal in Dtn 27 und Jos 8. Von Dtn 29 aus griff auch A. D. H. Mayes auf das Buch Josua hinüber (Jos 9). Dtn 29-30 wurden von A. Rofé (Jerusalem) analysiert. Mit dem Moselied hat sich neben P.-M. Bogaert (Louvain-la-Neuve) auch J. Luyten (Leuven) befaßt. Er untersuchte die eigengeprägten Urzeit- und Endzeitvorstellungen des Lieds.

Nicht nur M. Anbar und A. D. H. Mayes griffen auf die *deuteronomistische Literatur* aus. H.-J. Fabry (Bonn) sprach über Spuren des Pentateuchredaktors in Jos 4,21 ff. C. F. Whitley äußerte neuartige Ideen über das nach 2 Kön 22 im Tempel gefundene Gesetzbuch. Ich selbst hatte in meinem Einführungsreferat zur jüngeren Forschung über 2 Kön 22-23 auch einiges zu den neuen Bestreitungen und Weiterführungen der Theorie Noths vom «Deuteronomistischen Geschichtswerk» gesagt. Hier schlossen sich die Ausführungen von G. Vanoni (Wien-Mödling) an. Er brachte neue Gründe dafür bei, daß bis gegen Ende von 2 Kön 23 ein vorexilischer, von dort an dann ein ergänzender nachexilischer «Deuteronomist» anzunehmen ist. W. L. Holladay (Newton Centre) schlug schließlich die Brücke vom Deuteronomium zu Jeremia. Er verband die Vorschrift von Dtn 31,10-13 mit wichtigen Punkten in dem von ihm rekonstruierten Lebenslauf Jeremias.

Der in der neueren Deuteronomiumsexegese oft vernachlässigte *juristische Gesichtspunkt* trat erfreulicherweise mehrfach in den Vordergrund. J. Halbe (Preetz) brachte bei uns bisher unbekannte Kategorien der neueren Rechtssoziologie und -ethnologie ein. H. Cazelles (Paris) ging bei der Rekonstruktion der institutionellen Welt des Deuteronomiums und der ihr zugeordneten Rollenträger von modernen Theorien des internationalen und nationalen Rechts aus. G. Braulik (Wien) lehnte sich methodisch an die neueren keilschriftrechtlichen Arbeiten über die antiken Methoden der Gesetzesdisposition an. C. Locher (Zürich und Chur) wertete im orientalistischen Rechtsvergleich nicht nur legislative Texte, sondern auch Dokumente aus der Rechtspraxis aus.

Sprache und Stil des Deuteronomiums kamen beiläufig mehrfach zu ihrem Recht. Doch zwei Beiträge legten neue, bisher ungewohnte Gesichtspunkte vor. D. L. Christensen (Berkeley) trug dem englischen Seminar die These vor, das Deuteronomium sei nicht in Prosa, nicht einmal in «Kunstprosa», sondern in streng metrisch geordneter Sprache verfaßt, die zu mündlichem Vortrag mit Musikbegleitung geeignet gewesen sei. Für die Anordnung der «Verse» und «Versgruppen» lassen sich dann «konzentrische» Strukturen beobachten. C. J. Labuschagne (Groningen) stieß bei der Analyse der im Deuteronomium zitierten Gottesreden auf immer wieder neu vorkommende Zahlenverhältnisse, sowohl für die Gottesreden selbst als auch für ihre Einführungsformeln und die jeweiligen Wortmengen. Er zeigte dann noch an Beispielen, daß sich ähnliche numerische Kompositionsschemata auch in den anderen Textbereichen des Buches nachweisen lassen. Beide Kollegen bereiten Kommentare vor, für die sie uns eine Analyse des gesamten Textes unter ihren besonderen Gesichtspunkten versprechen.

Keinen sehr breiten Raum nahm der *theologische Aspekt* ein. Selbstverständlich ergaben sich bei manchen Referaten theologische Ausblicke.

Im übrigen sprach I. Mihalik (New Orleans), vor allem von den Belegen für den Gottesnamen «El» her, über die Gottesbezeichnungen im Deuteronomium. S. Amsler (Lausanne) stellte aus dem Selbstverständnis des Deuteronomiums Beobachtungen für den Fragenbereich «Schrift und Tradition» zusammen. Vielleicht ist das geringe theologische Interesse zufällig. Aber ich glaube eher, daß es unsere augenblickliche Situation kennzeichnet. Wir befinden uns in der Ablösung von einer vorangehenden Epoche, deren prominentester Vertreter der große Theologe Gerhard von Rad war. Wir sind wieder weitgehend auf Vorfragen zurückgeworfen, ja — auch wenn wir es gar nicht gern sehen — auf Fragen nach der rechten Methode. Dieser Situation können wir uns nicht durch einen vorschnellen Sprung über Abgründe hinweg in ein theologisches Jenseits entziehen.

Da zur Zeit an mehreren großen und kleinen *Kommentaren zum Deuteronomium* gearbeitet wird, die Pentateuchdiskussion ständig mit einem keineswegs geklärten *Begriff des «Deuteronomischen»* arbeitet und bezüglich des «*Deuteronomistischen Geschichtswerks*» neue und einander gegenseitig aufhebende Theorien entwickelt worden sind, ist damit zu rechnen, daß auch in den kommenden Jahren viel über das Deuteronomium gearbeitet werden wird. Vielleicht kann diese Dokumentation unseres *Colloquiums* dabei eine kleine Hilfe sein, indem sie zeigt, wo wir stehen und wieviel noch zu tun ist.

Offenbacher Ldstr. 224
D-6000 Frankfurt a.M. 70

Norbert LOHFINK

ERSTER TEIL

FORSCHUNGSGESCHICHTE

HILKIAH AND THE LAW (2 KINGS 22) IN THE 17TH AND 18TH CENTURIES

SOME INFLUENCES ON W. M. L. DE WETTE

It is widely known that de Wette thought the book of the law, found by Hilkiah, was Deuteronomy, written shortly before. In this short paper I want to answer three questions:

1) Who identified in the previous centuries the law in 2 Kings 22 with Deuteronomy?
2) Who suggested earlier that the law was not only found, but also written at the time of Josiah?
3) Is there any traceable influence in this respect on de Wette?

1. Hilkiah found Deuteronomy

G. E. Lessing wrote between 1771 and 1774 a short article about Hilkiah. In it he says that the most and excellent exegetes are of the opinion that the book which was found, contained the main parts of the second law [1] (i.e. Deuteronomy). J. Hempel who called attention to this article of Lessing, thinks the appeal to the Consensus doctorum is only a mask [2]. But I think it is only a little exaggeration, because there are some exegetes who have expressed the just mentioned opinion.

R. Smend in his excellent study about de Wette mentions some interpreters of the early church, and of later time Lessing and Th. Hobbes [3], who identified the law with Deuteronomy[4]. But there are more scholars who have done this. The tradition of the early church is preserved in the Middle Ages, e.g. by Alphonsus Tostatus [5]. When in 1642 in his commentary on 2 Kings Cornelius a Lapide speaks about the identity of the book, he tells us that Chrysostomus, Athanasius and Tostatus thought it was Deuteronomy [6]. J. S. Menochius, another

1. After his death his brother KARL published it for the first time in *Der Theologische Nachlass*, 1784. K. LACHMANN (ed.), *G. E. Lessings Sämtliche Schriften*, vol. 16, Leipzig, 1902, p. 245.

2. J. HEMPEL, *Chronik*, in *ZAW* 51 (1933), p. 299.

3. TH. HOBBES, *Leviathan*, 1651, ch. 42.

4. R. SMEND, *Wilhelm Martin Leberecht de Wettes Arbeit am Alten und Neuen Testament*, Basel, 1958, p. 36.

5. A. TOSTATUS or ABULENSIS (1455 †), *Commentaria*, vol. 7, Coloniae Agrippinae, 1613, pp. 378-379 (2 Kings 22).

6. C. A LAPIDE, *Commentaria* (ed. A. CRAMPON), vol. 4, Paris, 1877, p. 81.

Roman-catholic exegete, made the same choice, saying that there are many interpreters who held this view [7].

In Germany Hermann von der Hardt wrote his *Dulcia arva Virgilii* in 1740. He supposes that the whole of Deuteronomy comes from the highpriest Hilkiah [8]. In the Jewish tradition there is suggested, when Josiah opened the Scriptures, the first verse to strike his eye was the one in Deuteronomy: «The Lord will bring you, and your king whom you set over you, to a nation that neither you nor your fathers have known» (Dt 28,36) [9]. So the book contained at least part of Deuteronomy. This tradition is preserved too, e.g. by Grotius [10]. With a slight variation Calmet thinks that the book consists of the chapters 28-31 of Deuteronomy [11].

The English philosopher Lord Bolingbroke writes: «That the book, thus found, contained nothing but the law of Moses, strictly so called, or than the recapitulation of it, made in Deuteronomy, not the mosaical history, we may, nay we must conclude, from the little time that the reading in the presence of the king, and before it was sent by his order to the prophetes Huldah, took up» [12].

So it is clear that de Wette was not the first to identify the book of the law found by Hilkiah with Deuteronomy.

2. *Deuteronomy written in the 7th century B.C.*

Our second question is: «Who suggested earlier that the law was not only found, but also written at the time of Hilkiah?» In 1814 in his *Recherches nouvelles sur l'histoire ancienne* C.F. Comte De Volney attributed the final redaction of the Pentateuch to Hilkiah, very likely without reading the work of de Wette [13]. Is this accidental, or are the same ideas advanced earlier? The first time — as far as I know — some doubts are issued about the integrity of Hilkiah is in 1693 by the Deist Charles Blount in his *Oracles of Reason*. About the finding of the law he

7. J.S. MENOCHIUS (1594†), *Brevis Explicatio Sensus Literalis Totius S. Scripturae*, vol. 1, Coloniae Agrippinae, 1630, p. 515.

8. H. VON DER HARDT, *Dulcia arva Virgilii, Quintilius Varus, in tertium typographiae jubilaeum*, 1740. See H. MOELLER, *Hermann von der Hardt als Alttestamentler*, Theologische Habilitationsschrift, Leipzig, 1962, pp. 426 and 453 (unpublished); *Neue Deutsche Biographie*, vol. 7, pp. 668-669 (art. of H. BARDTKE).

9. *Yoma* 52b.

10. H. GROTIUS, *Annotationes ad Vetus Testamentum*, in *Opera Omnia Theologica*, vol. 1, Basel, 1732, p. 173 (2 Kings 22,10).

11. A. CALMET, *Commentaire littéral*, vol. 2, Paris, 1724, p. 924 (2 Kings 22,8).

12. *The Works of Henry St. John, Lord Viscount Bolingbroke*, vol. 3, London, 1754, pp. 276-277.

13. C.F. COMTE DE VOLNEY, *Recherches nouvelles sur l'histoire ancienne*, vol. 1: *Examen de l'histoire des Juifs jusqu'à la captivité de Babylone*, Paris, 1814, pp. 67-93. A. WESTPHAL, *Les Sources du Pentateuque. Étude de Critique et d'Histoire*, vol. 1: *Le Problème Littéraire*, Paris, 1888, pp. 158-160.

says: «We have only Helkiah's Word for it» [14]. Nearly 50 years later the bookseller Samuel Parvish concludes «that the Whole depends only on Hilkiah: Of whose Ability and Honesty we know nothing; but whose Interest it was to have a Law, either genuine or spurious» [15]. In France Voltaire confidently rejected a Mosaic Pentateuch, but he is less certain about the alternative. Sometimes he puts forward the theory that the scroll discovered in the temple included the modern Pentateuch, written for the occasion by the Levites [16]. In *Dieu et les Hommes* Voltaire hides himself behind others: «The scholars have strongly suspected the priest Hilkiah for having himself compiled the book» [17].

So we may say that in the circle of the Deists and Rationalists the integrity of Hilkiah was questioned [18]. It was one of their arguments to attack the reliability of the Bible.

Let us now consider two well known Old Testament scholars at the end of the 18th century: Eichhorn and Michaelis. In his *Einleitung in das Alte Testament* Eichhorn defends that neither the priests in the time of Josiah, nor the priest sent to the Samaritans invented the Pentateuch. In connection with the first opinion he gives no names. Is it because he didn't like to mention Freethinkers? He only speaks about «enemies of these books» [19]. In his book *Einleitung in die göttliche Schriften des Alten Bundes* Michaelis sums up some questions as: Are the Books of Moses from Esra? Are they from David? And then: Are the Books of Moses from Hilkiah? In five pages he firmly rejects this view [20]. Regrettably he too doesn't mention any name.

3. *Influences on de Wette*

In 1805 de Wette published his thesis [21]. His main purpose is to show that Deuteronomy stands apart from the other four books of the

14. Ch. BLOUNT, *The Oracles of Reason*, London, 1693. Reprinted in *The Miscellaneous Works*, 1695, pp. 17-18. C. HOUTMAN, *Inleiding in de Pentateuch*, Supplement, Kampen, 1980, p. 33, note 3.

15. S. PARVISH, *An Inquiry into the Jewish and Christian Revelation*, London, 1739. P. KLEINERT, *Das Deuteronomium und der Deuteronomiker*, Bielefeld und Leipzig, 1872, p. 2.

16. *La Bible enfin expliquée par plusieurs aumoniers de S.M.L.R.D.P.*, Londres, 17777, p. 103 (anonymous, but written by VOLTAIRE).

17. *Dieu et les Hommes*, Londres, 1770, ch. 19, p. 52. B.E. SCHWARZBACH, *Voltaire's Old Testament Criticism*, Genève, 1971, p. 87.

18. I have already mentioned H. VON DER HARDT. In his last years he went away from the pietistic movement and became more rationalistic.

19. J.G. EICHHORN, *Einleitung in das Alte Testament*, vol. 2, Leipzig, 1781, pp. 229vv. (3rd impr., 1803, pp. 257vv.).

20. J.D. MICHAELIS, *Einleitung die göttlichen Schriften des Alten Bundes*, vol. 1/1, Hamburg, 1787, pp. 201-205.

21. W.M.L. DE WETTE, *Dissertatio critico-exegetica qua Deuteronomium a prioribus pentateuchi libris diversum, alius cuiusdam recentioris auctoris opus demonstratur*, Jena,

Pentateuch. In a footnote he suggests that the book found by Hilkiah may have been Deuteronomy. But this suggestion is only touched upon in passing, and it does not look like a new suggestion, but no names are mentioned. His greatest concern is the centralisation of the cult. Deuteronomy demands centralisation. Attracted by the idea of a late origin of the Pentateuch de Wette seeks to demonstrate the late origin of Deuteronomy, and not so much the link with Josiah, which became so very important in later research[22]. In his *Beiträge zur Einleitung in das Alte Testament* he adds many arguments. This work is intended to elaborate the small thesis. Now de Wette clearly shows that Deuteronomy is not only found, but also written in the time of Josiah. Possibly it is a fraud of Hilkiah himself, but he is not sure about that[23]. So it seems de Wette is brought to his conclusion only by his exegetical insights. But many of the exegetical insights are noted earlier. So the tension between Ex 20 and Dt 12 is felt by Michaelis[24] and many others. But they are less critical than de Wette and usually defend a Mosaic origin of the Pentateuch. The identification of the book with Deuteronomy did not lead the exegetes in previous centuries to the assumption that the book was originated from the 7th century. That assumption came from the Rationalists and Freethinkers. At least via Eichhorn and Michaelis he must have known this. When we look at the religious conviction of de Wette, we see that it was a very rationalistic one. Not in the sense od declaring miracles as naturally possible, but in giving the Ratio a very prominent place. Influenced by Herder he was a Romantic too. He sought after a very radical criticism: We cannot read the Bible as our forefathers did. Once the criticism has begun, it has to go to the end. The Bible is not a historical book; it contains myth in each book. Only in this way the path shall be opened to read the deeplying message of the Bible[25]. So it is explainable de Wette felt very much attracted to philosophers like Voltaire, directly or indirectly.

Therefore I think we have to look to the philosophical and theological position of de Wette and the influence of it on his great discovery, more than is usually done[26].

Shawzijde 86 M.J. PAUL
NL-2725 PZ Zoetermeer

1805. The title of the reprint in G.M.L. DE WETTE, *Opuscula Theologica*, Berlin, 1830, pp. 151-168, is slightly different: *Dissertatio critica qua a prioribus Deuteronomium Pentateuchi libris diversum*, etc.

22. R. SMEND, *De Wettes Arbeit*, pp. 32-36. G.J. WENHAM, *The Structure and Date of Deuteronomy*, Unpublished thesis, London, 1970, pp. 29-37.

23. W.M.L. DE WETTE, *Beiträge zur Einleitung in das Alte Testament*, vol. 2, Halle, 1807, p. 179.

24. J.D. MICHAELIS, *Mosaisches Recht*, vol. 3, Reutlingen, 1785, pp. 42-50.

25. R. SMEND, *De Wettes Arbeit*, pp. 30-31. G.J. WENHAM, *Deuteronomy*, pp. 22-26.

26. In my thesis about Josiah and the centralisation of the cult I hope to investigate this subject more extensively.

A. VAN HOONACKER AND DEUTERONOMY

A. Van Hoonacker died 50 years ago, the 1st of November 1933. His adult life had been one long devotion to the study and teaching of the Old Testament. With him began the era of critical exegesis at the Catholic University of Leuven [1]. His main fields of interest were: first, the questions pertaining to the Hexateuch and the critical hypotheses of A. Kuenen and J. Wellhausen [2]; second, the chronology of the period after the Exile, with Ezra and Nehemiah [3]; third, the prophetic literature [4]. There is no need for a new biography of A. Van Hoonacker. His successor, J. Coppens, provided us with ample information concerning his life and his works [5]. To a certain extent, there was one domain which was left unexplored, that of his relations with Rome and the Biblical Commission. Recently, F. Neirynck was able to publish some relevant data concerning the threats emanating from the Congregation of the Index in the years 1913-1914 [6]. Though further research could be done in

1. J. COPPENS, *L'enseignement de l'Écriture Sainte à l'université de Louvain*, in *ETL* 9 (1932) 613-614.

2. In an Appendix (pp. 363-367) we reproduce with some additions *Van Hoonacker's bibliography* published by J. Coppens in *Le chanoine Albin Van Hoonacker. Son enseignement, son œuvre et sa méthode exégétiques*, Paris-Gembloux, 1935, p. XII-XX. As far as the questions concerning the Hexateuch are concerned we may refer especially to n°s 2.3.4. 5.6.15.20.21.28.29.34.

3. See Appendix n°s 9.10.11.13.14.24.26.35.96.99.100. His important contributions to the study of the Aramaic Papyri from Elephantine may also be referred to in this context: see n°s 48.50.51.63.75.76.93.

4. See the Appendix n°s 38.39.41.42.43.44.45.46.47.49.52.54.55.56.58.59.60.71.73.77.80. 86.90.92.95.98.102.108.109.113.

5. J. COPPENS, *Prof. Dr. Mgr. Alb. Van Hoonacker*, in *Ons Volk ontwaakt* 12 (1926) 689-692; *Le Ve Centenaire de la Faculté de théologie de Louvain, 1432-1932. Liber memorialis*, Brugge, 1932, p. 26-32, *L'enseignement de la théologie à l'université de Louvain depuis sa restauration en 1834. L'écriture sainte.* in *ETL* 9 (1932) 608-634, p. 613-620; *Albin Van Hoonacker*, in *Le Muséon* 47 (1934) 365-366; *Le chanoine Albin Van Hoonacker. Son enseignement, son œuvre et sa méthode exégétiques*, Paris-Gembloux, 1935; *M. le chanoine A. Van Hoonacker, professeur émérite de la Faculté de théologie*, in *Université Cath. de Louvain. Kathol. Universiteit te Leuven. Annuaire-Jaarboek 1934-1936*, Leuven, 1937, p. LI-LXXXIX; *A propos de l'œuvre exégétique du chanoine Van Hoonacker*, in *ETL* 16 (1939) 225-228; *Hoonacker (Albin Van)*, in *Dict. de la Bible*, *Suppl. 4*, Paris, 1949, c. 123-128; *Id.*, in *Catholicisme*, Paris, 1959, c. 937-938; *Id.*, in *Encicl. Cattolica*, 6, Rome, 1951, c. 1478. Other biographic notices were written by E. DE KNEVETT, *Professor Van Hoonacker*, in *Exp. Times* 20 (1909) 165-166; H. POELS, *Manifestation - Huldebetoon J. Forget - J. de Becker - A. Van Hoonacker*, Leuven, 1928, p. 47-57; J. SALSMANS, *Levensbericht van Kan. Prof. Albinus Van Hoonacker*, in *Hand. Vl. Acad. Jaarboek 1934*, Gent, 1934, p. 99-100.

6. F. NEIRYNCK, *Albin Van Hoonacker et l'Index*, in *ETL* 57 (1981) 293-297; Idem,

this area[7], on the occasion of the present Colloquium Biblicum, an exposition of A. Van Hoonacker's views on Deuteronomy may be more appropriate.

His thoughts concerning Deuteronomy can be rubricated as follows: (1) The literary unity of the Book; (2) The relative date of Deuteronomy in comparison with the date of the Priestly Code; (3) The absolute date of Deuteronomy. These three rubrics roughly correspond to three subsequent periods in the author's scholarly work. The following pages will be subdivided accordingly.

* * *

At the very beginning of his academic career, in 1889, A. Van Hoonacker composed a lengthy article on the connection of the first four chapters of Deuteronomy with the rest of the book[8]. The author's views attracted great attention: S. R. Driver, for instance, devoted several pages of his authoritative Commentary on Deuteronomy to A. Van Hoonacker's dissertation[9]. J. Coppens appreciated not only its high scholarly character but also, and perhaps even more so, its literary qualities: «A certains égards, c'est l'étude littéraire la plus délicate qu'il ait écrite»[10].

Against the majority of critics, the author intends to show that chapters 1-4 of Deuteronomy were written by the same hand as chapters 5 ff. It is not easy to summarize his arguments which are always formulated as an answer to the theses of his opponents.

1. While his opponents bring to the fore the occurrence of some expressions in chapters 1-4, absent elsewhere in Deuteronomy, A. Van Hoonacker insists on the similarity of style and terminology throughout the book. He does not deny that some expressions are typical of chapters 1-4. Certainly the most remarkable one is *jršh* (possession)[11]. In this case, he refers to the frequent occurrence of the verb *jrš* in the other sections. In the case of the other expressions he alleges that there was no occasion for their use in chapters 5 ff.

2. The basic objections against the unity are the historical inconsistencies alleged to exist between chapters 1-4 and chapter 5 ff.

A. Van Hoonacker, het Boek Jona en Rome, in *Academiae Analecta, Mededelingen van de Kon. Ac. voor Wet. Lett. en Sch. Kunsten, Klasse der Letteren* 44 (1982) 75-100.

7. See our notice in *ETL* 59 (1983) 331-332: *A Letter from M.J. Lagrange to A. Van Hoonacker*.

8. *L'origine des quatre premiers chapitres du Deutéronome*, Leuven, 1889; first published in *Le Muséon* 7 (1888) 464-482; 8 (1889) 67-85; 141-149.

9. S. R. DRIVER, *Deuteronomy* (ICC), Edinburgh, 1895, p. LXVII-LXXII.

10. *Le chanoine A. Van Hoonacker*, p. 27.

11. Compare with N. LOHFINK, *Kerygmata des Deuteronomischen Geschichtswerks*, in *Die Botschaft und die Boten, Fs. H. W. Wolff*, Neukirchen, 1981, p. 87-100.

a) In 2,14-16 it is said that all the generation which rebelled at Kadesh had perished in the wilderness, but in 5,2ff. and 11,2-7 those whom Moses is addressing are supposed to be witnesses of the Exodus. A. Van Hoonacker replies: The terms of 2,14-16 are limited to the «men of war», i.e. the adult males. A fair proportion of the younger ones would still be alive at the time of Moses' allocution in Moab. b) The Moabites and Edomites, who are placed on the same footing in 2,29 are put on a different footing in 23,4f.8f. A. Van Hoonacker answers first, that the facts reported in 2,29 are anterior to those mentioned in 23,4ff. and second, that 23,5a, which might seem to be in contradiction with 2,29, refers to the Ammonites only, and not to the Moabites, the latter being referred to in 23,5b.6. c) The note on the cities of refuge in chapter 4,41-43 is in contradiction with the one in chapter 19. A. Van Hoonacker retorts as follows: The writer in 4,41-43 mentions three cities of refuge appointed in the East of Jordan. In chapter 19 the same writer notices that three additional cities of refuge are to be instituted in Canaan. In chapter 19 he confines himself to those three and does not have to refer explicitly to the ones already dealt with in chapter 4.

3. Another objection against the unity is found in the presence of two superscriptions: 1,1-2.4-5 and 4,44-49, which appear to be mutually exclusive. A. Van Hoonacker answers that the second heading in 4,44-49 is rendered necessary by the interruption occasioned by 4,41-43, the short section dealing with the cities of refuge.

4. As regards 4,1-40, it is urged that the connection with chapters 1-3 is loose and that 4,1-40 is in no way a sequel of chapter 3. A. Van Hoonacker points out that chapter 4 begins just where chapter 3 breaks off. He admits that chapters 1-3 have rather historical character, whereas chapter 4 is more parenetic, but rejects the statement that chapters 1-3 are not at all parenetic. Moreover, he wonders whether it is necessary that one author should have used the same style everywhere.

5. According to several critics, the introduction to the promulgation of the laws (chapters 1-11) is too long and cannot be from one author. A. Van Hoonacker argues that the author presupposes an earlier promulgation of the law as explicitly stated in chapter 4,5. This presupposition allows the author to insist upon lengthy parenetic recommendations before giving a summary of the law.

It is remarkable that A. Van Hoonacker argued that even chapter 4,25ff is the work of the same author as, say, chapter 30,3ff. As far as I can see, in this early exposition, he failed to compare chapter 4,25ff with chapter 30,3-4, which he did do at a later time. Both passages appear to imply a reference to the *diaspora* and even to a return from the *diaspora*. They must be the result of a very late redaction.

On the other hand, in his article, A. Van Hoonacker never explicitly states the Mosaic authorship of Deuteronomy. This is remarkable for a catholic author in this period. In his later works it becomes clear that he envisages a Mosaic authorship as far as the basic contents are concerned. The composition of the book, however, is due to an author working in the period of Josiah or even later, during the exile. This may explain how an extremely critical scholar like Van Hoonacker could attribute some obviously late sections to the author who composed the book as a whole.

*
* *

Later, around 1894, while working out his ideas on the cultic institutions in Israel [12], A. Van Hoonacker reached some important conclusions concerning the date of Deuteronomy and its relations with the other Law codices. He demonstrated that the unity of sanctuary in Israel, far from dating merely from the reforms of Josiah, was attested throughout the entire legislation of the Israelites and could be proven to be a matter of fact all through Israel's history. On the other hand, he convincingly argued that there had been an evolution concerning the legality of the altars outside the central cultic area. Whereas the Book of the Covenant and the Priestly Code admitted the existence of local altars, the Holiness Code and Deuteronomy rejected this phenomenon. From this evolution, A. Van Hoonacker deduced that the Priestly Code must be older than Deuteronomy. With some hesitation he accepted the widely spread view that Deuteronomy was to be connected with the Josian Reform. The Priestly Code had to be earlier. In the argumentation, the role of Ex 20,24 ff. is preponderant [13]. It is stressed that this passage does not deal with the regulations of the official public worship in the temple but rather with the rules concerning private worship and domestic altars [14]. Deuteronomy, when urging the centralization of the public cult in one temple (12,5), is not in contradiction with the prescriptions of Ex 20,24 ff. On the other hand, Deuteronomy brings about a renovation when it forbids the erection of local altars.

His investigations concerning the Levitic priesthood [15] confirmed these views. In the priestly code, the title «priest» is reserved to the sons of Aaron; the title «levite» is used to name the other members of the Levitic tribe. In Deuteronomy all the Levites receive the priestly title [16]. This change reflects the growing influence of the Levites. The reasoning roughly sketched here, is underpinned by a detailed argumentation.

In 1901, A. Van Hoonacker was nominated as one of the first members of the Biblical Commission in Rome [17]. The questions sub-

12. See Appendix 20.21.29.
13. See *Le lieu du culte*, 19-32 (bibl. app. 20).
14. *Ibid.*, p. 27.
15. *Le sacerdoce lévitique*, bibl. app. 29.
16. *Op. cit.*, p. 173ff.
17. He received the news in a letter dated September 18, 1901, written by the secretary

mitted by the Commission to its members [18] invited him to reformulate his views concerning Deuteronomy within the context of the Pentateuch or Hexateuch. His answers to these questions, or better, a series of notes very similar to them, have been published posthumously by J. Coppens [19]. As far as Deuteronomy is concerned, the author rephrases the views which he exposed earlier and develops them further. He reaffirms his thoughts on the unity of style in both chapters 1-4 and in chapter 5ff, but no longer insists on the unity of the authorship of both sections. He merely states that if chapters 1-4 have been written by an author different from the one responsible for the core of the book, then he must have carefully imitated the style of the original author [20].

of the Commission D. Fleming. A. Van Hoonacker must have had some doubts concerning the authenticity of the message marked with the seal, not of the Vatican, but of the *Ordo Fratrum Minorum*, to which D. Fleming belonged. In a second letter, dated November 20, 1901, D. Fleming reassures the critical professor. I was able to consult these and other documents through the kindness of M. Van Hoonacker in Brugge.

18. The first letter mentions 10 members; the second one announces that two more members have been named: H. Poels and R. Clarke. This confirms the tentative list given by J. Coppens in *Paulin Ladeuze, orientalist en exegeet*, in *Versl. en Mededelingen. Kon Vl. Acad. Wet. Lett. en Schone Kunsten, Kl. der Letteren*, Brussel, 1941, p. 105. In 1903, 28 new members were added to the Commission.

19. *A. Van Hoonacker. De compositione litteraria et de origine mosaica hexateuchi disquisitio historico critica* (= *De compositione*). See our bibliographical appendix n° 116. In his introduction, J. Coppens mentions that he received the manuscript from friends, after the death of his predecessor (p. 8). The manuscript perished in the second World War, *secundo bello oecumenico* (p. 17). However, J. Coppens had transcribed it before the disaster. He reworked it, being faithful to the author's intentions (p. 8) and did not feel the need to tell us where exactly he changed the original. The text published by J. Coppens is to a large extent identical with the «Votum R.^{mi} D. A. Van Hoonacker» answering the «Quaestio IV^{a} ad X^{am} Seriei I^{ae}» dated September 1905. Printed copies of this votum are preserved in A. Van Hoonacker's legacy. One copy can be found in the archives of M. Van Hoonacker and an other in J. Coppens' archives. The front page of J. Coppens' copy has two handwritten notices obviously written by the owner. The first one simply states: «Trouvé parmi les papiers du Chan. Van Hoonacker». The second one, written with different ink, continues the first one: «et remis à M. Coppens après la publication de son traité inédit de Van Hoonacker sur la même question, reconstitué d'après des notes manuscrites. Il verra que son texte est une préparation ou une refonte de ce mémoire». The second part of the note may contain some mild form of pious fraud. The envelope in which J. Coppens stored away the «Votum» bears the postal date of July 14, 1939. It is very unlikely that he would have used an envelope dating from 1939 as a file for a document given to him after the publication of the manuscript on the Hexateuch in 1949. He must have received this document earlier and must have known that his manuscript was identical to it, or a first draft of it. For some reason he must have thought it wise not to mention this in his publication. His introduction leads some of his readers to the assumption that A. Van Hoonacker's manuscript was merely a set of class notes. Thus e.g. H. J. KRAUS, *Geschichte der historisch-kritischen Erforschung des A.T.*, Neukirchen, 1962^{2}, p. 524. Compare with C. HOUTMAN, *Inleiding in de pentateuch*, Kampen, 1980, p. 106 and *ibidem suppl.*, p. 18 note 101.

20. *Votum*, p. 63; = *De compositione*, p. 63.

He is more categorical concerning chapter 33, which is to be interpreted as a late insert preserving an old song [21], and concerning chapter 27,11-26, which is an equally late section giving a literal and material interpretation to the figurative command in 11,29: «You shall set the blessing on Mount Gerizim and the curse on Mount Ebal» [22]. He also restates that the Priestly Code is prior to Deuteronomy. The discrepancy in the laws concerning the altars and the Levitic priesthood are again the ground for this presumption [23].

The questions of the Biblical Commission also forced him to reveal his views concerning Mosaic authorship. Faithful to his earlier conclusions he frankly rejected the Mosaic authorship of the Hexateuch and thus of Deuteronomy in its present form [24]. On the other hand, he strongly insisted on the authentic Mosaic character of a great deal of its contents [25]. Several redactors successively worked at the book. Their activity is not to be considered as being inspired [26]. Its final redaction took place after the exile. Its core consisting of the law codex with the benedictions and maledictions in chapter 28 was composed not too long before 622, the date of its promulgation by Josiah [27].

* * *

The enlarged Biblical Commission [28] did not accept the views of its «advanced» [29] members among whom A. Van Hoonacker excelled.

21. *Votum*, p. 63; = *De compositione*, p. 63; compare with *Notes sur le texte de la Bénédiction de Moïse (Deut. 33)*, in *Le Muséon* 42 (1929) 42-60 (app. bibl. n° 107).

22. *Votum*, p. 64; = *De compositione*, p. 64. Deut. 27,1-8 is also a late insert.

23. *Votum*, p. 26-34; = *De compositione*, p. 33-37.39-40.

24. *Votum*, p. 3-18; compare with *De compositione*, p. 19-30.82-84. The latter sections are heavily reworked by J. Coppens. Obviously, the final decree of the Biblical Commission concerning the Hexateuch, promulgated in 1906 did not accept this view and some others of A. Van Hoonacker. The professor must have had strong presentiments. On repeated occasions the secretary D. Fleming had to reassure him. As an example we quote his letter dated November 7, 1902: «Je puis vous rassurer quant aux réponses données aux questions posées aux Consulteurs. Personne ne les connais jusqu'à présent. Tout reste sous le secret le plus vigoureux encore. Soyez donc tranquil de ce côté-là ... Travaillez courageusement pour la bonne cause ... Ecrivez franchement ... Rien ne pourra jamais nuire aux Consulteurs».

25. *Votum*, p. 78.

26. «Ex quo sequitur *redactores* qui huiusmodi documentis 'redigendis' incubuissent, non fore ut inspiratos considerandos»: *Votum*, p. 75. In J. Coppens' copy the passage is marked in the margin with four question-marks and equally as many exclamation-marks. It is not reprinted in *De compositione*.

27. *Votum*, p. 94-95; compare with *De compositione*, p. 76-77.

28. See note 18.

29. According to D. Fleming in a letter dated February 10, 1903, addressed to Van Hoonacker, the Commission was to be enlarged for several reasons. One of them, and obviously the major one, was that the first members «étaient à quelques exceptions près, tous des *avancés*». D. Fleming emphasized «avancés».

After the promulgation of the *Responsum de Mosaica authentia Pentateuchi*[30] in 1906 he never explicitly returned to this topic. However, indirectly and on several occasions he confirmed or nuanced his opinion concerning the date of publication of Deuteronomy. This happened especially in his major work on «The Twelve Prophets» and more specifically in the introduction to the commentary on Malachi. He points out the affinities of Malachi with Deuteronomy and its discrepancies with the Priestly Code concerning divorce and the Levitic priesthood. From these data he deduces the suggestion that the Law proclaimed by Nehemiah in Jerusalem[31] shortly after Malachi's preaching, was not the Priestly Code but rather Deuteronomy[32].

In an unpublished note destined to function as a supplement to the introduction to Malachi[33], he digs deeper into a question brought up by the comparison between Malachi and Deuteronomy. If Deuteronomy stands close to Malachi, is it then reasonable to say that Deuteronomy, or at least its core, was already proclaimed by Josiah? With some hesitation, the author defends the following answer. The law proclaimed by Josiah was not Deuteronomy but rather the Holiness Code or Lev 17-26. Deuteronomy is an exilic composition, at least in its present form. The latter affirmation solves the problems caused by the fact that on the one hand several sections in Moses' last discourse and also in the introductory part, e.g. chapter 4,29f., presuppose an exilic setting, and that on the other hand these sections display the same style as the rest of the book. The first affirmation is supported by the fact that the Holiness Code offers a good basis for the reformation performed by Josiah in 2 Kings 23. Before giving an analysis of the argumentation, we briefly turn to the questions concerning the originality of Van Hoonacker's proposal. Finally we will try to answer the question why he did not publish it.

30. The *Responsum* can be found in the *Enchiridion Biblicum*, Neapoli-Roma, 1954^2, p. 72-73.

31. Neh 8.

32. *Les douze petits prophètes*, p. 700-702. See also p. 665; *Une communauté Judéo-Araméenne à Eléphantine* (bibl. app. 75), p. 17-20.

33. Through the care of F. Neirynck the notice has recently been published in *ETL* 59 (1983) 86-90, under the title *Le rapprochement entre le Deutéronome et Malachie. Une notice inédite de A. Van Hoonacker (1908)*. The note was originally destined to be printed in the author's commentary on the Twelve Prophets (see our bibl. app. 47) as a supplement to the introduction to Malachi. As far as I could discover, the notice having the form of galley-proofs, has been preserved in four copies, one in J. Coppens' volume of Van Hoonacker's Commentary on the Twelve Prophets; two others in the author's own volume of the same book on the prophets to be found in the archives of M. Van Hoonacker, and a last one in the archives of the Library of the Faculty of Theology at Leuven in the fourth volume of the Varia A. Van Hoonacker. A handwritten comparison in three columns between 2 Kings 22-23, Deut. and the Holiness Code goes with A. Van Hoonacker's own copies of the notice.

Several critics advocated an exilic or postexilic date for Deuteronomy prior to A. Van Hoonacker. L.B. Paton [34] refers to C.P.W. Gramberg in 1829, to W. Vatke in 1835, L. Seinecke in 1876, G. D'Eichtal in 1886; M. Vernes and L. Horst in 1887, S.A. Fries and J. Cullen in 1903 and R.H. Kennet in 1906. We may add H. Reimarus and H. Preiss to this list [35]. None of these works attracted much attention at the time of their publication. In 1920, the exilic or postexilic theory of Deuteronomy was taken up again by G.R. Berry and R.H. Kennet and in 1922 by G. Hölscher with reference to Berry and Kennet. In 1923, F. Horst enthusiastically supported Hölscher's views [36].

Only a small minority of these authors drew the conclusion that the book of the Law discovered by Josiah should be identified with the Holiness Code. So far as I know, the first to do so was W. Vatke [37]. He was followed by H. Preiss [38], who explicitly builds his theory on W. Vatke, and later by G.R. Berry [39]. In his earlier publications, A. Van Hoonacker had adopted the more common view that the Law proclaimed by Josiah was to be identified with the core of Deuteronomy. However, it should be noted that already in his *Votum* for the Biblical Commission he pondered the possibility that the Book found in the temple and brought to Josiah was nothing but the Holiness Code [40]. It is not certain whether he knew his predecessors. Though he usually made frequent reference to his sources, in this case none are given. It may be that he had found the incentives for his thinking in a rather vague suggestion given by S.R. Driver [41] in which case no reference was needed. It is more likely however that the introductory character of his notice on Malachi did not allow the insertion of extensive bibliographic notes.

34. L.B. PATON, *The Case for the Post-exilic Origin of Deuteronomy*, in *JBL* 47 (1928) 322.

35. H. PREISS, *Zum Deuteronomium. Ein Beitrag zur Kritik des Pentateuchs*, Berlin, 1892; H.S. REIMARUS, *Apologie oder Schutzschrift für die vernünftige Verehrer Gottes*, 18th cent., see C. HOUTMAN, *Inleiding in de pentateuch*, Kampen, 1980, vol. I, p. 59-60. H.S. Reimarus' work was edited posthumously. A recent edition has been published in Frankfurt, 1972.

36. See L.B. PATON, *art. cit.*, p. 323f. F.C. BURKITT (1921) and S. SPIEGELBERG (1923) accepted the late dating. Compare with F. NEIRYNCK, *Albin Van Hoonacker et l'Index*, p. 293, note 2; J. COPPENS, *La réforme de Josias*, in *ETL* 5 (1928) 581-598, p. 595.

37. *Die Religion des AT*, vol. I. According to this author, Josiah's book consisted not only of Lev 17-20.26 but also of some other Law codices. W. Vatke's book was not available to me. The above data are taken from H. PREISS, *op. cit.*, p. 13.

38. See notes 35 and 37.

39. *The Code Found in the Temple*, in *JBL* 39 (1920) 44-51. Berry's views are severely criticized by A. FREED, *The Code Spoken of in 2 Kings 22-23*, in *JBL* 40 (1921) 76-80.

40. *Votum*, p. 22 note 2; *De compositione*, p. 56: «Utique partim etiam Lev. XVII-XXVI convenire possent».

41. *Deuteronomy*, p. XLV.

The argumentation primarily deals with content rather than with style and terminology. In a first series of remarks the author argues that the characteristics of the «Book of the Law» found by Josiah correspond to those of the Holiness Code equally well or even better than to those of Deuteronomy. After listing a number of examples [42] he elaborates upon the following element in Josiah's reform which has a good basis in the Holiness Code but not in Deuteronomy. Josiah destroys all the altars outside the temple of Jerusalem: 2 Kings 23,8.13.15; he does so in perfect agreement with the prescriptions of Lev 17,1f; Deuteronomy, however, presupposes this reform. In a second series of remarks the author defends the thesis of preexilic origin of the Holiness Code and of an exilic or postexilic date for the redaction of Deuteronomy. Since Josiah was a preexilic king, he may have known the former but not the latter book of the law. The chronological priority of the Holiness Code is deduced from the character of its official altar which is the preexilic altar of the tabernacle made of wood overlaid with bronze (Ex 27,1-2). The altar in Deuteronomy on the other hand is built with stones (Deut 27,5) like the one in the postexilic temple (1 Macc 4,44-47). Other data confirm the postexilic origin of Deuteronomy: the law forbidding foreign kings in Israel (Deut 17,14f); the law concerning the cities of refuge (Deut 19,2.7f); the law of the tithes (Deut 12,6-11; 14,22-27; comp. Mal 3,10); the law dealing with «bastards» (*mamzer*: Deut 23,2; comp. Zech 9,6).

In his first major contribution as A. Van Hoonacker's successor, J. Coppens continued the debate concerning Josiah and the Book of the Law [43]. He summarized the argumentation of his predecessor's unpublished notice and criticized it. It is remarkable that he downplays A. Van Hoonacker's strong stand in favor of the exilic or postexilic character of Deuteronomy: «M. Van Hoonacker ajoutait que le Deutéronome contient quelques éléments rédactionels, qui datent peut-être d'après l'exil» [44]. In his criticism he does not really answer A. Van Hoonacker's objections against the identification of Josiah's code with Deuteronomy. He merely refers to the arguments in favor of such an identification, adduced by A. Šanda who evidently ignores Van Hoonacker's theory. In addition J. Coppens draws attention to the passover festival in 2 Kings 23,21-23 which corresponds very well with Deut 16,1-8 and to Josiah's convocation of all the priests from Judah into Jerusalem reminiscent of Deut 18,1-8 [45]. However, he does not mention that Lev 23,5-8 also provides prescriptions concerning the

42. A full list is given in the handwritten sheet referred to in note 33.

43. *La réforme de Josias. L'objet de la réforme de Josias et la loi trouvée par Helcias*, in *ETL* 5 (1928) 581-598.

44. *Art. cit.*, p. 595. J. Coppens must have thought it wise not to emphasize A. Van Hoonacker's stands concerning the date of composition of Deuteronomy.

45. *Art. cit.*, p. 596-597.

passover festival; moreover he has to admit that Deut 18,1-8 does not correspond exactly with 2 Kings 23,8-9.

Although succinct, A. Van Hoonacker's reasoning is prudent and solid, at least on the level of the institutions in Israel. It fits in with his general theory set up against the Graf-Wellhausen hypothesis and accepting an earlier date of origin for P than for D. A renewed criticism of A. Van Hoonacker's positions concerning the Code of the law and Josiah would have to take into account questions of style and terminology. Moreover, it would have to deal with the history of the redaction of 2 Kings 22-23. A. Van Hoonacker's thesis rests on the hypothesis of the historical character of the story of Josiah. However, if the narrative proves to be an exilic or postexilic Deuteronomistic composition, this thesis is undermined [46].

Why did he not publish the notice? In *Le chanoine A. Van Hoonacker*, J. Coppens remarks that he had to omit it because of the ecclesiastic censorship [47]. He corrected this view when he discovered that the notice was withdrawn at the demand of M. J. Lagrange O. P. who had warned A. Van Hoonacker that the notice was of a nature which would provoke problems. J. Coppens' informer in this matter was J. Vosté [48].

We are not well informed concerning the character of the problems threatening A. Van Hoonacker at the eve of the publication of his commentary on the Twelve Prophets. They may have been caused by his views on the date of the composition of Deuteronomy. The decree of the Biblical Commission concerning the Hexateuch did not accept such opinion. One may be inclined to think that those difficulties were avoided through the removal of the supplementary note on Malachi. However, the remaining introduction to Malachi leaves no doubts concerning the author's convictions on the late dating of the promulgation of Deuteronomy. The same convictions are formulated in the author's commentary on Zech 9,5-7 [49]. It is true that these statements are more veiled than the supplementary notice on Malachi, but would they have escaped the Index if they had been offensive? It is not at all certain that the galley-proofs on Malachi, although more explicit, contain more offensive utterances. Like the other notices concerning the same matter they are mainly meant to support the chronological priority of P and of

46. See H. D. HOFFMANN, *Reform und Reformen* (AThANT), Zürich, 1980.

47. *Op. cit.*, p. 63.74. He repeated this remark in later notes. See F. NEIRYNCK, *Albin Van Hoonacker et l'Index*, p. 283-294. This conviction may explain why J. Coppens, after his promising article in 1928, never again treated the subject of Josiah and the code of the law.

48. See F. NEIRYNCK, *art. cit.*, p. 294, with reference to *ANL* 10 (1955) 213-215.

49. *Les douze petits prophètes*, p. 665. Later on he restated his view in his book on the Aramaic papyri from Elephantine: *Une communauté Judéo-Araméenne à Eléphantine*, 1915, p. 17-20, 54.

the Holiness Code over Deuteronomy. They do not deny the Mosaic authorship.

One wonders whether one of the reasons of the withdrawal of the notice could not have been the author's own indecision. He may not have been entirely convinced concerning the identification of Josiah's book with the Holiness Code. The notice itself betrays some hesitation: «Ce n'est pas notre intention d'émettre en ce moment aucune affirmation catégorique. Mais s'il fallait, de deux hypothèses l'une, choisir entre le Deutéronome et le recueil Lév. XVII-XXII, *comme composition d'origine exilienne*, nous nous demandons s'il ne serait pas plus commode de rapporter à l'époque de la captivité la rédaction ou la composition de notre Deutéronome ... et d'identifier le livre de la Loi dont il est question en 2 R XXII s. avec Lév. XVII-XXVI» [50]. It is the affirmation concerning the identification of Josiah's Law Book with the Holiness Code which disappears from the commentary and from A. Van Hoonacker's later writings, not the statements concerning the late date of Deuteronomy.

Van 't Sestichstraat 34 J. LUST
B-3000 Leuven

50. Third paragraph of the supplementary note. The italics are by the original author.

ZUR NEUEREN DISKUSSION ÜBER 2 KÖN 22-23[1]

Als wir dieses Colloquium vor drei Jahren planten, war Joseph Coppens noch unter uns, und die Wahl des Themas ging vor allem auch auf sein Drängen zurück. Erst später habe ich entdeckt, daß er sich praktisch im ersten Jahr seiner Lehrtätigkeit hier in Löwen, 1927/28, sehr gründlich mit 2 Kön 22-23 beschäftigt hat[2]. Im Jahre 1928 veröffentlichte er dann in den *Ephemerides Theologicae Lovanienses* den Artikel «La réforme de Josias. L'objet de la réforme de Josias et la loi trouvée par Helcias»[3]. Dieser Artikel scheint mir höchst aufschlußreich für die innerkatholische Geschichte der Bibelwissenschaft zu sein. Er läßt sich durchaus in Parallele stellen zu Walter Baumgartners Artikel «Der Kampf um das Deuteronomium», der im darauf folgenden Jahr 1929 die Neue Folge der *Theologischen Rundschau* eröffnete[4]. Wenn Baumgartners Beitrag eine Art Zusammenfassung und Schlußstrich für die heftige Auseinandersetzung der zwanziger Jahre um die Auslegung von 2 Kön 22-23 und um das Alter des Deuteronomiums bedeutete, so brachte der Beitrag von Coppens den damals weithin abseits stehenden katholischen Exegeten diesen Kampf überhaupt erst voll zur Kenntnis und legte Lösungen nahe, die sich von denen Baumgartners eigentlich nur im Detail unterschieden[5]. Es ist schön, daß ich an diese Anfänge des verehrten Gründers des *Colloquium Biblicum Lovaniense* anknüpfen kann.

1. 1928/29 flaute also der «Kampf um das Deuteronomium» langsam ab. Die beiden markantesten Vorkämpfer waren Östreicher und

1. Dieser Beitrag war der Einleitungsvortrag des Kongresses. Ich hatte den Versuch, in die gesamte Deuteronomiumsforschung einzuführen, bald aufgegeben und mich auf das in der Überschrift angezeigte Teilthema beschränkt. Dies war umso leichter möglich, als wir jetzt die größte jemals gedruckte Bibliographie zur Deuteronomiumsforschung besitzen: H. D. PREUSS, *Deuteronomium* (Erträge der Forschung, 164), Darmstadt, 1982, pp. 203-243. Sie ist gut gegliedert, mit vielen Querverweisen versehen und durch ein Autorenverzeichnis (pp. 245-258) und ein Bibelstellenverzeichnis (pp. 259-269) gut erschlossen. Die vorangehende Einführung in den Forschungsstand (pp. 1-201) enthält noch eine Reihe zusätzlicher Titel. Zum ganzen Buch vgl. meine Besprechung in *TLZ* 108 (1983) 349-353.

2. Wie mir die Universitätsbibliothek Löwen aus ihren Akten freundlich mitteilte, las J. Coppens im 2. Semester dieses Schuljahrs freitags und samstags über «*Le Deutéronome*». Wie die auf diese Vorlesung zurückgreifenden Prüfungsfragen aus den Jahren 1928-1930 zeigen, handelte er dabei über die Probleme der Herkunft und des Alters des Deuteronomiums.

3. *ETL* 5 (1928) 581-598.

4. *TR* NF 1 (1929) 7-25.

5. Zur Absetzung von den Annahmen seines Lehrers und Vorgängers A. Van Hoonacker vgl. den Beitrag von J. LUST in diesem Band.

Hölscher gewesen[6]. Theodor Östreicher in Bethel hatte die seit de Wette in ihren historischen Auskünften fragwürdige chronistische Darstellung der Joschija-Geschichte[7] wieder ernst genommen und sich von ihr anregen lassen, in 2 Kön 22-23 zwei ursprünglich nicht zusammenhängende Vorlagen anzunehmen, einen Buchauffindungsbericht[8] und einen Reformbericht[9]. So konnte er die kultischen Reformen Joschijas von der Auffindung des Gesetzbuches unabhängig machen. Sie wurden stufenweise durchgeführt, gewissermaßen als Signale der stufenweise gelingenden Befreiung von der assyrischen Oberherrschaft. Was in dem aufgefundenen Buch stand, war dann nicht mehr so wichtig. Für Östreicher war es nicht mehr das Deuteronomium allein, und dieses konnte er aus anderen Gründen als ein sehr altes Buch ansehen. Damit hatte er dem Wellhausenschen System den archimedischen Punkt genommen.

Gustav Hölscher in Marburg hatte auf völlig andere Weise das Gleiche getan. Seine Analyse des Deuteronomiums hatte ergeben, daß dieses ein nachexilisches utopisches Programm war. Auch in den Königsbüchern sah er ein von den berichteten Ereignissen zeitlich wie inhaltlich schon weit entferntes exilisch-nachexilisches Werk. Joschija und das Deuteronomium hingen weiter zusammen, aber nur auf der Ebene der Literatur.

Um diese beiden Hauptfiguren waren Mitstreiter und Vermittler verschiedenster Art gruppiert. Andere schauten zu und blieben vorerst bei de Wette und Wellhausen. Es gab weder Sieger noch Verlierer, sondern am Ende stand die allgemeine Ermüdung[10].

Eine neue Generation beschloß, bei der Frage nach dem Deuteronomium und nach der Geschichte Joschijas den Text in 2 Kön 22-23 aus dem Zentrum der Auseinandersetzung zu schieben und sich auf andere Quellenbereiche und Fragestellungen zu konzentrieren. Historiker wie Albrecht Alt suchten nach neuen Quellenbereichen, territorialgeschichtlich auswertbaren Texten etwa oder Ergebnissen archäologischer Ausgrabungen. Exegeten wie Gerhard von Rad fragten neu nach den

6. Für die Titel, auch von ÖSTREICHER und HÖLSCHER, sei auf BAUMGARTNERS Forschungsbericht (v.s. Anm. 4), pp. 7f., verwiesen.

7. 2 Chr 34-35. Vgl. W. M. L. DE WETTE, *Kritischer Versuch über die Glaubwürdigkeit der Bücher der Chronik mit Hinsicht auf die Geschichte der Mosaischen Bücher und Gesetzgebung* (Beiträge zur Einleitung in das Alte Testament, Erstes Bändchen), Halle, 1806, pp. 56f., 67-73, 106, 115f., vgl. auch 168-179.

8. 2 Kön 22,3-23,3.16-18.20-24.

9. 2 Kön 23,4-14.14.19.

10. Neben BAUMGARTNERS Referat (Anm. 4) seien noch folgende forschungsgeschichtliche Darstellungen empfohlen: S. LOERSCH, *Das Deuteronomium und seine Deutungen* (SBS, 22), Stuttgart, 1967; pp. 50-68; W. DIETRICH, *Josia und das Gesetzbuch (2 Reg. XXII)*, in *VT* 27 (1977), 13-35, esp. pp. 13-18; H. SPIECKERMANN, *Juda unter Assur in der Sargonidenzeit* (FRLANT, 129), Göttingen, 1982, pp. 18-24.

Inhalten des Deuteronomiums und entwickelten traditionsgeschichtliche Fragestellungen [11].

Um 2 Kön 22-23 wurde es still. Wie still — das zeigt der von Ernst Jenni in der *Theologischen Rundschau* von 1961 veröffentlichte, 82 Seiten starke Forschungsbericht über «Zwei Jahrzehnte Forschung über Josua bis Könige» [12]. Auf der allerletzten Seite hat er gerade *auch* noch zwei Autoren zu nennen, die nach ihm in seiner Berichtszeit von diesen beiden Kapiteln in eigenen Veröffentlichungen gehandelt haben: Alfred Jepsen und Rudolf Meyer [13]. Hier irrt er zwar, aber erheblich ließe sich die Zahl nicht vermehren [14].

Wie sehr sich dann die Situation verändert hat, zeigen neuere Zahlen. Ich zähle — sicher nicht vollständig — seit 1960 zu 2 Kön 22-23, zu einzelnen Passagen und Themen daraus und zu Joschija ungefähr 50 Titel [15]. Natürlich kommen in den letzten zwei Jahrzehnten auch noch viele Arbeiten über andere Gegenstände auf 2 Kön 22-23, auf Joschija und auf die Frage der Herkunft des Deuteronomiums zu sprechen. Was ist geschehen? Ich würde sagen: Alle ungelösten Fragen der zwanziger Jahre und auch fast alle verschiedenen Weisen von damals, die Fragen anzugehen, sind wieder auferstanden. Es hat nichts genutzt, sie ungelöst am Wege liegen zu lassen. Oder vielleicht doch, zumindest ein wenig und in einigen Bereichen.

2. Inzwischen scheint zum Beispiel einigermaßen klar zu sein, wie weit Joschija in den letzten Jahren seiner Regierung die Grenzen seiner Herrschaft nach Norden ausgedehnt hat: gar nicht sehr weit [16]. Eher

11. Näheres bei SPIECKERMANN, *op. cit.*, pp. 24-26.

12. *TR* 27 (1961) 1-32 und 97-140.

13. R. MEYER, *Auffallender Erzählungsstil in einem angeblichen Auszug aus der «Chronik der Könige von Juda»*, in *FS Friedrich Baumgärtel zum 70. Geburtstag* (Erlanger Forschungen, A 10), Erlangen, 1959, pp. 114-123; A. JEPSEN, *Die Reform des Josia*, ebd., pp. 97-108.

14. Z. KARL, *Die Auffindung der Tora in den Tagen Josias* (hebr.), in *Tarbiz* 22 (1950/51) 129-135; D. W. B. ROBINSON, *Josiah's Reform and the Book of the Law*, London, 1951; F. M. CROSS-D. N. FREEDMAN, *Josiah's Revolt against Assyria*, in *JNES* 12 (1953) 56-58 — das ist alles, was ich zusätzlich zu nennen hätte.

15. Vgl. unten Anm. 60.

16. P. WELTEN, *Die Königs-Stempel. Ein Beitrag zur Militärpolitik Judas unter Hiskia und Josia*, Wiesbaden, 1969; D. LANCE, *The Royal Stamps and the Kingdom of Josiah*, in *HTR* 64 (1971) 315-332; A. MALAMAT, *Josiah's Bid for Armageddon: The Background of the Judean-Egyptian Encounter in 609 B.D.*, in *JANES* 5 (1973) 267-279 (= FS Gaster); M. COGAN, *Imperialism and Religion: Assyria, Judah and Israel in the Eighth and Seventh Centuries B.C.E.* (SBL Monograph Series, 19), Missoula, 1974, p. 71; M. ROSE, *Der Ausschließlichkeitsanspruch Jahwes. Deuteronomische Schultheologie und die Volksfrömmigkeit in der späten Königszeit* (BWANT 106), Stuttgart, 1975, pp. 156-159; E. WÜRTHWEIN, *Die Josianische Reform und das Deuteronomium*, in *ZTK* 73 (1976) 395-423; H. BARTH, *Die Jesaja-Worte in der Josiazeit. Israel und Assur als Thema einer produktiven Neuinterpretation der Jesajaüberlieferung* (WMANT, 48), Neukirchen, 1977, pp. 255-260;

ist er nach Westen bis zum Meer vorgestoßen. Die Basis für den breiten Konsens in dieser Meinung bilden die inzwischen rund tausend Königs-Stempel auf Vorratskrügen und deren stratigraphische und geographische Verteilung. Ferner Ausgrabungen, vor allem in Mezad Chaschavyahu[17].

Die Archäologie[18] hat uns auch in der Frage des historischen Ansatzes der Kultzentralisation weitergebracht, vor allem Yohanan Aharonis Ausgrabungen von Arad und Beerscheba[19]. Zwar läßt sich Aharonis anfängliche Meinung, er könnte die Nichtwiedererrichtung des Altars im Jahweheiligtum von Arad mit einer Opferzentralisation unter Hiskija und die Nichtwiedererrichtung des ganzen Heiligtums nach einer weiteren Zerstörung mit einer radikalen Vernichtung aller Heiligtümer außer dem Tempel von Jerusalem unter Joschija synchronisieren, inzwischen stratigraphisch nicht mehr halten. Aber die Entscheidung zum Nichtwiederaufbau des Heiligtums von Arad liegt jetzt noch vor der Zeit von Joschija[20]. Wir können also auf jeden Fall den Abbau von Jahweheiligtümern nicht mehr als etwas betrachten, was erstmalig

G. S. OGDEN, *The Northern Extent of Josiah's Reforms*, in *ABR* 26 (1978) 26-34; H. CAZELLES, *La vie de Jérémie dans son contexte national et international*, in *Le livre de Jérémie. Le prophète et son milieu, les oracles et leur transmission* (BETL, 54), Leuven, 1981, pp. 21-39, esp. pp. 29-31; SPIECKERMANN, *Juda unter Assur* (v.s. Anm. 10), pp. 114-118. Unter diesen Autoren rechnet eigentlich nur noch COGAN mit voller Ausdehnung des Reichs nach Norden. ROSE läßt das Zeugnis der Königs-Stempel nur für die Grenzen der Zivilverwaltung gelten, in deren Bereich die Truppen aus Krongütern ernährt werden. Für die Ausdehnung militärischer Besetzung weiter nach Norden folge daraus nichts. MALAMAT argumentiert dafür, daß Megiddo direkt von assyrischer in ägyptische Hand überging. CAZELLES rechnet für die Zeit nach 622 mit einverständlicher Gebietsaufteilung zwischen Ägypten und Juda: Ägypten hatte Megiddo, Juda das Bergland. Im übrigen hat sich WELTEN durchgesetzt.

17. Hierzu zusammenfassend: *Encyclopedia of Archaeological Excavations in the Holy Land* (4 Bde), London, 1975-1978, III 872f; O. KEEL/M. KÜCHLER, *Orte und Landschaften der Bibel*, Bd. 2, Zürich/Göttingen, 1982, pp. 32f.

18. Als Einführung vgl. immer noch: E. STERN, *Israel at the Close of the Period of the Monarchy: An Archaeological Survey*, in *BA* 38 (1975) 26-54.

19. Vgl. seine eigenen Darstellungen: Y. AHARONI, *Arad*, in *BA* 31 (1968), 2-32; *Israelite Temples in the Period of the Monarchy*, in *Proceedings of the Fifth World Congress of Jewish Studies*, I, Jerusalem, 1969, 69-74; *The Horned Altar of Beer-sheba*, in *BA* 37 (1974) 2-6. Zu Letzterem genauer: Z. HERZOG, A. F. RAINEY, S. MOSHKOVITZ, *The Stratigraphy at Beer-sheba and the Location of the Sanctuary*, in BASOR 225 (1977) 49-58. Zu den Ausgrabungen in Arad und Beerscheba vgl. jetzt KEEL/KÜCHLER, *Orte und Landschaften* 2 (v.s. Anm. 17), pp. 209-233 und 185-209. Ein sehr vorsichtiger Bericht darüber ist D. CONRAD, *Einige (archäologische) Miszellen zur Kultgeschichte Judas in der Königszeit*, in *Textgemäß. Aufsätze und Beiträge zur Hermeneutik des Alten Testaments* (FS E. Würthwein), Göttingen, 1979, pp. 28-32.

20. Vgl. den Mitausgräber V. FRITZ, *Tempel und Zelt. Studien zum Tempelbau in Israel und zu dem Zeltheiligtum der Priesterschrift* (WMANT, 47), Neukirchen-Vluyn, 1977, p. 41, n. 5. Zu einer anderen ernsthaften Schwierigkeit gegenüber Aharoni vgl. F. M. CROSS, *Two Offering Dishes with Phoenician Inscriptions from the Sanctuary of ʿARAD*, in *BASOR* 235 (1979) 75-78.

unter Joschija stattfand. Außerdem könnte Rut Amiran im Gebiet des heutigen westlichen Jerusalem einige von Joschija kultunfähig gemachte Opferhöhen ausgegraben haben [21].

Hans-Detlev Hoffmann will noch 1980 das Hulda-Orakel dadurch als nachexilische Konstruktion erweisen, daß er behauptet, in der Zeit Joschijas habe es keine Neustadt (*mišnāh*), in der Hulda nach 2 Kön 22,14 gewohnt haben soll, gegeben [22]. Deshalb möchte ich ausdrücklich darauf hinweisen, daß Nigel Avigad in den Ausgrabungen im jüdischen Viertel 1969-1971 die Besiedlung des Südwesthügels von Jerusalem seit dem 8. Jahrhundert nachgewiesen hat. Frühestens seit Hiskija [23], spätestens seit Joschija [24] war diese Neustadt auch von einer Mauer geschützt, von der ein Stück heute durch jeden Touristen besichtigt werden kann.

Auch die umfassenderen politischen und militärischen Vorgänge, die einzelnen Phasen des assyrischen Machtzerfalls, die Rolle Babyloniens einerseits, Ägyptens andererseits lassen sich heute wesentlich genauer bestimmen als vor einem halben Jahrhundert [25]. Noch wichtiger aber ist, daß die Unterwerfungs- und Beherrschungstechniken der Assyrer in den ihrem Reich als Provinzen einverleibten oder als Vasallenstaaten angegliederten Gebieten inzwischen gründlicher erforscht sind [26]. Die

21. R. AMIRAN, *The Tumuli West of Jerusalem*, in *IEJ* 8 (1958) 206-227; Deutung auf von Joschija zerstörte Jahwe-Höhen: Y. ELITZUR, *The Josiade Reform in the Light of Jerusalem Archaeology* (hebr.), in *Proceedings of the Fifth World Congress of Jewish Studies*, I, Jerusalem, 1969, 92-97. Doch ist der Sachverhalt nicht ganz eindeutig. Vgl. noch FRITZ, *Tempel und Zeit* (v.s. Anm. 20), p. 73.

22. H.-D. HOFFMANN, *Reform und Reformen. Untersuchungen zu einem Grundtheme der deuteronomistischen Geschichtsschreibung* (ATANT, 66), Zürich, 1980, p. 199, n. 30. Seine archäologischen Gewährsleute reichen nicht über Dame Kenyon hinaus.

23. So N. AVIGAD selbst in *Jerusalem Revealed: Archaeology in the Holy City 1968-1974* (Ed. Y. YADIN), New Haven, 1976, p. 44.

24. So E. OTTO, *Jerusalem - die Geschichte der Heiligen Stadt: Von den Anfängen bis zur Kreuzfahrerzeit* (Urban-Taschenbücher, 308), Stuttgart, 1980, p. 68.

25. In den letzten beiden Jahrzehnten hat sich vor allem A. MALAMAT immer wieder neu zur Geschichte der Joschija-Zeit geäßert, und bei ihm kann man leicht zu weiterer Literatur finden. Ich nenne: *The Historical Background of the Assassination of Amon, King of Judah*, in *IEJ* 3 (1953) 26-29; *The Last Kings of Judah and the Fall of Jerusalem*, in *IEJ* 18 (1968) 137-156; *Josiah's Bid for Armageddon* (v.s. Anm. 16); *Megiddo, 609 B.C.: The Conflict Re-Examined*, in *Acta Antiqua Academiae Scientiarum Hungaricae* 22 (1974) 445-449; *The Twilight of Judah: In the Egyptian-Babylonian Maelstrom*, in *Congress Volume Edinburgh 1974* (VTSuppl 28), Leiden, 1975, pp. 123-145. Vgl. ferner M. ELAT, *The Political Status of the Kingdom of Judah within the Assyrian Empire in the 7th Century B.C.*, in *Investigations at Lachish: The Sanctuary and the Residence* (Lachish, V; ed. Y. AHARONI), Tel Aviv, 1975, 61-70; BARTH, *Jesaja-Worte* (v.s. Anm. 16), pp. 242-250; B. OTZEN, *Israel under the Assyrians: Reflections on 'Imperial Policy in Palestine*, in *ASTI* 11 (1977/78) 96-110; S. BULBACH, *Judah in the Reign of Manasseh as Evidenced in Texts during the Neo-Assyrian Period and in the Archaeology of the Iron Age* (Ph. D. Dissertation, New York, 1981); CAZELLES, *La vie de Jérémie* (v.s. Anm. 16), pp. 29ff.; SPIECKERMANN, *Juda unter Assur* (v.s. Anm. 10), pp. 139-143 und passim.

26. COGAN, *Imperialism and Religion* (v.s. Anm. 16); G. BEGRICH, *Der wirtschaftliche*

Techniken der Kontrolle und der wirtschaftlichen Ausbeutung sind untersucht, vor allem aber auch die Frage des ausgeübten religiösen Zwangs. Hierzu hat es im vergangenen Jahrzehnt eine Reihe umfassender Arbeiten gegeben. Während John William McKay 1973 eher mit religiöser Großzügigkeit Assurs gegenüber unterworfenen Völkern rechnete [27], hat schon Morton Cogan 1974 ein wesentlich düstereres Bild gezeichnet, aber noch einen starken Unterschied zwischen Gebieten, die zur assyrischen Provinz gemacht wurden, und Vasallenstaaten aufrechterhalten [28]. Durch die im Jahre 1982 erschienene, sehr breit angelegte und gründlichst dokumentierte Monographie von Hermann Spieckermann, «Juda unter Assur in der Sargonidenzeit», wird auch diese letzte Unterscheidung in mehrfacher Hinsicht in Frage gestellt [29]. Wir müssen damit rechnen, daß assyrische Kulte sich in Jerusalem und Juda keineswegs nur auf dem Weg des Kulturdrucks ausbreiteten, sondern, vor allem in Jerusalem selbst, offiziell auferlegt waren. Von der assyrischen Praxis her spricht alles dafür, daß Joschijas kultische Reformen zu einem großen Teil in der Abschaffung assyrischer Religionsformen bestanden, auch wenn die biblischen Texte den betreffenden Gottheiten zum Teil kanaanäische Namen geben [30].

Spieckermanns Buch ist vor allem auch deshalb wichtig, weil er aufweist, daß Assurs plötzlicher Untergang zu Lebzeiten Joschijas von Juda letztlich auf eine tiefe religiöse Identitätskrise in Assur zurückgeht, die auch durch immer intensiveren Ausbau der Divination und des Rituals nicht aufzufangen war [31]. Man würde sich in diesem Zusammenhang eine ähnlich umfassende Untersuchung der hohen Rolle des Eid- und Verpflichtungswesens für die immer prekärer werdende Erhaltung der inneren Konsistenz Assurs wünschen [32], da bestimmte Aspekte der

Einfluß Assyriens auf Südsyrien und Palästina (Dissertation Berlin, 1975). Vgl. die folgenden Anmerkungen.

27. J. W. McKay, *Religion in Judah under the Assyrians* (Studies in Biblical Theology, II, 26), London, 1973, esp. pp. 28-44.

28. *Imperialism and Religion* (v.s. Anm. 16), esp. pp. 42-86.

29. *Juda unter Assur* (v.s. Anm. 10), esp. pp. 200-225 und 307-372.

30. So schon H. Gressmann, *Josia und das Deuteronomium. Ein kritisches Referat vom Herausgeber*, in *ZAW* 42 (1924) 313-337, esp. pp. 321-327.

31. L.c., pp. 227-306.

32. Vgl. vorläufig Cogan, *Imperialism and Religion* (v.s. Anm. 16), pp. 42-44. Die beiden Aspekte der Absicherung — Intensivierung der Religion und der Eidleistungen — überschneiden sich da, wo gegenüber der Gottheit selbst «vertragliche» Verpflichtungen beschworen werden. Zu Zeugnissen hierfür vgl. N. Lohfink, *Gott im Buch Deuteronomium*, in *La notion biblique de Dieu* (BETL, 41), Leuven, 1976, pp. 101-126, esp. p. 115, n. 52 (Bund zwischen dem Gott Assur und dem Volk von Assur zugunsten von Asarhaddon, vermittelt durch die Göttin Ischtar); Z. Zevit, *A Phoenician Inscription and Biblical Covenant Theology*, in *IEJ* 27 (1977) 110-118, esp. pp. 114-118 (Bund einer Gruppe mit dem Gott Assur, den «Gottessöhnen» und dem «Anführer der Versammlung aller Heiligen»), falls diese Inschrift echt ist. Zur Berichterstattung von Preuss, *Deuteronomium* (v.s. Anm. 1), p. 68, über diesen Sachverhalt vgl. meine Besprechung (v.s. Anm. 1), p. 352.

deuteronomischen Sprache und Theologie davon durchaus beeinflußt sein könnten [33]. Sehr viele Einzeluntersuchungen sind in diesem Zusammenhang allerdings schon geleistet, vor allem durch Moshe Weinfeld [34].

So können wir dich nicht sagen, daß beim Umgang mit dem Text von 2 Kön 22-23 alles noch genau so wäre wie in den zwanziger Jahren. Wir wissen ganz anders über den Kontext Bescheid, in dem das stand, wovon diese beiden Kapitel sprechen [35]. Die faktischen Ereignisse, die materielle Kultur, die politischen Großvorgänge, die gesellschaftlichen und ideologischen Verschiebungen — all dies tritt deutlicher hervor. Trotzdem: 2 Kön 22-23 ist ein Text. Die neuen Einsichten in dessen historischen Kontext mögen unsere frei vagabundierende Fantasie daran hindern, bestimmten Richtungen des Verständnisses weiter nachzulaufen. Letztlich muß der Text zunächst einmal als Text verstanden und eingeordnet werden. Und im übrigen bleibt er unsere Hauptquelle für die Epoche und

33. Vgl. N. LOHFINK, *Culture Shock and Theology. A Discussion of Theology as a Cultural and a Sociological Phenomenon Based on the Example of Deuteronomic Law*, in *BTB* 7 (1977) 12-22. Die beiden einflußreichsten Monographien zur alttestamentlichen «Bundestheologie» aus dem Berichtszeitraum gehen auf diese Zusammenhänge wohl zu wenig ein: L. PERLITT, *Bundestheologie im Alten Testament* (WMANT, 36), Neukirchen-Vluyn, 1969; E. KUTSCH, *Verheißung und Gesetz. Untersuchungen zum sogenannten «Bund» im Alten Testament* (BZAW, 131), Berlin, 1972. Bei PERLITT vgl. aber die positive, wenn auch knappe Ausführung ganz am Ende des Buches, pp. 282f.

34. Gründlichste Gesamtdarstellung: D. J. MCCARTHY, *Treaty and Covenant: A Study in Form in the Ancient Oriental Documents and in the Old Testament* (New Edition completely rewritten; AB, 21A), Rom, 1978. Neueste Literaturverweise finden sich in D. J. WISEMAN, *«Is it Peace?» — Covenant and Diplomacy*, in *VT* 32 (1982) 311-326. Am Anfang war die Diskussion zu sehr auf den Vergleich mit hethitischen Vasallenverträgen, ja mit Verträgen überhaupt eingegrenzt. In der Ausweitung der Gesichtspunkte nach verschiedenen Richtungen hin besteht gerade die Leistung von M. WEINFELD. Von ihm vgl. etwa: *The Covenant of Grant in the old Testament and in the Ancient Near East*, in *JAOS* 90 (1970) 184-203; *Deuteronomy and the Deuteronomic School*, Oxford, 1972; *Covenant Terminology in the Ancient Near East and its Influence upon the West*, in *JAOS* 93 (1973) 190-199; *B^erit - Covenant vs. Obligation*, in *Bib* 56 (1975) 120-128; *The Loyalty Oath in the Ancient Near East*, in *Ugarit-Forschungen* 8 (1976) 379-414.

35. In zwei Fragen scheint kaum ein neuer Geschichtpunkt hinzugetreten zu sein. 1. Begannen die Kultreformen Joschijas schon vor der Buchauffindung, oder sind sie erst durch sie ausgelöst? Hier stehen Autoren, die wie de Wette und Wellhausen nur den Königsbüchern trauen, gegen andere, die wie Östreicher in der Konstruktion der Chronik doch ein Wahrheitskörnchen finden. Wirklich neue Argumente entdeckte ich nicht. 2. War das gefundene Buch das Deuteronomium, und, wenn ja, in welchem Sinn? Der Konsens geht weiter auf das Deuteronomium in irgendeiner Form. Aus ihm springen nur J. MAIER, *Bemerkungen zur Fachsprache und Religionspolitik im Königreich Juda*, in *Judaica* 26 (1970) 89-105, esp. pp. 101-105 (ein Buch «auf der Linie der priesterschriftlichen Tradition»), und J. R. LUNDBOM, *The Lawbook of the Josianic Reform*, in *CBQ* 38 (1976) 293-302 («the lawbook is the song of Moses in Deut 32»), hinaus. Interessant ist M. ROSE, *Bemerkungen zum historischen Fundament des Josia-Bildes in 2 Reg 22f*, in *ZAW* 89 (1977) 50-63, esp. p. 56, n. 26, der aus 2 Kön 22,19 *dibbarti* folgert, daß damals Dtn noch nicht «als Mose-Rede stilisiert» war, sondern «als Jahwe-Rede».

den Bereich von Juda, vieles an historischer Einsicht hängt letztlich auch wieder an seiner Deutung. Für 2 Kön 22-23 als Text sind trotz allem die ungelösten Fragen der zwanziger Jahre wieder auferstanden.

Ja, in mancher Hinsicht haben sie sich verkompliziert. Denn nun ist noch für den umfassenderen Textzusammenhang, die biblischen Bücher von Deuteronomium bis 2 Könige, Martin Noths Theorie vom «Deuteronomistischen Geschichtswerk» dazwischengekommen [36]. Bei der Auseinandersetzung mit ihr bilden unsere beiden Kapitel eine strategische Stelle. Und auch diese Auseinandersetzung ist in vollem Gang.

3. In den zwanziger Jahren war man zwar über die Quellenstruktur der Königsbücher uneins, doch war man sich einig in der Annahme einer deuteronomistischen Redaktion dieser Bücher. Seit Abraham Kuenen [37], der selbst an Heinrich August Ewald anknüpfte, unterschied man auch weithin zwischen zwei Phasen dieser Redaktion: einer vorexilischen, die mit Joschija oder mit Jojakim endete, und einer über den Untergang Jerusalems hinaus ergänzenden exilischen. Diese Doppelung der Redaktion stellte die Richtung von Hölscher [38] allerdings in Frage, indem sie das ganze Werk, ja schon seine Hauptquellen, in die exilische und nachexilische Zeit versetzte. Sieht man diese Theoriekonstellation der zwanziger Jahre, dann wird zumindest einer der Herkunftsbereiche von Martin Noth deutlich. Er hat nicht nur — was er selbst am meisten in den Vordergrund stellt — aus deuteronomistischen «Redaktoren» einen echten «Autor» gemacht [39] und dessen Werk als in sich stehende Einheit vom anders zu beurteilenden Tetrateuch deutlich getrennt [40]. Er hat vielmehr, zusammen mit Hölscher, die deuteronomistische Literaturproduktion konsequent hinter den Untergang Jerusalems geschoben [41] — wenn auch nicht ganz so weit weg wie Hölscher und wenn auch so, daß er gleichzeitig mit vorexilischem Quellenmaterial seines Deuteronomisten rechnete. So selbstsicher Noth sich ausdrückt, seine Theorie

36. Entwickelt in *Überlieferungsgeschichtliche Studien. Die sammelnden und bearbeitenden Geschichtswerke im Alten Testament*, Tübingen, [2]1957.

37. *Historisch-kritische Einleitung in die Bücher des Alten Testaments hinsichtlich ihrer Entstehung und Sammlung*, I, 2, Leipzig, 1890, pp. 90-96. Die Hauptvertreter der Theorie der doppelten Redaktion der Königsbücher präsentiert kurz R. D. NELSON, *The Double Redaction of the Deuteronomistic History* (JSOT, Suppl. Series, 18), Sheffield, 1981, 14-19.

38. Zu Vorläufern Hölschers im französisch- und englisch-sprachigen Raum vgl. SPIECKERMANN, *Juda unter Assur* (v.s. Anm. 10), p. 18, n. 7. Ferner den Beitrag von J. LUST in diesem Band.

39. Vgl. etwa den gesperrt gedruckten Text in den *Überlieferungsgeschichtlichen Studien* (v.s. Anm. 36), p. 11.

40. *L.c.*, pp. 180-216.

41. *L.c.*, pp. 91-95 und p. 110, n. 1. Noth scheint sich subjektiv des Alters und des forschungsgeschichtlichen Gewichts der Theorie von der doppelten Redaktion der Königsbücher nicht ganz bewußt gewesen zu sein. Wenigstens sagt er l.c., p. 91, n. 1, «neuerdings» denke man gern an so etwas. Diese Formulierung hätte er ja wohl kaum benutzt, wenn er vor Augen gehabt hätte, daß schon Kuenen und Wellhausen die Theorie vertreten haben.

ist im Grunde ein äußerst gefährdeter Balanceakt. Wenn man die Anmerkungen der «Überlieferungsgeschichtlichen Studien» genau besieht, stellt man ja auch bald fest, daß er seinen *einen* Deuteronomisten nur durchhalten konnte, indem er recht viele Unstimmigkeiten entweder in die Diskrepanz des übernommenen Quellenmaterials oder in reichlich angenommene spätere Zusätze abschob.

Die Reaktion der Kollegen ließ erstaunlich lange auf sich warten, von einzelnen Freunden des Alterarbeiteten [42] und dem sofort hellsichtigen Gerhard von Rad abgesehen, der aber so vorsichtig und höflich formulierte, daß sein Dissens kaum auffiel [43]. Noths «Deuteronomistisches Geschichtswerk» wurde fast allgemein rezipiert [44]. Erst in den letzten beiden Jahrzehnten hat die wirkliche Auseinandersetzung mit ihm begonnen, und sie ist noch voll im Gang [45]. Dabei entwickelten sich zwei Richtungen, die zunächst ohne jede Kommunikation untereinander die gleichen Probleme auf zwei verschiedene Weisen zu lösen versuchten. Ich verbinde sie am besten wieder mit zwei Namen, obwohl das an sich eine ungebührliche Vereinfachung ist. Wir können von der «Richtung Cross» von der «Richtung Smend» sprechen.

Rudolf Smend [46] und seine Schüler [47] bleiben bei Noths exilischem

42. Auffallend ist, daß gerade die Verfasser von Kommentaren und Einleitungswerken Noth gegenüber zur Vorsicht geneigt waren, offenbar weil sie das Gewicht der vorangehenden Forschung stärker spürten und zum Teil wohl auch schon an ihren Werken gearbeitet hatten, bevor Noths Theorie bekannt wurde. An Kommentatoren vgl. J.A. MONTGOMERY/H.S. GEHMAN, *A Critical and Exegetical Commentary on the Books of the Kings* (ICC), Edinburgh, 1951; J. GRAY, *I & II Kings: A Commentary* (OT Library), London, 1964; an «Einleitungen» vgl. R.H. PFEIFFER, *Introduction to the Old Testament*, Revised Ed., New York, 1948; O. EISSFELDT, *Einleitung in das Alte Testament*, 3., neuarbeitete Auflage, Tübingen, 1964; G. FOHRER, *Einleitung in das Alte Testament. Begründet von Ernst Sellin*, Heidelberg, [10]1965. EISSFELDT hatte zunächst monographisch reagiert: *Geschichtsschreibung im Alten Testament. Ein kritischer Bericht über die neueste Literatur dazu*, Berlin, 1948. Einzelnes zu den frühen Reaktionen auf NOTHS Theorie bei JENNI, *Zwei Jahrzehnte Forschung* (v.s. Anm. 12), pp. 97-118.

43. *Die deuteronomistische Geschichtstheologie in den Königsbüchern*, in *Deuteronomium-Studien* (FRLANT, 58), Göttingen, 1947, pp. 52-64.

44. Typisch dürften etwa die einfühlsame Darstellung bei G. MINETTE DE TILLESSE, *Martin Noth et la Redaktionsgeschichte des livres historiques*, in *Aux grands carrefours de la révélation et de l'exégèse de l'Ancien Testament* (Ed. Ch. HAURET; Recherches Bibliques, 8), Bruges, 1967, pp. 51-75, oder der fest von NOTHS Theorie überzeugte Forschungsbericht von A.N. RADJAWANE, *Das deuteronomistische Geschichtswerk. Ein Forschungsbericht*, in *TR* 38 (1974) 177-216, sein.

45. Als deren neueste Darstellung vgl. R. RENDTORFF, *Das Alte Testament. Eine Einführung*, Neukirchen-Vluyn, 1983, pp. 194-199. RENDTORFF plädiert für zwei Hauptredaktionen, eine joschijanische und eine exilische.

46. R. SMEND, *Das Gesetz und die Völker. Ein Beitrag zur deuteronomistischen Redaktionsgeschichte*, in *Probleme biblischer Theologie. Gerhard von Rad zum 70. Geburtstag*, München, 1971, pp. 494-509. Hier arbeitete er eine zweite dtr Schicht in Jos und Ri heraus,die er DtrN nannte. Die Annahmen seiner Schüler, die vor allem im Bereich von Sam und Kön arbeiteten, machte er sich in seinem Lehrbuch *Die Entstehung des Alten Testaments* (Theologische Wissenschaft, 1), Stuttgart, 1978, im wesentlichen zu eigen.

47. Vgl. vor allem W. DIETRICH, *Prophetie und Geschichte. Eine redaktionsgeschichtliche*

Zeitansatz, holen aber Noths Anmerkungen gewissermaßen in den Text, indem sie mit mehreren übereinanderliegenden deuteronomistischen Redaktionsschichten rechnen. Hier werden Siglen vom Typ «DtrH», «DtrP» und «DtrN» gebraucht: deuteronomistischer Geschichtsschreiber, prophetischer Deuteronomist, nomistischer Deuteronomist[48]. Frank Moore Cross[49] und seine Schüler[50] knüpfen an der Kritik Gerhard von Rads an. Dieser hatte gegen Noths Deutung des Werks als einer im Endeffekt jeder Zukunftshoffnung baren Rechtfertigung der eingetretenen Katastrophe Israels auf die hoffnungsträchtige Rolle der Davidsverheißung in den Königsbüchern hingewiesen. Diese offenbar im jetzigen Werk fest eingebaute Spannung zwischen zwei verschiedenen Kerygmata verbindet Cross nun mit der alten Anschauung von zwei Redaktionen, einer vorexilischen, hoffnungsgeladen in der Gestalt und dem Werk Joschijas gipfelnden, und einer ergänzenden und vom Faktum des Untergangs Jerusalems her umdeutenden exilischen Redaktion. Im Gegensatz zu den älteren Auffassungen billigt er jedoch seinem joschijanischen Deuteronomisten in Anlehnung an Noths Konzeption in ganz anderem Ausmaß den Charakter eines Autors zu. Ähnliche Ansätze wie

Untersuchung zum deuteronomistischen Geschichtswerk (FRLANT, 108), Göttingen, 1972; T. VEIJOLA, *Die ewige Dynastie. David und die Entstehung seiner Dynastie nach der deuteronomistischen Darstellung* (STAT, 193), Helsinki, 1975; ders., *Das Königtum in der Beurteilung der deuteronomistischen Historiographie* (STAT, 198), Helsinki, 1978; SPIECKERMANN, *Juda unter Assur* (v.s. Anm. 10). Vgl. ebenfalls L. J. HOPPE, *The Origins of Deuteronomy* (Ph.D. Dissertation, Northwestern University, 1978), pp. 325f.; C. LEVIN, *Der Sturz der Königin Atalja. Ein Kapitel zur Geschichte Judas im 9. Jahrhundert v. Chr.* (SBS, 105), Stuttgart, 1982; R. STAHL, *Aspekte der Geschichte deuteronomistischer Theologie. Zur Traditionsgeschichte der Terminologie und zur Redaktionsgeschichte der Redekompositionen* (Habilitationsschrift, Jena, 1982).

48. Im einzelnen gibt es innerhalb der Schule (und noch mehr, wo die Ansätze nur locker übernommen werden) mancherlei Diskrepanzen. Es wäre einmal zu prüfen, in welchem Maß die parallel zu Noth erarbeitete Theorie von A. JEPSEN, *Die Quellen des Königsbuches*, Halle, 1953, für die ganze Schule anregend gewesen ist.

49. *The Structure of the Deuteronomic History*, in *Perspectives of Jewish Learning*, III (Annual of the College of Jewish Studies), Chicago, 1968, pp. 9-24; aufgenommen als Kapitel in ders., *Canaanite Myth and Hebrew Epic: Essays in the History of the Religion of Israel*, Cambridge, MA, 1973, pp. 274-289 (The Themes of the Book of Kings and the Structure of the Deuteronomistic History).

50. R.D. NELSON, *The Redactional Duality of the Deuteronomistic History* (Th.D. Dissertation, Union Theological Seminary in Virginia, 1973), leicht überarbeitet veröffentlicht als *The Double Redaction of the Deuteronomistic History* (JSOT, Suppl. Series, 18), Sheffield, 1981; J.D. LEVENSON, *Who Inserted the Book of the Torah?*, in *HTR* 68 (1975) 203-233; R.E. FRIEDMAN, *From Egypt to Egypt: Dtr*[1] *and Dtr*[2], in *Traditions in Transformation: Turning-Points in Biblical Faith* (FS F. M. Cross), Winona Lake, 1981, pp. 167-192, eingearbeitet in ders., *The Exile and Biblical Narrative. The Formation of the Deuteronomistic and Priestly Works* (Harvard Semitic Monographs, 22), Chico, CA, 1981. Zu RENDTORFF vgl. oben, Anm. 45. Von NELSON vgl. noch *Josiah in the Book of Joshua*, in *JBL* 100 (1981) 531-540.

die von Cross haben sich auch unabhängig von ihm gemeldet, etwa bei Wolfgang Richter [51] und Helga Weippert [52].

Versuche, die beiden Schulen miteinander zu konfrontieren und einen Kompromiß zwischen den beiden Ansätzen auszuarbeiten, haben gerade erst begonnen. Das erste umfassendere Zeugnis dafür ist das soeben erschienene Buch von Andrew D. H. Mayes, The Story of Israel between Settlement and Exile [53]. Für die Auslegung unseres Textes in 2 Kön 22f, der für beide Theorien Schlüsselpositionen einnimmt, bedeutet dies, daß man fast notwendig in umfassendere Fragestellungen hineingezogen wird und in die Gefahr gerät, exegetische Einzelfragen von woanders her zu entscheiden.

Dies gilt natürlich genau so, wenn man einfach von der Konzeption Noths aus arbeitet. Diese wird im übrigen zur Zeit gewissermaßen auf ihrer eigenen Linie radikalisiert. In seinem Buch «Reform und Reformen» macht Hans-Detlev Hoffmann Noth den Vorwurf, seine eigene These von einem wirklichen deuteronomistischen «Autor» nicht konsequent genug durchgehalten zu haben [54]. Das versucht er selbst dann zu tun, indem er die Frage nach rekonstruierbaren Quellen praktisch aufgibt und — auf der Linie Hölschers — die ganze deuteronomistische Arbeit als eine einzige Unternehmung in nachexilischer Zeit konzipiert. Man muß hier eine dritte Linie der Weiterführung des Werkes von Martin Noth sehen, die gerade erst beginnt, sich voll zu artikulieren [55].

51. *Die Bearbeitungen des «Retterbuches» in der deuteronomistischen Epoche* (BBB, 21), Bonn, 1964.

52. *Die «deuteronomistischen» Beurteilungen der Könige von Israel und Juda und das Problem der Redaktion der Königsbücher*, in *Bib* 53 (1972) 301-339; dazu W. B. BARRICK, *On the «Removal of the 'High-Places'» in 1-2 Kings*, in *Bib* 55 (1974) 257-259; E. CORTESE, *Lo schema deuteronomistico per i re di Giuda e d'Israele*, in *Bib* 56 (1975) 37-52; NELSON, *Double Redaction* (v.s. Anm. 37), p. 31.

53. *A Redactional Study of the Deuteronomistic History*, London, 1983. MAYES war schon früher, und zwar offensichtlich noch unabhängig von CROSS, zur Annahme einer ersten, vorexilischen Redaktion gekommen: vgl. sein *Deuteronomy* (New Century Bible Commentary), Grand Rapids, 1979, und den Vorabdruck aus der Einleitung dieses Kommentars *King and covenant: a study of 2 Kings chs 22-23*, in *Harmathena* 125 (1978) 34-47, esp. p. 37. Meine eigenen Denkversuche laufen auf joschianische Abfassung von Vorstadien des exilischen DtrG hinaus, jedoch eher in Einzelstücken, noch nicht in einem einzigen Werk. Das exilische DtrG dürfte noch mehrere Überarbeitungen gehabt haben, darunter den von SMEND in Jos und Ri herausgearbeiteten DtrN. Vgl. zuletzt N. LOHFINK, *Kerygmata des deuteronomistischen Geschichtswerks*, in *Die Botschaft und die Boten* (FS H. W. Wolff) Neukirchen-Vluyn, 1981, pp. 87-100.

54. V.s. Anm. 22, pp. 17-21. Er bezeichnet sein eigenes Programm dann als «konsequent überlieferungsgeschichtliche Analyse» (p. 21).

55. Vgl. vor allem das Einleitungswerk von O. KAISER, *Einleitung in das Alte Testament. Eine Einführung in ihre Ergebnisse und Probleme*, Gütersloh, 1969, in seinen verschiedenen Auflagen. Schon in der ersten wird — mit allen Folgen für alles Deuteronomistische überhaupt, vgl. p. 140 — die Annahme bevorzugt, «das Deuteronomium sei erst in der Zeit der sich konsolidierenden jüdischen Gemeinde in Palästina entstanden» (p. 109). Seit längerer Zeit wird eine ähnliche Annahme — verbunden mit der Idee rein literarischen

Sie läßt sich natürlich nur durchführen, wenn man mit einer höchst «extensiven Deuteronomismusdefinition» [56] arbeitet, durch die die Differenzen und Spannungen, die die anderen Forscher beunruhigen, kein Problem mehr darstellen, und wenn man die Verlagerung des ganzen Geschichtswerkes in so späte Zeit für plausibel halten kann [57].

Das Buch von Hoffmann enthält im übrigen eine der ausführlichsten und originellsten Analysen von 2 Kön 22-23, die bisher geschrieben wurden (101 Seiten) [58]. Ihr ist an Umfang und Gründlichkeit eigentlich nur noch *eine* andere, gerade erschienene an die Seite zu stellen: diejenige von Spieckermann in seinem Buch «Juda unter Assur in der Sargonidenzeit» (130 Seiten) [59]. Sie gehört in den Bereich der Schule von Smend. Aus der Schule von Cross liegt eine Analyse vergleichbarer Intensität leider nicht vor. So möchte ich im folgenden diese beiden Autoren ein wenig vorstellen und sie auf ihre jeweils besondere Leistung und ihre Grenzen hin interpretieren. Sie mögen stellvertretend für die eigentlich literarische Arbeit an 2 Kön 22-23 stehen, die in den letzten beiden Jahrzehnten wieder so heftig in Gang gekommen ist [60].

Charakters des deuteronomischen Gesetzes — in zahlreichen Buchbesprechungen von J. BECKER dem Leser nahegelegt. Er sieht die Zeit voraus, wo in der Bibelwissenschaft «das Deuteronomistische samt dem Deuteronomium seinen ausschließlichen Platz in der exilisch-nachexilischen Restauration erhält» (Besprechung von F.I. ANDERSEN-D.N. FREEDMAN, *Hosea*, in *Bib* 63, 1982, 583-587, esp. p. 585). Konkrete Durchführung an einem Teiltext: WÜRTHWEIN, *Die josianische Reform* (v.s. Anm. 16). Vgl. auch HOPPE, *Origins* (v.s. Anm. 47); C. LEVIN, *Noch einmal: Die Anfänge des Propheten Jeremia*, in *VT* 31 (1981) 428-440, esp. p. 434, n. 9 (zu 2 Kön 22f.: da «spiegelt» schon die älteste Schicht «die Zeit des zweiten Tempels»).

56. So kritisch SPIECKERMANN, *Juda unter Assur* (v.s. Anm. 10), p. 119.

57. Für mich fehlt es an Plausibilität, weil der Abschluß des Werks in 2 Kön 25,27-30 doch viel eher das letzte, gerade noch berichtbare Ereignis ist als ein aus weiter Distanz ausgesuchter Erzählungsabschluß eines Werkes, das bewußt nur eine frühere Epoche darstellen will und die Erzählung nicht bis an die Gegenwart des Autors heranführen möchte. Ferner wirken jene wenigen Texte, die ein Ende des Exils ins Auge fassen (ich denke vor allem an Dtn 4,1-40 und 30,1-10), eher als letzte Lichter, die auf ein an sich durchaus anders konstruiertes Werk aufgesetzt worden sind — selbst wenn sie mit dem Stichwort «Umkehr» schon ihre Basis in älteren Schichten des Werkes haben (hierzu vgl. grundlegend H.W. WOLFF, *Das Kerygma des deuteronomistischen Geschichtswerks*, in *ZAW* 73, 1961, 171-186). Die Zukunftserwartung der «Deuteronomisten», die das Jeremiabuch gestaltet haben, wird hier in einer letzten Kraftanstrengung gerade noch erreicht. Und selbst diese scheint mir noch ganz und gar exilisch, nicht aber nachexilisch zu sein. Zum Verhältnis des Schlusses des DtrG zum Jeremiahbuch vgl. zuletzt K.F. POHLMANN, *Erwägungen zum Schlußkapitel des deuteronomistischen Geschichtswerkes. Oder: Warum wird der Prophet Jeremia in 2 Kön 22-25 nicht erwähnt?*, in *Textgemäß. Aufsätze und Beiträge zur Hermeneutik des Alten Testaments* (FS E. Würthwein), Göttingen, 1979, pp. 94-109.

58. HOFFMANN, *l.c.*, pp. 169-270.

59. SPIECKERMANN, *l.c.*, pp. 30-160.

60. Eine Behandlungen aller Arbeiten seit 1960 zu den beiden Kapiteln oder zu Passagen daraus ist in diesem Zusammenhang leider ganz unmöglich. Deshalb seien — ohne Anspruch auf Vollständigkeit — die bisher nicht erwähnten Titel voll, die anderen mit Kurztitel

4. Ich beginne mit Hoffmann. Für ihn scheinen mir, schon ganz von außen her kommend, zwei Dinge typisch zu sein. Einmal stehen seiner auch für ihn zentralen Analyse von 2 Kön 22-23 schon mehrere andere

zusammengestellt. Da die Arbeiten nur zum geringeren Teil aufeinander Bezug nehmen, dürfte die alphabetische Anordnung praktischer sein. J. ALONSO DIAZ, *La muerte de Josias en la redaccion deuteronomica del libro de loš reyes como anticipo de la teologia del libro de Job*, in *Homenaje a J. Prado*, Madrid, 1975, pp. 167-177; O. BÄCHLI, *Israel und die Völker. Eine Studie zum Deuteronomium* (ATANT, 41), Zürich, 1962, pp. 208ff.; K. BALTZER, *Das Bundesformular* (WMANT, 4), Neukirchen, 1960, pp. 60-62; G. BRAULIK, *Gesetz als Evangelium. Rechtfertigung und Begnadigung nach der deuteronomischen Tora*, in *ZTK* 79 (1982) 127-160, esp. pp. 131-135; W. E. CLABURN, *The Fiscal Basis of Josiah's Reform*, in *JBL* 92 (1973) 11-12; M. DELCOR, *Les cultes étrangers en Israël au moment de la réforme de Josias d'après 2R 23*, in *Mélanges bibliques et orientaux en L'honneur de M. Henri Cazelles* (AOAT, 212) Kevelaer - Neukirchen-Vluyn, 1981, pp. 91-123; ders., *Reflexions sur la pâque du temps de Josias d'après 2 Rois 23,21-23*, in *Henoch* 4 (1982) 205-219; DIETRICH, *Josia und das Gesetzbuch* (v.s. Anm. 10); S. B. FROST, *The Death of Josiah: A Conspiracy of Silence*, in *JBL* 87 (1968) 169-182; Y. M. GRINTZ, *The Josianic Reform and the Book of Deuteronomy*, in *Studies in Early Biblical Ethnology and History*, 1969, pp. 222-241; A. H. J. GUNNEWEG, *Leviten und Priester* (FRLANT, 89), Göttingen, 1965, pp. 118ff.; HOFFMANN, *Reform und Reformen* (v.s. Anm. 22), pp. 169-270; H. HOLLENSTEIN, *Literarkritische Erwägungen zum Bericht über die Reformmaßnahmen Josias 2 Kön xxiii 4ff.*, in *VT* 27 (1977) 321-336; HOPPE, *Origins* (v.s. Anm. 47), pp. 322-328; C. D. ISBELL, *2 Kings 22:3-23:4 and Jeremiah 36: A Stilistic Comparison*, in *JSOT* 8 (1978) 33-45; LEVIN, *Die Anfänge* (v.s. Anm. 55), p. 434, n. 9; J. LINDBLOM, *Erwägungen zur Herkunft der josianischen Tempelurkunde*, Lund, 1971; N. LOHFINK, *Die Bundesurkunde des Königs Josias (Eine Frage an die Deuteronomiumsforschung)*, in *Bib* 44 (1963) 261-288 und 461-498; ders., *Die Gattung der «Historischen Kurzgeschichte» in den letzten Jahren von Juda und in der Zeit des babylonischen Exils*, in *ZAW* 90 (1978) 319-347; J. LUNDBOM, *Lawbook* (v.s. Anm. 35); B. Z. LURIA, *Joshua, Governer of the City, and the High Places of the Gates*, in *Beth Mikra* 23 (1977/78) 136-138; MAIER, *Fachsprache und Religionspolitik* (v.s. Anm. 35); MAYES, *King and Covenant* (v.s. Anm. 53); ders., *Story of Israel* (v.s. Anm. 53), pp. 128-131; J. W. MCKAY, *Further Light on the Horses and Chariot of the Sun in the Jerusalem Temple (2 Kings 23.11)*, in *PEQ* 105 (1973) 167-169; R. P. MERENDINO, *Zu 2 Kön 22,3-23,15: Eine Erwiderung*, in *BZ* 25 (1981) 249-255; NELSON, *Josiah* (v.s. Anm. 50); ders., *Double Redaction* (v.s. Anm. 37), pp. 76-85; E. W. NICHOLSON, *The Centralisation of the Cult in Deuteronomy*, in *VT* 13 (1963) 380-389; ders., *II Kings XXII 18 - A Simple Restoration*, in *Hermathena* 97 (1963) 96-98; ders., *Josiah's Reforms and Deuteronomy*, in *Transactions of the Glasgow University Oriental Society* 20 (1965) 77-84; ders., *Deuteronomy and Tradition*, Oxford, 1967, pp. 1ff.; G. ODASSO, *La famiglia di Shafan e la funzione di «'ašer 'al habbayiṯ»* (Diss., Universitas S. Thomae Aqu., Rom, 1978); M. OR, *I have Found the Book of the Law in the House of the Lord*, in *Beth Mikra* 23 (1977/78) 218-220; PERLITT, *Bundestheologie* (v.s. Anm. 33), pp. 8-12; G. PFEIFER, *Die Begegnung zwischen Pharao Necho und König Josia bei Megiddo*, in *MiOr* 15 (1968) 297-307; D. PLATAROTI, *Zum Gebrauch des Wortes* mlk *im Alten Testament*, in *VT* 28 (1978) 286-300; N. POULSSEN, *König und Tempel im Glaubenszeugnis des Alten Testaments* (SBM, 3) Stuttgart, 1967, pp. 101-118; PREUSS, *Deuteronomium* (v.s. Anm. 1), pp. 1-19; J. PRIEST, *Huldah's Oracle*, in *VT* 30 (1980) 366-368; H. REVIV, *The Pattern of the Pan-Tribal Assembly in the Old Testament*, in *JNES* 8 (1980) 85-94; ROSE, *Ausschließlichkeitsanspruch* (v.s. Anm. 16), pp. 163-165; ders., *Bemerkungen* (v.s. Anm. 35); L. ROST, *Josias Passa*, in *Theologie in Geschichte und Kunst* (FS W. Elliger), Witten, 1968, pp. 169-175; ders., *Zur Vorgeschichte der Kultusreform des Josia*, in *VT* 19 (1969) 113-120; J. SCHARBERT, *Jeremia und die Reform des Joschija*, in *Le livre de Jérémie* (v.s. Anm. 16, unter

Dinge voran. Er hat schon untersucht, wie die Königsbücher grundsätzlich die Geschichte der einzelnen Könige zu bauen pflegen[61]. Ebenfalls hat er die Motive und Motivkomplexe beschrieben, die sich durch alle Berichte über Kultmaßnamen der Könige quer hindurchziehen und so ein großes Beziehungsgeflecht herstellen[62]. Schließlich hat er die Grundlegung der Kultpolitik in der Darstellung Salomos, Jerobeams und Rehabeams und die einzelnen Modellfälle der Kultreform in der Darstellung der restlichen Königszeit bis zu Joschija analysiert[63]. Er tritt also mit voller Aufarbeitung dessen an die Analyse von 2 Kön 22-23 heran, was der Leser an Wissen, Urteil und Erwartung schon mit sich bringt, wenn er zur Lektüre dieses Textes kommt[64]. Zweitens verweist Hoffmann bei der Analyse des Textes in den Anmerkungen ständig auf einen sehr umfangreichen Anhang, der «Die deuteronomisch-deuteronomistische Kultsprache» statistisch aufarbeitet[65]. Er bietet hier Listen, die die an sich schon sehr guten und umfassenden Listen von Moshe Weinfeld[66] beträchtlich ergänzen, vor allem auch durch ihre sorgfältige Kommentierung.

Von diesen breiten Voraussetzungen her versucht er nun, den jetzt vorliegenden Text als einheitliches Aussagesystem zu erschließen. Das

CAZELLES), pp. 40-57, esp. pp. 48f.; M. SEKINE, *Beobachtungen zu der josianischen Reform*, in *VT* 22 (1972) 361-368; R. SMEND, *Die Bundesformel* (TS, 68), Zürich, 1963, pp. 8-10; E.J. SMIT, *Death and Burial Formulas in Kings and Chronicles Relating to the Kings of Judah*, in *Biblical Essays: Proceedings of the Ninth Meeting of Die Ou Testamentiese Werkgemeenskap in Suid-Afrika*, Potchefstroom, 1966, pp. 173-177; SPIECKERMANN, *Juda unter Assur* (v.s. Anm. 10), pp. 30-160; P.H. VAUGHAN, *The Meaning of «bāmâ» in the Old Testament: A Study of Etymological, Textual and Archeological Evidence* (SOTS, Monograph Series, 3), Cambridge, 1974; M. WEINFELD, *Cult Centralisation in Israel in the Light of a Neo-Babylonian Analogy*, in *JNES* 23 (1964) 202-212, esp. pp. 211f.; P. WELTEN, *Kulthöhe und Jahwetempel*, in *ZDPV* 88 (1972) 19-37, esp. p. 32; H.G.M. WILLIAMSON, *The Death of Josiah and the Continuing Development of the Deuteronomic History*, in *VT* 32 (1982) 242-248; WISEMAN, *Is it Peace?* (v.s. Anm. 34), esp. p. 325; H.W. WOLFF, *Das Ende des Heiligtums in Bethel*, in *Archäologie und Altes Testament. FS Kurt Galling*, Tübingen, 1970, 287-298; WÜRTHWEIN, *Josianische Reform* (v.s. Anm. 16). Die wichtigsten literarischen Analysen beider Kapitel oder größerer Teile daraus sind die Arbeiten von DIETRICH, HOFFMANN, HOLLENSTEIN, LOHFINK, MAYES, NELSON, ROSE, SPIECKERMANN und WÜRTHWEIN.

61. HOFFMANN, *Reform und Reformen* (v.s. Anm. 22), pp. 33-38.

62. *L.c.*, pp. 38-46.

63. *L.c.*, pp. 47-167.

64. Hierhin passende grundsätzliche Überlegungen über den allmählichen Aufbau der Autor-Leser-Kommunikation in Großtexten und deren Bedeutung für die redaktionsgeschichtliche Arbeit finden sich bei R. OBERFORCHER, *Die Flutprologe als Kompositionsschlüssel der biblischen Urgeschichte. Ein Beitrag zur Redaktionskritik* (Innsbrucker theologische Studien, 8), Innsbruck, 1981, pp. 11-86. Beim Vergleich wird allerdings deutlich, daß HOFFMANN hinter der hier erreichten Fragedifferenzierung zurückbleibt.

65. *L.c.*, pp. 323-366.

66. WEINFELD, *Deuteronomy* (v.s. Anm. 34), pp. 320-365. Ein mehrfach bemerkter Mangel dieser Listen war die Ausklammerung von Gen-Num.

gelingt ihm in sehr hohem Ausmaß. Es ist eine Freude, mit ihm immer neue Querbeziehungen, Anspielungen, Wiederaufnahmen, Baustrukturen zu entdecken, auf die in der bisherigen, wahrlich nicht geringen Literatur noch nie oder doch nicht unter einer das Verständnis der Endfassung fördernden Rücksicht aufmerksam gemacht wurde[67]. Ich glaube, wir sollten Hoffmanns Buch genau studieren. Er gibt uns sehr viel zu lernen.

Leider kann ich seine Ergebnisse hier natürlich nicht ausbreiten. Ich möchte vielmehr, ohne von dem bisher Gesagten etwas zurückzunehmen, sofort zu zwei kritischen Bemerkungen kommen.

Die erste stellt sich gewissermaßen auf seinen eigenen Standpunkt und verfolgt sein bisher gekennzeichnetes Hauptinteresse. Ich glaube, trotz seiner immensen Arbeit hat er an manchen Stellen den Text immer noch nicht genügend erfaßt und beschrieben. Seine Arbeit müßte weitergeführt werden.

So hat er zum Beispiel beobachtet, wie bei der Darstellung der Kultmaßnahmen Joschijas im Gebiet Samariens die eigentlichen Reformnotizen (2 Kön 23,15 und 19) rahmend um die Prophetenlegende 23,16-18 herumgelegt sind[68]:

1. Betel (15)
   2. *Erfüllungserzählung zu 1 Kön 13* (16-18)
3. Die anderen «Höhen» des Nordens (19f.)

Ein analoges Phänomen findet sich aber auch zuvor schon bei der Darstellung der Kultmaßnahmen im Gebiet von Juda:

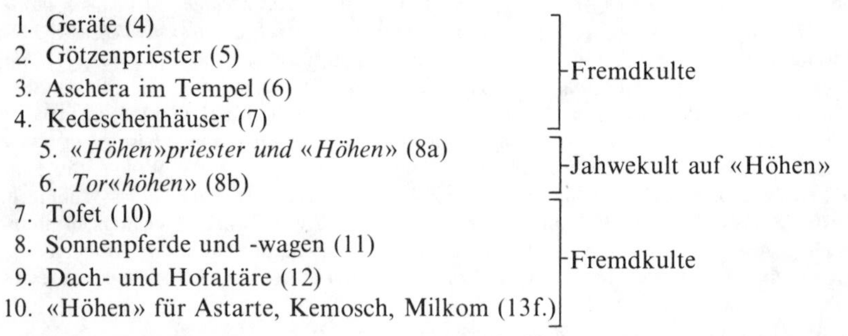

Es gibt hier insgesamt 10 Reformnotizen[69]. Von ihnen beziehen sich genau die beiden mittleren auf die Zentralisation des Jahwekultes in

67. Meist leitete bisher der Gesichtspunkt der Abhebung von Deuteronomischem, oder innerhalb von Deuteronomischem die weitere Zuteilung zu verschiedenen Schichten und Händen.

68. *L.c.*, p. 219 (Schema).

69. Diese Zählung setzt die m.E. gute Analyse des Baus dieser Notizen durch HOFFMANN (pp. 220-223) voraus, vgl. die hilfreiche Übersicht, pp. 226f., in die sich allerdings einige kleine Ungenauigkeiten eingeschlichen haben.

Jerusalem [70], während die vier ersten und die vier letzten die Beseitigung von Fremdkulten behandeln. Daraus folgt natürlich, daß hier weder eine historisch richtige Reihenfolge gesucht werden darf [71] noch daß der Unterschied zwischen Kultreinigung und Kultzentralisation verwischt werden soll [72]. Vielmehr ist die Aussage über die Kultzentralisation in die zentrale Position des rhetorischen Aufbaus gerückt [73] — im übrigen genau analog zu den Aufbauverhältnissen in Dtn 12 [74].

Für den Gesamtaufbau der Joschijadarstellung hat Hoffmann zwar gut die Rahmung durch 2 Kön 22,1-2 und 23,25-30 beschrieben, für das Umrahmte dann aber auf die alten literarkritischen Begriffe «Auffindungsbericht» und «Reformbericht» zurückgegriffen. Dabei geriet er in Schwierigkeiten bei der Festlegung der Grenzen zwischen den beiden «Berichten» und deklarierte außerdem noch ohne jede Begründung das Huldaorakel zur «Mitte der gesamten Komposition» [75]. Es ist jedoch offensichtlich, daß der jetzige Text in 5 Aktionseinheiten gegliedert ist, an deren Anfang jeweils eine «Sendung» oder ein «Befehl» steht, die vom König ausgehen (22,3; 22,12; 23,1; 23,4 und 23,21).

1. Einführungsformel (22,1)
   2. Wertung (22,2)
      3. *KORPUS (22,3-23,24 - Datierung in 22,3 und 23,23f* [76]*)*
         I. 22,3 «König Joschija sandte» *Tempel, Buch, Buße*
         II. 23,12 «Der König befahl» *Hulda-Befragung*

70. Die dazugehörige, chiastisch eingebundene Notiz über die Behandlung der Höhenpriester in Jerusalem gibt diesem Mittelstück sogar ein wenig erzählerische Verbreiterung — parallel zu der noch viel umfangreicheren in 23,16-18. Zum Chiasmus «Priester - 'Höhen' - 'Höhen' - Priester» vgl. HOFFMANN, p. 213.

71. Dies ist die alte, einst wie selbstverständlich gemachte Voraussetzung, derentwegen zum Beispiel noch JEPSEN, *Reform* (v.s. Anm. 13), zu Versumstellungen gegriffen hatte.

72. Auch HOFFMANN, p. 214, meint, die deuteronomistische Kultkritik unterscheide «niemals reinlich zwischen Jahwehöhen und Fremdgötterhöhen». Der Höhenkult werde vielmehr «stets zum Fremdgötterkult». Zweifellos wird ab Salomo der Höhenkult immer in den Bereich des Ersten Gebots gezogen — dennoch gibt es Fälle, wo die anderen Götter mit Namen genannt werden, und andere, wo dies nicht geschieht.

73. HOFFMANN bleibt im Recht, wenn er die Absicht vermutet, durch die «Fülle der Aktionen» Joschijas solle der «Eindruck totaler, restloser Vollständigkeit aller nur denkbaren Reformaktionen» hervorgerufen werden (p. 219), ferner solle der Bericht als größte aller Zusammenstellungen von Kultnotizen im ganzen Werk «gleichsam *alle* bisherigen Kultreformationen in *einer* Reform zusammenfassen» (p. 251). Doch hat diese Reform darüber hinaus noch eine Spitze, die ins Zentrum gestellt ist.

74. Dtn 12,2-3 (gegen fremde Heiligtümer) — 12,4-28 (Opferkult für Jahwe an einem einzigen Heiligtum) — 12,29-31 (gegen fremde Kulte).

75. *L.c.*, p. 169. An dieser methodisch nicht sehr konsequenten Kompositionsanalyse hängt dann praktisch die eher verwirrende Disposition der folgenden 100 Seiten des Buches.

76. Die genaue Entsprechung zur Datierung von 22,3 findet sich in 23,23, aber 23,24 gehört noch einmal mit zur Rahmung des Korpus, da es durch den Namen Hilkija und die Erwähnung der Buchauffindung auf 22,4 und 8 zurückgreift. Eine literarkritische Analyse

III. 23,1 «Der König sandte» *BUNDESSCHLUSS*
IV. 23,4 «Der König befahl» [77] *Kultreformen*
V. 23,21 «Der König befahl» *Passa in Jerusalem*
4. Wertung (23,25-27)
5. Schlußformel (23,28ff.)

Die äußersten Einheiten handeln von Joschijas Sorge für den Tempel, von dem dort gefundenen Buch, von Joschijas Bekehrung bei der Begegnung mit dem Buch (I) und von dem in Anlehnung an dieses Buch im Tempel neu eingerichteten Festgottesdienst (V). Das Zentrum (III) erzählt, wie König und Volk sich vor Jahwe auf dieses Buch verpflichten — durchaus eine Art Gegenpol zum «Bundesschluß in Moab», den das Buch Deuteronomium am Anfang des Geschichtswerkes (vgl. besonders Dtn 28,29) darstellte — wobei es zugleich den Inhalt des Buches mitteilte. Die beiden Zwischenstücke (II und IV) verweisen, chiastisch, nach vorn und hinten in der Geschichte. Das Hulda-Orakel kündet das doppelte, später im Buch geschilderte Ende an: das Ende Joschijas und das Ende Judas [78]. Die Kultreform läßt zurückerinnern: an die Forderung des deuteronomischen Gesetzes, die jetzt endlich erfüllt wird (Reform in Juda), und an die endgültige Aufhebung der für die Geschichte so entscheidenden kultischen Sünde, der Sünde Jerobeams (Reform im Norden). Die geographische Bewegung der Reform entspricht im Übrigen der geographischen Bewegung Israels bei der Landnahme unter Josua: von einem Bereich der Mitte her zunächst der Süden und dann der Norden. Allein von der Baustruktur her faßt 2 Kön 22-23 das ganze deuteronomistische Geschichtswerk wie in einem Brennpunkt zusammen.

Auf diese und ähnliche Weise ließe sich die Arbeit von Hoffmann sicher auch noch an anderen Stellen in seinem eigenen Sinne weiterführen — und doch ist das alles offenbar nur halb in seinem Sinne. Ich komme damit zu meiner zweiten kritischen Einlassung.

Hoffmann sieht diese Analyse des definitiven deuteronomistischen Geschichtswerks dann doch nur als eine Art Sprungbrett an. Er wirft

hätte hier natürlich sehr viel zu bedenken. Doch wenn 23,24 relativ spät hinzugefügt worden ist, dann ist in unserem Zusammenhang zu fragen, inwiefern sein Ergänzer den Vers als die Struktur keineswegs sprengend, eher sogar verdeutlichend empfunden haben könnte.

77. Offensichtlich stört 23,4 eine ohne diesen Vers gegebene schöne Alternanz zwischen den Verben «senden» und «befehlen» in 22,3.12; 23,1.21. Daraus kann man literarkritische Schlüsse ziehen, und man wird sie ziehen müssen. Aber auf der Ebene des Endtextes genügte offenbar eine Anpassung an die anderen erkennbaren Neuansätze. Daß sie jedoch beabsichtigt war, zeigt die Notiz von der Rückkehr nach Jerusalem in 23,20. Sie entspricht der Beobachtung, daß auch die vorangehenden Handlungseinheiten immer nicht nur vom König ausgehen, sondern stets auch beim König in Jerusalem enden — vgl. LOHFINK, *Bundesurkunde* (v.s. Anm. 60), 267-271.

78. Es sollte nicht unbeobachtet bleiben, daß die Doppelstruktur des Hulda-Orakels der Doppelstruktur des «Reformberichts» entspricht.

anderen vor, zu sehr der Literarkritik verhaftet zu sein [79]. Aber er selbst möchte dann «Überlieferungsgeschichte» treiben — und das ist ja ganz genau so Rückfrage hinter den jetzt gegebenen Text in seine Vorgeschichte. Entsprechend diskutiert er regelmäßig die Frage, woher der deuteronomistische Autor seine Kenntnisse gewonnen habe und was letztlich an historischer Faktizität dahinterstehe. Zumeist steht nach Hoffmann nicht viel dahinter. Seine neuen Einsichten in das jetzige Textgefüge werden ihm meistens zum Argument dafür, keine verarbeiteten oder gar eingearbeiteten Vorlagen annehmen zu müssen. So ist er sehr schnell bei der Annahme einer sehr selbständigen schriftstellerischen Arbeit, oft nur unter Benutzung eines Wissens über die Vergangenheit, das aus dem Hörensagen stammt. Und in diesem Zusammenhang wird man nicht an einer sehr kritischen Besichtigung seiner Beweise vorbeikommen. Die höchst erstaunlich funktionierende Endgestalt des deuteronomistischen Geschichtswerk schließt ja keineswegs aus, daß es eine komplizierte Vorgeschichte gehabt hat und daß man diese sogar noch durch Analyse des Textes zumindest teilweise rekonstruieren kann [80].

Mit dem, was Hoffmann an Neuem und Eigenem in die Betrachtung des deuteronomistischen Gesichtswerks eingebracht hat, führt er, vermutlich ohne sich selbst darüber im klaren zu sein, so etwas wie ein neues Paradigma in diesen Forschungsbereich ein. Von seinem Ansatz her wäre eine konsequent synchrone Auslegung der geschichtlichen Bücher möglich. Auch wenn er sich selbst als Vertreter eines diachronen Ansatzes verstehen möchte, sollte der bei ihm implizierte synchrone Ansatz aufgegriffen werden [81]. Dabei steht von vornherein fest, daß es

79. *L.c.*, pp. 18f., wirft er dabei wohl zu Unrecht die Annahme von Redaktionsschichten mit der Rekonstruktion von «Quellenfäden» in einen Topf.

80. Die Einzelkritik an den «überlieferungsgeschichtlichen» Argumenten von HOFFMANN kann hier natürlich nicht geleistet werden. Ein kleines Beispiel klang anfangs an, im Zusammenhang mit der Frage nach der Existenz einer Jerusalemer Neustadt zur Zeit Joschijas (vgl. oben bei Anm. 22-24).

81. Analysen des Endtextes des deuteronomistischen Geschichtswerks, wie HOFFMANN, sie vorlegt, sind erst ein Anfang «synchroner» literarkritischer Analyse. Ganz andere Fragen müßten dann hinzukommen, etwa Fragen der Art, wie R. POLZIN, *Moses and the Deuteronomist: A Literary Study of the Deuteronomic History, I, Deuteronomy, Joshua, Judges*, New York, 1980, sie stellt. Das Zusammenspiel zwischen der «berichtenden» Rede (des Autors) und der «berichteten» Rede (Moses, verschiedener Propheten und Könige, Gottes selbst) erreicht gerade in 2 Kön 22-23 eine letzte Krise. Wer hat am Ende recht — der um das Orakel fragende König, das Orakel der Prophetin, der nicht mehr durch einen Propheten, ja eigentlich nur noch zu sich selbst sprechende Gott von 23,27, der ihn in 23,26 schon im voraus bestätigende und dann die Erfüllung aberzählende Autor? Oder gibt es noch andere «berichtete» Rede aus dem Anfang des Werkes, etwa aus Dtn 4 und Dtn 30, die über all das unberührt hinausragt und noch durch kein erzähltes Geschehen ausgelöscht ist, ja durch das seltsam offene Schlußstück des Autors in 2 Kön 25,27-30 in eine noch unerzählbare Zukunft hineingehalten wird? Dabei ist zu beachten, daß in solchen

ein letztes Entweder-Oder zwischen den beiden Ansätzen nicht geben kann. Beide Fragen ergänzen einander [82]. Nur haben wir bisher zu wenig synchron gefragt, und die diachrone Frage muß nicht notwendig jenen Typ von Antworten hervorrufen, den Hoffmann als «konsequent überlieferungsgeschichtlich» bezeichnet. Diachron ansetzende Untersuchungen, die sich selbst vor der Feststellung mehrfacher Schichtung von Texten nicht fürchten, sind weiterhin willkommen [83].

5. Das gilt zum Beispiel von der Analyse der Joschija-Kapitel durch Spieckermann, der ich mich nun zuwende [84]. Spieckermann ist auf das aus, was er mehrfach als das «literarhistorische Gefüge» des Textes bezeichnet. Letztlich will er die historische Nachricht. Hat er sie, dann wertet er sie sofort aus. Im Gang seiner den Text entlangwandernden Analyse rekonstruiert er immer sofort schon unter Herbeiziehung aller anderen Geschichtsquellen die historischen Vorgänge.

Zusammenhängen der Begriff «Autor» nicht auf einen historischen Verfasser und dessen subjektive Intention verweist, sondern ein Element im Sinngefüge des Werkes selbst meint, den im Text selbst sich präsentierenden «Autor». POLZIN, l.c., p. 18, sagt das mit aller wünschenswerten Klarheit: «There may actually have been no single individual or recognizable group to whom this term refers. I use it heuristically to designate that imagined personification of a combination of literary features that seem to constitute the literary composition of the Deuteronomic History. For me, the text creates the Deuteronomist's features as much as it creates those of Moses. The Deuteronomist is the 'implied author' of this work».

82. Eine Reihenfolge, in der man nacheinander fragen müßte, scheint mir nicht festlegbar zu sein. Die beiden Aspekte bedingen sich gegenseitig. Wohl ist in der augenblicklichen Forschungssituation zu vermuten, daß intensivere synchrone Textanalyse allzu leichtsinnige Schweifzüge der literarkritischen Fantasie ein wenig erschweren würde. Es wäre vielleicht in manchen Fällen nicht mehr ganz so einfach, literarkritisch relevante Spannungen, Widersprüche und Doppelungen zu entdecken — und das sind ja die Beobachtungen, die einer nachprüfbaren Literarkritik zugrundeliegen müßten.

83. Es muß natürlich stets mit der Möglichkeit gerechnet werden, daß ein konkreter, der Untersuchung vorgelegter Text *keine* «Vorgeschichte» hat, sondern so, wie er vorliegt, von einem einzigen Verfasser stammt. Mir scheint zum Beispiel Dtn 4,1-40 keinerlei «literarhistorisches Gefüge» aufzuweisen. Doch schließt eine solche Feststellung in keiner Weise diachrone Fragestellungen aus. Denn es ist zunächst einmal sinnvoll, den Text mit den üblichen Methoden daraufhin zu untersuchen, *ob* er «geschichtet» ist. Ist die Antwort negativ, dann hat man dennoch diachron gefragt. Das hat für diesen Text mit diesem Ergebnis z.B. G. BRAULIK, *Literarkritik und archäologische Stratigraphie. Zu S. Mittmanns Analyse von Dt 4,1-40*, in *Bib* 59 (1978) 351-383, getan — eine andere Lektüre dieser Arbeit ginge von einem Mißverständnis des Titels aus und müßte in einer Fehlinterpretation der Arbeit enden. Eine solche Arbeit ist jederzeit mit literarkritischen Argumenten falsifizierbar, falls solche sich auftreiben lassen. Hat sich aber einmal ergeben, daß ein Text wie Dtn 4,1-40 literarisch aus einem Guß ist, dann ist immer noch kein Ende mit diachronen Fragemöglichkeiten. Man muß nach vorausliegenden Inhalten und Formen, vielleicht sogar nach Texten fragen, mit denen dieser Text ein Gespräch führt. Schließlich hat der umfassendere Kontext, in diesem Fall das Deuteronomium und das Deuteronomistische Geschichtswerk, eine Entstehungsgeschichte, und innerhalb ihrer muß der Ort des Textes bestimmt werden. Alle diese Fragen sind diachron orientiert und von synchroner Textanalyse zu unterscheiden.

84. SPIECKERMANN, *Juda unter Assur* (v.s. Anm. 10), pp. 30-160.

Man mag fragen, ob diese Darstellungstechnik die Durchsichtigkeit der Textanalyse fördert. Doch wird man bestätigen müssen, daß Spieckermann sich fast immer gründlich mit der bisherigen Forschung auseinandersetzt. Ganz nebenbei liefert er zum Beispiel die meines Wissens bisher ausführlichste Untersuchung des Problems der *w^{e}qaṭal*-Narrative [85], die ja eine altbekannte Crux bei der Analyse des sogenannten Reformberichts zwischen 23,4 und 23,15 darstellen [86]. Er setzt sich an entscheidenden Stellen, vor allem beim Hulda-Orakel, vom Smend-Schüler Walter Dietrich ab [87], doch am Ende ergibt sich auch bei ihm ein Bild der Textschichtung, das der an Smend anknüpfenden Richtung zuzuordnen ist [88]. Eine Quelle, die nacheinander von Tempelreparatur [89], Buchfund, Buße des Königs, Hulda-Orakel, Bundesschluß und Kultreformen in Jerusalem und Juda erzählte, ist ausführlich verwertet und weithin erhalten. Der «DtrH» umrahmte sie ganz schmal in 2 Kön 22,2 und 23,28, setzte dem Reformbericht einige Lichter auf und ließ die Reformmaßnahmen in 23,15 bis nach Betel reichen. Der «DtrP» fügte die Friedhofszene in 23,16-20 hinzu. Dann haben noch zwei verschiedene «DtrN» das Hulda-Orakel überarbeitet und umge-

85. *L.c.*, pp. 120-130. Dort weitere Literaturangaben. Zu ergänzen wäre: W. GROSS, OTTO RÖSSLER und die Diskussion um das althebräische Verbalsystem, in *BN* 18 (1982) 28-78, esp. pp. 68f. (mit weiterer Literatur).

86. Das Phänomen wurde literarkritisch zum erstenmal voll ausgewertet durch B. STADE, *Anmerkungen zu 2 Kö. 10-14*, in *ZAW* 5 (1885) 275-297. Im Berichtzeitraum wurde es neu benutzt durch HOLLENSTEIN (v.s. Anm. 60), dem sich andere anschlossen. SPIECKERMANN kommt zu dem Ergebnis, daß man seit dem 8. Jahrhundert mit *w^{e}qaṭal*-Narrativen rechnen darf und deshalb mit literarkritischer Auswertung sehr zurückhaltend sein muß. Hierin ist ihm wohl zuzustimmen, soweit es um die Annahme sehr später und jeweils einzelner Zusätze geht. Doch bleibt es auch bei grundzätzlicher Möglichkeit der Form im 7. und 6. Jahrhundert ein literarkritisch beachtlicher Befund, wenn die Belege der Form innerhalb eines genau umgrenzbaren Textstückes sich häufen, während sie im Rest der beiden Kapitel völlig fehlen.

87. Für DIETRICH, *Prophetie und Geschichte* (v.s. Anm. 47), pp. 55-58, wurde eine Vorlage durch «DtrP» und «DtrN» überarbeitet, für SPIECKERMANN, pp. 58-71, nur durch «DtrN». Aus den in Anm. 60 genannten Autoren haben sich mit dem Hulda-Orakel insbesondere noch HOFFMANN (pp. 170-189), MAYES (*King and Covenant*, pp. 38-45; *Story of Israel*, pp. 128-130), NELSON (*Double Redaction*, pp. 76-79), NICHOLSON (*Deuteronomy and Tradition*, pp. 14f.), PRIEST, ROSE (*Bemerkungen*) und WÜRTHWEIN (pp. 402-496) befaßt. Vgl. ferner LOHFINK, *Kurzgeschichte* (v.s. Anm. 60), p. 320, n. 8, und p. 340, n. 53; CROSS, *Canaanite Myth* (v.s. Anm. 49), p. 286, n. 46. An der Divergenz der Meinungen und der Art ihrer Begründung wird deutlich, daß der Sachverhalt mit den uns zur Verfügung stehenden Mitteln wohl nie mehr überzeugend erhellt werden kann. Die Gründe, mit einer umdeutenden Überarbeitung im Licht von Megiddo und vom Ende Jerusalems zu rechnen, bleiben aber bestehen, selbst wenn man auf Rekonstruktion eines älteren Textes verzichten muß. Die Rekonstruktion SPIECKERMANNS bleibt eine unter vielen Denkmöglichkeiten.

88. Die folgenden Angaben vergröbern etwas. Genaueres ist aus den übersichtlichen «Textrekonstruktionen» im «Appendix» zu entnehmen: vgl. dort pp. 423-429.

89. Hierzu hat SPIECKERMANN, pp. 179-182, eine ausgezeichnete Diskussion der Frage des Verhältnisses zu 2 Kön 12, die HOFFMANNS Analyse (l.c., pp. 118-125) schlicht aussticht.

deutet, die Bundesschlußpassage mit deuteronomischen Sprachelementen versehen, in 23,21-23 die Passa-Feier eingesetzt, in 23,24 eine weitere Reformtat angehängt und vor allem die Geschichtsdeutung in 23,25-27 geschaffen, die Joschija zwar über alle seine Vorgänger erhebt, aber Gottes Zorn wegen der Sünden Manasses doch noch größer sein läßt. Schließlich gab es noch später kleinere Erweiterungen verschiedener Art.

Meine erste Frage an Spieckermann lautet, ob er mit den drei Smendschen Deuteronomisten dem Befund vor allem in der zweiten Hälfte von Kapitel 23 wirklich gerecht wird oder nicht doch ein vorgegebenes System in den Text einträgt. Ist es wirklich das Naheliegende, daß der Versuch einer Erklärung dafür, daß der fromme Joschija seine Reformen vergebens durchgeführt habe und Jerusalem und Juda trotzdem untergangen seien, weder von dem schon mehr als zwei Jahrzehnte nach der Zerstörung Jerusalems schreibenden «DtrH» noch von einem ihn ergänzenden «DtrP», sondern erst von einem nochmals späteren «DtrN» gemacht wurde — indem nämlich er erst das Hulda-Orakel überarbeitete und die geschichtsdeutende Notiz in 23,25-27 einsetzte? Die Rede von «*diesem* Bundesdokument» in 23,21 klingt so, als habe sie einmal recht nah an 23,3 gestanden, beide Verse kennen Mose nicht, in 23,3 ist nur von den Geboten, Satzungen und Gesetzen *Jahwes* die Rede. Diese beiden Verse sollen also verschiedenen Händen zugeteilt werden, aber die Rede von *Jahwes* Geboten, Satzungen, und Gesetzen in 23,3 dann ausgerechnet jenem «DtrN», der in 23,25 das gefundene Dokument nicht als Wort Jahwes kennzeichnet, sondern mit anderer Begrifflichkeit nun gerade von der «Tora *Moses*» redet? In 23,3 soll auch genau jener deuteronomisch oder deuteronomistisch niemals belegbare Ausdruck «aus ganzem Herzen und aus ganzer Seele» (ohne Suffixe!) von der gleichen Hand eingetragen sein, die sich in 23,25 des präzisen Ausdrucks aus Dtn 6,5 bediente: «aus *seinem* ganzen Herzen und aus *seiner* ganzen Seele und *aus seiner ganzen Kraft*». Wo sind die gewichtigen Gründe, die zu so wenig plausiblen Annahmen zwingen könnten? Muß außerdem für die Prophetengeschichte in 23,16-18 eine eigene Redaktionsschicht angenommen werden? Sprechen in 23,25 und 23,26f. die sehr verschiedenen Urteile über Joschija und das, was auf ihn folgte, nicht doch eher dafür, daß zunächst das eine Urteil dastand und später das andere, einschränkend und umwendend, aufgrund der faktischen Ereignisse hinzugefügt werden mußte? Dieser Textbereich ist zweifellos nicht in einem Zug verfaßt worden. Und viele Beobachtungen weisen dann auf anderes hin als das, was Spieckermann als seine Schichtung behauptet. Er wußte wohl doch schon zu genau im voraus, daß es die Größen «DtrH», «DtrP» und «DtrN» gibt und von welcher Art das sein muß, was man ihnen jeweils zuzuteilen hat [90].

90. Man vergleiche etwa die Art, auf die «DtrN» *l.c.*, pp. 43-46, eingeführt wird.

Ich möchte demgegenüber die Verse über Joschijas Passa weiterhin zu den Vorlagen rechnen [91]. Ferner scheint mir, daß sich gerade im Bereich von 23,25 ab eine der Stellen der Königsbücher findet, wo die Entscheidung zwischen Smend und Cross fallen muß — weshalb man hier viel sorgfältiger und mit viel größerer Reflexion über mögliche Alternativen argumentieren müßte [92]. Ich vermute, daß am Ende die Entscheidung für die alte Annahme Kuenens von einer vorexilischen und einer exilischen Ausgabe des Geschichtswerks herauskommen wird [93].

91. In diesem Punkt halte ich an meiner Rekonstruktion des Quellentextes 22,3-23,3.21-23 fest: vgl. *Bundesurkunde* und *Kurzgeschichte* (v.s. Anm. 60). Weder SPIECKERMANN noch andere Autoren der Zwischenzeit haben meine Beobachtungen, die für die Zugehörigkeit von 23,21-23 zum Grundbestand von 22,3-23,3 sprechen, erwähnt und diskutiert. Das einzige diskussionswürdige Argument gegen eine Zuteilung von 23,21-23 zu einer zeitgenössischen Quelle wäre das kalendarische: Das 18. Jahr Joschijas, in dem sowohl Buchfund wie Passafest anzusetzen seien, falls der Text zeitgenössisch ist, habe im Frühjahr begonnen, sodaß zwischen Buchfund und Passa keine Zeit für die Kultreformen bleibe. Doch dieses Argument gilt nur, wenn man — literarisch — auch den «Reformbericht» zur gleichen Quelle rechnet oder — historisch — alle Reformen hinter den Buchfund und vor das Passa Joschijas setzt. Beides ist bestreitbar. Ferner setzt es als gesichert voraus, daß die hier verwendete Jahreszählung mit Frühjahrsjahren arbeitete. WÜRTHWEIN, *Josianische Reform* (v.s. Anm. 16), p. 408, schreibt zwar: «Von allen Sachverständigen, die sich mit der alttestamentlichen Chronologie beschäftigt haben, wird als sicher angenommen, daß der Jahresbeginn zur Zeit Josias im Frühjahr lag.» Aber diese Behauptung beweist höchstens, daß WÜRTHWEIN zumindest einen Teil dieser «Sachverständigen» nicht konsultiert hat. Er gibt nicht weiter an, auf wen er sich eigentlich stützt. Seit der Veröffentlichung von Nebukadnezzars Chronik ist die Frage des Jahresbeginns sowieso wieder neu eröffnet. Ein Teil der «Sachverständigen» hat auch vorher stets für die Zeit Josias noch mit Herbstjahren gerechnet. Dabei war 2 Kön 23,23 zugegebenermaßen eines ihrer Argumente. Wenn man jedoch weiß, wie spärlich die Anhaltspunkte sind, mit denen kalendarische Überlegungen arbeiten müssen, sollte man zunächst einmal denen mißtrauen, die eine mögliche Informationsquelle ausschalten, weil sie nicht in ihr schon bestehendes System paßt. Und die literarkritischen Probleme sollte man zunächst einmal mit literarkritischen Argumenten angehen. Ein anderes Argument gegen den Quellencharakter von 23,21-23 ist der Ausdruck «seit den Tagen der Richter, die Israel gerichtet haben». Eine «Richterzeit» sei erst ein deuteronomistisches Konstrukt. Nun ist der Ausdruck unmöglich als deuteronomistisch nachweisbar, denn er ist als ganzer einmalig (man vergleiche die vergleichbarsten Texte: 2 Sam 7,11 und Rut 1,1). Daß man in der Umgebung Joschijas, in der zur gleichen Zeit möglicherweise die erste deuteronomistische Ausgabe des Richterbuchs angefertigt wurde, wirklich die vorkönigliche Zeit Israels nicht so bezeichnen konnte, wäre positiv zu beweisen.

92. Vgl. dazu jetzt in diesem Band den Beitrag von G. VANONI.

93. Als Werk der exilischen Redaktion betrachte ich, so wie ich die Dinge im Augenblick sehe, die Überarbeitung des Huldaorakels (mit der Hinleitung in 22,13b), vielleicht einige Ergänzungen im Bereich des «Reformberichts», dann 23,26ff., möglicherweise auch 23,24. Nimmt man diese Teile aus dem Text heraus, dann ist die oben in der Auseinandersetzung mit HOFFMANN aufgewiesene Gesamtstruktur von 2 Kön 22-23 eher noch deutlicher zu erkennen (wobei das dann positive Hulda-Orakel in eine offene Zukunft verwiese). Der eigentliche Bau des Textes geschah demnach durch den vorexilischen Deuteronomisten, der in 23,25 das aufgefundene Buch schon klar als die «Tora Moses» bezeichnet hat. Das läßt Fragen hinsichtlich einer speziellen «nomistischen» Redaktion aufkommen, zumindest hier am Ende der Königsbücher.

Meine zweite Frage an Spieckermann bezieht sich auf die Vorlage, die der älteste Deuteronomist (gleichgültig, ob man ihn vorexilisch oder exilisch ansetzt) benutzt hat. Spieckermann nimmt die literarische Einheit der Verse, die er einer Vorlage zuteilt, an. Ich meine, so etwas müßte er positiv nachweisen, zumal durch längere Zeit hindurch die gegenteilige Annahme üblich war.

Ursprünglich kommt die Unterscheidung eines «Auffindungsberichtes» und eines «Reformberichtes» von Östreicher[94]. Er war zweifellos von der Disposition des Stoffes in der Chronik zu seiner Annahme geführt worden, doch hatte er sie mit Beobachtungen am Text unterbaut. Diese haben dann viele Autoren überzeugt, die ihm in seiner Einschätzung der Chronik nicht ohne weiteres folgten[95]. Mit dem Hauptargument, dem stilistischen Unterschied zwischen dem «Auffindungs-» und dem «Reformbericht», setzt sich Spieckermann auseinander. Er gibt ihn zu, hält ihn aber für unwichtig, da gegenstandsbedingt[96]. Seltsamerweise argumentiert er dann allerdings bei 23,16-18 für eine andere Schicht damit, daß hier «die Auflistung von Reformobjekten durch eine im Erzählstil vorgetragene Episode abgelöst» werde[97]. Warum, was hier ein Kriterium ist, dort nicht als solches gelten darf, erklärt er nicht.

Es mag für die historische Betrachtung unbefriedigender sein, wenn der sachlich durchaus wahrscheinliche Zusammenhang zwischen Torafund, Bundesschluß und Kultzentralisation (vielleicht sogar auch Kultreinigung) literarisch erst vom ersten Deuteronomisten hergestellt wurde und nicht schon in dessen Quellenbereich greifbar ist[98]. Aber das müßte

94. Vgl. für seine Abgrenzungen oben Anm. 8 und 9.

95. Zu ihnen gehörten etwa ALT, GRAY, JEPSEN, NOTH — für Stellenangaben vgl. DIETRICH, *Josia und das Gesetzbuch* (v.s. Anm. 10), p. 15, nn. 9 und 10. Im Berichtszeitraum: BARTH, *Jesaja-Worte* (v.s. Anm. 16), p. 251; LOHFINK, *Bundesurkunde* (v.s. Anm. 60), pp. 265-267; NELSON, *Double Redaction* (v.s. Anm. 37), pp. 76-85.

96. *L.c.*, p. 79.

97. *L.c.*, p. 116.

98. Das gilt auch im Fall von Theorien, die nur bei dem «Reformbericht» mit einer schriftlichen Quelle rechnen und die Darstellung von Buchfund, Hulda-Befragung und Bundesschluß erst als Werk eines «Deuteronomisten» (der dann meist auch noch sehr spät angesetzt wird) betrachten: vgl. etwa WÜRTHWEIN (v.s. Anm. 16), HOPPE (v.s. Anm. 47), MAYES (mit 2 Varianten; v.s. Anm. 53). Der Sache nach halte ich diese Position kaum für möglich. Wenn sich eine Quelle im Bereich von 2 Kön 22-23 rekonstruieren läßt, dann hinter der sehr eigengeprägten Erzählung von Tempelerneuerungsbeflissenheit des Königs, Buchfund, königlicher Buße, Prophetenbefragung, Bundesschluß und Passa-Feier. Das anscheinend «Deuteronomistische» in diesem Bereich erweist sich bei genauerem Zusehen gerade als nichtdeuternomistisch, wenn auch ganz in der Nähe befindlich. Die Erzähltechnik ist recht subtil und zeigt eher Verwandtschaft zu erzählenden Stücken im Jeremiabuch als zu redaktionell verfaßten «deuteronomistischen» Texten in Dtn — 2 Kön (hierzu LOHFINK, *Kurzgeschichte*, v.s. Anm. 60). Das muß jedoch nicht notwendig ein Indiz für die Entstehungszeit sein, sondern kann auch auf ähnliche ursprüngliche Zweckbestimmung oder auf Herkunft aus dem Umkreis der Schafanfamilie weisen. Der

man aushalten können, falls die Textanalyse es nahelegt. Durch die Beobachtungen an 2 Kön 23,5-14, die oben bei der Auseinandersetzung mit Hoffmann gemacht wurden, wird die Annahme, der Deuteronomist wolle hier irgendetwas chronologisch ordnen, sowieso noch mehr geschwächt [99]. Auch das müßte man aushalten können, vor allem, weil der Verfasser bei allem chronologischen Desinteresse doch offenbar Wert darauf legt, Fakten mitzuteilen. Und es muß ihn dem Historiker noch einmal sympathischer machen, wenn er davon ausgehen kann, daß die erste deuteronomische Hand schon vorexilisch, also praktisch zeitgenössisch ist.

Ich breche hier ab. Spieckermanns monumentales Buch, in dem die Analyse von 2 Kön 22-23 ja nur einen einzigen Baustein darstellt, holt so viel an bisheriger Diskussion über Joschija und seine Zeit, auch über das Buch Deuteronomium, zusammen, daß es gut zu einem Ausgangspunkt der weiteren Diskussion werden kann. Ausgangspunkt neuer Diskussion muß es allerdings werden. Denn es ist zu sehr in die noch keineswegs entschiedene Diskussion verwickelt, wie heute eigentlich Noths Theorie vom Deuteronomistischen Geschichtswerk abgewandelt aufrechterhalten werden könnte.

6. Diese Diskussion, und überhaupt alles, was über 2 Kön 22-23 gearbeitet wird, ist bedeutsam für die Erforschung des Deuterononiums selbst. Denn hier werden die Weichen gestellt. Hier entscheidet sich, wohin das Deuteronomium historisch gehört — und daran hängt wieder vieles in der Auslegung des Buches. Da das Buch Deuteronomium ein Teil des deuteronomistischen Geschichtswerkes sein könnte, sind Hypothesen über die Redaktionsgeschichte dieses Werkes auch immer zugleich Fragen, wo und wie im Deuteronomium selbst die gleichen redaktionellen Schichten gefunden werden könnten. Derartiges wird zwar schon lange für die Rahmenteile des Deuteronomiums diskutiert, aber noch recht selten für das Mittelstück [100]. Auch vieles über die Sprache und die literarische Technik des Deuteronomiums läßt sich nicht am Deuteronomium allein entscheiden. Schließlich müßten methodo-

«Reformbericht» dagegen enthält sehr viele «deuteronomistische» Merkmale, und zwar solche, die in den Horizont der deuteronomistischen Königsbücher gehören.

99. Ich halte es kaum für beweisbar, daß er hier eine schriftlich vorliegende Quelle benutzte — vgl. Anm. 98. Daß ihm eine vorlag, ist natürlich möglich. Daß er sie, wenn sie ihm vorlag, relativ frei benutzte, ist wahrscheinlich. Daß er — speziell wenn er noch zu Lebzeiten von Joschija schrieb — sich einfach nur auf persönliche Erinnerung und allgemein zuhandenes Wissen stützte, ist ebenso möglich.

100. Das mag damit zusammenhängen, daß nach NOTH der «Deuteronomist» Dtn 5-30 als Block in sein Werk eingefügt hat. Erste Fragen hierzu äußerte 1961 WOLFF, *Kerygma* (v.s. Anm. 57), pp. 180-182, dann ging als erster G. MINETTE DE TILESSE, *Sections «tu» et sections «vous» dans le Deutéronome*, in *VT* 12 (1962) 29-87, die Frage im Sinne einer Differenzierung von NOTHS Position an. Mein letzter Beitrag zur Frage: *Kerygmata* (v.s. Anm. 53).

logische Einsichten, etwa die, daß sowohl diachrone als auch synchrone Textanalyse notwendig ist, auch bei der Arbeit am Deuteronomium selbst ganz anders als bisher zum Zuge kommen.

Offenbacher Landstraße 224 Norbert LOHFINK
D-6000 Frankfurt am Main 70

ZWEITER TEIL

DAS DEUTERONOMISCHE PHÄNOMEN UND DAS BUCH ALS GANZES

LOI ORALE ET LOI ÉCRITE DANS LE DEUTÉRONOME

A la différence des contrats de vassalité qui se présentent eux-mêmes, tôt ou tard, comme des «paroles et serment inscrits sur cette tablette» [1], le testament de Moïse dans le Deutéronome est une collection d'enseignements oraux. Cette activité orale de Moïse recouvre la totalité du livre, depuis la suscription de 1,1 jusqu'à la conclusion du chapitre 30, par dessus les cérémonies du chapitre 27. Elle englobe même les appendices que sont d'une part le cantique du chapitre 32 que «Moïse prononce aux oreilles de toute l'assemblée d'Israël» (31,30; 32,44.45) — d'autre part la bénédiction du chapitre 33 que Moïse «dit» (33,2). Il faut attendre le chapitre 31 — outre la courte notice de 4,41-43 sur les trois villes de refuge — pour voir le Moïse du Deutéronome remplir sa mission autrement que par la parole. Aussi, après avoir parlé, il ne lui reste plus qu'à monter sur la montagne pour mourir (34,1.5).

Seules font exception à cette image deux notices narratives du chapitre 31: en vue de l'époque qui suivra sa mort, il est dit que Moïse «écrivit cette tôra et la donna aux prêtres fils de Lévi» (v. 9 et 24) en leur ordonnant de «déposer ce livre de la tôra à côté de l'arche de l'alliance de YHWH» (v. 25s), lui-même étant d'ailleurs pressé de s'adresser encore une dernière fois *par la parole* aux chefs des tribus (v. 28). C'est d'autre part, dans ce même chapitre, la mention que Moïse «écrivit ce cantique» sur ordre de Dieu (v. 19 et 22). On sait les problèmes littéraires particuliers posés par ce chapitre, qui met en œuvre des thèmes non-deutéronomiens (investiture de Josué, théophanie dans la colonne de nuée, à l'entrée de la tente, etc. ...). Je prends provisoirement la liberté de traiter ces deux mentions marginales comme les exceptions qui confirment la règle: pour le Deutéronome lui-même, Moïse n'écrit rien, il parle. Comme tel, il est le chef et le modèle des Lévites qui, eux aussi, enseignent la loi oralement (17,9ss; 27,9.14; 33,10).

Ce trait mérite d'être souligné et apprécié théologiquement. Car d'une part le Deutéronome a été aussi mis par écrit — c'est notre chance! — à travers un processus rédactionnel qui excite notre curiosité. Mais surtout, la tradition, on le sait, n'a pas tardé à transformer cette image deutéronomienne d'un enseignement oral de Moïse pour lui donner la forme d'un écrit, le *sepher-hattôrâ* (Jos 1,8) ou *sepher-tôrat-Moshe* (Jos 8,31; cf. 23,6; I R 2,3; 2 R 14,6; 2 Ch 23,18; 25,4 etc.... Esd 3,2; Né 8,14; Dn 9,11-13).

1. Cf. Traité de Murshilish II avec Duppi-Teshup d'Amourrou, formules finales, *ANET* p. 205.

Ce passage de l'oral à l'écrit, postérieur à la couche rédactionnelle principale du Deutéronome, est pourtant déjà amorcé par quelques données du témoignage deutéronomien lui-même qui montrent, me semble-t-il, comment s'articulent loi orale et loi écrite, articulation qui a son importance pour notre conception de l'Écriture, justement aujourd'hui où la communication écrite est débordée de toutes parts, voire supplantée par l'explosion des media de la communication orale!

1. Je me contente de mentionner d'abord deux passages, de rédaction deutéronomiste visiblement tardive, où Moïse ne quitte pas son rôle de prédicateur, mais qui savent que la loi enseignée par Moïse prendra aussi une forme écrite, dans un *sepher*: en 28,58 dans les développements secondaires des malédictions (v. 47ss); et en 30,10a dans la prédication dtr d'appel à revenir à YHWH (30,1ss)[2].

2. Plus significatif est le fait que l'imprécation (*'alah*) qui accompagne la *berit* prend forme écrite, grâce à quoi elle demeure active contre les transgresseurs: «toute l'imprécation écrite dans ce livre l'assaillira» (29,19[3]; voir aussi 29,26 et 28,61). Ainsi la face menaçante de l'enseignement oral de Moïse doit prendre forme écrite pour conserver son efficacité, une efficacité que le temps risque d'enlever à la parole orale.

3. Au chapitre 27, Moïse ordonne au peuple, lorsqu'il aura passé le Jourdain, de dresser de grandes pierres, de les enduire de chaux et «tu écriras sur elles toutes les paroles de cette *tôra*» (v. 2s). «Tu dresseras ces pierres sur le mont Ebal» (v. 4), «tu écriras sur les pierres toutes les paroles de cette *tôra*» (v. 8). On peut se demander si le Deutéronome ne ré-interprète pas ici une tradition d'alliance instituant des stèles-témoins, à la manière des douze pierres d'Ex 24,4 ou de celle de Jos 24,26, pour faire de ces pierres des stèles écrites, à la manière des codes royaux de Mésopotamie. Car, s'il s'agit d'un simple support d'écriture, pourquoi dresser plusieurs stèles au même lieu? Plus instructif est le fait que, selon cette réinterprétation, Moïse veille à assurer ainsi l'avenir de son enseignement oral, si du moins nous comprenons bien les deux derniers mots du v. 8 qui ré-activent l'enseignement oral de Moïse (cf. 1,5)[4]. On sait que le Dtr rapporte l'accomplissement de cet ordre par Josué (Jos 8,32-35), avec la lecture orale de «toutes les paroles de la *tôra*, bénédiction et malédiction, selon tout ce qui est écrit dans le livre de la

2. La formule «les paroles de cette *tôra*, écrites dans ce livre» rappelle directement celle des contrats diplomatiques, cf. *supra*, note 1.

3. En 29,20 TM rapporte la formule «écrite dans ce livre de la *tôra*» à la *berit* et non aux imprécations (f.pl.) comme au v. 19. Le m.pl. de Sam et Syr, qui pensent peut-être à *devarim*, n'est pas plus satisfaisant. LXX hésite entre le sing. et le pl.

4. En 1,5b on remarque que le verbe *bē'ēr* introduit une déclaration orale en *lē'mōr*. Il est vrai qu'en Hab 2,2a le même verbe, explicité par «sur les tablettes», est mis en parallèle avec *katav*. Mais la fin du verset, en 2,2b, montre qu'il s'agit de faciliter ainsi une lecture orale: *qōrē'*. Ce rapprochement pourrait donner à la formule *ba'ēr hēytēv* de Dt 27,8 la nuance d'une écriture soignée, ou d'un commentaire accompagnant ce qui est écrit.

tôra». La fixation de l'oral par l'écrit vise donc à assurer la perennité de la loi orale.

4. Dans la loi sur le roi (17,14-20), la loi est orale, puisque le roi la reçoit de la bouche des prêtres lévites (*milliphné*-). Mais le roi est exposé, plus que tout israélite, à l'oublier. Aussi la rédaction dtr tardive ajoute-t-elle qu'il en fera de sa main une copie écrite pour lui permettre d'être son propre catéchète, en la lisant oralement chaque jour (v. 18-20). L'écrit sert ainsi de relais entre l'oral de l'enseignement des Lévites et *l'oral* de la lecture quotidienne qu'en fera le roi. On se doute que ce programme idéalisé du roi est susceptible de se généraliser un jour pour chaque israélite!

5. Est-ce à quoi l'on assiste dans la prescription des *tefillîm* (6,9; 11,20)? Que le commandement soit à comprendre, dès l'origine, au sens rituel que lui a donné la piété juive, ou plutôt, ce que je crois, au sens imagé d'une polémique contre le port d'amulettes ou d'inscriptions magiques dans le monde ambiant, on remarquera que le but est de maintenir en toutes circonstances les paroles de la *tôra* vivantes «sur ton cœur» dans une oralité lucide et décisionnelle. Quant à l'ordre d'inscrire les commandements sur le montant des portes de la maison et de la ville, c'est une manière d'indiquer que les commandements s'appliquent à toute la vie familiale et sociale de la cité israélite, bien plus qu'une intention de fixer la *tôra* par écrit.

6. Reste une dernière mention, la plus importante au plan théologique, et qui pourrait bien être un témoignage inédit de la tradition deutéronomienne: ce sont «les deux tables de pierre, écrites du doigt de Dieu» (9,10 cf. Ex 31,18) [5], ces deux tables que Moïse à brisées, mais qu'il reçoit l'ordre de remplacer, afin que YHWH puisse à nouveau «y écrire les paroles qui étaient sur les premières tables» (10,2 et 4). Il s'agit des paroles du Décalogue, comme le laisse entendre la description de la théophanie de l'Horeb, au chapitre 5, où la liste a été intercalée plus ou moins adroitement (cf. 5,22 *in fine*) [6]. C'est ce que précise explicitement la prédication plus récente du chapitre 4 (v. 12-14).

Deux remarques s'imposent ici: ces fameuses «dix paroles» (4,13; 10,4), YHWH les a d'abord «dites pour vous, sur la montagne» (*dibber*:

5. D'où vient cette formule, où *Elohim* est employé seul, sans l'accompagnement du nom YHWH, ce qui est relativement rare dans le Dt (cf. 4,32.33.34; 5,24.26; 21,23; 25,18)? Serait-ce une formule de la tradition élohiste (Ex 31,18; cf. 24,12; 32,16; 34,1) reprise par Dt? Mais on sait que l'Exode atteste aussi une autre tradition selon laquelle c'est Moïse qui écrit sur les tables les paroles de la *berit* (Ex 24,4; 34,27; cf 34,28 où le sujet est incertain), et ce pourrait bien être la tradition plus ancienne. En outre 31,18a sert de transition rédactionnelle entre l'institution du sanctuaire (ch. 25-31) et l'affaire du veau d'or (ch. 32-34); on y reconnaît le vocabulaire de P (*Sinaï, les tables de la charte*). Il est donc plus probable que la formulation de 31,18b, unique dans Ex, soit une surcharge dtr tirée du Dt.

6. Sur les problèmes littéraires du Décalogue dans ses deux contextes, cf. F.-L. HOSSFELD, *Der Dekalog, seine späten Fassungen, die originale Komposition und seine Vorstufen*, Fribourg-Göttingen 1982 (OBO 45), p. 163ss.

10,4), il les a «dites à toute votre assemblée» (*dibber*: 5,22), et «il vous a communiqué son alliance» (*wayaggēd*: 4,13a). L'écriture sur les deux tables n'intervient que dans un acte second, au service de l'acte premier de la proclamation par la voix de YHWH lui-même, exactement comme le protocole du contract de vassalité est établi après la proclamation de la relation de vassalité par le suzerain lui-même.

Seconde remarque: le rappel de l'affaire du veau d'or, dans 9,7 à 10,5, mentionne justement la suppression de la loi *sous sa forme écrite*, et non sous la forme orale initiale: Moïse brise les tables *écrites*, mais rien n'est supprimé des paroles que YHWH avait dites (10,4), puisque ce sont ces paroles-là que YHWH écrit sur les nouvelles tables. Paradoxalement, la loi écrite est donc, à certains égards, plus fragile que la loi orale qui reste maîtresse d'elle-même, quels que soient les avatars de sa forme écrite.

Concluons: La tradition deutéronomienne pourrait bien être la première à avoir introduit dans la représentation de la révélation de la *tôra* le motif d'une mise par écrit par YHWH, selon le modèle littéraire du contrat de vassalité conservé sous forme de protocole. Mais cette mise par écrit, limitée à la liste des dix paroles — liste que je suis de plus en plus enclin à attribuer au Deutéronome lui-même [7] — reste entièrement au service de la loi orale, celle que YHWH a lui-même prononcée et celle qu'il a chargé Moïse d'enseigner de vive voix. Les deux tables écrites, on le sait, n'ont pas été données au peuple, mais à Moïse, afin qu'il enseigne le peuple de vive voix.

Lorsqu'un jour, les Lévites du Nord réfugiés en Juda chercheront à surmonter la résistance officielle et populaire à leur prédication, ils se serviront de ce précédant divin: de même que YHWH a écrit jadis les deux tables sur l'Horeb, de même il veut que toute la *tôra* soit maintenant mise par écrit. C'est d'ailleurs, expliquent-ils, ce qu'a déjà fait Moïse lui-même (31,9-13); et c'est ce que nous, les Lévites, nous faisons en son nom. Ainsi mettent-ils par écrit l'enseignement oral de Moïse, tel qu'ils l'avaient transmis et réinterprété à travers les siècles, non pour remplacer leur prédication par un texte, mais pour conserver à cette prédication, grâce au texte écrit, son actualité de parole vivante.

Tel est, et tel reste dans la vie du peuple de Dieu, le rôle de la Sainte Écriture.

68 Av. de Rumine
CH-1005 Lausanne

Samuel AMSLER

7. J'ai l'intention de reprendre ce problème ailleurs.

«GEMEINSCHAFT, DIE WELT UNTERBRICHT»

Grundfragen und -inhalte deuteronomischer Theologie und Überlieferungsbildung im Lichte der Ursprungsbedingungen alttestamentlichen Rechts

I. Ausgangspunkt und Fragestellung

Die «Grundfragen und -inhalte deuteronomischer Theologie und Überlieferungsbildung», um die es hier gehen soll, sind solche des *Rechts*, vorab des im Buch Deuteronomium selbst uns überkommenen Rechts.

Diesem Gegenstand — 'Recht' — entspricht die Art unserer Fragestellung. Sie zu entwickeln, zwei allgemeinere Erwägungen vorweg [1]:

1. Wo es um Recht geht, geht es um Alternativen möglichen Lebens und Handelns: 'Dies soll sein, das soll nicht sein'. Im Recht, noch ehe es Entscheidungen begründet, sind Entscheidungen getroffen. Seine Funktion, so gesehen, ist *Selektion*: Auswahl im Blick auf die Alternativen, die die Welt derer, denen es gilt, ihnen als Möglichkeit bietet. 'Recht' daher hat nicht nur 'Welt', sondern hat 'Welt' zum Problem: 'Welt' als den gleichzeitig offenen Raum abweichend möglichen Lebens und Handelns, ja sogar abweichend möglichen Rechts. Es wäre nicht Recht, bestimmte es nicht, was darauf bezogen 'in Auswahl', in konkreter *Unterscheidung* also, 'recht' sein soll: 'so und nicht anders!'.

2. In seiner Selektionsfunktion ist Recht nicht souverän. Es ist angewiesen auf *Zustimmung* derer, denen es gilt, und verlangt Modi der *Stabilisierung*: 'Recht muß Recht bleiben' (können) — nämlich angesichts widersprechender Ereignisse oder alternativer Optionen. Es braucht 'Evidenz' — und zwar so, daß auch der Ausschluß von Alternativen miteinleuchtet; und es muß sich stützen können auf Mittel und Rahmenbedingungen, die seinen Normen 'Durchhaltbarkeit' bei Normenverletzungen sichern. In beiden Aspekten — 'Evidenz' und 'Durchhaltbarkeit' — melden sich aber nur wieder Probleme, die unmittelbar zusammenhängen mit der selektiven Grundfunktion von Recht. Bezogen, und eben selektiv bezogen auf 'Welt' als Problem, ist es zugleich im Verhältnis zur Welt, die ihm entsprechen soll, selbst ein Problem: problematisch als Ordnung des Lebens und Handelns, die Zustimmung braucht und Bestand haben will — trotz sich eröffnender, aber durchs Recht eben verschlossener Alternativen.

1. Vgl. dazu grundlegend und umfassend N. LUHMANN, *Rechtssoziologie 1.2* (rororo studium, 1.2), Reinbek, 1972. Ergänzend auch DERS., *Gesellschaftsstruktur und Semantik. Studien zur Wissenssoziologie der modernen Gesellschaft I. II*, Frankfurt/M, 1980. 1981.

So viel vorweg. — Wohin es uns führt, ist wiederum doppelt zu fassen:

Zum einen — es geht uns um 'Recht' in funktionaler Betrachtung, das heißt: um Recht in seinem Weltbezug. Dies so, daß wir Recht zu verstehen versuchen als problematisch im Blick auf Probleme — in einem *Gegenüber* also zu Zeit und Gesellschaft, denen es gilt, das nicht (in welcher Richtung immer!) kausal bestimmt und zu analysieren ist, sondern als ein reziprok offenes Verhältnis, in dem 'Welt' und 'Recht' füreinander Problem und so aufeinander bezogen sind.

Zum zweiten — über die Weise, in der 'Welt' und 'Recht' füreinander Problem sind, lassen sich Aussagen machen: unabhängig vom jeweils konkret geschichtlich gegebenen Fall. Mit den Stichworten 'Selektivität', 'Evidenz' und 'Durchhaltbarkeit' haben wir dies angedeutet. Sie verweisen konvergent auf *Spannungen* im Verhältnis von 'Welt' und 'Recht', die nicht eine Frage von Störungen dieses Verhältnisses sind, sondern ihm selbst inhärent. Wie immer auch die Betroffenen sie erleben mögen — ohne sie, ohne diese Spannungen gibt es kein Recht, das auf 'Welt' angelegt, und keine 'Welt', die durch Recht geordnet wäre.

Dies nun vorausgesetzt, ist es uns möglich, Fragestellung und Vorgehensweise im Rahmen unseres Themas zu konkretisieren:

Zuerst und grundlegend wird es uns darum gehen, das *Spezifische* deuteronomischen Rechts zu erkennen: das Spezifische nämlich *in seinem Weltbezug*. Wodurch zeichnet es sich aus — nicht im Kontext anderer Texte, sondern als Ordnung des Lebens und Handelns, die Alternativen negiert — und darin selbst auf sie verweist?

Derart zu fragen, heißt: ansetzen bei den *Spannungen im Weltverhältnis* deuteronomischen Rechts. — Ihnen gilt der nächste Abschnitt (II).

Darin zugleich aber auch ist dann die Wendung zum zweiten Aspekt unseres Themas vorbereitet: zur Frage der Eigenart deuteronomischer Rechtsgestaltung «im Lichte der Ursprungsbedingungen alttestamentlichen Rechts» überhaupt. Denn genau an den Spannungen im Weltverhältnis deuteronomischen Rechts wird sich die Frage entzünden, ob sich womöglich — und wie sich — darin *durchhält*, was alttestamentliches Recht 'immer schon' prägt — und 'immer schon' heißt: von den «Ursprungsbedingungen» her, in seinem primären Weltbezug also.

Wir widmen dieser Frage einen dritten Teil (III). — Ein vierter wird dann nur in Ansätzen noch — zurückkehrend gleichsam auf dem beschrittenen Weg — die Richtung bezeichnen, in der wir die Eigenart deuteronomischen Rechts sich herausbilden sehen (IV).

II. Spannungen im Weltverhältnis deuteronomischen Rechts

Ein Leitwort mag helfen zusammenzufassen, worum es dem Recht deuteronomischer Prägung in Spannung zur Welt, der es gilt, grundlegend und bis ins einzelne geht: Es geht um '*Gemeinschaft, die Welt unterbricht*'.

An prominenter Stelle einmal (26,18f.) und wiederholt auch sonst (7,6; 14,2.21; 28,9) bringt deuteronomische Sprache selber die Sache auf den Begriff: ein «heiliges Volk» ist Israel — nicht von sich aus 'heilig', sondern heilig Jahwe, seinem Gott: Volk seiner Wahl, Volk seines 'Eigentums'. — Gemeinschaft ist *Jahwe*-Gemeinschaft: und so erst, von da her geordnet, menschliches Miteinander — bis ins Verhältnis zum Ochsen, der drischt (25,4).

Weil das so ist — und unumkehrbar so! —, ist die Gemeinschaft, um die es hier geht, eine, die 'Welt unterbricht'.

Was das bedeutet und einschließt, ist nicht besser zu entfalten als im Durchgang durchs Deuteronomium selbst. Hinweise aber müssen hier reichen. Sie ordnen Bekanntes — und stellen Ergänzungen frei.

'Unterbrechung von Welt':

Schon die Einkleidung des Rechts in die Form der Mose-Rede spricht Bände. Sie ruft das Israel der späten Königszeit (ich bleibe bei dieser Datierung) heraus aus seiner Alltagswelt, sogar aus seiner Sonntagswelt — und stellt es ins 'Heute' des Anfangs. Eines Anfangs voller Spannung: bestimmt durchs 'Schon jetzt' der Horeb-*b^{e}rît*, bestimmt durchs 'Noch nicht' der Ankunft, erst recht des 'Ruhens' im Land. Das 'Hören' in diesem 'Heute' versetzt in Horeb-Gegenwart: trotz Horeb-Distanz (Dtn 5); versetzt auf den Weg hin ins Land: trotz Sitzens darin.

Spiel mit der Zeit, das Zeit unterbricht: 'Heute'!

Den Kern der Sache erschließt *Dtn 6,4-5*: eine Einheit, gefügt nach syntaktischem Schema:

I a	Interjektion	—	שמע ישראל
b	Feststellungssatz	—	יהוה אלהינו יהוה אחד
II	Aufforderung	—	ואהבת את יהוה אלהיך ...

Das Schema ist geläufig[2]: Es bindet Verhaltenserwartung an Verhaltensgrund. Was gefordert wird, ist nur zu fordern — und ist erfüllbar nur! — in und kraft der Wirklichkeit, die als 'gegeben' zugesprochen wird — und in Form des Zuspruchs in der Tat 'gegeben'. — Zum Vergleich (Gn 20,15):

I a	Siehe,	Höre, Israel,
b	mein Land — vor dir:	JHWH — unser Gott, JHWH einzig:
II	siedle, wo es dir gefällt!	so liebe JHWH, deinen Gott ...

Nur eine Differenz wiegt schwer: Abweichend vom durchgängig Typischen in der Verwendung des Schemas heißt es im Einsatz nicht «Siehe!» (הִנֵּה, רְאֵה), sondern «Höre!» (שְׁמַע). — Und wirklich (Dtn 5,

2. Vgl. zuerst N. LOHFINK, *Darstellungskunst und Theologie in Dt 1,6-3,29*, in *Bib* 41 (1960) 105-134, pp. 124-125. Dann J. HALBE, *Das Privilegrecht Jahwes Ex 34,10-26. Gestalt und Wesen, Herkunft und Wirken in vordeuteronomischer Zeit* (FRLANT, 114), Göttingen 1975, pp. 98f. 100ff. — Beziehungen zu Dtn 6,4-5 sind bisher m.W. nicht aufgefallen.

in sehr prinzipieller hermeneutischer Funktion, reflektiert die Gründe): es gibt nichts zu 'sehen', nicht im 'Heute' der Mose-Rede; denn was dieses 'Heute' bestimmt, ja dieses 'Heute' erst werden läßt: unabhängig von laufender Zeit, — das ist die Gegenwart Jahwes im Wort, im Wort seines 'Mose'! Welt unterbrechende Gegenwart — darum worthaft; Zeit unterbrechende Gegenwart — darum 'Heute': alle versammelnd im 'Hören'; jeden versammelnd aus seinen Bindungen — zu «homologischer Existenz» (G. Ebeling)[3]: zu Leben und Handeln 'ex auditu'; wortgemäß; Jahwe entsprechend, daß nichts draußen bleibt: «mit all deinem Herzen und all deiner Seele und all deiner Kraft» (6,5).

Unterbrechung von Welt!

Wir haben hier so etwas wie den Fluchtpunkt der Perspektive, in der alles weitere liegt. Denn diese Struktur: herausgerufenen, 'hörenden', in Liebe zu Jahwe versammelten Lebens, — diese Struktur, sozusagen, ist Form- und Materialprinzip deuteronomischer Rechtsgestaltung im ganzen.

Das gilt für das dreifache 'ein': *ein Gott*, *ein Heiligtum*, *eine Tora*: Ruf — heraus aus Lebensbindungen, aus Alternativen, in denen sich Jahwe-Gemeinschaft 'verläuft' (durchaus im doppelten Sinn).

— Ruf hinein in ein «Leben im Heute» (G. Ebeling)[4], das Leben in ungeteilter Jahwe-Verbundenheit ist;
— Ruf zu einem Gottesdienst an keinem Ort sonst — und mit keinem Ort sonst — als in der 'Namens'-Gegenwart Jahwes;
— Ruf zum Halten der Gebote, die leicht sind, nicht schwer; die nah sind, nicht fern; eine Wohltat Jahwes (לְטוֹב לָךְ: 10,13) — und Jahwe genug (13,1; vgl. 4,2)![5]

Welt unterbrechend, 'diese Tora', gerade auch hierin! Gerade auch darin, daß niemandem sonst Gesetzgebungsrecht über Israel zukommt. — Was es braucht, hat es: in 'dieser Tora'.

Wir werden uns dessen erinnern.

Zuvor aber noch einen anderen Aspekt: die '*Weltlichkeit*' dieses Rechts, dem kein Gitter am Dach zu banal (22,8) — und noch die Vogelmutter schutzbedürftig ist: «auf daß es dir wohl ergehe und du lange lebest» (22,6-7). In engem Zusammenhang damit: seine *Menschenfreundlichkeit* — das, was die 'Humanität' in diesem Recht genannt worden ist; aber worum es sich handelt, ist — bezogen und begrenzt auf das Israel Jahwes — durchaus konkret, durchaus 'weltlich' jedermanns

3. G. EBELING, *Theologie und Verkündigung. Ein Gespräch mit Rudolf Bultmann* (HUT, 1), Tübingen, 1962, pp. 83ff., auch pp. 93ff.

4. Ebd. (Anm. 3).

5. Vgl. S. HERRMANN, *Die konstruktive Restauration. Das Deuteronomium als Mitte biblischer Theologie*, in H. W. WOLFF (ed.), *Probleme biblischer Theologie*. Fs G.v. Rad, München, 1971, pp. 155-170, speziell zur sog. «Wortlautformel» p. 157.165 mit n. 24.

Pflicht zu Beistand, Fürsorge, Freigebigkeit: denen zugut, die sie brauchen (bes. Dtn 15 und verstreut Kap. 22ff.)[6].

Auch diese Züge verbinden sich klar mit der genannten Struktur 'hörenden' Lebens im 'Heute'; ich brauche das nur anzudeuten: Das Leben, das alles von Jahwe empfängt: sich selber und alles (mit fälligem Stichwort:) — als 'Segen', dies Leben kann aufatmen. Und nicht nur selbst: es kann aufatmen lassen. Es ist von den Bindungen frei, die es hindern, Menschen und Dingen frei zu begegnen. Herausgerufen aus allem, was ist, erhält es dies alles zurück: neu, anders; 'weltlich', weil Welt unterbrechend — als Gabe.

Und diese Gabe verpflichtet — zur Hilfe, die Aufhelfen ist (15,1-18!); zu Beistand und offener Hand.

Der Gedanke ist klar: theologisch wie anthropologisch. — Was aber gibt ihm in diesem Recht das Gewicht, das ihm zukommt?

G. v. Rad, seiner Zeit, antwortete mit dem Hinweis auf das «Idealisrael», das dem Deuteronomium vorschwebt[7]: «Gerade das Dt., das so entschlossen in dem Gesamtisrael das Gottesvolk erkannt hat und also in dem Gesamtvolk den Anwärter auf Gottes Segnung sieht, mußte» darauf drängen, «auch die armen Volksgenossen nach Kräften teilhaben zu lassen»[8]. Und weiter, den ausschließlichen «Gnadencharakter» der Gaben Jahwes einbeziehend: «Keiner ist ihrer würdig. Beschenkt aber Gott trotzdem sein Volk, so gilt gleiches Recht für alle»[9].

Das ist mehr und greift tiefer als allfällige Hinweise auf die Einflüsse prophetischer Predigt[10]. Gleichwohl — die Erklärung ist theologisch so voraussetzungsvoll und so voraussetzungsvoll theologisch, daß die Frage bleibt, ob wir damit an der Wurzel sind. Das Thema 'Beistandspflicht, Fürsorge, Freigebigkeit im deuteronomischen Recht' ist mit alledem eher aufgeworfen als erledigt.

Wir halten dies fest und kommen darauf im nächsten Abschnitt zurück; denn vorher noch fehlt uns ein weiterer Schritt:

Wir haben skizziert, wie 'diese Tora', wie deuteronomisches Recht *in sich selber begründet*, was das Verhältnis zu ihm bestimmt: 'Hören';

6. Vgl. nur G.v. RAD, *Das Gottesvolk im Deuteronomium* (BWANT, 3.F.11), Stuttgart 1929, jetzt in DERS., *Gesammelte Studien zum Alten Testament II* (TB, 48), München, 1973, pp. 9-108, hier pp. 45ff.; L. PERLITT, *«Ein einzig Volk von Brüdern». Zur deuteronomischen Herkunft der biblischen Bezeichnung «Bruder»*, in D. LÜHRMANN, G. STRECKER, *Kirche. Fs. G. Bornkamm*, Tübingen, 1980, pp. 27-52.

7. *Gottesvolk*, p. 58, vgl. pp. 50ff.57ff.

8. Ebd., p. 52.

9. Ebd.

10. L. PERLITT, *«Ein einzig Volk von Brüdern»*, pp. 50-51. — Aber: Auf welcher Basis ihrerseits stehen die Propheten? — Vgl. W. ZIMMERLI, *Das Gottesrecht bei den Propheten Amos, Hosea und Jesaja*, in R. ALBERTZ, H.-P. MÜLLER, H.W. WOLFF, W. ZIMMERLI (ed.), *Werden und Wirken des Alten Testaments, Fs C. Westermann*, Göttingen-Neukirchen-Vluyn, 1980, pp. 216-235.

und aus 'Hören': 'Lieben'. Jahwe lieben mit der ganzen Existenz. Amor ex auditu; 'Leben im Heute': Welt unterbrechende Folge Welt unterbrechenden Worts.

Wir könnten nun weiter verfolgen, wie sich von hier aus, vom 'Heute' Jahwes her — Jahwe-Geschichte erschließt: sein irrationales Erwählen; sein Herausführen aus dem Sklavenzwinger — Welt unterbrechend auch dies, gerade dies!

Wir könnten verfolgen , wie sich von hier aus, wie sich vom 'Heute' her — Zukunft eröffnet: Zukunft, die Jahwe entspricht; reine Gabe, Segen; Welt unterbrechend wie seine Gegenwart selbst. — Und Fluch. Verfluchte Möglichkeit des Abfalls. Möglichkeit aber, die überhaupt erst mit 'dieser Tora' in die Welt kommt — als zu vermeidende nämlich. Auch über sie, über 'Leben' und 'Tod', fällt die Entscheidung im 'Heute' (28,1.15; 30,15-20)!

Wir könnten so fortfahren. Wichtig jedoch im Sinn unseres Themas und der uns leitenden Frage ist etwas anderes: nicht rechtsimmanent die Entfaltung des Ansatzes, von dem her dies Recht sich gestaltet, verstanden und gelebt werden will; sondern, im Weltbezug, was dieser Ansatz — ausschlägt, negiert. Was er als Möglichkeit *nicht* akzeptiert: und zwar als Möglichkeit nicht nur *im* Recht, sondern bereits der *Begründung* von Recht.

Welche Spannung zur Welt reißt es auf, dies Rufen ins 'Heute' als Rufen ins Recht?

Zuerst und vor allem: es verzichtet darauf, sich über *Herrschaft* zu legitimieren. Sei es Königsherrschaft, sei es Priesterherrschaft: es verzichtet darauf.

Dabei: der Hinweis ist noch provinziell, daß das Doppelinteresse, Herrschaft durch Recht und umgekehrt Recht durch Herrschaft zu legitimieren, überall altorientalisch begegnet; so auch in Israel selbst (vgl. nur Ps 72). Es ist da, wo überhaupt Herrschaft ist — und aus nicht fraglichen Gründen[11].

11. Vgl. allgemein G. DUX, *Rechtssoziologie. Eine Einführung* (UB, 241), Stuttgart u.a., 1978, pp. 121-125; K. EDER, *Die Entstehung staatlich organisierter Gesellschaften. Ein Beitrag zu einer Theorie sozialer Evolution*, Frankfurt/M, 1976, pp. 79ff.82ff.98ff.158ff. — Im Blick auf die altvorderorientalische Welt: J. KLÍMA, *Die juristischen Gegebenheiten in den Prologen und Epilogen der mesopotamischen Gesetzeswerke*, in *Travels in the World of the Old Testament. Fs M.A. Beek*, Assen, 1974, pp. 146-169, esp. p. 150f.155-159.167f.; R. HAASE, *Einführung in das Studium keilschriftlicher Rechtsquellen*, Wiesbaden, 1965, pp. 16ff.36ff.; E.A. SPEISER, *Authority and Law in Mesopotamia*, in *JAOS.S* 17 (1954) 8-15; H.G. GÜTERBOCK, *Authority and Law in the Hittite Kingdom*, in *JAOS.S* 17 (1954) 16-24; J. GROTHUS, *Die Rechtsordnung der Hethiter*, Wiesbaden, 1973, pp. 17-18; J.A. WILSON, *Authority and Law in Ancient Egypt*, in *JAOS.S* 17 (1954) 1-7; J.M. LURJE, *Studien zum altägyptischen Recht* (FRR,30), Weimar, 1971, pp. 22ff.126ff.; E. SZLECHTER, *Le Droit Egyptien dans le Cadre du Droit Comparé* (*Droit Babylonien*), in A. THÉODORIDÈS (ed.), *Le droit égyptien ancien. Colloque organisé par l'Institut des Hautes Etudes de Belgique 18 et 19 mars 1974*, Brüssel, 1974, pp. 207-216; A. THÉODORIDÈS, *A propos de la loi dans*

Hier dagegen: womöglich noch schlimmer als völliges Schweigen — ein 'Königsgesetz' (17,14-20), das den Herrscher eher diszipliniert als legitimiert und ihm jedenfalls nicht einmal mehr die Stellung und Rolle läßt, die der König im Rechtswesen Israels gehabt haben dürfte: Stellung und Rolle des 'Herrscher-Richters', der ohne allgemein legislative Kompetenz und mit nur geringen Möglichkeiten eigener Einflußnahme (bes. in Heer, Residenz und Verwaltung) 'Repräsentant' des institutionellen Rahmens ist, innerhalb dessen das Rechtsleben sich auf traditionaler Normengrundlage relativ eigenständig entfaltet [12]. — Nicht einmal dies (vgl. in dtn 'Gewaltenteilung' 16,18-20; 17,8-13)! Die 'Zentralisierung' im Sinn deuteronomischen Rechts, seine 'Einheits'-Forderung (wie besprochen), ist 'Zentralisierung' am König vorbei!

Das ist nicht nur ein Politikum; das ist es auch: im durchaus ja auch politischen Sinn deuteronomischer 'Ämterordnung'. Doch hängt damit mehr zusammen: empirisch, sowohl wie ideologisch.

Zur empirischen Seite der Sache: Nicht nur wir wissen (dank der auf diesem Gebiet intensiveren Forschung der letzten Jahre ist das bekannter geworden), welch tiefgreifende Umbrüche die Herausbildung zentralisierter Gewalt und die Institutionalisierung von Herrschaft als 'Zentralinstanz' für primär verwandtschaftlich organisierte Gesellschaften bedeutet: Umbrüche bis hinein in die Grundstrukturen von Interaktion und Erfahrung [13]. Israel wußte das auch. Es hatte es erfahren. Jahr-

l'Egypte pharaonique, in *RIDA Sér. 3*, 14 (1967) 107-152; S. MORENZ, *Ägyptische Religion* (RM, 8), Stuttgart u.a., 1960, pp. 12f.63-66.120ff. — Zusammenfassend: H. J. BOECKER, *Recht und Gesetz im Alten Testament und im Alten Orient* (NSB, 10), Neukirchen-Vluyn, 1976, pp. 44ff.; W. SCHOTTROFF, *Zum alttestamentlichen Recht*, in *VF* 22 (1977) 3-29, pp. 12ff.

12. Vgl. zu diesem Typus K. EDER, *Entstehung*, p. 87, und s. entsprechend G.C. MACHOLZ, *Die Stellung des Königs in der israelitischen Gerichtsverfassung*, in *ZAW* 84 (1972) 157-182; ergänzend DERS., *Zur Geschichte der Justizorganisation in Juda*, *in* ZAW 84 (1972) 314-340. Ferner auch H. J. BOECKER, *Recht*, pp. 20ff.32ff.75f.123.

13. Vgl. umfassend C. SIGRIST, *Regulierte Anarchie. Untersuchungen zum Fehlen und zur Entstehung politischer Herrschaft in segmentären Gesellschaften Afrikas*, Olten, 1967 (2.A. Frankfurt/M, 1979); F. KRAMER, C. SIGRIST (ed.), *Gesellschaften ohne Staat 1.2*, Frankfurt/M, 1978; P. CLASTRES, *Staatsfeinde. Studien zur politischen Anthropologie*, Frankfurt/M, 1976; K. EDER, *Seminar: Die Entstehung von Klassengesellschaften* (stw, 30), Frankfurt/M, 1973; DERS., *Entstehung*. — Für Israel namentlich F. CRÜSEMANN, *Der Widerstand gegen das Königtum. Die antiköniglichen Texte des Alten Testaments und der Kampf um den frühen israelitischen Staat* (WMANT, 49), Neukirchen-Vluyn, 1978; auch C. SCHÄFER-LICHTENBERGER, *Stadt und Eidgenossenschaft im Alten Testament. Eine Auseinandersetzung mit Max Webers Studie «Das antike Judentum»* (BZAW, 156), Berlin-New York, 1983, pp. 329ff.369ff. — Berichtend N. LOHFINK, *Die segmentären Gesellschaften Afrikas als neue Analogie für das vorstaatliche Israel*, in *Bibel und Kirche* 38 (1983) 55-58; H.-W. JÜNGLING, *Die egalitäre Gesellschaft der Stämme Jahwes*, in *Bibel und Kirche* 38 (1983) 59-64; DERS., *Propaganda für das Königtum*, ebd., p. 64f.; vgl. DERS., *Richter 19 — Ein Plädoyer für das Königtum. Stilistische Analyse der Tendenzerzählung Ri 19,1-30a;21,25* (AB, 84), Rom, 1981.

hunderte zwar vorm Deuteronomium. Aber es gab viele Gründe, die Erinnerung daran nicht ganz zu verlieren. Einer davon, der im Laufe der Zeit nicht weniger, sondern im Gegenteil zunehmend wichtig wurde, lag in den Erfahrungen, die es mit Königtum machte: Erfahrungen sozialer und politischer Krisen und Deformationen, die ihre Zeit brauchten, aber desto brisanter, desto katastrophaler wurden, je näher die Zeit des Deuteronomiums rückte [14]. Sieht man auf die Verhältnisse, die uns die Prophetie des 8. und 7. Jahrhunderts beleuchtet, so steht dazu das deuteronomische Recht mit seiner Verpflichtung zu Beistand, Fürsorge, Freigebigkeit nicht nur in Spannung, sondern in Alternative. Das erledigt noch nicht unsere Frage von früher: nach Kontext und Implikationen dieser Verpflichtung als eines Themas im Recht. Hier geht es nur darum: diesem Thema Raum zu schaffen — Raum im Leben Israels —, setzt 'diese Tora' nicht aufs Königtum. Und mit empirischem Grund!

Der zweite, der ideologische Zusammenhang, den der Verzicht deuteronomischen Rechts auf die Bindung ans Königtum zu bedenken gibt, ist der folgende: Bindung des Rechtes an Herrschaft bedeutet zugleich immer auch — legitimierende Integration des Rechtes in Herrschaftsideologie. Das besagt konkret für Israel (wenn auch aufs Typische reduziert, das auch fürs Königtum anderer Kulturen typisch ist): Integration des Rechts in ein Konzept von 'Welt als Ordnung', das Herrschaft und Herrschaftsfunktionen schöpfungsmythisch legitimiert (ich verweise hier nur auf Ps 72 im Kontext der 'Königspsalmen') [15].

Wie, buchstäblich, himmelweit davon geschieden sich deuteronomisches Recht konzipiert, ist sofort evident. Eben nicht Gemeinschaft in 'Welt-als-Schöpfung', in 'Welt-als-Ordnung' ist sein Thema; sondern 'Gemeinschaft, die Welt unterbricht'! Pointiert gesagt: Was im Licht dieses Rechts 'Welt' ist — *ohne* Unterbrechung im 'Heute', '*un*unterbrochene Welt', — das zeigt der deuteronomische Fluch!

Zurückgewendet auf unsere Eingangsbeobachtungen in diesem Teil: Die Einkleidung deuteronomischen Rechts in die Form der Mose-Rede unterläuft wie gezielt eben die Legimitationsfigur, die die Bindung ans Königtum anbieten würde: die Herleitung aus schöpfungsmythischer Ur-Zeit. Nicht einmal um hohes Alter geht es! Dabei läge mindestens

14. Vgl. nach wie vor A. ALT, *Der Anteil des Königtums an der sozialen Entwicklung in den Reichen Israel und Juda*, in M. NOTH (ed.), *Kleine Schriften zur Geschichte des Volkes Israel von A. Alt III*, München, 1959, pp. 348-372. — Inzwischen K. KOCH, *Die Entstehung der sozialen Kritik bei den Profeten*, in H.W. WOLFF (ed.), *Probleme biblischer Theologie. Fs G.v. Rad*, München, 1971, pp. 236-257.

15. Vgl. die Hinweise in Anm. 11 und s. die vielfältigen Studien, die H.H. SCHMID diesem Sachverhalt gewidmet hat: aufgeführt und (bes. im Hinblick aufs alttestamentliche Recht) kritisch besprochen bei J. HALBE, *«Altorientalisches Weltordnungsdenken» und alttestamentliche Theologie*, in *ZTK* 76 (1979) 381-418.

dies, vergleicht man die Rechte verwandter Kulturen, nahe. Denn Heiligkeit und Alter symbolisieren, was sie stützt: das Nicht-anders-Mögliche, Nicht-Disponible, ja — in schöpfungsmythischen Bezügen — das welttragend Gültige rechtlicher Ordnung [16]. — Nichts davon hier: Nicht ein 'Damals', sondern das 'Heute'; nicht ein 'Seit je', sondern 'Hören' je jetzt; nicht ein Schöpfungswort am Anfang, sondern Jahwe in Wort-Gegenwart begründet den Anspruch — und: ermöglicht Erfüllung.

Spannung im Weltbezug deuteronomischen Rechts: auch dies; dies zumal!

Wir können zusammenfassen:

1. Deuteronomisches Recht stützt sich nicht auf 'Welt' als 'Ordnung', sondern ruft heraus aus Welt — zum Leben, das im Mose-Wort alles hat: Jahwe im 'Heute' — und *so* Ordnung.

2. 'Aus Welt heraus' heißt konkret (soweit wir gesehen haben):
— Heraus aus Alternativen, die Alternativen zu Jahwe sind: dem einen; dem in 'Namens'-Gegenwart; dem dieser einen Tora.
— Heraus aus Bindungen, die Herz und Hand binden: in ein Leben, das Segen verteilt.
— Heraus aus Königtum legitimierender, selber durchs Königtum legitimierter Ordnung von Menschsein und Welt.

3. 'Aus Welt heraus' heißt in diesen Aspekten: Spannung zum Wirklichen; mehr: Alternative zu ihm.

Wir fragen jetzt weiter: ob sich womöglich — und wie sich — darin durchhalten mag, was von den Ursprungsbedingungen her für Israels Rechtsbildung wesentlich ist.

III. Strukturen und Strukturprobleme frühisraelitischen Rechts

Die gestellte Frage stellt sich ja im Ernst von selbst: Denken wir deuteronomisches Recht überhaupt angelegt auf eine Welt, die ihm entsprechen; auf Zustimmung, die es finden; auf Gesellschaft, die an ihm festhalten soll: auch im enttäuschenden Fall der Mißachtung (s.o. I), — dann ist die Frage da: die Frage nach der *Evidenz*, mit der dies Recht sich seiner Zeit und Wirklichkeit entgegensetzt. Und 'Evidenz' sollte heißen: einleuchtend so, daß auch der Ausschluß von Alternativen miteinleuchtet (S. 55).

Unser Versuch zu antworten geht — wie naheliegend — aus vom Bundesbuch, speziell von Ex 23,1-9 (vgl. Dtn 16,18-20; 19,16-21; 22,1-4; 24,17f.).

16. Vgl. dazu H. M. KLINKENBERG, *Die Theorie der Veränderbarkeit des Rechtes im frühen und hohen Mittelalter*, in P. WILPERT (ed.), *Lex et Sacramentum im Mittelalter* (Miscellanea Mediaevalia, 6), Berlin, 1969, pp. 157-188; H. SCHELSKY, *Systemfunktionaler, anthropologischer und personfunktionaler Ansatz der Rechtssoziologie* (Jahrbuch für Rechtssoziologie und Rechtstheorie, 1), Düsseldorf, 1970, pp. 37-89, esp. p. 73; N. LUHMANN, *Rechtssoziologie 1*, pp. 193ff. Ferner auch die Hinweise Anm. 11.

Zunächst (I) der Text, ohne v. 9[17] mit Umstellung von v. 8 vor v. 7 und in einer Anordnung, die die Komposition sichtbar machen soll[18]:

v. 1: Verbreite nicht leeres Gerücht! Du darfst deine Hand nicht dem Frevler reichen, daß du Zeuge zu Gewalttat würdest!

  v. 2: Schließe dich nicht einer Mehrheit an zum Bösen und sage in einem Rechtsstreit nicht aus, nach der Mehrheit zu neigen, (das Recht) zu beugen!

    v. 3: Auch den Geringen bevorzuge nicht in seinem Rechtsstreit!

      v. 4: Wenn du das Rind deines Feindes oder seinen Esel verirrt antriffst: brings ihm zurück, unbedingt!

      v. 5: Wenn du den Esel deines Hassers unter seiner Last erliegen siehst, so laß dich nicht ankommen, ihms zu überlassen: hilf ihm auf, unbedingt!

    v. 6: Beuge das Recht deines Armen nicht in seinem Rechtsstreit!

  v. 8: Und Bestechung nimm nicht an; denn die Bestechung macht Sehende blind und verdreht die Sache der Gerechten.

v. 7: Von betrügerischer Sache halte dich fern! Und einen Schuldlosen und Gerechten darfst du nicht umbringen (helfen)!

Denn: Ich spreche nicht gerecht einen Frevler.

Diesem Text (I) liegt eine Prohibitiv-Reihe (II) zugrunde. Die Korrespondenz-Struktur in den Satzpaaren blieb in der chiastischen Komposition des erweiterten Textes erhalten[19]:

17. V.9 gehört einer anderen Schicht, bei deren Ergänzung v.8 hinter v.7 gestellt wurde.

18. Zu Einzelheiten der Begründung vgl. meine Analysen in *Privilegrecht*, pp. 413ff. 423ff., esp. pp. 430ff. — Die Entsprechungsstruktur im Aufbau wurde oft empfunden, aber als Gestaltungsprinzip nicht transparent. Vgl. bezeichnend für beides die Kommentierungen von M. NOTH, *Das zweite Buch Mose*. Exodus (ATD, 5), Göttingen, 1961^{2}, p. 153; U. CASSUTO, *A Commentary on the Book of Exodus*, Jerusalem, 1967, pp. 296-299, und B. S. CHILDS, *Exodus. A Commentary* (OTL), London, 1974, pp. 480-482, esp. p. 482: «Verses 6-8 are not really different in kind from vv. 1-3». Wenn CHILDS dann im Anschluß an H. FREY meint, v. 1-3 gelte eher den Zeugen, v. 6-8 eher den Richtern (p. 480.482), so scheitert das an v.3 (par. v.6) und wohl auch an v. 7abα (par. v.1). Vollends bleiben v.4/5 unklar (p. 480); s.u.!

19. Nur anmerkungsweise zur Rekonstruktion:
(*1.*) *V.1.7:* In beiden Fällen wird der Prohibitiv (v.1a.7a) durch einen Vetitiv ergänzt, der als solcher formal abgesetzt ist, thematisch in beiden Fällen die Prohibitive nur mahnend unterstreicht und der Kontextstellung wie auch der Tatsache nach, daß er im ganzen Bundesbuch überhaupt nur hier — also auffällig genug — vorkommt, *der* Hand zuzusprechen sein dürfte, die v. 1-8 komponierte. Vgl. mit weiterer Literatur J. HALBE, *Privilegrecht*, p. 431-433.
(*2.*) *V.2.8:* V.2b (in sich kompliziert, aber kaum durch Streichungen zu glätten: mit B. S. CHILDS, *Exodus*, p. 450, gegen W. RICHTER, *Recht und Ethos. Versuch einer Ortung des weisheitlichen Mahnspruches* [SANT, 15], München, 1966, p. 121, u. dort gen. andere) unterstreicht den Prohibitiv v.2a ganz so, wie dies für die Vetitive v.1b.7b gilt. Gewollt wird mit Worten gespielt: *hajā ăḥ*^{a}*rê-răbbîm l*^{e}*ra*^{c}*ot / lin*^{e}*ṭot ăḥ*^{a}*rê răbbîm l*^{e}*hăṭṭot*, — auch dies ein Zug, der an v. 1 (*lo' tiśśa / 'al-tašæt*) wie an v.7 erinnert (*tir*^{e}*ḥaq / tăh*^{a}*rog*). Beides zusammen läßt daran denken, daß v.2b von derselben Hand wie v.1b.7b stammt. — V.8b

v. 1a: *lo' tiśśa' šemă' šaw'*
v. 7a: *midd^{e}băr-šaeqaer tirḥaq* (3 + 2)

v. 2a: *lo'-tih^{e}jae ăḥ^{a}rê-răbbîm l^{e}ra^{c}ot*
v. 8a: *w^{e}šoḥăd lo' tiqqaḥ* (3 + 2)

v. 6*: *lo' tăṭṭae mišpăṭ 'aebjon^{e}ka*
*v. 3**: *w^{e}dal lo' taehdăr* (3 + 2)

Es ist schließlich auf Zentral-Sätze (III) hinzuweisen, die aufzunehmen das 'zentrale' Anliegen des Bearbeiters war:

— Wenn du das Rind deines *Feindes* oder seinen Esel verirrt antriffst: brings ihm zurück, unbedingt!

— Wenn du den Esel deines *Hassers* unter seiner Last erliegen siehst ...: hilf ihm auf, unbedingt!

Die Inversion bei Auflösung des dritten Prohibitiv-Paars v. 6*/3* hängt mit dieser Einfügung zusammen [20].

Wir gehen nun aus von der Prohibitiv-Reihe (II): Sie führt mitten hinein in Strukturen und Strukturprobleme frühisraelitischen Rechts.

ist sprichwörtliches, aber, wie der Vergleich mit Dtn 16,19b erweist (Austausch *piq^{e}ḥîm* / *ḥ^{a}kamîm*), nicht schon ausgeprägt 'weisheitliches' Interpretament (vgl. W. RICHTER, *Recht*, pp. 114.142f., der freilich die Erkenntnis, daß der Ausdruck Ex 23,8 «singulär in der weisheitlichen Schule» ist [p. 143], zugunsten seiner 'Schulthese' unzulässig neutralisiert: ebd. und p. 119.133). Ohne das verbindende *kî* konnte das Element volkstümlich umlaufen: ohne Bindung an «Schule» und «vornehmen Stand» (gegen W. RICHTER, ebd., p. 122).
(*3.*) *V.3.6: w^{e}dal* v.3 ist ursprünglich (vgl. J. HALBE, *Privilegrecht*, p. 430; B. S. CHILDS, *Exodus*, pp. 450.481). Kaum aber auch das *b^{e}rîbô*, das einträgt, was selbstverständlich ist (vgl. W. RICHTER, *Recht*, p. 121, n. 4), und nur gebraucht wird, um v.3 mit v.6 durch dieses Stichwort zu verbinden. In v.6 aber ist es erst recht redundant. An beiden Stellen ergänzt der Gestalter im Sinn und Interesse seiner Gesamtkomposition, die auf Entsprechungsstrukturen aufbaut.
Redaktion und Grundbestand der Prohibitive sind also leicht zu trennen. Dieser Grundbestand ergibt in der *überlieferten* Reihenfolge der Sätze ein wenig einheitliches Bild. Das ändert sich sofort, wenn man die Einzelglieder im Sinn der Entsprechungsstruktur der heutigen Textanlage *paarweise* zusammenstellt: Sechs Verbote in drei Paaren, deren jedes chiastisch geschlossen, rhythmisch ausgewogen und inhaltlich klar strukturiert ist! — Die Umstellung von v. 6 vor v. 3 hatte kompositorisch-sachliche Gründe; sie wurde bei Schaffung der heutigen Textanlage vorgenommen (wir kommen darauf zurück).

20. So ratlos die Forschung diesen Sätzen im gegebenen Kontext gegenübersteht (vgl. das resignierte Referat bei B. S. CHILDS, *Exodus*, pp. 480-481), so klar ist zumindest formal ihre Schlüsselfunktion: Alles in der Anlage des Textes konvergiert dahin, sie hervorzuheben — und umgekehrt, von dieser Mitte her, das Ganze zu beleuchten. Dennoch muß das Satzpaar nicht selbst vom Bearbeiter stammen, sondern kann übernommen sein: vgl. H.W. GILMER, *The If-You Form in Israelite Law* (SBL Dissertation Series, 15), Missoula/Mont., 1975, pp. 46ff.102ff. Wie weit noch der Weg bis zum Dtn ist, zeigt der Vergleich mit Dtn 22,1-4 (L. PERLITT, *«Ein einzig Volk von Brüdern»*, p. 39, n. 39, streift diesen Abschnitt nur anmerkungsweise. Aber gerade auch seine Beobachtungen schlagen hier zu Buch; s. bes. ebd. p. 43). — Zur ursprünglichen Form von v. 5 vgl. J. HALBE, *Privilegrecht*, p. 430, n. 26.

Ich zähle auf und kommentiere möglichst kurz (als Hintergrundbild empfehle ich Ri 17-18/*19-21 — Kapitel, die zwar tendenziös, aber kenntnisreich parodieren [21]):

1. Grundlegend fürs ganze ist rechtssoziologisch: eine Gesellschaft, die sich in Strukturen von *Abstammung und Verwandschaft* und auf *Nachbarschaftsbasis* in relativ autonomen Gruppen organisiert (Großfamilien, Sippen; Ortschaften) [22]. — Dazu, nebenbei: Verwandtschaftsorganisation ist keine nur 'nomadische', Nachbarschaftsbindung keine nur 'sedentäre' Erscheinung. Beides begegnet in Mischung, und dies nicht zuletzt in dem Sinn, daß primär verwandtschaftsgebundene Einstellungen und Erwartungen häufig auf enge Nachbarschaftsbindungen 'ausgedehnt' bzw. übertragen werden [23]

2. *Gruppenbindung* ist die Basis von Rechtsgeltung und Rechtshandeln. Beides, m.a.W., ist nicht 'abstrakt' institutionalisiert, nicht unabhängig von der sozialen Struktur und der darin angelegten Machtverteilung, sondern gebunden an sie. Man kann bei «Rechtsstreitigkeiten nicht davon absehen, wer die direkt oder indirekt Beteiligten sind in bezug auf Ahnen und Eigentum, Ansehen und Gefolgschaft» [24]. Die Befriedungs- und Schlichtungsfunktion des Rechts hängt darum wesentlich ab vom Einigungszwang auf der Basis *gleicher Verteilung von Macht* zwischen den interagierenden Gruppen. Und entsprechend, nur die andere Seite der Medaille: Gewaltbereitschaft im Rahmen von Selbsthilfe färbt den Horizont des Rechtshandelns [25]. — Daher das Glück des

21. Vgl. die Anm. 13 gen. Arbeiten von H.-W. JÜNGLING.

22. Vgl. etwa J. PEDERSEN, *Israel. Its Life and Culture I.II*, London-Kopenhagen, 1926 (1959), pp. 29ff.; C. H. J. DE GEUS, *The Tribes of Israel* (SSN, 18), Assen-Amsterdam, 1976, esp. pp. 124-164; W. THIEL, *Die soziale Entwicklung Israels in vorstaatlicher Zeit*, Neukirchen-Vluyn, 1980; C. SCHÄFER-LICHTENBERGER, *Stadt*, passim; dazu auch die Hinweise Anm. 13 und speziell in Rechtszusammenhängen G. LIEDKE, *Gestalt und Bezeichnung alttestamentlicher Rechtssätze. Eine formgeschichtlich-terminologische Studie* (WMANT, 39), Neukirchen-Vluyn, 1971, pp. 39ff., sowie die verschiedenen Studien zur Erforschung der atl. Rechtsgattungen seit E. GERSTENBERGER, *Wesen und Herkunft des «apodiktischen Rechts»* (WMANT,20), Neukirchen-Vluyn, 1965. Zusammenfassend H. J. BOECKER, *Recht*, passim; W. SCHOTTROFF, *Recht*.

23. Vgl. C. SIGRIST, *Anarchie*, pp. 60ff.; C. H. J. DE GEUS, *Tribes*, pp. 124ff.150ff. 171ff.; N. K. GOTTWALD, *The Tribes of Yahweh. A Sociology of the Religion of Liberated Israel 1250-1050 B.C.E.*, Maryknoll/NY, 1979, passim. — Speziell zur 'Ausdehnung' bzw. 'Übertragung' von Verwandtschaft auf Nachbarschaft vgl. nur M. FORTES, *Verwandtschaft und das Axiom der Amity*, in F. KRAMER, C. SIGRIST (ed.), *Gesellschaften ohne Staat 2*, Frankfurt/M 1978, pp. 120-164, esp. pp. 147ff. Mit zu bedenken ist dabei, daß sich in Israels Siedlungen (jedenfalls der älteren Zeit) 'Verwandtschaft' und 'Nachbarschaft' weitgehend deckten: E. NEUFELD, *The Emergence of Royal-Urban Society in Ancient Israel*, in *HUCA* 31 (1960) 31-53, pp. 35ff., H. J. BOECKER, *Recht*, p. 23.

24. N. LUHMANN, *Rechtssoziologie 1*, p. 149.

25. Vgl. zu beiden Aspekten, die konstitutiv zum Funktionieren einer «Rechtsgemeinschaft» in akephalen Gesellschaften gehören, C. SIGRIST, *Anarchie*, pp. 60ff.112ff.118ff., esp. pp. 123-125; M. BARKUN, *Law without Sanctions. Order in Primitive Societies and the World Community*, New Haven-London, 1968, pp. 17ff.65ff.; J. CHELHOD, *Le Droit*

mit Söhnen gesegneten Mannes: «Er wird nicht zuschanden, wenn er redet mit Feinden im Tor» (Ps 127,5). Und aufs 'Reden im Tor' bezieht sich unsere Prohibitiv-Reihe.

Sie verdeutlicht zunächst:

3. *Verfahren* sind institutionalisiert [26]. Interessenwahrung ist nur noch in selber schon rechtlich geregelten Ausnahmefällen der unmittelbaren Geschädigtenreaktion und also dem direkten Kräftemessen der Parteien überlassen (z.B. Blutrache; Spurfolge Ri 18,13ff.; oder im Bundesbuch der Fall Ex 22,1-2) [27]. Statt dessen gibt es Schiedsorgane: Ad-hoc-Versammlungen der Ältesten, später aller Vollbürger eines Ortes. — Ihnen gelten unsere Prohibitive.

4. *Schlichtungsmittel* sind Beilegungsvorschläge dieser Schiedsversammlungen (sie sind eingegangen ins uns überlieferte 'kasuistische' Recht: G. Liedke). — Unsere Prohibitive haben also wohl einen anderen 'Sitz im Leben' als das 'kasuistische' Recht; sie entstammen aber demselben Milieu.

5. *Stabilisierungsmodus* ist primär die *Armut an Alternativen*, nicht die Sanktion. — Das heißt: die Annahme schiedsgerichtlicher Beilegungsvorschläge ist erwartbar trotz Fehlens einer zum Zweck der Erzwingung eigens organisierten Gewalt [28]; — und sie ist erwartbar mangels Alternativen [29]. Wer sich verweigert, riskiert nicht allein Gewaltreaktionen des

dans la Société Bédouine. Recherches ethnologiques sur le 'orf ou droit coutumier des Bédouins (PBSI, Sér.A), Paris, 1971, pp. 369ff.; A. S. DIAMOND, *Primitive Law, Past and Present*, London, 1971, pp. 237ff.261ff.279ff.293f. und passim; F. KRAMER-C. SIGRIST (ed.), *Gesellschaften ohne Staat 1*, Frankfurt/M, 1978, passim. Vor diesem Hintergrund u.a. D. DAUBE, *Studies in Biblical Law*, Cambridge, 1947, pp. 201-220; E. NEUFELD, *The Prohibitions Against Loans at Interest in Ancient Hebrew Laws*, in *HUCA* 26 (1955) 355-412; B. S. JACKSON, *Theft in Early Jewish Law*, Oxford 1972, p. 6ff.180f.212f.215f. und ch. 9 (pp. 203ff.) im ganzen; G. LIEDKE, *Gestalt*, ch. I.u.III; C. H. J. DE GEUS, *Tribes*, ch. III.

26. Vgl. zum folgenden v.a. G. LIEDKE, *Gestalt*, pp. 31ff.; H. J. BOECKER, *Recht*, pp. 20ff.

27. Vgl. dazu H. J. BOECKER, *Recht*, pp. 28-29; D. DAUBE, *Studies*, pp. 202ff.235ff.257-259 u.ff.; B. S. JACKSON, *Theft*, pp. 215ff., bes. zu Ex 22,1-2 (vgl. Jer 2,34) pp. 203ff., esp. p. 206: worum es an dieser Stelle geht, ist «the regulation of selfhelp, not the imposition of penalties»! Und genau dies: der Regulierungsbedarf im Hinblick auf gewaltbereite Selbsthilfe ist das zentrale Bezugsproblem, das durch die Institutionalisierung ortsgerichtlicher Schiedsverfahren und des aus ihnen hervorgegangenen 'kasuistischen Rechts' (G. LIEDKE, *Gestalt*, pp. 39ff.) gelöst werden konnte und worden ist. Vgl. zu diesem Problem D. DAUBE, *Studies*, pp. 203ff.; B. S. JACKSON, *Theft*, pp. 150.155ff.203.205f. 212f.215 u.ö.

28. Zu diesem entscheidenden Sachverhalt vgl. bes. G. LIEDKE, *Gestalt*, pp. 40ff.; vgl. pp. 88ff. und die treffende Formulierung p. 125, hinter dem kasuistischen Rechtssatz stehe «nur die Autorität des Einverständnisses aller Beteiligten». Zu kurz nur kommt dabei die Frage, wie denn mit diesem «Einverständnis» gerechnet werden konnte.

29. Vgl. dazu umfassender (mit weiterer Lit.) J. HALBE, *«Altorientalisches Weltordnungsdenken»*, pp. 396-398. — Alternativenarmut des sozialen Systems ist der das reiche Vergleichsmaterial verbindende Grundsachverhalt: vgl. N. LUHMANN, *Rechtssoziologie 1*,

Gegners, sondern er sieht sich vor allem der Ablehnungsfront der Männer im Tor gegenüber, die die Gesamtheit des Ortes vertreten! Eine ausweglose Situation, deren Absehbarkeit jenen Beilegungsvorschlägen 'konkret' verleiht, was ihnen 'abstrakt' nicht zukommt: rechtliche 'Geltung'. — Das eben auch erklärt unsere Prohibitive, die Sanktionslosigkeit dieser Gattung. Sie taugt für enge, überschaubare, alternativenarme Gemeinschaft. Ja, unter dieser Bedingung ist die Sanktionslosigkeit wirksamer, weil bedrohlicher, als das rationale Mittel eigens normierter Fallregulierung via Sanktion. Sanktion erwirkt Neuanfang; Sanktionslosigkeit bringt Hos 7,2 in den Blick: «Jetzt umzingeln sie ihre Taten, / vor meinem Angesicht leben sie auf.» Wobei zu bedenken ist, freilich: Was den Taten Macht verleiht, den Täter zu 'umzingeln', das ist — auch ohne das 'Angesicht' Jahwes — in enger, überschaubarer Gemeinschaft zuerst und konkret — das Auge der Öffentlichkeit, einer Leben und Handeln hautnah begleitenden, unentrinnbaren Öffentlichkeit. Im Hinblick auf sie gilt empirisch, nicht nur als Redensart, daß 'sich unmöglich macht', wer sich 'unmöglich' verhält [30]. Einer mag auswandern aus 'Vaterhaus und Verwandtschaft'; wohl. Aber — selbst Abraham wagte das nicht auf eigene Faust, und zum Kondottiere David hat nicht jedermann das Zeug. — Der Lossagungsfluch ist ein schreckliches Mittel!

6. Dies alles jedoch wird nicht vergessen machen, wie *störungsanfällig* solche allein durch 'social control', durch soziale Kontrolle gesicherte Rechtspraxis ist. 'Gerechtigkeit' (als Rechtssicherheit) ist nur so lange und nur in dem Maß gewährleistet, wie beides gegeben ist:

a: Abgeschlossenheit und Enge des Lebens- und Bewegungsraums bei ebenso geringer wie indisponibler Differenzierung der Rollen im Medium von Verwandtschaft und Nachbarschaft;

b: eine Sozialstruktur, die aufbaut auf Prinzipien von Gleichheit und Gegenseitigkeit im Verhältnis der Gruppen zueinander.

pp. 148-150, dazu ebd. pp. 27f., n. 3; 97.105f.; M. BARKUN, *Law*, passim; M. GLUCKMAN, *Politics, Law and Ritual in Tribal Society*, Oxford 1971, pp. 178ff.202ff.; S.F. NADEL, *Social Control and Self-Regulation*, in *Social Forces* 31 (1953) 265-273; E.E. EVANS-PRITCHARD, *Die Nuer im südlichen Sudan*, in F. KRAMER, C. SIGRIST (ed.), *Gesellschaften ohne Staat 1*, Frankfurt/M, 1978, pp. 175-200, esp. pp. 194ff.199; L. BOHANNAN, *Politische Aspekte der sozialen Organisation der Tiv*, in F. KRAMER, C. SIGRIST (ed.), *Gesellschaften ohne Staat 1*, Frankfurt/M, 1978, pp. 201-236, esp. pp. 220ff.226!

30. Vgl. bes. eindrücklich S.F. NADEL, *Social Control*. Des weiteren H. SCHELSKY, *Ansatz*, pp. 51.54; N. LUHMANN, *Rechtssoziologie 2*, pp. 282ff.; L. BOHANNAN, *Politische Aspekte*, p. 226. — Vgl. daneben L. KÖHLER, *Der hebräische Mensch. Eine Skizze*, (Tübingen, 1953) Darmstadt 1976, pp. 56f.82f.; O. KEEL, *Feinde und Gottesleugner. Studien zum Image der Widersacher in den Individualpsalmen* (SBM,7), Stuttgart, 1969, pp. 36ff.; J. HALBE, *«Altorientalisches Weltordnungsdenken»*, pp. 408f., n. 161.

Was 'los ist', wenn eines von beidem — oder beides — fehlt, hat (in verdichteter Szene) vor Augen, wer das Mißgeschick Michas verfolgt (Ri 18, 15ff.): der Teufel ist los. — Und natürlich, wenn auch ganz anders, gehört Amos hierher! Die Rechtsklage der Propheten ... Klage auf den Trümmern einer Ordnung, deren empirische Basis verloren war: die Basis von Gleichheit und Gegenseitigkeit im Zusammenleben 'ebenbürtiger' Gruppen bei nur geringen Möglichkeiten auszuweichen, Leben und Handeln alternativ zu gestalten.

Ja, es entscheidet sich viel — an dieser Stelle: nicht nur für uns und unser Thema, sondern, ich denke, für das Verständnis der Bildung und Geschichte israelitischen Rechts insgesamt.

Darum: im Augen behalten, diese beiden zuletzt genannten Punkte — und zurück zu unsern Prohibitiven! Denn ging es bisher eher darum, sie einzuordnen, so können sie jetzt führen.

Worum sie kämpfen, versteht sich nur scheinbar von selbst. Gewiß, sie wehren dem Lügenprozeß, der Beeinflussung, der Rechtsbeugung — und schützen so das Recht im Tor. Aber bedenken wir das konkret: einbezogen die Welt gruppengebundenen Lebens in Verwandtschaft und Nachbarschaft; einbezogen die Tatsache, daß ohne die Sicherung von Gleichheit und Gegenseitigkeit im Verhältnis der Gruppen — Recht nicht zu sichern ist! Dann ergibt sich zu v. 1a.7a: Substanzlos bezichtigt, wer Einfluß genug hat, auch zu obsiegen, das heißt: Leute genug, die sich *nicht* «fernhalten *midd*^{e}*băr-šaeqaer*». Isebel, um Nabot zu legen, nahm sich «Älteste und Edle», Leute mit Anhang und Geld (1 Kö 21,8.11 in v. 8-14).

Eben um Anhang und Geld geht es denn auch v.2a.8a. Die Gefahr, der gewehrt wird, natürlich, ist auch die des Unrechts im einzelnen Fall. Aber ebenso — und hier dann erst zeigt sich die ganze, die fundamentale Bedeutung dieser Normen —, ebenso geht es darum zu verhindern, daß faktische Ungleichheit in der Verteilung von Einfluß und Mitteln durchschlägt aufs Recht — und damit das Recht nicht nur selbst korrumpiert, sondern es instrumentalisiert: zum Werkzeug macht der Sicherung und noch des Ausbaus dieser Ungleichheit. Am Recht soll sich faktische Ungleichheit brechen!

Und dies denn auch ist die Pointe in v.6* und 3*: die Pointe, die die Textkommentierung von v.3 nicht mehr verstanden und verdorben [31], die aber dem Bearbeiter so am Herzen gelegen hat, daß er in seiner Komposition v.3* vor v.6* einordnete und ihm so einen Platz gab, an dem er auffällt — sperrig, überraschend: «Auch den Geringen bevorzuge nicht in seinem Rechtsstreit!»

Dasselbe Thema: Ungleichheit und Recht! Nun aber mit einem Akzent, der auffällig *ist*, nicht nur auffallen *soll*: Aus Mitleid keine Rücksichtnahme!

31. Vgl. BKH und BHS z.St.; J. HALBE, *Privilegrecht*, p. 430, n. 27.

Um dies zu verstehen, und zwar in einer Reihe von Verboten, die nicht zufälligen Regungen, sondern typisch erwartbaren Gefahren gelten, ein Zitat: zu finden in einem besonders wichtigen Buch des ebenso wichtigen Anthropologen Meyer Fortes [32]:

«Obwohl die strukturale Konnotation, die an den Begriff der Verwandtschaft gebunden ist, stark variiert, ist die darauf bezogene zentrale Wertsetzung gleichförmig. Verwandtschaft prädiziert das Axiom der Amity, den präskriptiven Altruismus, dargestellt in der Ethik der Großzügigkeit. Besonders eindrucksvolle Beispiele finden sich in Studien über Stammesrecht. ... Von Verwandten wird erwartet, daß sie liebevoll, gerecht und großzügig zueinander sind und voneinander keine streng äquivalenten Gegengaben fordern. Da Dorfgenossen meistens zugleich Verwandte sind, *kollidieren* auf politisch-rechtliche Beziehungen gegründete, *legale Ansprüche oft mit der Ethik der Großzügigkeit*, wie sie für den familiären Bereich vorgeschrieben ist».

Das genau ist hier der springende Punkt: Kollision von Beistands- und Großzügigkeitserwartungen, wie sie verwandtschaftlich eingelebt werden, Kollision von «Amity» — mit Recht. Was innerfamilial, im engsten Verwandtschaftskreis hingehen mag — daß Solidarität vor Recht, Amity vor Anspruch geht: 'es bleibt ja in der Familie' (vgl. Ri 17,1-6!) —, das würde auf ortsgemeindlicher Ebene, also im Rechtshandeln *zwischen* Gruppen, aufheben, was die zentrale Errungenschaft ortsgerichtlicher Schiedspraxis ist: zu hindern, daß faktische Ungleichgewichte in der Verteilung von Reichtum und Macht aufs Recht und über das Recht auf die Sozialstruktur insgesamt durchschlagen. Nicht nur die Macht der Mächtigen hat ihre Grenze im Recht; auch die im Anspruch auf Beistandsbereitschaft ('Amity', Freundlichkeit) mächtige Macht der Machtlosen ist in der hier zu erschließenden Welt eine Bedrohung der rechtlich zu wahrenden Gleichheit und damit der Basis der Rechtswahrung selbst!

Dies vorausgesetzt, erinnert an die *Grenzen* des 'Amity-Rechts', des Rechtes auf 'Amity' nämlich, erreicht man nach Willen und Disposition des Bearbeiters unserer Verbotsreihe — das Zentrum seiner Komposition: die Verse 4 und 5.

Sie setzen den Gegenakzent, nein — mehr: als Sätze des Rechts verlangen sie Handeln, das — *unterbricht*. Sehr konkret: Feindschaft, Gegnerschaft, Rechtsgegnerschaft (vgl. Ps 127,5) — unterbricht. Unterbrechung der Allwirksamkeit des Gesetzes strikter Entsprechung von 'Tun' und 'Ergehen'. Unterbrechung durch 'Amity'-Logik — *im Recht*!

32. *Kinship and the Social Order*, Chicago, 1969; darin: *Kinship and the Axiom of Amity*, pp. 219-249; hier zitiert nach M. FORTES, *Verwandtschaft und das Axiom der Amity*, in F. KRAMER, C. SIGRIST (ed.), *Gesellschaften ohne Staat 2*, Frankfurt/M, 1978, pp. 120-164, esp. p. 142 (Hervorhebung von mir).

Gefordert ist Hilfeleistung. Gefordert ist Beistandsbereitschaft. Gefordert ist: *mehr geben, denn erwarten zu bekommen.*

Es lohnt sich, hier innezuhalten. Denn das Gesagte hat Kontext, der mindestens angedeutet werden muß.

1. 'Großzügigkeit': «*Axiom* der Amity» kann Meyer Fortes sagen, weil dies zum Grundgerüst der Lebens- und Verhaltensorientierungen in 'Gesellschaften ohne Staat', in sogenannten 'segmentären' Gesellschaften gehört: in Gesellschaften also wie der des vorstaatlichen Israel[33].

2. «Axiom» aber auch darum, weil es in verschiedensten Zusammenhängen sozialen Lebens Gültigkeit hat — besonders (und besonders gründlich untersucht) in der Ökonomie gentiler Gesellschaften 'ohne Staat'[34]. Hier auch wird am konkretesten greifbar, welche pragmatische Logik darin verankert ist. Man hat diese Gesellschaften simplifizierend 'egalitär' genannt[35]. Schon der Hinweis auf das Verbot der Zinsnahme

33. Vgl. die Lit. in Anm. 13.22.

34. Vgl. außer M. FORTES selbst (*l.c.*) beispielhaft G. ELWERT, *Die Elemente der traditionellen Solidarität. Eine Fallstudie in Westafrika*, in *Kölner Zeitschrift für Soziologie und Sozialpsychologie* 32 (1980) 681-704; ferner R. FIRTH, *Der Soziale Rahmen der ökonomischen Organisation*, in F. KRAMER, C. SIGRIST (ed.), *Gesellschaften ohne Staat 1*, Frankfurt/M, 1978, pp. 101-131, esp. pp. (112ff.) 118ff.; M. GLUCKMAN, *Politics*, pp. 50-54.58.70-74; C.SIGRIST, *Anarchie*, pp. 176-179; last not least M. MAUSS, *Die Gabe. Form und Funktion des Austausches in archaischen Gesellschaften*, in DERS., *Soziologie und Anthropologie II* (Ullstein Buch 3491), Frankfurt/M-Berlin-Wien, 1978, pp. 9-144, esp. ch. 2 (pp. 38ff.). — Eine besondere Rolle spielen Freigebigkeits- und Fürsorgenormen bezeichnenderweise, wo es um den Erwerb und schließlich die Stabilisierung politischer Macht in primär verwandtschaftlich strukturierten Gesellschaften geht: Nur, wer denen, die weniger haben, großzügig abgibt und so für sie sorgt, kann legitim Führer, Häuptling, ja König sein! Wobei zu bedenken ist: Solange das Machtprivileg *konkret* an Freigebigkeit, d.h. an die Verteilung eigenen *materiellen* Reichtums gebunden ist, wirken dieselben Normen, die (Vor-)Herrschaft legitimieren, dahin, sie — abzubauen (vgl. M. GLUCKMAN, *Politics*, pp. 15-17.124-128; G. BALANDIER, *Politische Anthropologie* [dtv WR, 4191], München, 1976, pp. 47f.72.83f.156; C. SIGRIST, *Anarchie*, pp. 225.233; A.S. DIAMOND, *Primitive Law*, pp. 162f.165f.207f.283.328f.; G. LENSKI, *Macht und Privileg. Eine Theorie der sozialen Schichtung* [stw, 183], Frankfurt/M, 1977, pp. 146.148.185-187.224). — Es sei hier zumindest angedeutet, was eigenständig zu entfalten wäre: Wir begegnen genau den hier erwähnten 'frühen' Legitimationsmustern im Rahmen der altvorderorientalischen Königsideologie, freilich unter der Voraussetzung einer sozialstrukturell wesentlich weiter ausdifferenzierten und politisch verselbständigten, daher eine entsprechend 'abstraktere' Legitimation erfordernden Form von Herrschaft: An die Stelle *konkreter* Freigebigkeit und Fürsorge sind die abstrakteren Sinnversprechen durchs Königtum garantierter Fruchtbarkeit, Wohlfahrt und Rechtssicherheit (speziell auch für die Personen minderen Rechtes) getreten (vgl. Ps 72 u.s. J. KLÍMA, *Die juristischen Gegebenheiten*, pp. 154ff.159f.169, sowie mit weiterer Lit. J. HALBE, *Privilegrecht*, p. 456, n. 15). Was damit erreicht ist, liegt auf der Hand: Diese abstrakten Güter sind 'unbezahlbar' — nämlich auch in dem Sinn, daß sie den Herrscher nichts kosten, oder — wo doch — ihm Gefolgschaft, Klientel und Arbeitskräfte sichern. Ökonomische Macht wird in *diesem* Rahmen nicht mehr ab-, sondern ausgebaut.

35. Vgl. dazu (und zum folgenden) mit wichtigen Klarstellungen C. SIGRIST, *Gesellschaften ohne Staat und die Entdeckungen der* social anthropology, in F. KRAMER, C. SIGRIST (ed.), *Gesellschaften ohne Staat 1*, Frankfurt/M, 1978, pp. 28-44, esp. p. 43f., n. 1. Vor diesem Hintergrund (und durch ihn relativiert) dann auch B. STRECK, T. ZITELMANN,

bei Darlehen, das zentral in den hier fraglichen Zusammenhang gehört und rechtsethnologisch entsprechend universal begegnet (vgl. im Bundesbuch, stark redigiert, Ex 22,24-26!)[36], — schon dieser Hinweis genügt, um die Realität hervorzuholen: Es *gibt* Arme und Reiche. Das entscheidende ist die Einstellung dazu, die Reaktion der Gesellschaft. Ist es, mit J. Habermas zu reden, das Problem *staatlicher* Gesellschaften, Arbeit und Reichtum «*ungleich* und doch *legitim* zu verteilen»[37], so geht es hier, in Gesellschaften '*ohne Staat*' um den laufenden *Abbau* entstehender Ungleichgewichte in der Verteilung von Einfluß und Mitteln. Sie sind förmlich darauf hin organisiert, Gleichheit in der Machtverteilung zwischen Gruppen immer wieder herzustellen. Ein verzweigter Zusammenhang sich unterstützender 'äußerer' Institutionen ebensowohl wie 'innerer' Grundüberzeugungen ist darauf gerichtet. «Amity»: mehr geben, als erwarten zu bekommen, ist darin die Grundfigur. Wer weggibt, ohne strikt äquivalente Gegengaben erwarten zu dürfen, — hilft auf und gibt weg, was ihm Macht sichern könnte!

Damit schließt sich ein Kreis:

— Eine Sozialstruktur, die aufbaut auf Prinzipien von Gleichheit und Gegenseitigkeit zwischen Verwandtschaftsgruppen, sagten wir früher, gehöre zu den Funktionsbedingungen frühisraelitischen Rechts.

— 'Amity' als der zentrale Wert enger Verbundenheit zwischen Verwandten und als verwandt sich erlebenden Menschen soll Mitte und Basis des Umgangs in der Gemeinschaft sein: sagt das Recht des Bundesbuches in der betrachteten Komposition (23,4-5).

— Und 'Amity' — hat die Funktion, Ungleichheit abzubauen: abzubauen, was keinen Einfluß aufs Recht haben soll, damit nicht am Ende Recht und Gericht selber die Mittel sind, Reichtum und Macht «*ungleich* und doch *legitim* zu verteilen», nach Herrschaftslogik: das sagt die Reihe der Prohibitive und, darauf basierend, der Bundesbuch-Abschnitt, den wir betrachten, im ganzen.

Geschlossen, dieser Kreis! Ohne — Jahwe!

Die Herrschaft der Blutsbande. Vorstudien zu einer Kritik der gentilen Produktionsweise (Argumentationen, 43), Giessen, 1979, pp. 95ff.117ff.

36. Vgl. zu diesem Komplex E. NEUFELD, *Prohibitions*, pp. 359ff.383ff.394-399 (Lit.!) und s. bes. auch R. FIRTH, *Der soziale Rahmen*, pp. 112f.123-128, der zugleich den Horizont weiterer, gleichgerichteter Regeln und Institutionen segmentärer Gesellschaften zur «Beseitigung oder Verringerung der Ungleichheiten im Kapitalbesitz» andeutet (p. 113). — Noch grundlegender wäre in diesem Zusammenhang das Bodenrecht Israels zu bedenken: Unveräußerlichkeit des Sippengrundes; Restitutionsregeln und -institutionen. Beides wehrt der Konzentration ökonomischer Macht in wenigen Händen — und damit der Transformation dieser Macht in politische Herrschaft.

37. J. HABERMAS, *Technik und Wissenschaft als 'Ideologie'*, in D. KÄSLER (ed.), *Max Weber. Sein Werk und seine Wirkung* (ntw, 3), München, 1972, pp. 89-127, esp. p. 101.

Und doch gehört er zum Text: «Denn ich spreche nicht gerecht einen Frevler!»[38] «Ich»: Jahwe.

Dieses «Ich» allein schon ließe nach ihm fragen. Aber es kommt noch hinzu: ein Problem ist offen — eines, das in den Prämissen israelitischer Rechtsbildung liegt und noch bedacht werden muß[39]:

Wir sahen: entscheidend für die Entstehung und die Funktionsfähigkeit nicht nur des Rechts in den Prohibitiven, sondern im selben Maß auch des 'kasuistischen' Rechts ist die Begrenztheit und Enge, die Überschaubarkeit und Alternativenarmut der Lebenszusammenhänge, innerhalb derer es praktisch gebraucht und durchhaltbar angewandt wurde. Keine Frage, in beiderlei Gattung konnten sich Rechtstraditionen entwickeln — *ohne* die Bindung an Jahwe. Aber sie konnten dies nur partikular; begrenzt nur auf enge Gemeinschaft! Die mochte auskommen mit diesem Recht. — Aber: kam Jahwe aus — damit?

Die Frage ist rhetorisch. Was sie bewußt machen kann, ist, daß sich hier in engster Verbindung mit dem soeben geschlossenen Kreis ein zweiter, nicht minder geschlossener auftut:

Jahwe beanspruchte Israel ganz — in allen 'Bereichen' des Lebens und Handelns: auch (und ich meine: von früher Zeit an) in dem seines Rechts.

Gleichzeitig, andererseits: in diesem Recht lag eine Schwierigkeit; wenn man so will, ein latentes Zwar — Aber, das aufbrechen mußte, als — und in dem Maß, in dem — Israel zusammenwuchs, ja auch nur partikular zu größeren Einheiten fand. Welche Basis sollte haben, was *allen* auf Dauer identisch als Recht gelten sollte? — 'Zwar': eine Antwort zu finden, wurde wichtig. 'Aber': *eine* war ausgeschlossen — bei Strafe der Selbstpreisgabe dieses Rechts! Ausgeschlossen war die Institutionalisierung auf der Basis legitimierter Ungleichheit, auf der Basis von Herrschaft.

Die Alternative war Jahwe. Und Jahwe, den eines vor allem auszeichnet: mehr geben, als erwarten zu bekommen. Handeln von Ägypten her; Handeln wie dies:

> «Wenn du den Esel deines Hassers unter seiner Last erliegen siehst: hilf ihm auf, unbedingt!» (Ex 23,5*)

Wie diese Alternative ergriffen und wie umgekehrt vom Jahweglauben her an ihr gearbeitet wurde, — das sind Fragen, die zu beantworten uns zurückführen würde ins Bundesbuch und seine Traditionszusammenhänge, aber auch etwa hin zu Dtn 27,16-25, einer im hier entfalteten Kontext besonders bedeutsamen Einheit.

38. Vgl. zu diesem Element und seiner Funktion im Kontext J. HALBE, *Privilegrecht*, pp. 432ff.

39. Vgl. dazu eingehender auch J. HALBE, *«Altorientalisches Weltordnungsdeken»*, pp. 396ff.

Doch wir brechen ab. Genug zu erinnern, daß zu den 'Ursprungsbedingungen' israelitischen Rechts auch dies gehört: die sachliche Nähe des dieses Recht prägenden, tief im Gemeinschaftsleben verwurzelten 'Amity'-Geistes zur Jahwe-Religion. Genauer, zum Zentrum der Jahwe-Erfahrung: daß er sich Israel annimmt — rettend, befreiend; vor allem: nicht nach der Logik strenger Entsprechung von 'Tun' und 'Ergehen'. Sondern 'zuvorkommend'. Das selber heißt: diese Logik — unterbrechend.

War Gemeinschaft möglich, Gemeinschaft 'Israels': ohne den Preis der Legitimierung zentralisierter Gewalt? — Sie war möglich. Als eine des Rechts.

Doch nicht auf der Basis des Rechtes allein. Sondern des Rechts, sofern es als Wille des *einen*, für *alle* 'zuvorkommend' handelnden Gottes, Jahwes, erfahren und eingelebt wurde.

Was bleibt, ist für uns: zusammenzufassen. Ein Blick zurück; zugleich aber auch — voraus auf das Werden des Rechts, das zum 'deuteronomischen' wurde.

IV. Blick zurück und voraus

Mit welcher Evidenz, war eine unserer Fragen, setzt deuteronomisches Recht sich seiner Zeit und Gesellschaft entgegen, wie es dies tut? Mit welcher Erwartung, Zustimmung zu finden — auch in dem, was es *nicht* akzeptiert? Nicht nur im einzelnen nicht akzeptiert, sondern als Basis von Recht?

Ich denke, die Antwort ist klar: In ihm lebt der Geist eines Rechts, das tief in Vergangenheit wurzelt.

Ein Geist, der in früher, in nicht schon vom 'Staat' geordneter Welt seine Grundlagen hat. Der ein Geist war: des Lebens des Volkes.

Nirgendwann später konnte er wachsen wie hier: aus dem gegebenen Leben heraus: gestaltend, was *war*; konkret einleuchtend. Auch streitend mit 'Welt', darum Recht; streitend mit 'Welt' als der Rechtswille Jahwes. — Aber mit Anschluß in ihr!

Als eine Krise, die tief, die ins Leben ging, mußte im Sinn dieses Rechts, dieses alten, das Aufkommen des Königtums erlebt werden: Ungleichheit — legitimiert!

Durchbrochen dies eine, grundlegende: daß Reichtum nicht heißen darf: 'Verfügungsgewalt über viel', sondern: 'im Hinblick auf viel — Verpflichtung zu Beistand und Großzügigkeit'.

Zerschlagen die Grundstruktur von Gegenseitigkeit und Ebenbürtigkeit im Verkehr von Familien und Sippen.

Zerschlagen im Blick auf die Ordnung des ganzen. — Nicht gänzlich zerschlagen vor Ort. Nicht sogleich! Hier konnte — und gerade im Medium des Rechts, der Versammlung der Männer im Tor! — altes Wissen, alter Sinn festgehalten werden. — Aber das Ganze, das Volk?

Hier beim Alten zu bleiben, war nur mehr möglich im Gegenentwurf. War nur möglich, wenn selber das Ganze, das Volk, gegen die Wirklichkeit neu gedacht wurde. 'Abstrakt' — nämlich frei *gegenüber* der Welt.

Das Thema des Deuteronomiums!

Und so denn auch seine Antwort:

Jahwe! Frei gegenüber der Welt — und so auch Gemeinschaft mit ihm.

'Bruderschaft' — nun aber nicht mehr gestützt auf Verwandtschafts- und Nachbarschaftsbindung (L. Perlitt hat das gezeigt)[40]. Sondern davon 'abstrahiert': Bruderschaft im Jahwe-Volk.

Volk mit Vätern. — Aber mit Vätern, die wichtig sind nicht, weil die Linie des Blutes sich durchhält. (Dtn 5,3 ist sagbar: «Nicht mit unsern Vätern ...»!) Sondern weil Jahwe sich durchhält, sich treu bleibt in seiner Verheißung und Wahl.

Gemeinschaft, horribile dictu, mit einem König. — Aber mit einem, der ist, was jeder im Gottesvolk ist: 'Bruder'. «Nur daß er sich nicht viele Rosse halte ... Er soll sich auch nicht viele Frauen nehmen ... auch Silber und Gold soll er nicht zu viel sammeln!» (17,16f.) — Königsrecht: das!

Ein Recht, zweifellos, das Welt, wie sie ist — unterbricht.

Kielerstraße 30 Jörn HALBE
D-2308 Preetz

40. L. PERLITT, *«Ein einzig Volk von Brüdern»*, esp. pp. 42ff.50ff.

THE EMERGENCE OF THE DEUTERONOMIC MOVEMENT
THE HISTORICAL ANTECEDENTS

'*The place where the Lord will choose to establish his name there*' occupies — as is well known — a central place in the book of Deuteronomy, and from the time of Josiah, at least, there was no doubt that Jerusalem was the place. It is interesting, however, that the very book that considers Jerusalem the chosen place, so admires the place of Shechem at *Alonei-Moreh*, near Mt. Gerizim and Mt. Ebal (Deut 11,30, compare Gen. 12,6) [1]. The theme of blessings and curses at Gerizim and Ebal appears at the opening of the code and at its conclusion, and thus forms a kind of *inclusio* for the Deuteronomic law (Deut 11,26-30; 27). What is more, 'the words of the Torah', that is Deuteronomy [2], are written on the stones which are to be erected at Mt. Ebal (Deut 27,4,6).

The connection between the Deuteronomic Plains of Moab tradition and the tradition of Mt. Gerizim and Mt. Ebal is illustrated by the linking of Moses' sermon at the Plains of Moab to the ceremonies at Mt. Gerizim and Mt. Ebal. Moses' proclamations about Israel *becoming a people this day* are interwoven with these ceremonies: the first proclamation in Deut 26,16-19 comes before the command about the erection of the stones and building the altar at Ebal, while the second proclamation in 27,9-10 comes before the blessings and the curses at Gerizim and Ebal (27,11-26). By this combination the composer (I use purposely a vague expression in order not to commit myself) of Deuteronomy makes it clear that the establishment of the people of Israel at the Plains of Moab cannot be dissociated from their crossing the Jordan and erecting the stones and the altar at Mt. Ebal. In fact, what we have before us in Deuteronomy 26,16-28,69 is a description of the act of Israel's foundation at its entrance into Canaan. Moses' farewell address in Deuteronomy is a kind of preparation for the ceremony at Gerizim and Ebal.

1. It seems that the sacred site was outside the city somewhere between Mt. Gerizim and Mt. Ebal, cf. M. HARAN, *Shechem Studies* in *Zion* 38 (1973), pp. 6-9 (Hebrew). However it should not be separated from the city. The covenantal ceremonies are described as taking place «in Shechem», see Jos. 24,25, and compare Judges 9,6: «the terebinth of the pillar (אלון מצב) *at Shechem*». This terebinth is to be identified with the *Elon-meonnim* in Judg. 9,37 and with the terebinth in Gen. 35,4 and Jos. 24,26. Cf. recently B. MAZAR, *Canaan and Israel*, Jerusalem, 1974, pp. 148-150 (Hebrew).

2. This phrase occurs only in Deuteronomy and in the Deuteronomic literature (cf. M. WEINFELD, *Deuteronomy and the Deuteronomic School*, p. 339, no. 23) and solely refers to the book of Deuteronomy.

This conception contradicts the traditions in Exodus, according to which the foundation of the people of Israel — also involving erecting pillars, building an altar and writing the Laws (Exod 24,3-8) — took place at Sinai. In contrast to the view in Exodus chap. 24, according to which all the words of God were given to Israel at Sinai, Deuteronomy distinguishes between the Decalogue given to Israel at Horeb (5,19) and the other laws given to them just before they enter the promised land (6,1). The people turn into the people of God only when they take upon themselves the laws of Deuteronomy at the plains of Moab [3] as it says:

> This day the Lord your God commands you to observe these laws ... this day you have made God declare (האמרת) that he will be your God ... and that you will walk in his ways ... and God made you declare (האמירך) that you will be his people ... which shall observe all his commandments and that he will set you ... high above all the nations (26,16-19) [4].

This actually constitutes the solemn mutual proclamation, the *verba solemnia* of the bond between God and Israel [5].

Similar mutual declarations are reflected in Hosea, where we shall find other affinities to Deuteronomy. In Hosea we find that at the moment of the reestablishment of the relations between God and Israel, God says: «*I will say* to Lo-ammi: you are my people, and *he will say*: (you are) my God». At the rupture of the relationship, the divorce, as it were, the opposite is declared:

> «Call him Lo-ammi, because you are not my people and I will not be your (God)» (1,9, comp. Zech. 13,9) [6].

These declarations, playing on a background image of divorce and marriage [7], strengthen the view that the formula «I will be your God and

3. The laws themselves were revealed to Moses at Sinai (Deut. 5,28), but were disclosed to the Israelites only at the Plains of Moab (Deut. 6,1ff.).

4. For a thorough analysis of this passage cf. N. LOHFINK, *Dt. 26,17-19 und die «Bundesformel»*, in *Zeitschrift für katholische Theologie* 91 (1969) pp. 517-553.

5. Each declaration implies in itself the declaration of the other party. God declares that he will be the God of Israel and therefore Israel must keep his commandments whereas Israel declares that it will be the people of God and therefore God will guarantee its superiority, cf., with slight differences, the article of LOHFINK (previous note).

6. Recently M. E. FRIEDMAN (*JBL* 99 [1980], pp. 199-204) suggested that Hosea 2,17 וענתה שמה כימי נעוריה «and there she shall respond as in the days of her youth», refers to the formula of commitment recited by the wife to her husband: «You are my husband», which is very likely.

7. See the commentary of RASHBAM (RABBI SAMUEL B. MEIR, ed. D. ROSIN, p. 222): «You caused the Holy One, blessed be He, to say that He consents to be unto you a God, and He also caused you to say that you consent to be unto Him a people. האמרת = *fais dire* in foreign language (= French)». I do not consider this interpretation blasphemy, as does A. B. EHRLICH, *Peshuto shel Miqra*, v. 1, p. 362 (Heb.). On the contrary, the interpretation cited by EHRLICH (which he heard in his youth) that the root אמר here is to be understood in light of Rabbinic usage: עשה בה מאמר = he betrothed her unto her» (Mishnah Yeb. 2,1, 3,6, etc.) only strengthens R. Samuel's contention.

you will be my people» in Priestly and Deuteronomic literature are rooted in the legal sphere of marriage and adoption, as I have elsewhere observed [8].

The mutual declarations found in Deut 26,17-19 remind us of the declarations in Ex 19,6ff. where God says: «You will be a precious people to me, etc. ...», and the people respond: «We shall do all that the Lord has spoken» (19,8, cf. 24,7). However, whereas the declaration in the book of Exodus belongs to the Sinai covenantal cycle, the declarations in Deuteronomy belong to the Plains of Moab context; this, as indicated, is interwoven into the Shechemite tradition of Gerizim and Ebal. The shift from Sinai to the covenantal scene of the Plains of Moab becomes clearer when we compare Deut 26,16-19 to Ex 34,10-11. In both places one finds an enjoinder to observe the command of God, «which he commands this day» (מצוך היום), the proclamation of the establishment of relations between God and Israel, and, finally, God's promise to exalt Israel and distinguish it from other peoples on the face of the earth (comp. Ex 34,10; 33,14 with Deut 26,19). But whereas in Exodus the act of establishment takes place at Sinai, in Deuteronomy it happens on the plains of Moab and is associated with the ceremonies of Gerizim and Ebal [9].

In this light, it is clear that according to Deuteronomy the establishment of Israel as God's people occured not at Sinai but in Transjordan, with linkage to the sacred place at Shechem. Indeed, according to Jos 24, Joshua made a divine covenant at Shechem, erected a stone in testimony thereof, and recorded law in the book of God's Torah, as Moses did at Sinai (vv. 25.26).

In ancient Israel, in short, two views prevailed regarding the establishment of Israel as a people. According to one view this happened in Sinai at Moses' initiative; according to the other, it occured at Shechem, under Joshua's leadership [10]. The author of Deuteronomy adopted in principle the Shechemite version, but did not abandon altogether the Sinaitic one. He took the line of compromise: Horeb has been preserved as the place of the first revelation and the giving of the ten commandments, while Arboth-Moab on the border of the promised land has been chosen as the place of the establishment of the nation. In this manner he managed to preserve the position of the founder for Moses. He did not ascribe it to Joshua as did the author of Jos. 24. One could try to reconcile the two

8. Cf. my article in *VT* 27 (1977), pp. 188-189. Since the formula is so clearly expressed in Hosea it is possible that it is of Northern provenance like the other ideas of Deuteronomy (see below).

9. In the Qumran Temple Scroll the Deuteronomic laws uttered — according to tradition — by Moses at the Plains of Moab were put in the mouth of God and thus the setting of all the laws is shifted back to Sinai. See my article in *Shnaton, An Annual for Biblical and Ancient Near Eastern Studies* 3 (1978-9), pp. 218-219 (Hebrew).

10. For these divergent views cf. M. J. BIN GORION, *Sinai und Garizim*, 1926, pp. 311ff.

divergent traditions by the supposition that the covenant at Shechem constitutes the renewal of the Sinaitic covenant. However, this supposition cannot be upheld since Deut 26,16-18; 27,9 say explicitly that Israel became a nation «this day», i.e. standing at the plains of Moab, in contrast to the previous traditions which say explicitly that Israel became God's nation at Sinai (Ex 6,7; 19,4-8; 34,10-11).

Deuteronomy preserved then a very old tradition about the establishment of the nation at Shechem, the capital of the house of Joseph. Foundation stories of the Greek world [11] indicate that settlers whose colonization was based on divine instigation [12] used to perform ceremonies accompanied by blessings and curses [13] and by writing the oath [14] on stone [15]. Identical elements are found in the ceremony described in Deut. 27. Here we find:

1) erecting stones on Mt. Ebal in order to write upon them the words of the covenant (vv. 1-4,8)
2) building an altar (vv. 5-7) [16]
3) the proclamation of the act of foundation (vv. 9-10) [17]
4) blessings and curses (vv. 11-13, cf. 28,3-6, 16-19).

In addition to these we find there curses for transgressors who perpetrate crimes clandestinely (vv. 14-26).
The blessings and curses in vv. 11-13 refer to Deut 28,3-6, 16-19:

> Blessed shall you be in the city and blessed shall you be in the country.
> Blessed shall be the fruit of your womb, the fruit of your soil and the offspring of your cattle, the calving of your herd, and the lambing of your flock.
> Blessed shall be your basket and your kneading bowl.
> Blessed shall you be in your comings and blessed shall be in your goings.

11. See especially the inscription about the foundation of Cyrene (late seventh century BCE) in R. MEIGGS, D. LEWIS, *A Selection of Greek Historical Inscriptions to the End of the Fifth Century BC*, 1969, no. 5, pp. 5-9.

12. Cf. in the above mentioned document (previous note): ἐπεὶ Ἀπόλλων αὐτομάτιζεν «as Apollo expressed his own will (by oracle)», see LIDDEL-SCOTT-JONES, *Addenda s.v.* αὐτοματίζω and H. W. PARKE in *Journal of Hellenic Studies*, 82 (1962), 145f.

13. For the curses in the foundation decree of Cyrene and their dramatization by moulding wax images, a phenomenon well attested in the ancient Near East, see my article in *UF* 8 (1976), pp. 400-401.

14. About settlers of Cyrene it says: ὅρκια ἐποιήσαντο which means they established a treaty; see my article in *JAOS* 43 (1973), pp. 191 n. 9, 192 n. 47.

15. *Ibid., p. 198.*

16. An instructive parallel for this in the Greek tradition is to be found in THUCYDIDES 6,3:7 about the founders of Sicily who built an altar to Apollo. The altar stood in his time outside the city not unlike the altar of Mt. Ebal which is located outside the city of Shechem.

17. For the understanding of these verses as proclaiming the foundation of the nation cf. J. LICHT, in *Shnaton — An Annual for Biblical and Ancient Near Eastern Studies* IV (1980), pp. 98ff.

Their reversal, i.e. the curses:

> Cursed shall you be in the city etc.

That the ceremony of blessing and cursing on Mt. Gerizim and Mt. Ebal respectively refers to the series of blessings and curses in Deut 28,3-6.16-19 was already observed by Ibn Esra. It was also Ibn Esra who saw that the curse proclamations in Deut 27,14-26 apply to transgressions perpetrated in secrecy.

It is indeed interesting that both types of public anathema — cursing the violaters of the oath and banning transgressors — are attested in Greek covenantal oaths.

Thus, for instance, in the oath taken by the members of the amphictyony against Cirrha (the first «holy war», 590 BCE) we read [18]:

> If anyone should violate this, whether city, private man or tribe[19] let them be under the curse ... *that their land bear no fruit*; that their wives bear children not like those who begat them, but monsters; that *their flocks yield not their natural increase*; that *defeat await* them *in camp and court and their gathering place*.

Similarly in the Greek's oath at Plataeia before the battle with the Persians (479 BCE[20]):

> If I observe what is written in the oath my city will be *free of disease* : if not it shall be sick ...; and *my* (*land*) *shall bear* (*fruits*): if not it shall be barren; and the *women shall bear children* like their parents: if not they shall bear monsters; and *the flock shall bear like the flock*: if not (they shall be) monsters.

These blessings and curses are strikingly similar to the series of blessings and curses in Deut 28,3-6.16-19 quoted above.

As in the Greek oath at Plataeia every blessing in Deut 28,16-19 has its corresponding curse. And the content of the series is identical with that of the Greek oath: fertility of the soil, women and the flock. The element of *comming and going* in Deuteronomy is identical with the element of success or failure in *camp, court and agora* in the Greek oath[21]. Furthermore the element of sickness which occurs in the oath of Plateia appears in an identical series of blessings and curses in the ancient epilogue to the Covenant Code in Ex 23,25f.:

> I shall remove illness from your midst.
> None will miscarry or go barren in your land.

18. AESCHINES III 109-111.

19. Compare Deut. 29,17 in connection with the oath at the Plains of Moab: «perchance there is among you some man or woman or some clan or tribe». In Deut. 13 we also find warnings against instigators from a family or a city. For similar warnings in Ancient Near Eastern treaties see in my book *Deuteronomy*, pp. 91ff.

20. Cf. P. SIEWERT, *Der Eid von Plataiai* 1972, pp. 5-7.

21. The comings and goings (צאת ובוא) in Deut. 28,6.19 refer to war activities (Num. 27,17, Jos. 14,11, 1 Sam. 18,16, 29,6) as well as to participation in judicial procedure (Gen. 23,18, 34,24).

This is elaborated in Deut 7,13ff. in a chapter which depends on the peroration in Ex 23,20ff. [22]. Here we read:

> «He will bless the fruit of your womb and the fruit of your soil ... the increase of your herds, and your flocks of sheep ... there will be neither male nor female barren among you and your live-stock. And the LORD will remove from you all sickness.»

To all appearance, this genre of blessings and curses has its origin in the tribal confederation based on covenant; hence the similarity to the blessings and curses of the amphictyonic oaths in Greece. The stereotyped series of blessings and curses in Deut 28,3-6.16-19 thus belongs to the ancient Shechemite covenant ceremony which is elaborated by the Deuteronomic author of 28,7-14.20-68. These deuteronomic expansions have a lot in common with the Assyrian and Aramaean treaties of the 8-7th cent. BCE [23] and thus are clearly later than the short stereotypic blessings and curses which have their parallels in the Greek tribal milieu.

The «curses» in 27,14-26 represent a different genre. These are not threats of punishment as are those in 28,16-19, but legal proclamations accompanied by a curse and addressed to those who commit crimes clandestinely which cannot be punished by the authorities. Such «curses» are also attested in the Greek tribal culture. In Greece those who violated the law were reviled by the leaders and priests of the polity and were made «accursed» (*eparatos*). So, for example, it is related of Alcibiades (PLUTARCH, *Alcibiades* 22) that he was found liable at law for desecrating the sacra of Demeter. After placing his property under the «ban», his judges decided that the priests and priestesses should curse him. Aristides is said to have suggested that the priests should cast curses on anyone who abandoned the war-treaty with the Greeks (PLUTARCH, *Aristides* 10). As in Greece so in Israel it is the sacred group (the Levites) who have the authority to «revile», i.e. excommunicate the transgressors.

However, early Israel's affinities to the Greek tradition are most clearly expressed in the foundation ceremony found in Deut. 27. As indicated above oath taking and erecting stones during foundation ceremonies is attested in Greek colonization. Indeed, the Greeks as well as the Israelites had elaborate foundation traditions. Israel nurtured divergent traditions about their first settlements in the land. Besides the Shechemite tradition recounted in Deuteronomy 27 we find other versions describing foundation ceremonies linked to other places. According to a cycle of traditions crystallized at Gilgal, the children of Israel crossed the Jordan at Gilgal and erected stones there (Jos. 3-4) [24]. Instead of a written covenant we find there the ceremony of circumcision

22. See my book *Deuteronomy* pp. 46ff.
23. *Ibid.*, pp. 116ff.
24. According to the Rabbis (*Tosefta* Sotah 8,6) stones were erected at three sites: the plains of Moab, Gilgal and Mt. Ebal.

which is considered the sign of the covenant in Genesis 17 and the celebration of the Passover which is the oldest ritual connected with the Exodus.

Another sacred place which claimed for itself the tradition of foundation was Shiloh, and — as will be presently shown — the tradition of this sanctuary's foundation is even closer to the Greek *Ktisis* stories than the others. Priestly circles, especially those from the house of Eli, saw in the sanctuary of Shiloh the point of departure for the settlement of the Israelites in Canaan. According to this tradition, after arriving to the land of Canaan the Israelites set up the Tent of Meeting in Shiloh. From there Joshua dispatched men to divide the land in accordance with the lots cast before the Lord (Jos 18). This tradition has clear echoes in the Greek tradition of colonization.

Thus we read in Odyss. VI, 2ff. that Nausithos settled in Scheria, surrounded the city with a wall, built houses, *made temples of the gods* and divided the land. Similarly, we read in Jos 18,1ff. that the Israelites gathered in Shiloh after the land was conquered and set up the tent of Meeting there. After the Tabernacle is established, Joshua sends out men (three from each tribe) to measure the land and then casts the lot and divides the land according to tribe.

A similar procedure is found in a decree about the foundation of an Athenian colony at Brea (445 BCE)[25]. The decree provides for the selection of geo-nomoi for allocation of land; and like in Joshua they are selected according to clans (phyle): «Geonomoi shall be elected, 10 men, one from each phyle, these shall allocate the land».

An instructive analogy to Joshua's enterprise may be found in the Laws of Plato 745, where the matter of founding a colony is discussed. The plan of a new colony, according to Plato, should be as following:

> The city should be founded in the center of the new settled country. A temple should be erected and surrounded with a wall. Then the whole land is to be divided into twelve sections with a corresponding division of the countryside and twelve allotments for each of the twelve gods.

This is strikingly similar to what is said about the division of the land in Jos 18,1-10. Furthermore, as Biblical law prohibits the sale (Lev 25,23) or transfer of land (Numbers 36,7) because the land is the Lord's, so we read in Plato's Law that land should be kept in the family (740) and that since the land is holy to the gods it should not be sold (742).

The various traditions about the establishment of Israel in its land belong then to the pattern prevalent in the Eastern Mediterraenean after the destruction of Troy. As I shall try to show elsewhere, the small nations emerging at the end of the second millenium BCE in the Eastern Mediterreanean were concerned with their identity and the legitimacy of

25. MEIGGS-LEWIS, *Greek Historical Inscriptions* 1969 no. 49.

their settlements, and the foundation stories supplied the answers to the problems. As we have seen, in ancient Israel three versions of such stories were preserved: the Shechemite version, the Gilgal version and the priestly one about Shiloh. Deuteronomy has chosen the Shechemite tradition and sees the act of establishment of Israel against the background of the ceremony at Gerizim and Ebal. Judah did not preserve any such tradition of foundation and the Deuteronomist could only rely on the northern heritage in this matter. For this purpose he chose neither Gilgal nor Shiloh [26], but Shechem, and it seems that the Shechemite northern tradition left its imprint on other aspects of the ideology of Deuteronomy. The Shechemite tradition seems indeed to be the most ancient one, and this may now be corroborated by archaeological evidence. We are lastly informed about a plan of Mt. Ebal excavations. This plan shows an altar (9 × 7 m) overlooking the Jordan valley with numerous ovens and a temenos around the area. According to the excavator, Adam Zaretal, the finds are of the 12th cent. BCE and there is no sign of any continuation of the later times. We may surmise that the site with its installation reveals something of the Israelite cult at Mt. Ebal; what is very significant is that the place overlooks the Jordan valley, which may explain the linkage of the Mt. Ebal ceremony to the crossing of the Jordan (at Damiyeh) and arriving for Shechem by Wadi Farʿah.

The ideology of Deuteronomy and its northern roots

The purification of Israel's cult from pagan elements including the abolishment of the high places, associated with the Hezekianic-Josianic reforms, has its roots also in northern Israel.

The struggle with Baal worship started in the North in the period of Ahab, and in the time of Jehu the Baal was extirpated from Israel (2 Kings 10,28). From the struggle with the Baal apparently evolved the polemic against the golden calves which is expressed by Hosea (10,5, 13,2). As is well known, the sins of the Baal and of the golden calves are, in Deuteronomic historiography, the two decisive sins of Israel. Both sins were condemned in Northern Israel (see especially Hosea), before the rise of the Deuteronomic movement.

Furthermore, it seems that the condemnation of the astral worship so characteristic of the Deuteronomic writings has its roots in the North. Amos 5,26 refers vaguely to this sin [27], but the assault is more clearly expressed in the Septuagint version of Hosea. In the framework of the

26. Priestly circles in Judah may have preserved the tradition of Shiloh as the establishment site. Cf. Jeremiah 7,12. Jeremiah was a priest of Anatoth, and thus a descendent of Abiathar, from the house of Eli.

27. Cf. my article in *UF* 4 (1972), pp. 149-150.

admonition against pagan worship in Hos 13,1-4 we find a short doxology which according to the LXX reads as follows:

> I am the Lord your God who forms the heavens and creates the earth, whose hand created all the host of heavens and I did not fix them for you to go after them. I am the God who brought you out of Egypt etc.

We find here affinites to Deut 17,3:

> «a man or women who turned to worship ... of the heavenly host, something that I never commanded»

and other passages in Deuteronomy which speak about astral worship as having been assigned to other peoples but not to Israel (Deut 4,19, 29,25). As has recently been argued by several scholars [28] there is no basis for denying the authenticity of the doxologies of Amos and Hosea.

Another interesting short doxology in Hos 12,6 polemicises against popular religious views. As H. L. Ginsberg recognized [29], Hos. 12,4-5 contains criticism of the notion of Jacob wrestling with the angel (comp. Gen 32,25f). Hosea seems to imply here that one should not rely upon angels because God himself is the savior and none else: «Yet the Lord, the God of Hosts, must be invoked as Lord» (NJPS) (and not any of the angelic hosts). The same attitude is to be recognized in the book of Deuteronomy. As I have shown in my book [30], Deuteronomy chap. 7 purposely omits the angel encountered in the old Exodus traditions of Ex 23, on which it relies. A similar omission occurs in Deut 26,8 which is verbally dependent on Num 20,15-16, where the angel appears as bringing out the people from Egypt. This anti-angelolistic view comes clearly to expression in Deut 4,37:

> «He himself (בפניו) took you out of Egypt»

For this meaning of פנים cf. Exod 33,14-15; 2 Sam 17,11. It seems that aversion towards belief in angels as mediators is a characteristic feature of Deuteronomy. This accords with the facts that the Urim and Tummim are not mentioned at all in Deuteronomy and that the ark in Deuteronomy does not function as the seat of the Lord but only as a receptacle for the tablets [31].

The polemic against the worship of stone and wood which is so salient in Deuteronomy and the Deuteronomic literature (4,25; 27,15; 28,36.63; 29,16; 31,29) is already found in Hosea and appears there in phraseology identical with that of Deuteronomy. In Hosea 13,2 we find מעשה חרשים, «craftsman work», which is identical with מעשה ידי חרש in Deut 27,15. Similary the word מעשה ידי אדם «handiwork of man» in Hosea 14,4 is

28. See the discussion in J. L. CRENSHAW, *Hymnic Affirmation of Divine Justice*, (SBL Dissert. Series 24) 1975.
29. *JBL* 80 (1961), pp. 339-347.
30. *Deuteronomy* etc. pp. 33-34.
31. *Ibid.*, pp. 208-209.

most characteristic of Deuteronomic literature. It seems to me that we ought not speak about the influence only of Hosea on the Deuteronomic school but about an iconolastic tendency originating in the North which pervaded Judah after the destruction of Samaria. It was this tendency which caused Hezekiah to smash the bronze serpent in Jerusalem (2 Kings 18,4). The Chronicle which recounts this event speaks also about the removal of the high-places, the breaking of the pillars and the cutting down of the Asherah: it is not by chance that all these are mentioned together. We have to do here with deeds intended to purge from Israelite religion pagan elements. As is well known, the Canaanite cult was based on high-places, which contained stone pillars and wooden symbols, and it seems that the iconoclastic stream which started in the North developed the struggle not only against the golden calves but also against high-places, pillars and Asheroth. In the final stage, all provincial altars were prohibited as the doctrine of centralization of the cult reflects. This process too finds its echo in the book of Hosea. Let us adduce the evidence.

Like Deut 12,2 which prohibits worship on highplaces because this is the way the pagans worship their gods, «on lofty mountains and on hills or under any luxuriant tree», Hosea admonishes his generation for worshipping «on mountaintops, on hills ... and under trees whose shade is pleasant» (4,13). The condemnation of trees in worship joins the condemnation of stone worship, as in the Deuteronomic literature:

> «he made altars a plenty, cult pillars abounded ... their heart is divided, they feel guilty, he will pull apart his altars, he will smash his pillars» (Hos 10,1-2)

There is no reference here to idolatry but to the multiplying of altars and pillars[32]. Israel is guilty because of serving God with divided heart — false and insincere — in contrast to the «wholeheartedness» (בכל לב) much stressed in the Deuteronomic writings:

The same tendency is reflected in Hos. 8,11-13:

> For Ephraim ... has multiplied altars
> altars have become his sin ...
> they love sacrifices,
> let them slaughter and eat meat (יזבחו בשר ויאכלו)
> the Lord has not accepted them.

This kind of reservation about altars and sacrifices is also found in Amos. He says:

> Come to Bethel and transgress,
> Come to Gilgal and multiply transgressions,
> present your sacrifices every morning,
> because this is what you love, o Israelites (4,4-5).

32. Contra RUDOLPH (KAT 1966) in his commentary on these verses.

The sacrifices as such are seen here as transgressions and their multiplication means multiplying sin, as Hosea sees in the multiplication of altars multiplication of sin. Hosea and Amos see the sacrifices as means for the gratification of the desire to eat flesh; therefore the proclamation: «Let them slaughter and eat meat, the Lord has not accepted them». A similar phrase is found in Jerem 7,21:

> «Add your burnt offerings to the other sacrifices and eat meat»

It is this very language which Deuteronomy uses when allowing profane slaughter:

> «wherever (or whenever) you desire you may slaughter and eat meat» (12,15) [33].

This is the view that took root in Judah during the days of Hezekiah and paved the way for the reform.

It is true, it was not ideology alone that brought the revolutionary change. As I indicated years ago [34] the Hezekian reform was born out of dire circumstances at the time of Sennacherib's expedition against Judah, when only Jerusalem was left free. It was therefore easy to proclaim Jerusalem as the only legitimate place of worship. However, the Northern opposition to multiplying sacrifices could well have served as the ideological support for the decree of centralization. One must add that the fact that Jerusalem was saved by miracle from Sennacherib's assault added a glorious dimension to the decree of centralization [35].

The objection to provincial sites created the proper atmosphere for spiritualization of worship. The temple in Jerusalem in the Deuteronomic school was conceived not as the physical house of the Lord but as the house in which God established *his name*. The deuteronomic writer never says that God dwells in the house but always — in consistent manner — that God causes his name to be there [36]. Deuteronomy too, deals with the cult in an indirect way. It is not said what one does in the house of the Lord, but what one ought not to do. We do not find commands about communal sacrifices, festival offerings, kindling the lamps, burning, sacrificing the daily sacrifice (תמיד) etc. There is no doubt that the

33. See H. L. GINZBERG, *The Israelian Heritage of Judaism*, New York 1982, p. 21; J. JEREMIAS, *Hosea* (ATD) 1983, p. 111, n. 21.

34. Cf. my article in *JNES* 23 (1964), pp. 202-212.

35. If M. HARAN is correct in assuming that Lev. 17 demands centralization of worship (cf. his article in *Beer-Sheva* I [1973], 114ff. [Heb.]) and that P was crystallized in the days of Ahaz and Hezekiah (*Zion* 45 [1980], pp. 10-12 [Heb.]), then the most appropriate time for the execution of the reformation was the eve of Sennacheribs siege, when the cities of Judah were in the hands of the enemy [2 Kings 18,13] and only Jerusalem remained under Judean sovereignty. Jerusalem's salvation was interpreted by the people as a sign that God did not abandon his legitimate holy dwelling-place, while abandoning other cities of whose altars he disapproved. For the miracle of the salvation of Jerusalem as the background for the centralization ideology cf. V. MAAG in *VT* 6 (1956), pp. 10-18.

36. Cf. my discussion in *Deuteronomy* etc. pp. 193ff.

author of Deuteronomy takes it for granted that such cultic acts were performed in the temple (cf. e.g. 2 Kings 16,15); however, he does not find it necessary to prescribe them. The only ritual performances he is interested in are those of the first fruits, the removal of the tithe and the ceremony of the unknown murder: this is because these are accompanied by prayer (Deut 26,5-10.13-15; 21,7-9) and prayer is what he is concerned with. Indeed the Shema' and the Ten Commandments both of which turned into standard prayers in the second Temple (Mishnah Tamid 5:1) occur in Deuteronomy one next to the other (5,6-6,9). It is even possible that already in Deuteronomy both were intended to serve as a Credo.

We do not know whether this spiritualized understanding of the religion existed in Northern Israel or is the outcome of inner development in Judah in the time of Hezekiah-Josiah. One thing is clear: that it confines the line of development which started in Israel during the time of Ahab and went on down to the period of Hosea the prophet. This brings us to the feelings of guilt and the expression of repentance so characteristic of the Deuteronomic movement but which have their incipits in the book of Hosea.

The return to God and the return to the Lord

The exile of Israelite population which started in 732 with the invasion of Tiglath Pileser III into Galilee (2 Kgs 15,29) deeply shocked the nation of Israel. It seems that this is the time when the faithful of the nation began to ponder Israel's destiny. They saw in the national catastrophe divine punishment for their syncretism: the worship of the Baal and the golden calves. Because of these sins Hosea indeed predicts dispersion into Egypt and Assyria (8,9-13; 9,3; 11,5). Especially striking in these predictions is the phrase: «they will go back to Egypt», «and Ephraim will go back to Egypt», which reminds us the conclusion of the threats in Deuteronomy 28,68:

> «and God will bring you back to Egypt with ships».

At the time of Hosea, the prophet, when the kingdom of Samaria disintegrated, Israel, as well as Judah had close relationship with Egypt (2 Kgs 17,4; Isa 18,2; 30,1ff.; 31,1ff.) and as the Assyrian danger approached, Israelites sought Asylum in Egypt. The Israelite diaspora in Egypt in this period is mentioned in Isaiah 11which is about an exile in *Egypt, Patros and Cush* (v. 11). We have no right to see this verse as post-exilic — as some assume — since these three territorial units appear in the same order in the Esarhaddon inscriptions and this topographical combination does not occur elsewhere[37]. It seems that the Jewish

37. Cf. S. PARPOLA, *Neo-Assyrian Toponyms* (AOAT 6), 1970.

diaspora in upper Egypt — *pꜣ-tꜣ-rsy* = the land of the southerner (Patros) — started in this period and continued there until the time of Jeremiah (Jer 44,1.15). Hosea, who lived and acted before the fall of Samaria, speaks therefore about the descent to Egypt no less than about the ascent to Assyria (8,9). In general he speaks about wandering amongst nations (9,17; 7,8; 8,8).

The phenomenon of exile brought with it naturally the longing for return to the homeland and hence the current term for return, שוב שבות, which is prevalent in the Deuteronomic literature but is first mentioned in Hosea. In fact, the idea of returning from exile or returning from captivity is not particular to Israel and Judah. It is also attested in Aramaic texts of this period, in the Sefire inscriptions:

> And now the gods have brought about the return (השבו שיבת) of my father's house ... and the return of Talayim (III, 24-25) [38].

However in Hosea [39] and in the Deuteronomic writings the return to the land is combined with the return to God. Hosea speaks about God who brings about the return of his people and heals Israel: «When I would bring about the restoration of my people, when I would heal Israel» (6,11-7,1) [40]. Similarly we read in 14,2-5 «Return, O Israel, to the Lord your God, for you have fallen because of your sin ... I will heal their apostasy. I will take them back in love». The return to God is then conditioned by healing caused by God out of generous love, an idea which occurs in Deut 30,1-10. This, like Hos 14,2-10, comes after a list of threats (28,29,9-28). As in Hos. 14,2, in Deut. 30,2 we find the expression «to return to God» (שוב עד ה') as well as the expression שב השבות (ו. 3). Here, also, it is accompanied by the idea of divine help in enabling the people to repent: «The Lord will circumcise your heart ... to love the Lord your God» (v. 6). Circumcision of heart here parallels the healing of apostasy in Hosea. The same idea appears in Jeremiah:

> «Return to me you apostate sons, I will heal your apostasy» (3,22)
> «I will heal and cure Judah and Israel ... I will restore their fortunes, I will cleanse them of all the wickedness and sin» (33,2f.)

In another instance dealing with restoration and repentance we find more verbal congruence between Deuteronomy and Hosea:

Hosea 5,15-6,1	Deut. 4,29-30
In their distress (בצר להם) they will seek me: [41] «come let us return to the Lord».	You will seek the Lord ... when you are in distress (בצר לן) ... you will turn back to the Lord

38. Cf. J.A. FITZMYER, *The Aramaic Inscriptions of Sefire*, 1967. For the other minorities in Syria striving to return to their homeland cf. J. EPHAL, 'The Western Minorities in Babylonia in the 6th-5th Centuries BC', in *Orientalia* 47 (1978), pp. 74-90.

39. For a thorough analysis of the theme of repentence in Hosea see A. BIRAM, in *A. Urbach Festschrift* (5715), pp. 116-139 (Heb.).

40. The end of 6,11 is to be joined to the beginning of 7,1.

41. Similar verbage is attested in wisdom passages (Prov. 1,27-28) which have affinities to Deuteronomy and Hosea, cf. my book *Deuteronomy* etc. p. 369.

Deut. chaps. 30 and 4 are usually believed to be post-exilic. But in light of the fact that the ideas of repentance and return occur already in Hosea we may legitimately suppose that these ideas started to crystallize in Northern Israel and were later adopted in Judah and applied to the exile of Judah (cf. Jer 29,13-14; 1 Kgs 8,47f.).

The affinities between Hosea and Deuteronomy may also be found in other areas of theology: Thus the concept of the love of God to Israel is expressed very clearly in Hosea as well as in Deuteronomy (Hos 11,1-8; 14,5; Deut 1,31; 10,15 and cf. Jer. 31,2). The same applies to the concept of *berith* connected to *Torah* which is central in the Deuteronomic literature but is clearly attested in Hosea (8,1, comp. 6,7; 8,12). There is no justification for denying the authenticity of these verses in Hosea since the concept *Torah of the Lord* occurs also in Isa. 5,24; 30,9, undisputed Isaianic verses[42].

The most striking point of contact between Hosea and Deuteronomy is the formulation of the idea of hybris. The concept of forgetting the Lord out of affluence and satiety which occurs also in other Biblical sources (Deut 32,10f., cf. wisdom literature)[43] is expressed in Hosea and Deuteronomy in a particularly idiosyncratic manner: man eats his fill and his heart grows haughty and forgets God:

Hosea 13,6	Deut. 8,12-14
They were filled,	Lest, when you have eaten and are dull …
their heart was lifted up,	your heart be lifted up
therefore they forgot me.	and you forget the Lord your god.

The verbs are identical in both sources: שׂבע, רום לב, שׂכח. The idea as such occurs in the song of Moses (Deut. 32,10ff.), in the framework of the description of leaving the desert and coming into the affluent land. It is interesting to note that in Hosea verse 13,6 follows a mention of God guiding the Israelites in the desert.

How are we to explain the contact between northern prophecy and the Book of Deuteronomy which became the basis for Jerusalemite theology in the period of Hezekiah-Josiah?

The national renaissance at the times of Hezekiah and Josiah

After the fall of Samaria, Hezekiah, King of Judah, made efforts to draw the northern population towards Jerusalem as may be learned from 2 Chr 30. Although the book of Chronicles is a tendentious work we

42. L. PERLITT argues that מאס תורת יהוה in Is. 5,24, as well as in Amos 2,4, is deuteronomistic (*Bundestheologie im Alten Testament* 1969, p. 147). But this phrase is not attested in Deuteronomic literature. Cf. the list of idioms and indices in my book *Deuteronomy etc.* pp. 320ff. On the authenticity of the oracle against Judah in Amos 2,4-5 cf. S. M. PAUL, *A Literary Reinvestigation of the Authenticity of the Oracles against the Nations of Amos*, in *De la Torah au Messie, Mélanges H. Cazelles*, 1981, pp. 144ff.

43. Cf. M. WEINFELD, *Deuteronomy* p. 281.

have no right to see the event itself as fiction. The flow of Northerners to Jerusalem in those days is now attested archaeologically. At the end of the eight century BCE Jerusalem underwent an expansion never encountered before; the same applies to the territory of Judah. As shown by Avigad [44], Jerusalem of that time included the western hill of the city, now the Jewish quarter. By the same token the settlement of Judah grew immensely at this period and the population doubled [45]. The only explanation for this situation is that after the fall of the northern kingdom Israelites began to migrate to the south to the territories under the control of their brethren [46]. That people from the North were attached after the fall of the northern kingdom to Jerusalem and its cult may be learned from the fact that after the destruction of the Temple of Jerusalem people from *Shechem, Siloh and Samaria* made pilgrimages to the Temple site (Jer. 41,5). It seems that in this period, the hatred between Judah and Israel vanished and some kind of symbiosis between the sister nations was established. This is reflected perhaps in Isaiah's consolation oracle of this time:

> «Ephraim's jealousy shall vanish and Judah's enmity shall end, Ephraim shall not envy Judah and Judah shall not harass Ephraim» (11,13)

In the continuation of this oracle we read about the expansion of Israel and Judah towards the Philistine territory in the west on the one hand and Ammon, Moab and Edom in the east on the other (v. 14). The period of Hezekiah was indeed a period of great expansion. In 2 Kgs 18,8 we hear about Hezekiah overrunning Philistia as far as Gaza and from 1 Chr 4,41-43 we learn about his incursion towards Seir in the south. It is this period that «the remnant of Israel ... and the house of Jacob» return to the Lord and to «mighty God» (אל גבור) [47] (Isa 10,20-21). As has been recently seen by H. Cazelles the remnant which returns, שאר ישוב, represents the Israelites from the North who join Judah and accept the authority of Hezekiah, styled (among other things) «El Gibbor» (cf. Isa 9,5) [48]. The same imagery is found in Micah 5,1. Micah speaks about the youngest of the clans of Judah, who will rule Israel; then the rest of his brethren will return to the children of Israel (5,1-2). This rectifies the earlier situation when Judah was cut off from the other tribes (cf. Deut 33,7: «Hear, O Lord, the voice of Judah and bring him back to

44. *The Upper City of Jerusalem*, 1980, pp. 23ff. (Heb.).

45. Cf. *Judaea, Samaria and the Golan, Archaeological Survey* 1967-1968, ed. M. KOCHAVI 1972, pp. 20-21 (Heb.)

46. Cf. M. BROSHI, *Expansion of Jerusalem under Hezekiah and Manaseh*, in *IEJ* 24 (1974), pp. 23-26.

47. This equals חזקיה and seems to allude to King Hezekiah.

48. *Le nom de Shear Yashub* etc., in *Proceedings of the Eighth World Congress of Jewish Studies*, Division A, 1982, pp. 47-50.

his people»)[49]. Micah goes on to say that the leader of Judah will stand and shepherd by the might of the Lord ... Assyria with the sword (vv. 3-5). This suits Hezekiah, who rebelled against the king of Assyria and expanded the territory of his kingdom (before the invasion of Sennacherib).

This period of national revival may explain the nationalistic and patriotic atmosphere prevailing in Deuteronomy and Deuteronomic literature. The book of Deuteronomy abounds with military speeches aimed at strengthening the people in their future wars with their enemies[50]. These in fact reflect the national fervor of the times of Hezekiah-Josiah[51]. Remarks such as «be strong and courageous» (חזק ואמץ), «no man shall be able to stand against you» (לא יתיצב איש בפניכם), «every spot on which your foot treads shall be yours», «the Lord your God will put the dread and the fear on you over the land in which you set foot» (11,24-25) seem to express the national enthusiasm of the period of Hezekiah-Josiah. I refer to the Hezekiah or Josianic period because it is very hard to date the various layers of Deuteronomic literature. Since the book of Deuteronomy was discovered in the days of Josiah (622 BCE) we must suppose that the main layout of the book was existent long before that time — that is, at the time of Hezekiah. However, we still do not know what belongs to later Josianic elaboration and what existed before.

The idea of the ban on all Canaanite population also seems to have crystallized at this time. According to the book of Deuteronomy the Israelites are commanded to exterminate all the Canaanites and not to leave a soul of them living (Deut. 20,16-17). Such a rigorous policy, obliging the extermination of the whole population of the land whether fighting or passive is utopian and is indeed unheard of in the historical accounts of Israel[52]. On the contrary, from 1 Kgs 9,21 we learn that the Israelites were unable to annihilate the inhabitants of Canaan and Solomon subjected them to corvée labor. Rabbinic sources[53] preserved a tradition according to which Joshua sent out three messages to the Canaanites: 'Whoever wants to make peace let him make peace, whoever wants to evacuate let him evacuate and whoever wants to fight let him

49. H. CAZELLES, *ibid.*

50. Cf. WEINFELD, *Deuteronomy* etc. pp. 45ff.

51. Josiah's audacity in confronting the Egyptian king as he set out for the Euphrates (2 King 23,29) is rooted in this nationalist fervor.

52. According to A. BIRAM (*Tarbiz* 23 [1952], p. 138) the main kernel of the law (Deut. 20,10-14) which commands call for peace originally referred to the Canaanite cities and it was the Deuteronomic editor who applied it to the non-Canaanites. Indeed the words כן תעשה «thus you shall do» in v. 15 constitute an exegetical clause, compare וכן תעשה in Deut. 22,3.

53. Cf. *Palest. Talmud Shebi'ith* 6:1, 36,c; *Debarim Rabah, Šopetim* 14 (ed. LIEBERMAN p. 101).

fight'; Judaism could not conceive a massive slaughter by command of God. The command of *Herem* of all the Canaanites in Deuteronomy is an utopian program which reflects the bitter struggle with the Canaanite religion and culture ongoing from the time of Elijah until the time of Josiah. Indeed the reason for the annihilation of the Canaanites in Deut 20,18 is one of *Kulturkampf*:

> «lest they (the Canaanites) lead you into doing all the abominable things that they have done for their gods and you shall be sinful to the Lord your God».

One should acknowledge that the Herem as such was practiced in ancient Israel as elsewhere in the ancient world (cf. Mesha inscriptions). It is found in connection with Jericho (Jos 6,17), Amalek (1 Sam. 15) and is also applied to apostate or treacherous cities within Israel such as the city condemned for idolatry in Deut 13,16 and the cities of Benjamin which were banned because of the sin at Gibea (Judg 20,40.48). It seems that Deuteronomy adopted the ancient doctrine of Herem from the North (cf. also 1 Kgs 20,42) and applied it theoretically towards the seven nations of the land of Canaan. The original Herem referred to hostile cities banned by means of votive proclamations (Jos 6,17; Numb 21,2-3) whereas Deuteronomy conceived Herem as an automatic decree which applied to a whole country and its inhabitants. This sort of Herem is not dependent on any vow or dedication, but is an a priori decree which belongs more to theory than to practice.

The national patriotic attitude of Deuteronomy may also be recognized in its conception of the extent of the promised land. According to the ancient sources of the Pentateuch, and especially the list of boundaries in Num 34,1-15, Transjordan was not part of the land of Israel. The request of the Gadites and Reubenites to settle in Transjordan was considered by Moses as a sin (Num 32,14), and from Jos 22,19 we may deduce that Transjordan was considered impure land. The stories of the conquest in Jos 2-9 also make it clear that the conquest started with the crossing of the Jordan: the passage of the Jordan and the erecting of the stones at Gilgal actually commemorate the entrance into the promised land (Jos 3,10; 5,1, etc.). This old conception about the Jordan being the border of the land was not accepted by Deuteronomy. According to Deut. 1-3 the conquest of the land started with the crossing of the river Arnon (Deut 2,24) at the border between Moab and the Mishor, the territory of King Sihon. In accordance with this view the Israelites apply the law of Herem to these territories (2,34; 3,6) just as they are commanded to do to the peoples of the Western side of the Jordan (Deut 20,16-17). The conquered territories of the eastern side of the Jordan are divided among the tribes as are the other parts of the promised land, and are not just a gift on condition as in Num 32. The author of Deuteronomy accepted the ideal borders of Gen 15,18, which reflect the borders of the Davidic kingdom, as binding borders (see Deut 1,7; 11,24); for him, therefore, Transjordan was an integral part of the land (cf. Deut 34,1). In his manner, the author of Deuteronomy affords Transjordan a status equal with that of Cisjordan; this works like an endeavor to restore Israel to its ideal borders of the Davidic-Solomonic period [54].

The national resurgence of the period of Hezekiah or Josiah explains the feelings of superiority expressed in Deuteronomy. Israel is promised exaltation above all nations of the earth (26,19) to be always at the top and never at the bottom (28,13); people who hear the laws of Israel will say: «That great nation is a wise and understanding people» (4,6); «Israel will rule many nations but they will not rule it» (15,6). The book of Deuteronomy depicts Israel as a proud nation unfearful but feared. In accordance with this, it changes and reworks old sources. In Numbers, the Israelites asked permission from Edom to cross its territory. The Edomites refuse and went out against the Israelites in force (Num 20,14-21). In the book of Deuteronomy, the opposite happens: Not only do the Israelites pass Edom and buy food there (2,6.29), but the Edomites fear the Israelites and the Israelites are asked not exploit this fact in order to provoke the Edomites (2,4-5) [55].

The national pride prevailing in Deuteronomy comes to bold expression in the account of Moses' appointing officers for judging the people. According to Exod. 18 the appointment arose from the advice of Jethro the priest of Midian. In Deut 1,13-17, Moses appoints the officers on his own initiative. Jethro is not mentioned at all because — as A. B. Ehrlich says [56] — 'in the Deuteronomist's days it was not glorious to tell the people that a foreigner contrived such a plan'.

Deuteronomic historiography

The national consciousness which developed in the periods of Hezekiah and Josiah set in motion the work of Deuteronomic historiography which pretends to present the nation's history from the Exodus to the end of the monarchic period [57]. The alleged restoration of old Israel at this time awakened a new interest in the past of the nation. In order to implement the task it was necessary to collect various traditions from the

54. See M. WEINFELD, *The Extent of the Promised Land — the Status of Transjordan*, in *Das Land Israel in biblischer Zeit* (ed. G. STRECKER), Göttingen, 1983, pp. 59-75.

55. See M. WEINFELD, *The Awakening of National Consciousness in Israel in the 7th Century BC*, in *Oz LeDavid: D. Ben-Gurion Jub. Vol.*, 1967, pp. 412ff. (Heb.).

56. *Randglossen zur hebräischen Bibel*, 1908, to Deut. 1,9.

57. The project was begun during the period of Hezekiah-Josiah but deuteronomistic scribes continued it until after the destruction of Jerusalem. Many posit the existence of two deuteronomistic strata: pre-destruction and post-destruction, but it is difficult to establish the extent and nature of these strata.

great Israel in the North, and this was done with the help of the people from the North who migrated to the revived capital (see above). The scribes who were engaged in this work divided the history into three periods: conquest, judges and monarchy, a division accepted until our days. However this schematic division is the product of the systematic thought of the scribes. The material was presented in a way that would suit the tripartite division of the history of Israel in its land; the material itself, however, can not be subjected to such division. The conquest — as is well known — continued during the time of the Judges and was not limited to the days of Joshua.

In order to present the period of the conquest, these scribes collected traditions from Northern sanctuaries such as Gilgal, Shechem and Shiloh (not from Bethel and not from Dan which were associated with the cult of the golden calves) and these were preferred to that of the Judaic tradition of Judges 1. I have tried to show elsewhere that Judges 1 constitutes a tendentious Judahite document about the conquest which ignores the achievement of the Ephraimites under the aegis of Joshua. This tradition was not incorporated in the original Deuteronomic historiography, which completes the conquest with the farewell speech of Joshua in Josh. 23 and opens the period of the Judges with the sermon in Judg 2,6ff. Judg 1,1-2,5 contains, on the other hand, ancient material which was added as an appendix in later times.

The deuteronomic scribes utilized Northern traditions in order to render an ideal picture of total conquest of the land under Joshua, the leader of the house of Joseph. The traditions themselves do not draw such a picture since the wars described are limited to the area of Benjamin, and to the valley of Ayalon south-west of Mt. Ephraim on the one hand and to the battle of the waters of Merom on the other. The scribes, however, arranged the traditions in such a way as to create the impression of a systematic military operation: a battle in the center with its ramification to the south which enabled the conquest of the center and the south; and a battle in the North, which completed the conquest of the whole land from Baal Gad in the valley of Lebanon down to Mt. Halaq at Mt. Seir in the south (Jos. 11,16-17). The individual traditions themselves utilized by the author do not feature such a Blitz.

In order to describe the settlement of the tribes in the various parts of the land the deuteronomic scribes utilized various administrative lists from various periods, and retrojected them to the time of Joshua. Thus, for example, the list of settlements used to present Joshua's allotment of Judah (chap. 15) is actually an administrative list of Judah from the time of Josiah [58]. Analysis of the list shows that it could not have been composed before the times of Josiah. Thus, for example, the city of

58. For the Josianic background of this list see A. ALT, *Kleine Schriften* II, pp. 276-288.

En Gedi mentioned in the list (v. 62) was nonexistent before the 7th century[59]. Most of the lists are from the time of the monarchy and the delineations of the tribes' border as well as the list of the Levitical cities are from the time of the united monarchy[60]. They were used by the scribes anachronistically as descriptions of settlements at the beginning of the Israelites' settlement in the land of Canaan.

It is hardly necessary to mention that the presentation of the period of Judges is mainly based on documents and traditions from the North. For the period of David and Solomon the scribes drew from the Jerusalemite archives but for the Israelite kingdom they were dependent on northern material including prophetic stories. Only when they reached the period of Hezekiah and Josiah did they use Judean material again (2 Kgs 18-25). The large proportion of northern material in the deuteronomic historiography teaches us that the writers availed themselves of contacts with the North in their work. In fact the bulk of Tetrateuchal traditions also originated in the North; but these had already crystallized before the deuteronomic movement started its activity. The author of Deuteronomy used these traditions and reworked them according to his proclivities.

The school of scribes

The character of the circle involved in the deuteronomic creation emerges from the fact that the school could not conceive a regime without a king. In contrast to the other law codes in the Tetrateuch in which no indication of a monarchic regime can be found, Deuteronomy presents law which reflect a typical monarchic rule. We find here not only the law of the king but a whole set of legal pericopes reflecting a monarchic state: laws about courts of justice and the supreme court, priesthood and prophecy and laws about the military. It is true, all these laws still preserve the old premonarchic reality, as has been seen by M. Noth[61]; but their manner of presentation reflects the Hezekianic-Josianic period.

The cultic laws in chapters 12-18 are all presented in a revised form, in the light of the centralization which was put in practice by royal initiative in the period discussed here. The laws about the tithe, the firstborn, Passover and the festivals are in fact brought up in order to stress the innovation following the reform.

On the whole the deuteronomic code constitutes, to my mind, a manual for the king and its people. Sacred matters are dealt with here insofar as they touch the religious-social aspect of national life. Methods of sacrifice and performance of the sacral service, which are so exten-

59. Cf. B. Mazar, *Cities and districts in Eretz-Israel*, 1975, pp. 65-90 (Hebrew).

60. Cf. Z. Kallai, *The Tribes of Israel*, 1967 (Hebrew).

61. *Die Gesetze im Pentateuch, Ihre Voraussetzungen und ihr Sinn*, in *Schriften der Königsberger Gelehrten Gesellschaft*, *Geisteswissenschaftliche Klasse*, 17. Jahr (1940) Heft 2 = *Gesammelte Studien zum Alten Testament*, 1957, pp. 9-141.

sively discussed in the Priestly code, are altogether missing in Deuteronomy. This is not the concern of the author of the book, whose main interest is the education of the king and his people. The educational vein stems, as I have argued for years [62], from the scribal circles which were interested in those days not only in secular, but also in religious education. Confirmation is to be found in Jer 8,8, where wise men and scribes are mentioned as involved in the Torah of Y. It is interesting to note in this context that the verb «to learn», למד, which is so characteristic of wisdom literature is not found at all in the Tetrateuch and yet is prominent in Deuteronomy. Furthermore the Torah is here defined as wisdom and understanding (4,6); it is no wonder therefore that this book speaks so often about writing on stones (27,1-8), doorframes (6,9; 11,20), books (31,9) etc. Deuteronomy is the only book of the Pentateuch which refers to a written Torah as comprising the divine will. The most interesting item, however, in this context is the copy of the law which the king is obliged to write for himself in Deut 17,18-19 [63].

Recently I have had the opportunity to study the so called *peri basileias* literary genre that is the type of educational literature designed for kings [64]. It has become clear to me that this type of literature, so prevalent in the Hellenistic period, has its roots in the cultures of the Ancient Near East. In Mesopotamia as well as in Egypt, we find instructions (some kind of Torah = *sbꜣyt* in Egyptian) for the king written by court counsellors and scribes. Prominent topics in this instruction were: just behavior and warnings against greediness and against the oppression of his subjects. Most instructive is the so called «Advice to the Prince» (Fürstenspiegel) in the Mesopotamian literature from the library of Ashurbanipal (the 7th cent. BCE). Here the king is warned to listen to his counsellors, not to covet money and not to mobilize into the army people of Nippur, Sippar and Babylon. As has been most recently shown by E. Reiner [65] this text was canonical in Mesopotamia; we find it quoted in a middle-Babylonian text from the twelfth cent. BCE, which says that the ancestors handed down these tablets where it is written that people of Nippur, Babylon and Sippar should not be mistreated [66]. In this text provision is made to a foreigner (*nakru*) who is nominated, which brings to mind the commandment not to appoint a foreigner as king (Deut. 17,15). In a recently discovered

62. Cf. *Deuteronomy and the Deuteronomic School* pp. 244ff.

63. These verses are an addition which disturb the flow of the passage, but this in no way reflects upon the date of the verses themselves.

64. Cf. *Shnaton — An Annual for Biblical and Ancient Near Eastern Studies* 3 (1978), pp. 224ff.; *Journal of Jewish Studies, Y. Yadin Festschrift* 33 (1982), pp. 189-194.

65. *The Babylonian Fürstenspiegel in Practice*, in *Societies and Languages of the Ancient Near East, Festschrift I. M. Diakonoff* 1980, pp. 320ff.

66. E. WEIDNER, in *Archiv fuer Orientforschung* 10 (1935), pp. 5ff.; B. LANDSBERGER, in *AFO* 10 (1935), pp. 141-142.

letter to Esarhaddon [67], king of Assyria, the author cited the rights of the cities Sippar, Nippur and Babylon and says: «let the Lord of Kings ... look up the tablets: 'if the king does not give heed to justice'», which is the beginning of the *Fürstenspiegel*; the writer goes on to say, that the tablet is true (*ṭuppu kīnu*) and that they should read it to the king.

What is more, the colophon to the «Advice to the Prince», the *Fürstenspiegel*, says on behalf of the king: «I wrote it in tablets ... and put it in my palace to my constant reading» [68]. Similar colophons are attached to other ritual texts, which may indicate that the Assyrian king was obliged — as it were — to read texts pertaining to religious behavior and apparently having to do with national cultic-religious policy. The Hittite kings also had to comply with the instructions written in the books. Thus we hear Muwatalish, the Hittite king, saying: «whatever I find written in the tablets ... I will do», and similarly Muršiliš: «what concerns laws/covenants of the temple ... the scribes started to violate them and I have written them anew» [69]. This reminds us of Josiah's eagerness to fulfill the words written in the book of the Torah discovered in the Temple. In Egypt too we hear about the king being subjected to instructions written in a book. Hecataius of Abdera (300 BCE) tells us that the Egyptian king had to obey instructions written in the books and that he had to listen to recitations from holy books in order to practice the fear of god [70]. This reminds us of the law of the king in Deut 17,19:

> «and he shall read out of the copy of the Torah all his days of life so that he will learn to fear the Lord ...»

From Deut 31,10-13 we learn that the leader — according to the Mishnah: the king — ought to recite the Deuteronomic code every seventh year before the assembled people. It is thus clear that the same book that the king read for himself was also recited before the people. This means that the book of Deuteronomy was a manual for the king as well as for the people, which seems to be a particular Israelite phenomenon. Would it be legitimate to suppose that the scribes of the courts of Hezekiah and Josiah are responsible for this transition: from a book for the king to a book for the whole people? One thing is clear: this book turned out to be the binding law code for the next generations — not the priestly or Holiness code — perhaps because Josiah put it in practice by means of a solemn covenant in Jerusalem (2 Kgs 23,1-3).

67. Cf. the article by E. REINER quoted above n. 65.

68. *ina tuppāni ašṭur ... abrēma ana tamarti šitassiya qereb ekalliya ukīn*, cf. H. HUNGER, *Babyl. und Assyr. Kolophone*, (AOAT 2), 1968, no. 319.

69. For these sources cf. M. WEINFELD, *Social and Cultic Institutions in the Priestly Source*, in *Proceedings of the Eighth World Congress of Jewish Studies*, Panel Sessions, Bible Studies and Hebrew Language, Jerusalem 1983, pp. 98-99.

70. *Diodorus Siculus* I, 70. For this source and its parallels in Deut 17,19 and the Temple Scroll from Qumran (Y. YADIN, מגילת המקדש 57:1ff.), see my article in *RB* 87 (1980), pp. 394-396.

Were it not for his initiative the history of Israelite and monotheistic religions would have been different: Monotheists would have continued to sacrifice until our day. It was the law of centralization which caused the liquidation of provincial cult and with the destruction of the Temple sacrifices vanished, because of the limitations of cult to one place. Instead of sacrifice came synagogue and church based on Book and Prayer. Deuteronomy has thus acquired great significance for the history of world religions.

Hebrew University
Jerusalem

M. WEINFELD

DROIT PUBLIC DANS LE DEUTÉRONOME

Telles les autres parties de la Torah, le Deutéronome a surtout été étudié comme la révélation des actes prescrits par Dieu aux membres de son peuple afin qu'ils acquièrent vie et bonheur. De plus l'humanisation de certaines lois, par exemple, sur les femmes, l'esclave, la guerre, ainsi que l'appel à l'amour de Dieu, faisaient de ce Deutéronome un lieu privilégié de l'étude des préparations de la loi et de la morale évangélique [1].

Mais on peut également examiner les structures sociales que suppose une législation: d'une part les rapports entre individus et familles dans une société donnée, avec ses autorités responsables législatives, exécutives et judiciaires; d'autre part, le statut de cette société au milieu de ses voisins. Le premier est le droit public national, le second le droit public international. Ce n'est généralement pas sous cet angle que les spécialistes actuels ont abordé leurs nombreuses études sur le Deutéronome [2] et on ne peut que leur donner raison, car ce concept de droit national ou international n'est ni deutéronomiste ni même biblique. Mais, quitte à employer un langage plus sociologique, ne serait-ce pas une voie apte à introduire nos contemporains, et surtout les juristes, aux questions d'exégèse? Dans les incertitudes actuelles à propos du Pentateuque, ne serait-ce pas un complément utile aux approches stylistiques, littéraires et théologiques de ce domaine? Ne serait-ce pas une sorte de ressourcement? Le Pentateuque n'était-il pas considéré comme une Torah, un *nomos*? Et la force de l'exégèse Graf-Kuenen-Wellhausen ne venait-elle pas de la comparaison des lois [3] dans les codes, beaucoup plus que dans l'analyse des récits? Essayons donc d'analyser le Deutéronome en

1. G. VON RAD, *Das Gottesvolk im Deuteronomium*, Stuttgart, 1929.

2. Voir par exemple O. KAISER, *Einleitung in das Alte Testament*, 4ᵉ éd. 1978, Gütersloh pp. 113-127; R. SMEND, *Die Entstehung des A.T.*, Stuttgart 1978, pp. 69-81; H. D. PREUSS, *Das Deuteronomium*, Darmstadt 1982, pp. 121-144. On peut voir combien est courte la bibliographie proposeée par B. LANG, *Biblische Notizen* 20, 1983, pp. 39s. Il en est de même des études publiées dans *The Jewish Law Annual*, Leiden, 1979sq, même celle de M. CHIGIER, *Codification of Jewish Law*, II, 3-33.

3. Il est toujours utile de réétudier les anciens articles de l'*Encyclopaedia Biblica* (éd. Cheyne, Londres, 1901) II, 2045-2058, du *Hastings Dictionary of the Bible* III, 64b-72 (cf le tableau I,863), et les *Introductions à l'A.T.* du début du siècle, en particulier L. GAUTHIER et S. DRIVER (9ᵉ éd 1920, p. 1-103 et ses tableaux). Le récent article de J. VAN SETERS, *The Place of the Yahvist in the History of Passover and Massot* dans *ZAW* 95 (1983) pp. 167-181 a fait un effort en ce sens, en citant J. Wellhausen, mais encore déficient, car il est trop porté sur l'analyse littéraire et pas assez sur l'analyse du contexte socio-politique que supposent des termes comme *maṣṣôt*; il ignore complètement l'étude de J. HENNINGER sur *Les fêtes de printemps chez les Sémites et la Pâque Israélite*, Paris, 1975.

fonction des catégories du droit national et international, en choisissant peut-être un autre titre, quelque chose comme «Les structures sociales, externes et internes d'Israël selon le Deutéronome».

A. Sur les «structures externes» ou le «droit international», on pourrait être relativement bref car, selon certains passages du livre, Israël devait vivre dans un splendide isolement comme l'Angleterre victorienne. Toute alliance avec les différents peuples de Canaan est interdite (7,2-4). D'une manière générale, il s'agit des Amorites (1,7.19.20.27.44; 2,8; 3,8; 4,47; 31,4)[4]. En conformité avec les conventions du livre où le discours est mis dans la bouche de Moïse avant la conquête, il n'est pas question de l'Assyrien, du Tyrien, de l'Araméen ou du Babylonien. On pourrait croire que l'interdiction est absolue vis-à-vis de tout Etat, de même que la répulsion d'Osée pour l'appel à l'Égypte et le passage en Assyrie (Os 7,11 cf. 9,3 plus 5,11; 11,1 et Jér 2,18). L'Égypte n'est-elle pas la «maison des esclaves»[5] d'où est «sorti»[6] Israël qu'il opprimait (26,6)? C'est contre elle que le Dieu d'Israël a lutté (1,30; 4,34; 6,22; 7,15.18; 11,3.4; 28,27.60; 29,1; 34,11). En ce temps où les traités de vassalité sont nombreux et les traités entre égaux très rares, au point qu'on peut douter de l'existence d'un véritable droit international[7], on peut se demander si le Deutéronome était disposé à reconnaître des droits aux peuples étrangers. Sidon n'est mentionné qu'en passant (3,9). Edom n'est pas nommé, sauf sous la forme personnelle «l'édomite» (23,8), et directement sous l'appellation «fils d'Esaü ou Séïr». Moab est une désignation géographique (1,5; 2,8-9,18; 28,69; 32,49; 34,1.5.6.8), rarement ethnique (2,11.29; 23,4), jamais comme un Etat. On peut en dire autant des Ammonites, et les Philistins ne sont jamais nommés.

Quand le Deutéronome reconnaît un droit à l'Edomite et à l'Égyptien, droit qu'il refuse au Moabite ou à l'Ammonite (23,8 cf 3), ce n'est même pas ce que l'on appellerait du droit international privé. C'est une loi interne permettant d'incorporer un non-Israélite au *qâhâl* de YHWH, l'un à titre de frère, l'autre en raison de l'hospitalité qu'il a témoignée en faveur d'un réfugié, un *ger*. Il en est de même des lois dites humanitaires en cas de guerre: traitement des captives (21,10-14), des villes adverses

4. Mais dans les listes, ce n'est qu'un élément ethnique entre autres (7,1; 20,17) englobant Og du Bashan en 4,47, mais d'habitude distinct (1,4: 2,24; 3,2-9; 4,46).

5. 7 fois: 5,6; 6,12; 7,8; 8,14; 13,6.11.

6. Expression typiquement deutéronomique à la différence de «monter du pays d'Égypte». 21 fois dans le Deutéronome. La connotation socio-politique n'est pas la même.

7. V. KOROŠEC, *Ueber die Entwicklung von völkerrechtlichen Beziehungen in der El-Amarna-Zeit*, dans *Revue Internationale des Droits de l'Antiquité*, 3e série, Tome xxii, Bruxelles, 1975, pp. 47-70; G. KESTEMONT, *Diplomatique et droit international en Asie Occidentale (1600-1200 av JC)*, Louvain, 1974; *Les grands principes du droit international régissant les traités entre les États proche-orientaux des XVe-xviiie s. av. JC)*, dans *xxv Rencontre Assyriologique internationale*, (1978), Berlin, 1982, pp. 269-279; *Accords internationaux relatifs aux ligues hittites (1600-1200 av JC)*, dans *Or. Per. Lov.* 12 (1981), pp. 15-78.

et de la végétation qui les entoure, exemptions de l'appel au combat (20,1-9). Le Deutéronome ne connaît pas de droit international. Il est dépositaire d'une sagesse admirée des peuples sans qu'ils y aient part (4,6), car le Dieu national, «Yahve ton Dieu», a donné à son peuple des lois justes, qui sont les stipulations d'une alliance entre lui et son peuple à l'exclusion de toute autre alliance; celle-ci impliquerait reconnaissance de la puissance d'un dieu étranger, du dieu national de chacun des autres peuples que Dieu a laissés comme part aux fils d'El (Dt 32,8, LXX et Qumrân). Il y a plus de droit international dans les deux premiers chapitres d'Amos, où le Dieu d'Israël juge les peuples étrangers, que dans le Deutéronome aux prises avec ses gros problèmes internes liés à la décadence et à la chute de Samarie.

B. Le discours et la législation deutéronomiques s'adressent à un Israël apparemment collectif[8]. Mais quel est l'Israël concret discernable derrière cet Israël que l'on voudrait unifié, mais qui ne l'est pas?

a) Faut-il songer au roi, responsable de la nation devant Dieu du fait de son élection? Certainement pas car la «Loi royale» ne s'adresse pas à lui et elle est rédigée à la 3e personne.

b) Il en va de même des paragraphes concernant les prêtres-lévites, (18,1-8), les prophètes (18,9-22) et jusqu'à ceux qui traitent du juge central (17,8-11), ou encore, semble-t-il, du juge local (16,18). Mais, dans ce dernier cas, la situation est plus complexe. Certes, le v. 16 (cf. 18) semble distinguer le juge que l'Israélite doit établir «dans toutes tes portes pour toutes tes tribus» et cet Israélite lui-même. Mais, dès les vv 19-20, c'est à l'Israélite lui-même que «YHWH ton Dieu» donne des règles de justice. Puis, dès 17.8, dans le paragraphe relatif au juge central, c'est à un juge local que s'adresse le discours: «S'il est trop difficile pour *toi* de juger ...»

c) C'est donc à une personnalité locale influente que pense le discours. Cette personnalité peut avoir à juger; il doit le faire conformément aux règles qui lui viennent du juge et des prêtres lévites qui siègent au «lieu choisi par le Seigneur ton Dieu» (17,8-11).

Cette personnalité locale influente est un riche propriétaire foncier. Non seulement il a des revenus agricoles importants sur lesquels il peut prélever une dîme annuelle et une dîme triennale (14,22-29), non seulement il a femme et enfants, serviteurs et servantes, mais il a en plus la charge des économiquement faibles; la veuve, l'orphelin, le réfugié (*gér*), et surtout le lévite local dépossédé par la centralisation du culte au «lieu choisi par le Seigneur» (14,29; 16,11.14; 12.12.19).

Cet Israélite a des revenus agricoles abondants qu'il peut convertir en argent (14,25), mais, en outre, il est riche et il a de quoi prêter (15,6.8). Il est vraiment de ces quelque 60.000 *gibbôrey-ḥaïl*, hommes de valeur, sur

8. G. von Rad, op. cit., p. 17.

lesquels Menahem fit peser l'impôt de capitation de 50 sicles, de manière à acquitter son tribut de 1000 talents d'argent envers Téglath-Phalazar III (II R. 15,19-20). Ce chiffre ne concerne que le royaume du Nord. Un point supplémentaire est à signaler. Selon l'ancien code de l'alliance, tous les 7 ans, le propriétaire devait abandonner sa récolte au profit des pauvres, voire des animaux sauvages (Ex 23,11). C'est ce que prévoit le Deutéronome pour la dîme triennale, mais il ne s'agit plus que de la dîme et non de la récolte entière, vigne et oliviers compris. Le rythme est accéléré, et le quota fort diminué. La *shemiṭṭah* de 7 ans ne vise plus les produits agricoles, mais les dettes. Le propriétaire foncier qui vit (et fait vivre) de la production agricole plus que des troupeaux ne semble pas trouver d'inconvénients à l'offrande des premiers-nés, aux holocaustes, sacrifices et offrandes volontaires traditionnelles (15,19; 12,6), à la dîme triennale, vestige de l'ancienne *shemiṭṭah*; mais, d'après la manière dont s'exprime le législateur, on le voit beaucoup plus réticent vis-à-vis de l'extinction des dettes au bout de six ans (15,6-10). C'était une mesure exceptionnelle en Orient, lors de l'avènement de certains rois (les édits *mesharu*), et on en a des traces dans le *derôr* (acc. *anduraru*) qui concerne bien d'autres cas de libération d'esclaves et de remises de dettes (nombreux exemples dans l'*Assyrian Dictionary of Chicago* A,II,115b-117b). C'est un *derôr* qui sera proclamé pour l'affranchissement des esclaves au temps de Jérémie (34,8). Le décret s'appuie sur Dt 15,12, mais le terme de *derôr* n'y apparaît pas, tandis que Lév 25,10 l'emploie pour la libération des hommes et des terres lors de l'année jubilaire. Le Deutéronome (et à sa suite le Lévitique) lie deux institutions que le Code de l'alliance distinguait: libération de l'esclave (Ex 21,2) et la *shemiṭṭah* agricole de l'année sabbatique (23,10). En joignant ces deux institutions, le Deutéronome s'adresse à un riche propriétaire, créancier de son frère pauvre (15,7) qu'il peut réduire en esclavage pour dette (15,12) après l'avoir obligé à vendre sa terre; nous savons par les prophètes que ce fut la situation au 8ᵉ s. (Am 2,6; Mi 2,8-9; 3,1-4; Is 5,8 cf Pr 22,22...). En langage moderne, c'est là que se trouve la classe dirigante et le pouvoir, ce «peuple du pays» (*ʿam hâʾareç*) que paraît ignorer le Deutéronome, mais que connaissent bien Jérémie (cf 34,19) et le livre des Rois; il est assez puissant pour contrecarrer les desseins de la cour, ainsi lors du meurtre (II Reg 21,23-24) du roi Amon.

C. Quelle est l'autorité publique qui parle ainsi à ces puissants propriétaires qui constituent l'armature économique du pays? On peut difficilement y voir le roi dont les pouvoirs sont étrangement restreints dans la Loi royale (17,14-19), si l'on compare avec les usages du temps, même à Jérusalem (cf. Achaz en II Reg 16). Ce n'est pas non plus un prophète en tant que tel: ce n'est ni le style des oracles prophétiques, ni l'affirmation d'une autorité divine inconditionnée, puisque la loi sur les prophètes va établir des distinctions entre prophètes et prophètes. L'autorité invoquée est celle de Moïse et l'on peut penser au milieu des Lévites du Nord (von Rad)[9] venus à Jérusalem après la chute de Samarie, ou mieux au clergé de Dan descendant de Moïse. Mais, de par sa rhétorique et son vocabulaire, ce discours doit aussi beaucoup au milieu des sages[10]. On ne peut qu'être frappé de ce que les fonctions des juges associés à Moïse, confiées à des militaires, officiers de 1000, 100 et 50 dans l'histoire prophétique (E, Ex 18,25) sont maintenant confiées à des chefs de tribus «sages et éprouvés» (Dt 1,13.15; 16,19: «le cadeau aveugle les yeux des sages»). Josué, héritier de Moïse aura un esprit de «sagesse» (34,9). Nous avons vu comment le Deutéronome définit ses lois envers l'étranger comme une «sagesse» (4,6).

Or les sages à cette époque sont des conseillers du roi (P. de Boer); à la cour, ils excercent des fonctions administratives, politiques (Is 29,14) ou judiciaires (Jér 9,8-9; Is 5,21; 10,1ss) et sont formés à cet effet dans des écoles de sagesse (Pr 1,2-5; cf le prologue d'Amenemopé). On y enseigne une sagesse administrative digne de Salomon, aux yeux de la reine de Saba (I R 10,4), et tout d'abord il faut apprendre à compter, à écrire, à rédiger des rapports et à juger (I Reg 3). On apprend à écrire grâce à des abécédaires (Lemaire)[11] et à compter à la manière égyptienne (voir l'ostracon de Cadès Barnéa trouvé par R. Cohen et les ostraca de Arad). Or, près des autorités judiciaires et administratives, le Deutéronome et la littérature deutéronomique placent souvent des *šôṭerîm*. C'est un terme, connu surtout de l'araméen (Nippur, Elephantine, Wadi Daliyeh), mais déjà de l'ancien assyrien et de l'ancien babylonien (AHw, 1103s) avec le sens d'«enregistrer» (voir SVT XV, 104s). Dans l'historiographie prédeutéronomique (Ex 5,6ss; Num 11,16), ils ont ce que M. Weinfeld appelle «des fonctions de secrétariat» (*Isr. Oriental St.* VII, Tel Aviv, 1977, p. 83). Ce sont des scribes qui enregistrent un recensement (avec les dispenses avant un engagement militaire cf 20,5.8.9, Jos 1,10; 3,2), de la comptabilité, mais aussi des jugements (Dt 1,16). La littérature post-deutéronomique en gardera la trace à propos des institutions monarchiques (Pr 6,7; I Chr 26,29; 26,11; 27,1). Associés aux juges (Dt 16,18), aux prêtres lévites (II Chr 19,1), aux anciens (21,2), aux conseillers (Is 1,26), leur présence discrète, mais appréciée, dans le Deutéronome nous indique que c'est dans ce milieu que se rédige le discours deutérono-

9. G. VON RAD, *Deuteronomium-Studien*, 2e éd., Göttingen, 1948.

10. M. WEINFELD, *Deuteronomy and the Deuteronomic School*, Oxford 1972; J. BLENKINSOPP, *Wisdom and Law in the O.T.*, Oxford, 1983, pp. 92-101: «Deuteronomy, the watershed».

11. A. LEMAIRE, *Abécédaires et exercices d'écolier en épigraphie nord-ouest sémitique*, dans *Jour. Asiatique* 266 (1978) pp. 221-235; *Les Écoles et la formation de la Bible dans l'Ancien Israël*, Göttingen, 1981; je ne m'associerai pas à la critique de G. GARBINI, *Le serie alfabetiche semitiche e il loro significato*, dans *AIO (Napoli)* 42 (1972), pp. 104-411, surtout 405, qui veut voir dans ces abécédaires un symbolisme d'éternité, ni même aux hésitations de J. NAVEH, *Graffiti and dedications*, in *BASOR* 235 (1979) p. 30, qui se demande si certains de ces abécédaires n'auraient pas une connotation magique.

mique. Ces «notaires» (de Vaux) ne sont pas les ministres, mais ils constituent le milieu où ceux-ci peuvent être recrutés, quitte à appartenir à un parti opposé. Ils connaissent les rouages de l'administration centrale et ses défauts, aussi bien que les intérêts des propriétaires fonciers, attachés à leurs habitudes et qui ne voient pas la menace de la domination étrangère.

D. Dans les structures de la société deutéronomique, les autorités locales sont encore très puissantes et très peu favorables à la centralisation que va s'efforcer d'établir le mouvement deutéronomique. Il y a des cités fortifiées que le Deutéronome appelle des «portes» (déjà à Ugarit: RS 34126; Dt 5,14; 12,17 ... 16 fois «tes portes», beaucoup plus fréquent que *ʿyr*, ville; une seule fois «tes villes» 13,13). Comme de nos jours, pour des raisons d'approvisionnement en eau (la source) et de sécurité, l'Israélite du pays n'habite pas dans une ferme, mais dans ce qu'il conviendrait d'appeler un bourg, assez différent des enclos ou *ḥaṣerim* du sud et de l'est. Il en sort pour les travaux des champs et y rentre le soir; ainsi les gens de Sichem au temps d'Abimelek. Certes, cet Israélite avait du bétail et l'on voit mal ce bétail rentrer le soir dans ces bourgs exigus. Comme encore récemment en Palestine, il y avait des campements dans les terres en friche entre les bourgs, mais le Deutéronome est très discret sur le dimorphisme de cette époque que reflétaient encore les rapports entre Israélites et Sichémites en Gen 34. Il ne connaît le camp ou campement qu'en 23,10-15; le camp est ici le campement de l'armée face à l'ennemi et non le campement de tribu semi-nomade. Quant à la tente, *'ôhel*, c'est un vestige du passé, qu'il s'agisse des tentes des Israélites avant l'occupation (1,27; 5,27; 11,6), ou de la tente de réunion (31,15), exceptionnellement de la tente qui abrite le pèlerin de Pâque au sanctuaire central (16,7). Tout en se limitant aux textes avec *ʿyr*, Don Carlos Benjamin a soutenu en 1981 à Claremont une thèse intéressante sur la vie de la cité dans le Deutéronome. C'est la cité qui compte.

Nous avons vu qu'à ces portes il y avait des juges assistés de scribes (16,18). C'est une autorité locale. Mais il y a aussi des *Anciens* comme les *shibutu* de Mari. Ils ont à intervenir dans des litiges qui opposent des familles (22,16; 25,7.9, affaires de mariage, 19,12; ou de famille 21,19.20; 21,3.4.6, affaire de meurtre). Certains textes gardent leur connexion avec l'antique institution tribale (29,9; 31,28 cf 9). Comme Num 11,16, Dt 31,28 leur accole des scribes. C'est une antique institution [12]. L'his-

12. Elle a été étudiée par J. R. KUPPER, A. FINET, H. LIMET et J. BOTTÉRO dans *La voix de l'opposition en Mésopotamie*, Bruxelles, 1973, pp. 23, 77, 137, 169s (cf. *Pouvoirs Locaux en Mésopotamie et dans les régions adjacentes*, Bruxelles, 1980=1982, p. 148), par H. KLENGEL (*Or* 29, 1960, pp. 357-375). Pour Ebla cf A. ARCHI, *I rapporti tra Ebla et Mari*, dans *St. Ebl.* 4 (1981) p. 139 et passim. Elle peut se référer à une structure tribale (H. REVIV, *Elders and Saviors*, dans *Or. Ant.* 16 [1977] pp. 201-204), mais aussi à des communautés de village (M. LIVERANI, *JESHO* 18, 1975, p. 154) et surtout à des cités (H. REVIV, *Elders and Men of the City in Syria and Palestine*, dans *Studies in the History of the Jewish People*, III,

toriographie prophétique (E)[13] admet l'existence de cette institution avant la conquête mais, dans le Deutéronome, elle est beaucoup plus urbaine que tribale. Coordonnée sémantiquement en Babylonie aux «témoins» (*šibutu* également), elle l'est davantage dans le Deutéronome aux «juges»[14]; nous pouvons préciser: «juges locaux» aux «portes». Nous retrouvons en effet ici le problème: juges locaux, et juges de la capitale. Il est posé par le texte même du code deutéronomique qui sépare le paragraphe sur les juges locaux des quatre grandes institutions: juges (en tête), rois, prêtres-lévites, prophètes (17,8-18,22). Y avait-il un représentant de l'autorité centrale près des autorités locales que sont les anciens des villes pourvus de pouvoirs judiciaires?

E. La centralisation est une donnée fondamentale de la législation deutéronomique, même si l'on admet plusieurs strates dans cette législation[15]. On en parle surtout à propos du culte, et certains exégètes ne sont pas disposés à admettre l'historicité de la notice du livre des Chroniques (II Chr 19,5) selon laquelle Josaphat aurait institué des juges dans toutes les villes fortifiées de Juda. On pourrait se demander si les *šôṭerîm* accolés aux juges en 1,16; 16,18 et aux anciens en 21,2 ne seraient pas des scribes formés aux écoles de Jérusalem, et envoyés par la cour pour contrôler le juge local. Mais la découverte d'abécédaires ailleurs qu'à Jérusalem[16] est un indice qu'il y avait des écoles de scribes ailleurs qu'à Jérusalem. Une vie urbaine et commerçante comme celle des cités de Juda demandait des scribes. Ce qui est plus sûr, c'est que les rois de Juda comme Roboam s'occupèrent de fortifier des villes, d'où une présence d'autorités militaires qui expliquent l'octroi des fonctions judiciaires aux militaires en Ex 18. On a noté (de Vaux) la connexion fréquente des *šôṭerîm* avec l'armée, non pour le combat, mais pour l'enrôlement et l'intendance. Nous avons vu que le Deutéronome avait tendance à substituer les scribes «sages» aux militaires. C'est que les militaires dépendaient très directement de l'autorité royale et que le Deutéronome se défie du roi.

Ce n'est toutefois pas aux «sages» qu'il confie le contrôle des institutions centralisatrices par lesquelles il affronte le puissant propriétaire foncier et les autorités locales trop attachées aux vieilles coutumes des cités cananéennes. Ce sont les prêtres-lévites qui devraient assurer le

1975, pp. 15-29). Pour la période néobabylonienne cf M.A. DANDAMAYEV, dans *Societies and Languages of the Ancient Near East, Studies in Honour of I. M. Diakonoff*, Warminster, 1982, pp. 38-41.

13. Cf H. Cazelles, *Rédactions et traditions dans l'Exode*, dans *Studien zum Pentateuch. W. Kornfeld zum 60. Geburtstag*, Wien, 1977, pp. 14s.

14. S.M. WARNER, *The Judges within the Structure of Israel ... the Office of the Elder*, dans *HUCA* 47, 1967, pp. 61s.

15. B. HALPERN, *The Centralization Formula in Deuteronomy*, dans *VT*, 31 [1981], pp. 20-38.

16. A. LEMAIRE, dans *JA*, 1978, pp. 230-234.

contrôle parce qu'ils sont les dépositaires de la Torah (31,9). Ils ne sont que la troisième grande institution, après les juges qui viennent en tête, et après le roi. Mais ils contrôlent l'institution judiciaire, puisque le juge en fonction dans la capitale est juxtaposé aux prêtres-lévites (17,9 cf 19,17). Comme vis-à-vis des juges d'Ex 18, ils ont le contrôle des sentences en cas difficile, pour que ces sentences soient en conformité avec la Torah. Ils contrôlent le roi, puisque celui-ci doit écrire une copie (*mishneh*) de cette Torah «devant les prêtres-Lévites» (17,18) et la lire tous les jours pour n'en dévier à droite et à gauche (17,20 cf 17,11 pour les juges). Enfin ils contrôlent les prophètes, puisque chaque prophète doit être un prophète «comme Moïse» (18,15), conformément aux paroles divines prononcées à l'Horeb (18,16 cf 5,22-31).

Conclusion. Dans le code deutéronomique, c'est donc non le roi, ni même le juge qui est la clé de voûte du droit public, c'est le prêtre-lévite. Cette vue était un peu théorique puisque la même loi de centralisation faisait du lévite un économiquement faible. Ce ne sont pas les lévites qui allaient entretenir les routes pour assurer le droit d'asile (19,3). Certes, pour le Deutéronome, le clergé de Jérusalem faisait partie de ces prêtres-lévites; il était puissant depuis l'action de Joyada lors de l'avènement de Joas auquel il avait imposé une *berit* (II Reg 11,17). Mais ce même Joas devenu grand avait secoué le joug à la mort de Joyada (II Reg 12,3 cf II Chr 24,15-22), et, au temps d'Achaz, le prêtre Uriya est très soumis aux volontés du roi Achaz. Michée au temps d'Achaz et peut-être d'Ezéchias sera aussi dur pour les prêtres que pour les prophètes et les «chefs» (3,11). C'est peut-être là que se trouve la cause profonde de l'échec de la réforme deutéronomique, soit au temps d'Ezechias, soit après Josias au temps de Joyaqim. En fait, jusqu'à Sédécias, c'est le roi et ses conseillers qui restent les maîtres dans le droit public d'Israël.

21 rue d'Assas
F-75006 Paris

H. CAZELLES

JERUSALEM IN THE DEUTERONOMISTIC HISTORY

The Book of Deuteronomy — or at least its core — has been associated with Josiah's reforms as described in the Deuteronomistic History (2 Kgs 22-23). While the bulk of these reforms were aimed at ridding Yahwistic cult of foreign accretions, apparently Josiah also tried to abolish all worship of the Lord outside of the temple in Jerusalem (2 Kgs 23,1-30). Both this purification and unification of Yahwistic cult were ostensibly religious in nature; however, there were political and cultural issues at stake as well [1]. The association of Deuteronomy with these reforms has been made primarily due to the portions of the book (e.g. Deut 12,2-28) which envision a single sanctuary that was to be the sole center of pure, authentic and legitimate Yahwistic worship [2]. This conclusion, of course, needs to be tempered with the observation that the centralization of worship is not as fundamental to Deuteronomy as is often assumed. Although von Rad may have been wrong when he asserted that centralization was a late and secondary addition to the book [3], it is nonetheless true that singificant portions of Deuteronomy do not seem to be aware of the requirement of a single sanctuary.

Attempts at evaluating the hypothesis of an association between the Book of Deuteronomy and Josiah's Reform generally revolve around analysis of relevant passages in the Deuteronomistic History — principally 2 Kgs 22-23. This paper will take a similar tack by looking at the portrait of Jerusalem in the historical work. Such an analysis will reveal that despite the apparent attempts by Josiah to make Jerusalem the sole legitimate place of Yahwistic cult, the city and its temple never acquired such a unique status before the exile. The reforms of Josiah had little significant or lasting effect. It is the thesis of this paper that Deuteronomy's cult centralization is a reflection of the exilic situation and is an attempt to make virtue out of necessity. Jerusalem barely survived the havoc of the Babylonian devastation of Judah, yet it was able to serve

1. See N. LOHFINK, *Culture Shock and Theology*, in *Biblical Theology Bulletin* 7 (1977), 12-22, and M. WEINFELD, *Cult Centralization in the Light of a Neo-Babylonian Analogy*, in *JNES* 22 (1964), 200-212. There are some who do not see Josiah's reform as part of his revolt against Assyria. See A. ROFÉ, *The Strata of the Law about the Centralization of Worship in Deuteronomy and the History of the Deuteronomic Movement*, in *VT Supp*. 22, Leiden, 1972, pp. 221, no. 1.

2. Though De Wette's thesis has proven quite durable, there are some who demur. Among the most recent to do so is A. D. H. MAYES, *King and Covenant: A Study of 2 Kings chs 22-23*, in *Hermathena* 125 (1978), 34-47.

3. G. VON RAD, *The Provenance of Deuteronomy*, in his *Studies in Deuteronomy*, London, 1953, p. 67.

as a cultic center though its temple was in ruins (see Jer 41,5). Judah itself was nothing more than an appendage to the Babylonian province of Samaria. Jerusalem, the area's one important population center, provided a logical site for whatever truncated form of worship that the exilic situation allowed. The Deuteronomist sees this limitation of worship to Jerusalem as a sign of the divine will and makes it a component of Judah's future.

The requirement of a single sanctuary caused a practical problem for the final redaction of the Deuteronomistic History. Deuteronomy presents itself as the work of Moses and its requirements as being known from his time on. As a consequence the Deuteronomistic History had to evaluate the kings of Israel and Judah in accordance with this requirement. On the other hand, the finding of the lawbook is presented in such a way that a prophetess had to be consulted as to the valitdity of the book's contents (2 Kgs 22,11-20).

To help unravel some of the problems surrounding 2 Kgs 22-23, Deuteronomy's concern for the centralization of worship and the date of Deuteronomy we will look at the portrait of Jerusalem in the Deuteronomistic History. 2 Sam 5,6-7 makes it clear that Jerusalem did not become incorporated into Israel until the time of David. Before then Jerusalem was a Jebusite enclave in which no Israelite would dare spend the night (Judg 19,10-12). The strategic location of the city made it an effective barrier between the northern tribes and Judah. It was an obstacle hindering a genuine sense of unity from developing among the Israelite tribes. Saul's failure to enlist the groups that made up the tribe of Judah into the new enterprise that was the monarchy probably doomed the new kingdom. These groups were cut off from direct communication with the northern tribes by Jerusalem and did not feel compelled to join Saul. The subsequent rise of the two kingdoms of Judah and Israel was no doubt the consequence of this long standing situation caused by the presence of a Canaanite Jerusalem in the heart of the Israelite tribes.

When David became king of Judah and later of Israel, he was determined to transform Jerusalem from being a barrier to unity into a source of unity among the tribes. He accomplished this by capturing the city and then making it his capital (2 Sam 5,6-9). David made no significant changes in the city except to build himself a palace there (2 Sam 5,11). He did, of course, bring the ark to Jerusalem (2 Sam 6,1-15). David thereby associated the traditions of the Mosaic period to his new capital and made the city a cultic site like other Israelite cities which housed the ark at one time or other. The city's importance then rested on two pillars: it was the city where David was enthroned and it was also the place where the Lord was enthroned upon the cherubim of the ark. These two pillars drew closer together because of Solomon who constructed his own palace and a temple to the Lord in a single architectural complex. The temple and its ritual became inextricably linked with the dynasty. Yahweh became the God of the Solomonic Empire and Jerusalem became the pre-eminent cultic site. Solomon's achievement then was his fusion of the political and religious dimensions of Jerusalem. As the sanctuary of the Davidic dynasty, the Jerusalem temple and sacrificial worship outside of Jerusalem was considered legitimate even in the Deuteronomistic History as the story of Elijah plainly shows. Here the staunchest of Yahwists and the greatest upholder of Mosaic tradition is presented as erecting an altar of sacrifice outside of Jerusalem (see I Kgs 18,32).

One event that served to enhance Jerusalem's status was the failure of Sennacherib's siege of the city in 701 B.C. (2 Kgs 18,13-19,37). This episode served to underscore the unique character of the city and its temple so that Jerusalem's inviolability became tantamount to an article of faith (see Jer 7,4). The last important modification of Jerusalem's status came with Josiah's reforms (2 Kgs 22-23). The king tried to eliminate all non-Yahwistic elements in Judah's cult. His efforts were successful only as long as he was in power. Centralization of worship in Jerusalem was probably not at the heart of Josiah's reform since Jeremiah makes no allusion to it though he admired and supported Josiah (see Jer 11,1-8; 22,15-16). Whatever cultic reforms took place in Jerusalem were temporary measures which met with considerable resistance even in Josiah's own life time (2 Kgs 23,8-9).

With the fall of Jerusalem in 587 B.C., the Davidic dynasty fell never to rise again. One of the props supporting Jerusalem's unique status was gone. The other prop, the temple, survived only in ruins. The Deuteronomistic History interpreted these disasters as God's judgement on the sins of Judah (2 Kgs 23,26-27). Despite the harshness of the judgement, both Deuteronomy and the Deuteronomistic History are testimonies to a profound and almost incomprehensible hope in a future time of salvation. Jerusalem was the once focus of hope when all the rest of Judah's institutions were dead or dying (see Ps 137). Jerusalem could serve as such a focus of hope because the city in effect replaced the actual temple structure as the place of God's dwelling just as the temple itself replaced the ark in Deuteronomic theology. The temple *per se* was no longer of critical importance; the very city of Jerusalem was the sacrament of the Lord's presence.

In the postexilic period, the restored community in Jerusalem was essentially a cultic community. When the actual temple was rebuilt in 515 B.C., it too was different since it was no longer a royal possession. The temple belonged to the people as the focal point of their religious life.

More fundamental to Deuteronomy than cult centralization is the book's underlying assumption that Judah's future is absolutely dependent upon her obedience to traditional moral and religious obligations which are found in the collection of law which comprise the book's core. Some of these laws are ancient practices whose origin and significance are obscure yet nonetheless remain valid (e.g. 21,1-9). Other laws are updated and humanized versions of traditional observances (e.g. Deut 5,12-15). Still other are Deuteronomic innovations such as the law of centralization (12,2-8). What binds all these together is the Deuteronomic perception that obedience is the key to Israel's future.

There is little doubt that the Deuteronomic tradition envisions Jerusalem as the central sanctuary [4]. A survey of the Deuteronomistic History leads to the conclusion that while Jerusalem did have unique status in Judah and Israel, it never was the sole legitimate site of Yahwistic cult. Even Josiah's attempt to make it such was resisted and ultimately failed. It was only with the fall of Judah that Jerusalem became practically speaking the one place where God might be worshipped; hence, Deuteronomy presented this reality as the divine will. Acceptance was on way that Judah might show its submission in obedience. It was Judah's obedience to the Lord that will secure her future.

5401 S. Cornell Ave.
Chicago, IL 60615, U.S.A.

Leslie J. HOPPE

4. R.E. CLEMENTS, *Deuteronomy and the Jerusalem Cult Tradition*, in *VT* 15 (1965), 300-213; E. NICHOLSON, *The Centralization of the Cult in Deuteronomy*, in *VT* 13 (1963), 380-385; A. ROFÉ, *op. cit.*; G.J. WENHAM, *Deuteronomy and the Central Sanctuary*, in *Tyndale Bulletin* 22 (1971), 103-118.

DIVINE SPEECH IN DEUTERONOMY

The book of Deuteronomy contains 30 passages phrased as words spoken by God, divine speeches (henceforth DS). They are distributed as follows: 10DSs in Deut 1-3; 8DSs in Deut 4-11 and 2 DSs in Deut 12-26 (= 10DSs in Deut 4-26), and once again 10DSs in Deut 27-34. It is not difficult to identify them, for, except in one instance, they are all ushered in by introductory formulas (henceforth DSF) qualifying them as divine speech.

The only exception, which is unique in the Pentateuch, is in a poetic passage, the Song of Moses in Deut 32. As I have shown elsewhere [1], the over-all structure of the song is such that the poet alternates several DSs with his own comments. The first DS in the Song is the monologue in vv. 20-27, the only one in Deuteronomy [2]. This divine self-resolution is followed by the poet's comments in vv. 28-31, easily recognizable by the fact that in the second part of this passage (vv. 30-31) the poet refers to God in the third person and uses the name YHWH and the term 'our Rock'. This passage, which is a well-balanced literary unit in itself [3], is followed by a second DS in vv. 32-35, which can be identified as such by the use of the first person singular in the second part of the speech (vv. 34-35). The following verse, v. 36, does not belong to the DS, for here the poet expresses his hope that YHWH will give his people justice, and he refers to YHWH in the third person singular. The last DS in the Song (vv. 37-42) is introduced by *wayyō'mèr*, and is followed by the final comment of the poet in v. 43.

Returning to the disguised DS in vv. 32-35, I might refer to the literary form to which Meir Weiss drew our attention 20 years ago [4], the so-called 'performative speech' (in German 'die erlebte Rede') also known as the 'interior monologue'. It differs from the ordinary direct speech because it lacks an introductory formula. In this literary device the

1. See C.J. LABUSCHAGNE, *The Song of Moses: its Framework and Structure*, in I.H. EYBERS, F.C. FENSHAM, C.J. LABUSCHAGNE, W.C. VAN WYK, A.H. VAN ZYL (Ed.), *De Fructu Oris Sui, Essays in Honour of Adrianus van Selms* (Pretoria Oriental Series, 11), Leiden, 1971, pp. 85-98.

2. For the monologues in the Pentateuch see my paper read at the 11th Congress of the IOSOT at Salamanca 1983, C.J. LABUSCHAGNE, *The Literary and Theological Function of Divine Speech in the Pentateuch*, in *VTSuppl* (forthcoming).

3. This passage consists of 34 words, a number that is used frequently in the Pentateuch as a composition device. See further below, and cf. the paper referred to in the previous note.

4. See M. WEISS, *Einiges über die Bauformen des Erzählens in der Bibel*, in *VT* 13 (1963), pp. 456-475, esp. 460ff.

author writes from the viewpoint of the subject, or character in question and uses direct speech. In my opinion, a more suitable term would be 'subjective speech'. There are several examples of such 'subjective speech' in the Pentateuch, but this is the only instance where it is employed with regard to God [5]. The lack of the introducing DSF here can easily be explained as being in accordance with the composition technique in the Song where the poet's comments also have the form of 'subjective speech'.

Once one has identified the DSs, it is relatively easy to determine and delimit precisely the words to be regarded as divine speech. There are, however, two problems; first, the question whether the words phrased in the 3rd person singular in Deut 1,8b.36; 2,12.21 and 5,11-16 belong to the *oratio recta*; and second, the problem whether the so-called 'ethnographic notices' in Deut 2,10-12 and 20-23 should be considered part of the DS in which they occur. In order to determine the exact scope of the DSs, we have to solve these two problems.

As to the first, it is important to note that the use of the 3rd person singular in divine speech is not exceptional; it occurs many times elsewhere in the Pentateuch (e.g. in Gen 9,16; 16,11; 18,19; 19,13f.; 21,17; Ex 3,12; 4,5; 19,21f.24; 20,7.10-12; 24,1; 30,11-16.34-38; 31,15; 34,10.14.23f.26). As a matter of fact the greater part of the DSs in the book of Leviticus is phrased in the 3rd person singular, and so is a large section of the Decalogue in both versions (Ex 20,7.10-12; Deut 5,11.12.14-16), which no commentator, so far as I am aware, would want to delete as secondary additions. On the whole Deuteronomy commentators seem to be at a loss with regard to the 3rd person wording in the DSs, e.g. S. R. Driver [6] considers 1,8b an 'addition'; P. C. Craigie, and before him C. Steuernagel [7] prefer the reading of the Samaritan Pentateuch and the LXX, which is phrased in the 1st person. Others skip the problem without comment [8]. As to 1,36 neither Driver nor Craigie give any comment, leaving the 3rd person wording as it is. The two references in 2,12 and 21 are situated in the two 'ethnographic notices', which we shall discuss presently. The 3rd person wording in the Decalogue is tacitly accepted by all commentators as an integral part of the direct address of God.

5. Cf. Gen 26,7.9; 32,31; 41,51.52. See also R. GORDIS, *Quotations as a literary Usage in Biblical, Oriental and Rabbinical Literature*, in *HUCA* 22 (1949), pp. 157-219, and R. GORDIS, *Kohelet — The Man and his Work*, New York, 1951, pp. 95-101.

6. S. R. DRIVER, *Deuteronomy* in *The International Critical Commentary*, Edinburgh, 1895, p. 14.

7. P. C. CRAIGIE, *The Book of Deuteronomy* in *The New International Commentary on the Old Testament*, Grand Rapids, 1976, p. 96; C. STEUERNAGEL, *Deuteronomium und Josua*, in *HAT*, Göttingen, 1900, p. 3.

8. See e.g. K. Fr. KRÄMER, *Numeri und Deuteronomium* in *Herders Bibelkommentar*, *Die Heilige Schrift für das Leben erklärt*, II/1, Freiburg, 1955, p. 234 and J. RIDDERBOS, *Het Boek Deuteronomium*, in *Korte Verklaring der Heilige Schrift*, Kampen, 1963, p. 59.

The real question is of course whether 3rd person wording may be used as a criterion for determining the scope of direct speech. In my opinion it should not. The considerable number of examples given above, including the Decalogue and the book of Leviticus, proves that 3rd person wording in the *oratio recta* was an accepted practice for biblical writers. These passages can all be explained as a kind of 'subjective speech' in a direct speech i.e. phrased from the viewpoint of the listener. They are part and parcel of the *oratio recta*[9]. If this is correct, we have no reason to disavow the legitimacy of the 3rd person singular passages in the DSs in Deuteronomy, or elsewhere in the Pentateuch. I shall support my argument by adducing additional evidence further below.

This brings us to the second problem: the question as to the legitimacy of the so-called 'antiquarian notices' (Driver), or better, the 'ethnographic sections' in 2,10-12 and 20-23. Since we cannot discuss the whole problem in any detail here, it must suffice to say that all the 'ethnographic', 'geographic', 'prehistoric' and 'historic' notices in 1,2.3; 2,10-12.20-23; 3,9.11.13b.14; 10,6-7 and 11,30 belong to the same category, and that the point at issue is whether we regard this type of information as loose, disconnected notices inserted here and there by one or several successive interpolators, or whether such notices should be considered integral parts of the text. I myself am convinced that such notices belong structurally to the text into which they have been integrated.

For a detailed discussion of these matters, I must refer to my forthcoming commentary on Deuteronomy. I restrict myself here to the two 'ethnographic notices' about which there seems to be general agreement among commentators that they should be regarded as (late) explanatory notes, which have been inserted into the text. This may be so, but whoever 'inserted' these notices must have done it in such a way that the structural balance of the text was not disturbed.

Both notices are enveloped in divine commands: in 2,9-13 it is between God's command to Moses with regard to territory God has assigned to the Moabites, phrased in 2nd person *singular* (v. 9) and God's command to the people, in 2nd person *plural* wording, to get ready and cross the border, the Zared (v. 13a); in 2,17-24 the notice is situated between God's command to Moses with regard to territory assigned to the Ammonites, phrased in 2nd person *singular* (v. 18f.) and God's command to the people, in 2nd person *plural* wording, to get ready and cross the border, the Arnon (v. 24).

In both cases the 'ethnographic notice' serves to bridge the gap created by the contrast between the command to Moses and that to the people. Neither in v. 13 nor in v. 24 is there any word that has this bridging

9. See note 4 of my paper cited in note 2 above. The reasons for the use of 3rd person singular in a direct speech is a subject for further study.

function between the 2nd person *singular* and 2nd person *plural* commands. In 1,37-40 there is a divine decision concerning Joshua and the young generation phrased in 2nd person *plural* between God's address to Moses and his command to the people; however the emphatic *wᵉʼattèm* (v. 40) marks the change to 2nd person *plural* command. In 2,3-5 the contrast between God's command to the people in 2nd person *plural* (v. 3) and the command to Moses in 2nd person *singular* (v. 4) is bridged by the peculiar phrasing of the words *wᵉʼèt-hāʽām ṣaw*.

My conclusion is that the 'ethnographic notices' simply cannot be missed in their context. Therefore they should be regarded as an integral part of their context. They are certainly not late interpolations inserted haphazardly into the text. In their present context they are meant to be part of the DSs in which they are situated, and cannot be missed there.

Another problem, peculiar to the DSs in Deut 1-3, is the question as to the exact function of the two forms of address: 2nd person *singular* and 2nd person *plural*. More precisely, is there any system in the use of the two forms in the DSs? Before we address ourselves to this problem, it is important to note that there is on the whole no doubt concerning the identity of the addressed, except in 2,24b.25. Contrary to the rule that Moses is addressed by God in the 2nd person *singular*, and the people (including Moses) in the 2nd person *plural*, here in 2,24b.25 the people are addressed in the *singular* form. This can be explained as a stylistic device to emphasize the importance of the divine command to Israel to begin with the occupation of the promised land. The sudden change of number here, can be compared with the abrupt transition from *plural* to *singular* in 2,7, where the change of number also indicates the end of God's message Moses had to bring over to the people.

If we examine the very conspicuous 2nd person *plural* imperatives, we can detect the system: God addresses the people directly when it concerns the five crucial turning-points during the journey from Horeb to the Arnon:

(i) 1,6-8 the command to set out in order to occupy the land (*dibbèr* and *lēʼmōr* are for extra emphasis)
(ii) 1,40 the command to turn back and set out for the wilderness
(iii) 2,3 the command to turn definitely towards the north
(iv) 2,13a the command to cross the Zared (*lēʼmōr* is for extra emphasis)
(v) 2,24 the command to cross the Arnon.

God addresses Moses with regard to things that concern him personally (1,37f.; 3,26-28) and when he is charged to convey a specific, already formulated message to the people (1,42; 2,4ff.) and also with regard to the relations with Moab (2,9) and Ammon (2,17ff.; *lēʼmōr* is for emphasis) and with regard to the occupation of the land of Sihon (2,31) and of Og (3,2). The people are included in the adress by the use of 2nd person *plural* in 1,6-8 (the only instance the preposition *'ēlênû* is used in a DSF) where God commands them to set out from Horeb. In 1,35ff., where God announces his decision about entrance into the land, the people are once more included in the address. Finally, the people are adressed in 2,24b.25, where God commands them (in the 2nd person *singular*!) to begin with the occupation of the promised land. Our conclusion is: there is a system and the exception to the rule serves the purpose of emphasis.

The 10 DSs in 1-3 show a distinct structure: the most crucial divine commands are marked by the three phrases beginning with *rab-lākèm/lāk*, in 1,6; 2,3; 3,26. They form the framework of the over-all structure of chapters 1-3. The other seven DSs are situated between them in a 3 + 4 pattern. We get the following scheme:

A. 1,6-8 *DS to people and Moses* at HOREB: «*Enough* ...!»
I 1,35f. DS to people and Moses about entrance into the land
II 1,37ff. DS to Moses and people about entrance into the land
III 1,42 DS to Moses about the people's decision to attack
B. 2,2ff. *DS to Moses and the people* at SEIR: «*Enough* ...!»
IV 2,9 DS to Moses with regard to Moab and his land
V 2,17ff. DS to Moses about Ammon and his land
VI 2,31 DS to Moses concerning Sihon and his land
VII 3,2 DS to Moses concerning Og and his land
C. 3,26-28 *DS to Moses about himself and Joshua* at PISGAH: «*Enough*...!»

This is a beautiful example of the use of a series of 10, of which many other examples can be given, some of which I have already drawn attention to [10].

We shall now examine the DSFs. In my first publication on the subject of divine speech in the Pentateuch [11], I dealt with the Deuteronomy material very summarily. Since then I have addressed myself more thoroughly to this material and studied the DSFs and the DSs with regard to their number, their distribution in distinct series, their pattern and their function. The revised Synopsis, in which I account for every DSF, shall be presented and discussed presently. I find it very useful to study formulas as these in synopsis. It was by means of such a synopsis that I first discovered the pattern of the DSFs in the Tetrateuch.

It is necessary to distinguish between introducing and referring DSF, the latter of which have been studied by D. E. Skweres [12]. We shall first

10. See C. J. LABUSCHAGNE, *The Pattern of the Divine Speech Formulas in the Pentateuch — The Key to its Literary Structure*, in *VT* 32 (1982), pp. 268-296, esp. pp. 279f. In Deut 1-3 *YHWH 'ĕlōhênû* occurs 10 × and likewise 10 × in 4-6; in the 'we-sections' there are two series of 10 verbs in 1st person plural, the first in 1,19; 2,1.8.13b-15 and the second in 2,32-36; 3,1.3-17.29; the Decalogue is divided into 10 commandements and the name YHWH occurs 10 × in it. For the series of 10 DSs and DSFs see the Synopsis below.

11. See my article cited in the previous note, pp. 279f.

12. D. E. SKWERES, *Die Rückverweise im Buch Deuteronomium*, in *Analecta Biblica*, 79, Rome, 1979.

deal with these briefly and supply additional information concerning their use in Deuteronomy: *ṣiwwāh, nišba*ʿ, *dibbèr* and *'āmar*. Significantly enough the verb *ṣiwwāh* is exclusively used as a referring DSF, never as a formula introducing DS like in Gen 2,16 and 3,17. The verb *nišba*ʿ, on the other hand is used twice (with *lēmōr*) to introduce DS (1,34; 34,4b). Another difference between the two verbs is that *ṣiwwāh* is frequently (15 ×) used with a variety of epitetha accompanying the divine name, such as *'ᵉlōhay*, *'ᵉlōhênû* (1 + 4 = 5 ×), *'ᵉlōhêkā* and *'ᵉlōhêkèm* (7 + 3 = 10 ×), while *nišba*ʿ lacks all such epitheta. As to their frequency: *ṣiwwāh* with YHWH as subject occurs 34 (2 × 17) times in Deuteronomy (with Moses as subject 52 times = 2 × 26) 23 times with the name YHWH and 11 times without, 15 × with epitheta and 8 times without. I mention these numbers explicitly, for we shall come across them time and again. The book of Deuteronomy is full to the brim of number symbolism! The verb *nišba*ʿ with YHWH as subject occurs 31 times in Deuteronomy, of which 11 times with the divine name, 11 times with *lātēt lᵉ*, 11 times in the phrase *(ka)'ᵃšèr nišba*ʿ *(YHWH) la'ᵃbōtêkā* which attests to the frequent use of the number 11, occurring very often, particularly in Genesis, as I have shown elsewhere [13].

I need not discuss the contents of these '*Rückverweise*' any further now, since Skweres has dealt extensively with this subject. I confine myself here to discussing the statistics of the two other verbs used in the referring DSFs, *'āmar* and *dibbèr*. At this stage, we must consult the synopsis. We note the following:

a. There are 10 references to God's speaking from the fire, *mittôk hā'ēš* of which 8 instances contain some form of the verb *dibbèr* and 2 instances refer to '*his words*' (4,36) and '*his voice*' (5,24). These series of 10 and 8 are typical of Deuteronomy — we shall find them again and again.

b. The term *par excellence* for introducing direct speech, *lē'mōr*, occurs 10 times with God as the speaker: 5 × with *verba dicendi* and 5 × without (the latter are 1,34; 1,37; 2,5; 9,23; and 34,4b) [14].

c. The partly stereotyped phrase *ka'ᵃšèr dibbèr (YHWH)* is found in two series of 8: the first series (marked *ka'ᵃšèr*$^{1\text{-}8}$) occurs in chapters 1-11;

13. In addition to the article cited in note 10 above, see also C. L. LABUSCHAGNE, *Additional Remarks on the Pattern of the Divine Speech Formulas in the Pentateuch*, in *VT* 34 (1984), pp. 91-95, where more examples of the 7+4 pattern are adduced. It is most significant that this pattern (7+4 = 11) occurs in the book of Genesis containing the promises to the fathers, and that the number 11 can be found frequently in connection with the verb *nišba*ʿ in Deuteronomy. This cannot be a coincidence. The significance of the (undoubtedly symbolic) number eleven is a subject for further study. It is interesting to note that the eleven instances of *nišba*ʿ connected with the divine name YHWH are divided into 7+4 (seven instances in chapters 1-11 and four in the rest of the book — see the Synopsis).

14. With Moses as speaker it occurs 15 × (8 × in chapters 1-3 and 7 × in 4-31). With the people as speakers it occurs another 15 times.

the other series (marked *ka'ᵃšèr*[1'-8']) occurs in chapters 12,1-31,13. In the two series together, 8 instances contain the name YHWH (marked YHWH[1-8]) and 8 do not (marked *dibbèr*[1-8]), and the preposition *lāk* (marked *lāk*[1-8]) is used 8 times, in the ratio: 3 × in the first series and 5 × in the second. A peculiarity of the first series is that it has the preposition *lākèm* (1,11 and 11,25) in the first, and again in the last instance.

This intricate, but nevertheless well-balanced, structure of the partly stereotyped phrase clearly shows that the words were carefully weighed, selected and counted in order to get these structures and series. It did not surprise me, when I assessed the total number of words in them (i.e. the smallest syntactical units) to find that the first series have 34 (2 × 17) words (see 1-11: Total Ref. DSF = 34), and that the second series yield 26 words (see 12,1-31,13: Total Ref. DSF = 26). Here we encounter once more the numbers 17 and 26 (and their multiples — see above where we discussed *ṣiwwāh*). They both represent the divine name YHWH: 26 is the sum of the letter value (Y=10 + H=5 + W=6 + H=5 = 26) while 17 is the sum of the digits (1 + 0 + 5 + 6 + 5 = 17).

For a fuller discussion of these divine numbers and their significance I refer to my paper read at the congress of the IOSOT in Salamanca [15]. Here I must restrict myself to saying that I discovered that certain parts of the Tetrateuch (Genesis and the 'Deuteronomistic sections' of the Tetrateuch) and the book of Deuteronomy are literally teeming with these numbers in one way or the other. The use of these divine numbers (and their multiples) is the hall-mark, the distinguishing characteristic of Deuteronomy and, in my opinion, of the Deuteronomistic redaction of the Tetrateuch. I realize that this has enormous consequences for the study of the whole Pentateuch problem, but at this stage of my investigation of the divine speech material I have to refrain from drawing any further conclusions.

d. Let us continue our discussion of the synopsis and turn to the 10 remaining phrases referring to God's speaking, which form the last series of Ref. DSFs starting at 5,24b (marked *dbr*/*'mr*[1-10]). They cover a variety of situations in which God has reportedly spoken. When I constituted the synopsis I naturally scanned the concordances, looking for the *verba dicendi* with YHWH as subject. Having accounted for all phrases occurring in the series I have just described, there were *nine* left, which was suspect, because I expected another series of either *eight* or *ten*. Realizing that the special merit of a series is that it sustains itself, I continued the search until at last, I found the tenth in Deut 26,17, the *Hiph'il* of the verb *'āmar* with *Israel* as (the grammatical) subject: *'èt-YHWH hè'ᵉmartā hayyôm lihyôt lᵉkā lē'lōhîm* «You have made

15. See note 2 above.

YHWH say today that he will be God to you». I was quite sure that this was the missing reference to God's speaking only when I discovered that in transitive *Hiph'il* forms the *grammatical* subject is not necessarily the *logical* subject of the verb, and that the biblical writers considered the logical subject as the real subject, i.e. the actual performer of the action [16]. Therefore YHWH must be regarded as the *logical* subject of the verb here: Israel makes him say and accepts his declaration, but it is YHWH who declares that he'll be her God. In the long debate on this passage, and especially on the meaning of the *Hiph'il* of *'āmar* [17], I have chosen for the literal meaning and find YHWHs declaration in v. 17 and that of the people in v. 18f. There YHWH is the *grammatical* subject of the verb: «He has made you say today ...», but it is Israel who is the *logical* subject, who declares that she'll be God's special people as he had said. If one chooses for the meaning 'proclaim', then of course we get the converse: Israel's declaration in v. 17 and YHWH's in v. 18f. But this does not make the passage any clearer or the syntax any smoother, for in both declarations there is a change in person, which, in my opinion, serves the purpose of emphasis.

Having accounted for every DSF referring to God's speaking, we now turn to the introducing formulas and to the DSs. The Synopsis shows that the 10DSs in chapters 1-3 are ushered in by 8DSFs containing the verbs *dibbèr* and *'āmar* (numbered 1-8) and by *lē'mōr* in the 2 instances where there are no *verba dicendi*. The total number of words (underlined) in the DSFs is 31; and the DSs yield 463, which add up to 494, which is a multiple of the divine number 26 (19 × 26). The 8 instances of the preposition *'ēlay*, of which the second one occurs in a referring DSF, seem to have the function of joining the introducing and the referring DSFs together.

The second series of 10 DSs we find in chapters 4-26. The first 8 occur in chapters 4-11 (marked DS$^{4-11}$ (marked DS$^{1-8}$) and the other 2 in the 'law section' chapters 12-26 (marked DS$^{9/1-10/2}$).

Of the first series of 8 in chapters 4-11, six are introduced by *verba dicendi* with *'ēlay* (both marked 1-6) and two are ushered in by *lē'mōr* (marked *lē'mōr*$^{6.8}$ - *lē'mōr*^{7} is part of the fuller DSF). The total number of words (underlined) in these 8 DSFs introducing DS is 21, which brings

16. The fact that this phrase belongs to the DSFs clearly shows that the actual performer of the caused action was considered to be the real subject of the verb, in spite of the fact that the grammatical subject is someone else. Another example in Deuteronomy can be found in 7,19 where YHWH is the grammatical subject of the verb *yṣ'* and Israel the logical subject and performer of the action of going out; see the arguments in my forthcoming commentary on Deuteronomy in the Dutch series *De Prediking van het Oude Testament*.

17. See *THAT*, I, Sp. 214; *TWAT*, I, Sp. 353f. For a detailed study of the passage, see N. LOHFINK, *Dt. 26:17-19 und die Bundesformel*, in *Zeitschrift für katholische Theologie*, 91 (1969), pp. 517-553.

the total number of words in the DSFs of chapters 1-11 to 52 (i.e. 31 + 21), once again a multiple of the divine number 26 (2 × 26). The DSs in these series of 8 yield 358. Together with the DSFs they have 379 words. As we have noted before, the total number of words constituting the 8 *ka'ᵃšèr dibbèr* phrases, amounts to 34, a multiple of the divine number 17 (2 × 17).

The first of the 2DSs in the 'law section' (marked $DS^{9/1}$ in 17,16) is introduced by the only Ref. DSF having an introducing function, which is phrased conspicuously differently and is accompanied by *lākèm*, obviously for the sake of emphasis. The second DS (marked $DS^{10/2}$) is introduced by the 7th regular introducing DSF in the series of eight, which contains the 7th *'ēlay*. The total number of words in this 10th DS is 51, once again a multiple of the divine number 17 (3 × 17). The grand total of words in the DSFs and DSs together in the 'law section' is 63 (a number that seems to have been associated with law) [18]. When we assess the grand total of words in the DSFs and DSs in chapters 4-26, we get 379 + 63 = 442, which is a multiple of *both* 17 *and* 26 (17 × 26)! Finally, in the whole book so far, chapters 1-26, the words constituting the DSFs are 58 (31 + 21 + 6 = 58), the number that represents the numerical value of *kᵉbôd YHWH*, which occurs several times [19].

The last series of 10 DSs begin in 31,2 where the first DS is ushered in by the remarkable formula *wᵉ YHWH 'āmar 'ēlay* (phrased so to make it emphatic?), the 8th and last in that series of 8 DSFs, here accompanied by the 8th *'ēlay* (marked *'ēlay*$^{8'}$). Is it a coincidence that the DSF and the DS have 8 words? The function of this second series of 8 prepositions (marked *'ēlay*$^{1'-8'}$) is evidently to form a bracket joining all the material in the chapters 4,1-31,13 together, a function similar to that of the stereotyped phrases in the books of Exodus — Numbers, as I have illustrated elsewhere [20].

The second DS in the series is in 31,14, the beginning of the concluding chapters of the book, 31,14-34,12. Here again we may note the bracketing function of the series of 10, which join the concluding section of the book to the preceding sections. As a matter of fact the last 3 instances of the series of 34 × *ṣiwwāh* and the last two occurrences of the series of 10 × *lē'mōr* have the same bracketing function. I have already remarked that the DS in 32,32-35 lacks an introducing DSF. Would an extra *wayyō'mèr* here have disturbed the numerical balance of the nine

18. It is well known that the Mishnah and Talmud have 63 tractates, but it is worth while to note that the first pericope of the 'law-section' in Deuteronomy (12,1-3) is made up of 63 words and so is the last pericope (26,16-19).

19. See C. SCHEDL, *Baupläne des Wortes, Einführung in die biblische Logotechnik*, Wien, 1974, pp. 50, 192. Cf. also my paper refered to in note 2 above, footnote 10. For further examples of 58 representing the *kᵉbōd YHWH* see Deut 5,28b-31 where the DS consists of 58 words and 9,26b-29 where the prayer of Moses is likewise made up of 58 words.

20. See the article cited in note 10 above, *op. cit.*, esp. pp. 270ff.

introducing formulas in this series, which have exactly 26 words? And was this the reason for the use of the literary device of the 'subjective speech' in the Song of Moses? Moreover, was it because of this numerical balance that the 4th instance of the DSFs with *wayyō'mèr* referring to Moses in the 3rd person (34,4a) reads *'ēlāw* (one word) instead of *'èl-mōšèh* (two words)? Was it for the sake of getting 26 words that the DSFs in 32,48 are so exceptionally long? And does this type of numerical structure explain the variety in wording and in length of the so-called stereotyped phrases occurring in series: *ka'ašèr dibbèr* (2 words); *ka'ašèr dibbèr lākèm* (3 words); *ka'ašèr dibbèr YHWH 'ēlay* (4 words); *ka'ašèr dibbèr YHWH 'èlōhêkā lô* (5 words) and *ka'ašèr dibbèr YHWH 'èlōhê 'abōtêkā lāk* (6 words)? What is more, doesn't this account for the remarkable baroque-like language so typical of Deuteronomy, with its extraordinary ability to expand and contract itself and to be kneaded in the numerical structures? And finally, does the numerical system explain the inclusion of the 'ethnographic notices' in the DSs in chapter 2, and does it also account for the remarkable structure of 1,1-5 with its presumably suspect 'geographic notice' in vs. 2?

We do not know the answers to all these questions yet, but so much is certain, that we can state that the evidence for number symbolism and numerical structures as determining factors with regard to the wording, the phrasing and the scope of literary compositions in Deuteronomy is conclusive.

The fact that the grand total of words constituting all DSs in the whole book of Deuteronomy is 1343, a multiple of the divine number 17 (79 × 17) attests to the use of this type of number symbolism in the entire book [21]. What we found in the subsections of the book, supports this conclusion.

What I have put forward up till now, is only the tip of the iceberg. There is an overwhelming amount of evidence to show that the use of the divine numbers is a vital part of the composition technique employed by the Deuteronomist(s). The words constituting the DSFs and the DSs themselves were carefully weighed and meticulously counted in order to fit them into patterns conforming to the rules of this numerical system, dominated by the divine name numbers 17 and 26. The purpose of the writer(s) seems to have been to let the divine name manifest itself in the words expressing divine speech, by means of the divine numbers and their multiples.

If we look beyond the tip of the iceberg, we find that the whole book of Deuteronomy is literally teeming with these numbers, not only in the texts referring to divine speech, but also elsewhere throughout the book. In my analysis of the first eleven chapters (to be published in the

21. Cf. remark c) in note 39 of the article cited in note 2 above.

forthcoming commentary in the Dutch series *De Prediking van het Oude Testament*) I have not come across a single section that totally lacks a numerical structure. When, as a result of my study of the DSFs in the Pentateuch I first came to realize that the biblical writers meticulously *counted* not only the formulas (7 + 4 etc., and 7 + 7 etc.) but also the *words* of these formulas in order to let them fit into premeditated patterns and to make them conform to the rules of numerical structures, I was convinced that we have to take their counting seriously if we want to understand the anatomy of their writings. This is how I learned to appreciate the worth and excellence of the method for analysing biblical texts advanced by the Austrian scholar Claus Schedl[22]. This method, known as logotechnical analysis (*Logotechnik*), involves the counting of the smallest syntactical units and assessing their number in the main clauses, subordinate clauses, sentences, pericopes and larger literary units. Up to the present time, for some reason or other this method, which is extremely objective and accurate, has not yet been appreciated, let alone employed by biblical scholars. In my opinion, this method is a very helpful, essential and indispensible tool for analysing biblical texts.

A logotechnical analysis enables us to detect concealed structures in the text that were not discovered up till now by traditional methods of literary analysis. Let me give two examples:

First, Deut 3,21-22: this pericope has 34 (2 × 17) words. A superficial logotechnical analysis shows that it consists of two parts: a) vs. 21, Moses' address to Joshua, phrased in 2nd person singular, which yields 26 words, and b) vs. 22, Moses' address to the people, phrased in 2nd person plural, which has 8 words (26 + 8 = 34). A deeper analysis shows that there are four main clauses:

(i) *wᵉ'èt-yᵉhôšûᵃᶜ ṣiwwêtî bā'ēt hahî' lē'mōr* (6)
(ii) *ʿênêkā hārō'ōt 'ēt kol* (4)
(iii) *kēn yaʿᵃśèh YHWH lᵉkol-hammamlākōt* (5)
(iv) *lō' tîrā'ûm* (2),

which are made up of 17 words. There are three subordinate clauses introduced by *'ᵃšèr* and *kî*:

(i) *'ᵃšèr ʿāśāh YHWH 'ᵉlōhêkèm lišᵉnê hammᵉlākîm hā'ēllèh* (7)
(ii) *'ᵃšèr 'attāh ʿōbēr šāmmāh* (4)
(iii) *kî YHWH 'ᵉlōhêkèm hû' hannilḥām lākèm* (6),

which yield once again 17 words[23].

Second, Deut 1,34-40: this pericope is made up of 95 words grouped in seven *pᵉsukîm* as follows:

22. See his book referred to in note 19 above.

23. The *four* main clauses and the *three* subordinate clauses show the 4+3=7 pattern; this pattern is repeated in the verbal forms: *four* verba finita and *three* participia.

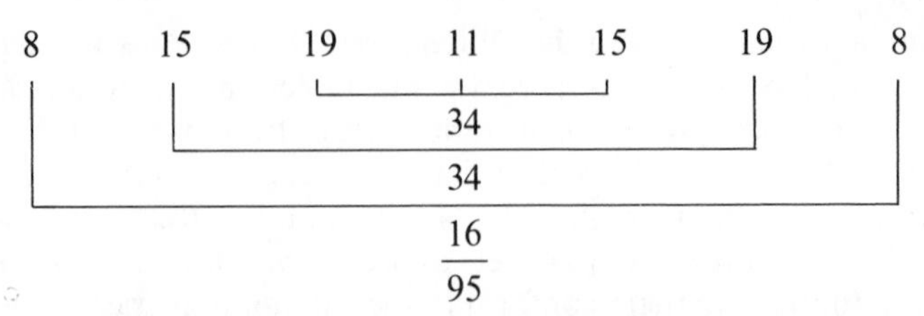

This is a typical example of the menorah-structure, of which there are several instances[24]. The first DS, in vv. 35-36, about entrance into the land, addressed to the people and phrased in 2nd person *plural*, consists of 34 words: the introduction to the second DS and that part of the DS phrased in 2nd person *singular*, addressed to Moses, are made up of 26 (11 + 15) words (vv. 37-38); the entire second DS consists of 5 words expressing God's refusal to let Moses enter the land and 34 expressing his approval of the entrance of Joshua and the young generation into the land (together = 39 = *YHWH 'èḥād*). Finally it may be noted that the concluding part of this adress, v. 39, is phrased in 2nd person *plural*, which means that the people are once again included in the address. The further analysis of the pericope will take us too far; it might suffice to say that the main clauses together are made up of exactly 68 words, a multiple of 17 (4 × 17).

I have selected these two examples more or less at random, but every pericope could have been selected to illustrate how the numerical system, based on the divine numbers 17 and 26 and their multiples, works.

It stands to reason that the use of these numbers as a vital part of the composition technique employed in Deuteronomy has now been firmly established. The weight of the evidence proves beyond any doubt that the book of Deuteronomy was not written in an off-hand way, but was carefully constructed according to premeditated schemes and structures dictated by number symbolism. The creating of this literary master-piece is comparable to the making of a vast crossword puzzle or to the weaving of a Persian carpet. This regards not only the smaller literary units and sub-sections, but also the larger sections, in fact the whole book. The last redaction must have been more thorough and painstaking than we ever thought. The whole book is pervaded by this numerical system representing symbolically the presence of God. It bears witness to the extreme care with which the authors surrounded their writing about God's speaking.

This sheds new light on the command in Deut 4,2 and 13,1 not to add nor detract from «the word I command you». The real purpose of this so-called 'canonical formula' is a twofold one: first, to protect the law

24. Sofar as I know C. SCHEDL was the first to focus attention upon this remarkable structure when he discovered it in Deut 5,14. See C. SCHEDL, *Op. cit.*, p. 172. For more examples I must refer to my forthcoming Deuteronomy commentary.

against tampering with it, and second, to preserve the intricate, latent-theological structures of the text, which obtained a sacred character.

It is in this light, in my opinion, that the difficult text in Deut 29,28 should be interpreted:

> *hannistārōt l^{e} YHWH $^{\grave{e}}$lōhênû w^{e}hanniglōt lānû ûl^{e}bānênû ʿad-ʿôlām lá^{ca}śôt ʾèt-kol-dibrê hattôrah hazzôʾt*
>
> «The hidden things are for YHWH our God, but the revealed things are for us and our children for ever, that we may do all the words of this law».

Here again the plain meaning of the text refers to its immediate context where it is spoken of national disaster as a consequence of disobedience. But at the same time it has another message: the concealed things, the esoteric knowledge with regard to the written text of the law, the sacred numerical structures, are for the benefit of God, to his glory, but the text of the law in its straight, plain language is for the benefit of the people. It is a coded message to the ordinary people, to the uninitiated, who do not know the hidden intricacies of the text, to obey the law in its plain meaning.

The key to the code is in the two words *hannistārōt* and *w^{e}hanniglōt*, both written defectively (a fact signalized in the massora). Their Gematria yields the following:

The sum of the digits of their letter value:

h=5 + n=50 + s=60 + t=400 + r=200 + t=400 = 26
w=6 + h=5 + n=50 + g=3 + l=30 + t=400 = 26

The sum of the digits of their alphabet value:

h=5 + n=14 + s=15 + t=22 + r=20 + t=22 = 26
w=6 + h=5 + n=14 + g=3 + l=12 + t=22 = 26.

The discovery of hidden things gives birth to true knowledge. May this knowledge lead us to real understanding.

Perklaan 22 C. J. LABUSCHAGNE
NL-9752 GP Haren (Gr.)

SYNOPSIS OF DIVINE SPEECH IN DEUTERONOMY

1-3

1,3	k^{e}kōl ʾ^{a}šèr ṣiwwāh[1]YHWH ʾōtô ʾ^{a}lēhèm	
1,6ff.	*YHWH ʾ$^{\grave{e}}$lōhênû dibbèr[1] ʾēlênû b^{e}ḥōrēb lēʾmōr[1]*	
		DS[1] 48 (DSF 6 + DS 48 = 54)
1,8	ʾèt-hāʾārèṣ ʾ^{a}šèr nišbaʿ YHWH laʾ^{a}bōtêkèm l^{e}ʾabrāhām l^{e}yiṣḥāq ûl^{e}ya^{ca}qōb lātēt lāhèm ûl^{e}zarʿām ʾaḥ^{a}rêhèm	
1,11	kaʾ^{a}šèr[1] dibbèr[1] lākèm	(*Ref. DSF* 3)
1,19	kaʾ^{a}šèr ṣiwwāh[2] YHWH ʾ$^{\grave{e}}$lōhēnû ʾōtānû	
1,21	kaʾ^{a}šèr[2] dibbèr YHWH[1] ʾ$^{\grave{e}}$lōhê ʾ^{a}bōtèka lāk[1]	(*Ref. DSF* 6)

1,34ff.	(wayyiqṣōp wayyiššāba') *lē'mōr*[2]	DS[2] 34 (DSF 1 + DS 34 = 35)
1,35	'ēt hā'areṣ haṭṭôbāh '^{a}šèr nišba'tî lātēt la'^{a}bōtêkèm	
1,37ff.	(gam-bî hit'annap YHWH biglalkèm) *lē'mōr*[3]	DS[3] 47 (DSF 1 + DS 47 = 48)
1,41	k^{e}kōl '^{a}šèr-ṣiwwnû[3] YHWH '^{è}lōhēnû	
1,42	*wayyō'mèr*[2] *YHWH 'ēlay*[1]	DS[4] 13 (DSF 3 + DS 13 = 16)
2,1	ka'^{a}šèr[3] dibbèr YHWH[2] 'ēlay[2]	(*Ref. DSF* 4)
2,2ff.	*wayyō'mèr*[3] *YHWH 'ēlay*[3] *lē'mōr*[4]	DS[5] 55 (DSF 4 + DS 55 = 59)
2,9ff.	*wayyō'mèr*[4] *YHWH 'ēlay*[4]	DS[6] 66 (DSF 3 + DS 66 = 69)
2,14	ka'^{a}šèr nišba' YHWH lāhēm	
2,17ff.	*way^{e}dabbēr*[5] *YHWH 'ēlay*[5] *lēmōr*[5]	DS[7] 121 (DSF 4 + DS 121 = 125)
2,31	*wayyō'mèr*[6] *YHWH 'ēlay*[6]	DS[8] 13 (DSF 3 + DS 13 = 16)
2,37	w^{e}kōl '^{a}šèr-ṣiwwāh[4] YHWH '^{è}lōhēnû	
3,2	*wayyō'mèr*[7] *YHWH 'ēlay*[7]	DS[9] 22 (DSF 3 + DS 22 = 25)
3,26ff.	*wayyō'mèr*[8] *YHWH 'ēlay*[8]	DS[10] 44 (DSF 3 + DS 44 = 47)
	1-3: Total: DSF 31 + DS 463 = 494 (19×26).	
4-11		
4,5	ka'^{a}šèr ṣiwwanî[5] YHWH '^{è}lōhāy	
4,10	*bè'^{è}mōr*[1] *YHWH 'ēlay*[1']	DS[1] 21 (DSF 3 + DS 21 = 24)
4,12	wayy^{e}d abbēr YHWH '^{a}lêkèm mittôk hā'ēš[1]	
4,13	'^{a}šèr ṣiwwāh[6] 'ètkèm la^{ca}śôt	
4,14	w^{e}'ōtî ṣiwwāh[7] YHWH bā'ēt hahî'	
4,15	b^{e}yôm dibbèr YHWH '^{a}lêkèm b^{e}ḥōrēb mittôk hā'ēš[2]	
4,21	wayyiššāba' l^{e}biltî 'obrî 'èt-hayyardēn	
4,23	'^{a}šèr ṣiwwāh[8] YHWH '^{è}lōhêkā	
4,31	'èt-b^{e}rît '^{a}bōtêkā '^{a}šèr nišba' lāhèm	
4,33	qôl ELOHIM dabbēr mittôk ha'ēš[3]	
4,36	ûd^{e}bārāw šāma'tā mittôk ha'ēš[4]	
5,4	dibbèr YHWH 'immākèm bāhār mittôk ha'ēš[5]	
5,2.5ff.	(YHWH '^{è}lōhênû kārat 'immānû b^{e}rît b^{e}ḥōrēb ...) *lē'mōr*[6]	DS[2] 189 (DSF 1 + DS 189 = 190)
5,12	ka'^{a}šèr ṣiww^{e}kā[9] YHWH '^{è}lōhêkā	
5,15	'al-kēn ṣiww^{e}kā[10] YHWH '^{è}lōhêkā	
5,16	ka'^{a}šèr ṣiww^{e}kā[11] YHWH '^{è}lōhêkā	
5,22	dibbèr YHWH ... mittôk hā'ēš[6]	
5,24a	w^{e}'èt-qōlô šāma'nû mittôk hā'ēš[7]	
5,24b	kî y^{e} dabbēr[1)] 'ELOHIM 'èt-hā'ādām	
5,26	qôl 'ELOHIM ḥayyîm m^{e} dabbēr mittôk-hā'ēš[8]	
5,27a	'ēt kol-'^{a}šèr yō'mar[2)] YHWH '^{è}lōhênû	
5,27b	'ēt kol-'^{a}šèr y^{e}dabbēr[3)] YHWH '^{è}lōhênû 'ēlêkā	
5,28ff.	*wayyō'mèr*[2] *YHWH 'ēlay*[2']	DS[3] 58 (DSF 3 + DS 58 = 61)
5,31	wa'^{a}dabb^{e}rāh[4)] 'ēlêkā 'ēt kol-hammiṣwāh	
5,32	ka'^{a}šèr ṣiwwāh[12] YHWH '^{è}lōhêkèm 'ètkèm	
5,33	'^{a}šèr ṣiwwāh[13] YHWH '^{è}lōhêkèm 'ètkèm	
6,1	'^{a}šèr ṣiwwāh[14] YHWH '^{è}lōhêkèm	
6,3	ka'^{a}šèr[4] dibbèr YHWH[3] '^{è}lōhê '^{a}bōtêkā lāk[2]	(*Ref. DSF* 6)
6,10	'el-hā'ārèṣ '^{a}šèr nišba' la'^{a}botêkā l^{e}'abrāhām l^{e}yiṣḥāq ûl^{e}ya^{ca}qōb lātēt lāk	
6,17	'^{a}šèr ṣiww^{e}kā[15]	
6,18	'èt-hā'ārèṣ haṭṭōbāh '^{a}šèr-nišba' YHWH la'^{a}botêkā	

6,19 ka'[a]šèr[5] dibbèr YHWH[4] (*Ref. DSF* 3)
6,20 '[a]šèr ṣiwwāh[16] YHWH '[è]lōhênû 'ètkèm
6,23 'èt-hā'ārèṣ '[a]šèr nišba' la'[a]bōtênû
6,24 way[e]ṣawwênû[17] YHWH
6,25 ka'[a]šèr ṣiwwānû[18]
7,8 'èt-hašš[e]bu'āh '[a]šèr nišba' la'[a]bōtêkèm
7,12 'èt-habberît we'èt-haḥèsèd '[a]šèr nišba' la'[a]bōtêkā
7,13 'al-hā'[a]dāmāh '[a]šèr-nišba' la'[a]bōtêkā lātēt lāk
8,1 'èt-hā'ārèṣ '[a]šèr-nišba' YHWH la'bōtêkèm
8,18 'èt-b[e]rîtô '[a]šèr-nišba' la'[a]bōtêkā kayyôm hazzèh
9,3 ka'[a]šèr[6] dibbèr YHWH[5] lāk[3] (*Ref. DSF* 4)
9,5 'èt-haddābār '[a]šèr nišba' YHWH la'[a]bōtêkā l[e]'abrāhām l[e]yiṣḥāq ûl[e]ya[ca]qōb
9,10 '[a]šèr dibbèr YHWH 'immākèm bāhār mittôk hā'ēš[9] ...
9,12a *wayyō'mèr[3] YHWH 'ēlay[3']* DS[4] *19 (DSF 3* + DS 19 = 22)
9,12b '[a]šèr ṣiwwîtim[19]
9,13f. *wayyō'mèr[4] YHWH 'ēlay[4'] lē'mōr[7]* DS[5] 23 (DSF 4 + DS 23 = 27)
9,16 '[a]šèr ṣiwwāh[20] YHWH 'ètkèm
9,23 (biš[e]lōaḥ YHWH 'ètkèm ...) *lē'mōr[8]* DS[6] 7 (DSF 1 + DS 7 = 8)
9,25 kî 'āmar[5)] YHWH l[e]hašmîd 'ètkèm
9,28 'el-hā'ārèṣ '[a]šèr dibbèr[6)] lāhèm
10,1f. (*bā'ēt hahî'*) *'āmar[5] YHWH 'ēlay[5']* DS[7] 27 (DSF 3 + DS 27 = 30)
10,4 '[a]šèr dibbèr YHWH '[a]lēkèm bāhār mittôk hā'ēš[10] ...
10,5 ka'[a]šèr ṣiwwanî[21] YHWH
10,9 ka'[a]šèr[7] dibbèr YHWH[6] '[è]lōhêkā lô (*Ref. DSF* 5)
10,11a *wayyō'mèr[6] YHWH 'ēlay[6']* DS[8] 14 (DSF 3 + DS 14 = 17)
10,11b 'èt-hā'ārèṣ '[a]šèr nišba'tî la'[a]bōtām lātēt lāhèm
11,9 'al-hā'[a]dāmāh '[a]šèr nišba' YHWH la'[a]bōtêkèm lātēt lāhèm ûl[e]zar'ām
11,21 'al-hā'[a]dāmāh '[a]šèr nišba' YHWH la'[a]bōtêkèm lātēt lāhèm
11,25 ka'[a]šèr[8] dibbèr[2] lākèm (*Ref. DSF* 3)

4-11: Total: DSF 21 + DS 358 = 379
1-11: Total DSF: 31 + 21 = 52
1-11: Total *Ref. DSF* = 34

12-26

12,20 ka'[a]šèr[1'] dibbèr[3] lāk[4] (*Ref. DSF* 3)
13,6 '[a]šèr ṣiww[e]kā[22] YHWH '[è]lōhêkā
13,18 ka'[a]šèr nišba' la'[a]bōtêkā
15,6 ka'[a]šèr[2'] dibbèr[4] lāk[5] (*Ref. DSF* 3)
17,16 w[e] YHWH 'āmar[7)] lākèm DS[9/1] 6 (DSF 3 + DS 6 = 9)
18,2 ka'[a]šèr[3'] dibbèr[5] lô *(Ref. DSF 3)*
18,17ff. *wayyō'mèr[7] YHWH 'ēlay[7']* DS[10/2] 51 (DSF 3 + DS 51 = 54)
18,18 'ēt kol-'[a]šèr '[a]ṣawwènnû[23]
18,20 'ēt '[a]šèr lō'-ṣiwwîtîw[24] l[e]dabbēr
19,8a ka'[a]šèr nišba' la'[a]bōtêkā
19,8b 'ēt-kol-hā'ārèṣ '[a]šèr dibbèr[8)] YHWH lātēt la'[a]bōtêkā
20,17 ka'[a]šèr ṣiww[e]kā[25] YHWH '[e]lōhêkā
26,3 'èl-hā'ārèṣ '[a]šèr nišba' YHWH la'[a]bōtênû lātēt lânû
26,13 '[a]šèr ṣiwwîtānî[26]

26,14 k^{e}kōl ʼ^{a}šèr ṣiwwîtānî[27]
26,15 kaʼ^{a}šèr nišbaʻtā laʼ^{a}bōtênû
26,16 hayyôm hazzèh YHWH ʼ^{è}lōhêkā m^{e}ṣaww^{e}kā[28]
26,17 ʼèt-YHWH hèʼ^{e}martā[9)] hayyôm
26,18 kaʼ^{a}šèr[4ʼ] dibbèr[6] lāk[6] (*Ref. DSF* 3)
26,19 kaʼ^{a}šèr[5ʼ] dibbèr[7] (*Ref. DSF* 2)

12-26: Total: DSF 6 + DS 57 = 63
4-26: Total DSF and DS (379+63) = 442 (17×26)
1-26: Total DSF: 31 + 21 + 6 = 58

27,1-31,13

27,3 ʼèrèṣ...kaʼ^{a}šèr[6ʼ] dibbèr YHWH[7] ʼ^{è}lōhê ʼ^{a}bōtèkā lāk[7] (*Ref. DSF* 6)
28,8 y^{e}ṣaw[29] YHWH ʼitt^{e}kā ʼèt-habb^{e}rākāh
28,9 kaʼ^{a}šèr nišbaʻ lāk
28,11 ʻal-hāʼ^{a}dāmāh ʼ^{a}šèr nišbaʻ YHWH laʼ^{a}bōtêkā lātēt lāk
28,45 ʼ^{a}šèr ṣiwwāk[30]
28,68 ʼ^{a}šèr ʼāmartî[10)] l^{e}kā
28,69 ʼ^{a}šèr ṣiwwāh[31] YHWH ʼèt-mōšèh
29,12a kaʼ^{a}šèr[7ʼ] dibbèr[8] lāk[8] (*Ref. DSF* 3)
29,12b w^{e}kaʼ^{a}šèr nišbaʻ laʼ^{a}bōtêkā l^{e}ʼabrāhām l^{e}yiṣḥāq ûl^{e}ya^{ca}qōb
30,20 ʻal-hāʼ^{a}dāmāh ʼ^{a}šèr nišbaʻ YHWH laʼ^{a}bōtêkā l^{e}ʼabrāhām l^{e}yiṣḥāq ûl^{e}ya^{ca}qōb lātēt lāhèm
31,2 *w^{e}YHWH[8] ʼamar ʼēlay[8ʼ]* DS[1] 5 (DSF 3 + DS 5 = 8)
31,3 kaʼ^{a}šèr[8ʼ] dibbèr YHWH[8] (*Ref. DSF* 3)
31,7 ʼèl-hāʼārèṣ ʼ^{a}šèr nišbaʻ YHWH laʼ^{a}bōtām lātēt lāhèm

12,1-31,13: Total *Ref. DSF* = 26

31,14-34,12

31,14a *wayyōʼmèr[1] YHWH ʼèl-mōšèh[1]* DS[2] 11 (DSF 4 + DS 11 = 15)
31,14b waʼ^{a}ṣawwènû[32]
31,16ff. *wayyōʼmèr[2] YHWH ʼèl-mōšèh[2]* DS[3] 140 (DSF 4 + DS 140 = 144)
31,20 ʼèl-haʼ^{a}dāmāh ʼ^{a}šèr nišbaʻtî laʼ^{a}bōtāw
31,21 ʼèl-hāʼārèṣ ʼ^{a}šèr nišbaʻtî
31,23a way^{e}ṣaww[33] ʼèt-y^{e}hôšu^{ac} bin-nûn
31,23b *wayyōʼmèr[3]* DS[4] 16 (DSF 1 + DS 16 = 17)
31,23c ʼèl-hāʼārèṣ ʼ^{a}šèr nišbaʻtî lāhèm
32,20ff. *wayyōʼmèr[4]*] DS[5] 95 (including *ʼāmartî*): (DSF 1 + DS 95 = 96)
32,26 (ʼāmartî)]
32,32-5 > DSF! DS[6] 37 (DSF 0 + DS 37 = 37)
32,37ff. *w^{e}ʼāmar[5]*] DS[7] 68 (incl. *ʼāmartî*) = 4×17 (DSF 1 + DS 68 = 69)
32,40 (w^{e}ʼāmartî)]
32,48ff. *way^{e}dabbēr YHWH ʼèl-mōšèh[3] b^{e}ʻèṣèm hayyôm hazzèh lēʼmōr[9]*
DS[8] 77 (DSF 8 + DS 77 = 85 = 5×17)
33,27 *wayyōʼmèr[7]* DS[9] 1 (DSF 1 + DS 1 = 2)
34,4a *wayyōʼmèr[8] YHWH ʼēlāw* DS[10] 15 (DSF 3 + DS 15 = 18)
34,4b zōt hāʼārèṣ ʼ^{a}šèr nišbaʻtî l^{e}ʼabrāhām l^{e}yiṣḥāq ûl^{e}ya^{ca}qōb lēʼmōr[10]
(DS is part of DS[10]!)
34,9 kaʼ^{a}šèr ṣiwwah[34] YHWH ʼèt-mōšeh[4]

27-34: Total: DSF 26 + DS 465 = 491
1-34: Grand total: DSF 84 + DS 1343 (79×17) = 1427

DRITTER TEIL

TEXTE UND EINZELPROBLEME IM DEUTERONOMIUM

LA SEPTANTE DE DT 1-11

POUR UNE ÉTUDE DU «TEXTE» *

Les versions anciennes ne sont-elles que des traductions plus ou moins fidèles d'un même texte hébreu? Quand doit-on avoir recours à la LXX pour «corriger» le texte hébreu? Comment la LXX peut-elle témoigner du «texte hébreu»? La pratique des exégètes varie passablement, on le sait: les éditions de BHK, celle de BHS, les grands commentaires du XXe s., montrent que la LXX n'est pas tellement étudiée pour elle-même.

Comparant la LXX de la Gn à celle du Dt, J. W. Wevers signale que Gn est plus libre que Dt. Par voie de conséquence, Gn est d'un grec meilleur. Chaque livre biblique doit être étudié pour lui-même. Wevers insiste, à juste titre, sur le fait que, lors de la traduction de la LXX, le canon n'était pas encore fixé. Le Pentateuque samaritain est parfois le témoin d'un texte hébreu différent du TM, qui a continué à évoluer [1]. Cette évolution du TM, il faut bien le dire, n'est pas suffisamment prise en considération.

La Vulgate peut paraître peu utile pour une étude «textuelle». Rappelons toutefois que s. Jérôme a mis en application le principe selon lequel la «veritas hebraica» fait loi. De fait, neuf fois sur dix (pour donner un ordre de proportion), la Vg traduit un texte «pré-massorétique». La tradition juive du texte paraît virtuellement fixée à l'époque de s. Jérôme. On peut déduire qu'il est important de noter les rares cas où la Vg rejoint la LXX, les fragments de Qumrân, les targums, là où le TM lira autre chose.

Un mot sur la méthode suivie dans cet essai: avant d'étudier en détail la LXX de l'un ou l'autre chapitre du Dt, j'ai lu (pour mieux établir les comparaisons) le TM, la Vg, le targum Neofiti et le Pseudo-Jonathan. Les variantes attestées à Qumrân ont été examinées, puis, à partir des exemples retenus pour cet essai, les variantes possibles attestées par l'araméen des targums (Neofiti I, Pseudo-Jonathan, Onqelos) et par le Pentateuque samaritain ont été considérées [2].

* Abréviations: TM: texte massorétique; LXX: Septante; Samar: Pentateuque samaritain; Vg: Vulgate; N: Targum Neofiti I; BHK: *Biblia Hebraica*, ed. Kittel; BHS: *Biblia Hebraica Stuttgartensia*; DJD: *Discoveries in the Judaean Desert*; TOB: *Traduction Œcuménique de la Bible*.

1. J.W. WEVERS, *The Attitude of the Greek Translator of Deuteronomy towards his Parent Text*, in H. DONNER, R. HANHART, R. SMEND (éd.), *Beiträge zur Alttestamentlichen Theologie. Festschrift für Walther Zimmerli zum 70. Geburtstag*, Göttingen, 1977, 498-505, pp. 408-499.

2. Ouvrages consultés: *Biblia Hebraica Stuttgartensia* (J. HEMPEL: Dt, 1972); J.W.

On peut dire que les différences entre LXX et TM, dans le Dt, sont minimes. De plus, le style répétitif de ce livre prête flanc à des amplifications nullement imputables à un texte hébreu a priori différent. Lorsque des ajouts ou des «omissions» se retrouvent dans la LXX, à Qumrân, dans le targum N, il faut faire attention aux conclusions qu'on en tire. La transmission du texte par la tradition massorétique n'est pas indemne de retouches, si limitées soient-elles. Les variantes anciennes connues nous obligent à briser l'équivalence: texte de l'AT = texte massorétique des Ben Asher = texte «canonique» [3].

Une comparaison globale entre LXX et TM est éclairante: pour les ch. 1-3 du Dt (soit pour 112 versets), on a 49 versets absolument identiques dans la LXX et le TM (choix de mots, ordre des mots, etc.). À cela, il faut ajouter que les différences sont minimes pour plusieurs autres versets, différences parfois attribuables à des remaniements internes. Mais des différences subsistent, qui laissent voir des formes textuelles divergentes. Ce sont des exemples de tels cas que nous voulons examiner ici.

1) L'expression *hayyôm* («ce jour»/«aujourd'hui»). L'actualisation, si appréciée du deutéronomiste pourrait avoir donné lieu à des ajouts fortuits, là où la LXX nous offre un *sêmeron* non attesté dans le TM. Ainsi pour 4, 1 et 2. Au v. 1a, la syriaque [4] pourrait avoir été influencée par la LXX, là où elle ajoute son «aujourd'hui», et la LXX pourrait avoir introduit cette «actualisation» tant au v. 1 qu'au v. 2. Mais, alors, comment expliquer la rencontre LXX — Samar pour le v. 2?

WEVERS, *Deuteronomium* (Septuaginta ... III,2), Göttingen, 1977; M. BAILLET, J.T. MILIK, R. DE VAUX, O.P., avec une contribution de H.W. BAKER, *Les 'petites grottes' de Qumrân* [...] (DJD, III), Oxford, 1962, t.* Textes, t.** Planches; *Qumrân Grotte 4*. II, *I. Archéologie* par R. DE VAUX [...], *II. Tefillin, Mezuzot et Targums (4Q128-4Q157)* par J.T. MILIK (DJD, VI), Oxford, 1977; A. DÍEZ MACHO, *Neophyti 1, Targum Palestinense Ms de la Biblioteca Vaticana*, t.V, *Deuteronomio* [...], Madrid, 1978; R. LE DÉAUT, *Targum du Pentateuque* [...], t.IV: *Deutéronome* [...] (Sources Chrétiennes, 271), Paris, 1980; A. SPERBER, *The Bible in Aramaic Based on Old Manuscripts and Printed Texts*, Vol. I: *The Pentateuch According to Targum Onkelos*, Leiden, 1959; A. TAL, *The Samaritan Targum of the Pentateuch. A Critical Edition*. Part II: *Leviticus, Numeri, Deuteronomium* (Texts and Studies in the Hebrew Language and Related Subjects. V), Tel Aviv, 1981; M.H. GOSHEN-GOTTSTEIN (éd.), *The Bible in the Syropalestinian Version* [...], Part I: *Pentateuch and the Prophets* (Publications of the Hebrew University Bible Project, Mon. Ser., 4), Jerusalem, 1973. Je n'ai pas pu consulter l'ouvrage de D. RIEDER, *Pseudo-Jonathan. Targum Jonathan ben Uziel on the Pentateuch*, Jerusalem, 1974. Lorsqu'aucune autre précision n'est fournie, on renvoie aux éditions mentionnées, *ad locum*. Pour le texte araméen de N, voir l'*editio princeps* de DÍEZ MACHO; les citations en traduction française sont empruntées de l'ouvrage de LE DÉAUT, *Targum du Pentateuque, t. IV: Deutéronome*.

3. Au sujet de la relation entre le texte hébreu et ce que semble lire N, une remarque de R. LE DÉAUT risque d'être mal interprétée: «Les notes parfois signalent quelques mots du TM *omis* dans le Targum, *peut-être intentionellement*, et que nous n'avons pas restitués» ([c'est nous qui soulignons] *Targum du Pentateuque* ... t. I: *Genèse* ... [SC 245], p. 68). Mais qu'en est-il, si c'est la tradition massorétique qui a ajouté ces mots?

4. Voir l'apparat critique de BHS.

En 6,2b, le *sêmeron* rejoint le *hayyôm* de Qumrân et le *ywmn* de Samar [5]. En 11,7, le changement n'est pas limité au *sêmeron*. TM: «Car vos yeux ont vu toute l'œuvre grandiose de Yahvé, qu'il a faite». La LXX ajoute: «pour vous aujourd'hui» (*hymin sêmeron*). Curieusement, au moins deux textes de Qumrân attestent le «à vous» (*'tkmh*) [6]. De plus, là où TM lit «l'œuvre grandiose de Yahvé» (au sg.), à Qumrân, on lit le pl.: «les œuvres grandioses de Yahvé» [7], tout comme la LXX: *ta erga kyriou ta megala*, ce que confirme N: «toutes les œuvres grandioses que Yahvé a faites».

2) Très souvent, l'on trouve «mon/ton/notre/votre Dieu» ajouté au nom divin (Yahvé), phénomène non limité à la LXX, où elle se trouve en 1,41; 4,3.35.39; 6,12.18; 9.18; 10,13. Ne pas oublier qu'elle est ajoutée dans le TM en 4,5 et 9,5. Un cas curieux: en 2,30, là où TM et Vg lisent «ton Dieu», la LXX et la marge du N lisent «notre Dieu». Le cas de 10,13 est à noter: l'ajout *tou Theou sou* est attesté par deux textes de Qumrân [8]. En guise de complément, il est bon de savoir que Samar, tout comme la LXX, atteste la formule longue en 1,41; 6,12.18; 10,13 et se contente du seul nom divin en 9,5, comme la LXX. Il ne s'agit donc pas uniquement de fantaisie de la part de traducteurs grecs.

3) L'on sait comment il est difficile de voir clair dans l'alternance «tu/vous», lorsqu'on parle des sources du Dt. Je crois qu'une grande prudence s'impose. Si on veut se servir de cette alternance, j'aimerais que l'on tienne compte des divergences entre LXX et TM, car les changements par assimilation ou par dissimilation peuvent venir de l'une ou de l'autre tradition textuelle ou même remonter à des sources différentes. Voyons quelques cas intéressants:

a) 1,8 et 21. Au v. 8, le TM se lit: «*Vois*, je vous remets le pays ...» et au v. 21: « *Vois*, Yahvé ton Dieu te donne le pays ...». N a le pl., mais cela ne peut pas nous servir, car N donne, à quelques exceptions près, le «vous» partout où l'on aurait «tu» ou «vous» [9]. Par contre, tant en 1,8 qu'en 1,21, la LXX lit le pl. «voyez» (*idete*), leçon attestée par 2Q10 (pour le v. 8), où le *waw* de *r^{e}û* est net [10]. Le targum Onqelos a le pl. au v. 8 et le sg. au v. 21 (*ḥzw* et *ḥzy*) [11]. Même phénomène dans Samar. On

5. 8Q3, fragment 15 (DJD III, pp. 150 et 152).

6. Il s'agit de deux phylactères (A et K): 4Q128 et 4Q138 (DJD VI, pp. 48, 50 et 67, 69).

7. 4Q138: même s'il semble y avoir eu hésitation, la finale du pl. (*-îm*) ayant été ajoutée en contrebas du mot *gdwl* (DJD VI, pp. 67, 69 et Pl. XX).

8. *'lhyk*: 8Q3, phylactère (DJD III, pp. 152, 154, Pl. XXXII, fragment 18) et 8Q4, mezouza (DJD III, pp. 158, 160, Pl. XXIV).

9. Cela vaut aussi pour les autres targums. Seuls, les rares cas où le sg. est retenu («tu») méritent d'être étudiés.

10. DJD III, p. 60 et Pl. XII. La TOB indique en note qu'elle lit au v. 8 le sg. «Vois»; dans le texte, le pl. est employé («Voyez»), sans doute à cause du contexte, car aucune mention n'est faite de la LXX ni du texte de Qumrân.

11. A. SPERBER, *The Bible in Aramaic ...*, *ad locum*.

notera la même différence entre LXX et TM en 4,5, alors alors que 11,26 donne le sg., tant dans le TM que dans la LXX.

b) 3,21: «Alors à Josué, j'ai donné mes ordres: 'Tu as vu de *tes* propres yeux ...'»[12]. Y aurait-il eu adaptation au contexte, vu qu'il s'agit d'une parole adressée à Josué? Notons que la suite emploie «vous»: «tout ce que Yahvé *votre* Dieu a fait...» Le message est donc adressé à Josué, mais tout aussi bien à la communauté. De fait, la LXX s'adresse à la communauté: «*Vos* yeux ont vu tout ce que Yahvé *votre* Dieu a fait». Tant la LXX que le TM ont pu essayer à leur façon de tenir compte du contexte.

4) 11,14.15. Ce passage fait voir l'alternance «tu/vous», mais, ce qui est encore plus intéressant, l'alternance entre la 1e et la 3e personne. Cela semble avoir une portée théologique.

a) En 11,14, il est dit que Dieu donnera en son temps «la pluie à *votre* terre», là où la LXX lit *têi gêi sou*: « à *ta* terre», leçon que suppose samar: «et *il* donnera la pluie à *ta* terre en son temps ...»[13]. Dans la tradition massorétique, le texte est à la 1e personne, et au v. 14 et au v. 15: «*je* donnerai en son temps la pluie... *je* donnerai de l'herbe à tes bêtes...» (*ntty*)[14]. À ce propos, le commentaire de la TOB est intéressant: «Le discours prend subitement la forme d'une parole adressée directement par Dieu à son peuple (vv. 14-15), pour indiquer que Dieu se porte personnellement garant de la réalisation des promesses (cf. 28,20; 29,4)»[15].

b) Allons voir le texte de 29,4 auquel renvoie la TOB: «*Je* vous ai fait marcher...»; v. 5: «... c'est *moi* Yahvé votre Dieu». Pour ces quatre cas (Dt 11,14.15 et 29,4.5), il n'y a pas de doute que la LXX lit la 3e personne: *dôsei*... *dôsei*... *êgagen*... *houtos kyrios*... La TOB a-t-elle raison? Le commentaire est bon, mais peut-être la LXX ne lisait-elle pas encore la 1e personne dans son texte hébreu. Elle ne serait pas responsable du changement de personne. Se rappeler que la lecture de la 3e personne, tant au v. 14 qu'au v. 15, est attestée par 8Q4 (*wntn mṭr 'rṣkm*... *wntn*...) et, au v. 15, par 4Q128[16]. La Vg, pour sa part, suit fidèlement la leçon pré-massorétique: *dabo*...[17] *adduxi vos*... *ego sum*

12. TOB, selon le TM: *'ynyk hr'wt*.

13. Remarquer qu'au v. 15 Samar emploie la 3e personne («et *il* donnera...»), tout comme la LXX.

14. J. T. MILIK (DJD VI, p. 46) reconstitue le texte des versets 14-15 (*wntn mṭr 'rṣkh*... *wntn*...), en tenant compte du fait que 4Q128 (DJD VI, p. 50), au v. 15, emploie la 3e personne au début du verset (*wntn*). Sa reconstitution du v. 14 est très plausible (cf. LXX et Samar), la 3e personne (*wntn*) trouvant un appui dans 8Q4 (cf. DJD III, pp. 159 et 161, Pl. XXXIV). Pour le possessif sg. (*'rṣkh*) au lieu du pl. (*'rṣkm*), je n'ai pas trouvé de confirmation dans les textes de Qumrân.

15. TOB, édition intégrale: *Ancien Testament*, Paris, 1975, p. 358, note *h*.

16. Des variantes existaient déjà, car 4Q130 (phylactère C) et 4Q136 (phyl. I) lisent la 1e personne du sg. (DJD VI, pp. 55 et 63).

17. En 11,15, «dabo» semble laissé de côté, pour éviter la répétition.

Dominus.... Quant à la 1e personne du TM de 29,5, n'y aurait-il pas eu influence de la célèbre formule d'Ezéchiel: «car je suis le Seigneur votre Dieu»?[18].

5) Le changement de personne en 2,24-25 (TM) fait intervenir Dieu et non plus seulement les Hébreux. Il faudra aussi noter d'autres variantes intéressantes. Dans le TM, le verbe *ḥll* est à la 2e personne de l'impératif au v. 24 (*hḥl*: «Commence à en prendre possession» [TOB]) et à la 1e personne de l'«impératif» au v. 25 (*'ḥl*: «Je commence à mettre la terreur», Dieu aidant son peuple face à ses ennemis). On comprend que, en bonne théologie, on a là le Dieu qui répand la terreur (cf. le *puluḫtu* mésopotamien) et non le peuple. La LXX lit la 2e personne de l'impératif, tant au v. 24 qu'au v. 25: *enarchou*. V. 25: «*Commence* à mettre la terreur et la crainte sur le visage de *tous* les peuples sous le ciel, qui, en entendant *ton nom*, seront effrayés...» On peut bien suggérer, avec BHS et les commentateurs, que le *enarchou* du v. 25 est influencé par celui du v. 24 (là où Aquila lit *arxomai dounai*)[19]. Mais l'histoire de ce texte est plus complexe. Il se peut que, par scrupule théologique, on ait voulu souligner que c'est Dieu et non Israël qui jette la crainte au visage des ennemis (contexte de «guerre sainte»). Dans le targum N, la transition est faite, car on y lit: «je vais commencer...» Par contre, Samar lit la 2e personne du sg. et, en marge, dans N, on a senti le besoin d'indiquer une autre lecture: «Commencez...»[20]. La vetus latina en témoigne elle aussi: «inchoare»[21]. Je maintiens donc que le choix de la 1e ou de la 2e personne n'est pas attribuable à de simples erreurs de copistes ou de traducteurs. Pour la suite du même verset, noter que le *kl* (*tout*) n'est pas au même endroit dans la Vorlage de la LXX («tous les peuples») et dans le TM («tous les cieux»). Quant à la Vg, elle lit comme le TM: «incipiam» et «sub omni caelo», mais, pour ce qui suit, appuie la LXX: «ut audito *nomine* tuo» (*akousantes to onoma sou*), ce qui supposerait *'šr yšm'wn šmk* au lieu du *šm'i* du TM. Notons enfin la *lectio conflata* du Pseudo-Jonathan (27031): «sur tous les peuples qui se trouvent sous tous les cieux»[22].

6) En 2,37, on pourrait croire qu'en continuant d'employer la 1e personne du pl., la LXX adapte le texte au verset précédent: «Du pays des fils d'Ammon seul, *nous* ne nous sommes pas approchés» (*ou prosēlthomen*), alors que TM lit «*tu* ne t'es pas approché». Si le Pseudo-Jonathan lit la 2e personne du sg., noter toutefois que N lit: «nous ne nous sommes pas approchés», tout comme la Vorlage de la

18. Contrairement à ce qu'il fait en 11,14.15, Samar emploie la 1e personne en 29,4.5.

19. Voir l'apparat critique de WEVERS.

20. Je rappelle que les targums emploient presque toujours la 2e personne du pl., au lieu du sg. Pour N et les variantes dans la marge, cf. DÍEZ MACHO, *Neophyti I*..., p. 24 (en espagnol) et p. 312: «M: «commencez» (avec LXX *-enarchou-* et Samaritain *šry*)».

21. Voir l'apparat critique de la LXX: «Latcod 100»: manuscrit du VIIe s. (Lyon).

22. Voir LE DÉAUT, *Targum du Pentateuque*, t. IV, p. 35.

LXX. Cet accord avec la LXX n'est pas signalé par Le Déaut [23]. Enfin, l'exception est à noter, la Vulgate lit «ad quem non accessimus».

En conclusion, il faut reconnaître que notre approche du texte hébreu est fortement conditionnée par l'état définitif du texte fourni par la tradition massorétique. L'on risque alors d'oublier que le TM, lui aussi, a continué à évoluer sur certains points. Il me paraît important de retrouver ces rares éléments divergents dans le Dt, éléments qui permettent de voir comment un texte n'est pas à l'abri des «relectures», même si on veut le transmettre fidèlement. Point question de corriger selon la LXX au petit bonheur, point question non plus d'ignorer la LXX, sous prétexte de la valeur absolue de la tradition massorétique. Sur ce plan, l'effort consacré à expliquer chaque tradition pour elle-même est beaucoup plus profitable qu'un choix éclectique de corrections et de conjectures, uniquement lorsque le TM fait problème [24].

Université Saint-Paul
223, rue Main
Ottawa, Ont., Canada K1S 1C4

Léo LABERGE, O.M.I.

23. Cf. *Id.*, ibid., pp. 38-39. Cet accord n'est pas davantage mentionné dans l'*editio princeps* de DIÉZ MACHO.

24. La lecture de D. BARTHÉLEMY, *Critique textuelle de l'Ancien Testament*, 1. *Josué, Juges* [...] (Orbis Biblicus et Orientalis, 50/1), Fribourg/S et Göttingen, 1982, montre bien que ce genre de travail a sa place en exégèse.

FORM AND STRUCTURE IN DEUTERONOMY 1-11

The form-critical problem in regards the book of Deuteronomy as a whole remains unresolved. Though the book contains a collection of laws, it is clearly not a law code in its literary form. And though the book has many affinities to international treaty texts of the ancient Near East, Deuteronomy is not the text of a covenant treaty as such, as M. Weinfeld in particular has shown [1]. It may be correct to see, with von Rad, the book as shaped by Levitical preaching which was put in the form of a cult liturgy as a series of sermons on the lips of Moses shortly before his death [2]. But once again the model of the sermon is less than adequate to explain this remarkable literary work. And though the book is clearly a repository for ancient traditions, the concept of an archive is simply too pedantic to describe adequately a work of such remarkable literary quality [3].

First and foremost the book of Deuteronomy is a work of literary art. Anyone who reads the book aloud attentively — even in translation — cannot help but be moved emotionally by the language, especially in chs. 1-11. Thus, if we are looking for a model to explain the book, we would do well to turn our attention to fields which focus more directly on aesthetic dimensions, namely those of music and literature, for possible parallels.

It should be noted that music and poetry are a common medium for transmitting cultural tradition among virtually all so-called preliterate peoples. In light of this fact some missionaries and administraters of mission agencies are beginning to ask new questions about the translation of the Bible into previously unwritten languages. The model of the Wycliffe Bible translator has been seriously challenged in recent years, from within the ranks of some of these translators themselves, as the most effective means of communicating the «Word of God» in such situations. Should an individual scholar give virtually a life-time to the tedious task of reducing such a language to written form in order to translate the Bible into one more of the 2000 such languages which exist to the present time? Where this has been done, the Bible often remains as an external artefact which never really becomes a vital part of the cultural tradition of such tribal groups. Would it not be better to

1. M. WEINFELD, *Deuteronomy and the Deuteronomic School*, Oxford, 1972, pp. 146-157.

2. G. VON RAD, *Deuteronomy* (OTL), Philadelphia, 1966, pp. 23-27.

3. P. KLEINERT, *Das Deuteronomium und der Deuteronomiker*, Leipzig, 1872; and N. LOHFINK, *Lectures in Deuteronomy*, Rome, 1968, p. 7.

translate the Bible into media already present in such societies for the transmission of culture, namely into their own forms of music? Recent experiments with the oral communication of the Scripture in sub-Sahara Africa, as reported by Herbert Klem, suggest a positive answer to this question[4]. Moreover, it may well be that these experiments themselves provide a closer analogue to the actual historical situation in ancient Israel than any of the models advanced in recent years within the mainstream of the academic study of the Bible.

In short, it is the thesis of this paper that the book of Deuteronomy, in its present literary form, is best explained as a didactic poem, composed to be recited publicly to music in ancient Israel within a liturgical setting. The book is primarily a work of literary art designed to transmit a canonical body of tradition, as effectively as possible to a given people. It was composed for oral recitation and, as the models in the field of ethno-musicology suggest, was no doubt composed with music as an essential aspect of the tradition itself. Moreover, as a work of literary art, the book of Deuteronomy was consciously composed in what some would call an «epic style» which is similar in its structure to other epic texts in the world of ancient Near Eastern and classical literatures. Thus we ought not to be surprised to find concentric structural features which are also the subject of investigation on the part of students of such classics as Homer's *Iliad* and Virgil's *Aeneid*[5]. And indeed such features are present in the biblical text as witnessed by the spate of such observations emerging in our discipline on either side of both the Atlantic and Pacific oceans.

It should also be noted that concentric structural features are not only characteristic of liturgical expression, from so-called primitive peoples to the celebration of the Roman Catholic mass; they are also common to both musical composition and epic literature in general[6]. Such structuring devices are one of the means of achieving that feeling of balance and symmetry which is an essential aspect of making art appear beautiful to both the ear and the eye. The astute observer of modern cinematography will be struck with how well some of our modern film

4. H. KLEM, *Oral Communication of the Scriptures: Insights from African Oral Art*, Pasadena, 1982. I am grateful to Roberta King, an ethno-musicologist in Kenya, for calling my attention to this book.

5. This observation was called to my attention by a student in the classics department at Harvard University and confirmed by conversations with other scholars.

6. The concentric structure of ritual activity is sometimes explained by reference to the superstitious belief that the ritual will be nullified if the worshipper does not exit from the experience in the reverse order of his or her entry. A particular striking example of concentric structures in music is illustrated by a recent symphony by A. PANUFNIK which was commissioned by the Boston Symphony Orchestra as part of its centennial celebration. The composer explained in detail in the program for that occasion an intricate concentric design based on the number eight — since this was his eighth symphony.

makers have mastered this same technique in the composition of an art form for popular consumption.

I have argued elsewhere that the book of Deuteronomy is more than what is commonly conveyed in the term «Kunstprosa» or artistic prose [7]. The book is written in metrical language in which individual «verse-units» and groups of such metrical units are in turn arranged into larger, sometimes rather elaborate, concentric structures. This architectural structural design of the book may be delineated by means of a careful analysis of the received Masoretic text in terms of a system of prosodic scansion which combines the «counting of morae» (a unit of length in time) and «syntactic accentual stresses» (a unit of rhythm or metrical beat). And by definition, a literary work which is written in metrical language is in fact a form of poetry. My purpose here is not to present the method of prosodic analysis as such but rather to discuss some of the results of such a prosodic analysis in terms of the architectural structural design of the larger literary composition which such an analysis has uncovered in Deut 1-11.

For the most part, the following concentric structures were found inductively by a detailed prosodic analysis of the Hebrew text based on a «close reading» of the Masoretic accentual system as well as the received consonantal Hebrew text [8]. Each of the categories in the following outlines which is labelled with a letter of the alphabet in lower case represents an individual metrical unit (a «verse») or grouping of such units, in my analysis of the Hebrew text.

From a prosodic point of view the whole of Deut. 1-11 is divided into two major parts, chs. 1-3 and 4-11, each of which is itself in the form of an elaborate concentric structure which in turn contains still further such structures — as one colleague put it, a literary analogue to Ezekiel's vision of the «wheels within wheels»!

The largest such structural pattern, which embraces the book as a whole, may be outlined as follows:

A — THE OUTER FRAME: Part One — A Look Backwards (chs. 1-3)
  B — THE INNER FRAME: Part One — The Great Peroration (chs. 4-11)
    C — THE CENTRAL CORE — Covenant Stipulations (chs. 12-26)
  B' — THE INNER FRAME: Part Two — The Covenant Ceremony (chs. 27-30)
A' — THE OUTER FRAME: Part Two — A Look Forwards (chs. 31-34)

Each of these five major parts of the book may be analyzed into somewhat similar concentric structures. Thus the «Outer Frame» (chs. 1-3 and 31-34) consists of the following parallel structures:

7. See my article, *Prose and Poetry in the Bible: Narrative Poetics in Deut. 1:9-18*, in *ZAW* (forthcoming).

8. A preliminary description of this method of analysis is included in my article in *ZAW* (see note 7).

Deut. 1-3 THE OUTER FRAME: Part One — «A Look Backwards»
1:1-6a A —Superscription: Deuteronomy in Nuce
1:6b-8 B —Summons to Enter the Promised Land
1:9-18 C —Organization of the People for Life in the Land
1:19-2:1 D —Israel's Unholy War
2:2-25 E —The March to Conquest
2:26-3:11 D'—YHWH's Holy War
3:12-17 C'—Distribution of the Land in Trans-Jordan
3:18-22 B'—Summons to Take the Promised Land
3:23-29 A'—Transition: From Moses to Joshua (introduction to ch. 31)

Deut. 31-34 THE OUTER FRAME: Part Two — «A Look Forwards»
31:1-6 A —From Moses to Joshua: What YHWH Will Do
31:7-23 B —Moses and Joshua: the Torah and the Song
31:24-29 C —The Torah as Witness
31:30 D —Moses Spoke the Words of the Song
32:1-43 E —The Song of Moses
32:44 D'—Moses Spoke the Words of the Song
32:45-47 C'—The Torah as Witness
32:38-34:6 B'—Moses and YHWH: the Death of Moses
34:7-12 A'—From Moses to Joshua: What Moses Has Done

There is not space here to present the detailed arguments for the above analysis (and those to follow)[9]. My concern here is simply to present the results of that detailed study as an invitation to colleagues to test these structural patterns by whatever means available. A secondary objective is to gain a hearing for the rather complex and controversial method of analysis which was used to find these structures, namely a detailed metrical analysis of the received Masoretic text.

The «Inner Frame» (chs. 4-11 and 27-30) appears to be arranged in parallel structures as well but my analysis of chs. 27-30 is not yet complete. In this particular paper the focus of attention is the first part of both the «Outer and Inner Frames» (i.e., chs. 1-3 and 4-11). Within these sections similar structural patterns are to be found wherever a given unit is developed in any length. Thus the central elements of chs. 1-3 (D, E and D' above) may be outlined as follows:

D—Deut 1:19-2:1 ISRAEL'S UNHOLY WAR
1:19 a—Travel Notice: «We went from Horeb to Kadesh-barnea.»
1:20 b—Report: «You have reached the promised land.»
1:21 c—Summons to Possess the Land
1:22 d—Israel's Sin: They Request Spies
1:23-24 e—Report: «I sent the spies.»
1:25-28 f—Report of the Spies and Israel's Rebellion
1) Spies: «It is a good land.»
2) Israel's Murmuring and Rebellion
3) Spies: «The people are too strong for us.»

9. The detailed analysis will appear in my commentary on Deuteronomy in the *Word Biblical Commentary*, Waco, Texas (forthcoming).

1:29-31 g — Summons Not for Fear
1:32-36 f' — Israel's Rebellion and YHWH's Judgment
1) Report of Moses: Israel's Lack of Trust
2) YHWH's Judgment: Postponement of Conquest
3) Report of Moses: The Exception of Caleb
1:37-39 e' — Report: «YHWH was angry with me.»
1) Joshua is to lead the Conquest.
2) The Land is to be possessed by your children.
1:40-41 d' — Israel's Sin: They Confess but Act Presumptuously
1:42 c' — Summons Not to Fight for the Land
1:43-44 b' — Report: «You failed to enter the land.»
1:45-2:1 a' — Travel Notice: «We went from Kadesh to Mount Seir.»

E — Deut 2:2-25 THE MARCH TO CONQUEST
2:2-4a a — Summons to Turn North (for Battle)
2:4b-6 b — Summons Not to Contend with the «Children of Esau»
2:7 c — A Look Backwards: the Exodus
2:8-9a d — Travel Notice and Summons Not to Contend with Moab
2:9b-11 e — The Emim Were Dispossessed by «Children of Lot»
2:12 e' — The Horites Were Dispossessed by «Children of Esau»
2:13-15 d' — Summons to Cross the Zered and Summary Travel Notice
2:16-18 c' — A Look Forwards: the Conquest
2:19-23 b' — Summons Not to Contend with the «Children of Ammon»
2:24-25 a' — Summons to Cross the Arnon (for Battle)

D' — Deut 2:26-3:11 YHWH'S HOLY WAR
2:26-30 a — Anecdote about Sihon: Refusal of Request for Safe-conduct
2:31-36 b — The Conquest of Heshbon
1) The Defeat of Sihon
2) Sihon's Kingdom Devoted to destruction at THAT TIME
2:37-3:1 c — Travel Notice: We turned toward Bashan against Og.
3:2 c' — Summons Not to Fear Og
3:3-10 b' — Conquest of Bashan
1) The Defeat of Og at THAT TIME
2) Og's Kingdom Devoted to Destruction
3) Summary of Conquest in Trans-Jordan at THAT TIME
3:11 a' — Anecdote about Og: the Last of the Rephaim

Some of the elements within these outlines are part of still other structures, some of which are not concentric in nature. As is the case in other works of art in both music and literature, no single analysis can possibly uncover all that is there. Works of art can seldom be reduced to a single structure. And even having uncovered dominant structural patterns, one is still a long way from describing what makes the resultant work aesthetically appealing. When the composer Panufnik described the intricate mathematical conceptual design of his eighth symphony, he also cautioned the reader about taking the design as such too seriously. He advised the reader to simply enjoy the music. Too much attention on the structure could detract from that experience. But for me personally, my first encounter with his symphony in 1982 was substantially enhanced by an awareness of the structure utilized by the artist in the composition of a truly beautiful work of art — conceived, incidentally, in terms of concentric structures not unlike both Deuteronomy and the book of Jonah [10].

The travel notices which serve as an envelope around the presentation of «Israel's Unholy War» (1:19-2:1) are part of a linear structure of such travel notices distributed throughout the «Outer Frame» (chs. 1-3 and 31-34). It is interesting to note the different ways in which this particular literary device is used in each of the three structures under discussion. In the presentation of «The March to Conquest» (2:2-25) such travel notices frame the central element rather than the structural entity as a whole (as in 1:19-2:1). In the presentation of «YHWH's Holy War» (2:26-3:11) the travel notice is placed in the center, along with the «Summons Not to Fear» which curiously is also the center of the corresponding structure (1:19-2:1) which highlights the same two elements, though in a different manner.

The use of the concentric structural design to enhance the theological message of the book itself is more clearly evident in the structure of chs. 4-11 which may be outlined as follows:

Deut 4-11 THE INNER FRAME: Part One — The Great Peroration

4:1-40	A — «And now, O Israel, obey YHWH's commandments.»
4:41-43	B — Moses set apart three (Levitical) cities of refuge.
4:44-6:3	C — «This is the Torah» — the Ten Words
6:4-7:11	D — «Hear, O Israel, YHWH is our God — YHWH alone.»
7:12-8:20	E — When you obey you will be blessed; when you disobey you will be destroyed.
9:1-29	D' — «Hear, O Israel, you are about to cross the Jordan.»
10:1-7	C' — «At THAT TIME YHWH spoke the Ten Words.»
10:8-11	B' — At THAT TIME YHWH set apart the tribe of Levi.
11:12-11:25	A' — «And now, O Israel, what does YHWH ask of you?»

Here the central aspect of the so-called Deuteronomic theology appears at the center of the larger concentric structure (7:12-8:20); namely, blessing is contingent on obedience to the «Law of Moses». A number of the concentric structures of the individual elements within this larger structure also highlight central theological concepts. Thus the structure of ch. 4:1-40 highlights the central message of the provisional nature of YHWH's blessing at the outer extremities and the meaning of the term *naḥălāh* («inheritance»), as it applies to both YHWH and Israel, at the center. At the same time the central elements (vss. 20-21) also pick up the Janus-like feature so dominant throughout Deuteronomy: the look backwards to the past (i.e. the Exodus) in order to look forwards to the present and future (i.e. the Conquest).

10. For a discussion of some of the concentric structures I have found in the book of Jonah see my article, *The Song of Jonah: A Metrical Analysis* in *JBL* (forthcoming).

A — «AND NOW, O ISRAEL, OBEY YHWH'S COMMANDMENTS (Deut 4:1-40)

4:1-4	a — Keep YHWH's commandments that you may live in the Land.
4:4-8	b — The uniqueness of Israel as shown in her Torah
4:9-10	c — Be careful not to forget what happened at Horeb.
4:11-15	d — Covenant stipulations — issued at Horeb
4:16-19	e — No images or astral deities
4:20	f — The Exodus made the people YHWH's «inheritance».
4:21	f' — The Conquest makes the Land Israel's «inheritance».
4:22-24	e' — No images for YHWH is a jealous God
4:25-27	d' — Covenant curses — in effect in the Land
4:28-34	c' — YHWH will not forget His covenant with your fathers.
4:35-39	b' — The uniqueness of YHWH as shown in the Exodus-Conquest
4:40	a' — Keep YHWH's commandments that you may live in the Land.

The structure of chs. 4:44-6:3 focuses on the command to «Keep the Sabbath» (5:12-15) as the central teaching of the «Torah» (4:44-48) which is indeed YHWH's «Commandment» (6:1-3).

C — «THIS IS THE TORAH» — THE TEN WORDS (Deut 4:44-6:3)

4:44-48	a — «This is the TORAH»
5:1-3	b — TODAY: «Hear, O Israel, the Law.»
5:4-5	c — THAT TIME: YHWH spoke out of the fire.
5:6-7	d — Commandment I: No Other Gods
5:8-10	e — Commandment II: Idolatry Forbidden
5:11	f — Commandment III: Honor YHWH's Name
5:12-15	g — Commandment IV: Keep the Sabbath
5:16	f' — Commandment V: Honor Your Parents
5:17-21	e' — Commandments VI-X: Ethical Morality
5:22	d' — Summary: No Other «WORDS»
5:23-31	c' — THAT TIME: YHWH spoke out of the fire.
5:32-33	b' — TODAY: Be careful to keep YHWH's commandments.
6:1-3	a' — «This is the COMMANDMENT»

The structure of chs. 6:4-7:11 highlights the *Shema'* (6:4) which is the central motivation for the command to obey YHWH's commandments (7:11). And once again, as was the case with ch. 4:1-40, the backwards-forwards orientation is at the center, though this time the look forwards extends well beyond the Conquest itself (6:20-25).

D — «HEAR, O ISRAEL, YHWH IS OUR GOD AND YOU ARE A HOLY PEOPLE» (Deut 6:4-7:11)

6:4-9	a — JHWH alone is our God; so love Him by keeping His words.
6:10-15	b — When YHWH brings you into the Land, be careful not to forget Him or He will destroy you.
6:16-19	c — A look backwards: Exodus-Conquest
6:20-25	c' — A look forwards: Post-Conquest
7:1-6	b' — When YHWH gives your enemies to you, destroy them utterly or YHWH will destroy you.
7:7-11	a' — YHWH's love for you is His way of keeping His word/oath to to your fathers; so keep the commandment.

The central section of chs. 4-11 (i.e. 7:12-8:20) presents a single theological message in that the center (8:1) and the outer boundaries (7:12-16 and 8:11-20) stress the same absolute necessity of obedience if the people are to experience YHWH's blessing in the land. The radical nature of this obedience is stressed still further in the disturbing command to destroy utterly those peoples already in the land. From a poetic point of view this is no doubt a way of stressing the radical nature of YHWH's holiness and of His demand for absolute obedience.

E — WHEN YOU OBEY YOU WILL BE BLESSED; WHEN YOU FORGET AND DISOBEY YOU WILL BE DESTROYED (Deut 7:12-8:20)

7:12-16 a — When you obey these laws you will be blessed in the Land; but you must destroy all these peoples.
7:17-24 b — Do not be afraid of them for YHWH will deliver them over to you that you may destroy them.
7:25-26 c — A Look Forwards: Destroy their gods or be destroyed.
8:1 d — Be careful to keep all the commandment that you may possess the Land.
8:2-5 c' — A Look Backwards: Remember YHWH's discipline those 40 years.
8:6-10 b' — Keep YHWH's commandments and praise Him for the Good Land He has given you
8:11-20 a' — When you forget YHWH and disobey His commandments you will be destroyed.

As one moves out of the center of the larger structure of chs. 4-11 as a whole, the first major section (9:1-29) is negative in tone. In the past Israel has proved to be a «stiff-necked people». They were even rebellious while Moses was on the mountain receiving the two stone tablets. Though deserving of destruction according to the terms of their own covenant relationship with YHWH, Moses was successful as an intercessor such that the Warrior-God remains faithful in His commitment to aid His «inheritance» (the people) as they cross the Jordan to take their «inheritance» (the land).

D' — HEAR, O ISRAEL, YOU ARE ABOUT TO CROSS THE JORDAN (Deut 9:1-29)

9:1-3 a — YHWH is crossing the Jordan as your vanguard to aid you in destroying the nations.
9:4-6 b — It is not because of your righteousness that YHWH is doing this; for you are a stiff-necked people.
9:7-10 c — You rebelled constantly in the wilderness, even while I was on the mountain receiving the two stone tablets.
9:11-12 d — While on the mountain YHWH told me what you had done in making a cast image.
9:13-14 d' — As YHWH put it: «They are a stiff-necked people — stand back while I destroy them.»
9:15-21 c' — When I came down and saw the calf, I shattered the tablets, interceded for you and Aaron, and crushed the image to dust.

9:22-24 b' — You rebelled time and again in the wilderness, as long as I have known you.
9:25-29 a' — I argued with YHWH: «Do not destroy Your people lest You tarnish Your reputation; for they are Your 'inheritence'.»

The central part of this structure is spatially oriented in chiastic fashion:

A — Moses want up the mountain to God (9:7-10).
B — Divine Speech on the Mountain:
«Go down quickly for your people have sinned!» (9:11-12)
B' — Divine Speech on the Mountain:
«I will destroy them and make of you a nation greater than they!» (9:13-14)
A' — Moses went down the mountain to the people (9:15-21).

This unit is in turn framed by parallel units which stress Israel's rebellious nature in times past (9:4-6 and 9:22-24). The structure as a whole is framed by a description of YHWH's redemptive power in the Conquest to come (9:1-3) which is the result of Moses' appeal for Him to show mercy again on his undeserving «inheritance» (9:25-29).

The final such structure to be presented here is parallel to that of ch. 4:1-40, both of which begin with the phrase, «And now, O Israel.» Whereas, the succeeding phrase in ch. 4:1 anticipates the *Shema'* of Deut. 6:4, the corresponding phrase here echoes a familiar theme among the eighth century prophets, namely: «What does YHWH your God require of you?»

A' — AND NOW, O ISRAEL, WHAT DOES YOUR GOD ASK OF YOU? (Deut 10:12-11:25)

10:12-15 a — Fear YHWH and keep His commandments for He has chosen you.
10:16-19 b — Circumcize your hearts and love the alien.
10:20-11:1 c — Fear YHWH and keep His commandments, for He has blessed you.
11:2-7 d — A Look Backwards: Your eyes have seen what YHWH has done.
11:8-9 e — Keep all the commandment that you may possess the land and remain in it.
11:10-12 d' — A Look Forwards: YHWH's eyes are upon the land to bless it.
11:13-15 c' — If you obey my commandments, I will bless you in your land.
11:16-21 b' — Do not serve other gods and keep my words before you that you may remain in the land.
11:22-25 a' — If you carefully observe these commandments, YHWH will dispossess nations and give you the whole land.

Both the center and the external boundaries of this structure stress the same central teaching of the book of Deuteronomy; namely, that continued blessing in the land is contingent on obedience to YHWH's commandments.

If these concentric structures are indeed in the text itself and not imposed on it, the implications are clear. The book of Deuteronomy has a structure rather different from the linear outlines presented in most of our commentaries. And that structure is curiously similar to a number of works of art, both from antiquity and the present — particularly in the fields of epic poetry and music. The reason for this similarity is apparently the simple fact that in its essential nature the book of Deuteronomy is itself a work of literary art in poetic form, subject to the restraints of the musical media to which it was originally composed.

American Baptist Seminary of the West Duane L. CHRISTENSEN
2515 Hillegass Ave.
Berkeley, CA 94704, U.S.A.

THE LITURGICAL SIGNIFICANCE OF THE DATE IN DT 1,3

In order to understand the significance of the date in Dt 1,3, «in the fortieth year, in the eleventh month, on the first day», I propose an examination on the whole time-structure in the Torah. Of the forty years from the deliverance from Egypt till the entry into the Promised Land, only three years are indicated, namely: the first year, that of the deliverance, in Exodus 12, the second year, «in the desert», in Numbers 1,1, and the fortieth year, in the land of Moab, in Dt 1,3, here under discussion. In this triennial time-structure — which must be the work of a late redactor — three Passovers are referred to: One in Egypt in Exodus 12, a second in Numbers 9, and a third one which appears outside the Pentateuch in Joshua 5. The thesis of this paper is that the date in Dt 1,3 means liturgically: the time of preparation of the next Passover [1].

These three Passovers together form the theme of the Passover-story, and of the later Passover Haggadah. We might go further: The Torah *is* a Passover-story, consisting of three Passovers, each contributing to the whole story. These three Passovers form, in my opinion, the basis of the «Poem of the Four Passovers», as known in the Jewish and Samaritan tradition [2]. And this triennial structure may have formed the basis of the later traditional reading of the Torah in three years.

However that may be, in the fortieth year, the year before the entry, the Torah commemorates the dying-out of the generation that came from Egypt: Miriam died in the first month [3], Aaron on the first day of the fifth month [4], and Moses on the same date as that mentioned in Dt. 1,3 [5]. This means that the book of Deuteronomy is presented as the Testament of Moses, to be read as a preparation for the Passover. Moses' death must remind the reader of Aaron's death [6]. It does not seem to be a coincidence that Moses died two and a half months before Passover, and Aaron two and a half months before Sukkoth, both being opposite days within the liturgical year-cycle.

When we take Deuteronomy and Joshua as a single composition, then it is clear that the day of preparation in Dt 1,3 looks forward to the Passover in Joshua 5 — the Passover in the land which is reflected in

1. See J. VAN GOUDOEVER, *Biblical Calendars*, Leiden, ^{2}1961; *Fêtes et Calendriers Bibliques*, Paris, ^{3}1967.

2. R. LE DÉAUT, *La Nuit Pascale*, Rome, 1963.

3. Nb 20,1.

4. Nb 33,38, and Nb 20,22-29.

5. Dt 32,48.

6. Dt 32,50.

Dt 26. Now this *story* in Deuteronomy-Joshua, with its preparation and Passover, is, I think, the actual theme of the Passover *celebrated* by king Josiah. When the highpriest Hilkiah found the Book of Law (an earlier form of Deuteronomy that already in some way referred to the coming Passover), king Josiah, on hearing the stirring message of Moses' testament and realising that the land was originally destined for all twelve tribes, for South and North, decided to celebrate the Passover to the Lord, as it was written in the book of the covenant found in the temple. By way of preparation the people, according to the book of Kings, made a covenant [7]. Such a Passover was never celebrated before, and was thus new [8]. By the liturgical and political celebration of king Josiah, the story in Deuteronomy-Joshua got its real function and meaning, that is to say it was a commemoration of the so-called past with a message for «today».

During and after the Babylonian Exile, the perspective of Dt 1,3 changed. The Torah of five books developed, of which Deuteronomy became the last one, the book of Joshua being no longer connected with it. From that time on, Deuteronomy, or the testament of Moses, looked forward to the land of the future to which the people would return (or better «turn»). This would become the new content of the «third Passover», being no longer a part of the Torah, but rather a perspective of the Torah.

We find a similar outlook in Deutero-Isaiah, and in the Greek version of Jeremiah 38,8 which states that the tribes will return to the land at Passover. If Psalms 104, 105, 106, and 107 actually belong together, then Psalm 104 praises the Creation, Psalms 105 and 106 the Exodus and journey through the desert, and Psalm 107 the return of the people from the four corners of the earth, i.e. the same perspective as the last book of the Torah. This coming Passover is part of the total Passover-story, as reflected in the Haggadah («next year in Jerusalem») and in the «Poem of the Four Passovers».

After the Exile, there developed a more closed concept. We are told that, after their return, the exiles kept the Passover once again in Jerusalem [9]. For the book of Esra, living again in the promised land was the realisation of the perspective of the Torah. All this is perhaps still clearer in Third Esra. There Esra celebrated the Passover before the Exile, and together with the returned exiles after the Exile [10], thus forming a new Passover-cycle. The Book of Jubilees, on the contrary, which is a re-written Torah, ends in an open-ended, almost apocalyptic, way [11].

7. II Ki 23,2-3.
8. II Ki 23,22.
9. Esra 6, 19.
10. III Esra 1,1; 7,10.
11. Jb 50,4-5.

A last remark, on the date itself: «the first day of the eleventh month». It seems that some time after the Exile the month of preparation for Passover shifted from the eleventh to the twelfth month. According to the Mishnah preparations for Passover should start in Adar [12]. The four Shabbaths in Adar have all a special significance in relation to the coming festival. Purim must be celebrated at any rate in the second Adar, thus underlining its relationship with Passover [13]. According to Josephus, Moses delivered his last speech thirty days before the end of the year [14]. In rabbinic tradition, Moses died on the 7th of Adar [15], the period of 30 days' mourning was over on the 7th of Nisan, three days before the crossing of the Jordan. But there are indications that formerly the month of Shebat was the month of preparation. The Mishnah calls the first or the fifteenth day of Shebat the «New Year of Trees» [16]. Purim could be kept in the first month of Adar, also in a leap year — so two months before Passover [17]. I think the festival of repentance that was held by the Qumran sect, and on which parts of Deuteronomy were read, was celebrated on the first day of the eleventh month, commemorating that once the people of Israel assembled in the land of Moab, before the crossing of the Jordan [18]. One of the Qumran scrolls, called the «Words of Moses», is dated, as in Dt 1,3, in the eleventh month, on the first day, giving a long quotation of Deuteronomy [19]. The Samaritans still celebrate the Zimmuth (the conjunction of sun and moon) of Passover two months before Passover, and the Zimmuth of Sukkoth, two months before Sukkoth. On the Zimmuth of Passover, they read the passage of the half-shekel which the Jews read on the first of Adar [20]. The Karaites preserve the probably older tradition of intercalating Shebat with Shebat [21]. The Falashas know in their calendar a kind of Purim in the eleventh month [22]. A similar shift from the eleventh to the twelfth month is to be observed in the Babylonian calendar [23]. Further research into the

12. MShek 1,1; Gn 8,5 (LXX).
13. MMeg 1,4; MEduoth 7,7.
14. Jos., Ant, IV, 176.327.
15. Seder Olam Rabba 16.
16. MRosh-Hashanah, 1.1.
17. MEduoth 7,7.
18. Cf. M. WEISE, *Kultzeiten und kultischer Bundesschluss in der Ordensregel vom Toten Meer*, Leiden, 1961.
19. Cf. A. DUPONT-SOMMER, *Les écrits esséniens découverts près de la Mer Morte*, Paris, 1960, pp. 320-323.
20. J. BOWMAN, *Is the Samaritan Calendar the old Zadokite one?* in *Pal. Expl. Quart.* 1958, 23-37.
21. JE VII 447; L. NEMOY, in HUCA VII (1930), p. 384; AL-BIRUNI, *Chronology of Ancient Nations*, ed. E. Edward Sachau, p. 69, about the Ananites.
22. W. LESLAU, *Falasha Anthology*, New Haven, ²1954, p. xxxi.
23. S. LANGDON, *Babylonian Menologies and the Semitic Calendars*, Schweich Lectures, 1933, p. 10.

origin of the Christian Lent may reveal how far the Jewish way and time of preparing Passover has influenced the Christian concept [24].

In conclusion, a general remark: Since the book of Deuteronomy probably is the most liturgical book of the Bible, it has various liturgical backgrounds [25]. The word «today» occurs 27 times in this book. In the liturgical context of Dt 1,3, this «today» can mean: «today», i.e. in the time of Moses, before the entry; «today», i.e. on the festal day the words are read and listened to, e.g. in the time of Josiah; «today», with the message for the future. The mutual cohesion of these three significances is typical of any liturgy.

Van IJsselsteinl. 28
NL-Amstelveen

JAN VAN GOUDOEVER

24. The oldest period of fasting in the Christian tradition is seven or eight weeks, e.g. in Egypt. As with the Samaritans, the early Christians commemorated during that time the plagues in Egypt.

25. So e.g. the sabbatical year, and the liturgical text in Dt 26,1-11, which is also of interest for the significance of Dt 1,3.

DEUTERONOMIUM 1-3
IM STREIT DER EXEGETISCHEN METHODEN

I

Der jüngste Beitrag zur Dtn-Forschung ist die im Mai 1983 erschienene Rezension von Lohfink [1] über die «Erträge» dieser Forschung von Preuss [2]. Da diese Besprechung aufs Grundsätzliche zielt, nehme ich sie zum Ausgangspunkt für meine Überlegungen zum gegenwärtigen Methodenstreit. Damit möchte ich zur Diskussion, eben zum «Colloquium Biblicum» beitragen. Dafür benutze ich Dtn 1-3 als exemplarischen Text.

Lohfink konstatiert also, daß es in der heutigen Dtn-Exegese «kaum einen Konsens» [3] gibt. Er spricht von einer «Theoriekrise der alttestamentlichen Wissenschaft», die «zu einem großen Teil mit der Beurteilung und zeitlichen Ansetzung des deuteronomischen Phänomens» zusammenhänge (349). Die ungewöhnlich scharfe Rezension [4] hält sich an Preuss, meint aber wohl, wie man im Deutschen sagt, die ganze Richtung, der die neuere Linguistik «noch fernzuliegen» scheint [5]. Ihr *peccatum grave*: das Buch von Preuss kreist «in einem erstaunlichen Ausmaß um die Fragen der Literarkritik, dazu um die des historischen Ansatzes». Das wäre vor nicht langer Zeit bekanntlich ein höchstes Lob gewesen. Aber Lohfink fährt fort: «Das sind die typischen Interessefixierungen der mitteleuropäischen Exegese» (352).

Demnach gibt es unter uns Forscher, die sich altmodisch der historischen Methoden bedienen, wie sie in der Geschichts- und Literaturwissenschaft mindestens seit B.G. Niebuhr [6] oder auch de Wette entwickelt und seit bald 200 Jahren erprobt sind; es gibt andere, die diese 'Interessefixierungen' überwunden oder doch überschritten haben — hin zu neuen Ufern einer literaturwissenschaftlichen Betrachtung, die nun als universal gilt. Darin also besteht die Theoriekrise, daß die einen 'schon'

1. *TLZ* 108 (1983) 349-353.
2. H.D. PREUSS, *Deuteronomium* (Erträge der Forschung, 164), Darmstadt, 1982.
3. *Ibid.*, p. 350. — Eindeutig auf das zitierte Werk bezogene Seitenzahlen stehen hinfort eingeklammert im Text.
4. Lohfink wirft dem Autor «Hilflosigkeit», «Desinteresse» und «erstaunliche Fehlurteile» vor (351).
5. Immerhin schrieb Preuss, wozu ich nicht bereit gewesen wäre, nämlich einen Forschungsbericht über die 'andere Richtung': H.D. PREUSS, *Linguistik - Literaturwissenschaft - Altes Testament*, in *VuF* 27 (H. 1/1982) 2-28.
6. Cf. dazu L. PERLITT, *Vatke und Wellhausen* (BZAW 94), Berlin, 1965, pp. 57ff.

dies tun und die anderen 'noch' oder 'noch immer' jenes [7]. Demgegenüber möchte ich hier ebenso für die mitteleuropäische Tradition des Forschungspluralismus plädieren wie für die Einsicht, daß diese Theoriekrise nicht durch methodischen 'Fortschritt', welchen auch immer, zu beheben ist.

Da die Dtn-Forschung nur das allgemeine Methodenproblem spiegelt, verweise ich einleitend auf zwei Werke, in denen sich die Differenzen nicht aphoristisch, sondern systematisch niederschlagen: die beiden neuesten, etwa gleichzeitig entstandenen «Einleitungen» von Childs [8] und Smend [9]. Beide Forscher verfügen über die herausragende Kenntnis der (mit Verlaub: mitteleuropäischen) Forschungsgeschichte, ohne die man sich zu diesen Fragen kaum äußern sollte.

Childs bricht mit der Tradition der 'klassischen' Einleitung: aus Sorge um den Verlust der Heiligen Schrift «as scripture». Er beschreibt die kanonische Gestalt einer Literatur, deren Gewordensein er nicht bestreitet, aber gleichsam der Vorgeschichte seiner Bemühungen zuordnet. Seine Arbeit verdankt sich nicht methodologischem Optimismus, sondern einer hermeneutischen Entscheidung [10]. Mit ihr gibt er, unbeabsichtigt, auch der 'neueren Literaturwissenschaft' den Text und das gute Gewissen. Seine Gründe sind respektabel: Die seit Eichhorn entwickelte historisch-kritische Einleitung analysierte nicht die kanonische Schrift der Synagoge und der Kirche, sondern die Entwicklungsgeschichte der hebräischen Literatur. Durch ihr «predominantly historical interest» übersah sie die besondere, beziehungsreiche Gesamtstruktur dieser Literatur [11] ebenso wie ihren Bezug auf die Gemeinschaft, «which treasured it as scripture» (41).

Dieser normativen Fixierung auf die Endgestalt der Texte müssen natürlich jene widersprechen, die, wie Childs selbst formuliert, die Aufdeckung der Tiefendimension für das Herzstück der exegetischen Arbeit halten (75). Zu ihnen zählt R. Smend. Er setzt — und das bitte ich zu beachten — überall bei dem ein, was Childs im Blick hat: beim «canonical shape» der biblischen Bücher. Es zeichnet diese Einleitung vor anderen aus, daß sie gerade nicht von «the critically reconstructed literature» [12] ausgeht, sondern von dem, was der Bibelleser vor Augen hat. Dazu zählt nun freilich auch das, was, von der alten Kirche an,

7. Mit diesen Epitheta stützte N. LOHFINK auch schon vor 20 Jahren das 'Neue' gegen das 'Alte': *Das Hauptgebot* (AB, 20), Rom, 1963, p. 177, n. 47; p. 179, n. 51.

8. B. S. CHILDS, *Introduction to the Old Testament as Scripture*, Philadelphia, 1979.

9. R. SMEND, *Die Entstehung des Alten Testaments*, Stuttgart, 1978.

10. Cf. die Diskussion mit Childs in *JOSOT* 16 (1980) sowie W. ZIMMERLI, *VT* 31 (1981) 235-244.

11. *Ibid.*, p. 40: «... the peculiar dynamics of Israel's religious literature, which has been greatly influenced by the process of establishing the scope of the literature, forming its particular shape and structuring its inner relationships.»

12. CHILDS, *op. cit.*, p. 40.

diesen Leser stutzig machte. So kam die 'kritische' Forschung in Gang — nicht im 20., sondern eher im 2. Jahrhundert. Der Rückgang durch die Entstehungsgeschichte kommt nicht aus dem Mutwillen der historistischen Epoche, sondern ist das Resultat aller der Rück-Fragen von Philo über Ibn Ezra und Spinoza bis zum Bibelleser der Neuzeit. Aus einfachen Fragen wurden methodisch geleitete Fragen. So entstand die Synthese aus alttestamentlicher Literatur-, Religions- und Theologiegeschichte. Also müssen wir uns heute fragen, ob es sich bei dieser «Hilfe der Vergangenheit»[13] um eine abgeschlossene oder um eine ihrem Wesen nach unabschließbare Geistesbemühung des Menschen und darum der Forschung handelt. Um aber vor künstlichen Alternativen zu warnen: auch der Literarhistoriker war nie gehindert, das Alte Testament als Heilige Schrift, als Predigttext und als literarisches Kunstwerk anzunehmen.

Beim Versuch, diese Vorbemerkungen nun näher auf die Erforschung von Dtn 1-3 zu beziehen, beschränke ich mich auf die Arbeit der letzten Jahre, etwa seit 1975. Aber es lohnt, ein paar Sätze in Erinnerung zu rufen, mit denen Lohfink in seinem «Hauptgebot» vor genau 20 Jahren diese neueste Phase eingeleitet hat. Sein Fazit zu der an Steuernagel[14] exemplifizierten literarkritischen Periode seit Wellhausen lautet kurz und bündig: «Ein Weg war zu Ende gegangen. Er hatte sich nicht bewährt» (35). Zwar hebt er auch die sorgfältige Textarbeit dieser 'Schule' hervor, aber das sind liebenswürdige Marginalien zu dem, was insgesamt ein Nachruf ist. Dem Grabgeläut entspricht das Morgengeläut — mit der richtigen Prämisse: «Die Neubearbeitung eines Problemkreises hat nur Sinn, wenn neue Tatsachen entdeckt sind ... oder wenn neue Methoden entwickelt wurden» (13). Beide Bedingungen sah der Autor glücklich erfüllt. Die 'neue Tatsache' war das sog. Bundesformular; dazu will ich mich nicht wiederholen[15]. Die 'neue Methode' aber bot die «neue Stilistik», der es gelang, «sich von Vor- und Hilfsmethoden ... abzusetzen» (13f.), und zu diesen zählen «Textkritik, Grammatik, Geschichtsforschung, Literaturgeschichte» etc. — kurzum alles, was die 'alte' Wissenschaft ausmachte.

Von dieser geradezu an Deuterojesaja geschulten, nämlich mit 'alt' und 'neu' chiffrierten Periodisierung möchte ich ausgehen und in zwei (weiteren) Hauptteilen das Problem erst näher an der Forschung, dann näher am Text selbst entfalten. Beide Hauptteile sind durch das Für und Wider in diesem Methodenstreit untergliedert.

13. So überschrieb N. LOHFINK (cf. n. 7, pp. 18-47) seine knappe Skizze der Forschungsgeschichte.

14. C. STEUERNAGEL, *Das Deuteronomium*, Göttingen, 1898; ^{2}1923.

15. Cf. L. PERLITT, *Bundestheologie im Alten Testament* (WMANT, 36), Neukirchen, 1969.

II

1. Childs [16] behandelt (auf zwei Seiten) Dtn 1-4 — wissend, daß schon diese Abtrennung eine These inkludiert. Deren Begründung muß der erste Satz tragen: «In spite of the different form and style of ch. 4, it now functions along with the first three chapters of the book as an introduction to the chapters which follow» (213). Geleitet vom Interesse der letzten Redaktoren verzichtet Childs so auf Literarkritik, Formgeschichte und sogar Stilistik. Aber auch die theologischen Unterschiede zwischen Dtn 1-3 und 4 verschwimmen dabei, denn jetzt führen die Kapitel 1-3 nicht mehr zur (weiteren) Geschichte, sondern zum Gesetz. Daß sie das, zumal mit der Lesehilfe von Dtn 1,5, *auch* tun, ist nicht zu bestreiten; daß sie das aber im Akt ihrer Entstehung vielleicht *nicht* tun, also ursprungshaft und darum wesenhaft *anders* gelesen sein wollten, ist nun kein Gegenstand legitimer Betrachtung mehr.

Damit ist ein halbes Jahrhundert Forschung widerrufen, und zwar keinesfalls nur M. Noths Grundthese, sondern z.B. auch Lohfinks schöne Betrachtung über «Darstellungskunst und Theologie in Dtn 1,6-3,29» die von Noths Konzeption ausging [17]. Das gilt dann aber auch für Brauliks rhetorische Analyse [18] von Dtn 4, die von Dtn 1-3 nicht beinahe gänzlich absehen dürfte, wenn der Zusammenhang von Dtn 1-4 jene letzte theologische Dignität hätte. Das gilt schließlich, wenn man in Dtn 4 so etwas wie einen Midrasch nicht auf Dtn 1-3, sondern auf Dtn 5 sähe. Hat Dtn 1-3 einmal vor und damit unabhängig von 4 existiert, dann beantwortet Childs nicht die Frage, mit welcher Absicht die Kapitel *geschrieben* wurden; er beantwortet aber auch die Frage, mit welcher Absicht Dtn 1-3 *kommentiert* wurde, nur unter der stillschweigenden Voraussetzung, daß Dtn 4 tatsächlich im Hinblick auf 1-3 entstand. Da aber der Verfasser von Dtn 1-3 selbst den Blick des Lesers auf Jos 1 ff. lenkt, indem er hier wie dort eindeutige Vor- bzw. Rückverweise unterbringt, muß man sein Werk gegen den Strich lesen, um dem Dogmatismus des Kanonprinzips zu entsprechen. Demgegenüber war schon Luther der bessere Exeget: «Et ita concludit hoc capitulo (sc. Dtn 3) narrationem coeptam, qua historiam totam recapitulavit. Sequenti capitulo incipit exhortari et legem explicare — et Deuteronomium orditur.» [19]

Ging Childs von der Würde des Kanons aus, so begegnen wir einer der Theorien der «New Literary History» in dem ein Jahr später publizierten

16. *Op. cit.* (n. 8), pp. 213-215.
17. *Bib* 41 (1960) 105-134, esp. p. 105, n. 2.
18. G. BRAULIK, *Die Mittel deuteronomischer Rhetorik - erhoben aus Deuteronomium 4,1-40* (AB, 68), Rom, 1978.
19. M. LUTHER, *Deuteronomion Mosi cum annotationibus* (1525), in *WA* 14, p. 579.

Werk von Polzin [20] über die erste Hälfte des DtrG. Seinen komplizierten theoretischen Voraussetzungen will ich hier nicht weiter nachgehen [21]. Er konstatiert jedenfalls, die gesamte Dtn-Forschung, von de Wette bis Noth, habe keine einzige Hypothese hervorgebracht, «that can be described as historically or literarily adequate» (13). Dieses aus der Zurückweisung alles Bisherigen gewonnene Novitätsbewußtsein hat für mich nur noch etwas Lächerliches. Da höre ich lieber den frommen und heiteren Wunsch des klugen Rechtshistorikers Bernard S. Jackson [22]: «Perhaps all we need are *halakhists*?» Ich habe in Polzins Buch, in dem sogar die Unterscheidung von dtn und dtr sowie jede historische Fragestellung überhaupt verweigert wird [23], keine einzige analytische Beobachtung zu Dtn 1-3 gefunden, die bei Driver oder Steuernagel nicht auch zu finden wäre. Wenn ich auf die historische Frage verzichten wollte, dann wäre mir Child's Achtung vor dem Kanon bedeutsamer als diese narrativen oder linguistischen Stilübungen, mit denen an den alten Text nicht *weniger*, sondern *mehr* modernes oder modisches Instrumentarium herangetragen wird als mit der gescholtenen Frage nach der Genese des Textes. Mit dem Grabgeläut für die Literarkritik wurde das von Lohfink [24] geforderte «Verständnis des Textes *als Text*» für mein Urteil nicht gefördert; und ein besseres Verständnis des *Werdens* von Dtn 1-3 wurde ja bei diesem methodischen Ansatz nicht einmal erstrebt.

2. So will ich nun Ihre Aufmerksamkeit auch auf jene Werke lenken, in denen Dtn 1-3 literarkritisch analysiert und dabei freilich 'als Text'

20. R. POLZIN, *Moses and the Deuteronomist, Part One: Deuteronomy, Joshua, Judges*, New York, 1980.

21. Polzin bezieht sich auf das brilliante Werk von H. FREI über Geschichte und Probleme der Hermeneutik (*The Eclipse of Biblical Narrative*, New Haven/London, 1974) sowie besonders auf die narrative Hermeneutik von F. KERMODE (*The Genesis of Secrecy: On the Interpretation of Narrative*, 1979). Zu beachten ist auch Polzins eigenes vorbereitendes Werk (*Biblical Structuralism*, Semeia, Suppl. 5, Philadelphia, 1977), in dem er die strukturale Textanalyse von vorstrukturalistischen Bemühungen wie Literarkritik, Formkritik und Traditionskritik abhob.

22. *Essays in Jewish and Comparative Legal History* (Studies in Judaism in Late Antiquity, 10), Leiden, 1975, p. 7.

23. In Anlehnung an V. N. VOLOSHINOV (= M. BAKHTIN), *Marxism and the Philosophy of Language*, New York, 1973, unterscheidet POLZIN in Dtn 1-3 zwischen «reported speech» und «reporting speech» (19) und gelangt dabei zu Einsichten, die jedem Schulkind möglich und langweilig wären: Mal spricht der Erzähler, mal zitiert er Mose, mal Jahwe. «Deuteronomy may be described therefore as the speech of the Deuteronomic narrator in which he directly quotes only two figures in the story, predominantly Moses and sometimes God» (26). Die bekannten 'antiquarischen Notizen' in Dtn 2f., die mit dem geographischen, literarischen und theologischen Duktus der Moserede wenig zu tun haben, veranlassen Polzin zu der Beobachtung, daß in Dtn 1,6-4,40 der Text fünfmal «abruptly shifts» von Moserede zum Erzählerkommentar und zurück (31). Darin sieht er eine besondere Raffinesse des (einen) Autors, «manipulating and programming his reader's responses» (31). Immerhin erkennt er aber auch mit seinen methodischen Mitteln die Unterschiede zwischen Dtn 1-3 und 4 (39-43).

24. *Op. cit.* (n. 7), p. 13.

auch destruiert wurde. Ich lasse also beiseite, was vor 1975 erschien [25] oder Dtn 1-3 nicht direkt betrifft [26], konstatiere aber, daß auch die jüngsten, in Göttingen entstandenen und 1982 publizierten Analysen dtr Texte sich penibelster, ja gelegentlich wirklich 'atomisierender' Literarkritik bedienen [27].

Näher zu betrachten ist natürlich vor allem Mittmanns [28] einschlägiges Werk. Um es vorab zu sagen: ich teile alle seine Fragen, nicht aber alle seine Antworten. Er hat wie nur wenige die Brüche und Spannungen in Dtn 1-3 gesehen, aber er hat dabei übersehen, was der Text m.E. nicht erst in einem Tertiärstadium, sondern bereits in seinem Primärstadium ist: eine spannungsvolle Ganzheit, in der manche Anstöße nichts anderes zeigen als die Nahtstellen der getreulich verarbeiteten Überlieferungen. Seine verblüffende Reduktion einer «Grundschicht» von Dtn 2f. auf 2,1-3.8b; 5,1 ff. verdankt sich einer 'außengeleiteten' Erkenntnis, nämlich der Hypothese, Dtn 1-3 sei, in diesem spärlichen Kern, nichts anderes als eine Hinführung zum Dekalog.

Mittmann zersplittert sogar den in pluralischer Anrede formulierten Haupttext in eine Grundschicht, zwei Ergänzungsschichten und noch eine weitere Redaktionsschicht. Ob man bei dieser Betrachtungsweise auf insgesamt fünf oder zehn Schichten kommt, ist beinahe gleichgültig wegen des generellen Mangels an Plausibilität. Man muß sich dabei auch fragen, ob die materielle Kultur des antiken Israel eine solche Vielzahl von Durchgängen und Anreicherungen auch nur wahrscheinlich macht. Wichtiger aber ist die andere Frage, was eigentlich Mittmanns «Grundschicht»-Autor beabsichtigte, der zwar in Dtn 1 die Kundschaftergeschichte aus dem Grundbestand von Num 13f. breit aufnahm, in Dtn 2f. aber die erzählerischen Äquivalente aus Num überging, für die sich dann freilich der 2. 'Pluralist' interessieren darf. Schließlich läßt diese Grundschicht Mose im geographischen 'Ungefähr' hängen, da 2,8b (der letzte Vers vor 5,1!) sein Weg nur «in Richtung auf die moabitische Steppe» führt; auch hier dürfen die genaueren Angaben zum ostjordanischen Standort der Abschiedsrede (3,27.29) erst durch Pl^2 gegeben werden. Wollte Mittmann die ostjordanische Eroberung aus

25. J.G. PLÖGER, *Literarkritische, formgeschichtliche und stilkritische Untersuchungen zum Deuteronomium* (BBB, 26), Bonn, 1967.

26. R.P. MERENDINO, *Das deuteronomische Gesetz. Eine literarkritische, gattungs- und überlieferungsgeschichtliche Untersuchung zu Dt 12-26* (BBB, 31), Bonn, 1969; F.-L. HOSSFELD, *Der Dekalog* (OBO, 45), Freiburg/Göttingen, 1982.

27. CHR. LEVIN, *Der Sturz der Königin Atalja* (SBS, 105), Stuttgart, 1982; H. SPIECKERMANN, *Juda unter Assur in der Sargonidenzeit* (FRLANT, 129), Göttingen, 1982. Zu nennen ist hier auch R. STAHL (*Aspekte der Geschichte deuteronomistischer Theologie*, Diss. theol. Jena, 1982), der die Flora der Siglen weiterwuchern läßt: DtrH, DtrP, $DtrN^{1-3}$, $DtrTh^{1-4}$!

28. S. MITTMANN, *Deuteronomium 1,1-6,3 literarkritisch und traditionsgeschichtlich untersucht* (BZAW, 139), Berlin, 1975.

seiner Grundschicht aussparen, so hätte er wenigstens Mose aus der Wüste herausführen müssen. Aber er bleibt seiner Annahme treu — um den Preis einer geographisch, erzählerisch und theologisch nichtssagenden Grundschicht. Ich bezweifle, daß die formgebende, alle Nachträge also erst stimulierende Grundschicht dieser Kapitel jemals derart aussagearm war, daß die den Zusammenhang konstituierende geographische Tendenz erst aus solcher Addition am besten zu begreifen wäre. Natürlich gibt es in Dtn 2f. Zusätze und mit ihnen Verschiebungen der Aussagerichtung; aber am Anfang, bei dem man für alle Literatur die gestaltgebende Phase sucht, stand kaum ein Entwurf von so atemberaubender Dürftigkeit, sondern ein kompositorischer Wille, der Spannungen zwischen den verarbeiteten Einzelüberlieferungen nicht aus-, sondern einschließt.

Natürlich ersetzen diese Andeutungen keine ernsthafte Auseinandersetzung mit Mittmann, zumal er zu den wenigen zählt, die diese Kapitel im ganzen analysiert haben; und unterhalb dieser Schwelle sind Lösungen nicht möglich. Darum werfe ich nur einen flüchtigen Blick auf zwei Monographien, die Dtn 1-3 nur im Rahmen ganz anderer Fragestellungen berühren. So stößt M. Wüst [29] bei seinen siedlungsgeographischen Untersuchungen im Kontext von Jos 12f. auch auf Dtn 2f. Sein spezielles Interesse entbindet ihn von einer Textanalyse, also auch von der erzählerischen Einbindung der geographischen Angaben; literarkritisch verläßt er sich zudem auf Mittmann. Bei seiner isolierten Beobachtung von Siedlungsnotizen bleibt das Hin und Her zwischen Erzählung/Liste/Erzählung und damit das Gesamtphänomen der Form von Dtn 1-3 unbeachtet [30]. Noths Annahme, daß in Jos rekapituliert wird, was in Dtn 2f. erzählt wurde, hat noch immer die Plausibilität des Unkomplizierten für sich, erscheint Wüst (4f.) aber als methodisch undifferenziert.

Überhaupt gibt es auf diesem Felde kaum eine neuere Untersuchung, die sich nicht mit vatermörderischer Emphase von M. Noth absetzte

29. M. WÜST, *Untersuchungen zu den siedlungsgeographischen Texten des Alten Testaments, I. Ostjordanland* (Beih. z. TAVO, Reihe B, Nr. 9), Wiesbaden, 1975.

30. Obwohl er — um die Sihon-Episode als Beispiel zu nehmen — konzediert, daß «Dtn 2,26-37 zumindest in seinem Gruldbestand auf Num 21,21-31 basiert» (12) und andererseits Jos 12,1-6* sowie die einschlägigen Verse in Jos 13 gestufte Einschübe in ihren Großkontext sind, rekonstruiert er auf der literarischen Ebene der Satzteile (Tab. 1) Abhängigkeitsverhältnisse von schwindelerregender Präzision. Soweit davon nur die historisch-geographischen Angaben selbst betroffen sind, kann das hier auf sich beruhen, da es sich insgesamt um literarisch junge Texte handelt, die über die fiktive Eroberung des Ostjordanlandes unter Mose weder Gutes noch Böses besagen. Aber die prinzipielle Gleichbehandlung von erzählerischen Zusammenhängen und listenartigen Rückblicken wirft noch einmal andere Probleme auf. Ohne Mittmanns Destruktion der erzählerischen Zusammenhänge in Dtn 2f. bedürfte Wüsts Vorstellung von den wechselseitigen Halbvers-Interdependenzen freilich einer eigenen Begründung auf der Ebene der Literarkritik wie der Überlieferungs- und Redaktionsgeschichte.

— seltsamerweise bei Bestreitern wie Benutzern der Literarkritik. So beginnt auch Martin Rose[31] seine Untersuchung «Deuteronomist und Jahwist» von 1981 mit der Selbstermunterung, die beinahe kanonische Geltung der Entwürfe Noths trete zurück. «Dabei scheint sich genau das, was einst ihre Faszination ausmachte, die phänomenale Komplexität und zugleich 'fundamentale Einfachheit'[32] ..., nun als ihre Schwäche zu erweisen» (9f.). Rose vergleicht nun in diesem Buch, in dem ca. 100 Seiten Dtn 1-3 berühren[33], ungefähr zehn Texte des DtrG mit ihren Tetrateuch-Parallelen — mit dem Resultat, das er im ganzen anzielt: Die 'jahwistischen' Texte in Num erscheinen «als erzählerische Umsetzungen dessen, was Dtn 1-3 in seiner ältesten literarischen Form ... bot» (323). So beim Beispiel Sihon: die Frage nach der Priorität von Num 21,21-31 oder Dtn 2,26-37 behandelt Rose knapp anhand einiger viel diskutierter sprachlicher Details[34], aber ohne Gesamtanalyse des Textes[35]. Da er generell das Ziel der Spätdatierung (s)eines 'Jahwisten' verfolgt, kann sein Urteil über den Einzeltext Dtn 2||Num 21 gar nicht anders lauten.

Der notgedrungen überaus flüchtige Durchgang durch diese neueren Arbeiten führte zunächst einmal zu dem belastenden Eindruck, daß die

31. M. ROSE (ATANT, 67), Zürich, 1981.

32. So mit R. SMEND, *Nachruf auf Martin Noth*, in H.W. WOLFF (ed.), M. NOTH, *Gesammelte Studien zum Alten Testament II* (TB, 39), München, 1969, pp. 139-165, esp. p. 147.

33. Schon in seiner Dissertation (*Der Ausschließlichkeitsanspruch Jahwes*, BWANT, 106, Stuttgart, 1975), behandelte Rose «die dtr Einleitung (Dtn 1,1-4,40)» auf zehn Seiten (146-156) mit der Devise, man könne die dtr Literatur nicht mehr «so undifferenziert» traktieren wie noch M. Noth (146), um gleich auf der nächsten Seite zu konzedieren: «In der Erhebung der Textgrundlage hierfür kann meist auf die literarkritischen Ergebnisse M. Noths zurückgegriffen werden.»

34. Ich greife das erste und wichtigste dieser Details heraus: den Titel Sihons. Dazu cf. J. VAN SETERS, *The Conquest of Sihon's Kingdom*, in *JBL* 91 (1972) 182-197; J. R. BARTLETT, *The Conquest of Sihon's Kingdom*, in *JBL* 97 (1978) 347-351; J. VAN SETERS, *Once again — the Conquest of Sihon's Kingdom*, in *JBL* 99 (1980) 117-119. Das Beispiel: in Dtn 2,26.30; 3,6 heißt Sihon «König von Heschbon». Das könnte sein wirklicher Titel gewesen sein. In Num 21,21 dagegen heißt er «König der Amoriter», und das war bestimmt niemals sein Titel. Darin findet Rose einen Hinweis auf die Priorität von Dtn 2f. Daß aber einerseits auch in Dtn 1-3 Sihon einer der preisgegebenen 'Amoriter' ist und darum im Dtn wie im DtrG mehrmals ebenso «Amoriterkönig» heißt, daß andererseits gerade und nur Num 21 in seinem Kern, dem Heschbon-Spruch, schlicht von Stadt und Residenz Sihons spricht, bedarf kaum der Erwähnung. Aber hier fehlt vor allem wieder die kontextuale Exegese: Niemand bestreitet, daß sich in Num 10-34 zahlreiche dtr Retuschen finden, und niemand bestreitet wohl, daß auch Dtn 2, wie alt oder jung auch immer im Gefüge der dtr Schichten, nicht den Schatten einer historischen Nachricht über Sihon bietet. Von ihm wissen wir nur das wenige, was der rätselhafte Heschbon-Spruch andeutet, und das steht, nicht zufällig, eben nur in Num 21.

35. Dazu cf. (ganz in den Spuren M. Noths und darum hier nicht weiter auszubreiten) auch U. KÖPPEL, *Das deuteronomistische Geschichtswerk und seine Quellen. Die Absicht der deuteronomistischen Geschichtsdarstellung aufgrund des Vergleichs zwischen Num 21,21-35 und Dtn 2,26-3,3* (Europäische Hochschulschriften, Reihe XXII, Bd. 122), Bern/Frankfurt, 1979.

meisten der zu Dtn 1-3 vertretenen Thesen untereinander gänzlich unvereinbar sind. Schon von daher ist es kein Wunder, daß in diesen letzten Jahren nichts so gefördert wurde wie das Methodengezänk. Mittmann [36] sah in Lohfinks Arbeit von (und seit) 1960 [37] der exegetischen Willkür Tor und Tür geöffnet, weil ästhetischer Subjektivismus zum Methodenprinzip erhoben wurde. Demgegenüber sah G. Braulik [38] in der literarkritischen Arbeit Mittmanns die «Diktatur eines Methodenmonismus» und erhob den Vorwurf, der heutzutage das Gewicht des Häresieverdachts zu haben scheint: «Mittmann reflektiert nirgends explizit über die von ihm angewandte literarkritische Methodik» (353). So entsteht der Eindruck, hier stünden Glaubensbekenntnisse einander gegenüber: Wo die historische Frage im Vordergrund steht, hat die Literatur-Ästhetik in der Tat nur den Rang eines Glasperlenspiels; umgekehrt kann, wer den Vorwurf der 'mitteleuropäischen' Blickverengung erhebt, die Literarkritik nur noch begrüßen wie Jacob Burckhardt den berühmten Kentauren am Waldesrand [39]. Bei Burckhardt könnte man immerhin lernen, was zu lernen heute wieder nötig scheint, wenn nicht diese ganze Methodenlyrik am Ende die wissenschaftliche Arbeit ersetzen soll: «Übrigens ist jede Methode bestreitbar und keine allgültig. Jedes betrachtende Individuum kommt auf *seinen* Wegen, die zugleich sein geistiger Lebensweg sein mögen, auf das riesige Thema zu und mag dann diesem Wege gemäß seine Methode bilden» [40]. Wellhausen sagte dasselbe bekanntlich kürzer: Es kommt nicht auf die Brille, sondern auf die Augen an! So versuche ich nun, auch hier im Für und Wider der Aspekte, mit den eigenen Augen auf Dtn 1-3 zu sehen. Dabei geht es mir nicht um Originalität, sondern um den Konsens über dem Bewährten. Selbstverständlich kann ich nur andeuten, was in einem Kommentar ausgeführt sein will.

III

1. Liest man Dtn 1-3 nur 'kanonisch', als Anfang des Buches Dtn, so ist für die Exegese noch nicht viel gewonnen, denn der Text lebt von weit

36. *Op. cit.* (n. 28), pp. 3-5.
37. *Op. cit.* (n. 17).
38. G. BRAULIK, *Literarkritik und archäologische Stratigraphie. Zu S. Mittmanns Analyse von Deuteronomium 4,1-40*, in *Bib* 59 (1978) 351-383, p. 351.
39. Was J. BURCKHARDT (*Weltgeschichtliche Betrachtungen*, Stuttgart, 1955, p. 6) auf die Geschichtsphilosophie münzte, kann man in der heute beschworenen 'nachkritischen' Ära beinahe auf die historisch-kritische Methode übertragen: «Immerhin ist man dem Kentauren den höchsten Dank schuldig und begrüßt ihn gerne hier und da an einem Waldesrand der geschichtlichen Studien. Welches auch sein Prinzip gewesen, er hat einzelne mächtige Ausblicke durch den Wald gehauen und Salz in die Geschichte gebracht.»
40. *Ibid.* (Hervorhebung von B.).

größeren Textblöcken, die nicht künstlich gesucht werden müssen, sondern ebenso 'kanonisch' naheliegen:

a. Es gibt hier keinen erzählenden Stoff ohne Parallele in Num.
b. Es gibt keine geographische Angabe (und in ihrer Gesamtheit bilden diese das historisch-geographische Rückgrat des Textes) ohne Parallele, Fortsetzung oder Zusammenfassung in Jos (und Ri).
c. Es gibt hier kaum ein theologisches Motiv ohne Bezug zum Kern des Dtn.

Darum inkludiert jede exegetische Aussage über Dtn 1-3 eine Aussage über drei ihrerseits höchst umstrittene Textbereiche:

a. über den Tetrateuch und dessen Quellen — denn die Num-Texte verlangen eine Deutung der Doppelüberlieferung.
b. über das DtrG, zumindest aber über den Hexateuch — denn die ausdrücklichen Bezüge auf Jos verlangen eine redaktionsgeschichtliche Erklärung.
c. über die Entstehungsgeschichte des Dtn selbst — denn im kanonischen Zusammenhang ist vorausgesetzt, daß der Leser von 1-3 in 4-34 eine sinnvolle Fortsetzung erkennen kann.

M. Noths umfassende Erklärung[41] aller dieser Phänomene wird jedenfalls durch keine Teil-Untersuchung ersetzt; nicht zufällig war Noth auch der Kommentator der entscheidenden Nachbarbücher Num und Jos[42]. Ohne Aufarbeitung des Großkontextes ist kein Urteil über einzelne Kapitel zugewinnen.

Da nun das Alte Testament selbst die Stoffe von Dtn 1-3 mehrfach und verschieden überliefert, wäre Verzicht auf literarhistorische Arbeit identisch mit dem Verzicht auf Beantwortung der Fragen, die sich jedem Bibelleser stellen, der von Num zu Dtn weiterliest. Wo in mehreren Anläufen dasselbe erzählt wird, wird in der Regel auch zu unterschiedlichen Zeiten erzählt: in der Absicht, anders und besser, in jedem Fall aber auf die Herausforderungen der je eigenen Zeit bezogen zu erzählen. Damit öffnet sich das Neben- und Nacheinander der Gestaltungen der literar*historischen* und sachlogisch eben auch der literar*kritischen* Betrachtung — und dies nicht zuletzt aus *theologischen* Gründen, denn es ist für das Verständnis dieser einzelnen Gestaltungen nicht gleichgültig, sondern entscheidend, auf welche ausgesprochenen oder meist unausgesprochen Fragen sie antworten, in welche geschichtliche Situation hinein sie theologisch sprechen wollen. Ohne literarhistorische Arbeit wird das Verständnis jeder dieser Gestaltungen also nicht tiefer, sondern flacher, nicht 'kanonischer', sondern 'unkanonischer'. Denn das Alte Testament selbst in seiner Fülle lehrt, daß Israel die großen Taten seines

41. *Überlieferungsgeschichtliche Studien*, Tübingen, ²1957.

42. *Numeri* (ATD, 7), Göttingen, 1966; *Das Buch Josua* (HAT, I 7), Tübingen, 1938; ²1953.

Gottes nicht einmal oder gar ein für allemal, sondern immer wieder neu und anders beschrieben, also geradezu *fort*geschrieben hat. Darum erschließt sich auch und gerade die Schönheit eines Textes nicht ohne 'kanonischen' Vergleich und die Berücksichtigung seines Werdens[43]. Wie in Israel die Volksgeschichte nicht stillstand, so auch nicht die Glaubensgeschichte, so und darum aber auch nicht die Literaturgeschichte. Die Stoffe von Dtn 1-3 haben wir gerade *nicht* in einer einzigen, kanonischen, sakrosankten Gestalt, sondern in Glauben und Leben bezeugender *diversitas*.

Ist dieser Prozeß zwischen Num, Dtn und Jos nun im *Großen* deutlich, so bedarf es keines anderen Gedankenschrittes, um ihn auch im *Kleinen* zu begreifen. Im Lehrhause der Deuteronomisten wurde mitnichten nur *einmal* geschrieben, sondern (und vielleicht über ein Jahrhundert hin) unablässig *fort*geschrieben. Das ist die natürliche und darum für den theologischen Exegeten nicht etwa gefährliche, sondern entschlüsselnde Beobachtung und Einsicht, die sich jedem eröffnet, der in Dtn 1-3 auch nur über die geringste literarische 'Merkwürdigkeit' stolpert. Es gibt also einerseits die Fortschreibung der Stoffe in einem gänzlich *neuen* Entwurf (darum wird Sihon in Num 21 *und* in Dtn 2 geschlagen); es gibt andererseits die Fortschreibung *desselben* Entwurfs. Ein Beispiel auch dafür: In der Hauptschicht der Erzählung von Dtn 2 erhält Mose die Siegeszusage an der 'richtigen' Stelle, nämlich nach der Weigerung Sihons: «Siehe, (jetzt) fange ich an, dir Sihon und sein Land preiszugeben» (2,31a). Mit demselben *ntn lfny* wird der Vollzug berichtet: «Da gab ihn Jahwe ... uns preis» (2,33a). In anderer Sprache (*ntn byd*) und an der 'falschen' Stelle, nämlich schon vor dem Friedensangebot an Sihon, steht in 2,24aß die Zusage: «Siehe, ich gebe Sihon, den König von Heschbon, den Amoriter, und sein Land in deine Hand.» Hier ist über Sihon im Himmel entschieden, was immer er dann auf Erden sagt oder tut. Diese Vorwegnahme (und Aufhebung der Spannung!) ist übrigens keine Anrede an Mose, sondern steht höchst sperrig in pluralischem Kontext: «Brecht auf und durchschreitet den Arnon — siehe, ich gebe Sihon ... in deine Hand» (2,24a). Das ist also der von Lohfink ersehnte

43. Es ist mir unbegreiflich, daß G. Braulik seiner rhetorischen Analyse von Dtn 4 (cf. n. 18) die literarkritische im Druck nicht vorangestellt hat. Würde sie irgendwo die Vermutung aufkommen lassen, daß das Kapitel nicht «aus einem Guß» ist (VII), dann fiele das Kartenhaus der rhetorischen Abschnitte und Strukturen in sich zusammen. Die Überprüfbarkeit in ein und derselben Monographie wäre wünschenwert gewesen.

H. D. PREUSS, *op. cit.* (n. 5), p. 20, schrieb zu Brauliks Buch: «B. versucht Dtn 4 als kunstvolle Einheit zu verstehen, sieht in den Spannungen und Brüchen ... nur Hinweise auf Abschnitte, übersieht dabei, daß eine thematische Einheit noch keine literarkritische sein muß und greift wohl auch daneben, wenn er einen so literarischen Text wie Dtn 4 von rhetorischen Sprechzeilen her interpretieren oder die Einheit Dtn 4,9-31 von der Struktur altorientalischer Staatsverträge her einleuchtend machen will.» Vielleicht hatte N. LOHFINK in seiner eingangs zitierten Rezension (cf. n. 1) auch diese Zurückweisung im Blick.

«Konvergenzbeweis»[44] für das literarkritische Gewicht des Numeruswechsels. Ich halte die sog. «Numerusmischung»[45] nicht für eine exegetische Problemlösung, sondern für ein Kapitulationsprogramm. In dieser Hinsicht machen mich weder die 1000 Seiten Forschungsgeschichte von Begg[46] noch neuerdings die 500 Seiten stilistischer Analyse des Numeruswechsels von Suzuki[47] wesentlich klüger, so hilfreich letztere gerade für das Verstehen von Motivkombinationen ist.

Am Text von Dtn 1-3 läßt sich die 'Fortschreibung' ebenso durch singularische Anreden und damit zusammenhängende Kontextspannungen wie durch theologische Differenzierungen deutlich zeigen: Der größeren Furcht wird die stärkere Zusage und der kräftigere Trost entgegengesetzt — so in 1,21.31a; 2,7.30b. Dabei nimmt das Interesse an der historisch-geographischen Längsspannung ab und die Tendenz zur Spiritualisierung der Geschichte zu. Ohne 'vertikale' Lektüre gerade dieser Kapitel macht man sich und das Alte Testament ärmer. Ich halte es auch in ästhetischer Hinsicht für ein Vergehen, die Bruchflächen zu verkleistern, die Israel selber funkeln ließ. Auch die 'neueste' Literaturwissenschaft (falls 'neu' ein Wert in sich ist) könnte dazu nur raten um den Preis einer *beatitudo* ohne Ecken und Kanten, also ohne Reiz. Die Tiefendimension der Texte ist mitnichten zu verbergen oder 'künstlerisch' — vielleicht doch nur: künstlich zu verwischen, sondern sie ist ein aufzudeckender Reichtum der Heiligen Schrift. Der Kanon ist geworden und gewachsen; das Lesen der Spuren dieses Wachstums ist ein Aspekt der Rezeptionsästhetik. Wer von der Kondeszendenz Gottes in die Geschichte Israels hinein redet, muß die diese Geschichte begleitende Kondeszendenz des Wortes in Literatur nicht verschweigen oder leugnen. Das wäre nicht nur ein historischer und literaturwissenschaftlicher Kunstfehler, sondern der Ansatz zu einer *theologia gloriae*, die nicht wahrhaben will oder nicht ertragen kann, daß wir auch diesen Schatz nur in irdenen Gefäßen haben.

2. Ebendieses Ja zur literarhistorischen Durchleuchtung dtr Texte bewegt mich nun dazu, die konzeptionelle Einheit von Dtn 1-3 zu verteidigen. Wer darin einen Widerspruch sieht, bejaht nicht die Mehrdimensionalität aller Geschichts- und Literaturwissenschaft, sondern den Methodenfanatismus.

Die Erzählungsstoffe von Dtn 1-3 finden sich also auch in Num — mit einem gravierenden Unterschied: Dort sind sie verstreut, ungeordnet,

44. *Das Hauptgebot* (n. 7), p. 31; cf. p. 204f.

45. *Ibid.*, p. 242f. Beim gewählten Beispiel von Dtn 2,24 kann man sich dann auch mit der lakonischen Bemerkung Augustins begnügen: «*Non dixit, in manus vestras, sed a plurali ad singularem transiit*» (*Locutiones de Deuteronomio*, MPL 34, p. 531).

46. Chr. BEGG, *Contributions to the Elucidation of the Composition of Deuteronomy with Special Attention to the Significance of the* Numeruswechsel, Diss. theol. Leuven, 1978.

47. Y. SUZUKI, *The* 'Numeruswechsel' *in Deuteronomy*, Diss. theol. Claremont, 1982.

mit legislativem Material vermischt, in mehrere nicht-dtr Schichten eingebettet und schließlich priesterschriftlich arrondiert. In Dtn 1-3 dagegen sind die literarisch komprimiert, geographisch orientiert, in der Redeform aneinander adaptiert und theologisch einheitlich akzentuiert. Wenn literarischer Vergleich überhaupt einen Sinn hat, dann gilt: das Ungeordnete geht dem Geordneten voraus, die Vielfalt der Formen geht deren Vereinheitlichung voraus — etc.

Dem entspricht der Prozeß der Theologisierung: In der Num-Version der Sihon-Erzählung kommt Jahwe nicht vor, weder in dem alten rhythmischen Spruch noch in der ihn bergenden Erzählung. In Dtn 2 dagegen ist Israel zuerst und zuletzt Empfänger der Gaben und Befehle Jahwes. Es ist undenkbar, daß der Weg der Überlieferung wie der Literatur von alledem weg und zum Gegenteil hin geführt hätte. So erweist sich uns der formgebende Verfasser von Dtn 1-3 als ein vollmächtiger Gestalter von Tradition(en).

Dieser Sicht entspricht die Redeform im ganzen: Dtn 1-3 will *expressis verbis* Nach-Erzählung, literarisch also: Sekundär-Gestaltung sein. Vom ersten Satz der Exposition in 1,6 erinnert Mose daran, daß alles, was folgt, allen bekannt ist. Die Moserede ist Vergegenwärtigung von gemeinsam Erlebtem durch den einen Augenzeugen für die anderen — ungeachtet der Generationenbrüche. Man darf mit Lohfink [48] vermuten, daß dieser Verfasser auf die älteren Gestaltungen anspielt, also mit 'Textkenntnis' rechnet. So haben wir es in beiden oder noch mehr Stadien mit 'Literatur' zu tun, die darum keinen Zugriff der Literaturwissenschaft ausschließt. Im Blick auf die Stoffe war dieser Verfasser 'Literaturproduzent' der zweiten oder dritten Stunde; im Blick auf das Ergebnis aber war er der Mann des schöpferischen Entwurfs, der umgreifenden literarischen Planung und Gestaltung. In seinen Grundlinien und -aussagen entstand Dtn 1-3 nicht durch Addition, sondern durch Konzeption. Dafür gibt es eine Fülle von Hinweisen.

Die südjudäisch orientierte Kundschaftergeschichte (1,19-46) steht in einem festen antithetischen Zusammenhang mit den ostjordanischen Begebenheiten (2,16-3,17). Dem Scheitern dort entspricht das Gelingen hier. Diese Gegensatz-Spannung exemplifiziert die dtr Predigt-Alternative [49] Ungehorsam/Gehorsam. Diese Gegenüberstellung der in Num 13f. und 21 noch isolierten Stoffe geschah *uno actu* und in theologischer Absicht.

Eine vergleichbare Spannung schafft das Gegenüber der Brudervölker und der Amoriter: Erstere sind zu verschonen, letztere zu bekämpfen. Wegen der mit den Brudervölkern vorgegebenen geographischen und historischen Überlieferungen muß auch diese Antithese *uno actu* ent-

48. *Darstellungskunst* (n. 17), p. 109f.

49. Cf. die «Alternativ-Predigt» der exilischen Zeit bei W. THIEL, *Die deuteronomistische Redaktion von Jeremia 1-25* (WMANT, 41), Neukirchen, 1973, pp. 290-295.

worfen sein; anders ist der geographische Gesamthorizont von Dtn 2f. nicht zu erklären. Dafür nimmt der Verfasser freilich den artifiziellen Begriff 'Amoriter' sowie die unhistorische Vorstellung einer kompletten Eroberung des Ostjordanlandes in Süd-Nord-Richtung in Kauf. So reicht sein ostjordanisches Israel vom Arnon bis zum Baschan — vom nachgetragenen Hermon gar nicht zu reden. Dabei sorgt die Gesamtplanung aber nicht nur nach 'außen', sondern auch nach 'innen' für herrische Komplettierung: Für die Südhälfte des Ostens steht Sihon, für die Nordhälfte ist Og eher erfunden als bezeugt. Daß das nördliche Ostjordanland zwischen Jabbok und Jarmuk vom Ausgang der mittleren Eisenzeit bis zum Ende der persischen Zeit nahezu unbesiedelt war, kann diesem Verfasser nicht die historisch-theologische Systematik verderben. Das alles aber setzt Übersicht und Absicht voraus, und dies kaum erst im 3. oder 4. Glied der Deuteronomisten, sondern im 1. und 2. Glied, denn die Leistung besteht in der unlösbaren Beziehung der Stoffe aufeinander.

Ein delikates Indiz dieser Planung ist schließlich die Synthese zweier nach Herkunft und Überlieferung verschiedener Elemente. Auf die Frage, warum das ostjordanische Amoriter-Land so flächendeckend auf Sihon und Og verteilt wird, antwortet 3,8ff. überraschend: Der Süden wurde Ruben und Gad, der Norden Halb-Manasse übergeben. Hier überschneiden sich also zwei Interessen: das fiktive eines Gesamtisrael und das faktische der Stämme. Geht man davon aus, daß spätestens in davidischer Zeit Teile der mittelpalästinischen Stämme sich nach Osten und dort nach Süden ausbreiteten, dann steht Dtn 2f. in stärkster Spannung zur Geschichte. Ich erwähne das, weil die Elemente der Stämmelisten gerne in den Bereich der tertiären Ergänzungen von Dtn 1-3 abgeschoben werden [50]. Nach meiner Ansicht gehört aber selbst diese Synthese zum Grund-Entwurf, denn der dtr Historiker entwirft ja mit dem Blick auf Josua. Hier wie dort erobert Israel wie ein einheitlicher Organismus, aber in Besitz nimmt es immer stammesmäßig. Also zielt bereits die künstliche Aufteilung des Landes auf die Vorbesitzer Sihon und Og von vornherein auf deren Ablösung durch *bestimmte* Israeliten: jene Stämme, die nach der Überlieferung dort ansässig waren, wann und wie lange auch immer. Mit der Resektion dieses 'Ergebnisses' der Landnahme fiele Dtn 2f. in sich zusammen, weil die Kapitel als Präludium und Kontrapunkt der westjordanischen Landnahme unter Josua verstanden werden sollen; und auch bei dieser wurde kein Quadratmeter Land anders als an Stämme verteilt. Auf die Kontrapunktik von Dtn 1-3 und Jos 1-11 bezieht sich das Fazit in Jos 12 in

50. Es muß hier ganz offen bleiben, was der 'Verzicht' auf das Ostjordanland in dem frühestens exilischen Stämme-Konzept von Ez 47,13-48,29 bedeutet. Offen bleiben muß auch die Frage nach der historischen Beziehung exilischer oder frühnachexilischer Hoffnungen auf Baschan und Gilead in Jer 50,19; Mi 7,14. Cf. H.W. WOLFF, *Dodekapropheton 4: Micha* (BKAT, XIV/4), Neukirchen, 1982, pp. 193f.; 202.

schöner Bestätigung. Mose präfiguriert Josua: Man kann Dtn 1-3 nur in seinem Großkontext auslegen.

So, nur so, konnte der dtr Historiker auch die beiden wichtigsten, weil alle Einzelheiten lenkenden Elemente der Überlieferung bruchlos in das Gesamtwerk einbauen: Mose kam nie über den Jordan; und: in Verbindung mit der westjordanischen, also der Landnahmetradition *in sensu stricto* stand Josua. Darum betet Mose am Ende von Dtn 1-3 ganz 'folgerichtig', d.h. mit dem Blick auf die in Jos folgenden Begebenheiten: «Herr Jahwe, du hast nun angefangen, deinen Knecht deine Größe ... sehen zu lassen» (3,24). Das wußte der Erzähler von 1,6 ab: Was hier anhebt, zielt auf eine große Geschichte — über das Gesetz hinweg, das zwischeneingekommen war.

Ich habe hier einem genialen geschichtstheologischen Verfasser von Literatur das Lied gesungen. Er wußte die Num-Texte hinter sich und die Jos-Texte vor sich. Daß er nicht der Letzte blieb, der in diesem sensiblen Bereich der Frühgeschichte Israels theologische Akzente setzte, beweisen die erkennbaren Umakzentuierungen, und zu ihnen gehört als bedeutendste, in 1,5 vorbereitet, die Vereinigung der Geschichte mit dem Gesetz. Daß aber ein Geschichtstheologe von Rang für alle ihm nachfolgenden 'Schüler' den Grund legte, lehrt das kunstvolle Gefüge des Textes, aus dem sich nur relativ wenige Steine herausbrechen lassen, ohne das Gebäude zum Einsturz zu bringen.

Wer sich die eine dieser beiden Lese-Arten, der 'vertikalen' und der 'horizontalen', meint ersparen zu können, verläßt mutwillig die Vielgestaltigkeit der Geschichts- und Literaturwissenschaft und hat, mir jedenfalls, nichts zu sagen.

Wilhelm-Weber-Str. 40
D-3400 Göttingen

Lothar PERLITT

DEUTERONOMY 5: ITS PLACE AND FUNCTION

This study presumes that 4,44ff. is not an introduction to ch. 5 but rather to the second speech of Moses as a whole. Therefore, it will not be considered here. The same applies to 6,1-3, which presupposes the text of ch. 5, reassumes some of its pronouncements and at the same time prepares 6,4ff. Thus these verses serve as a kind of transition between the two chapters and may be omitted from our present study. I will restrict myself, therefore, to 5,1-33. Further, it is not my intention to embark on a detailed study of all the problems posed by the Decalogue, which occupies such a prominent place in this chapter. I will restrict myself to the remainder of the chapter, although the function of the Decalogue in this chapter will be considered — indeed, it cannot be avoided.

The composition of ch. 5 is still at issue among scholars. Some defend its unity; others accept some expansions of the text; and others have proposed extremely complicated theories about its origin [1].

It seems obvious that there is an introduction in v. 1 and a conclusion in vv. 32-33. While the entire chapter is an attempt to explain Moses' position as the giver of the laws of Israel, v. 1 already presupposes that Moses has that authority. Moses is concerned in this verse with the people hearing these prescriptions, learning them, and fulfilling them. The text differs from the rest of the chapter in its paraenetic style, and it manifests several elements of what Lohfink has called the paraenetic scheme. There is no interest at all in the position of the Deuteronomic law relative to the Decalogue, its attention being focused only on the Deuteronomic law itself. Finally, the transition from the 2nd person plural to the 1st person plural in v. 2 may also be an indication that v. 1 should be distinguished from the rest of the chapter.

The same problems return with vv. 32-33. Whereas Yahweh speaks to Moses in vv. 28-31 and the people are spoken of in the 3rd person plural, v. 32 suddenly switches to the 2nd person plural, and it is Moses who is speaking to the people. We also leave the narrative style of the rest of the chapter and return to the paraenetic style of v. 1. These verses have the same paraenetic scheme, even in its complete form. There is no longer any mention of the Decalogue or the special task of Moses, and it is even stated that Yahweh himself commanded (*ṣiwwāh*) all that the people must do in the land.

1. The unity of the chapter has been defended by A. Bertholet, S.R. Driver, A.C. Welch, N. Lohfink, D. McCarthy, P. Jacobs. Some expansions are accepted by G. Seitz, A.D.H. Mayes. Extremely complicated solutions were offered very recently by R.P. Merendino, F.-L. Hossfeld and H.D. Preuss.

Thus, it would appear that v. 1 and vv. 32-33 are a redactional introduction and conclusion that have no direct significance with respect to the rest of the chapter. Rather, they situate vv. 2-31 in the Book of Deuteronomy. The real content of the chapter, therefore, must be sought in vv. 2-31. Two parts may be distinguished in these verses: the Decalogue and its framework (vv. 2-22) and the problem of its relation to the Deuteronomic law and the function of Moses with respect to that law (VV. 23-31).

The first part has its own introduction in vv. 2-5. I think that all scholars would agree that v. 5 (with the exception of the last word) does not fit at all with the remainder of the text and must be considered a later addition, and probably even a post-Deuteronomistic one. It defends the special position of Moses even at the proclamation of the Decalogue and so betrays the influence of the later, so dominant position he occupied. There could be some connection between Dt. 34,10 and our verse, because there it is said that only Moses knew the Lord face to face.

The last word of v. 5 could be the continuation of v. 2 or of v. 4, and scholars disagree on which of them belongs to the older form of the chapter. The disadvantage for those who think that v. 2 was the older introduction to the Decalogue is that they must consider v. 3 to be a later expansion, even though it is closely linked to v. 2[2]. There are, indeed, great differences between vv. 2-3, on the one hand, and v. 4, on the other. There is not only the 1st person plural speech in vv. 2-3 and the 2nd person plural in v. 4, there is also the fact that vv. 2-3 speak about the convenant at Horeb and its actualization, while v. 4 tells how the Lord spoke to the people. We could say, perhaps, that the problem of the rest of the chapter is introduced more properly by v. 4 than by vv. 2-3. Indeed, the covenant of vv. 2-3 does not return in the rest of the chapter, while v. 4 does introduce the themes of the speaking of Yahweh (see *dibbēr* in vv. 22.24.26.27.28.31) and the fire on the mountain (see *bāhār mittôk hā'ēš* in vv. 22.23.24.26). We may conclude that v. 4 seems the more proper and direct introduction to the chapter and that vv. 2-3 interpret the Decalogue as a covenantal text.

After the Decalogue immediately follows the conclusion of the first part. The primary points of v. 22 are that the words of the Decalogue were spoken directly by Yahweh to the people and that these were the only words thus communicated to them (*lô' yāsaf*). The first part of the verse also directs our attention to the circumstances of this speaking by God: it happened on the mountain from the midst of the fire; there were clouds and darkness; and God spoke with a mighty voice. All these

2. That v. 3 is a later addition was defended lately by A. D. H. MAYES, *Deuteronomy* (NCB), Grand Rapids-London, 1979, p. 161. See for the contrary opinion L. PERLITT, *Bundestheologie im Alten Testament* (WMANT 36), Neukirchen, 1969, p. 81.

elements form part of the conclusion of the first part of the chapter and, at the same time, prepare for the second. The position of *ʿānān weʿarāfel* in the sentence creates some grammatical problems, and, because it does not recur in the rest of the chapter, it may be a later expansion derived from 4,22. The reason could be that direct contact between Yahweh and the people was considered somehow intolerable, and therefore it must be softened. The same cannot be said of the expression *qôl gadôl*, although it does not recur in the rest of the chapter either. Because the rest of the chapter frequently mentions the *qôl* of Yahweh (vv. 23.24.25.26), *qôl gadôl* seems a very appropriate preparation for this aspect of the second part of the story. The question of whether *haddebarîm* at the beginning of the verse, which of course refers to the Decalogue, must be considered a technical term for the Decalogue is more difficult to decide. The fact that *debarîm* has this meaning elsewhere in Deuteronomy (4,12-13.36; 9,10; 10,2.4) is, of itself, insufficient proof because the formula in v. 22 seems to be a common wording of a reference to a previously cited text. Nevertheless, while v. 22b says that God wrote them (plural suffix) on tablets of stone, it may be argued that the beginning of v. 22 is more than a commonplace concluding formula.

The last words of v. 22a (*lô' yāsaf*) also prepare for the second half of the chapter. For if God proclaimed only the Decalogue directly to the people, the question of the position of the other laws of Israel arises. One could say, of course, that the people in the second part still expects God to speak to them again. But this need not have prevented the author from making it clear to his readers that this will not be the case.

We may conclude that v. 22a, although a conclusion of the first part of the narrative speech, at the same time prepares the second part. This shows very clearly that the two parts of the chapter belong together and that the one cannot be understood apart from the other.

At first sight, v. 22b seems much less important. That God wrote the Decalogue on stone tablets and handed them over to Moses plays no further role in the story. This seems to be the main reason why many scholar consider this second part or even the whole of the verse as a kind of gloss [3]. It is difficult to refute this opinion by treating our text as the concluding part of covenantal text, as Lohfink has done [4]. In his view, v. 3 gives a definition of the partners of the covenant; vv. 6-21 have the covenant text; and v. 22 concludes with the various juridical acts that are part of the conclusion of a covenant: proclamation (*dibbēr*), writing down to furnish a document (*kātab*), transmission of the text

3. E.g. PUUKKO, *Das Deuteronomium*, Leipzig, 1910, p. 130 note 1; C. STEUERNAGEL, *Das Deuteronomium* (HKAT), Göttingen², 1923, p. 72f.; H. D. PREUSS, *Deuteronomium* (Erträge der Forschung, 164), Darmstadt, 1982, p. 48; S. MITTMANN, *Deuteronomium 1,1-6,3 literarkritisch und traditionsgeschichtlich untersucht* (BZAW, 139), Berlin, 1975, p. 137; F.-L. HOSSFELD, *Der Dekalog* (OBO, 45). Freiburg-Göttingen, 1982, p. 226.

4. *Das Hauptgebot* (AnB 20), Rome, 1963, p. 143.

(*nātan*). One rather gets the impression that the author could not leave the Decalogue without mentioning what, according to the tradition, happened after its proclamation. In doing this, he creates an opportunity to emphasize that Moses, after all, had a role even with regard to the Decalogue. And because the entire chapter is very much concerned with the special task of Moses, this does not seem at all improbable. The thesis that these words are a proleptic preparation to chs. 9-10, as Steuernagel suggests, cannot be retained. But they undoubtedly present the Decalogue as an already existing document, written down in a fixed form, and underline its permanent validity, which was already implied in the *lô' yāsaf* of v. 22a.

Several scholars have seen the Decalogue as a secondary element in our chapter [5]. Most recently, H. D. Preuss has argued that the original continuation of v. 5c is vv. 23ff. (you were afraid of the fire and did not go up the mountain... but you approached me and said)[6]. To me it seems rather difficult to accept a form of our chapter in which the Decalogue was not present at all. When the whole question of the relation between the Decalogue and the Deuteronomic law is eliminated, the meaning of the chapter and its place in Deuteronomy are anything but clear to me. Indeed, the coherence of the chapter would be completely destroyed.

In another recent study, Hossfeld is inclined to consider the whole of v. 22 as a later redactional addition [7]. The following arguments are brought forward:

1. The redactor makes Israel into a religious community (*qāhāl*), which greatly differs from the community based on the law of 23,2ff., which is a war community.
2. He expands the theophany by adding «clouds and darkness» and «great voice».
3. He strictly delineates the Decalogue: nothing was added and it was written down and fixed forever.

The second and third arguments have already been dealt with. The idea of *qāhāl* may be different from that of ch. 23, and this may indicate that both texts are not the same layer of Deuteronomy, but this does not mean that it is a redactional element in our chapter. There are other places in which *qāhāl* occurs. Dt. 4,10 and 18,16 are almost quotations from ch. 5 and may be considered dependent on our chapter. The texts in 9,10 and 10,4 do not show the same connection with ch. 5, but they nevertheless use the word in the same context of the revelation at Horeb. Therefore, they may have the same origin.

We may conclude that v. 22, perhaps with the exception of some minor expansions, is best seen as part of the older form of our chapter.

5. C. STEUERNAGEL, *Deuteronomium*², p. 71.
6. *Deuteronomium*, p. 48.
7. *Der Dekalog*, p. 227f.

The second part of our chapter has a very clear structure, as has been shown by Lohfink:[8]

a. 23a: the reason for the following narrative and the reassumption of the preceding;
b. 23b-27: the initiative of the people, which contains: a description of the situation (24: the Horeb event), the reaction to this event, introduced by *w^e'attāh* (25-26), the proposal of the people to Moses (27);
c. 28-31: the acceptance of the proposal by God and a description of the task of Moses.

However, there remain some problems with regard to the composition of these verses. First of all, there are the last words of v. 23, «all the heads of your tribes and your elders», which sound a bit strange with the 2nd person plural of the rest of the verse and of the following narrative. Moreover, they do not appear again in the rest of the chapter. According to Lohfink and García López, these officials are mentioned explicitly here because they are public representatives of the people at the Horeb covenant[9]. This presupposes that our text represents a covenantal document with all its details, which is rather improbable as we have seen. It seems better here to follow the majority of scholars, who consider these words a later addition to the text[10].

The problem of vv. 24-26 is more complicated. These verses seem to say that man may hear the voice of God and live, while at the same time the people fear to die should they do so. Many scholars consider these elements contradictory and therefore accept later expansions of the text. According to Seitz and Mayes, vv. 24 and 26 are secondary elements; Mittmann considers 24b and 25a (but not *w^e'attāh*) as later additions; Hossfeld agrees with Mittmann but also accepts v. 26 as a later element[11]. If we agree that our narrative is based on the Yehowistic account of Ex 20,18ff.[12], we may ask what the Deuteronomic recension adds to this older tradition. The God-man opposition in 24b and the flesh-living God opposition in v. 26 certainly must be seen as further reflections of Ex 20,18ff. But that they are reflections, of itself, does not prove that they must be considered redactional elements in our chapter. It is pointed out that *bāśār* and *'elohîm ḥayyîm* occur only here in Deuteronomy. And *hā'ādām* is found in 4,28.32; 8,3; 20,19; and 32,8, which all seem to be rather late elements in the Deuteronomic tradition. Thus, since all of the terminology is rather exceptional, there are reasons for attributing these reflections to later redactions of the text. To this

8. *Das Hauptgebot*, p. 144.

9. LOHFINK, *Das Hauptgebot*, p. 144; F. GARCÍA LÓPEZ, *Analyse litéraire de Deut. 5-11*, in *RB* 85 (1978), p. 18.

10. S. MITTMANN, o.c., p. 137ff.; MAYES, *Deuteronomy*, p. 172; HOSSFELD, *o.c.*, p. 229.

11. Cf. preceding note.

12. L. PERLITT, o.c., p. 82, calls Dt. 5 a midrash of this older tradition.

must be added that these reflections are not very relevant to the story itself: they do not further or interrupt its continuation. The question in v. 26 *mî kol bāśār 'ašer* shows similarity with those of 4,7-8: *mî gôy gādôl 'ašer*. Such questions suggest that the special privileges given to Israel underline its particular position among the nations. Since this is the case also in v. 26, it does not seem to fit very well in the context of the rest of the chapter, and this verse could be a later addition, perhaps from the same school that produced ch. 4. I am not convinced that the same can be said for v. 24. It is not certain that the use of *kābôd* in this verse betrays priestly influence, as is often argued. In Ps. 29,28 the thunder is the voice of *'ēl kābôd*, Isaiah in his call vision sees the whole of the earth as full of Yahweh's *kābôd*. It seems, therefore, that theophany was seen as the revelation of the *kābôd* of God already in very ancient times. Moreover, our text lacks the specific elements of the priestly tradition connected with the *kābôd*[13]. That the *gôdel* of God is associated with the Horeb theophany only here is no reason to deny its authenticity, because in other texts it is also used for the manifestation of the great deeds of Yahweh. So v. 24 may very well be a Deuteronomic reflection based on the Yehowistic tradition of Ex. 20,18ff.

It is much more difficult to decide if there is some redactional reworking in v. 28. This has so many common Deuteronomic expressions that it seems quite possible. It is true, for example, that Moses is called the teacher of the people in rather late texts of Deuteronomy (4,1.5.14; 6,1; 31,19.22), but at least the texts of ch. 4 and of 6,1 may have been influenced by our chapter.

Looking back for a moment at the two parts of this chapter, we note a striking difference between them. The verbal forms in the first part are mainly perfect forms (*kārat* in vv. 2-3; *dibbēr* in vv. 4 and 22). Only the last two verbs of v. 22 show the narrative tense, and these are, as we have seen, a reference to older traditions and not so essential for the tendency of the chapter as a whole. In the second part, this narrative tense very clearly predominates (see vv. 23, 24, and 28). In my opinion, this is an indication that the first part of the chapter contains mainly introductory statements leading up to the narrative proper in the second part.

I would call attention here to another striking element of this chapter. The main verbs are those of speaking (*dibbēr* in vv. 4.22.24.26.27.28.30) and of hearing (*šāma'* in vv. 23.24.25.26.27.28.39). It is not said that the people saw Yahweh, only that they heard him speaking to them. This must be taken into account in considering v. 4, which states that Yahweh spoke to the people, *panîm b^{e}panîm*, which means that God is not seen but that he spoke to them directly and personally. From the analysis, I

13. Cf. M. WEINFELD, art. *kābôd* in *TWAT* IV, Stuttgart, 1982, col. 33-34; C. WESTERMANN, art. *kābôd*, in *THAT* I, München, 1971, col. 803-805.

14. See e.g. MAYES, *Deuteronomy*, p. 266.

am inclined to consider this chapter as a literary unit except for some later expansions in vv. 22.23.26 and perhaps in v. 31. The introductory v. 1 and the concluding vv. 32-33 situate it in the Book of Deuteronomy. More uncertain is the position of vv. 2-3 in the chapter, to which problem I will return to below.

After having the analysis of the chapter, we must now turn to its place in the composition of the Book as a whole. To begin with, we must confront the problem of the covenant at Horeb. This Horeb covenant is found in other places in Deuteronomy. In 4,13, Yahweh is said to have proclaimed his covenant there. The tablets of the covenant are mentioned in 9,9.10.15, and the ark of the covenant as the container of these tablets is referred to in 10,8 and 31,9.25.26. Finally, 28,69 mentions the covenant at Moab as coming after the covenant Yahweh concluded at Horeb. Now these texts occur in the rather late chapters 4 and 31 and in the narrative texts of chs. 5 and 9-10. The text of 28,69, like that of 4,13, contains a direct reference to 5,2-3. 4,13 is a kind of quotation and depends on ch. 5. Must the same be said of 28,69? The Horeb covenant in 5,2-3 is seen as operative for all future generations, and, although further prescriptions are to be given by Moses, there is no suggestion that a second covenant is needed. One may well ask what exactly is the place of vv. 2-3 in our chapter. All the emphasis of the text is on the speaking of God to the people and, in the future, to Moses, whereas the covenant idea is restricted to vv. 2-3. Are these verses not, therefore, a later element in this chapter and would they thus be closely related to 28,69, stemming perhaps from the same hand? Or is 28,69 only dependent on 5,2-3?

Even if 5,2-3 is an original part of ch. 5, it seems that the Horeb covenant does not belong to the older layers of the Book of Deuteronomy. In 7,9.12 and 8,3, *b^e^rît* is the gracious promise of God to the fathers, an idea that is not so very different from the oath to the fathers mentioned so frequently in Deuteronomy. Other texts in which *b^e^rît* occurs without any clear reference to Horeb are 4,23 (*škḥ b^e^rît*), 17,2 (*ʿbr b^e^rît*), 29,24 (*ʿzb b^e^rît*), and 31,16.20 (*hêfēr b^e^rît*). The only text in the corpus of the laws (17,2) belongs to 17,2-7, which are generally considered as a later redactional expansion that interrupts the law about judges in 16,18-20 and 17,8-13.14. All the other *b^e^rît* texts are certainly elements of later layers of the book. The texts in 29,8.11.13.20 all refer to the covenant ceremony at Moab. So the Horeb covenant does not belong to the older form of Deuteronomy, although it may belong to the original form of our chapter.

The name Horeb occurs in Dt 1,2.6.19; 4,10.15; 5,2; 9,8; 18,16 and 28.69. Again there is only one text in the corpus of the laws, and this text is a kind of quotation from our chapter and so depends on it. The same goes for 4,10.15, which verses are quotations from ch. 5. The only independent texts, therefore, seem to be those of ch. 1, which are all geographical notes concerning the departure or the journey of the people from Horeb, and 9,8, which says that the people provoked the anger of God at Horeb, Thus, one gets the impression that the older layers of Deuteronomy do not manifest very much interest in the Horeb event itself.

Now many scholars consider chs. 1-3 as the introduction to the Deuteronomistic history. After M. Noth, who defends the unity of the Deuteronomistic history, several scholars believe that we must accept more than one redaction of this work. After the introduction of the nomistic redaction by R. Smend, a prophetic redaction was discovered by W. Dietrich and taken over by T. Veijola [15] and others. Recently, N. Lohfink has discerned an older form of the Deuteronomic history comprehending only Deuteronomy and Joshua [16]. And in a recent German dissertation, the splitting up of these redactions was carried to the point of absurdity [17]. Alongside this German approach, there exists an American one that defends a double redaction of the Deuteronomic history, Josianic and Exilic. This was first defended by F. M. Cross, and it has been further developed by Nelson and Friedman [18]. For a certain time, these two exegetical traditions seemed to be not very much aware of each other, but the latest study of A. D. H. Mayes [19], although opting fundamentally for the American solution, tries to assimilate many of the insights gathered by the German studies.

Our ch. 5, because of its narrative style and its plural form of address, has been often associated with the Deuteronomistic edition of Deuteronomy. If one accepts a double redaction of this history with the Americans and assigns ch. 4 to this second redaction, then ch. 5 cannot be considered a part of that same redaction because, as we have seen several times, ch. 4 presupposes and utilizes ch. 5 for its own purposes. It identifies the covenant and the Decalogue (4,13) and uses the theophany at Horeb as a warning against the making of images of gods (4,15 ff.). If, however, ch. 5 does not belong to the same redaction as that of ch. 4, it could be part of the first Deuteronomic redaction.

15. R. SMEND, *Das Gesetz und die Völker*, in *Probleme biblischer Theologie*, Festschr. G. von Rad, München, 1971, p. 494-509; W. DIETRICH, *Prophetie und Geschichte* (FRLANT, 108), Göttingen, 1972; T. VEIJOLA, *Die ewige Dynastie*, Helsinki, 1972; id., *Das ewige Königtum*, Helsinki, 1975.

16. N. LOHFINK, *Kerygmata des Deuteronomistischen Geschichtswerkes*, in *Die Botschaft und die Boten*, Festschr. H. W. Wolff, Neukirchen, 1981, p. 87-100.

17. R. STAHL, *Aspekte der Geschichte deuteronomistischer Theologie* (Diss. Jena, 1982). Cf. *TLZ* 108 (1983) 74-76.

18. F. M. CROSS, *Canaanite Myth and Hebrew Epic*, Cambridge, 1973, pp. 274-289; R. N. NELSON, *The Double Redaction of the Deuteronomic History* (JSOT Suppl. 18), Sheffield, 1981 (revised from a 1973 dissertation); R. E. FRIEDMAN, *The Exile and Biblical Narrative* (HSM 22) Chico, 1982.

19. A. D. H. MAYES, *The Story of Israel between Settlement and Exile*, London 1983.

And such is the conclusion of Mayes, who holds that ch. 4 already presupposes the presence of the Decalogue and that the original introduction to Deuteronomy has a singular form of address, has no historical references, and is concerned only with the proclamation of the law on the border of the Promised Land and not with the events at Horeb. «It is therefore most probably to the deuteronomistic historian that we owe these insertions .»[20] In his commentary, he adds: «the original parenetic introduction does not refer to the Decalogue or presuppose its presence.»[21]

It seems to me that, even after all this, some problems remain. The first Deuteronomic historian begins his survey with the departure from Horeb, and from the very outset all his attention is directed to the land that Yahweh will give to Israel (1,7-8). Then he mentions the unsuccessful attack from the south and interprets the whole sojourn in the desert as a punishment for the unbelief of the people (1,17-46). He then tells of the conquest of Transjordan (chs. 2-3) and announces that Joshua will continue the conquest (3,28). Why then should this Deuteronomistic historian return to the events at Horeb in chs. 5 and 9? Older scholars suggested that the original place of these chapters must have been before ch. 1. Although we do not have to return to such a radical textual rearrangement, this opinion clearly indicates that there is a problem with this chapter, a problem confirmed by the present study since it revealed no reason to consider its terminology comparable with that of chs. 1-3.

To this must be added that the desert period is quite different in chs. 5 and 9 and in chs. 1-3. The first chapters of Deuteronomy interpret the forty years in the desert as the punishment for not conquering the Promised Land from the south, a punishment that endured until the unfaithful generation had completely passed away. In ch. 9, however, it is said that Israel was unfaithful from Egypt up to that very day. The failure to conquer the Promised Land from the south was added later on (v. 23) in the series of deeds of infidelity and thus becomes only one element of infidelity in that series. This again may be contrasted to 8,2 ff., where Yahweh is said to have tested the people in the desert, but where, nevertheless, the whole of the wilderness period is interpreted as a continuous grace of God. We may then conclude that the ideas of the desert period are very different from those of chs. 1-3. Indeed, I would agree with F.-L. Hossfeld: «Die Literarkritik zu Dtn. 5 hat keinen Tatbestand ergeben, das Kapitel van Dtn. 1-3 her zu verstehen.»[22] I would further add that some of the religious ideas in them are so different that it is difficult to ascribe them to the same hand.

20. *The Story of Israel*, p. 31-32 (quotation on p. 32).

21. *Deuteronomy* p. 161. See also id., *Deuteronomy 5 and the Decalogue*, in *Proceedings of the Irish Biblical Association* 4 (1980) 68-83.

22. *Der Dekalog*, p. 237.

It must be concluded, therefore, that ch. 5 is not a part of the older layers of Deuteronomy and that it can be ascribed either to the first or the second redaction of the Deuteronomistic history. It is better seen as one of the redactions of the Book of Deuteronomy. This redactor, who wished to interpret the law of Deuteronomy as an extension of the Decalogue, must have been convinced that the Decalogue was the most important law of Israel, and he could not himself have been the creator of this law. Otherwise, the right understanding of this chapter as a whole would be impossible. Whether the redactor who added this chapter to the Book of Deuteronomy reworked the rest of the Book in the same spirit is a matter for further study.

Platte Lostraat 71
B-3200 Leuven

Chr. BREKELMANS

LES SECTIONS NARRATIVES DE DEUT 5-11
ET LEUR RELATION À EX 19-34

Dans le foisonnement de la recherche actuelle, la formation de Deut 5-11 fait l'objet de deux types principaux d'hypothèses. Selon l'opinion la plus commune, qui connaît elle-même plusieurs variantes, l'élément de base de ces chapitres est de nature parénétique[1] et coïncide avec au moins certaines sections en «tu» adressées à Israël; les exhortations écrites à la deuxième personne du pluriel et surtout les éléments narratifs (5,1-31; 9,7-10,11) sont tenus pour autant d'additions qualifiées de «deutéronomistes»[2]. Une hypothèse presque inverse est cependant défendue par N. Lohfink: l'introduction primitive au Code législatif (Deut 12-26) comprenait le récit des événements de l'Horeb, avec le don du Décalogue (5,1-31) et l'épisode du veau d'or (9,9-10,5*) et, dans les deux cas, un commentaire de style parénétique (5,32-6,25*; 10,10-11,17*); les autres sections de Deut 5-11 seraient à considérer comme des commentaires plus récents, ajoutés au texte en plusieurs étapes[3]. En somme, les points d'accord quasi-unanime entre les exégètes sont peu nombreux: C'est dans les ch. 5 à 11 qu'il faut chercher l'introduction primitive au Code[4]. — Cette introduction remonte au moins à l'époque

1. Comme le note F. GARCÍA LÓPEZ, *Analyse littéraire de Deutéronome, V-XI*, dans *RB* 84 (1977) 481-522; 85 (1978) 5-49, «la dénomination 'sections parénétiques' et 'sections historiques' est (...) insuffisante» (p. 47). En effet, les sections «historiques» ou «narratives» contiennent souvent plus d'un élément de nature parénétique; voir par exemple le récit du veau d'or, placé sous le signe du «souvenir» et donc de la leçon à tirer (9,7). L'inverse est également vrai: la parénèse se fonde sur l'expérience historique. Pour des raisons évidentes de simplicité, je continuerai cependant à parler de «sections narratives» et de «sections parénétiques», comme le fait d'ailleurs F. García López.

2. Outre l'article de F. García López cité dans la note précédente, voir par exemple, parmi les travaux récents: E. NIELSEN, *«Weil Jahwe unser Gott ein Jahwe ist», Dtn 6,4f.*, dans *Festschrift W. Zimmerli*, Göttingen, 1977, pp. 288-301 (p. 289); H.D. PREUSS, *Deuteronomium* (ErtrForsch, 164), Darmstadt, 1982, p. 95. Certains auteurs dissocient cependant les ch. 5 et 9-10*: seuls ces derniers sont alors considérés comme «tardifs».

3. N. LOHFINK, *Das Hauptgebot. Eine Untersuchung literarischer Einleitungsfragen zu Dtn 5-11* (AnBibl, 20), Rome, 1963.

4. Les ch. 1-3 sont souvent considérés comme l'introduction originelle de l'«histoire deutéronomiste» (Josué-Rois), suivant la thèse de M. NOTH, *Überlieferungsgeschichtliche Studien I*, Halle, 1943; voir l'état de la question présenté par H. D. PREUSS, *Deuteronomium*, pp. 75-84, qui se rallie d'ailleurs à cette thèse tout en soulignant la complexité de la rédaction de ces chapitres. Deut 4,1-40 est habituellement considéré comme un morceau d'origine assez récente, lui-même complété par les vv. 41-43; seul le titre du v. 44 ou du v. 45 peut avoir fait partie de l'Ur-Deuteronomium; voir notamment F. GARCÍA LÓPEZ, *Analyse*, p. 506. Rappelons que certains auteurs anciens limitaient le recueil trouvé (ou produit) sous Josias à la partie proprement législative du Deutéronome: J.S. VATER,

de Josias. — L'appel à aimer Yahvé et lui seul (6,4-9) a fait partie du texte de base et y a joué un rôle important. — Ce texte de base a été enrichi à plusieurs reprises, les éléments les plus récents étant qualifiés de «deutéronomistes» (Dtr) et assignés à un ou plusieurs rédacteur(s) de l'époque exilique.

S'il est vrai que Deut 5-11 compte plusieurs strates littéraires, de quels critères disposons-nous pour en déterminer le nombre ainsi que la chronologie relative, le contenu précis et le *Sitz im Leben* concret de chacune? Comme l'a fait remarquer N. Lohfink dans un article récent [5], les analyses portant sur la langue et le vocabulaire ne sont ici guère décisives, car tous les textes se situent à l'intérieur d'une même école, et les relectures successives entraînent aussi la reprise d'éléments plus anciens; outre les indices de rupture stylistique, c'est donc le contenu même — le kérygme — du texte et son déplacement par rapport au message antérieur qui fournira le critère essentiel. Encore faut-il que ce kérygme puisse être lui-même situé. À cet égard, les sections narratives offrent a priori une meilleure prise que les sections parénétiques, car elles permettent la comparaison avec des passages parallèles en Ex 19-34. Comme ce dernier texte est lui-même controversé, je commencerai par exposer aussi brièvement que possible l'histoire probable de sa rédaction [6]. Je serai alors à pied d'œuvre pour entreprendre la lecture comparée des deux textes (Ex 19-34 et Deut 5,1-6,3+9,7-10,11), ce qui me permettra enfin de tirer quelques conclusions concernant la *Redaktionsgeschichte* du livre.

I. La formation d'Ex 19-34

A défaut d'une analyse littéraire complète du texte, évidemment impossible dans le cadre de cette étude, je me contenterai d'en résumer les conclusions, quitte à en justifier les points principaux.

Commentar über den Pentateuch, t. 3, Halle, 1805, p. 461; J. Wellhausen, *Die Composition des Hexateuch und der historischen Bücher des Alten Testaments*, 4e ed., Berlin, 1963; voir aussi, plus récemment, O. Eissfeldt, *Einleitung in das Alte Testament*, 3e éd., Tübingen, 1964, p. 309, qui fait remarquer l'absence d'introduction historique ou parénétique tant pour le *Bundesbuch* que pour Lév 17-26.

5. N. Lohfink, *Kerygmata des Deuteronomistischen Geschichtswerks*, dans J. Jeremias-L. Perlitt (éd.), *Die Botschaft und die Boten. Festschrift für H. W. Wolff*, Neukirchen, 1981, pp. 87-100 (p. 89).

6. En ce qui concerne Ex 32-34, j'ai exposé mon argumentation dans *L'affaire du veau d'or et ses conséquences. Une clé pour la «question deutéronomiste»?*, à paraître dans *ZAW* 96 (1984). On voudra bien s'y reporter pour tout ce qui concerne ces chapitres; je ne fais ici qu'en reprendre les grandes lignes.

1. *Le document J.*

Les études d'Ex 19-34 antérieures au grand bouleversement actuel de l'exégèse du Pentateuque assignent à J de larges sections du texte [7]. Pour ma part, je reste convaincu de l'existence d'un document J remontant à l'époque salomonienne [8], même s'il se confirme que le sigle «J» de l'exégèse classique confondait des matériaux de diverses origines et que le «vrai» J proposait sans doute un texte assez court [9]. En ce qui concerne Ex 19-34, aucun des passages traditionnellement assignés à J n'utilise le langage ni ne développe la pensée de cet auteur, sinon une seule phrase, conservée en 19,2a: «Ils partirent de Rephîdîm et atteignirent le désert du Sinaï, et ils campèrent dans le désert.» Cette phrase suit l'épisode du combat avec Amaleq à Rephîdîm (17,8-13* J) et semble trouver son prolongement immédiat en Nb 10,29-32. En d'autres termes, J paraît avoir ignoré les événements liés à la montagne sainte; pour lui, le Sinaï est une simple étape sur la route.

2. *L'apport de E.*

La base du récit des événements liés à la montagne divine remonte, semble-t-il, à la rédaction élohiste du VIIIe siècle [10]. Se révélant dans la

7. On assigne le plus souvent à J l'essentiel d'Ex 19 et la base des ch. 32-34; certains y ajoutent des éléments de la section 24,1-15. Les commentateurs insistent cependant sur la complexité de la question, et nombreux sont ceux qui renoncent à y voir clair; ainsi R. de VAUX, *Histoire ancienne d'Israël* (É B) t. 1, Paris, 1971, p. 374, à propos des passages pré-sacerdotaux: «La critique littéraire de ces pièces est à peu près désespérée». Elle l'est, en effet, si l'on ne sort pas des cadres de la théorie documentaire classique.

8. J. VERMEYLEN, *La formation du Pentateuque à la lumière de l'exégèse historico-critique*, dans *RTL* 12 (1981) 324-346. Voir aussi, dans le sens de la reconnaissance d'un J «salomonien», malgré les objections de H. H. Schmid, R. Rendtorff, M. Rose et d'autres: L. SCHMIDT, *Ueberlegungen zum Jahwisten*, dans *EvTh* 37 (1977) 230-247; F. CRÜSEMANN, *Der Widerstand gegen das Königtum* (WMANT, 49), Neukirchen, 1978, pp. 167-180; F. NIEDNER, *The Date of the Yahwist Source of the Pentateuch and its Role in the History of Israelite Tradition*, diss. Christ Sem.-Seminex, 1979 (cfr. DissAbstr 41 [1980-1981] 1657A); A.F. CAMPBELL, *The Yahwist Revisited*, dans *AustralBiblRev* 27 (1979) 2-14; W.H. SCHMIDT, *Ein Theologe in salomonischer Zeit? Plaidoyer für den Jahwisten*, dans *BZ* n.s. 25 (1981) 82-102; F. CRÜSEMANN, *Die Eigenständigkeit der Urgeschichte. Ein Beitrag zur Diskussion um den «Jahwisten»*, dans J. JEREMIAS - L. PERLITT (éd.), *Die Botschaft*, pp. 11-29; R. NORTH, *Can Geography save J from Rendtorff?*, dans *Bib* 63 (1982) 47-55; E. ZENGER, *Auf der Suche nach einem Weg aus der Pentateuchkrise*, dans *Theologische Revue* 78 (1982) 353-362.

9. Un grand nombre de passages réputés «J» sont en fait postérieurs; ceci ne préjuge pas de l'extension du récit à partir de Gen 2.

10. La question de l'apport élohiste au Pentateuque, très discutée autrefois, est aujourd'hui éclipsée par l'interrogation plus fondamentale portant sur J et sur l'ensemble de la formation du Pentateuque. Comme je l'ai expliqué brièvement dans l'article mentionné plus haut (voir *supra*, note 8), la consistance stylistique et théologique d'un ensemble de matériaux de type «E» me paraît assurée; je crois cependant que l'Elohiste ne forme pas une tradition indépendante de J. Dans la même ligne, voir H.-C. SCHMITT, *Die*

nuée et l'orage, Dieu s'entretient avec Moïse (19,2b-3a.16aβb-17.19) [11] et lui révèle le Décalogue (20,1-17*) [12]. Moïse invite le peuple qui se tient à

nichtpriesterliche Josephsgeschichte (BZAW, 154), Berlin-New York, 1980, pp. 177-184, qui situe cependant E après l'Exil, alors qu'on y retrouve plutôt le point de vue théologique des «prophètes de la conversion» de la seconde moitié du VIIIe siècle.

11. Les vv. 2b-3a s'appuient sur la notice J du v. 2a: E identifie le lieu du campement dans le désert avec la montagne de Dieu, qui est déjà celle du Buisson (3,1b* E); sur l'appartenance de ces vv. 2b-3a à E, voir notamment W. BEYERLIN, *Herkunft und Geschichte der ältesten Sinaitraditionen*, Tübingen, 1961, p. 13; H. CAZELLES, art. *Pentateuque*, dans *SupplDictBibl*, t. 7, Paris, 1966, c. 787; E. ZENGER, *Die Sinaitheophanie. Untersuchungen zum jahwistischen und elohistischen Geschichtswerk* (Fzb, 3), Würzburg-Stuttgart, 1971, pp. 149, 166. La répartition des strates à l'intérieur de la scène de la théophanie proprement dite est discutée. On y trouve au moins deux mains différentes, ainsi que l'attestent l'alternance des noms divins (Elohim: vv. 17,19; Yahvé: vv. 18,20a, 20b) et la double présentation des événements (orage: vv. 16,19; éruption volcanique: v. 18). L'usage du mot Elohim et le rapprochement avec 20,18-21 permettent d'attribuer les vv. 16aβ-17.19 à E; telle est d'ailleurs l'opinion classique, rappelée par H. H. SCHMID, *Der sogenannte Jahwist*, Zurich, 1976, p. 98. Les vv. 16aα (à mettre en relation directe avec le v. 15), 18 et 20 ne sont pas l'œuvre de J, comme on le propose généralement, mais plutôt celle de P. En effet, on retrouve aux vv. 18 et 20 la représentation de la «descente» (*yārad*) de Yahvé sur la montagne, comme au v. 11 et aussi en Ex 34,5 P; dans les traditions anciennes, contrairement à Ex 19, la descente de Yahvé a pour objet la destruction de ses ennemis, ainsi que le souligne F. SCHNUTTENHAUS, *Das Kommen und Erscheinen Gottes im Alten Testament*, dans *ZAW* 76 (1964) 1-22. Le rédacteur semble s'appuyer sur le récit E, qui ne pourrait donc être qu'antérieur. C'est ainsi que le tremblement (*wayyèḥᵉrad*, v. 18) de la montagne paraît être une transposition du tremblement (*wayyèḥᵉrad*, v. 16 E) du peuple terrorisé. De cette transposition résulte le passage du motif de la nuée (*ʿānan*, v. 16 E) à celui de la fumée (*ʿāšān*, v. 18). L'origine sacerdotale de ces versets est encore confirmée par l'emploi de l'expression *har sînay*, «mont Sinaï» (cfr Ex 19,11,23; 24,16; 31,18; 34,2,4,29,32; Nb 3,1; 28,6), et du mot *kibšān*, «fournaise, fourneau» (cfr Ex 9,8, 10 P). D'ailleurs, le rédacteur de Deut 5, qui s'appuie très probablement sur Ex 19-20, ne semble pas connaître les vv. 16aα,18,20.

12. On a depuis longtemps fait remarquer que les vv. 18-21 ne font pas référence à la proclamation des commandements, mais à la théophanie (19,16-19*); surtout, on n'y trouve aucune manifestation d'assentiment du peuple. Cette observation a conduit de nombreux auteurs à en conclure que le Décalogue était originellement placé après le v. 21; voir encore H. GESE, *Der Dekalog als Ganzheit betrachtet*, dans *ZThK* n.s. 64 (1967) 121-138 (p. 122); R. de VAUX, *Histoire*, t. 1, p. 373. Cette reconstruction est arbitraire et peu vraisemblable, car de tels déplacements sont très rares dans l'Ancien Testament, et on ne voit pas quel motif impérieux aurait pu le provoquer; aussi est-elle aujourd'hui de plus en plus abandonnée. Une autre solution est donc proposée: le Décalogue est une pièce indépendante insérée dans le récit par un rédacteur postérieur à E; voir notamment M. NOTH, *Das zweite Buch Mose*, p. 124; L. PERLITT, *Bundestheologie im Alten Testament* (WMANT, 36), Neukirchen, 1969, pp. 91-92; F.-L. HOSSFELD, *Der Dekalog* (OBO, 45), Fribourg-Göttingen, 1982, pp. 172-176. On se heurte cependant ici à une autre difficulté: sans le Décalogue, la théophanie n'a pas d'objet, ce qui serait probablement un cas unique dans l'Ancien Testament. En outre, le v. 1 — qui provient évidemment du rédacteur responsable de l'insertion du Décalogue dans on contexte actuel — comporte le nom divin *ʾᵉlōhîm*, qui ne semble pratiquement plus utilisé que par E au-delà d'Ex 6. Mieux vaut donc s'en tenir à l'hypothèse la plus simple: quelles que soient l'origine et la forme primitive du Décalogue, c'est E qui l'a inséré dans le récit de la théophanie, comme l'atteste le cadre rédactionnel formé par les vv. 1 et 20-21. Le rédacteur E aura repris le Décalogue préexistant pour en faire le centre de sa narration, et il est normal que les expressions de son

distance, à ne pas craindre; lui seul s'approchera de Dieu (20,21-22) [13]. Il gravit en effet la montagne et reçoit les Tables écrites de la main de Dieu, contenant le texte du Décalogue (31,18*; 32,15-16*) [14]. Le récit est donc très simple: il ne comprend qu'une seule ascension sur la montagne, avec le don d'une seule législation — le Décalogue primitif — et ne paraît pas connaître l'épisode du veau d'or.

3. *L'apport deutéronomiste*

La question des rédactions deutéronomistes d'Ex 19-34 est plus compliquée mais aussi plus décisive pour notre propos. Il faut, en effet, distinguer ici quatre niveaux différents, ainsi qu'en témoignent autant de points de vue sur l'histoire du veau d'or.

cadre rédactionnel se correspondent. L'absence d'adhésion du peuple ne doit pas étonner: un tel motif littéraire semble répondre avant tout au souci juridique de bien établir l'engagement conscient et unanime dans l'Alliance, et donc aussi sa culpabilité lors de la rupture de celle-ci (ch. 32-34); ce motif littéraire est deutéronomiste (Ex 19,8; 24,3,7; Jos 24,21-24). La question du Décalogue «primitif» et de ses remaniements sera abordée plus loin.

13. Ces versets forment la seconde partie du cadre E entourant le Décalogue; leur attribution classique à E se justifie par la mention répétée du nom *'ᵉlōhîm* et par les thèmes de l'épreuve (*nassôt*, v. 20a; cfr *nissāh*, Gen 22,1 E) et de la crainte de Dieu (*yir'ātô*, v. 20; cfr *yir'at 'ᵉlōhîm*, Gen 22,11 E), qui ne sont toutefois pas l'apanage de E. Contrairement à l'opinion habituelle, l'apport de E n'inclut pas les vv. 18-19. En effet, E. ZENGER, *Die Sinaitheophanie*, pp. 66-67, a fait remarquer que le v. 20 répond mal à la demande du peuple (v. 19) et que le nom divin *'ᵉlōhîm* est utilisé tantôt sans (v. 19) et tantôt avec l'article (vv. 20,21); voir aussi F.-L. HOSSFELD, *Der Dekalog*, p. 172, qui attribue en conséquence les vv. 18-19 à un rédacteur sacerdotal dépendant de Deut 5 (173-175). L'argument de l'article est sans doute insuffisant, car la même variation s'observe dans plusieurs autres péricopes élohistes; voir notamment Gen 20,6,13,17 (où les deux formes se succèdent); 22,1,3,8,9,12. Je crois cependant qu'il faut donner raison à F.-L. Hossfeld. En effet, le v. 18 emprunte au récit E plusieurs éléments de la théophanie: le tonnerre (*qôlōt*, cfr 19,16) et le son de trompe (*qôl haššōpʰār*, cfr 19,16,19); il y mêle cependant des données qui ne répondent plus, comme dans E, à la manifestation dans l'orage, mais à la description de l'éruption volcanique, comme en P: les torches (*lappîdîm*; cfr Gen 15,17; Jg 7,16,20; 15,4,5; etc.) et la montagne fumante (*hāhār 'āšén*, cfr 19,18). En outre, la littérature sacerdotale souligne plus que d'autres le danger mortel d'un contact trop immédiat avec Yahvé, comme au v. 18; voir notamment Ex 19,21; 33,20; Lév 16,2; Nb 4,20; Deut 5,26 P.

14. Ex 31,18 comporte des expressions sacerdotales: *bᵉhar sînay*, «sur le mont Sinai», et *šᵉnéy luḥōt hā'édut*, «les deux tables du pacte». Cette dernière expression fait cependant concurrence avec *luḥōt 'èbèn*, «les tables de pierre», si bien qu'il faut la considérer comme une addition probable. Débarrassé de ses surcharges P, le verset peut être considéré comme élohiste à cause de l'emploi du nom divin et de la nécessité du récit: la scène d'Ex 20,20-21 requiert une suite qu'on chercherait vainement ailleurs, et le don des Tables y convient tout-à-fait. On trouve en 32,15-16 la suite logique de 31,18* E et la conclusion du récit; ces versets utilisent l'expression *hāhar*, «la montagne» (v. 15; cfr 19,2b,16,17 E) et le nom divin *'ᵉlōhîm* (v. 16, deux fois), ce qui confirme l'origine élohiste. Encore une fois, le texte ancien a été surchargé par une glose sacerdotale (*šᵉnéy luḥōt hā'édut*, v. 15, cfr 31,18).

a. La première rédaction deutéronomiste (Dtr585) [15].

Dans une première version, Moïse intercède pour le peuple pécheur, et Yahvé concède un délai de grâce: il ne punira pas Israël immédiatement, mais au jour de sa Visite (32,34b); le rédacteur essaye sans doute d'expliquer ainsi pourquoi Yahvé semble avoir rejeté son peuple lors de la ruine de Jérusalem en 587 [16]. Il écrit vraisemblablement peu après la catastrophe, alors que Yahvé était accusé d'injustice envers les siens.

15. Au risque d'alimenter encore l'actuelle inflation en matière de sigles, je propose de distinguer les quatre rédactions deutéronomistes à l'aide de leurs dates présumées, à quelques années près; ces dates ne doivent évidemment pas être comprises comme des points de repère tout-à-fait précis. Ces sigles permettent d'éviter toute confusion avec d'autres systèmes, notamment ceux qui ont été proposés à propos de l'«histoire deutéronomiste» (F.-M. Cross: dtr I et dtr II; R. Smend: DtrG ou DtrH, DtrP, DtrN1, DtrN2); ils permettent en outre d'y ajouter, si nécessaire, des étapes intermédiaires.

16. Cette affirmation conditionne toute la suite de cette étude, aussi faut-il s'assurer de sa solidité. Lors de sa visite punitive, Yahvé va exécuter ce qu'il avait décidé au v. 10: exterminer (*kālāh*) son peuple. Ce texte se greffe sur le récit E et ne peut donc être antérieur au VIIIe siècle. Dans quel contexte a-t-on pu raconter une telle histoire, sinon au moment où Israël vivait un terrible malheur et éprouvait la nécessité de justifier la conduite de Yahvé par le recours au récit du «péché originel» du peuple au temps de Moïse? Ainsi, le châtiment n'est pas reporté à un futur indéterminé, comme on l'écrit trop souvent, mais à l'époque même où vit le narrateur; c'est ainsi seulement que le récit prend toute sa force. Remarquons qu'il n'est pas question d'une punition «médicinale», douloureuse mais en fin de compte salutaire: le v. 10 parle d'une destruction d'Israël en tant que tel, sans aucune perspective de renouveau ultérieur (la finale est un ajout plus récent), et, s'il la reporte à une époque ultérieure, le v. 34 n'atténue en rien cette perspective. Seul, le drame de 587 correspond à ce tableau: avec les horreurs du siège, la ruine du Temple, la fin de la monarchie davidique et la dispersion du peuple, il devait être clair que Yahvé rejetait Israël comme peuple élu et l'anéantissait en tant que nation; ce drame a d'ailleurs suscité une énorme vague de révolte contre un Dieu dont les actes paraissaient tout-à-coup monstrueux, et c'est en réponse aux accusations lancées contre Yahvé que l'école deutéronomiste a voulu répondre en montrant à travers toute l'histoire que la justice divine ne s'est jamais démentie. Ce souci de montrer la justice de Yahvé à des gens qui la contestent transparaît dans une foule de textes du début de la période exilique; voir notamment Deut 28,15-68; 29,21-27; 31,16-18; Jos 23,15-16; 24,19-27; Jg 2,11-19*; 1 Rois 9,1-9; 2 Rois 17,7-23; Is 5,1-7 Dtr; Jér 5,19; 16,10-13; 22,8-9 (tous Dtr). Remarquons en outre que le verbe *pāqad*, «visiter», est encore utilisé en Am 3,2 Dtr pour annoncer le grand châtiment d'Israël; sur l'origine deutéronomiste de ce verset, voir J. VERMEYLEN, *Du prophète Isaïe à l'apocalyptique* (ÉB), t. 2, Paris, 1978, pp. 543-544. On objectera: la chute de Samarie ne fournit-elle pas, elle aussi, un contexte historique approprié? Cette objection ne paraît pas devoir être retenue. En effet, s'il est vrai que les événements de 722 furent, eux aussi, dramatiques, ils ne mettaient en cause ni l'existence d'Israël en tant que peuple, ni la pérennité de son lien privilégié avec Yahvé, ce qui semble pourtant postulé par Ex 32,10 et 34*; il est significatif que la ruine de Samarie n'a provoqué aucun mouvement de contestation de Yahvé dont la Bible aurait gardé le souvenir; contemporains des événements, Isaïe et Michée ne semblent même pas avoir éprouvé le besoin de les commenter (Is 8,14 est antérieur à 722, de même que Mi 1,2-7*; voir par exemple B. RENAUD, *La formation du livre de Michée*, Paris, 1977, p. 58). Une première rédaction de l'histoire du veau d'or à la fin du VIIIe siècle est donc très improbable.

Il faut sans doute attribuer au même auteur les textes suivants, indispensables à la logique du récit:

20,2-6: Les deux premiers commandements du Décalogue, violés par l'adoration du veau d'or [17].

32,7-8a.9-10a: Sur la montagne, Yahvé révèle à Moïse le forfait d'Israel et exprime sa colère. (Le récit se poursuit en 32,15-16* E: Moïse descend de la montagne avec les Tables).

32,19-20abα: Moïse voit le veau et le culte qui lui est rendu: il brise les Tables, puis détruit l'idole.

32,30-32a.33aα.34aαb: Moïse intercède auprès de Yahvé, qui consent à retarder le châtiment mérité jusqu'au jour de sa Visite.

34,1.4*.28b*.29a*: Yahvé donne à Moïse de nouvelles Tables, écrites de sa main, avec les «dix paroles», c'est-à-dire le texte du Décalogue (20,2-17*).

17. Ainsi que l'a fait remarquer M. LESTIENNE, *Les dix «paroles» et le décalogue*, dans *RB* 69 (1972) 484-510, les vv. 2-6 se distinguent du reste du Décalogue par plusieurs caractéristiques propres: leur ton plus parénétique, leur parallélisme beaucoup plus strict avec Deut 5, leur présentation de Yahvé à la première personne (et non à la troisième, comme à partir du v. 7), leur destinataire (le «tu» vise Israël, et non l'individu) et surtout leur composition concentrique, alors que les vv. 7-17 se présentent comme une composition linéaire. Ils forment un tout bien construit, dont on n'exclura pas le v. 4, ainsi que le propose M. Lestienne: il y a correspondance entre les vv. 2 et 5b-6, qui comportent chaque fois l'autoprésentation de Yahvé et s'ouvrent par la même phrase *'ānōkî YHWH 'ᵉlōhéykā*; de même, il y a correspondance entre les vv. 3-4 et 5a, qui interdisent chaque fois le culte des autres dieux à l'aide de deux verbes. Il est possible que le v. 4 appartenait — en tout ou en partie — à une forme plus ancienne du Décalogue et visait alors l'interdiction des images, y compris celles de Yahvé, ce qui expliquerait la longueur plus grande de cet élément; dans le texte actuel, en tout cas, il est interprété dans le sens d'une interdiction des idoles païennes. Quoi qu'il en soit de ce dernier point, et malgré l'appel à la prudence de N. LOHFINK, *Die These vom «deuteronomischen» Dekaloganfang — ein fragwürdiges Ergebnis atomistischer Sprachstatistik*, dans G. BRAULIK (éd.), *Studien zum Pentateuch. W. Kornfeld zum 60. Geburtstag*, Vienne, 1977, pp.99-109, Ex 20,2-6 présente des affinités significatives, tant sur le plan de la phraséologie que sur celui du contenu, avec la littérature D/Dtr, ainsi que l'a souligné en particulier L. PERLITT, *Bundestheologie*, pp. 83-86. Il faut concéder à N. Lohfink que plusieurs textes parallèles mentionnés à l'appui de l'origine D/Dtr de la péricope doivent être considérés comme dépendants eux-mêmes du Décalogue et ne peuvent donc pas entrer en considération. D'autres part, l'origine de nombreux textes utilisant les mêmes expressions que la première partie du Décalogue est incertaine, car certains les considèrent comme proto-deutéronomiques et très anciens, et d'autres comme Dtr (sans doute souvent avec raison). Même en tenant compte de ces observations, c'est encore — et de très loin — avec la littérature D/Dtr qu'Ex 20,2-6 présente les affinités les plus évidentes, ce qui invite donc à situer leur composition dans le même milieu. On doit cependant tenir compte d'une autre donnée: le récit Dtr585 du veau d'or (Ex 32-34*) suppose l'interdiction solennelle du culte des idoles formulée au début du Décalogue; c'est donc de préférence à cette strate qu'on assignera Ex 20,2-6. Si l'on tient compte du fait que le rédacteur initial de Deut 5 semble dépendre d'Ex 20 (voir *infra*) et qu'il tire sans doute de ce texte les phrases identiques dans les deux sections, il faut encore assigner au même rédacteur Dtr585 les vv. 7b, 9-10 et 12b; ces éléments apparaissent en effet comme adventices au Décalogue primitif. La question de ces derniers versets n'a cependant qu'une importance mineure pour notre propos.

b. La deuxième rédaction deutéronomiste (Dtr575).

Le deuxième rédacteur fait état du pardon sans réticence apparente de Yahvé, alors que Moïse se trouve encore sur la montagne (32,14); il répond visiblement à une accusation lancée contre Yahvé: s'il a fait tant de mal à son peuple, c'est qu'il est un Dieu mauvais (32,12). Le rédacteur va donc insister sur l'extraordinaire générosité de Yahvé, qui n'a cessé de pardonner un peuple toujours rebelle, jusqu'au jour où le châtiment est devenu inévitable. On peut vraisemblablement lui assigner les textes suivants:

20,22-23,33*: Le vieux «livre de l'Alliance» est introduit dans le récit en complément du Décalogue, grâce à un cadre rédactionnel sans doute formé de 20,22aα.24-26 et 23,20.23 [18].

18. Comme l'a fait remarquer, après d'autres, H. H. SCHMID, *Der sogenannte Jahwist*, p. 96, le *Bundesbuch* n'a pu trouver place dans la péricope du Sinaï qu'après le Décalogue et ne peut donc y avoir été inséré avant 587. D'autre part, il n'est pas évident que cette insertion soit postérieure à la rédaction de Deut 5, qui ne parle que du Décalogue sans faire allusion au Livre de l'Alliance, ainsi que l'estiment J. L'HOUR, *L'Alliance à Sichem*, dans *RB* 69 (1962) 350-355 et R. DE VAUX, *Histoire*, t. 1, pp. 373-374; en effet, comme je l'expliquerai, le *Bundesbuch* a dans le Deutéronome sa contrepartie avec le Code des ch. 12-26. On reconnaît depuis longtemps la facture deutéronomiste d'Ex 23,20-33, qui constitue la conclusion rédactionelle du discours ouvert en 20,22 et fait ainsi partie du cadre du *Bundesbuch*. Cette section est elle-même composite, et son élément le plus ancien paraît constitué par les vv. 20 et 23, qui parlent de l'envoi par Yahvé de son Ange, comme en 32,34aβ et 33,2, textes Dtr575, ainsi que je l'ai montré dans *L'affaire du veau*; on y trouve d'ailleurs également la liste des peuples occupant la terre promise. A cette finale paraît correspondre la section initiale 20,22aα.24-26, où l'on retrouve le même «tu» adressé, semble-t-il, à Moïse. On considère généralement la loi sur l'autel comme un reste du *Bundesbuch* primitif, en contradiction avec la loi deutéronomique de la centralisation du culte (Deut 12). En réalité, ces versets se trouvent en dehors du cadre législatif introduit par la formule «voici les prescriptions que tu leur donneras» (21,1); en outre, ils ont pour objet le culte, alors que le Code s'ouvre par les règles de la vie sociale et s'achève par les dispositions proprement religieuses. Si donc les vv. 24-26 sont issus du Code de l'Alliance primitif, ils sont déplacés, et il faut expliquer par qui et pourquoi ils ont été mis en évidence, en tête de l'ensemble, opération peu imaginable avant l'insertion du recueil dans son cadre littéraire actuel; son auteur serait donc Dtr (ou un rédacteur plus récent), ce qui ramène au problème de la contradiction avec Deut 12, qui a joué un rôle déterminant dans la théorie wellhausénienne de la formation du Pentateuque. A ce sujet, il ne faut pas se faire de la théologie deutéronomiste une idée trop simple, comme si elle interdisait «en soi» tout autre lieu de culte que le Temple de Jérusalem. Au contraire, Dtr semble envisager plusieurs étapes dans l'histoire religieuse du peuple, comme le dit explicitement Deut 12,8-12, et il faut tenir compte d'une diversité de points de vue à l'intérieur de l'école deutéronomiste. Certains textes parlent d'une absence de sacrifices pendant le séjour au désert (2 Sam 7,6-7; Am 5,25; etc.). D'autres passages parlent de la construction d'un autel de pierres brutes (comme en Ex 20,25!) sur le mont Ébal: Deut 27,5-6; Jos 8,30-31 Dtr; voir également Jg 6,26; 13,19; 21,4; 1 Sam 7,9; 13,9. Il semble donc que, dans l'esprit d'un rédactuer deutéronomiste au moins, la construction du Temple de Salomon était précédée d'une période où il était permis d'offrir des sacrifices en différents lieux choisis par Yahvé. La loi sur l'autel trouve son application concrète en Ex 24,4-5 Dtr575, où Moïse bâtit un autel et fait offrir des holocaustes et des sacrifices de paix.

24,2-5.8: L'accord du peuple aux paroles divines est solennisé par la cérémonie de l'aspersion du sang [19].

24,12-13*: Sur l'ordre de Yahvé, Moïse gravit la montagne [20].

32,11-12.14: Avant de redescendre, Moïse intercède pour Israël, et Yahvé accorde son pardon.

33,2-4.12-17: Yahvé envoie Israël vers la terre promise et lui délègue son Ange. Moïse demande à Yahvé d'accompagner lui-même son peuple; encore une fois, le Dieu d'Israël se laisse fléchir.

33,21.22b; 34,6-7: Le passage de Yahvé devant Moïse, avec la formule kerygmatique inspirée par 20,5b-7, mais inversée et modifiée en vue de souligner la bonté divine.

c. La troisième rédaction deutéronomiste (Dtr560).

Alors que l'accent avait été placé précédemment sur le pardon divin, un troisième rédacteur parle cette fois d'un châtiment immédiat du peuple coupable (32,35abα), selon le principe énoncé au v. 33: «Celui qui a péché contre moi, c'est lui que j'effacerai de mon livre.» Ces additions font écho à la question de la seconde génération du temps de la ruine de Jérusalem: allons-nous payer pour les fautes de nos pères? Le rédacteur répond: seule, la génération coupable est punie, ce qui laisse

19. Comme je l'indiquerai plus loin, les vv. 6-7 semblent former une addition deutéronomiste plus récente, calquée sur les vv. 3 et 8. La partie plus ancienne de la péricope n'est pas pré-deutéronomiste pour autant. Ainsi, au v. 3a, Moïse fait rapport au peuple des *d^ebārîm* et des *mišpāṭîm*, c'est-à-dire respectivement du Décalogue (cfr *d^ebārîm*, 20,1) et du *Bundesbuch* (cfr *mišpāṭîm*, 21,1), qui viennent d'être énoncés; la péricope suit d'ailleurs immédiatement le Code de l'Alliance, car les vv. 1-2 sont plus récents. Ceci correspond à l'addition du *Bundesbuch* par Dtr575. De même aux vv. 4 et 5, la construction de l'autel ainsi que l'offrande des holocaustes et des sacrifices de communion répondent à 20,24-25, l'introduction Dtr575 du *Bundesbuch*. Ajoutons que la réponse du peuple formulée au v. 3b peut être rapprochée d'Ex 19,8a Dtr et de Jos 24,16-24 Dtr. L'érection de douze stèles, une par tribu, (v. 4) est analogue au placement des douze pierres lors de la traversée du Jourdain en Jos 4,1-9, texte dont la rédaction actuelle est deutéronomiste même si la péricope contient des matériaux plus anciens; on retrouve en Gen 31,44a.45 Dtr et Jos 24,25-27 Dtr les stèles érigées comme témoins d'un pacte. Le caractère rituel de la scène ne suffit pas à écarter l'origine deutéronomiste de la péricope, ainsi que l'estime E. W. NICHOLSON, *The Covenant Ritual in Exodus XXIV 3-8*, dans *VT* 32 (1982) 74-86 (pp. 81-82), à la suite de D. J. McCarthy et A. D. H. Mayes: le rite sert à souligner le caractère solennel, unanime et irrévocable de l'engagement d'Israël envers Yahvé et sa parole (*ʿal kol-d^ebārîm hāʾéllèh*, v. 8b); il ne doit pas être opposé au souci deutéronomiste d'une fidélité aux commandements; voir, en parallèle, l'évocation du rite d'auto-imprécation en Jér 34,18-20 Dtr.

20. Ces versets sont souvent attribués à E, à cause de l'expression *har hāʾ^elōhîm*, «la montagne de Dieu» (v. 13b); il faut cependant relever la mention de Yahvé au v. 12a, tandis que le mot *ʾ^elōhîm* peut ne pas être utilisé comme nom propre, mais comme substantif; il est possible que, seul, le v. 13b remonte à E, mais ce n'est même pas nécessaire car 20,21 E dit déjà que Moïse s'approche de la nuée obscure. Par ailleurs, on reconnaît en général, avec raison, deux gloses deutéronomistes: *w^ehattôrāh w^ehammiṣwāh* (v. 12b) et *wîhôšuaʿ m^ešārtô* (v. 13a); la mention de Josué est évidemment ajoutée, comme en témoigne le verbe au singulier (*wayyaʿal*, «il monta»). L'essentiel des vv. 12-13 semble donc être l'œuvre d'un des premiers rédacteurs Dtr, mais il est impossible de trancher avec certitude entre Dtr585, Dtr575 et Dtr560.

entrevoir une fin prochaine du malheur; voir, dans le même perspective, Deut 7,9-10. Cette problématique est encore celle du thème deutéronomiste du séjour de 40 ans au désert: telle est la durée nécessaire pour que la génération coupable ait péri; voir Nb 14,20-23.27-35; Deut 1,34-35.39; 2,14-16. Ceci suggère une date voisine de 560, soit une petite quarantaine d'années après le premier exil de 598 (voir aussi le signe de la réhabilitation de Yoyakin en 2 Rois 25,27-30). On peut attribuer à cette strate les additions que voici:

19,9: Yahvé annonce qu'il se manifestera afin que le peuple croie en Moïse [21].

23,21-22.24-33*: Conseils de fidélité au premier commandement et promesses conditionnelles de bonheur [22].

32,32b.33aβb.35abα: Yahvé punit immédiatement les coupables, et nul autre.

33,1: Moïse est invité à monter au pays promis, selon la promesse faite aux ancêtres (relecture du v. 2).

33,5-6: Israël redevient docile à la volonté divine et échappe ainsi à l'extermination (relecture des vv. 3-4).

33,12b-14: Prière de Moïse qui demande à Yahvé de lui faire connaître ses voies, et réponse favorable de Yahvé (relecture des vv. 12a.15-17).

34,8-10a.11-12.14-28a: En réponse à une nouvelle demande de Moïse, Yahvé renouvelle ses recommandations (insertion du «Décalogue cultuel»). On peut y reconnaître le style de la parénèse en «tu».

d. La quatrième rédaction deutéronomiste (Dtr525).

Un dernier rédacteur deutéronomiste, enfin, distingue un groupe de coupables, lié à Aaron, et un groupe fidèle à Yahvé, dont les champions sont Moïse et les lévites (32,1-6,25-29,35bβ). Cette rédaction, qui désigne Aaron et donc le sacerdoce qui se réclame de lui comme coupable, a pu voir le jour dans le contexte du retour des déportés, guidés précisément par les prêtres; c'est à cette époque (vers 525-520, selon S. Hermann) [23], que se manifeste, en effet, l'opposition des gens restés au pays contre le

21. Ce verset, qui a été attribué à toutes les traditions possibles, a pour fonction essentielle d'interpréter la théophanie comme suscitant la foi du peuple en Moïse. Cette même préoccupation. est exprimée en Ex 4,5 Dtr et surtout 14,31 Dtr. Selon toute vraisemblance, le v. 9 émane de l'école deutéronomiste qui commente le récit E, auquel il emprunte le motif de la nuée (*ʿānān*, cfr v. 16E); voir notamment H.-Chr. SCHMITT, *Redaktion des Pentateuch im Geiste der Prophetie*, dans *VT* 32 (1982) 170-189 (p. 177).

22. Ces versets commentent Ex 23,20.33 Dtr575 (voir la reprise partielle de la liste des peuples au v. 28) dans un sens surtout parénétique. On y reconnaît en général un texte deutéronomiste au moins en substance, car apparenté à Deut 7; voir par exemple M. NOTH, *Das zweite Buch Mose*, p. 140; H. HORN, *Traditionsschichten in Ex 23,10-33 und 34,10-26*, dans *BZ* n.s. 15 (1971) 203-222. Etant donné sa proche parenté avec Ex 34,10-26, on assignera de préférence ce texte à la même strate Dtr560. Ceci convient tout-à-fait: il est postérieur aux vv. 20 et 23 Dtr575 et lui-même glosé aux vv. 21 et 25a par des additions Dtr525 (voir *infra*).

23. S. HERRMANN, *Geschichte Israels in alttestamentlicher Zeit*, Munich, 1973, pp. 368-370; voir déjà A.H.J. GUNNEWEG, *Geschichte Israels bis Bar Kochba*, Stuttgart, 1972, p. 125.

projet de reconstruction du Temple, ainsi que contre l'autorité du davidide Zorobabel et du grand-prêtre Josué [24]. Encore une fois, cette rédaction semble avoir produit de nombreuses additions:

19,3b-8: Par l'intermédiaire de Moïse, Yahvé promet à Israël que celui-ci sera son peuple particulier, à condition qu'il garde son Alliance. Le peuple s'engage à la fidélité [25].

20,22aβ-23: Toujours par l'intermédiaire de Moïse, Yahvé rappelle au peuple l'interdiction du culte des idoles [26].

23,21bα et 25aα: Deux gloses qui soulignent la nécessité de servir Yahvé [27].

24,13aβ: La mention de Josué, qui accompagne Moïse, permet de le disculper: il n'était pas avec le peuple coupable; cfr 32,17-18 [28].

24. Voir Esdr 4,1-4, texte écrit cependant longtemps après les événements et déformant peut-être les faits dans une optique partisane. On remarquera, de même, que la Pâque de 515 est célébrée au Temple rebâti non par l'ensemble de la population, mais par les Juifs revenus d'Exil et ceux qui se sont rangés dans leur camp (Esdr 6,19-22). L'existence d'une opposition puissante à Zorobabel et Josué est postulée par l'insistance de Za 1,16; 3,1-10; 4,1-10; 6,9-15 et Ag 1,1-2,9; 2,20-23.

25. La rédaction deutéronomiste de cette section est admise par de nombreux auteurs; l'argumentation la plus complète a été présentée par L. PERLITT, *Bundestheologie*, pp. 167-181, et par F.-L. HOSSFELD, *Der Dekalog*, pp. 185-189. Ce dernier auteur précise: «Will man dabei weiter differenzieren, dann spricht vieles für eine der späteren dtr Redaktionen» (p. 188). Ceci rejoint d'une certaine façon l'opinion des auteurs qui, constatant les affinités de la péricope avec Dtr mais aussi la présence d'expressions propres parfois proches de P, lui assignent une origine post-deutéronomiste; voir en particulier M. HAELVOET, *La théophanie du Sinaï*, dans *ETL* 29 (1953) 374-397 (pp. 375-380); H. CAZELLES, *Alliance du Sinaï, Alliance de l'Horeb et renouvellement de l'Alliance*, dans *Beiträge zur alttestamentlichen Theologie. Festschrift W. Zimmerli*, Göttingen, 1977, pp. 69-79 (pp. 78-79). De toute manière, la péricope n'appartient pas à la même strate que le v. 9 Dtr560, car les vv. 8b et 9b sont presque identiques, ce qui dénote un phénomène de relecture. Remarquons la formulation du discours en «vous», qui correspond à 32,13 et 34,13 Dtr525.

26. L'origine deutéronomiste secondaire de ces versets est reconnue notamment par E. ZENGER, *Die Sinaithophanie*, pp. 109-110,117,213. Cette hypothèse peut s'appuyer sur des arguments de poids. Au v. 22a, la formule *kōh tō'mar 'èl-bᵉnéy yiśrā'él*, «tu parleras ainsi aux Israélites», résume l'expression double *kōh tō'mar lᵉbéyt ya'ᵃqōb wᵉtaggéyd libnéy yiśrā'él*, «tu parleras ainsi à la maison de Jacob, tu déclareras aux Israélites» (19,3b Dtr525). De même, le discours à transmettre s'ouvre au v. 22b comme en 19,4 Dtr525 par les mêmes mots *'attèm rᵉ'îtèm*, «vous avez vu vous-mêmes». La révélation du Décalogue «du haut du ciel» (v. 22b) ne correspond pas au récit ancien, où Dieu parlait de la montagne, mais à Deut 4,36. Enfin, le v. 23 rappelle l'interdiction des idoles (cfr 20,2-6), comme Deut 4,9-24.

27. Ces phrases se distinguent du contexte par leur emploi de la deuxième personne du pluriel, comme 34,13 Dtr525.

28. Comme il a déjà été noté, l'addition est d'autant plus évidente que le verbe *wayya'al* est au singulier. La montée de Josué n'est pas préparée par l'ordre divin du verset précédent, qui ne concerne que Moïse; elle n'est mentionnée que pour permettre l'insertion de 32,17-18 Dtr525. Au v. 12, les mots *wᵉhattôrāh wᵉhammiṣwāh* proviennent probablement du même rédacteur.

24,14-15a: Cette addition attire l'attention sur la présence d'Aaron comme responsable du peuple et prépare ainsi 32,1-6 [29].
32,1-6: La fabrication du veau, sous l'autorité d'Aaron.
32,8b: Glose harmonisante, qui reprend le v. 4b.
32,10b et 13: Ces additions soulignent la distinction entre Moïse et le peuple; elles réaffirment la promesse de multiplication faite aux patriarches.
32,17-18: Addition destinée à disculper Josué, qui sera le successeur de Moïse.
32,25-29: Envoyés par Moïse, les lévites massacrent 3000 coupables; la responsabilité d'Aaron est réaffirmée.
32,35bβ: Correction: c'est Aaron qui a fabriqué le veau.
34,10aβb: Annonce des merveilles que Yahvé réalisera pour son peuple.
34,13: Ordre de détruire les objets des cultes païens.

Ce me paraît important de remarquer, c'est qu'Ex 19-34 comporte un certain nombre de passages apparentés à la parénèse du Deutéronome: ils appartiennent tous à la troisième ou à la quatrième rédaction deutéronomiste.

4. *L'apport sacerdotal ou apparenté.*

Relevons enfin les matériaux d'origine sacerdotale ou apparentée; ceux-ci ne sont pas parfaitement unifiés. En mettant bout à bout les sections sacerdotales présumées «anciennes», on obtient un récit cohérent, qui suit, dans son ensemble, la trame de la narration JE et ne semble pas connaître l'apport deutéronomiste:
— Les Israélites arrivent au désert du Sinaï (19,1).
— Yahvé demande à Moïse que le peuple se sanctifie pour la théophanie et ne franchisse pas la limite (19,10-13a); ces ordres sont exécutés (19,14-15).
— Le surlendemain, Yahvé se manifeste dans l'éruption volcanique (19,6aα.18).
— La nuée couvre la montagne pendant six jours; le septième jour, Yahvé appelle Moïse, qui accède au sommet et demeure 40 jours (24,15b-18*). L'objet de cette convocation concerne essentiellement la Tente de la Rencontre (25,1-31,11) et le repos sabbatique, signe d'Alliance (31,12-17).
— Enfin, Moïse redescend de la montagne, le visage rayonnant de la Gloire divine (34,29-35*). Il transmet les consignes qu'il a reçues, et le peuple se met à les exécuter (35,1-40,38).

Outre cet ensemble, on relève en Ex 19-34 une série de compléments ou de commentaires sans doute plus récents encore (notamment 19,13b, 20-25; 20,11,18-19, 24,1-2,9-11; 32,21-24; 33,18-20,22a,23; 34,2-3,5). Ceux-ci proposent une structuration du peuple israélite en trois niveaux:

29. On notera ici le même procédé rédactionnel que pour la mention de Josué au v. 13, ainsi que la *Wiederaufnahme* (le v. 15 répète en d'autres mots le v. 13b).

seul Moïse accède au sommet de la montagne; les prêtres-notables montent à mi-hauteur; enfin le peuple reste en bas. Ceci répond à l'organisation concrète du Temple de Jérusalem après l'Exil, avec ses enceintes successives. Relevons aussi la tentative de mise hors cause d'Aaron, qui n'aurait aucune responsabilité dans la fabrication du veau (32,21-24).

II. Essai de lecture de Deut 5 et 9-10* en relation avec Ex 19-34

De ce qui précède, retenons surtout la présence en Ex 19-34 de quatre rédactions deutéronomistes successives, bien situées chronologiquement entre la ruine de Jérusalem en 587 et l'époque de Zorobabel (520), avec chaque fois des préoccupations et des thèmes caractéristiques. Comment se situent les textes parallèles de Deut 5 et 9-10* par rapport à ces rédactions?

1. *Observations générales.*

a) Deut 5 et 9-10* comportent à la fois des matériaux très semblables — voire identiques — à Ex 19-34 et des matériaux différents. Dressons l'inventaire des correspondances les plus remarquables.

1° En ce qui concerne Deut 5 et son équivalent en Ex 19-20, il faut distinguer la cadre narratif et parénétique du texte même du Décalogue.
— La première partie du Décalogue, qui forme un tout homogène, comme l'indique la construction par enveloppement [30], est identique dans les deux livres (Ex 20,2-6 = Deut 5,6-10), à deux détails près [31]; nous avons vu que ces versets ont été ajoutés en Ex 20 par Dtr585.
— La seconde partie du Décalogue, qui se présente plutôt sous la forme d'une énumération (Ex 20,7-17; Deut 5,11-21), se déroule selon le même ordre général d'exposition et avec une série d'éléments identiques de part et d'autre, mais aussi avec un certain nombre de différences; les plus importantes d'entre elles ne concernent pas le fond ancien du Décalogue, tel que E a dû le rapporter dans le récit de la théophanie, mais seulement des compléments [32].

30. Voir *supra*, note 17.

31. Il y a divergence quant à la place d'un *waw* en Ex 20,5 et Deut 5,8; en outre, *lmṣwty* en Ex 20,6 correspond à *lmṣwtw* (ketib) et *lmṣwty* (qere) en Deut 5,10; ces variantes sont imputables à des erreurs de scribe, comme l'a montré A. Lemaire, *Le Décalogue: essai d'histoire de la rédaction*, dans A. Caquot-M. Delcor (éd.), *Mélanges bibliques en l'honneur de M. Henri Cazelles* (AOAT, 212), Kevelaer-Neukirchen, 1981, pp. 259-295 (p. 267).

32. Les divergences les plus nettes portent sur les motivations du commandement du sabbat (Ex 20,11; Deut 5,14b-15) et du respect des parents (Ex 20,12; Deut 5,16), avec, en outre, l'addition de la formule *ka'ᵃšèr ṣiwwᵉkā YHWH 'ᵉ̀lōhéykā*, «comme te l'a commandé Yahvé ton Dieu» en Deut 5,12b et 16a. Les commandements positifs et les prohibitions, qui

— En revanche, on chercherait en vain un parallélisme strict dans le cadre narratif (Ex 19,16aβ-17.19; 20,1.18-21 E; Deut 5,4-5.22-31). C'est avec grande liberté que les rédacteurs de Deut 5 ont repris une série de motifs du récit élohiste de l'Exode: la crainte du peuple, sa place au bas de la montagne, la nuée (*'ānān*), la voix de Yahvé (*qôl*), les ténèbres (*'ᵃrāpʰèl*), la menace de mort. L'ordre de l'exposé est différent, et le texte n'est jamais repris littéralement. Ajoutons que la correspondence entre les deux textes devient presque nulle à partir de Deut 5,28.

2° On retrouve la même différence lorsqu'on compare Ex 32-34 et Deut 9-10*.

— Il y a correspondance étroite et le plus souvent littérale entre les sections suivantes, si l'on tient compte de la transposition du récit à la première personne, dans le cadre du discours de Moïse:

Ex	Deut	
Ex 31,18* et	Deut 9,10a	: Yahvé remet les Tables à Moïse.
32,7-8a	9,12	: Yahvé donne à Moïse l'ordre de descendre de la montagne et lui révèle le péché d'Israël.
32,9-10	9,13-14	: Yahvé exprime sa décision de détruire Israël.
32,15	9,15	: Moïse descend avec les Tables.
32,19a	9,16a	: Moïse voit le péché d'Israël.
32,19b	9,17	: Moïse brise les Tables.
32,20	9,21	: Moïse détruit le veau d'or.
34,1-4*	10,1-3	: Yahvé invite Moïse à tailler de nouvelles Tables et à gravir la montagne.
34,28b	10,4	: Yahvé écrit les dix Paroles sur les Tables.
34,29a*	10,5	: Moïse redescend de la montagne.

Remarquons que l'ordre d'exposition est identique et que, d'autre part, le texte du Deutéronome suit ici pas à pas le récit de l'Exode suivant sa rédaction E + Dtr585, mais semble ignorer les rédactions ultérieures.
— Certains motifs sont attestés dans les deux textes, mais à des places différentes dans le récit, et avec des formulations en général beaucoup moins convergentes:

La mise en cause personnelle d'Aaron (Ex 32,1-6,25,35bβ; Deut 9,20).

forment très vraisemblablement le noyau le plus ancien du Décalogue, comportent des variantes moins importantes. Tout d'abord, alors qu'Ex 20,8 invite à «se souvenir» (*zākar*) du sabbat, Deut 5,12 commande de l'«observer» (*šāmar*); cette dernière formulation est très fréquente dans le Deutéronome et peut se comprendre comme une correction, d'autant plus que l'appel au souvenir est moins contraignant en apparence que l'impératif *šāmôr*; voir en ce sens notamment N. LOHFINK, *Zur Dekalogfassung von Dt 5*, dans *BZ* n.s. 9 (1965) 17-32 (pp. 21-22). Ensuite, Ex 20,16 interdit le «témoignage de mensonge» (*'éd šāqèr*) et Deut 5,20 le «faux témoignage» (*'éd šāw'*); cette dernière formulation pourrait avoir été préférée pour établir un lien avec le troisième commandement, comme le propose, après d'autres, A. LEMAIRE, *Le Décalogue*, pp. 289-290. Le dixième commandement fait l'objet de différences nombreuses mais au total peu importantes (Ex 20,17; Deut 5,21); encore une fois, ces variantes peuvent s'expliquer comme autant de légères corrections deutéronomistes; voir A. LEMAIRE, *Le Décalogue*, p. 291.

L'intercession répétée de Moïse (Ex 32,11-13, 30-32; Deut 9,18-19a,20b,25-29; 10,10a); notons cependant que la prière d'Ex 32,30-32 correspond dans la suite du récit à celle de Deut 9,25-29, même si la formulation est différente.

Le pardon accordé par Yahvé (Ex 32,14; Deut, 9,19b; 10,10b).

L'ordre de partir avec le peuple vers la terre promise (Ex 32,34a; 33,1-3; Deut 10,11).

La mise en valeur des lévites (Ex 32,26-29; Deut 10,8-9).

Les quarante jours et les quarante nuits de jeûne (Ex 34,28a; Deut 9,9,11,18,25; 10,10).

— Certains épisodes, enfin, sont propres soit au récit pré-sacerdotal de l'Exode (notamment la fabrication du veau, le dépouillement des parures, la délégation de l'Ange et la présence de Yahvé lui-même au milieu de son peuple, le passage de Yahvé, le «Décalogue cultuel»), soit à celui du Deutéronome (les péchés d'Israël à Tab'ērāh, à Massāh, à Qibrōt hatta'awāh et à Qādēš Barnéa', 9,22-24; la mort d'Aaron et le départ vers Gudgōdāh et Yoṭbātāh, 10,6-7).

b) Hormis le texte du Décalogue, la correspondance la plus remarquable concerne le récit E + Dtr585 du veau d'or avec certaines parties de Deut 9-10. Cette correspondance est si étroite, à la fois quant à l'ordre d'exposition et quant à la formulation qu'elle postule une dépendance littéraire [33]. Dans quel sens? Le doute n'est pas permis: c'est le récit du Deutéronome qui dépend de celui de l'Exode. Ainsi que l'a souligné N. Lohfink [34], Deut 9-10* se distingue du texte de l'Exode par son caractère à la fois plus juridique et plus théologique: par exemple, Moïse voit «le péché» d'Israel (9,16), alors qu'en Ex 32,19, il voit «le veau» (on retrouve encore la même transposition en Deut 9,21); de même, Deut 9,17 précise — contrairement à Ex 32,19 — que Moïse brise les Tables «sous les yeux» des Israélites ou ajoute le motif de l'Arche comme réceptacle des Tables (10,1-5,8). Ajoutons que le rédacteur de Deut 9-10* renforce certains traits: la menace d'extermination divine (9,14a) est plus insistante (comparer avec Ex 32,10a), alors que la colère personelle de Moïse (Ex 32,19b) est omise; le mode de destruction du veau, déjà très sophistiqué en Ex 32,20, est encore renforcé en Deut 9,21 par l'addition du broyage.

33. Il faut, en effet, exclure la possibilité d'une tradition ancienne commune aux deux textes: l'histoire du veau d'or n'a pu, à elle seule, faire l'objet d'un récit populaire indépendant, car elle suppose les évènements qui précèdent, avec la révélation du Décalogue (interdiction du culte des idoles) et la montée solitaire de Moïse sur la montagne. En outre, le rédacteur Dtr585 d'Ex 32-34 réutilise la finale du récit E de la théophanie (32,15-16*).

34. N. LOHFINK, *Das Hauptgebot*, pp. 212-213. La dépendance de Deut 9-10* par rapport à Ex 32-34* est encore admise notamment par H. VALENTIN, *Aaron. Eine Studie zur vorpriesterschriftlichen Aaron-Ueberlieferung* (OBO, 18), Göttingen, 1978, pp. 269-270; F.-L. HOSSFELD, *Der Dekalog*, p. 148.

c) La dépendance littéraire du texte de base de Deut 9-10* par rapport à la rédaction Dtr585 d'Ex 32-34 correspond à un phénomène caractéristique: l'omission d'Ex 32,33aα.34aαb, qui rapporte la décision de Yahvé postposant le châtiment au jour de sa Visite. Comme je l'ai dit plus haut, ce dernier élément se trouve au cœur même du kérygme du premier rédacteur deutéronomiste d'Ex 32-34, qui n'est donc plus celui de Deut 9-10*. Dans ce dernier texte, en revanche, la prière de Moïse (9,25-29) reçoit pour réponse l'offre de nouvelles Tables (10,1-2), c'est-à-dire le renouement de l'Alliance brisée; on y trouve en outre par deux fois la proclamation du pardon total de Yahvé (9,19b; 10,10b); tout ceci correspond au message de Dtr575 (voir Ex 32,14). La conclusion s'impose: le texte de base de Deut 9-10*, qui ne connaît d'Ex 32-34 que sa rédaction Dtr585 et la transpose dans la perspective de Dtr575, est l'œuvre de ce dernier ou d'un rédacteur très proche de lui. Il est clair, cependant, que le texte actuel comporte des éléments encore plus récents et que les observations superficielles recueillies jusqu'ici doivent faire l'objet d'un examen plus approfondi.

d) On remarquera, dans la même ligne, que le rédacteur initial de Deut 5 connaît Ex 19-20 dans ses éditions E et Dtr585, mais qu'il semble en ignorer les éléments plus récents. De là à penser que le texte de base de Deut 5 + 9-10* provient d'un seul et unique rédacteur — Dtr 575, en l'occurrence — il n'y a qu'un pas. Celui-ci est confirmé par les rapports étroits qu'on peut constater entre les deux sections narratives de Deut 5-11 sur le plan de la terminologie et de la thématique [35]. Si cette hypothèse se vérifie, on constatera que, dans sa première rédaction, l'ensemble Deut 5 + 9-10* suit pas à pas Ex 19-34* E + Dtr585, sans en omettre aucune partie importante; comme je le montrerai plus loin, en plaçant Deut 9-10* à la suite de Deut 5* (dans leur rédaction initiale), on obtient un récit qui se poursuit sans faille, en parallèle étroit avec Ex 19-34* E + Dtr 585. Dès lors, il faut aller plus loin et se demander si, dans un premier stade, Deut 5* et 9-10* ne sont pas seulement l'œuvre d'un même rédacteur, mais formeraient ensemble un seul récit continu.

e) Cette hypothèse doit être mise en relation avec une observation faite plus haut: en Ex 19-34, les éléments de type parénétique appartiennent tous aux deux dernières strates deutéronomistes; plus précisément, la parénèse en «tu» semble remonter à Dtr560 (voir Ex 23,21-22.24-33*; 34,11-12.14-16), tandis que les exhortations en «vous» (Ex 19,3b-6; 20,22-23; 23,21bα,25a; 34,13), qui se greffent dans plus d'un cas sur les textes à la deuxième personne du singulier, semblent être l'œuvre de Dtr525. Si la grande masse des textes à dominante parénétique qui

35. Voir la conclusion de F. GARCÍA LÓPEZ, *Analyse*, pp. 30-31, malgré le caractère composite de chacune des deux sections.

séparent aujourd'hui Deut 5* et 9-10* (et ceux qui sont rapportés en Deut 10,12-11,32) proviennent également de Dtr560 et Dtr525, et ne remontent donc pas à une époque ancienne, on retrouve en Dtr575 un récit continu des événements de la montagne sainte, avec la révélation du Décalogue et l'histoire du veau d'or; en outre, ce récit qui remonte à la première génération de l'époque exilique précède immédiatement le Code 12-26*. Au temps de Josias, celui-ci ne comportait donc pas d'introduction, ce qui n'a d'ailleurs rien de surprenant: une introduction de style parénétique affaiblit la loi plus qu'elle ne la sert car, à force d'insister sur l'élément volontaire, c'est l'évidence de l'obligation absolue, indiscutable, qui se dissout.

f) L'introduction la plus ancienne au Code serait donc formée par le discours narratif de Moïse rapporté en Deut 5*.9-10*. Pourquoi cette introduction? Encore une fois, c'est le parallèle avec Ex 19-34 qui livre la réponse. Pour E et Dtr585, le seul recueil législatif révélé lors de la théophanie est le Décalogue. C'est le deuxième rédacteur exilique (Dtr575) qui a flanqué le Décalogue d'un deuxième ensemble législatif plus détaillé, le vieux *Bundesbuch* entouré par son cadre rédactionnel (20,22aα.24-26; 21,1; 23,20.23). Remarquons que le Décalogue est qualifié de *d^ebārîm*, «paroles», et attribué directement à Dieu (20,1; cfr 34,28b; voir aussi l'insistance placée sur l'écriture divine en 31,18; 32,16; 34,1), tandis que le Code de l'Alliance est présenté comme le recueil des prescriptions (*mišpāṭîm*) que Moïse donne au peuple (21,1). De même, au début de la scène d'engagement solennel du peuple (24,3-8), Moïse rappelle «toutes les paroles (*d^ebārîm*) de Yahvé» et «toutes les prescriptions (*mišpāṭim*)», c'est-à-dire respectivement le Décalogue et le *Bundesbuch* (v. 3a Dtr575). Autrement dit, le Décalogue est présenté comme la «loi fondamentale» d'origine divine immédiate et le Code de l'Alliance comme son application concrète à travers des lois «ordinaires» formulées par Moïse; on remarquera d'ailleurs que c'est sur la mise en pratique des «paroles de Yahvé» — et non celle des prescriptions — que le peuple s'engage (vv. 3b et 8 Dtr575). Dans le Deutéronome, on peut établir un rapport analogue entre le Décalogue (5,6-21) et le Code apparu sous Josias (12-26*): celui-ci apparaît ainsi comme la nouvelle législation qui concrétise le Décalogue pour le temps de la possession du pays, alors que le *Bundesbuch* livre les lois du temps des pérégrinations au désert; le rapport entre les deux législations est d'ailleurs clairement établi en Deut 12,8-12, qui répond au début du *Bundesbuch* (Ex 20,24-26 Dtr575). Ce n'est sans doute pas par hasard si la structure actuelle de Deut 12-26 correspond point par point à celle du Décalogue, comme l'a montré récemment S.A. Kaufmann[36]. Ainsi, le récit de l'Exode et celui du

36. S.A. KAUFMAN, *The Structure of the Deuteronomic Law*, dans *Maarav* 1 (1978-1979) 105-158.

Deutéronome appartiennent à un seul tout bien construit, ce qui explique pourquoi le Code de Deut 12-26 a été placé *après* l'épisode du veau d'or et non juste après le Décalogue comme en Ex 20-23: le Décalogue n'est donné qu'une fois et reste logiquement à sa place, mais le Code est présenté comme la législation qui applique concrètement le Décalogue pour le temps qui suit le péché d'Israël et le pardon de Yahvé.

J'aboutis ainsi à l'ébauche d'une nouvelle théorie sur la formation du Deutéronome. Il faut à présent en vérifier le bien-fondé et affiner l'analyse par une lecture attentive du texte. Puisqu'il ne m'est évidemment pas possible dans ce cadre d'effectuer un tel travail pour le Deutéronome entier, je propose d'examiner ici les deux sections narratives de Deut 5-11.

2. *Deut 5,1-6,3.*

a) La première question posée à l'exégèse est celle de l'introduction originelle de la section et — si mon hypothèse est exacte — de l'ensemble du livre. Il y a, en effet, concurrence entre 4,44; 4,45 et 5,1. Plusieurs auteurs récents ont pris option pour 4,45, qui aurait formé le titre le plus ancien du livre, suivi immédiatement par 6,4ss [37]. En effet, le titre de 4,44 serait deutéronomiste [38], tandis que 5,1 serait lié plus spécialement au ch. 5. Cette argumentation n'est cependant pas décisive, si l'on ne refuse pas a priori la présence en Deut 5-11 de plusieurs strates deutéronomistes. Si l'on considère que 4,45 paraît plutôt lié à la péricope secondaire 4,45-48, qui résume les ch. 1-3 [39], rien n'empêche de voir en 4,44 le titre général primitif, et l'on ne s'étonnera guère de devoir le qualifier de «deutéronomiste»: c'est l'ensemble de Deut 5-11 qui mérite sans doute ce qualificatif. Dans ce cas, le mot *tôrāh* convient parfaitement: l'objet du livre n'est autre que la révélation de la Loi divine, avec sa charte fondamentale (le Décalogue) et ses applications concrètes (le Code 12-26*).

b) Il faut distinguer en Deut 5,1 plusieurs éléments:

— La phrase d'introduction apparaît encore, identique, en Deut 29,1 et, transposée sur Josué, en Jos 23,2 Dtr. Il faut vraisemblablement

37. Voir par exemple F. GARCÍA LÓPEZ, *Analyse*, p. 506. F.-L. HOSSFELD, *Der Dekalog*, p. 219 n. 15, a cependant fait remarquer que le lien entre 4,45 et 6,20 est beaucoup plus fort, car on y retrouve les trois mêmes termes désignant les commandements (*hā'édōt wehaḥuqqîm wehammišpāṭîm*), ainsi que le «vous» (*'ètekèm*).

38. Voir en particulier G. SEITZ, *Redaktionsgeschichtliche Studien zum Deuteronomium* (BWANT, 93), Stuttgart-Berlin-Cologne, 1971, pp. 23-44.

39. Si les avis divergent quant au v. 45, il y a unanimité pour reconnaître aux vv. 46-49 (eux-même glosés) une section secondaire. Le v. 46aα, cependant, pourrait avoir formé la finale primitive de la phrase commencée au v. 44; l'introduction «ancienne» aurait ainsi été coupée par l'insertion postérieure du v. 45, lié au vv. 46aβ-49; voir S. MITTMANN, *Deuteronomium 1,1-6,3 literarkritisch und traditionsgeschichtlich untersucht* (BZAW, 139), Berlin-New York, 1975, pp. 128-130.

comprendre *kol-yiśrā'él*, «tout Israël», dans un sens distributif, comme en Jos 23,2, où elle est explicitée: «tout Israël: ses anciens, ses chefs, ses juges et ses scribes»; des énumérations analogues figurent encore, en liaison avec *kol-yiśrā'él*, en Deut 11,6 et 31,11-12 (voir aussi 29,9, dans le discours introduit par le v. 1a). Remarquons qu'une liste semblable est attestée en 5,23, ce qui pourrait être un indice de l'appartenance à la même strate littéraire que le v. 1aα. De toute manière, *kol-yiśrā'él* est ici l'équivalent d'un pluriel, comme l'indique l'expression *wayyō'mèr 'alèhèm*, «et il *leur* dit» (voir aussi 13,12).
— La formule *šᵉma' yiśrā'él*, «écoute, Israël» (v. 1aβ), en revanche, apparaît ailleurs comme l'introduction d'un discours de Moïse au singulier (6,4; 9,1; 27,9); ce n'est que dans la citation du discours rituel du prêtre avant le combat (20,3) qu'elle est accordée à une exhortation en «vous». En outre, cette formule est toujours utilisée ailleurs comme une phrase complète, sans aucun complément grammatical. Tout ceci invite à considérer la suite du verset comme une addition. Comme le note F. García López, «si on ôtait ce complément, on aurait en Deut, V,1aβ*, 2a le même *incipit* qu'en VI,4: *šm' yśr'l (...) yhwh 'lhynw*» [40].
— La suite du verset, rédigée en «vous», formerait donc un ajout plus récent, ce que tend à confirmer l'analyse du vocabulaire, avec notamment le verbe *lāmad*, «enseigner», en référence avec les commandements [41].

c) Les vv. 2-3 se distinguent du contexte par l'emploi répété de la première personne du pluriel. Ces versets appartiennent à la rédaction Dtr560, comme il ressort de plusieurs observations:
— Ces versets opposent avec insistance deux générations: celle des pères, qui ont péri pendant le séjour au désert, et celle des Israélites survivants, qui vont entrer dans la terre promise. Cette opposition se trouve au cœur même de la réflexion de Dtr560, comme je l'ai montré à propos d'Ex 32,33.35abα.
— On rapprochera en particulier le v. 3a avec Jér 31,31-34, qui développe la même problématique avec, encore une fois, l'opposition caractéristique entre la génération avec laquelle Yahvé refait Alliance et la génération des pères coupables [42].
— Le discours en «nous» doit être rapproché de Deut 1-3*, où le même «nous» est dominant. C'est précisément dans cette section qu'on trouve

40. F. García López, *Analyse*, p. 40.
41. Voir F. García López, *ibidem*.
42. Sur l'origine deutéronomiste de la péricope, voir S. Herrmann, *Die prophetischen Heilserwartungen im Alten Testament* (BWANT, 85), Stuttgart, 1965, pp. 179-185; Id., *Die konstruktive Restauration. Das Deuteronomium als Mitte biblischer Theologie*, dans *Probleme biblischer Theologie, G. von Rad zum 70. Geburtstag*, Munich, 1971, pp. 155-170 (pp. 167-168); S. Böhmer, *Heimkehr und neuer Bund*, Göttingen, 1976, pp. 74-79; W. Thiel, *Die deuteronomistische Redaktion von Jeremia 26-45* (WMANT, 52), Neukirchen, 1981, pp. 23-28.

à nouveau l'opposition entre les pères coupables et les fils innocents (1,35,39), mais aussi un large développement sur l'extermination nécessaire de la génération pécheresse (1,35; 2,14) et la fin de l'errance après 38 ou 40 ans (2,7,14)[43].
— La mention de l'Horeb (v. 2) confirme encore l'appartenance à la troisième rédaction deutéronomiste; voir Ex 33,6 Dtr560, ainsi que Deut 1,6.19.
— Ajoutons que ces vv. 2-3 peuvent avoir formé la suite directe de l'invitation du v. 1a *šᵉmaʿ yiśrāʾél*, ainsi qu'il a été signalé plus haut. Cela signifierait du même coup que la suite du v. 1 appartiendrait à Dtr525.

d) Quoique tous deux écrits en «vous», les vv. 4 et 5 n'appartiennent vraisemblablement pas à la même strate, car le premier parle d'une communication de Yahvé avec le peuple «face à face» et le second met au contraire l'accent sur la médiation de Moïse[44]. Cette dernière présentation est certainement la plus récente. Ainsi, l'adresse directe de Yahvé à Israël correspond à la teneur du récit E en Ex 19,16-19* et 20,18: ce n'est qu'ensuite que le peuple, terrorisé, demande la médiation de Moïse (20,19-21 E); le v. 5, en revanche, développe le même rôle médiateur de Moïse qu'Ex 19,3b-8 Dtr525 et 20,22-23 Dtr525[45]. Seul, le dernier mot de Deut 5,5 (*léʾmōr*, «en disant») appartient sans doute à la même rédaction que le v. 4, c'est-à-dire vraisemblablement Dtr575; en effet, il se rapporte avec difficulté au corps du v. 5, mais poursuit avec naturel le v. 4.

e) Le Décalogue (vv. 6-21), qui reprend point par point le texte E + Dtr585 d'Ex 20,2-17, appartient logiquement à la rédaction Dtr575, tout au moins en ce qui concerne le «texte de base» commun avec l'Exode. Comme il ne saurait être question de reprendre ici l'énorme dossier de la formation du Décalogue, je me contenterai de relever quelques points importants:

43. Ainsi que l'a fait remarquer F. GARCÍA LÓPEZ, *Analyse*, p. 10, il convient en outre de rapprocher Deut 5,2-3 de la section 29,11-14, également rédigée en «nous», où l'on trouve à la fois la même expression *kārat bᵉrît ʾèt*, «conclure une Alliance avec (quelqu'un)» (v. 13), la même construction *lōʾ ʾèt... kî ʾèt...* (vv. 13-14) et la même insistance sur l'«aujourd'hui» (*hayyôm*, 4 fois!) de l'Alliance. Notons que Deut 29,12 présente des analogies avec Ex 33,1 Dtr560 (motif du serment juré à Abraham, Isaac et Jacob) et avec Jér 31,33b Dtr560 (formule d'Alliance; sur l'histoire de ce texte, voir la note précédente).

44. Voir P. BUIS, *Le Deutéronome* (Verbum Salutis. Ancien Testament, 4), Paris, 1969, p. 110; S. MITTMANN, *Deuteronomium*, p. 132; F. GARCÍA LÓPEZ, *Analyse*, p. 11; F.-L. HOSSFELD, *Der Dekalog*, p. 225.

45. Sur le caractère plus récent du v. 5, voir la discussion de S. MITTMANN, *Deuteronomium*, pp. 132-133, avec L. Perlitt. F.-L. HOSSFELD, *Der Dekalog*, p. 225, attire l'attention sur le lien entre Deut 4,10-15 et 5,5. F. GARCÍA LÓPEZ, *Analyse*, pp. 11-12, souligne le caractère deutéronomiste de la phraséologie des deux versets, ce qui n'a rien d'incompatible avec la distinction de deux niveaux littéraires.

— Reprenant une option très répandue, P. Buis estime que l'insertion du Décalogue en Deut 5 est tardive; cette addition aurait été «jugée d'autant plus nécessaire que le livre le commente souvent, aussi bien dans les parties dogmatiques que dans le code»[46]. Il faut cependant faire remarquer que l'explication inverse — défendue en particulier par N. Lohfink — est bien plus facile: c'est la présence du Décalogue au ch. 5 qui a suscité les multiples commentaires des chapitres suivants. Quant à prétendre que le texte du Décalogue «déséquilibre le récit»[47], c'est là un pur postulat: il en forme, tout au contraire, à mon avis, le centre de gravité, comme en Ex 19-20* E.
— Le texte du Décalogue est parfaitement introduit par Deut 5,4 et par le dernier mot du v. 5, qui appartiennent tous deux à Dtr575 et postulent la citation d'un discours divin. L'utilisation de la forme «tu» dans le Décalogue par opposition au «vous» de l'introduction narrative[48] s'explique par la reprise du texte à partir du livre de l'Exode[49].
— Précisément, la question de la priorité du texte d'Ex 20 ou de Deut 5 fait aujourd'hui l'objet d'opinions contradictoires[50]. Pour la trancher, il ne faut pas s'appuyer sur les éléments très différents dans les deux textes, car ils peuvent s'expliquer par autant d'additions indépendantes postérieures à l'insertion du Décalogue de part et d'autre, mais sur les passages où les différences sont plus minimes. Si l'on s'en tient à l'examen de ces variantes, la priorité d'Ex 20 paraît s'imposer[51].
— Les phrases qui n'ont pas leur équivalent dans le texte d'Ex 20,2-17 s'expliquent au mieux comme autant d'additions deutéronomistes postérieures à Dtr575: les vv. 12b,14-15* et, au v. 16, les expressions *kaʾᵃšèr ṣiwwᵉkā YHWH*, «comme te l'a commandé Yahvé» (= v. 12b) et *ûlᵉmaʿan yîṭab lāk*, «et afin que tu sois heureux». La formule *kaʾᵃšèr ṣiwwᵉkā YHWH* est encore utilisée mot pour mot en Deut 20,17, dans un passage en «tu» où il est question de la liste des peuples voués à

46. P. BUIS, *Le Deutéronome*, p. 10.

47. P. BUIS, *ibidem*.

48. Voir E. W. NICHOLSON, *The Decalogue as the Direct Address of God*, dans *VT* 27 (1977) 422-433 (p. 425), qui s'appuie sur cette constatation pour affirmer le caractère secondaire du Décalogue par rapport au contexte narratif.

49. Quoiqu'usant du «tu», le Décalogue ne peut avoir figuré en Deut 5 sans les sections «vous» qui l'encadrent, ainsi que l'a fait remarquer G. MINETTE DE TILLESSE, *Sections «tu» et sections «vous» dans le Deutéronome*, dans *VT* 12 (1962) 29-87 (p. 35). Ainsi, si le critère du *Numeruswechsel* est opératoire pour une distinction des niveaux rédactionnels, il demande à être manié avec prudence et discernement.

50. Mentionnons, parmi les partisans de l'antériorité d'Ex 20,2-17*: H. G. REVENTLOW, *Gebot und Predigt im Dekalog*, Gütersloh, 1962, p. 95; N. LOHFINK, *Zur Dekalogfassung*; G. FOHRER, *Das sogenannte apodiktisch formulierte Recht und der Dekalog*, dans *Kerygma und Dogma* 11 (1965) 49-74 (p. 56); S. MITTMANN, *Deuteronomium*, pp. 134-136; A. LEMAIRE, *Le Décalogue*. Parmi les tenants de l'antériorité de Deut 5,6-21*: E. W. NICHOLSON, *The Decalogue*, p. 431; F.-L. HOSSFELD, *Der Dekalog*, pp. 21-162, 283-284.

51. Voir *supra*, note 32.

l'anathème, ce qui est caractéristique de Dtr560 [52]; voir aussi 6,25, en «nous» comme 5,2-3 Dtr560. Les éléments ajoutés aux vv. 14-15 doivent être rapprochés en particulier de Deut 15,15; 16,11-12; 24,14-18,22; tous ces textes sont écrits en «tu» et semblent être l'œuvre de Dtr560 [53]. Enfin, la formule *l*^{e}*maʿan yîṭab lāk* apparaît encore en Deut 4,40; 6,3,18; 12,25,28; 22,7; la plupart de ces textes attirent l'attention sur le passage des générations et doivent être attribués, encore une fois, à Dtr560.

f) Deut 5,22 correspond au v. 4, dans l'introduction au Décalogue: on y retrouve le même sujet («Yahvé»), le même destinataire («vous»), la même formule *bahar mittôk hāʾēš*, «sur la montagne, du milieu du feu». Surtout, on trouve dans les deux versets la même communication directe entre Yahvé et Israël, contrairement au v. 5. On assignera donc ce v. 22, comme le v. 4, à Dtr575 [54]. Remarquons aussi la correspondance avec le récit élohiste de la théophanie: le Décalogue est présenté comme *d*^{e}*bārîm*, «paroles», ainsi qu'en Ex 20,1; Yahvé a parlé depuis «la nuée et la ténèbre» (*heʿānān w*^{e}*hāʿ*^{a}*rāp*^{h}*èl*), ce qui répond à Ex 19,16 (*ʿānān*), et 20,21 (*haʿ*^{a}*rāp*^{h}*èl*); la «voix forte» (*qôl gādôl*) répond à l'emploi répété du mot *qôl* en Ex 19,16,19 (deux fois); 20,18 (deux fois). La finale du verset correspond à Ex 31,18* E. Remarquons encore l'insistance placée sur l'origine divine des paroles et de l'écriture, avec la précision: «il n'y ajouta rien»; cette phrase semble opposer le Décalogue comme loi fondamentale donnée par Yahvé lui-même aux prescriptions du Code 12-26, données par Moïse (cfr 11,32; 27,1).

g) La section 5,23-27 appartient en substance à la même strate littéraire:
— C'est la même narration à la deuxième personne du pluriel qui se poursuit. Le «nous» des vv. 24b-27 ne doit pas être rapproché des vv. 2-3 et ainsi faire illusion: contrairement à ce passage, il s'agit ici d'une citation du peuple, et la forme «nous» est empruntée à la *Vorlage* élohiste (Ex 20,19-20).
— Comme au v. 22, en effet, le rédacteur s'inspire directement du récit E de la théophanie, en l'occurrence Ex 20,18-21, avec la terreur du peuple, qui a peur de mourir, et la demande de médiation adressée à Moïse.

52. Voir Deut 2,34; 3,6 et surtout 7,1-2. Sur le caractère deutéronomiste de la liste des peuples et du motif du *ḥèrèm* dans ce dernier texte, voir F. GARCÍA LÓPEZ, *«Un peuple consacré». Analyse critique de Deutéronome VII*, dans *VT* 32 (1982) 438-463 (pp. 439-442).

53. Voir en particulier Deut 24,16, où le kérygme majeur de Dtr560 s'exprime en toute clarté, avec la distinction des générations tant pour la culpabilité que pour le châtiment; ce texte doit être rapproché d'Ex 32,33 Dtr560.

54. Les vv. 4 et 22 sont souvent attribués au même rédacteur; voir par exemple G. SEITZ, *Redaktionsgeschichtliche Studien*, p. 47. Les arguments présentés par S. MITTMANN, *Deuteronomium*, p. 137, et par F.-L. HOSSFELD, *Der Dekalog*, pp. 226-228, qui considèrent le v. 22 comme une addition postérieure, ne me paraissent pas déterminants; voir l'article de C. BREKELMANS dans ce même volume.

— Ainsi que je l'ai signalé plus haut, l'analogie avec Deut 11,6; 31,11-12 et Jos 23,2 invite à rapprocher l'énumération du v. 23b (*kol-ro'šéy šibṭéykèm w^e ziqnéykèm*) de l'expression *kol-yiśrā'él* au v. 1a Dtr575.
— Le v. 24b[55] affaiblit le discours du peuple et la portée du v. 25. On y verra de préférence une addition de Dtr560, qui insiste sur le temps de détresse comme épreuve dans l'ensemble positive, sous l'active protection d'un Dieu qui maintient les siens en vie; voir Deut 4,33; 8,2-6 Dtr560 (cfr aussi 29,4). Remarquons que le v. 24b n'offre aucun contact significatif avec Ex 20,18-21, mais correspond en revanche à Deut 5,3 Dtr560 («nous-mêmes qui sommes ici aujourd'hui tous vivants»). Sans doute le v. 25a, dont la teneur fait double emploi avec la finale du verset, appartient-il encore à la même strate littéraire[56].
— Le v. 26, qui n'a pas plus de lien avec Ex 20, pourrait former une nouvelle addition, qui prend cependant le contrepied du v. 24b et semble plutôt apparentée à la théologie sacerdotale; voir Gen 32,31; Ex 24,11; 33,20; Nb 4,20. Le même thème est cependant attesté dans la littérature deutéronomiste: Jg 6,22-23; 13,22. L'origine sacerdotale (ou apparentée) du verset est confirmée par l'emploi de l'expression *kol bāśār*, «toute chair»[57]. Le motif de la Gloire divine (*kābôd*), au v. 24a, insolite dans la littérature deutéronomiste, a pu être inséré par le même rédacteur[58].

h) A partir du v. 28, on retrouve le discours en «vous» de Moïse; cette fois, cependant, le parallélisme avec Ex 20 fait à peu près défaut; de plus, c'est Yahvé qui répond au peuple, qui s'était pourtant adressé à Moïse. La section 5,28-31 forme donc un commentaire plus récent, qui suppose évidemment les vv. 23-27*. Cette fois, l'accent est placé sur les conditions du bonheur et de la vie: l'observance des commandements. Remarquons comment cette réflexion se greffe sur l'inquiétude exposée un peu plus haut: alors que le peuple constatait: «Nous avons vu (...) l'homme rester en vie» (v. 24b Dtr560) et se demandait: «Et maintenant, pourquoi devrions-nous mourir?» (v. 25a, sans doute Dtr560), le v. 33 conclut: «... *alors*, vous vivrez, vous aurez bonheur et longue vie dans le pays dont vous allez prendre possession». On remarquera en outre que le début du v. 32 (*ûš^e martèm la^{ca}śôt*, «vous garderez pour mettre en pratique») est identique à la finale du v. 1 Dtr525. On attribuera donc les vv. 28-33 au même rédacteur[59]. Le discours se termine sans doute en 6,1,

55. Sur l'appartenance du v. 24b à une strate secondaire, voir S. MITTMANN, *Deuteronomium*, pp. 138-139; F.-L. HOSSFELD, *Der Dekalog*, pp. 229-230.

56. Comme le fait remarquer S. MITTMANN, *Deuteronomium*, p. 138, le v. 25 est hétérogène, car le peuple dit deux fois sa crainte de mourir, mais chaque fois pour un motif différent; voir aussi F.-L. HOSSFELD, *Der Dekalog*, p. 230. Un lien très fort est établi entre les vv. 24b et 25a par *w^{ec}attāh*, «et maintenant».

57. Voir Gen 6,12,13,17,19; 7,16,21; 8,17; 9,15,17; etc.

58. Voir P. BUIS, *Le Deutéronome*, p. 111.

59. On retrouve aux vv. 28-31 le rôle médiateur de Moïse, souligné au v. 5 Dtr525, mais

dont la formulation est proche de Deut 4,14, généralement considéré comme récent[60].

i) La section 6,2-3, enfin, donne à nouveau les conditions de la longue vie (v. 2b; cfr 5,33), mais à la deuxième personne du singulier. Ces versets appartiennent vraisemblablement à Dtr560, comme le montre la phraséologie[61], et se lisaient donc à l'origine à la suite immédiate de 5,27.

La première rédaction de Deut 5 est donc l'œuvre de Dtr575, qui transpose assez fidèlement le texte E + Dtr585 d'Ex 19-20 (4,44; 5,1aα.4.5bβ*.6-21*.23-24a.25b.27), en suivant de plus près les sections deutéronomistes que les passages élohistes. Le récit, qui a pour centre de gravité la révélation du Décalogue, ne comporte aucun élément parénétique, au contraire des deux rédactions deutéronomistes ultérieures (Dtr560 et Dtr525), qui se partagent le restant du texte. Notons l'usage du discours en «vous» tant en Dtr575 qu'en Dtr525, alors que Dtr560 préfère le «nous» et le «tu» adressé à Israël.

3. *Deut 9,7-10,11.*

Les nombreuses répétitions qui affectent cette section rendent l'analyse des rédactions du texte très difficile. Tentons cependant de nous y frayer un chemin, en tenant compte de la dépendance du rédacteur initial par rapport à Ex 32-34* Dtr585.

a) Deut 9,7 débute au singulier et se termine au pluriel. L'appel au souvenir est typique des passages en «tu» adressés à Israël (4,9; 5,15; 6,12; 7,18; 8,2,11,14,18,19; 24,18,22; 25,17,19) qui soulignent combien Yahvé a toujours protégé son peuple aux temps de détresse ou d'épreuve; voir en particulier 8,2, au début d'un développement typique de Dtr560 sur le sens providentiel du séjour au désert pendent 40 ans. Le texte au singulier de Deut 9,7* appartient à la même strate: à la protection constante de Yahvé depuis la sortie d'Égypte (5,15; 6,12; 7,18-19; 8,14; 24,18,22) et tout au long de la marche au désert (8,2-6,15-16) répond l'infidélité d'Israël «dans le désert, depuis le jour de (sa) sortie du pays

aussi en Ex 19,3b-8 Dtr525; 20,22aβ-23 Dtr525. Moïse est le type du vrai prophète, chargé de transmettre au peuple les paroles divines d'invitation à la fidélité.

60. On a remarqué depuis longtemps que Deut 4 appartient au moins en substance à une des strates les plus récentes du Deutéronome, datant sans doute de la fin de la période exilique; voir notamment H. D. PREUSS, *Deuteronomium*, pp. 85-86.

61. F. GARCÍA LÓPEZ, *Analyse*, pp. 17-18, a bien montré le caractère deutéronomiste de plusieurs tournures. Le passage du pluriel (v. 1) au singulier (vv. 2-3) trahit l'appartenance à une strate littéraire distincte, mais n'oblige pas à voir dans les vv. 2-3 un commentaire du v. 1, comme l'estiment F. GARCÍA LÓPEZ, *Analyse*, p. 18, et S. MITTMANN, *Deuteronomium*, p. 140. Le v. 2a trouve son plus proche parallèle en 1 Rois 8,40, dans une péricope deutéronomiste (vv. 37-40) qui insiste sur la rétribution de chacun selon sa conduite (cfr Ex 32,33 Dtr560).

d'Égypte»[62]. S'il faut considérer le changement de personne comme un critère de distinction des strates littéraires[63], la finale au pluriel du v. 7, qui continue la même phrase, doit être tenue pour un ajout plus récent, c'est-à-dire sans doute relevant de Dtr525[64]. Remarquons d'ailleurs que la formule finale *mamrîm hᵉyîtèm ʿim-YHWH*, «vous avez été rebelles envers Yahvé», semble former une reprise dans une formulation plus récente du début du verset (*hiqṣapʰtā 'èt-YHWH 'ᵉlōhéykā*, «tu as irrité Yahvé ton Dieu»). L'emploi de la forme «vous» se poursuivra jusqu'en 10,9, mais il est évidemment impossible de considérer l'ensemble de cette section comme une unité littéraire homogène.

b) A partir du v. 8, le rappel des événements évoqués en Deut 5 est explicite. Le v. 8 appartient, comme le v. 7b, à Dtr525:
— La formule *hiqṣapʰtèm 'et-YHWH*, «vous avez irrité Yahvé», reprend au pluriel *hiqṣapʰtā 'èt-YHWH* (v. 7a).
— Le verbe *'ānapʰ*, au hitp., ne se rencontre dans le Deutéronome que dans des textes appartenant à Dtr525: 1,37 et 4,21 opposent Moïse au peuple coupable (1,37-38 apparaît comme une addition au milieu d'un texte typique de Dtr560); enfin 9,20 parle de la colère de Yahvé contre Aaron, ce qui correspond au point de vue d'Ex 32,1-6,21-24,35bβ Dtr525.
— L'expression *wayyit'annapʰ YHWH bākèm*, «Yahvé se mit en colère contre vous», est complétée par *lᵉhašmîd 'ètkèm*, «à vous faire détruire»; ce n'est pas par hasard si l'on trouve le même lien en 9,20 (*lᵉhašmîdô*).

62. F. GARCÍA LÓPEZ, *Analyse*, p. 18, attire l'attention sur l'emploi de l'expression *lᵉmîn hayyôm 'ᵃšèr*, «depuis le jour où», dans des textes deutéronomistes tardifs (Deut 4,32; 2 Sam 7,11; Jér 7,25). L'appel au souvenir semble compléter l'impératif *šᵉmaʿ yiśrā'él*, «écoute, Israël» (v. 1), qui porte sur l'aujourd'hui (*hayyôm*, vv. 1,3,6); ainsi, les vv. 1-6 et 7a permettent de réinterpréter le récit plus ancien du péché d'Israël dans le cadre de la parénèse: la mémoire de la culpabilité passée et de la générosité divine doit encourager le peuple à adopter «aujourd'hui» une juste attitude d'humilité et de confiance en Yahvé. D'ailleurs la leçon du souvenir du grand péché est immédiatement tirée par le même rédacteur en 10,12-13. Le même lien entre l'impératif *šᵉmaʿ yiśrā'él* et l'appel à la mémoire peut encore s'observer en Deut 5,1aα.15 et 6,4.12, dans des textes qui utilisent tous la deuxième personne du singulier adressée à Israël.

63. Le vieux débat relatif au *Numeruswechsel* est loin d'être tranché de manière définitive, ainsi qu'en témoignent Chr. T. BEGG, *Contributions to the Elucidation of the Composition of Deuteronomy with Special Attention to the Numeruswechsel*, diss. Leuven, 1978: ID., *The Significance of the* Numeruswechsel *in Deuteronomy. The «Pre-History» of the Question*, dans *ETL* 55 (1979) 116-124; Y. SUZUKI, *The «Numeruswechsel» in Deuteronomy*, diss. Claremont, 1980-1981; W. HIGGS, *A Stylistic Analysis of the* Numeruswechsel *Sections of Deuteronomy*, diss. Southern Baptist Theological Seminary, 1982. Voir aussi la large confiance attribuée au critère du changement de nombre par H.D. PREUSS, *Deuteronomium*, pp. 35,84-85,93,94,103,107, confiance elle-même critiquée dans le compte-rendu de l'ouvrage par N. LOHFINK, dans *TLZ* 108 (1983) 349-353.

64. Sur le caractère tardif des expressions du v. 7b, voir F. GARCÍA LÓPEZ, *Analyse*, p. 18.

c) Les vv. 9-11 parlent de la remise des Tables. Ces versets ne sont pas homogènes.

— Le v. 9a peut être attribué à Dtr575, car ce même rédacteur utilise ailleurs les expressions *ʿālāh hāhārāh*, «gravir la montagne» (Ex 24,12), *lûḥōt hāʾᵃbānîm*, «les Tables de pierre» (Ex 24,12; Deut 5,22) et *habbᵉrît ʾᵃšèr kārat YHWH ʿimmākèm*, «l'Alliance que Yahvé a conclue avec vous» (Ex 24,8).

— Le v. 9b, en revanche, appartient à une strate plus récente, car le motif du jeûne de 40 jours et 40 nuits, sans doute dérivé de celui des 40 ans au désert, n'apparaît pas avant Dtr560 (Ex 34,28)[65].

— Le v. 10a se présente comme un décalque à la première personne d'Ex 31,18* E et appartient logiquement à Dtr575. Il en est de même pour la suite du verset, qui reprend presque mot pour mot 5,22 Dtr575[66].

— Le v. 11, qui reprend le motif des 40 jours, semble appartenir encore à Dtr560; la seconde partie du verset répète pour l'essentiel le v. 9a Dtr575[67].

d) Les vv. 12-17 suivent de très près le texte plus ancien d'Ex 32,7-8a.9-10a.15.19 Dtr585 et doivent être attribués en substance à Dtr575. Le texte ne s'écarte de sa *Vorlage* qu'aux vv. 14b et 16:

— Même si l'on trouve au v. 14b la même idée générale qu'en Ex 32,8b (au même endroit du récit), il faut sans doute considérer la phrase comme Dtr525, car le rédacteur oppose Moïse au peuple coupable.

— Le v. 16a reprend la matière d'Ex 32,19a, mais la formule en des termes plus théologiques, en insistant davantage sur la signification de l'adoration du veau (*wᵉhinnéh ḥᵃṭāʾtèm lᵃYHWH ʾᵉlōhéykèm*, «voici que

65. Le motif du séjour au désert pendant 40 ans n'est pas attesté dans la littérature antérieure à Dtr; voir notamment W. H. SCHMIDT, *Die deuteronomistische Redaktion des Amosbuches*, dans *ZAW* 77 (1965) 168-193 (p. 180). J'ai rappelé plus haut le lien de ce motif avec la problématique de la deuxième génération de l'époque exilique. En jeûnant 40 jours, Moïse vit symboliquement l'expérience de la faim et de la soif qui est celle du peuple au désert, mais il la vit dans la disponibilité à Yahvé et non dans la révolte, et cette épreuve aboutit à l'obtention de la grâce divine. Ainsi, le thème des 40 jours de jeûne paraît une réinterprétation de la grande détresse comme un temps d'épreuve positive, où l'homme découvre qu'il «ne vit pas seulement de pain», mais «de tout ce qui sort de la bouche de Yahvé» (Deut 8,3; voir l'ensemble des vv. 2-6); il n'a guère de fonction avant Dtr560.

66. L'expression finale *bᵉyôm haqqāhāl*, «au jour de l'Assemblée», qu'on ne retrouve qu'en Deut 10,4 et 18,16 Dtr560, pourrait appartenir à une strate littéraire plus récente; elle serait alors liée au motif des 40 jours (v. 9b), qui établit une distance temporelle avec les événements rapportés au ch. 5. Peut-être cependant ces mots appartiennent-ils tout simplement au «récit de base»; voir 5,22 Dtr575, où figure l'expression *kol-qᵉhalᵉkèm*, «toute votre assemblée».

67. Le lien avec le v. 9 est souligné en particulier par G. SEITZ, *Redaktionsgeschichtliche Studien*, p. 54, et par F.-L. HOSSFELD, *Der Dekalog*, p. 151. Il ne signifie pas, comme ces auteur l'estiment, que le v. 10 forme une addition: ce sont, au contraire, les vv. 9b et 11 qui sont secondaires.

vous aviez péché contre Yahvé votre Dieu») que sur sa matérialité. Par ailleurs, ce v. 16a est nécessaire pour la cohérence du récit; malgré la différence de formulation par rapport à Ex 32,19a, on l'attribuera donc à Dtr575.

— Le v. 16b n'a aucun parallèle dans la section correspondante d'Ex 32, mais répète presque littéralement le v. 12b; comme dans la première partie du verset, l'accent est placé sur la culpabilité d'Israël, qui contraste évidemment avec la générosité divine. C'est donc, encore une fois, à Dtr575 qu'on assignera la phrase.

e) Les vv. 18-19 rapportent la prière d'intercession de Moïse et la réponse favorable de Yahvé. A première vue, cette section exprime le kérygme de Dtr575 (cfr Ex 32,14) et doit appartenir au «récit de base» de Deut 9-10*. C'est là cependant, je crois, une illusion, car on trouve une nouvelle intercession de Moïse après la destruction de l'idole (vv. 25-29), conformément à la *Vorlage* d'Ex 32,30-32a, et le pardon déjà octroyé au v. 19 lui ôte tout objet. En réalité, ces versets doivent être attribués à Dtr525:

— La prosternation de Moïse (v. 18aα) est répétée en termes identiques au v. 25a, qui fait lui-même double emploi avec le v. 26a et doit être considéré comme une addition Dtr525 (voir *infra*).

— Le v. 18aβ reprend littéralement l'expression du v. 9b Dtr560 et y fait d'ailleurs allusion («comme la première fois»); il ne peut donc lui être antérieur, mais peut aussi avoir été ajouté par Dtr525.

— La phraséologie du v. 18b est, semble-t-il, celle de Dtr525 [68]. De même, le v. 19a est formulé en des termes très proches du v. 8: il est possible, a priori, que le v. 8 en dépende; cependant, vu le lien qui unit le v. 19a au v. 18b, il est plus probable que les deux textes soient l'œuvre du même rédacteur [69]. Notons l'effet de contraste avec le v. 18a: l'innocent fournit un effort considérable en vue de sauver des gens dont la culpabilité est écrasante; cette opposition correspond à la teneur du v. 14 et place Moïse dans la position du prophète intercesseur face au peuple enferré dans son péché; voir, en parallèle, le rôle de Moïse face à Pharaon en Ex 8,21-28; 9,27-30.33-34 Dtr.

— L'exaucement (v. 19b) est formulé en des termes identiques à 10,10bα; de plus, les derniers mots du verset (*gam bappaʿam hahûʾ*, «cette fois encore») ne se rapportent à aucun événement du passé; ils doivent avoir été écrits par analogie avec *kārîʾšōnāh*, «comme la première fois», au v. 18; peut-être faut-il y trouver l'écho de l'idée selon laquelle la prière du prophète est toujours exaucée [70].

68. F. GARCÍA LÓPEZ, *Analyse*, p. 21, en souligne l'origine deutéronomiste, c'est-à-dire, à l'entendre, son appartenance à une strate récente du Deutéronome.

69. Voir l'examen de la phraséologie par F. GARCÍA LÓPEZ, *Analyse*, p. 22.

70. Voir F.-L. HOSSFELD, *Der Dekalog*, p. 149: les vv. 18-19 constituent une section

f) Le v. 20, qui accuse Aaron en particulier, appartient à Dtr525[71]. Remarquons, encore une fois, la tournure *l^e^hašmîd*, «au point de détruire», comme aux vv. 8 et 19a.

g) Le v. 21 correspond à Ex 32,20 Dtr585 et remonte au «récit de base» de Deut 9-10*[72].

h) Comme on l'a remarqué depuis longtemps, les vv. 22-24 interrompent le fil du récit[73] et doivent, par ailleurs, être rapprochés des vv. 7b-8 Dtr525, tant sur le plan du contenu que sur celui de l'expression. Ces versets appartiennent à la même strate[74]. Remarquons la phrase finale, qui résume toutes les infidélités d'Israël et forme une sorte de conclusion des différents ajouts Dtr525 qui précèdent (voir les vv. 7aβb-8,18b-19a,20,22-23).

i) On retrouve aux vv. 25-29 l'intercession de Moïse, à laquelle répondra l'offre de nouvelles Tables (10,1-5); cette fois, la prière occupe dans la structure du récit la même place qu'Ex 32,30-32a Dtr585, même si la formulation est différente. On remarquera surtout la motivation donnée au v. 28, typique de Dtr575: l'accusation selon laquelle Yahvé aurait agi par haine envers son peuple (cfr Ex 32,12). L'essentiel de cette section appartient donc à cette rédaction. Encore une fois, cependant, il faut constater la présence d'éléments plus récents:
— Il y a concurrence entre le v. 25aα et le v. 26aα, qui parlent tous deux de la prosternation de Moïse en termes très semblables. La phrase la plus ancienne est sans doute la seconde, car le v. 25aα — formulé de manière identique au v. 18aα — semble servir avant tout à introduire le motif plus récent des 40 jours (cfr v. 18aβ). Le v. 25b reprend la phraséologie des vv. 8, 19a et 20, avec l'expression *l^e^hašmîd*. C'est donc l'ensemble du v. 25 qui paraît provenir de Dtr525.
— Dans la prière de Moïse, le v. 27 introduit un nouvel argument, qui brise la belle continuïté du motif de la sortie d'Égypte aux vv. 26 et 28, comme d'ailleurs en Ex 32,11-12 Dtr575. De plus, l'appel à la mémoire des patriarches correspond à l'addition du v. 13 Dtr525 dans le récit

secondaire qui ne correspond pas à Ex 32 et ne convient pas après les vv. 15-17, car la supplication a son lieu naturel sur la montagne.

71. Pour F.-L. HOSSFELD, *Der Dekalog*, p. 149, ce verset forme une addition aux vv. 18-19 et doit donc être très tardif.

72. Ainsi que le souligne F. GARCÍA LÓPEZ, *Analyse*, pp. 22-23, la formulation précise de Deut 9,21 est plus proche de 2 Rois 23,6,12 que d'Ex 32,20, «montrant par là son caractère secondaire vis-à-vis de cette tradition» (p. 23).

73. Voir, parmi d'autres, F.-L. HOSSFELD, *Der Dekalog*, p. 149.

74. Sur le lien avec les vv. 7-8, voir N. LOHFINK, *Das Hauptgebot*, pp. 210-211; P. BUIS, *Le Deutéronome*, pp. 163,166; F. GARCÍA LÓPEZ, *Analyse*, p. 23. N. LOHFINK, *Kerygmata*, p. 100, précise que les vv. 1-8 et 22-24 sont l'œuvre du dernier rédacteur deutéronomiste (DtrÜ).

parallèle d'Ex 32. Ce verset sera donc assigné à la même rédaction Dtr525 [75]; comme les vv. 7b-8,18b-20,22-24, il souligne d'ailleurs la culpabilité du peuple pour lequel Moïse intercède.

j) Deut 10,1-5 suit littéralement le récit Dtr585 d'Ex 34,1.4*.28b-29a* et appartient au texte de base de Deut 9-10 [76]. Les seuls éléments nouveaux par rapport à la *Vorlage* d'Ex 34 sont la fabrication de l'Arche — qui semble répondre au souci juridique que le rédacteur manifeste aussi en 9,10,17 [77] — et la relative *'ᵃšèr dibbèr YHWH 'ᵃléykèm bāhār mittôk hā'éš bᵉyôm haqqāhāl*, «que Yahvé vous a dites sur la montagne, du milieu du feu, au jour de l'Assemblée» (v. 4); cette phrase est presque identique à 9,10 (cfr 5,4), et rien n'empêche son appartenance à Dtr575 [78]. La remise des nouvelles Tables signifie la pardon divin et le rétablissement des liens antérieurs, en réponse à la supplication de Moïse (9,26.28-29).

k) La section 10,6-9 est généralement tenue pour secondaire [79]. Ces versets interrompent, en effet, le fil du récit, qui reprend aux vv. 10-11. Encore faut-il distinguer deux apports différents:
— Les vv. 8-9 commentent le dépôt des Tables dans l'Arche et s'y rattachent sans doute directement. Ces versets exaltent le rôle des lévites; comme Ex 32,25-29, ils appartiennent sans doute à Dtr525 [80].
— Les vv. 6-7, qui s'intercalent, sont apparentés à P par leur vocabulaire et leur contenu [81]. Ils s'expliquent au mieux par la volonté de rattacher les privilèges accordés à la tribu de Lévi à la figure d'Aaron. On assiste donc, comme en Ex 32,21-24, à une réhabilitation d'Aaron, qui ne peut provenir que de milieux se réclamant de lui.

75. L'appartenance du v. 27 à une strate plus récente que le texte de base de la prière de Moïse est soulignée par F.-L. HOSSFELD, *Der Dekalog*, p. 153.

76. Plusieurs auteurs tiennent la section 10,1-5 pour une addition au récit primitif de Deut 9-10*, écrite par analogie avec Ex 34. Voir G. SEITZ, *Redaktionsgeschichtliche Studien*, pp. 51-57; S. E. LOEWENSTAMM, *The Formula* בעת ההיא *in Deuteronomy*, dans *Tarbiz* 38 (1968-1969) 99-104; F.-L. HOSSFELD, *Der Dekalog*, p. 150, 155. Précisément, le parallèle étroit avec Ex 34 paraît être le signe le plus clair de l'appartenance de la section au récit de base!

77. Voir N. LOHFINK, *Das Hauptgebot*, p. 212.

78. L'expression *bᵉyôm haqqāhāl* pose le même problème qu'en 9,10; voir *supra*, note 66.

79. Le caractère additionnel de ces versets est admis même par des auteurs portés à défendre presque inconditionnellement l'unité du texte, comme P. C. CRAIGIE, *The Book of Deuteronomy*, Grand Rapids, 1976, p. 200.

80. N. LOHFINK, *Das Hauptgebot*, p. 209, note avec raison le lien de ces versets avec 9,20: on y retrouve la même expression *bā'ét hahî'* (voir aussi 10,1, cependant), mais aussi l'intérêt pour la question du sacerdoce légitime: alors qu'Aaron est tenu pour coupable et échappe de peu à la colère divine (9,20), la tribu de Lévi est mise à part et investie par Yahvé de la mission du service liturgique «jusqu'à ce jour» (v. 8). Cette dernière expression prend tout son sens dans le contexte d'une contestation du sacerdoce aaronide.

81. Voir F. GARCÍA LÓPEZ, *Analyse*, p. 30, n. 208.

l) Deut 10,10 reprend encore une fois le motif de l'intercession pendant 40 jours, suivi par l'exaucement. La formulation est presque identique à 9,18a.19b Dtr525, sauf la finale, qui semble inspirée par 9,26 (*šāḥat*, «détruire»). La prière de Moïse ne s'explique que si le peuple avait recommencé à pécher: on retrouve donc la préoccupation de souligner la culpabilité grave et répétée d'Israël, telle qu'elle se manifeste dans les additions de Dtr525.

m) Deut 10,11, enfin, pourrait avoir constitué la finale du «récit de base» des ch. 9-10. En effet, non seulement il se rattache sans difficulté au v. 5, mais en outre il reprend en substance Ex 32,34a Dtr585, que le rédacteur avait omis plus haut pour ne pas introduire le motif de la Visite punitive de Yahvé (voir aussi Ex 33,3,12 Dtr575). Remarquons l'absence de toute allusion à une interdiction faite à Moïse de franchir le Jourdain: le rédacteur semble ignorer Nb 20,12; Deut 1,37-38; 3,23-28; 32,48-52 [82]. La suite logique du récit se trouve en 12,1*, qui introduit le Code législatif.

Conclusion

Les textes examinés mériteraient sans doute une analyse plus fouillée. Voici néanmoins quelques conclusions provisoires, qui devront être confirmées par des enquêtes complémentaires:

1. Les hypothèses formulées plus haut quant à la formulation du Deutéronome s'écartent sur des points essentiels de l'opinion générale: ainsi, le livre apparu sous Josias n'aurait comporté à ce moment que le Code deutéronomique, sans introduction narrative ou parénétique; en outre, sous sa forme la plus ancienne, qui remonte au début de la période exilique, le Code aurait été introduit par le récit des événements de l'Horeb, avec la remise du Décalogue (ch. 5*) et l'affaire du veau d'or (ch. 9-10*); quant aux nombreux développements parénétiques du livre, ils seraient l'œuvre des deux derniers rédacteurs deutéronomistes, qui écrivaient respectivement vers 560 et à l'époque du retour des déportés. Aussi surprenantes que soient ces hypothèses, elles se trouvent confirmées par l'analyse particulière de Deut 5.9-10*, où elles fonctionnent sans difficulté.

2. L'introduction primitive du Deutéronome semble avoir comporté les éléments suivants: 4,44; 5,1aα.4.5bβ(*lē'mōr*).6-12a.13-14a.15b.16*.17-24a.25b-27; 9,9a.10.12-14a.15-17.21.26.28-29; 10,1-5.11. Ce texte, qui raconte la grande théophanie, avec la révélation du Décalogue, la remise des Tables, la constatation de l'apostasie d'Israël et le bris des Tables,

82. C'est dans ces textes où Moïse remet le pouvoir à Josué que Deut 10,11b est repris mot pour mot (Jos 1,6; cfr Deut. 31,7); ce n'est pas par hasard!

puis la prière de Moïse, le don de Tables nouvelles et l'envoi vers la terre promise, forme un récit continu, qui suit d'assez près, dans l'ensemble, le texte (continu, lui aussi) d'Ex 19-34 dans sa rédaction E + Dtr585. Le rédacteur veut sans doute présenter le Code deutéronomique comme l'ensemble des prescriptions qui appliquent la loi fondamentale du Décalogue pour le temps du séjour sur la terre promise. Par ailleurs, l'accent est placé sur la générosité de Yahvé: si le drame de l'an 587 a tout de même eu lieu, c'est parce qu'Israël, inattentif aux pardons successifs dont Yahvé le gratifiait, a refusé avec obstination le chemin de la fidélité; il a trahi son Dieu non seulement au temps du désert, mais aussi sur la bonne terre qu'il avait reçue en héritage. Ce texte ne comporte aucun élément parénétique, ce qui s'explique bien: les regards ne se tournent pas encore vers les conditions d'un bonheur à retrouver, mais restent fixés sur le scandale du rejet d'Israël; il s'agit de répondre à la révolte qui gronde contre Yahvé, d'où le souci juridique du rédacteur. Tout ceci convient au contexte des années 580-570 environ et correspond au profil de la rédaction Dtr575 d'Ex 19-34.

3. La deuxième rédaction du texte se caractérise par une lecture plutôt positive des événements douloureux que vit Israël. Après quarante ans de marche au désert — lisons en clair: après une quarantaine d'années de grandes épreuves au VIe siècle —, la génération nouvelle constate qu'elle a survécu (5,2-3,24b-25a); surtout, elle se met à réfléchir à la possibilité de retrouver le bonheur perdu («et que tu sois heureux», 5,16; «ce qui te rendra heureux», 6,3), d'où l'invitation répétée à la mémoire des événements passés («tu te souviendras», 5,15; «souviens-toi; n'oublie-toi; n'oublie pas», 9,7) et à l'obéissance («écoute, Israël», 5,1; «comme te l'a commandé Yahvé ton Dieu», 5,12b,16a; voir aussi 6,2-3), ainsi que l'emploi du conditionnel (6,2-3). Cette fois, l'élément parénétique devient dominant. Notons l'emploi des personnes: alors que, dans le récit de base, Moïse s'adressait à Israël à l'aide de la forme «vous»[83], Dtr560 utilise le «tu» pour la parénèse et le «nous» pour la constatation des faits du passé et du présent (5,2-3,24b-25a). Les nombreux passages parénétiques en «tu» de la section 6,4-9,6 pourraient appartenir à la même strate, ce qui demande évidemment vérification attentive; en tout cas, l'histoire du veau d'or est aujourd'hui séparée de celle du ch. 5 et précédée d'une introduction (9,7a) qui la place sous le signe du «souviens-toi» et l'englobe ainsi dans la parénèse. Tout ceci correspond aux préoccupations du rédacteur Dtr560 d'Ex 19-34.

4. La troisième rédaction de Deut 5.9-10* souligne plus encore que la précédente l'appel à la parfaite obéissance; contrairement à Dtr560, elle utilise pour sa parénèse la forme «vous» (5,1,28-33; 6,1), qui pourrait

83. Le Décalogue, repris à Ex 20, fait évidemment exception, mais il faut noter que son cadre rédactionnel est écrit à la forme «vous» (5,4,22).

correspondre à un glissement vers la perspective d'une rétribution plus individuelle que nationale. Par opposition à la strate précédente, on note aussi que Moïse est présenté comme médiateur entre Yahvé et Israël: il n'y a plus de communication directe, car le peuple est resté au bas de la montagne, et c'est Moïse qui doit transmettre les paroles divines (5,1,5,28-31). Dans les ch. 9-10, cette médiation s'exerce par la prière d'intercession efficace de Moïse (9,18-20,25; 10,10). Tout ceci contribue à opposer Moïse, champion de la fidélité, à tout le peuple idolâtre; on retrouve la même opposition dans la dernière strate deutéronomiste de l'histoire d'Élie, où le prophète reste le seul fidèle de Yahvé face au peuple qui adore Baal sous la conduite de Jézabel (voir 1 Rois 18,3b-4,13-14,19bβ; 19,1-10,15-17; 21,1-16*,23,25-26)[84]. Moïse est ainsi présenté comme le prophète par excellence, qui intercède avec puissance pour son peuple et l'appelle sans relâche à la fidélité aux commandements de Yahvé. D'autre part, c'est le même rédacteur qui souligne la culpabilité d'Aaron (9,20) et parle en termes positifs de la fonction sacerdotale des lévites (10,8-9). Il y a donc pour lui un clergé infidèle — celui qui a été déporté — et un clergé lié à Yahvé; peut-être oppose-t-il aussi de manière implicite le vrai prophète Moïse aux «prophètes de mensonge» des sections deutéronomistes en prose de Jérémie (voir en particulier Jér 26,11,16-19, où «prêtres et prophètes» veulent mettre à mort Jérémie, défendu par les princes et certains «anciens du pays»[85].

84. C'est surtout O.H. STECK, *Ueberlieferung und Zeitgeschichte in den Elia-Erzählungen* (WMANT, 22), Neukirchen, 1968, qui a montré que la stylisation actuelle du récit, avec son opposition entre Élie et Jézabel, provient d'une rédaction secondaire; celle-ci est identifiée avec DtrP (vers 580-560) par R. BOHLEN, *Der Fall Nabot* (Trierer Theologische Studien, 35), Trèves, 1978, p. 319. On peut cependant se demander si l'opposition Élie-Jézabel n'est pas l'œuvre d'une rédaction deutéronomiste plus récente. Prenons l'exemple de 1 Rois 18. On peut y discerner au moins trois niveaux rédactionnels. L'élément le plus ancien semble être le cadre du chapitre (vv. 1-2a et 41-46), dans lequel Élie n'entre pas en conflit avec le roi, mais réalise devant lui un prodige: il annonce, contre toute attente humaine, la venue de la pluie, et celle-ci vient en effet aussitôt. Une deuxième rédaction introduit la scène du Carmel (vv. 20-40; récit originellement indépendant?), précédée par le double épisode de la rencontre d'Élie avec Obadyahu et avec Achab (vv. 2b-19*). Cette fois, l'opposition entre le prophète et le roi est placée en évidence: les vv. 2b-19* font peser la responsabilité de la trahison de l'Alliance sur Achab, en conformité avec la notice de 1 Rois 16,30-33 Dtr; les 450 prophètes de Baal sont les créatures du roi, qui a «abandonné Yahvé et suivi les Baals» (v. 18b); en face d'Achab, persécuteur des prophètes authentiques, se trouvent Élie («C'est Yahvé qui est mon Dieu») et Obadyahu («Serviteur de Yahvé»), dont le rédacteur souligne le respect pour le vrai prophète (v. 7) et la crainte de Dieu (v. 12). Cette deuxième rédaction est deutéronomiste, comme en témoignent à la fois son kérygme et sa phraséologie. C'est une rédaction deutéronomiste secondaire qui a fait ensuite porter le poids de l'opposition à Yahvé et à son prophète sur Jézabel; cette relecture s'est traduite par l'addition des vv. 3b-4, 13-14 et 19bβ («qui mangent à la table de Jézabel»).

85. Jér 26 recèle une double présentation de l'attitude du peuple à l'égard de Jérémie: aux vv. 8-9 et 24, le peuple est hostile au prophète et veut le condamner à mort; au v. 16, au contraire, «les princes et le peuple entier» s'opposent à une telle mesure et

Le rédacteur paraît s'opposer ici au groupe des déportés guidés par les prêtres aaronides: ce groupe a été expulsé parce qu'il formait la partie coupable du peuple. Une telle polémique trouve son meilleur contexte historique au moment du retour des exilés, soit probablement vers les années 525-520[86]; on trouve les mêmes centres d'intérêt dans la strate Dtr525 d'Ex 19-34. Les éléments parénétiques en «vous» des autres sections du Deutéronome, éléments qui se greffent le plus souvent sur des textes au singulier, pourraient provenir du même rédacteur.

5. Signalons aussi la présence de quelques additions postexiliques, qui se situent dans la mouvance sacerdotale, notamment en 5,26 et 10,6-7; ce dernier texte a pour fonction de situer les lévites dans le prolongement d'Aaron. Une telle addition ne peut émaner que de milieux proches du sacerdoce aaronide.

6. Si ce qui précède est exact, au moins en substance, il en faut en tirer les conséquences dans d'autres domaines. Tout d'abord, l'existence de quatre rédacteurs deutéronomistes qui se succèdent de 587 au temps du retour[87] oblige à reconsidérer la question des soi-disant textes «pré-» ou «proto-deutéronomistes» de l'époque royale: ces textes peuvent probablement être expliqués par l'appartenance à l'une ou l'autre strate

protègent Jérémie contre les prêtres et les prophètes. On remarquera en outre que le v. 11 — formulé en termes presque identiques au v. 16 — fait état d'un discours des prêtres et des prophètes aux princes et à tout le peuple; or, aux vv. 12-15, c'est Jérémie qui répond, et en s'adressant «à tous les princes et à tout le peuple» ... qui n'ont pas pris la parole! Autrement dit, il semble que les vv. 11 et 16 (auxquels on ajoutera les vv. 17-19), formulés de manière assez stéréotypée, constituent deux additions complémentaires destinées à opposer, à l'intérieur de la population judéenne, deux groupes antagonistes. La première rédaction — postérieure au fond ancien de Jér 7 et elle-même deutéronomiste — parlait d'un rejet de Jérémie par toute la nation; c'est une rédaction deutéronomiste secondaire qui innocente le peuple comme tel ainsi que certains notables, mais accuse en particulier les prêtres et les prophètes hostiles à Jérémie, c'est-à-dire le groupe des exilés et ses leaders.

86. La date du retour des Juifs exilés à Babylone est controversée; je me rallie ici à l'hypothèse défendue par S. Herrmann (voir *supra*, note 23).

87. La succession de quatre rédactions deutéronomistes à l'époque exilique est défendue à propos de l'ensemble Josué-Rois par R. SMEND, *Die Entstehung des Alten Testaments*, Stuttgart, 1978, pp. 110-125; dans ses publications antérieures, l'auteur distinguait DtrG (appelé plus tard DtrH), DtrP et DtrN; il distingue à présent en outre DtrN1 et DtrN2 (p. 115). Les distinctions établies par R. Smend et son école (W. Dietrich, T. Veijola, etc.) ne correspondent pas à celles que j'établis en Ex 19-34 et Deut 5-11. Quoi qu'il en soit, la succession de quatre rédacteurs au temps de l'Exil n'a rien d'invraisemblable. On sait que les auteurs de l'Ancien Testament ont — le plus souvent, en tout cas — écrit parce que se posaient à eux et à leur entourage des questions vitales; la catastrophe de 587 a évidemment suscité parmi les Judéens les interrogations les plus douloureuses, et le flot des questions n'a pas dû se ralentir beaucoup durant les décennies qui ont suivi, notamment avec l'avènement d'une nouvelle génération qui s'estimait innocente du crime de ses devanciers, puis avec la confrontation avec les déportés rentrant au pays. C'est, assez logiquement, aux périodes où Israël subit les chocs les plus rudes et s'interroge avec angoisse à la fois sur l'attitude de Yahvé à son égard et sur son propre avenir en tant que peuple, que la réflexion sur l'histoire passée s'intensifie.

de l'époque exilique, qui permet de rendre compte de divergences avec ce qu'il est convaincu d'appeler «le» message deutèronomiste; l'hypothèse «pré-deutéronomiste» serait donc superflue. En second lieu, il faut peut-être renoncer à voir une continuïté profonde entre le «Code deutéronomique» dans sa forme originelle et l'«école deutéronomiste». Rien n'oblige à penser que le Code primitif ait été écrit dans une perspective théologique proche des milieux deutéronomistes; la loi de la centralisation du culte, en particulier, peut avoir été édictée pour des motifs politiques avant tout. Il est certain que les rédacteurs deutéronomistes y retrouvaient certaines de leurs préoccupations, sinon ils ne lui auraient pas donné une telle place; cependant on peut en dire autant du Décalogue et du *Bundesbuch*, dont l'origine est certainement indépendante de la mouvance deutéronomiste. Mais ce ne sont là que des conséquences possibles et lointaines de l'examen d'Ex 19-34 et Deut 5.9-10*: seule, l'étude attentive de l'ensemble des textes pourra les confirmer.

Avenue Henri Conscience, 156
B-1140 Bruxelles

Jacques VERMEYLEN

THE DESTRUCTION OF THE CALF

(Exod 32,20/Deut 9,21)

I. Introduction

The Old Testament devotes two rather extended segments to the affair of the «Golden Calf» and its sequels, i.e. Exod 32,1-34,28 and Deut 9,7(a)b-10,11[1]. Both accounts contain, as one of their climactic moments, a description of the various measures carried out by Moses against the calf. Within the version of Exod 32,20 five such measures may be distinguished, while the parallel Deut 9,21 enumerates four actions of Moses, compare:

Ex 32,20		*Dt 9,21*	
1)	ויקח את העגל	1)	ואת חטאתכם
	אשר עשו		אשר עשיתם את העגל לקחתי
2)	וישרף באש	2)	ואשרף אתו באש
3)	ויטחן	3)	ואכת אתו טחון היטב
	עד אשר דק		עד אשר דק לעפר
4)	ויזר	4)	ואשלך את עפרו
	על פני המים		אל הנחל הירד מן ההר
5)	וישק את בני ישראל		

The presentation of the above two verses might seem straightforward enough at first reading. And yet, even long before the «critical period» of Biblical study and right up until today, difficulties have been found with one or other feature of the two accounts — that of Exod 32,20 in particular. Here at the outset, then, it seems appropriate to briefly review the main problems which have emerged in the course of the history of research. Four such problems may be distinguished:

1) A first problem concerns the compatibility between Exod 32,20 and its context. Specifically, on a spontaneous understanding, the terms *śārap* and *ṭāḥan* in the former appear to refer to Moses' «burning» and «grinding» the calf respectively. But how then does his doing that square with the account of Aaron's fabrication of the calf in 32,4 where — again *prima facie* at least — the reference seems to be the fashioning of a molten calf of solid gold, seeing that, properly speaking, gold can be neither «burnt» nor «ground»?

1. Our delimitations of the two segments are approximate and rather conventional, but sufficient for our purposes. For more details, see the commentaries on Exodus and Deuteronomy.

2) Also taken for itself, Exod 32,20 (as likewise Deut 9,21) poses problems as regards the compatibility of the various measures of Moses it relates. Is it, e.g. conceivable that the same object which had first been «burnt» would thereafter still be capable of being «ground»?

3) What is the sense of Moses' final action as recounted in Exod 32,20, i.e. his having the people drink from «water» impregnated with the calf's remains?

4) How is the nature of the relationship between the two verses to be understood, given both their considerable verbal similarity, as well as their divergencies? Is the one literarily dependent on the other, and, if so, in which direction does the dependence lie? Under this head it is especially the absence in Deut 9,21 of anything corresponding to the «giving-to-drink motif» of Exod 32,20 which calls for explanation. Did the author of Deuteronomy deliberately eliminate that motif in his rewriting of the text of Exodus, or does it, rather, represent an amplification by the writer of Exod 32,20 (or by a later redactor of that verse) of an earlier, shorter formulation preserved in Deuteronomy?

In the history — stretching back to the *dicta* of the Talmudic authorities — of scholarly attempts at resolving the above questions, we may, with J. Hahn [2], distinguish two distinct periods. A first period extends until c. 1960 [3]. This period may be characterized and delimitated from the following one above all in negative terms [4]. In the first place, the account of Moses' actions in our two verses was, in this period, treated virtually without reference to the large (and ever-expanding) body of extra-Biblical ANE documentation concerned with the destruction/elimination of undesirable entities of all sorts, texts expressive of what U. Rüterswörden has called a « *Vernichtungssymbolik* » [5]. Likewise in this

2. J. HAHN, *Das «Goldene Kalb». Die Jahwe-Verehrung bei Stierbildern in der Geschichte Israels* (EHS XXIII/154), Frankfurt a.M., 1981, p. 196. This work is a revised version of the author's Tübingen dissertation of 1980. Rather remarkably, as may be noted, two other dissertations dealing with Exodus 32 appeared almost simultaneously with that of Hahn, i.e. A.J. MEENAN, *An Interpretative Study of the Narrative of the Golden Calf (Exodus 32)*, Edinburgh, 1980, and C. LAMBERT, *Le Veau d'or: étude critique et historique du chapitre 32 du livre de l'Exode*, 2 Vols., Université de la Sorbonne nouvelle (Paris III), 1982. Neither of these two latter works attempts to develop the problematic of Exod 32,20 (Deut 9,21) in the directions proposed in this paper.

3. It must, of course, be acknowledged that no absolute demarcation between pre- and post 1960 scholarship on the two verses can be made, since e.g. in various commentaries, monographs, etc. from the '60's and '70's our verses are treated in terms of the older questions and answers and without reference to the more recent approaches. This is the case e.g. with the following Deuteronomy commentaries of the last decade in their comments on Deut 9,21: A. PENNA, *Deuteronomio* (LSB), Torino-Roma, 1976; P.C. CRAIGIE, *The Book of Deuteronomy* (NICOT), London, 1976; A.D.H. MAYES, *Deuteronomy* (NCB), London, 1979.

4. For a detailed treatment of the handling of the two verses and the questions raised by them in the pre-1960 period, see HAHN, *Kalb*, pp. 95-208.

5. See the titles of his articles: *Vernichtungssymbolik in Ugarit*, in *Göttinger Miscellen* 19 (1976) 51-55; *Beiträge zur Vernichtungssymbolik*, in *BN 2* (1977) 16-22.

pre-1960 period of scholarship, no really systematic attempt was made to relate Moses' actions here with the full range of accounts elsewhere in the OT itself of the annihilation of offending cultic objects, just as relatively little effort was applied to exploiting the significant indications such a comparison can provide regarding the problem of the nature of the relationship between the two verses [6]. By contrast, post-1960 discussion of the two verses has been characterized by the attempt to bring their descriptions into connection with the extra-Biblical material on the one hand, and to investigate their affinities with other similar OT texts in an ever more thorough-going way on the other. Both these efforts have had a transforming effect on the whole approach to the various problems raised by the two verses as presented above. Both efforts are however, we believe, capable of further elaboration. In addition, it should be noted that the efforts have, to a large extent, been pursued in isolation from each other. Accordingly, our concern in this paper will be, not only to further extend each of the two contemporary approaches considered for itself, but also to promote their closer integration. In carrying out this aim, our procedure will be first to consider the extra-Biblical comparable material to the two Biblical verses. Thereafter, we shall examine the relationship of the two verses themselves; this investigation will, in turn, necessitate bringing into play the second approach mentioned above, i.e. an exploration of the affinities and differences between Exod 32,20/Deut 9,21 and a whole range of other OT texts speaking of the destruction of prohibited cultic objects. We shall then conclude with a few summary remarks concerning the integration of the two approaches.

II. Exod 32,20/Deut 9,21 and the extra-Biblical Comparative Material

A. *The State of the Question*

In the last 20 years, the two OT versions of Moses' destruction of the calf have been brought into connection, as indicated above, with a series of ANE texts speaking of the annihilation/elimination of various undesirable entities. In very general terms, the extra-Biblical materials adduced on this point may all be called mythological and/or magico-ritual in nature. In a first segment of this section of our paper we propose, as a kind of *status questionis*, to briefly review the documentation hitherto put forward by different authors, expanding it with references to like material where appropriate. We undertake this review on the consideration that the treatment given of this more recent

6. Such attempts were occasionally made in the earlier research, see e.g. K. H. Graf, *Die geschichtlichen Bücher des Alten Testaments*, Leipzig, 1866, p. 15 who cites 2 Kgs 23,6, 15 as comparative texts to Deut 9,21 which he views as a «freely reworked» version of Exod 32,20.

approach to the two Biblical verses in the monumental *forschungs-geschichtlich* survey of Exod 32 by J. Hahn is both rather summary and occasionally not altogether accurate [7]. Thereafter, we shall turn to a consideration of other types of ANE material which have not yet been brought into the discussion concerning the background to Exod 32,20/ Deut 9,21 but which are, in our view, of possible relevance to that discussion. In looking now first to the mythological and/or magico-ritual texts which have been cited as parallels to our verses by previous authors, we shall examine, in turn, material from the Ugaritic, Egyptian, Meso-potamian and Hittite spheres:

1) *Ugarit*: Of all the ANE «parallels» to the presentation of Exod 32,20/Deut 9,21 adduced in the last two decades, the first and most cited is the two-fold account, found within the Ugaritic «Ba'al-'Anat cycle», of 'Anat's assault on Mot, the murderer of her brother Ba'al, the first using the third person, the second having Mot himself relate, in the first person, and in somewhat different words, 'Anat's actions against him, compare:

KTU 1.6 II 30-37 [8]	*KTU 1.6 V 11-19* [9]
^{30}... *tiḫd* ^{31}*bn.ilm.mt.*	^{11}... *lk.bʿlm* ^{12}*pht.qlt.*
bḥrb ^{32}*tbqʿnn.*	*ʿlk.pht* ^{13}*dry.bḥrb*
bḫtr.tdry^{33}*nn.*	
bišt.tšrpnn	*ʿlk* ^{14}*pht.šrp.bišt*
^{34}*brḥm.tṭḥnn*	^{15}*ʿlk.* [*pht.ṭh*]*n brḥ* ^{16}*m.*
bšd ^{35}*tdrʿ.nn*	*ʿ*[*lk.*]*pht* [*.dr*]*y.bkbrt*
širh.ltikl ^{36}*ʿṣrm*	^{17}*ʿlk*[.] *pht.ǵly.*—^{18}*bšdm*
mnth.ltkly ^{37}*npr*[*m*].	*lk*[.] *pht* ^{19}*drʿ.bym.* ...
šir.lšir.yṣḥ	

Since their first publication in 1931 [10] these two passages have stimulated a whole series of (interrelated) controversies. These concern, first of all, the determination of the Ugaritic readings and their transla-tion. Likewise controverted is the understanding of Mot here — is he simply a hostile, destructive power («death») or does he represent (or also represent) rather the forces of fertility present in the grain? Finally, and above all, it has been debated whether or not a ritual is to be presupposed as the background of these «mythological» formulations — and if so, precisely what sort of ritual that would have been. We

7. For Hahn's treatment of post-1960 developments on Exod 32,20/Deut 9,21, see *Kalb*, pp. 208-212.

8. We cite the text as given by G. DEL OLMO LETE, *Mitos y Leyendas de Canaan*, Madrid, 1982, pp. 227-228.

9. DEL OLMO LETE, *Mitos*, p. 231.

10. C. VIROLLEAUD, *Un poème phénicien de Ras-Shamra*, in *Syria* 12 (1931) 193-224, pp. 205-206, 218-219.

cannot enter into these problems here [11]. We may, however, mention the rather surprising fact that it was not until thirty years after their first publication that these «Mot-passages» were first associated with the descriptions of Exod 32,20/Deut 9,21 [12]. That this connection should not have been made sooner is all the more surprising given what now appears as the quite obvious and striking affinities between the two sets of texts, as well as the fact that, in the interval, the Ugaritic passages had been treated by a number of OT scholars who did find links between them and other OT texts [13]. In any event, the first author to make the connection in print, albeit in a quite passing way, was S. E. Loewenstamm in 1962 [14]. Subsequently, the parallelism between the Ugaritic and Biblical calf-texts has been further elucidated, and its implications for our approach to the latter worked out by a whole series of authors — notably by Loewenstamm himself [15]. And while a few scholars have attempted to

11. From the vast literature on these questions we may cite the following (with emphasis on the more recent discussions): S. E. LOEWENSTAMM, *The Killing of Mot in Ugaritic Myth*, in *Orientalia* 41 (1972) 378-382; P. L. WATSON, *Mot, the God of Death at Ugarit and in the Old Testament*, Dissertation Yale, 1970, pp. 59, 63-64, 110-114, 122-123, 172-187, 205-213, nn. 1-60; *idem, The Death of «Death» in the Ugaritic Texts*, in *JAOS* 92 (1972) 60-64; A. CAQUOT-M. SZNYCER, *Textes ougaritiques*, t. 1: *Mythes et légendes*, Paris, 1974, pp. 229-234, 260, 266; B. MARGALIT, *A Matter of «Life» and «Death». A Study of the Baal-Mot Epic (CTA 4-5-6)* (AOAT, 206), Kevelaer/Neukirchen-Vluyn, 1980, pp. 158-162, 176, 181-184; DEL OLMO LETE, *Mitos*, pp. 138 and n. 199, 227-228, 231; LAMBERT, *Veau*, pp. 239-250; J. F. HEALEY, *Burning the Corn: New Light on the Killing of Motu*, in *Orientalia* 52 (1983) 248-251.

12. Somewhat analogous would be the delay of more than two decades by OT scholars in recognizing the significance of V. Korošec's account of the structure of the Hittite treaties for the study of OT «covenant texts».

13. Thus in one of the first studies of the Ugaritic passages, R. DUSSAUD, *La mythologie phénicienne d'après les tablettes de Ras Shamra*, in *RHR* 52 (1931) 353-408 linked these texts with the prescriptions concerning the offering of the fire-parched first fruits of the grain in Lev 2,14 (*Ibid.*, p. 391) and the depiction of the fate of the descendents of Saul in 2 Sam 21,1-10 whose corpses are exposed to consumption by birds and beasts (*Ibid.*, p. 392).

14. *The Ugaritic Fertility Myth - the Result of a Mistranslation*, in *IEJ* 12 (1962) 87-88, p. 87.

15. From among the numerous authors invoking the parallelism in the last two decades, we limit ourselves to the following studies which have been especially influential in working out that parallelism and its implications: S. E. LOEWENSTAMM, *The Making and Destruction of the Golden Calf*, in *Biblica* 48 (1967) 481-490, pp. 484-485; *idem, The Making and Destruction of the Golden Calf — A Rejoinder*, in *Biblica* 56 (1975) 330-348, pp. 338-340; F. C. FENSHAM, *The Burning of the Golden Calf and Ugarit*, in *IEJ* 16 (1966) 191-193, pp. 192-193; O. HVIDBERG-HANSEN, *Guldkaklvnes ødelaeggelse- en omformet frugtbarheidsrite?*, Licentiate Thesis Copenhagen, 1967, pp. 31-66, 96-97; *idem, Die Vernichtung des Goldenen Kalbes und der ugaritische Ernteritus*, in *Acta orientalia* 33 (1971) 5-46, pp. 23-33; WATSON, *Mot*, pp. 183-185; J. W. DAVENPORT, *A Study of the Golden Calf Tradition in Exodus 32*, Dissertation Princeton Theological Seminary, 1973, pp. 37-43.
In this connection we may note that Hahn's formulations in his account of the history of the question of the parallelism between the Ugaritic Mot texts and the Biblical calf narratives are somewhat misleading. In the body of his text, p. 208 he speaks of «von

downplay the affinities between them [16], it remains that the Ugaritic texts do represent the closest parallels — especially at the verbal level — to our Biblical passages yet adduced. In particular, we may note the following correspondences between them:

— In both a whole series of destructive actions are applied to one and the same entity. In both instances too the accumulation of these actions becomes problematic when taken as a straightforward account of an actual occurrence, e.g. if Mot were «burned», what would be left to be «eaten by the birds» as the first Ugaritic version relates?

— The Ugaritic and Biblical passages strikingly correspond in the sequence of and terms used for the annihilatory acts they relate. In the first Ugaritic version, as well as in both Biblical texts, the series opens with a verb referring to the destroyer's «getting hold» of the one to be annihilated (*tiḫd/lqḥ*). Subsequently, we have mention of a «burning» and a «grinding» of the reprobate entity, the Ugaritic and Hebrew terms used being cognates in both cases. Likewise the Ugaritic term *drʿ* used of the «scattering» of Mot's remains in the first version is generally taken as a cognate of the Hebrew *zārāh* in Exod 32,20. Again, the reference to the birds' «eating» Mot's remains with which the first Ugaritic version concludes can be compared with the people's «drinking» water laced with the calf grindings at the end of Exod 32,20. Finally, the mention of the «scattering» of Mot's remains, this time «in the sea», in the second Ugaritic version parallels the reference to Moses' casting the dust of the calf into a «brook» as the conclusion to the account of Deut 9,21.

How now does the fact of such striking correspondences between the Biblical and Ugaritic texts affect our approach to the various problems which have historically preoccupied scholars with regard to the former? In the first place, the parallelism would seem to indicate that the difficulties about the possibility of the actions related being actually performed on a calf of gold and the compatibility of the various actions among themselves, as well as the various attempts at resolving those difficulties which have been made are, in large part at least, inappro-

mehreren unabhängig von einander arbeitenden Exegeten» who have referred to this parallelism. In n. 67 to this allusion he lists a whole series of authors beginning with T. Worden in a VT article of 1953. Nowhere in that article, however, does Worden make a connection specifically between the Ugaritic texts and the Biblical calf accounts. The first to make such a connection, as indicated above in our text, was S. E. Loewenstamm, in an article we cite in n. 14. In his note Hahn does not mention this article of Loewenstamm on which the various authors whom he lists other than Worden did draw — whether directly or proximately — for their recognition of the parallelism, rather than coming to it independently as the wording of Hahn's text suggests.

16. E.g. L. G. PERDUE, *The Making and Destruction of the Golden Calf — a Reply*, in *Biblica* 54 (1973) 237-246, pp. 240-244; J. C. DE MOOR, *The Seasonal Pattern in the Ugaritic Myth of Baʿlu according to the Version of Ilmilku* (AOAT, 16), Kevelaer/Neukirchen-Vluyn, 1971, p. 213, n. 7.

priate to the intention of the texts themselves. In both the Biblical and Ugaritic material, the concern appears to be rather with heaping up every imaginable sort of destructive action without regard for the factual applicability of those actions to the object in question, or to the possibility of all the various actions being successively employed against one and the same entity. The significance of the Ugaritic parallel(s) would be then to suggest that the whole series of difficulties listed above under headings §1 and 2 are, ultimately, «non-problems».

Less clear-cut is the significance of the Ugaritic parallel(s) for the question of the meaning of the «drinking motif» in Exod 32,20. Thus we note that, among those who do invoke the parallelism, some hold that the comparable element in the first Ugaritic version, i.e. the consumption of Mot's remains by the birds precludes an «ordeal understanding» of Exod 32,20b^{b}, along the lines of the ritual prescribed in Nu 5,11-31 [17], the concluding notice in Exodus having to be seen, rather, like its Ugaritic counterpart, as one final eliminatory measure [18]. Other proponents of the parallelism, on the contrary, continue to view Exod 32,20 as speaking of an «ordeal» [19], while still others consciously leave the question unresolved [20], or do not state a clear view of their own concerning it [21].

Likewise somewhat ambiguous is the significance of the Ugaritic parallel(s) for the problem of the nature of the relationship between the two Biblical texts, a problem arising above all, as mentioned, from the divergence between them regarding the ultimate disposition of the calf's remains, i.e. a forced drinking by the people vs. a casting of the dust of the calf into a brook. But what, in any event, is certainly of interest in this connection is the observation that a quite analogous difference manifests itself in the two Ugaritic accounts where Mot's remains are one time said to be «eaten» by birds and the other to be «scattered in the sea». This latter divergence, occurring, as it does, within a single literary work, is of significance as suggesting that ANE authors felt both the need for and the freedom to vary their depictions of annihilatory happenings from one context to another by introducing alternative terms and descriptions — note too the other differences in wording between the two Ugaritic versions. And so, it may be that the problem of the discrepancy between

17. On the problematic of the relation between Exod 32,20 and Nu 5,11ff. in the earlier literature, see HAHN, *Kalb*, pp. 201-208.

18. So e.g. HVIDBERG-HANSEN, *Ødelaeggelse*, p. 96; *idem*, *Vernichtung*, p. 32; also H. VALENTIN, *Aaron. Eine Studie zur vor-priesterlichen Aaronüberlieferung* (OBO, 18), Freiburg/Göttingen, 1978, p. 241.

19. E.g. DAVENPORT, *Study*, p. 43.

20. E.g. FENSHAM, *Burning*, p. 193.

21. E.g. LOEWENSTAMM, *Making*, (1967), p. 485, n. 1, who cites the ordeal understanding of Exod 32,20b^{b} but does not explicitly commit himself on the question of its correctness.

the respective conclusions of Exod 32,20 and Deut 9,21 has been somewhat overstressed, and that we need not be unduly concerned to identify some profound contentual or theological motive which would have led the author of one text to so modify the presentation of the other. The difference between them may, on the evidence of the Ugaritic parallels, be reflective of nothing more than an interest in varying a familiar description by introducing an alternative formulation drawn from a large stock of available and standard annihilatory phraseology.

Finally, not only the similarities, but also the differences between the Biblical and Ugaritic accounts need also to be kept in mind. Two such differences might especially be underscored. However the nature of Mot may be conceived in the Ugaritic material, he is certainly not presented there as the man-made metal image with which the Biblical accounts are concerned. Secondly, whereas Moses' annihilatory measures do have the effect of definitely doing away with the object to which they are applied, this is not the case with 'Anat's actions against Mot who is depicted as very quickly reviving from her assault and, in fact, being able to describe his own «destruction» in the second account. In respect then both to the object to which they are applied and to their efficacy, the series of measures recounted in the Biblical and Ugaritic texts do differ, and the fact of this difference invites us to continue the search for extra-Biblical texts which might more closely parallel the two Biblical presentations in either or both regards.

Once an initial parallel to the Bible's descriptions of the destruction of the calf had been adduced, it was natural that the attempt should be made to identify additional extra-Biblical analogues to the Biblical (and *a fortiori* the Ugaritic) accounts. These efforts have been pursued particularly by two authors, i.e. U. Rüterswörden [22] and P. L. Watson [23], the latter drawing largely on the earlier research of E. Nielsen [24]. In their investigations Watson and Rüterswörden point to parallels to one or other element in the Biblical and/or Ugaritic descriptions of the annihilation of an unwanted being from Egyptian, Mesopotamian and Hittite mythological and/or magico-ritual materials. Here we shall in turn briefly review the evidence adduced by them from the three cultural spheres, expatiating on their references where appropriate.

2) *Egypt*: As Watson and Rüterswörden between them bring out, there does exist a large body of Egyptian material which speaks of

22. See n. 2.

23. WATSON, *Mot*, pp. 182-183, 185-187; *idem*, *Death*, p. 63.

24. E. NIELSEN, *The Burial of the Foreign Gods*, in ST 8 (1954) 103-122. In this article which attempts to identify extra-Biblical parallels to Jacob's action in burying the «foreign gods» of his household at Shechem in Gen 35,4, Nielsen does amass a considerable number of Egyptian and Mesopotamian references to practices involving the destruction of unwanted entities. Curiously, however, he nowhere brings these texts into connection with the Biblical accounts of the annihilation of the calf (or of other illicit cult objects).

the application, to various undesirable entities, of one of the major annihilatory measures inflicted on both the calf and on Mot, i.e. «burning». In our Egyptian documentation this measure is characteristically coupled with various other destructive actions, above all that of «cutting up» — just as «burning» and «splitting with a sword» appear together in the Mot accounts. The beings who undergo such measures in the Egyptian material include the mythical serpent Apophis [25], the god Seth [26], the wicked dead [27], and sacrificial animal victims which symbolize the enemies of both Pharaoh and the gods [28]. In all these cases, that of the sacrificial victims obviously excepted, the application of the various annihilatory procedures to the being in question does not, as with Mot, but in contrast to the calf, result in the definitive elimination of that being. Rather, Apophis, Seth and the damned dead are depicted as instantaneously reviving and then facing the same or similar set of destructive procedures once again.

Beyond the foregoing references to «burning», Rüterswörden and Watson likewise point to Egyptian parallels to several of the other measures directed against the calf and/or Mot. Watson cites the case of the god Osiris who, in various traditions concerning him, is said to have suffered both dismemberment and being cast into water by his enemies [29]. Rüterswörden, for his part, alludes to a Hellenistic notice concerning a ritual that involved the burning and subsequent scattering of the remains of persons called «Typonians» as substitutes for the malevolent deity Seth [30], comparing this with the fate of Mot «burned» and «scattered in the field» in the first Ugaritic version.

The foregoing are the instances of a «*Vernichtungssymbolik*» adduced by Watson and Rüterswörden from the Egyptian mythological and/or magico-ritual material. Their references may, however, very readily be amplified with other texts of the same character which parallel either the individual annihilatory measures spoken of in the Biblical and Ugaritic passages and/or their combinations. Simply by way of illustration on this point, we note the following examples of such additional parallels: In «Utterance 700» of the «Pyramid Texts» there is this summons to a god

25. On Apophis, see the texts cited by WATSON, *Mot*, pp. 183, 210-211, n. 46.

26. On Seth, see the material cited by NIELSEN, *Burial*, pp. 105-107 to which WATSON, *Mot*, pp. 185-186 refers.

27. On the punishments of the wicked dead, see the references given by RÜTERSWÖRDEN, *Vernichtungssymbolik*, p. 52.

28. On the sacrificial victims, see the remarks of RÜTERSWÖRDEN, *Vernichtungssymbolik*, p. 53 and p. 55, nn. 12-14; see also H. KEES, *Bemerkungen zum Tieropfer der Ägypter und seiner Symbolik* (NAWG, phil.-hist. Klasse, Jahrgang 1942, Nr. 2), Göttingen 1942, 71-82.

29. On the various traditions concerning the fate of Osiris, see J.G. GRIFFITHS, *The Origins of Osiris and his Cult* (Studies in the History of Religions, Suppls. to *Numen* 40), Leiden, 1980, pp. 8-10, 22-25.

30. See the references in RÜTERSWÖRDEN, *Vernichtungssymbolik*, p. 55, n. 15.

regarding his enemies: «throw them in the lake; throw them in the sea» [31]. Nor is the «grinding» cited as a destructive measure in both the Biblical and Ugaritic passages unknown in the Egyptian material. Apophis [32], the dammed dead [33] and the followers of Seth [34] are all threatened with this fate. Again, among the penalties inflicted on the damned is that of being «consumed» by assorted underworld monsters [35], this being reminiscent of the «consuming motif» in Exod 32,20 and the first Ugaritic account. Likewise to be noted here are instances where annihilatory actions are combined in a way similar to the Biblical and Ugaritic patterns. Thus H. Kees cites a ritual prescription from the temple of Edfou regarding an ass symbolic of Seth: «Seine Knochen sind im Feuer, und was von ihm übrig bleibt, gehöre den Hunden» [36]. Similarly, among the rituals of the Hellenistic temple of Esna there is one involving the burning of fish, symbolic of various hostile beings, followed by their being thrown into a canal [37].

In summary, we may note that the Egyptian evidence offers parallels to virtually the whole range of measures applied to the calf and/or Mot, i.e. burning, cutting up, grinding, devouring by other beings, and casting into water. In addition, as we have seen, these various actions are typically found in combination just as they are in the OT and Ugaritic texts.

3) *Mesopotamia*: Watson and Rüterswörden likewise call attention to a variety of Mesopotamian ritual-magical texts paralleling one or other of the measures inflicted on the calf and/or Mot, in particular the burning procedure. Thus Watson adduces a ritual from the Babylonian Akitu-festival in which two figurines fashioned of wood and bedecked with gold and precious stones are beheaded and then cast into the fire [38]. To this reference we may add the mention of another ritual from the

31. S. A. B. MERCER, *The Pyramid Texts in Translation and Commentary*, New York, 1952, p. 317.

32. The reference occurs in the third hour, the upper register of the «*Amduat*» as published by E. HORNUNG, *Das Amduat oder die Schrift des verborgenen Raumes*, Bd. II (AA, 7/2), Wiesbaden, 1963, p. 64 where the deities depicted receive the directive «den Widersacher [Apophis] zu zermalen (*nḏ*)».

33. The reference occurs in the fifth hour, fifth scene of HORNUNG, *Amduat*, p. 98 where various underworld deities receive the summons: «Zermalt (*nḏ*) die Feinde, (indem) ihr die Toten vernichtet und die Schatten der Vernichteten niedermetzelt! Straft alle(?) eure Toten!»

34. I.e. in the ritual of the temple of Denderah. See the reference in J. G. GRIFFITHS, *The Meaning of* nḏ *and* nḏ-ḥr, in *JEA* 37 (1951) 31-37, p. 36.

35. For references see e.g. E. HORNUNG, *Altägyptische Höllenvorstellungen* (ASAW zu Leipzig, phil.-hist. Klasse, 59/3), Berlin, 1968, p. 31.

36. KEES, *Bemerkungen*, p. 84.

37. For the texts see S. SAUNERON, *Les fêtes religieuses d'Esna* (Esna, V), Cairo, 1962, pp. 24-25.

38. WATSON, *Death*, p. 63. The text is translated by A. SACHS, in *ANET*, Princeton, [3]1969, pp. 331-332.

same festival in which the carcass of a sheep which had been employed in the purification of the temple is thrown into the river [39]. Comparable to the burning of the figurines at the Akitu-festival is a potency ritual cited by Rüterswörden in which images fabricated from various substances are burned to the accompaniment of an appeal to Ishtar to remove the sufferer's enchantment [40]. «Burning» also figures in the acted-out curses of the treaty texts to which both Watson and Rüterswörden allude. In the Sefire treaty there is reference to a burning of wax signifying the fate of Mati'el in case of infidelity [41]. In the Esarhaddon treaty wax images are both burned and «dissolved in water» as graphic depictions of what awaits the disloyal vassal [42] — compare the association of burning and casting into water in the Biblical and Ugaritic texts. Finally, Rüterswörden refers, in rather cursory fashion, to the practices prescribed in the magical collections *Šurpu* [43] and *Maqlu* [44]. For our purposes, however, this material is worth a more detailed consideration, and so we pause to further develop Rüterswörden's brief allusions to it. As the names of the two collections suggest, the practice they cite most frequently is the «burning» of objects and images representing the evil forces and the magicians who had activated those forces which the collections are designed to combat. Often, this ritual burning is accompanied by an appeal to some deity to likewise «burn» the magician who had afflicted the sufferer [45]. Not infrequently, moreover, these appeals to the gods for retaliatory action against the culprit speak not only of such «burning», but also of destructive activities involving «water» or «the river» [46], or a divine «consuming» and «drinking» of the guilty magi-

39. See SACHS, in *ANET*, p. 333.

40. RÜTERSWÖRDEN, *Beiträge*, p. 21. He cites the text as published by R.D. BRIGGS, *ŠÀ.ZI.GA. Ancient Mesopotamian Potency Incantations* (TCS, II), Locust Valley, N.Y., 1967, p. 28.

41. «As this wax is consumed by fire, thus Matti[el] shall be consumed by fire». Translation by F. ROSENTHAL, in *ANET*, p. 660.

42. «Just as one burns a wax figurine in fire, dissolves a clay one in water, so may they burns your figure in fire, submerge it in water». Translation by E. REINER, in *ANET*, p. 540, §89.

43. This collection has been published by E. REINER, *Šurpu. A Collection of Sumerian and Akkadian Incantations* (AfO Beiheft, 11), Graz, 1958.

44. This collection has been published by G. MEIER, *Die assyrische Beschwörungssammlung Maqlu* (AfO Beiheft, 2), Berlin, 1937.

45. See e.g. REINER, Tablet I, ll. 18-23 (p. 11); tablets V-VI, ll. 60-138 (pp. 31-33); MEIER, *Maqlu*, Tablet I, ll. 135-143 (p. 12); Tablet II, l. 15 (p. 13). In the last text cited we find this summons to Ṇusku: «verbrenne meinen Zauberer und meine Zauberin!»

46. See e.g. this appeal in MEIER, *Maqlu*, tablet III, ll. 84-87 (p. 24): «... möge die Zaubereien, Hexereien, den Spuk meiner Zauberin, meines Alps Gilbil verbrennen! Der reine Fluss zerbreche ihr Herz, das reine Wasser löse ihre Zauberei». See too *Maqlu*, tablet III, ll. 100-101 (p. 25) where there is an appeal to Sin to deal with the hostile magicians as follows: «Sin... vernichte deinen Leib und werfe dich in einen Schlund von Wasser und Feuer».

cians' hands [47]. Likewise to be noted is the long series of charges made against hostile magicians in Tablet IV of the *Maqlu* series; among those charges is the accusation that the magicians have given images of the sufferer to a dog, a pig and to birds for them to eat, just as they have thrown his image «into the river» [48]. This association of the two sorts of descriptive procedures is of interest given the fact that in both our Biblical and Ugaritic passages such a «consumption» by some living being and a casting into a body of water stand as alternative final eliminatory operations. The fact of their coupling here in a Mesopotamian text provides, it seems, a suggestive indication as to why the Biblical and Ugaritic writers, having one of the measures in question before them in a first account, would have substituted precisely the other of them when they came to renarrate the same event. Finally, reference should be made to the following incantation from the *Šurpu* series for the conception of the function of «water» with regard to «sin» which it articulates — a conception which may well be the background to the presentation of Moses' action in tossing the dust of the «calf» into the «brook» in Deut 9,21. The passage reads: «May the record of his sins, errors, crimes, oaths (all) that is sworn, be thrown into the water» [49].

The foregoing are the various categories of Mesopotamian magico-ritual texts adduced by Watson and Rüterswörden. Their references may, however, readily be supplemented with like materials in which mention is made of various of the same annihilatory measures as in the Biblical and Ugaritic accounts. Characteristic e.g. for the *Namburbi* magical series [50] is the casting into a river of objects, mostly fabricated images, representing the evil portent which had appeared and which this particular series is designed to counteract [51]. In several instances this ritual is accompanied by prayers addressed to the river appealing to it to remove the evil announced by the portent [52]. The same practice of

47. See MEIER, *Maqlu*, Tablet III, ll. 165-166 (p. 27): «Zauberer und Zauberin, eure Hand verbrenne Gira, verzehre Gira, trinke Gira, schaffe Gira fort!»

48. See MEIER, *Maqlu*, Tablet IV, ll. 42-33 (p. 30): «Figuren, [Ab]bilder(?) meines Gesichts und meiner Gestalt habt ihr angefertigt [und] einen Hund fres[sen] lassen, ein Schwein fressen lassen, die Vögel des Himmels fressen lassen, in den Fluss geworfen».

49. REINER, *Šurpu*, Tablet IV, ll. 79-80 (p. 27).

50. A representative selection of this material is available in R.I. CAPLICE, *The Akkadian Namburbu Texts: An Introduction* (SANE, 1/1), Malibu, 1974.

51. See e.g. CAPLICE, *Namburbu*, Text 6 (p. 16): «Ritual for the evil of a monstrous birth»: «You throw tamarisk, Dilbat-plant, *shalalu*-reed, a date-palm shoot, (and) the misborn creature, together with provisions and its gifts into the river...» See likewise Text 7 (pp. 16-17): «Ritual for the evil of a dog» where a clay image of a dog is to be cast into the river.

52. See CAPLICE, *Namburbu*, Text 13 (pp. 21-22): «Ritual for the evil of evil signs and portents». Here, the River is addressed as follows: «Take that evil away! Take it down to your depths!» Thereafter, it is directed that the «image and likeness» of the frightening portent be thrown into the river. Subsequently, we have this prescription: «a man lays hold on the sins of that man(?), then you gather (them) into a piece of clay,

casting an image to which malevolent forces had been transferred into water occurs in the «Incantation ritual to Ishtar and Dumuzi» published by W. Farber which prescribes that an image of the sick person be wrapped in a cloth and this be tossed into the river [53]. Again, in a text designed to effect reconciliation with one who has been angered, published by E. Ebeling, a clay image of a steer and its rider (the angry man) is to be «buried» in the river [54]. Similarly, in a «rite for the opening of the mouth» a whole collection of objects, including a crocodile made of gold and silver has to be cast into the river [55].

A combination of fire and water as agents of destruction occurs in another «ritual for the opening of the mouth» in which several images made of tallow and wax are burned in a stove and then the stove itself is thrown into the river [56]. Reference should likewise be made here to an «incantation against the enemy and the evil eye» where the smashing of a new pot and its being ground to dust is prescribed [57], an indication that, also in Mesopotamia, the act of «grinding» as an annihilatory procedure was not unknown. Finally, we might refer to various Mesopotamian prayers in which different animals are cited as agents who remove evil influences by «consuming» them, or alternatively, as tools of malevolent magicians who feed images of an afflicted person to these animals as a means of effecting the sufferer's destruction. Interestingly, these references to such functions on the part of animals are, several times, associated with a mention of a casting into water procedure in a way reminiscent of the *Maqlu* tablet cited above [58].

and that man recites as follows. I have removed my evils, I have stripped off my sins. May this day receive from the evil of the signs (and) portents which have been placed on me and send (it) across the river!... When he has recited this, he throws the evil of those things into the river».

53. «Diese (d.h. des Kranken) Figur wickelst du in ein Tuch... 'Er ist gerettet, er ist ohne Vorwurf: Samas ist Richter!', sagst du, und wirfst (das Bündel) in den Fluss». W. FARBER, *Beschwörungsrituale an Istar und Dumuzi*, Wiesbaden, 1977, p. 241.

54. E. EBELING, *Aus dem Tagewerk eines assyrischen Zauberpriesters* (MAG, 5/3), Leipzig, 1931, p. 23.

55. E. EBELING, *Tod und Leben nach den Vorstellungen der Babylonier*, I. Teil: *Texte*, Berlin-Leipzig, 1931, p. 103.

56. EBELING, *Tod*, pp. 119-120.

57. E. EBELING, *Beschwörung gegen den Feind und den bösen Blick aus dem Zweistromlande*, in AO 17 (1949) 178-211, p. 194: «Darnach sollst du einen... Topf [nehmen] zerschlagen [mit Weihwass]er [reinigen (und) (zu Staub) zermalen]...»

58. See e.g. the followin appeal to Shamash concerning a hostile sorcerer: «celui qui... a fait des figurines de moi, soit en argile, soit en pâte, soit en suif, soit en cire, les a données à manger à un chien, ou les a données à manger à un porc, ou les a données à manger à un oiseau, ou les a données à manger à un poisson, ou les a jetées au fleuve...». M.-J. SEUX, *Hymnes et prières aux dieux de Babylonie et d'Assyrie* (Littératures anciennes du proche Orient), Paris, 1976, p. 395. In another such prayer to Shamash it is said of the sorcerers: «... m'ont donné à manger à un poisson, m'ont donné à boire dans de l'eau à des animaux» (*Ibid.*, p. 398). Compare this appeal directed to a «personal god» and the complementary

4) *Hittite material*: As a Hittite analogue to the accounts of the destruction of the calf and of Mot, Rüterswörden adduces an enacted curse associated with the Hittite military oath (compare the acted-out curses of the treaty-texts referred to above). Here, hops are «ground with a millstone», then mixed with water, cooked and mashed as an illustration of what awaits the soldier who violates his oath [59]. Beyond this one instance, however, there exist several further parallels to the different measures recounted in our Biblical and Ugaritic annihilation accounts. In e.g. a «ritual for the purification of god and man» a boat containing small «oaths» and «curses» fabricated of gold and silver is launched into a river with a prayer that, like the boat that disappears down the river, so also any wrong committed by the one for whom the rite is being performed will be removed [60]. In another such ritual a cloak which has been cast over a «barbarian man» so as to communicate the sufferer's impurity to him is thrown into the river [61]. Again, in the «Tunnawi Ritual», various items which had been applied to the person undergoing the rite are cast into the river [62], while subsequently in the same ritual a dog and a pig which had been raised over the sufferer are «burnt» [63]. «Burning» also figures in a «ritual against domestic quarrel» in which stone pillars which had been erected are kicked over and thrown into the fire, following a prayer that just as the pillars «totter», so will the quarrelsome words the two parties had spoken to each other [64]. Finally, in a «ritual to counteract sorcery» the woman conducting the rite throws threads into the fire with the petition that the sorcerer's words will likewise be extinguished [65].

In summary, it appears that the Hittite magico-ritual texts make the same extensive use of «burning» and «throwing into water» as means of annihilation as do the Ugaritic, Egyptian and Mesopotamian materials surveyed. And this, in turn, suggests that when Exod 32,20 and Deut 9,21 speak of Moses' «burning» the calf and associate this with his consigning its remains to water, they are making use of some of the most typical items in the ANE repertoire of annihilatory measures.

function of the animals and of the water in the removal of unwanted substances to which it refers: «Qu'un poisson emporte mon trouble, que le fleuve l'emmène. Que le bétail de la steppe le reçoive de moi, que l'eau courante du fleuve me lave». (*Ibid*., p. 210).

59. RÜTERSWÖRDEN, *Beiträge*, p. 18. Rüterswörden cites the text as published by N. OETTINGER, *Die militärischen Eide der Hethiter* (STBoT, 22) Wiesbaden, 1976, pp. 10-11.

60. The text is translated by A. GOETZE, in ANET, p. 346.

61. V. HAAS and H. J. THIEL, *Die Beschwörungsrituale der Allaiturah(h)i und verwandte Texte* (AOAT, 31), Kevelaer/Neukirchen-Vluyn, 1978, pp. 135-137.

62. A. GOETZE and E. H. STURTEVANT, *The Hittite Ritual of Tunnawi* (AO Series, 14), New Haven, 1938, p. 17.

63. *Ibid.*

64. The text is translated by A. GOETZE, in ANET, p. 351.

65. Translation by A. GOETZE, in *ANET*, p. 347.

B. *Additional Types of Comparative Material*

Up till this point, we have been reviewing — and in some cases extending — the results of other authors who have brought forward texts of a mythological and/or magico-ritual character from the various cultures of Israel's environment which parallel one or other of the measures which Moses is said to employ against the calf in Exod 32,20/Deut 9,21. It should be noted, however, that comparable measures are by no means confined, in our ANE documentation, to texts of this type. In fact, as we now propose to show, such measures recur in a wide variety of other kinds of extra-Biblical texts:

1) A first group of such texts is comprised of admonitions, directives, and narratives in which various of the annihilatory measures we have been considering are threatened, prescribed or said to have been carried out against human enemies and wrongdoers as this-worldly punishments, generally at the hands of human agents. So e.g. Egyptian texts allude to the burning of evildoers [66], their being thrown into water [67], consumption by beasts [68], and, occasionally, a combination of burning and scattering on water [69]. Likewise the Assyrian royal inscriptions frequently refer to the burning of captured enemies [70], as also, though less often, to the throwing of their bodies into rivers [71] and the feeding of their corpses to beasts [72].

66. See the references given by HORNUNG, *Höllenvorstellungen*, p. 22.

67. See the references in A. HERMANN, *Ertrinken*, in *RCLA*, Bd. VI, ed. by T. Klausner, Stuttgart, 1966, 370-409, pp. 372-373.

68. So e.g. in the «Story of the Two Brothers» a wife who had attempted to seduce her brother-in-law and who, when unsuccessful, made false accusations against him, is killed by her husband and her body «thrown out to the dogs». The text is translated by J.A. WILSON, in ANET, p. 25.

69. See e.g. A. ERMAN, *Die Märchen des Papyrus Westcar*, Berlin, 1890, p. 8, where an adulterous wife is burned and her ashes thrown into the stream. (The latter element is a conjectural restoration of the text by Erman). See too the curse pronounced against negligent officials in an inscription of Amenhotep III as translated by A.R. BREASTED, *Ancient Records of Egypt*, Vol. II, Chicago, 1906, p. 378, §925: «He (Amon) shall deliver them into the flaming wrath of the king on the day of his anger; his serpent-diadem shall spit fire upon their heads, shall consume their limbs, shall devour their bodies, they shall become like Apophis on the morning of New Year's Day. They shall be engulfed in the sea, it shall hide their corpses».

70. E.g. in his Annals Assur-nasir-pal states that in the city of Hulai «3,000 captives I burned with fire». D.D. LUCKENBILL, *Ancient Records of Assyria and Babylonia* (hereafter ARAB), Vol. I, Chicago, 1926, rpt., New York, 1968, p. 146, §445. For further references to the «burning» of captured enemies, see e.g. *Ibid.* p. 150, §450, p. 156, §463, p. 180, §449.

71. See e.g. the notice on a statue of Shalmaneser III: «The rest of his [i.e. of Hadad-ezer, king of Aram] armies I cast (lit., poured) into the Orontes River». LUCKENBILL, ARAB, I, pp. 245-246, §681. For other similar references, see e.g. *Ibid.*, II, p. 333, §863; p. 398, §1072.

72. «Their [i.e. the supporters of Shamash-shum-ukin] dismembered bodies (lit., flesh)

2) A second group of texts to be looked at are those that might be called the «document clauses» of various sorts of ancient Mesopotamian records. These «document clauses» warn against the destruction of the object on which the matter recorded is set down, enumerating various possible modes of destruction in some detail. These enumerations are fairly stereotyped, recurring from one text and from period to another. Among the destructive actions cited some of the most typical are «burning», casting of the recorded object into water/a river/a well and its «breaking in pieces» — compare *kātat* in Deut 9,21. Quite frequently too, the first two of these measures are coupled, just as they are closely associated in the Biblical calf texts. Instances of such formulations can be found in the texts of building inscriptions from the Assyrian royal annals [73], Mesopotamian boundary stones [74], and the vassal treaties of Esarhaddon [75].

3) Finally, it remains to consider a group of texts which are of particular interest as parallels to Exod 32,20/Deut 9,21 given the nature of the objects whose destruction they record, i.e. artefacts/structures of cultic significance. In turning now to this body of documentation, we wish to develop a hint put forward by J. Hahn. Hahn concludes his account of various proposed ANE parallels to the depiction of Exod 32,20 with the statement:

> Daß sich grundsätzlich im Bereich des Alten Orients etliche Texte finden lassen, die die Zerstörung von Götterbildern oder anderen kultischen Gegenständen oder Einrichtungen beschreiben, verwundert nicht [76].

I fed to the dogs, swine, wolves and eagles, to the birds of heaven, and the fish of the deep». LUCKENBILL, ARAB, II, p. 304, §795. See further *Ibid.*, p. 404, §1109.

73. See e.g. the «Stele of Bel-Harran-Bel-usur»: «And as for (this stele), do not remove it from its place... do not break it to pieces, do not cover it with dust, do not throw it into the water, do not burn it with fire...». LUCKENBILL, ARAB, I. p. 296, §826. For other similarly worded warnings as part of royal building inscriptions, see *Ibid.*, I, p. 17, §46; p. 28, §76; pp. 90-91, §276; p. 176, §495, p. 193, §529, II, p. 227, §581. In this connection we might also cite the curse pronounced in a building inscription of Arik-den-ilu for the combination it evidences: «their images (steles?) may he(?) burn with fire... their torch may he plunge into the water». *Ibid.*, I, p. 26, §71.

74. See e.g. L.W. KING, *Babylonian Boundary-Stones and Memorial Tablets in the British Museum*, London, 1912, Text V, c. II, ll. 35-36 (p. 35): «(Whoever) shall smash this memorial with a stone, or put it in the fire, or put it in the river, or hide it in a field where it cannot be seen...». For other similar formulations, see *Ibid.*, Text III, c. V, ll. 43-46 (p. 17); Text IV, c. III, ll. 2-7 (p. 22), Text VI, c. II, ll. 33-36 (p. 35), text VII, c. II, ll. 8-12 (p. 41); Text VIII, c. I, ll. 2-5 (p. 48); Text IX, c. V, ll. 1-5 (p. 69); Text X, Rev., ll. 36-37 (p. 74), c. II, ll. 20-21 (p. 78).

75. «If you remove it, consign it to fire, throw it into water, bury it in dust, or by some trick, destroy, annihilate, or turn it face down...». Translation by E. REINER, in *ANET*, p. 538, §36.

76. HAHN, *Kalb*, p. 211.

Hahn himself simply alludes to this possibility, without adducing any actual instances of such texts, although he does cite an oft-anthologized depiction from the reign of Sargon II portraying Assyrian soldiers smashing an image of the god Chaldia of the city of Muzazir with axes (compare the use of the term *kātat* in Deut 9,21)[77]. In fact, however, the sort of texts to which Hahn alludes do exist, and, considering that they concern the destruction specifically of cultic objects, they seem well worth examining in our survey of possible ANE parallels/background to the account of Exod 32,20/Deut 9,21. Our evidence here derives from both Sumerian and Assyrian royal inscriptions:

a) *Sumerian material*: A text, preserved on boulders, from the time of Eanatum of Lagash (c. 2450 B.C.), relating to the border conflict between Lagash and Umma, records that the leader of Umma «smashed» (compare *kātat* in Deut 9,21) the boundary «monuments» erected by the Lagashites[78]. A text dealing with a later stage of the same conflict states that Urlumma ruler of Umma penetrated into territory under control of Lagash where «he set fire to their monuments and smashed them, and destroyed the established chapels of the gods that were built on the (boundary-levee called) Namnundakigara»[79]. To be noted in this formulation is its mention of the application of several distinct destructive measures to the Lagash «monuments», among them the «burning» employed against the calf (as well as many other condemned cult objects) in the OT[80]. Of particular interest is finally the extended account of the devastation of numerous Lagash cult centers by Lugalzagesi, ruler of Umma in c. 2360 B.C.[81] This account speaks of Lugalzagesi's «burning» various temples, and his carrying off of their precious stones and metals. It further states that he «destroyed» the

77. HAHN, *Kalb*, p. 211, n. 85. This representation is most readily accessible in O. KEEL, *Die Welt der altorientalischen Bildsymbolik und das Alte Testament. Am Beispiel der Psalmen*, Einsiedeln/Neukirchen-Vluyn, 1972, p. 212, §317.

78. J. S. COOPER, *Reconstructing History from Ancient Inscriptions: the Lagash-Umma Border Conflict* (SANE, 2/1), Malibu, 1983, Text 3 (p. 48).

79. COOPER, *Inscriptions*, Text 6 (p. 50). It should be noted that there is some question as to the correct rendering of the Sumerian term rendered «smashed» by Cooper here (as well as in the text cited in the previous note); in the recent publication of H. STEIBLE and H. BEHRENS, *Die altsumerischen Bau- und Weihinschriften*, Teil I: *Inschriften aus «Lagas»* (FOS, 5), Wiesbaden, 1982, p. 237 the rendering is rather «... hat sie [i.e. die Stelen] ausgerissen».

80. On the significance of the act of «burning» applied to the boundary markers in this text, see the remark of A. POEBEL, *Der Konflikt zwischen Lagas und Umma zur Zeit Enanantums I und Entemenas*, in *Oriental Studies dedicated to Paul Haupt*, Baltimore-Leipzig, 1926, 220-267, p. 242: «Ur-Lumma begnügt sich... nicht damit, die Stelen lediglich zu entfernen und zu zerschlagen, sondern sich auch jeden Rest ihrer Inschriften dadurch gründlichst zu vertilgen, dass er die Oberflächen der Stelen durch die Glut des Feuers zerspringen und sich zersetzen lässt».

81. COOPER, *Inscriptions*, Text 9 (p. 52).

statuary of the shrine Eana of Inana, and threw the precious metals of the temple of Amageshtinana (or the temple statue itself)[82] «into a well». There is some uncertainty among translators with regard to this last notice. If it can be accepted, however, it would provide a noteworthy parallel to Moses' action in consigning the remains of the calf to water in our Biblical accounts. It would likewise be comparable to the archeological discovery of a broken relief depicting the god Assur found in an ash-filled well in the temple of that god at Assur[83], as well as to the *kudurru* warnings about putting a boundary stone «in a well» as cited above.

b) *Assyrian material*: The Assyrian royal inscriptions contain numerous references to the treatment accorded the temples, cultic objects, etc. of conquered peoples. More frequently, what is recorded is the «deportation» of cultic images and artefacts to Assyria, whence, in a number of instances, they were subsequently returned[84]. In a few cases, however, an actual destruction of these objects is mentioned. Beyond the sculptural representation from the time of Sargon II alluded to by Hahn, we may note the following attestations for this practice: In his «letter to Assur» concerning his eighth campaign, the same Sargon II states: «The temple of Haldia, his god, I set on fire like brush and destroyed his shrine (sanctuary)»[85]. Again, in his «Bavian inscription» Sennacherib reports concerning his conquest of Babylon: «The gods dwelling therein, — the hands of my people took them, and smashed them»[86]. He further states:

> The city and (its) houses, from its foundations to its top, I destroyed, I burned with fire. The wall and outer wall, *temples and gods*, temple towers of brick and earth, as many as there were, I razed and dumped them into the Arahtu Canal[87].

This last notice is of interest for its coupling of «burning» and «throwing into water», and as yet another attestation of a seemingly rather widespread ANE practice of disposing of reprobate cult objects by consigning them to some body of water.

82. Thus STEIBLE-BEHRENS, *Inschriften*, p. 337: «(und) hat (die Statue?) dort in den Brunnen geworfen».

83. On this relief, see W. ANDRAE, *Kultrelief aus dem Brunnen des Assurtempels zu Assur* (WVDOG, 53), Leipzig, 1931, pp. 1, 5 and G. MARTINY, *Die Gegensätze im babylonischen und assyrischen Tempelbau* (AKM, 21/3), Leipzig, 1936, pp. 34-35.

84. For the most recent discussion of this practice, see H. SPIECKERMANN, *Juda unter Assur in der Sargonidenzeit* (FRLANT, 129), Göttingen, 1982, pp. 347-354.

85. LUCKENBILL, ARAB, II, p. 91, §165. On this text see M. COGAN, *Imperialism and Religion. Assyria, Judah and Israel in the Eighth and Seventh Centuries B.C.E.* (SBLMS, 19), Missoula, Mont., 1974, p. 24: «... the wrecking of a temple... reported... implies the destruction of the god (i.e. his statue) along with the cult center».

86. LUCKENBILL, ARAB, II, p. 152, §340.

87. LUCKENBILL, ARAB, II, p. 152, §341.

Also to be noted is the report of Assurbanipal's campaign against Elam from the «Rassam Cylinder»: Of various captured cities of Elam he recounts: «I smashed their gods and pacified the divine heart of the lord of lords» [88]. The report continues with a notice on the devastation of the Elamite capital Susa: «The zikkurat of Susa... I destroyed. (Its) pinnacles (lit., horns)... I broke down» [89]. There follows this general summary:

> The sanctuaries of Elam I destroyed totally (lit., to non-existence). Its gods and goddesses I scattered (lit., counted) to the wind(s). Their secret groves... my soldiers... set them on fire... The sepulchers of their earlier and later kings... I destroyed, I devastated, I exposed to the sun [90].

Likewise to be cited in this connection as similar in many respects to the descriptions of the destruction of cultic structures/objects in the Sumerian and Assyrian royal inscriptions is the account of the devastating of the temple (Ekur) of the god Enlil at Nippur by king Naramsin in the Sumerian historiographical poem «The Curse of Agade» [91]. In this text, Naramsin, losing patience with the prolonged divine refusal to respond to his plans, levels the Enlil-temple, throws its «*laḥama*-figures» into the fire, has smiths beat out its various metals and stones, and removes its treasures from Nippur by ship [92].

Finally, we may note that the notion of a destruction of cultic objects is not foreign to Egyptian literature, either. In the mythological context of an account of the conflict between Horus and Seth, the «Papyrus Jumilhac» refers to Thoth's (son and ally of Horus) «breaking in pieces» all the statues of Seth [93].

To our knowledge, no OT scholar has yet made the attempt to relate the Biblical accounts of destruction of cultic objects — and that of the calf in particular — to the series of Mesopotamian texts dealing with the annihilation of various cult structures and objects just cited [94], whereas a first effort has been made in this direction from the Sumeriological-Assyriological side by M. Brandes in an article on «destruction and

88. LUCKENBILL, ARAB, II, p. 308, §808.

89. LUCKENBILL, ARAB, II, p. 309, §810.

90. LUCKENBILL, ARAB, II, p. 309, §810.

91. For the most recent edition of this text, see J.S. COOPER, *The Curse of Agade*, Baltimore, 1983, pp. 50-63.

92. See *Ibid.*, pp. 55-57.

93. J. VANDIER, *Le papyrus Jumilhac*, Paris, s.d., p. 129. On the possible background to this «mythological» formulation in historical outbursts of iconoclasm in Egypt, see H. TE VELDE, *Seth, God of Confusion. A Study of his Role in Egyptian Religion* (PdA, 6), Leiden, 1967, pp. 146-147.

94. This is the case notwithstanding the fact that especially in recent years there has been considerable interest in and study of the Assyrian documentation relating to Assyria's politico-religious policies towards Israel and Judah, on which see the works of Cogan (n. 85) and Spieckermann (n. 84).

mutilation of statues in Mesopotamia» in which he gives a rather general comparison between some of the texts we have quoted and the «iconoclastic» measures of Josiah in 2 Kgs 23,4-20[95]. In terms of identifying extra-Biblical parallels/analogues to, as well as possible «sources» for the OT presentations on the destruction of cult objects, however, it seems to us that a detailed comparison of the two sets of material is very much in order. First of all, in contrast to the various texts which have been adduced as parallels to the Biblical passages by previous authors, these texts do deal specifically with the annihilation of objects and structures connected with the cult. In that sense, they represent closer parallels to the Biblical texts than do the other materials cited. But there are additional reasons which make the comparison of significance. As we have seen, correspondences in detail do exist in the formulations of the two groups of texts; both speak of the burning, smashing and consigning to water of the various cultic objects they mention. Again, in the case of the Assyrian royal inscriptions (which, in turn, have affinities with the Sumerian ones), we are dealing with texts stemming from approximately the same (8th-6th century B.C.) period as does the «Deuteronomic» (using the term in a very broad sense) material of the OT to which we would reckon the bulk of the pre-Chronistic accounts of the destruction of offending cult objects. As such these Assyrian texts have a temporal proximity to our OT material lacking in many of the extra-Biblical passages cited hitherto which are either considerably earlier (so the Ugaritic and Hittite texts), or much later (so a good deal of the Egyptian evidence which, in its present form, derives from Ptolemaic times) than the Biblical documentation. What makes this consideration of further importance is the observation that, as studies of the last two decades make clear, the «Deuteronomic» material of the OT does evidence much familiarity with the formulations of Assyrian texts of various sorts[96]. Hence, it is well conceivable that the «Deuteronomic» passages dealing with the destruction of cult objects could likewise have been influenced by Assyrian reports on this subject. Such a supposition receives added plausibility when it is noted that, in fact, the OT evidences awareness of the (occasional) Assyrian practice of destroying the divine images of enemy peoples. The relevant text here is 2 Kgs 19,18a (= Is 37,19) where, in the context of his prayer in the face of the Assyrian threat, Hezekiah is made to say «(the kings of Assyria 19,17) have cast their (i.e. those of the «nations» referred to in v. 17) gods into the fire». This reference has not attracted much attention from the commentators,

95. M. BRANDES, *Destruction et mutilation de statues en Mésopotamie*, in *Akkadia* 16 (1980), 28-41.

96. On this point see e.g.: R. FRANKENA, *The Vassal Treaties of Esarhaddon and the Dating of Deuteronomy*, in *OTS* 14 (1965) 122-154 and M. WEINFELD, *Deuteronomy and the Deuteronomic School*, Oxford, 1972, rpt. 1983, pp. 59-146.

although H. Wildberger, in his treatment of the parallel passage in Isaiah, does, quite appropriately, refer to the Sennacherib inscription cited above (p. 225) by way of background to Hezekiah's statement[97]. But if now, as 2 Kgs 19,18/Is 37,19 attest, the «Deuteronomic» authors of the OT did know the (occasional) Assyrian practice of destroying the cult objects of their enemies, is it not further thinkable that they likewise knew the Assyrian literary formulations on the subject and were influenced by them in their own presentations of comparable happenings, just as they were clearly influenced by Assyrian phraseology and imagery in other respects?

It is not possible for us to further pursue the comparison between the Biblical and extra-Biblical accounts relating to the destruction of cult objects here. A fuller treatment of this point remains a *desideratum*, however. Such a study would have to take into account various factors which we have left largely out of consideration in our discussion, e.g. the fact that all the extra-Biblical texts cited, in contrast to the Biblical passages, concern the destruction of cult objects pertaining to the worship of other (and hostile) cities/peoples, not those which figured within the cult of the destroyer himself, i.e. unlike the OT instances, the extra-Biblical measures cited were not motivated by a rejection of images as such. The study we envisage would also have to pay closer attention to the individual extra-Biblical texts, asking in each instance, about the factors prompting the destruction related (e.g. simple rapacity; particular animosity towards the people so treated — as would seem to be the case with the handling of the cult objects of the Babylonians and Elamites by Sennacherib and Assurbanipal, respectively), keeping in mind that, for the Assyrians at least, such destruction was not standard practice with regard to temples, images, etc. which fell into their hands. Here, however, we have simply wished to call attention to the existence of the various affinities between the Biblical and extra-Biblical accounts of the destruction of cult objects which make of the latter significant, but hitherto (virtually) overlooked, analogues to Exod 32,20/Deut 9,21 (and related) OT texts.

Conclusion: The foregoing survey which takes up and extends the work of previous authors indicates that the OT's descriptions of Moses' actions against the calf can indeed be related to a wide range of ANE presentations dealing with the elimination of undesirable entities. Each of the measures spoken of in Exod 32,20/Deut 9,21, i.e. burning, grinding, breaking in pieces, casting into water and «consumption» by some living being can be paralleled from various texts of the Ugaritic, Egyptian, Mesopotamian and Hittite cultures. Not only geographically, however, but also temporally, the extra-Biblical comparative material

97. H. WILDBERGER, *Jesaja* (BK, X), Neukirchen-Vluyn, 1982, p. 1427.

extends over a wide range. References to acts similar to those performed by Moses against the calf are met in Ugaritic and Hittite texts antedating the Biblical accounts. They recur in material from Ptolemaic Egypt, further in the Mishna which prescribes that idolatrous images be «ground and scattered to the wind or thrown into the salt-sea» [98], and still later in the 10th century A.D. Arab historian En-Nedim who relates the practice among the Sabian women of Haran of lamenting the murdered god Ta-wouz (Tammuz) whose «bones had been ground in a mill and dispersed to the wind» [99]. The two versions of the calf's destruction likewise have in common with a number of the ANE texts cited their accumulation of a range of destructive measures seemingly without regard to the question of whether or not those measures can, in fact, be one and all applied to the entity in question, given the nature of that entity. This last feature suggests that the Biblical authors, like those of the extra-Biblical passages were not primarily — if at all — concerned with the «realistic» considerations which have long troubled interpreters of the calf accounts, Exod 32,20 in particular. Rather, both the Biblical and extra-Biblical writers wanted above all to underscore, by their piling up of a whole series of destructive acts that the reprobate being described was, in fact, thoroughly, utterly annihilated. And if this be so, then a great deal of what, historically, has been found to be a difficulty with the presentation of Exod 32,20/Deut 9,21 as well as the responses developed thereto, has to be seen as the reflection of inappropriate expectations and approaches on the part of interpreters.

EXCURSUS

A further possible sense for Exod 32,20b^b in light of Biblical/extra-Biblical materials

One question which remains not fully resolved in the newer investigations of Exod 32,20, any more than it was in older studies of the verse, is that concerning the meaning of Moses' final action with regard to the calf here, i.e. his making the Israelites drink of the water on which he had scattered the grindings of the calf (see *supra*, p. 209, §3). In particular, uncertainty continues to prevail as to whether or not the «drinking» in Exod 32,20 should be seen as somehow analogous to the «ordeal procedure» of Nu 5,11-31 in which a drinking of water strewn with «dust» from the sanctuary floor serves to determine the guilt or innocence of a woman suspected of adultery, and, in case of the former, to effect her punishment. The evidence of the extra-Biblical material cited

98. Aboda Zara III:3: *šōḥēq wᵉzōrēh lārūaḥ ʾō mēṭīl layyām*. We cite the text as given by H. L. STRACK, *ʾAboda Zara. Der Mišnatraktat «Götzendienst»* (Schriften des Institutum Judaicum in Berlin, 5), Leipzig, ²1909, p. 14*.
99. Reference in DUSSAUD, *Mythologie*, p. 391.

above in which an undesirable entity is fed or given in drink to birds, animals and fish — as also that of several OT texts where a like fate is mentioned for enemies or malefactors [100] — might seem now to suggest that Moses' final action in Exod 32,20 has to be viewed simply as one last eliminatory measure designed to remove the remains of the calf from the scene once and for all. In other words, the people, their guilt and punishment — in contrast to the case of Nu 5 — would not be in focus in Exod 32,20b[b], any more than are the birds in the first Ugaritic version of Mot's destruction; they are simply the available agents for the disposition of the calf's remains (comparable in this to the «brook» and to the «sea» in Deut 9,21 and the second Ugaritic Mot account, respectively). Now, on the basis of both the Biblical and extra-Biblical parallels, it can certainly be accepted that the «drinking motif» in Exod 32,20 does have a destructive-eliminatory function. The question may be raised, though, whether this exhausts the significance of Moses' action here. The question arises given the difference between those who do the consuming (drinking) in this verse on the one hand and in the other Biblical and extra-Biblical texts where such a «consumption» is spoken of on the other. In the former, the «consumers» are sinful human beings, the object which they are made to ingest being a kind of embodiment of their «sin», whereas this is, obviously, not the case with the brutes mentioned in the latter. Accordingly, it might be suggested that the «drinking» in 32,20 is intended to effect, not only the removal of the calf's remains, but also a punishment of the people for their sin. Such a supposition takes on an added plausibility in light of a number of passages, both Biblical and extra-Biblical, which speak of the use of «water» as a means of bringing harm on people. Within these we may distinguish between those where the one manipulating the harm-effecting water is a god, and those where it is rather a fellow human being. In the first instance, the gods make use of water — or are called upon to do so — for the punishment of evildoers, whereas in the latter case we have to do with operations by magicians directed against an innocent party who, for his part, appeals to the gods to deliver him from such magical machinations and to punish their perpetuators.

Let us consider the former group of texts first. One such text occurs among the curses invoked against violators of the oath in the Vassal Treaty of Esarhaddon; it runs: «May Ea, king of the apsu, lord of the springs, give you deadly water to drink, and fill you with dropsy» [101]. The association made here between the divine administration of the

100. E.g. 1 Sam 17,44; 2 Sam 21,10; 1 Kgs 14,11; 16,4; 2 Kgs 9,10.

101. Translation by E. REINER, in *ANET*, p. 539, §60. See, in addition, the notice on the treaty-breaker Nabu-Shum-eresh from Assurbanipal's «Cylinder B»: «Nabu-shum-eresh... who had not kept his oath-dropsy carried him off». LUCKENBILL, ARAB, II, p. 330, §857.

«deadly water» and the swelling of the culprit's body with dropsy suggests that it is by way of the former action that the latter condition is induced. The curse of dropsy spoken of in this treaty-text is likewise called down upon those who venture to tamper with boundary stones in several *kudurru* inscriptions; here, Marduk is summoned to fill the culprit's body with the bloating of that disease [102]. Similarly from the Hittite sphere we have an acted-out curse as an element of the military oath in which the soldier taking the oath is presented with a water-filled figure as a graphic illustration of how the gods will cause his own belly to swell should he prove disloyal [103]. As N. Öttinger notes, references to the gods' smiting oath-breakers with dropsy are also known from ancient India; this observation leads him to the supposition that such a conception of dropsy as *the* divine punishment for oath-breaking was an element of the primordial Indo-Germanic religion [104]. But, in any case, within the OT itself we have three texts in the Book of Jeremiah, i.e. 8,14; 9,14; 23,15 where, in striking parallelism to the Esarhaddon treaty curse cited above, there is mention of Yahweh's giving the people «poisoned water (*mē rō'š*)» to drink, in each instance his doing so being motivated by a reference to the people's sins against him [105]. It is only rather infrequently that scholars have made a connection between these three texts and Exod 32,20b[b]. R. Press, for one, does, however, view Jer 8,14 as a «direct allusion» to the Exodus passage, just as the reference to Yahweh's sending snakes to bite the people in the context of 8,14 in 8,17 would be a reference to another Pentateuchal passage, i.e. Nu 21,4ff. [106]. Possibly, the direction of the influence is the reverse of that postulated by Press (*vide infra*), but in any case the affinities between the two sets of texts are worth further consideration. Reference should also be made in this connection to a further series of OT Texts, i.e. those which have been called «the cup of wrath passages»; here, there is mention of Yahweh's various peoples (both Israelites and foreigners) drink of a «cup» with various harmful consequences being envisaged as a result of this [107].

In view of the documentation it appears that the notion of a deity punishing individuals and groups guilty of wrongdoing through the agency of some «fluid» (characteristically water) which the god causes

102. «May Marduk... with dropsy, the bond of which cannot be loosened, fill his body». KING, *Boundary-Stones*, Text VII, c. II, ll. 25-26 (p. 41); see likewise *Ibid.*, Text VIII, c. III, ll. 31-32 (p. 46); Text IX, c. I, ll. 40-41 (p. 61).

103. OETTINGER, *Eide*, Rs III, ll. 12-22 (p. 13).

104. OETTINGER, *Eide*, pp. 71-73.

105. On these texts see W. MCKANE, *Poison, Trial by Ordeal and the Cup of Wrath*, in *VT* 30 (1980) 474-492, pp. 478-487.

106. R. PRESS, *Das Ordal im Alten Israel*, I, in *ZAW* 51 (1933) 121-140, p. 126.

107. I.e. Is 51,17,22; Jer 25,15ff.; 49,12; 51,7,39; Lam 4,21; Ezek 23,31ff.; Oba 16; Hab 2,16; Zech 12,2; Ps 11,6; 75,9; Job 21,20. On these texts see MCKANE, *Poison*, pp. 487-492.

to become present in the body of the culprit(s) (typically by a forced drinking) was rather well known both in Israel and its ANE environment (as well as even further afield, see India). Might it not be suggested then the motif of Moses' making the people drink in Exod 32,20b[b] represents a kind of historicization of this «mythological» motif in which Moses functions as Yahweh's agent in imparting the harm-laden water to the apostate people - compare the role of the priest in Nu 5 who presents the potion to the suspect woman.

Supplementary evidence regarding an ANE conception of forced drinking as a means of bringing harm on those so made to drink is provided by a number of anti-sorcery texts from Mesopotamia. In these texts a person who believes himself to be the victim of machinations by hostile magicians is made to recite (or has recited for him) a series of somewhat formalized charges against those magicians. Among such charges there occurs several times one concerning a procedure involving water. Thus e.g., in the *Maqlu* series we read: «(the magicians) bezaubertes Wasser mich trinken liessen» [108]. Moses, we may suggest, functions rather similarly in Exod 32,20b[b], his intention in administering the water to the people being likewise to thereby bring harm on them.

Finally, and parenthetically, we might refer here to another set of Mesopotamian texts which concern a magical rite of giving to drink, although now for a positive rather than a negative purpose, i.e. the potency rituals published by R.D. Briggs. These texts are of interest in that their description of the procedures for preparing the potion that is to be administered are quite reminiscent of the sequence of Moses' «grinding» the calf, scattering the grindings on the water and then giving that water to the people to drink in Exod 32,20. So e.g. we read this prescription:

> you dry and pound up a male partridge(?)
> you put (it) into water...
> and give it to drink [109]

A similar ritual runs:

> you pluck a *diqdiqqu*-bird,
> you dress (it), rub it with salt (and)
> «mountain-plant»,
> you dry (and) crush (it)
> you mix (it) in flour of roasted grain and
> you give (it) to him to drink... [110]

108. Translation by MEIER, *Maqlu*, Tablet I, l. 104, p. 11; see further Tablet II, l. 167 (p. 19) where the charge is made against the magicians «wie mit Schmutzwasser die Wandleiste, so mich anzufüllen». See too E. EBELING, *Quellen zur Kenntnis der babylonischen Religion* (MVAG, 23/1-2), Leipzig, 1918-1919, p. 34 where the charge against the magicians is that they «mir Brot von Zauberen zu essen gegeben, Wasser von Zauberen mir zu trinken gegeben haben».

109. BRIGGS, *Incantations*, c. I, ll. 8-10 (p. 56).

110. BRIGGS, *Incantations*, c. I, ll. 23-27 (p. 57).

By way of conclusion to this excursus, we would suggest that the drinking motif in Exod 32,20b[b] has a two-fold significance. It points to both a final, definitive mode of eliminating all traces of the calf, and to a punishment of the Israelites who function as «consumers» of the calf for their sin in causing it to be made. In both senses Moses' final action here can, as we have seen, be paralleled from both Biblical and extra-Biblical material. We may further note that neither sense of his action is spelled out as such in the text itself (unless the reference to Yahweh's sending a plague among the people in Exod 32,35 is to be seen as a development of the punishment aspect of the drinking procedure). Rather, it is the author's expectation that those meanings would be obvious to his Israelite readers for whom the notions of «consumption as means of elimination» and forced drinking as a mode of conveying bodily harm and as punishment for wrongdoing were familiar conceptions — just as they were among Israel's neighbors. Finally, we would state, in light of the above, that the long-standing effort to make a connection between the people's forced drinking in Exod 32,20 and the rite with the «water of bitterness» in Nu 5,11-31 does have a certain validity in that the latter text exhibits the same notion of an imposed drinking of water as a means of bringing harm and punishment to the drinker which we have seen to lie behind the Exodus passage. This communality remains even if the ordeal/testing dimension of Nu 5 be lacking in Exod 32,20.

III. The Nature of the Relationship between Exod 32,20 and Deut 9,21: Considerations and Consequences

Of the four major questions raised in the history of research concerning the Bible's two versions of the destruction of the calf (see *supra*, p. 208 s.), there now remains still unresolved by the foregoing discussion that regarding the nature of the relation between those two versions, i.e. is there a literary dependence between Exod 32,20 and Deut 9,21, and if so, which text is dependent on which? As will emerge, this question is worth a somewhat detailed investigation in that its resolution can provide various significant indications with regard to a number of wider questions which are much controverted today.

Initially, it does seem clear that we should reckon with a literary dependence — in whatever direction it may be — between the two verses. Thus we note first the contentual correspondence between them in the various actions of Moses related and the sequence of those actions (apart, of course, from his final measure in Exodus which has nothing parallel to it in Deuteronomy) — see the breakdown of the two verses into their respective elements on p. 208. In both Moses first gets hold of the calf, then burns it, reduces it to a powder and places that powder into a body of water. More significantly, the two verses exhibit a whole series of noteworthy verbal correspondences which do strongly suggest that the author of one formulated his text with the wording of the other before him.

— both use the verb *lāqaḥ* with «the calf» as object
— both contain a relative clause employing the verb *ʿāśāh* with the people («they/you») as subject.
— both use the phrase *śārap bāʾēš*.
— both employ a form of the verb *ṭāḥan* with reference to Moses' third action against the calf. This common feature takes on greater significance when it is noted that the verb *ṭāḥan* occurs a total of only seven times in the OT and that our two texts are the only cases where it is used with «images» as object [111].
— both make use of the construction *ʿad ʾᵃšer dāq* to designate the result of Moses' third action against the calf. Once again, the uniqueness of this common formulation *vis-à-vis* the usage of the OT as a whole lends it a heightened significance. Specifically, these are the only occurrences of the verb *dāqaq* in a qal infinitive construction with the phrase *ʿad ʾᵃšer*, just as it is only here that *dāqaq* qal is employed with reference to the «crushing fine» of illicit cult objects [112].

If, in view of the foregoing significant verbal correspondences between them, we do admit a relation of literary dependence between the two verses, we have next to raise the question of the direction of that dependence. In order to resolve that question, attention must now be focussed on the differences between the two verses. Apart from their employment of the third and first person formulation (which they have in common with their contexts) respectively, Exod 32,20 and Deut 9,21 diverge in their wording in the following respects:

— in Exod 32,20 Moses' initial action with respect to the calf is formulated «and he took the calf which they had made», while Deut 9,21 reads «and your sin, which ye had made, even the calf, I took».
— in the case of Moses' second action, the burning, Deut 9,21 has *wāʾeśrōp ʾōtō bāʾēš* for Exodus' *wayyiśrōp bāʾēš*.
— in Exodus Moses' third action reads «and he ground [it], until [it] was crushed fine» as against Deuteronomy's «and he beat *it* in pieces, grinding [it] well, until [it] was crushed fine into dust».
— for Moses' fourth action Exodus has: «he strewed (*wayyizer*) [it] upon the water», Deuteronomy: «and I cast (*wāʾašlik*) *its dust* into the stream that descended out of the mount».
— finally, Deuteronomy lacks all parallel to what in Exodus is Moses' fifth and final measure, i.e. «(he) made the children of Israel drink [of it].»

111. The remaining instances are: Nu 11,8; Judg 16,21; Is 3,15; 47,2; Job 31,10. With the exception of Is 3,15 where the verb is used metaphorically of the «grinding of the face of the poor», the reference in all these texts is to the domestic operation involved in the preparation of bread (or a bread-like substance).

112. The only other uses of the qal in the OT are Is 28,28 (object: bread grain) and 41,15 (object: the mountains). The hiphil is used with reference to the destruction of illicit cult objects in 2 Kgs 23,6,15; 2 Chron 15,16; 34,4,7 and then in other connections in Exod 30, 36; 2 Sam 22,43; Mic 4,13; Is 28,28.

An initial inspection of the above differences makes clear that, for what concerns the first four measures of Moses which they have in common, the formulations of Deuteronomy are consistently more verbose, elaborate and specificatory than the corresponding elements in Exodus. Thus while Exodus uses five words to relate Moses' first measure, Deuteronomy has seven, just as his third measure requires seven words in Deuteronomy as compared to only four in Exodus. In the case of the second, third and fourth measures of Moses, Deuteronomy provides an explicit mention of the object (see *'ōtō, bis* and *'et ʿapārō*) of the given action that is lacking in Exodus. Similarly, Exodus' quite indeterminate «upon the face of the water» as the place where Moses disposes the powder from the calf in his fourth measure becomes a more definite «into the stream that descended out of the mount» in Deuteronomy in which the particular nature of the body of water in question as well as its place of origin is specified. Further, it is obvious that the description of Moses' first and third actions with the calf are fuller-blown in Deuteronomy than in Exodus. In the case of the first action, this is so for what concerns the object which Moses is said to «take», whereas in the third the amplification has to do with the description of the process employed by Moses. Particularly to be noted here is the difference between Exodus' «objective» opening reference to the being with which Moses has to deal: «I took the calf which they made» and Deuteronomy's emphatically negative qualification «and your sin which you had made...» which precedes any mention of the «calf» itself.

All the above observations seem to point clearly to the same conclusion, i.e. Deut 9,21 is secondary with regard to Exod 32,20 of which it represents an amplifying and specifying rewriting. Conversely, the opposite supposition, that i.e. in Exod 32,20 the presentation of Deut 9,21 has been rendered deliberately less definite, less expansive, and less theologically qualified is patently implausible. At the same time, however, it must be admitted that there is one feature of Deut 9,21 as compared with Exod 32,20 which does seem to militate against that otherwise obvious conclusion, i.e. the absence in the former of any parallel to the latter's «drinking motif». Here, in contrast to its otherwise consistent tendency, Deut 9,21 appears less, not more, expansive than Exod 32,20. Have we then to suppose, as do some authors, that at least this final element of the Exodus verse is to be considered secondary *vis-à-vis* Deut 9,21 [113]?

The resolution of the above difficulty is best approached in somewhat round-about fashion, by widening our perspective to include an additional factor. This «detour» does, however, as will emerge, promise

113. Authors of this persuasion are listed by HAHN, *Kalb*, p. 242, n. 219.

significant clarifications not only concerning the problem of the divergent conclusions of our two verses, but also with regard to the whole range of verbal differences between them as enumerated above, just as it will enable us to bring into play the second major development in contemporary study of the two verses as cited above, i.e. the comparison between them and other OT texts recounting the destruction of forbidden cultic objects. The factor to be adduced now is M. Noth's theory of the Deuteronomistic History (hereafter Dtr) and its subsequent refinements. As is well known, Noth proposed, on the basis, particularly, of the contentual links between them, to ascribe portions of Deut 1-3(4), 31, 34 to one and the same author, i.e. the Deuteronomist, as the Deuteronomic-like passages in the books Joshua-Kings [114]. As is likewise well known, G. Minette de Tillesse, some twenty years after Noth's work of 1943, suggested, in consideration of the correspondences of theme and terminology between them and a range of passages in Joshua-Kings, that also the sections written in the second person plural in Deut 5-11 be reckoned to Noth's Deuteronomist [115]. Chief among such sections is Deuteronomy's calf account, 9,7b-10,11. In arguing for a derivation of this pericope from the Deuteronomist, Minette de Tillesse noted e.g. that while Deut 9,21 diverges from Exod 32,20 in having Moses terminate his measures against the calf by throwing its remains into a «brook» rather than in a making the people drink, precisely in so doing it serves, very much in the manner of Noth's Deuteronomist in Deut 1-3, etc., to prepare an event to be related in the subsequent Historical Books, i.e. Josiah's casting dust from the illicit altars he had pulverized «into the brook Kidron» in 2 Kgs 23,12 (cf. 23,6) [116]. Several subsequent authors have extended Minette de Tillesse's comparison of Deut 9,21 and 2 Kgs 23,12 (cf. 23,6) to include further passages from the Book of Kings [117]. What emerges from the investigations of these authors is that, not only in its introduction of a «brook» as the place where the calf's remains are disposed, but also in a whole series of other instances where its wording diverges from that of Exod 32,20, Deut 9,21 evidences verbal links with a wide range of texts in Kings recounting significant moments (both positive and negative) in the cultic history of Israel, so that the verse appears as a very deliberate rewriting of the text of Exodus with a view to setting up and fore-shadowing those various later moments. Let us now, making use of, while further expanding, the

114. M. Noth, *Überlieferungsgeschichtliche Studien*, Halle, 1943.

115. G. Minette de Tillesse, *Sections « tu » et sections « vous » dans le Deutéronome*, in *VT* 12 (1962) 28-87.

116. Minette de Tillesse, *Sections*, p. 60.

117. See in particular H.-D. Hoffmann, *Reform und Reformen. Untersuchungen zu einem Grundthema der deuteronomistischen Geschichtsschreibung* (AThANT, 66) Zürich, 1980, pp. 310-311 and Spieckermann, *Juda*, p. 91.

results of previous authors, examine the evidence on this point in greater detail:

1) Deuteronomy's qualification of the calf as «your sin (*ḥaṭṭatᵉkem*)», a qualification not found in Exod 32,20, serves to underscore the connection between the Mosaic calf and those of Jeroboam in that the same term is used repeatedly in Deuteronomistic references in Kings to Jeroboam's act in setting up the calves [118].

2) In Exod 32,20 the main verb used in connection with Moses' third action against the calf is *ṭāḥan*. Deut 9,21 does also employ *ṭāḥan* in this connection, not, however, as main verb, this being rather *kātat* to which the infinitive absolute *ṭāḥōn* functions as a kind of apposition. But now, this use of the term *kātat* (in the qal) in Deuteronomy's account does serve to establish a link between Moses' action here and another important moment in Judah's cultic history, i.e. the reform of Hezekiah. Specifically, in 2 Kgs 18,4b the piel of the same verb is used of Hezekiah's destruction of «Nehushtan»: «and he broke in pieces (*wᵉkittat*) the bronze serpent that Moses had made...» [119]. This correspondence takes on added significance when it is noted that in only two other of the 17 total uses of the verb *kātat* in the OT is it employed with an idolatrous entity as object, i.e. (the late) 2 Chron 34,7 (piel) and (the equally late) Mic 1,7 (hophal) [120].

3) Likewise of significance is another term proper to Deuteronomy's account of Moses' third action against the calf, i.e. the hiphil infinitive absolute *hēṭēb*. Already S. R. Driver noted that, in its adverbial usage in the sense «thoroughly», this form is characteristic of the *Sprachgebrauch* of the book of Deuteronomy, being used there, apart from our text, four other times in this sense, i.e. 13,15; 17,4; 19,18; 27,8, and then only once elsewhere in the entire OT in this way, i.e. 2 Kgs 11,18 [121]. This last text which reads, in the translation of NAB, «they shattered its (i.e. the Ba'al temple's) altars and images completely (*hēṭēb*)» has, however, a still greater interest for our purposes in that, with Deut 9,21, this is the only instance in the OT where an (itself already rather distinctive) use of the form *hēṭēb* is employed with reference to a «thorough-going» destruction specifically of forbidden cult objects. And given this consideration, it

118. I.e. 1 Kgs 12,30; 13,34; 14,16,22; 15,3, 26,30,34; 16,2,13,19 (*bis*), 26,31; 2 Kgs 3,3; 13,2,6,11; 14,24; 15,9,18,24,28; 17,22.

119. On 2 Kgs 18,4b see HOFFMANN, *Reform*, pp. 147-148, 311 and SPIECKERMANN, *Juda*, pp. 173-174, 420. For Hoffmann the text is Deuteronomistic, whereas Spieckermann refers it to the pre-Deuteronomistic *Vorlage*.

120. Mic 1,7 is of particular interest in that it contains the same combination of the verbs *kātat* and *śārap* as applied to cultic objects (persons) as does Deut 9,21. The text is widely regarded as deriving from a late (Exilic) «Deuteronomistic» redaction of the book of Micah by contemporary authors e.g. H. W. WOLFF, *Dodekapropheton: Micha* (BK, XIV/2), Neukirchen-Vluyn, 1980, p. 22.

121. S. R. DRIVER, *Deuteronomy* (ICC), Edinburgh, 1895, p. lxxxi, §43.

becomes very plausible to suppose that the term has been deliberately introduced in the formulation of Deut 9,21 with a view to setting up a link with and preparation for yet another of Dtr's subsequent cultic reform episodes, i.e. the elimination of the Baʿal cult from Judah as related in 2 Kgs 11,18 [122].

4) In Deut 9,21 the phrase *ʿad ʾᵃšer dāq* which it does have in common with Exod 32,20, receives an intensifying expansion, i.e. the word *lᵉʿapār*. This additional element, in turn, serves to link Deut 9,21 with two formulations in the account of Josiah's reforms in 2 Kgs 23,4ff. where the same term is appended to a hiphil — contrast the qal in Deut 9,21 and Exod 32,20 — form of the verb *dāqaq*, i.e. 23,6b[a] (of the Asherim) [123] and 23,15b[a] (of the Bethel *bāmāh*). In this connection we may further note that the only uses of the term *ʿapār* with reference specifically to the «dust» of illicit cultic objects in the OT are in Deut 9,21 and then in 2 Kgs 23,4ff., i.e. vv. 4,6 (*bis*), 12 and 15.

5) As noted by Minette de Tillesse, the formulation used of Moses' fourth measure in Deut 9,21, precisely in its divergence from that of Exod 32,20, serves to establish a further verbal connection between Moses' actions here and those of Josiah in 2 Kgs 23,4ff. Specifically, the identical full formulation *hišlik ʾet ʿapār ʾel naḥal* employed in 9,21 recurs in 2 Kgs 23,12 where the reference is to the disposition of the illicit altars, while in 2 Kgs 23,6 the construction *hišlik ʾet ʿapār* likewise appears, although with a different site being indicated as the place where Josiah «casts» the dust of the Asherah spoken of in this verse, i.e. «the graves of the common people». In this connection we might likewise mention that these three texts are the only instances in the OT where the verb *hišlik* is used specifically with *ʿapār* (= «dust» of pulverized cultic entities) as its object [124]. Conversely, the term *zārāh* used in Exod 32,20's account of Moses' fourth measure nowhere figures in the vast repertoire of expressions employed in Dtr for speaking of the elimination of forbidden cultic objects [125]. The conclusion seems rather clear then that

122. On 2 Kgs 11,18b see HOFFMANN, *Reform*, pp. 109-110 who calls it «Deuteronomistic» and SPIECKERMANN, *Juda*, pp. 178, 414, who designates it as «late Deuteronomistic». See too C. LEVIN, *Der Stürz der Königin Atalja* (SBS 105), Stuttgart, 1982, pp. 61-62 and n. 8 who refers 11,18b to what he calls the «bundestheologische Bearbeitung» of 2 Kgs 11 — a stratum which he further qualifies (*Ibid.*, pp. 72 and 95) as «late Deuteronomistic».

123. On this and related texts, see SPIECKERMANN, *Juda*, pp. 90-91.

124. The term is used several times elsewhere of a «casting away» specifically of idolatrous objects, i.e. Is 2,20; Ezek 20,7,8; 2 Chron 30,14; 33,15. Likewise somewhat comparable is the usage in Lev 14,40 and Ezek 5,4 where a «casting» of undesirable objects is spoken of. In none of these texts, however, is *hišlik* used with *ʿapār* as its object as such, nor is there reference to a «stream» (or a «grave») as the place into which the object is cast, as is the case with the above three texts.

125. This term is used once elsewhere in the OT with idolatrous entities as object, i.e. Is 30,22 «Then you will defile your silver-covered graven images and your gold-plated molten images. You will scatter them (*tizrēm*) as unclean things; you will say to them, 'Begone'».

the formulation of Moses' fourth action in Exod 32,20 has been deliberately modified in Deut 9,21 with a view to further conforming the presentation of Moses' action here to those of Josiah later on.

6) Closely related to the foregoing point is a further one, i.e. the difference between Exodus and Deuteronomy regarding their respective designations of the place where Moses disperses the ground remains of the calf. In the former, this is «on the face of the water», in the latter «into the brook coming down from the mount». Here too, it seems that the difference has to be accounted for in terms of the author of Deuteronomy's wanting to establish links with the presentation of the following books. Specifically, as just mentioned, 2 Kgs 23,12 speaks, in a formulation closely corresponding to that of Deut 9,21, of Josiah's casting the dust of the pulverized altars «into the brook Kidron». But it has further to be noted that also elsewhere when Dtr refers to the destruction of forbidden cult objects, a «brook», and specifically «the brook Kidron», figures prominently. Thus in 1 Kgs 15,13 Asa burns the «image» of his mother «at the brook Kidron» — this mention of a «brook» in connection with an iconoclastic action constituting a link between Deut 9,21 and yet another subsequent reform in Dtr, i.e. that of Asa (see 1 Kgs 15:12-14) [126]. Likewise, in a formulation identical to that of 1 Kgs 15,13, Josiah is said to «burn» the Asherah «at the brook Kidron» in 2 Kgs 23,6. Also to be compared here is the reference to Josiah's burning the vessels pertaining to the cult of various divinities «in the fields (*beṣadmōt*) of the Kidron» in 2 Kgs 23,4. Elsewhere in the OT, a «brook», and specifically «the brook Kidron» is mentioned as the place at which the destruction of cultic objects is carried out or into which the remains of such objects are cast only in 2 Chron 29,16 and 30 — both texts undoubtedly inspired by the formulations of Dtr [127].

At the same time, we should not leave this point without acknowledging the difference between the definite «brook Kidron» in Kings and the indeterminate «the brook coming down from the mount» in Deut 9,21. This difficulty need not at all, however, militate against our

Various commentators have made a connection between the formulations of Exod 32,20 and Is 30,22, some suggesting that the latter is literarily dependent on the former, so e.g. B. DUHM, *Das Buch Jesaja* (HKAT, 3/1), Göttingen, ²1902, p. 193. A somewhat comparable use of the term occurs in Ezek 5,2 in which the prophet receives the directive *tizrēh lāruaḥ* with regard to a portion of his hair which symbolizes the doomed people — see E. J. SMIT, *The Concepts of Obliteration in Ezek 5,1-4*, in *JNWSL* 1 (1971) 46-50. The same formulation as in Ezek 5,2, used this time of the prescribed handling of idolatrous objects, recurs in the Mishna text cited in n. 98.

126. On 1 Kgs 15,13, see HOFFMANN, *Reform*, p. 88 and SPIECKERMANN, *Juda*, pp. 168 and 412. Both authors view the verse as «Deuteronomistic», Spieckermann referring it to «DtrH».

127. On the significance of the «brook» in the cultic reform accounts of Dtr, see HOFFMANN, *Reform*, p. 244, n. 7, and SPIECKERMANN, *Juda*, p. 187.

supposition that the «brook» has been introduced in Deut 9,21 in place of the «water» of Exod 32,20 with the formulations of the Kings' passages in view. With those passages before him, the author of Deuteronomy was, on the one hand, anxious to have Moses' actions with the calf — like those of Asa and Josiah after him — take place, not just at any body of «water» (so Exodus), but precisely in proximity to a «brook». On the other hand, however, we may readily suppose that, whereas he was very familiar with the Kidron as *the* brook of Jerusalem, he would not have known the name of the «brook» at the far-off site Mt. Horeb where he localizes the calf incident — if, indeed, such a brook existed at all. Given, however, his situating the affair at a «mountain» (see Deut 9,8, 9, 10, 15, etc.), he does specify that «brook» which he wants to introduce here, as best he may, by designating it «the brook coming down from the mountain» [128].

7) With the above indications in mind, we now turn to our earlier difficulty as to how the absence in Deut 9,21 of a fifth measure of Moses, comparable to the drinking motif at the end of Exod 32,20, can be made intelligible on the (otherwise plausible) supposition that the latter text is literarily dependent on the former. In light of what we have just seen to be the consistent tendency in Deut 9,21, i.e. its modifying the wording of Exod 32,20 so as to bring that wording into conformity with the formulations to be encountered subsequently in Dtr in connection with developments in the cultic history of Israel (Judah), we would propose the following on this point. Nowhere in the many and varied accounts of post-Mosaic cultic reforms in Dtr do we find anything comparable to the concluding notice of Exod 32,20 according to which the people had to ingest the remains of the illicit cult object they had made. But now, as we have been noting in a whole series of instances, the major concern of the author of Deut 9,21 seems to be precisely to make his version of the calf's destruction as comprehensive a preparation as possible to the terminology and motifs employed in those various subsequent cult reform accounts. Given, however, the peculiarity of the concluding notice in Exod 32,20 that notice was simply unusable for such purposes. And accordingly, the author of Deut 9,21 just passed it over, having his version end rather with a feature which does correspond to the presen-

128. Another possible influence behind the introduction of the «brook» into the depiction of Deut 9,21 is the law concerning the case of a person murdered by an unknown hand in Deut 21,1-9. That law prescribes that the throat of a heifer be cut at «a wadi (*naḥal*) with an ever-flowing stream» (21,4, NAB), the idea being, apparently, that the «stream» will carry away the heifer's blood — which itself functions as a substitute for that of the murdered person — from the community affected. The author of Deut 9,21 could have been inspired by the law of 21,1ff. to introduce a «brook» into his presentation which would have the same function *vis-à-vis* the remains of the calf as does the *naḥal* with regard to the blood of the heifer. A connection between Deut 9,21 and 21,1ff. is made, e.g. by MAYES, *Deuteronomy*, p. 201.

tation of several of the following cult reform notices in Dtr, i.e. the bringing of the object which is to be eliminated into connection with a «brook». And thus, the «abbreviation» of the conclusion of Exod 32,20 in Deut 9,21 — which at first sight seems to run counter to the whole tendency of the latter in relation to the former and so to militate against the dependence of Deuteronomy on Exodus (rather than *vice versa*) — does appear capable of explanation on that supposition once the theory of «Dtr» and specifically a comparison between Deut 9,21, in its various differences with Exod 32,20, and the cult reform notices of Kings is brought to bear on the problem.

The immediately preceding investigation of the verbal contacts between Deut 9,21 and a whole series of passages relating to cultic developments in the book of Kings on the one hand, and against Exod 32,20 on the other, further enables us to make more precise our earlier remarks concerning the «tendencies» exhibited by Deut 9,21 in comparison with Exod 32,20. We spoke above of Deuteronomy's elaborating, specifying and theologically qualifying the presentation of Exodus. What now becomes clear, however, is that the particular terms and formulations in which those tendencies find expression have not at all been selected randomly or capriciously. Rather, each particular term/motif proper to Deut 9,21 has been chosen with a view to setting up a definite verbal contact between its account of the destruction of the calf and various significant cultic developments in the period of the divided monarchy, i.e. Jeroboam's fatal offense in erecting the calves (1 Kgs 12,26ff. etc.) and then the four major Judean cultic reforms of Asa (see 1 Kgs 15,13), Joas (see 2 Kgs 11,18b), Hezekiah (see 2 Kgs 18,4b) and Josiah (see 2 Kgs 23,4ff., *passim*). And it is, we propose, the same all-dominant interest on the part of the author of Deut 9,21 which explains why he simply passes over the (unusable) concluding notice of Exod 32,20 in his presentation.

Beyond the just-mentioned «literary» interest in setting up a series of verbal *Vorspiele* to subsequent accounts, however, there may be, as we might now note, several other factors which might be of relevance in explaining the divergencies between Exod 32,20 and Deut 9,21, above all the problem of the missing parallel to the conclusion of the former in the latter. Here we can draw on suggestions of various earlier authors. S. E. Loewenstamm, e.g. discerns a consistent tendency to «rationalize» the presentation of Exod 32,20 in the version of Deut 9,21. Thus while Deuteronomy does retain the term *ṭāḥan* of Exod 32,20, it would, on the consideration that a gold object cannot, in fact, be «ground», have preceded that term with the verb *kātat*, thereby intimating that *ṭāḥan* here is to be understood along the lines of a «breaking in pieces». Again, the introduction of the reference to «the brook coming down from the mountain» in Deut 9,21 would reflect a rationalizing concern with making somehow plausible the presence of «water» (so Exod 32,20) in the desert locale of Horeb. But this «rationalization» would, in its turn, engender another, still further-going modification of the Exodus-presentation, i.e. since a «brook» would very rapidly carry off the gold dust thrown into it, a drinking like that spoken of in Exod 32,20b[b] becomes an impossibility, and so Deuteronomy eliminates any mention of it[129].

In addition to the more *sachlich* «rationalizations» which Loewenstamm identifies as operative in Deuteronomy's recasting of the account of Exodus, we might also think in terms of possible ideological/ theological «rationalizations» at work here. Specifically, several authors have seen a theological objection on the part of the author of Deuteronomy to the primitive magical ordeal practice to which Exod 32,20b[b] would allude as the reason for the absence of this feature in his version[130]. Now, it is not, in fact, clear that Exod 32,20b[b] does, as such, concern an «ordeal»[131]. Perhaps, however, the idea of these authors that the writer of Deut 9,21 found some conceptual difficulty with the drinking procedure as narrated in Exodus can be retained, reformulated in somewhat more cautious terms as follows: it was not so much that the author of Deut 9,21 was opposed to what he found related in Exodus, as that, like so many subsequent commentators, he was simply unclear as to the sense of the reference. But then, the easiest solution to the problem posed by the obscurity of the concluding notice in Exod 32,20b would be for him to simply eliminate that problematic notice in his own presentation—a course that he might all the more easily adopt in that, as noted above, the notice did not offer anything usable to him as regards his primary concern, i.e. to make the various moments of Moses' destruction of the calf all so many presentiments of later cultic developments in Israel's history.

A further consideration that might be of relevance here is the suggestion put forward by D. Hoffmann in his Deuteronomy commentary of 1913[132]. Hoffmann views the drinking to which the people are subjected in Exodus as an act of punishment. The author of Deuteronomy would then, according to him, have eliminated such a notice in line with his consistent tendency, exhibited throughout his retelling of the calf account, of passing over the various punishments of the people related in the version of Exodus. In this connection Hoffmann

129. LOEWENSTAMM, *Rejoinder*, p. 339.

130. HAHN, *Kalb*, p. 205, n. 53 lists J. Loza and E.F. de Waard as advocates of this understanding. To this list we may add: J. MORGENSTERN, *Trial by Ordeal among the Semites and in Ancient Israel*, in *Hebrew Union College Jubilee Volume*, Cincinatti, 1925, 113-143, p. 140; P. BUIS-J. LECLERCQ, *Le Deutéronome* (SB), Paris, 1969, p. 89 and WEINFELD, *Deuteronomy*, p. 234, n. 2.

131. On the problematic here, see HAHN, *Kalb*, pp. 201-208.

132. D. HOFFMANN, *Das Buch Deuteronomium*, Berlin, 1913, p. 109.

cites the absence in Deuteronomy of anything parallel to the bloody intervention of the Levites recounted in Exod 32,25-29, and to this we may add the consideration that Deuteronomy likewise has nothing corresponding to the mention of Yahweh's sending a plague among the people in Exod 32,35. We proposed above that, against the background of other texts, both Biblical and extra-Biblical, that a «punishment dimension» is indeed, as Hoffmann affirms, also present in the drinking notice of Exod 32,20. And if this be admitted, then Hoffmann's suggestion provides us with yet another factor helping to make plausible why the author of Deuteronomy might readily have passed over that notice in his own version.

In concluding our treatment of the problem as to why there should be no parallel to the concluding notice of Exod 32,20 in Deut 9,21 we may now state, on the basis of the foregoing considerations, that the affirmation of W. Rudolph according to which the author of Deuteronomy would have had «no reason» for not taking up the notice of Exod 32,20b^{b} if, in fact, that notice were part of the text of Exodus available to him[133] seems not at all on target. Indeed, one might very well reverse Rudolph's claim and say that the author of Deuteronomy had, rather, every reason — its uselessness for the wider literary purposes he was pursuing with his account, the difficulties of versimilitude and of comprehension he may have found with it, as well as his set intention of eliminating all mention of a punishment of the people for their sin with the calf, and finally the simple desire for variation as discussed above — for just passing over the notice of Exod 32,20b^{b} — notwithstanding its presence in his source which he otherwise follows quite closely. But if this be so, then the one major obstacle to seeing Deut 9,21 as a rewriting of Exod 32,20 in its present extent and wording is effectively disposed of. And so, given the abundant converging evidence furnished by the comparison of the remainder of the two verses in favor of that supposition, it ought certainly to be accepted.

Finally, by way of rounding off the foregoing discussion, we might briefly take up here the conceptions of several authors who do regard the concluding notice of Exod 32,20 as secondary *vis-à-vis* Deut 9,21 in order to see if an effective response can be made to their views. A first such author is the just-cited W. Rudolph. For him Exod 32,20b^{b} represents a secondary assimilation of an earlier text which would have terminated (more or less) like the present Deut 9,21, to the ordeal procedure of Nu 5,11-31. This development further, has had as its consequence that the original «brook» of the Exodus text (so Deut 9,21) was changed to «water» on the consideration that it was only a standing body of water — not a brook — which would make possible the «drinking» referred

133. W. RUDOLPH, *Der «Elohist» von Exodus bis Josua* (BZAW, 68), Berlin, 1938, p. 51.

to in the appended notice. With regard to such a view, however, one can only wonder why the hypothetical «redactor» of Exod 32,20 has not made the connection with the ritual of Nu 5 somewhat more obvious in his reworking of the existing Exodus verse. Even leaving aside the problem of the lack of any clear-cut reference to the effects of the purported ordeal on the people corresponding to the indications provided in Nu 5,19-22, 27-28 in Exodus 32, there is the difficulty as to why, given Rudolph's supposition that the redactor did feel free to change the wording of the original Exodus text (i.e. modifying an earlier «brook» to the present «water»), he did not go further and conform the terminology of the verse more thoroughly to that of Nu 5 in the interests of underscoring and making more obvious the connection between the two passages. Specifically, we might refer here to the curious fact that, whereas Deut 9,21 does contain the term *ʿapār* used in the prescription concerning the preparation of the ordeal drink in Nu 5,16, it is precisely rather Exod 32,20 which lacks this word. Again, how is it that while Nu 5,16 employs the verb *nātan* of the priest's mixing of the «dust» with the «water», Exod 32,20 uses, not this verb, but rather *zārāh* for the somewhat comparable action of Moses? And finally, why would not a redactor, rewriting an earlier form of Exod 32,20 with the presentation of Nu 5,11 ff. in mind, have introduced into the former a mention of the «earthen vessel» spoken of in Nu 5,16 as the container for the water to be used in the ordeal — this all the more so in that the presence of such a «vessel» (or vessels) would certainly render more readily conceivable the drinking procedure which he has (purportedly) introduced in Exod 32,20. All these considerations raise doubts as to the correctness of Rudolph's claim that Exod 32,20b^{b} is intended to assimilate Moses' actions with the calf to the ordeal procedure of Nu 5, and *a fortiori* to his view that this assimilation represents a secondary development *vis-à-vis* the formulation of Deut 9,21.

A second author to be cited here is E. Zenger. According to him the present conclusion of Exod 32,20 was secondarily appended to an earlier form of the verse which ended, approximately as Deut 9,21 now does, with Moses strewing powder from the calf on «water». The purpose of this addition was to provide an answer to a question which would have been raised, but left unresolved, by that earlier conclusion, i.e. why, with what intention, did Moses throw the powder into the water? The response supplied by the added v. 20b^{b} is that he did so with a view to preparing the «drink» which he would subsequently force on the people[134]. Given, however, the numerous references to the practice of casting objects into water as a way of effecting their disappearance in ANE literature as cited above, we can only ask whether, in fact, a

134. E. ZENGER, *Die Sinaitheophanie. Untersuchungen zum jahwistischen und elohistischen Geschichtswerk* (FzB, 3), Würzburg, 1971, p. 106.

presentation like that of the hypothetical earlier form of Exod 32,20 (and the present Deut 9,21) would have occasioned questions (and eventually added explanations) about its sense as Zenger suggests. Rather, it seems that the meaning of Moses' action in casting the calf's remains into water would have been immediately evident to the ancient hearer/reader.

A final proponent of the secondary character of Exod 32,20b[b] with regard to Deut 9,21 is R. Gradwohl. For him this notice was added in order to underscore the worthlessness of the calf as an object which could only passively undergo being thus «consumed» by its own worshippers. With this intention the notice would reflect the same sort of anti-idol polemic articulated e.g. in Is 44,9-17, and so would represent an Exilic interpolation within the Exodus calf account[135]. Various difficulties suggest themselves against such a conception, however. First, we note that the different anti-idol passages of the OT (e.g. Is 40,18-20; 42,17; Ps 115,3-7; 135,15-17; Jer 10,2-9) do employ a number of recurring satirical motifs in their denigration of idols, e.g. fabrication of the idols by the very ones who worship them, the inability of the idols to perform the most elementary sensory functions. Among these *topoi* we find nothing parallel, however, to the supposed derogatorily intended depiction of the «consumption» of the calf's remains in Exod 32,20b[b], and so we can only wonder whether, in fact, that depiction does have such a purpose. Again, on Gradwohl's understanding of the notice, we would have to suppose that the redactor has introduced 32,20b[b] — in which an idolatrous object would simply be held up to ridicule — quite against the whole tenor of Exod 32 where the calf and its making is treated as a matter of utmost gravity — much in contrast to the polemics of Deutero-Isaiah for whom idols and their fabrication are merely something to be laughed at. Is such an obliviousness by a redactor to the character of the context in which he makes his insertion really plausible? Finally, alternative understandings of the sense of the notice of 32,20b[b] are available (*vide supra*), and given the evidence of both Biblical and extra-Biblical comparative material can, in fact, claim a far greater degree of plausibility than that proposed by Gradwohl for whose interpretation confirmatory parallels are lacking. And so we conclude that neither Gradwohl's interpretation of Exod 32,20b[b] nor his claim regarding the affinities of this notice with the anti-idol polemics of Deutero-Isaiah (and the dating for the notice such affinities would suggest) can be regarded as particularly satisfactory. But if so, then the same has to be said concerning Gradwohl's qualification of the notice as secondary and posterior to Deut 9,21 — a position to which he comes on the basis of his understanding of its sense and purported affinities.

It thus appears that all the various attempts to understand and make

135. R. GRADWOHL, *Die Verbrennung des Jungstiers*, in ThZ 19 (1963) 50-53, p. 53.

sense of Exod 32,20b[b] as a secondary appendix involve difficulties which are not readily resolvable by their proponents. And that recognition, in turn, lends added credence to the view for which we have argued on positive grounds above, i.e. the author of Deut 9,21 had as his source Exod 32,20 in its present wording and extent.

We have dealt as such length with the question of how the relationship between the two versions of the destruction of the calf is to be understood because, as indicated initially, it is our conviction that assured results on this point of detail — which are themselves attainable only through the sort of thorough-going weighing of evidence *pro* and *con* attempted above — can provide significant indications with regard to a whole series of broader questions which are in contention in contemporary scholarship. Here in the final segment of our paper we wish to briefly explicate the implications of our findings on the Deut 9,21 — Exod 32,20 relationship for these wider questions under four headings. In doing so we are, of course, fully aware that our evidential base is very small; a resolution of these questions, in so far as it can be attained at all, would require a detailed examination of all the component elements in Exod 32,1-34,28 and Deut 9,7b-10,11 both for themselves and in comparison with each other and with conscious attention to the various alternative explanations available in each particular case. Perhaps, however, the following presentation, narrowly based as it is, may stimulate just such a comprehensive investigation which, to our knowledge, has yet to be carried out with the requisite thoroughness.

1) In the first place, a detailed comparison of Exod 32,20 and Deut 9,21 does suggest that there is a relation of literary dependence between the two calf accounts of which these verses are clearly integral elements. In the case of our verses such a supposition — as opposed to the idea that they are simply independent developments of an older tradition — finds support in their common use of several quite distinctive expressions, i.e. the verb *ṭāḥan* as applied to illicit cult objects and the formula *ʿad ʾašer dāq*. In the face of such communalities, it is, clearly, simpler and less needlessly hypothetical to view one verse as literarily dependent on the other than to suppose that they both draw on a tradition — whether oral or written — which is no longer extant. The wider conclusion to which that finding points, i.e. that a relation of literary dependence does ordain between the respective overall accounts of which those verses are an integral part is, of course, in line with the long-standing dominant scholarly view. As a detailed substantiation of such a supposition our finding may, however, usefully serve to counteract the general questionings of that view which have been emitted from time to time[136].

136. Scholars opting for dependence rather on a common tradition are e.g. J. RENNES, *Le Deutéronome*, Genève, 1967, p. 56 and PENNA, *Deuteronomio*, p. 134.

2) Our finding with regard to the literary dependence of Deut 9,21 on Exod 32,20, in particular our showing that each and every divergence in wording and content between them can plausibly be explained as a deliberate, purposeful modification of the text of Exod 32,20 by the author of Deut 9,21 (whereas the reverse supposition can hardly be made so plausible) further suggests that the direction of the existing literary dependence for the respective contexts of these verses is from Exod 32,1-34,28 to Deut 9,7b-10,11, rather than *vice versa*. Once again, such a conclusion accords with what has long been the dominant view on the question. At the same time, though, such detailed support for that view as our investigation affords is not without significance in view of some contemporary scholarship which might appear to call it into question. We think here particularly of the recent work of M. Rose, *Deuteronomist und Jahwist*[137]. Rose does not, as such, address the problem of the relationship between the two calf pericopes. He does, however, make an elaborate attempt to demonstrate that the standard conception that it is Deut 1-3 which is literarily dependent on the «Jahwistic» (i.e. pre-P) material in Nu 10-21 needs to be reversed[138]. But given now the affinities between the Deuteronomistic Deut 1-3 and the equally Deuteronomistic Deut 9,7b-10,11 (see following point), as well as the widespread supposition that the core of Exod 32,1-34,28 derives from the same hand(s) as the pre-P (JE) material in Nu 10-21, it is only natural that Rose's thesis will and should be tested out also in regard to the calf accounts of Exodus and Deuteronomy. And, as a matter of fact, writing simultaneously with Rose, and so independently of him, J. van Seters did argue for a dependence of Exod 32 on Deut 9 (and 1 Kgs 12,26ff.), rather than the reverse[139]. Van Seters' presentation on this point remains at a quite general level in which individual verses of the two accounts are not subjected to any detailed analysis as regards their similarities and differences and how those are best to be accounted for. In a more thorough-going argumentation, however, Van Seters' theory would need to be confronted with the rather clear indication afforded by a detailed comparison of Exod 32,20 and Deut 9,21 that the direction of the dependence between the calf accounts in their entirety is, in fact, the opposite of that proposed by him.

3) The verbal affinities between Deut 9,21 and a whole series of formulations relating to subsequent moments in Israel's cultic history as presented above, several of these being quite distinctive within the language of the OT as a whole (see e.g. *hēṭēb* in Deut 9,21 and

137. M. ROSE, *Deuteronomist und Jahwist. Untersuchungen zu den Berührungspunkten beider Literaturwerke* (AThANT, 67), Zürich, 1981.

138. ROSE, *Deuteronomist*, pp. 221-319.

139. J. VAN SETERS, *Histories and Historians of the Ancient Near East: The Israelites*, in *Orientalia* 50 (1981) 137-185, pp. 173-174.

2 Kgs 11,18), do lend credence to an authorship of the verse by the Deuteronomist, that writer who, in the conception of M. Noth, expanded an earlier form of the book of Deuteronomy with material of his own composition with a view to thereby preparing subsequent events in Israel's history as he would relate these in the books Joshua-Kings. But now, given the key function of 9,21 within the narrative of Deut 9,7b-10,11 as a whole, the identification of the verse as «Deuteronomistic» constitutes an important indicator of a like Deuteronomistic provenance of the entire unit, as this was initially advocated by G. Minette de Tillesse and then further substantiated by a whole series of subsequent authors. In fact, in our view, this «Deuteronomistic» origin of Deut 9,7bff. — for which the evidence presented on 9,21 provides rather compelling confirmation — represents the best-assured result in the literary/redaction criticism of Deuteronomy in the last c. 25 years and one which may be taken as a given for future research. Perhaps at this stage, however, the time has come for scholarship to attempt to become more specific regarding this «Deuteronomistic» character of Deut 9,7b-10,11. Specifically, there is need for an investigation as to how (or if) 9,7bff. relates to the various, competing conceptions concerning the stratification of the material in Deuteronomy-Kings which may be called «Deuteronomistic» in the broad sense, i.e. the two strata model (pre-Exilic basic strand, Exilic expansion of this) of the «American school» of F.M. Cross, R.E. Friedman, R.N. Nelson, etc. [140] as opposed to the three-layer theory (exilic DtrH, DtrP, DtrN) of the «German (Göttingen) school» of R. Smend, W. Dietrich, T. Veijola, H. Spieckermann, etc., or the still more complicated view of R. Stahl [141]. Conversely, it needs to be asked whether the unit does not perhaps, rather, lend credence to H.-D. Hoffmann's case for a return to Noth's unitary Deuteronomist. Here we might only remark that the elaborateness of the description of the annihilation of the calf in 9,21 and the way in which it contrives to verbally foreshadow so many distinct moments in the subsequent history of Israel could suggest that the verse — and so likewise the unit of which it is an integral element — is the work of a late Deuteronomistic hand which had before it a whole range of earlier, less developed Deuteronomistic (or in some cases possibly pre-Deuteronomistic) formulations standing in various contexts which it has deliberately selected and

140. For a recent presentation in the line of the «American school», see A.D.H. MAYES, *The Story of Israel between Settlement and Exile. A Redactional Study of the Deuteronomistic History*, London, 1983.

141. R. STAHL, *Aspekte der Geschichte deuteronomistischer Theologie. Zur Traditionsgeschichte der Terminologie und Redaktionsgeschichte der Redekompositionen*, Dissertation Jena, 1982. See the author's own *précis* of his work in TLZ 108 (1983) 74-76. Stahl distinguishes ho less than nine distinct Deuteronomistic strands, i.e. DtrH, DtrP, $DtrN^1$, $DtrN^2$, $DtrN^3$, $DtrTh^1$, $DtrTh^2$, $DtrTh^3$, $DtrTh^4$.

combined [142]. Such a supposition obviously, however, requires a more detailed substantiation than we can give it here.

4) We have just identified Deut 9,21, as well as the unit in which it stands as «Deuteronomistic» — however much in need of further specification that appelation may be. At the same time, we have also determined that Exod 32,30 is both prior to and the source for the Deuteronomistic Deut 9,21 just as we have indicated that in several respects (e.g. use of *zārāh* for Moses' action with the grindings of the calf, the concluding «drinking motif») the Exodus verse evidences peculiarities which set it apart from the whole wide range of formulations relating to the destruction of illicit cult objects in Dtr. But given these considerations, it simply does not seem helpful or senseful to qualify Exod 32,20 as itself «Deuteronomistic». Nor, *a fortiori*, does such a designation seem appropriate for the core narrative in Exod 32,1-34,28 of which that verse is clearly an integral element. We say this in conscious opposition to a continuing tendency — also in the most recent discussions — to designate the core of Exod 32 (33-34) and v. 20 in particular as «Deuteronomistic» [143]. With regard to that tendency we can only re-echo the strictures pronounced some years ago by C. H. W. Brekelmans concerning the over-facile use of the term «Deuteronomistic» with reference to a whole series of passages in the Hexateuch [144]. In our view, the basic narrative in Exod 32-34*, to which 32,20 would certainly belong, is better denominated with the term favored by Brekelmans and others for those Hexateuchal passages frequently labelled «Deuteronomistic», e.g. Exod 12,24-27; 13,3-16; 19,3-8; 23,20-33; 34,11-16; Jos 24, i.e. «proto-Deuteronomic». Such a designation is appropriate in that, in their wording and theological emphases, Exod 32-34*, and 32,20 in particular, approximate, but do not attain, the fullness, and fixity of the Deuteronomic and Deuteronomistic strata in Deuteronomy and the Former Prophets. In any event, it seems clearly desirable, in consideration of both its peculiarities and anteriority in regard to the certainly Deuteronomistic Deut 9,21 (and its context), that Exod 32,20 (together with the core material in Exod 32-34*) be designated by some other term than «Deuteronomistic».

142. For a proposal along these lines, see W. DIETRICH, *Prophetie und Geschichte* (FRLANT, 109), Göttingen, 1972, p. 96. Dietrich affirms, in passing, that «allem Anschein nach» Deut 9,7-21 was composed by «DtrN», i.e. the third and latest of the Deuteronomistic redactors distinguished by him.

143. Thus HOFFMANN, *Reform*, p. 307 and n. 50, qualifies Exod 32 as a whole as Exilic-Deuteronomistic. Likewise according to SPIECKERMANN, *Juda*, p. 91, n. 121, it was «ein Dtr» who gave Exod 32,20 its present form. See further J. VAN SETERS, *In Search of History. Historiography in the Ancient World and the Origins of Biblical History*, New Haven, 1983, p. 313, n. 76, who designates Exod 32 as «Dtr or post-Dtr».

144. C. H. W. BREKELMANS, *Die sogenannten deuteronomistischen Elemente in Gen-Num. Ein Beitrag zur Vorgeschichte des Deuteronomiums* (SVT Suppl, 15), Leiden, 1965, 90-96.

We may now very briefly sum up what we have presented above under our four headings with regard to the implications of our findings concerning Exod 32,20/Deut 9,21 for the question of the literary/redaction-critical status of and relationship between the respective contexts of those two verses taken as a whole. Those implications are:

1) There is a relation of literary dependence between Exod 32,1-34,28 and Deut 9,7b-10,11.
2) The dependence runs from the account of Exodus to that of Deuteronomy, not *vice versa*.
3) Deut 9,7b-10,11 is to be seen as the work of a (or the) Deuteronomist.
4) The core narrative in Exod 32-34 should not be called «Deuteronomistic».

Finally, we might conclude with a remark on the desirability of a more conscious and thorough-going integration of the various contemporary approaches to the study of the accounts of the calf's destruction in Exod 32,20 and Deut 9,21. As indicated at the outset, post-1960 scholarship on these two accounts has been characterized, on the one hand by attention to their possible extra-Biblical parallels/background, and on the other by a more systematic comparison between them and various descriptions of the annihilation of illegitimate cult objects elsewhere in the OT, above all in Dtr. Each of these developments of the last 20+ years, taken for itself, represents a helpful contribution, serving to advance the problematic of the two verses, in its various dimensions, beyond what earlier scholarship, with its much more limited perspectives, was able to attain. Thus, the adducing of the extra-Biblical comparative material has led to a realization that the controversies concerning the actual applicability of the measures related to a calf of the sort described in Exod 32,4 as well as those about the mutual compatibility of the measures enumerated have to be regarded simply as largely not *ad rem*. Similarly, the intensive investigation of the affinities and differences between Exod 32,20/Deut 9,21 and other like Biblical texts has, we believe, helped scholarship arrive at a better-assured result concerning the traditional problem as to the nature of the relationship between the two verses. At the same time, however, it must be observed that the two approaches have, to their mutual detriment, been pursued rather largely in isolation. Thus we note that neither H.-D. Hoffmann nor H. Spieckermann, two recent authors who have concerned themselves particularly with the intra-Biblical parallels to Exod 32,20/Deut 9,21, nowhere even allude to the whole extended discussion concerning the Ugaritic and other ANE parallels to those verses that has developed over the last 20+ years[145]. Likewise

145. Any reference to the comparative extra-Biblical material is likewise absent in the analysis of Exod 32,20 by W. RESENHÖFFT, *Die Quellenberichte im Josef-Sinai-Komplex* (*Gen 37 bis Exod 24 mit 32-34*), (EHS, XXIII/199), Frankfurt a.M., 1983, pp. 140, 249-250, whose insistence on the criterion of «*Sachlogik*» leads him to distinguish 20a[a] and 20a[b]b as deriving respectively from E and a «third Jahwistic stratum» which he denotes «Z».

whereas such exponents of the extra-Biblical parallels as the key to the right understanding of our verses as S. E. Loewenstamm and O. Hvidberg-Hansen do offer some treatment of the affinities between those verses and the relevant texts in Kings, their handling of the point is either quite summary (so Loewenstamm) or largely inaccessible (Hvidberg-Hansen's more extended study of the question is to be found in his unpublished licentiate thesis written in Danish) [146]. But now, it seems clear to us that the two approaches in view both should and can rather readily be integrated in a more conscious and thorough-going way than has been attempted hitherto. Such an integration will, on the one side, serve to make clear that the fixity of formulation and the tendency to the heaping up of such fixed formulations in the Biblical accounts of the annihilation of prohibited cult objects, which has been noted particularly by H.-D. Hoffmann, is not something unique to the literature of the OT. Rather, those features have to be seen as part of an extended ANE *Vernichtungssymbolik* wherein various standardized destructive actions are applied, frequently in combination, to a very wide range of undesirable entities with a view to underscoring the thoroughness of their annihilation. At the same time, the integration suggested would help surface the question of the distinctiveness of the Biblical material under discussion *vis-à-vis* the whole body of relevant ANE evidence. It would do so in terms both of the particular annihilatory actions and their combinations recounted and of the objects to which those actions are said to be applied, as well as of the reasons for such peculiarities of the Biblical passages which do exist, e.g. how is it that the OT speaks of iconoclastic actions directed against objects pertaining to Israel's own cult, whereas in our extra-Biblical evidence such actions are reported only in relation to «foreign» cult objects? In any case, however, we believe that it is such a working together of the two contemporary approaches to the problematic of Exod 32,20/ Deut 9,21 and the following out of the further questions to which that integration will give rise that offers the most promise for the still further elucidation of these two verses which have so longe beguiled scholarship.

Caldwell Hall, Box 151
Catholic University of America
Washington D.C. 20064, U.S.A.

Christopher T. Begg

146. Hvidberg-Hansen, *Ødelaeggelse*, pp. 98-110.

DIE ABFOLGE DER GESETZE IN DEUTERONOMIUM 12-26 UND DER DEKALOG

1. Der Dekalog bildet für das Dtn den Inbegriff des «Bundes», den Jahwe mit Israel am Horeb geschlossen hat (in 5,2.3 mit Mose als Partner des Volkes, in 28,69 ohne ihn). Bund und Dekalog werden sogar direkt miteinander identifiziert (4,13; 9,9.11). Nach dtn Theorie hat Gott nur diese Worte unmittelbar zur ganzen Versammlung gesprochen (5,22). Das macht ihre unüberbietbare Dignität aus. Trotzdem bedurfte auch diese Offenbarung eines Mittlers: des Mose (5,5). Jahwe schrieb die «zehn Worte» auf zwei Steintafeln (4,13; 10,4) und übergab sie ihm (5,22; 10,4). Auf Einspruch des Volkes hin, den Jahwe akzeptierte, empfängt Israel von damals an alle weiteren Willensäußerungen Jahwes nur vermittelt durch Mose (5,23-31). Mose seinerseits übergibt diese Tora dann nach ihrer Niederschrift den Priestern (vgl. 10,4 mit 31,9), damit sie neben den Dekalogtafeln in der Bundeslade aufbewahrt werde (vgl. 10,5 mit 31,26). Für die künftige Vermittlung des jeweils aktuellen Gotteswortes aber wird Jahwe einen Propheten wie Mose erstehen lassen (18,15-18).

Das Dtn erklärt die Mittlerfunktion des Mose auf doppelte Weise. 5,31 zufolge hat Jahwe selbst ihm bereits «das ganze Gebot, die Gesetze und Rechtsvorschriften» (*kol hammiṣwâ haḥuqqîm wᵉhammišpāṭîm*) mitgeteilt, die er Israel lehren soll. Dagegen hat er nach 4,14 (vgl. V. 5) dem Mose nur befohlen, das Volk «Gesetze und Rechtsvorschriften» (*ḥuqqîm ûmišpāṭîm* — ohne Artikel) zu lehren, nicht aber ein neben dem Dekalog noch eigens mitgeteiltes Jahwegesetz zu wiederholen [1]. Wenn die Berichte vom Horebgeschehen die göttliche Zusatzoffenbarung an Mose bzw. seinen Lehrauftrag örtlich (5,31) wie zeitlich (4,14) direkt mit der Dekalogspromulgation Jahwes verbinden, legen sie damit nahe, in den «Gesetzen und Rechtsvorschriften» eine informative (5,31) bzw. autoritative (4,14) Interpretation des Dekalogs, etwas wie Durchführungsbestimmungen für eine konkrete Situation zu sehen. Denn der Dekalog verpflichtet immer und überall, die Gesetze dagegen gelten nur in Israels eigenem Land (4,5; 12,1) [2]. Bestätigt das Dtn ein solches Selbstver-

1. Der Nachdruck liegt hier also auf dem Daß mosaischer Gesetzeslehre. In ähnlicher Weise betont 4,13 die Niederschrift des Dekalogs, schweigt aber im Gegensatz zu 5,22 von einer Übergabe der beiden Tafeln an Mose.

2. Vgl. G. BRAULIK, *Weisheit, Gottesnähe und Gesetz — Zum Kerygma von Deuteronomium 4,5-8*, in G. BRAULIK (ed.), *Studien zum Pentateuch. Fs. W. Kornfeld*, Wien, 1977, 165-195, pp. 171-172.

ständnis der Gesetzesverkündigung als einer «Auslegung» zuvor ergangener Jahwegebote?

2. Tatsächlich gibt der Gebrauch des pluralischen Doppelausdrucks «Gesetze und Rechtsvorschriften» (*haḥuqqîm w^e^hammišpāṭîm*) einen ersten Hinweis, um das Verhältnis von Dekalog und dtn Einzelgesetzen zu klären. Seine ältesten Belege finden sich erst im Dtn, lassen also auf ein Proprium dieses Buches bei der Verwendung dieses Ausdrucks schließen. In der zweiten Moserede wird er (außerhalb von unechten Reihen) nur als Struktursignal eingesetzt [3]. Als solches rahmt er in 5,1 und 11,32 die dtn Paränese, in 12,1 und 26,16 den Kodex der Einzelbestimmungen. Das heißt aber: Wenn Mose «Gesetze und Rechtsvorschriften» vorträgt (5,1), beinhalten diese — trotz des Neueinsatzes in 6,1 — zuerst den an die Spitze gestellten Dekalogstext selbst (5,6-21); dann Paränesen, in denen der Text des Dekaloganfangs eine zentrale Rolle spielt und in Form von Paraphrasen (6,10-15; 7,8-11), ja sogar in der einer Paraphrase einer Dekalogsparaphrase (8,7-20) kommentiert wird [4]. Innerhalb des dtn Gesetzeskorpus aber umfassen sie neben anderen Gesetzen auch kasuistische Entfaltungen der meisten Dekalogsgebote (13,2-6.7-12.13-19; 17,2-7;19,11-13.16-19; 21,1-9.18-21; 22,113-21.22.23-27; 24,7).

Die Frage nach dem Dekalogsbezug verschärft sich, sollte der Doppelausdruck letztlich nur 12-26,16 meinen [5]. Genau genommen kündigt Mose in 5,1 ja bloß an, er wolle «Gesetze und Rechtsvorschriften» empfehlen; 11,31-32 aber blickt er nicht zurück, sondern weist voraus. Erst die Überschrift in 12,1 leitet mit dem Doppelausdruck auch tatsächlich «Gesetze und Rechtsvorschriften» ein, wobei hier der zu erwartende Promulgationssatz überhaupt fehlt. In 26,16 aber befiehlt nicht Mose, sondern Jahwe, obwohl der Gesetzessprecher sonst stets ein Mensch und nicht, wie beim Dekalog, Gott selber ist. Sollte also durch «Gesetze und Rechtsvorschriften» der dtn Kodex (12-26,16) als Aus-

3. N. LOHFINK, *Das Hauptgebot. Eine Untersuchung literarischer Einleitungsfragen zu Dtn 5-11* (AB, 20), Rom, 1963, pp. 56-57.

4. N. LOHFINK, *Die These vom «deuteronomistischen» Dekaloganfang — ein fragwürdiges Ergebnis atomistischer Sprachstatistik*, in Braulik, *Studien* (vgl. Anm. 2), 99-109, pp. 101-104. Auch die Dekalogparaphrase in 4,15-20 ist Teil der «Gesetze und Rechtsvorschriften», die Mose lehrt (V. 1.5).

5. Bei einer Begrenzung der «Gesetze und Rechtsvorschriften» auf das Gesetzeskorpus müßte allerdings die auffallende Auswahl von Promulgationsverben geklärt werden, die mit diesem Doppelausdruck verbunden sind. In der Überschrift 4,45, in 6,1, ebenfalls einer Art Überschrift, ferner in 5,1 und 11,32, wo der Terminus als Struktursignal dient, aber aber auch noch an anderen Stellen wird nämlich nicht *ṣwh*-pi. gebraucht wie sonst in den meisten Promulgationssätzen. Daß dies möglich gewesen wäre, beweist 7,11. S. dazu G. BRAULIK, *Die Ausdrücke für «Gesetz» im Buch Deuteronomium*, in *Bib* 51 (197p) 39-66, p. 62. Diese Eigentümlichkeit dürfte darauf hindeuten, daß Mose mit den «Gesetzen und Rechtvorschriften» nicht nur Gesetze autoritativ promulgiert, sondern auch Paränese verkündet wird, also das, was sich innerhalb der Kap. 5-11, dem zuerst gerahmten Teil, findet. Speziell für 5,1 und 11,32s. Lohfink, *Hauptgebot* (vgl. Anm. 3), p. 275.

legung des Dekalogs angedeutet werden, dann genügen die relativ wenigen, oben genannten kasuistischen Entfaltungen von Dekalogsgeboten wohl nicht, um den strukturierenden Gebrauch des Doppelausdrucks zu rechtfertigen. Wenn er über sie hinaus keine weitere Beziehung des dtn Kodex zum Dekalog signalisierte, würde der Terminus «Gesetze und Rechtsvorschriften» mehr Gesetze rahmen, die keine Verbindung mit dem Dekalog aufweisen, als solche, die ihn konkretisieren. Ein solches Mißverhältnis ist bei der Exaktheit dtn Systematisierens von vornherein unwahrscheinlich.

3. Besonders F. Horst[6] hat versucht, die redaktionelle Funktion des Doppelausdrucks in 12,1 als einen Hinweis auf zweierlei Art von Rechtsmaterial und auf dessen Disposition zu erklären. Die *ḥuqqîm* bezeichneten demnach ein «Privilegrecht Jahwes», das sich innerhalb der Kap. 12-18 finde, die *mišpāṭîm* hingegen das Zivilrecht in den Kap. 19-25. Bei den von Horst erschlossenen privilegrechtlichen Bestimmungen handelt es sich zwar um eine selbständige Sammlung von zehn Rechtssätzen, also um einen zweiten Dekalog. Er bleibt aber völlig hypothetisch und hat auch mit dem Horebdekalog inhaltlich nichts gemeinsam. Gegen eine Aufteilung von «Gesetzen» und «Rechtsnormen» auf zwei exklusive Gattungsbezeichnungen, die bestimmte Gesetzesgruppen ankündigen oder deren Anordnung anzeigen, sprechen jedoch erstens die Weise, wie der Doppelausdruck sonst im Dtn verwendet wird, und zweitens das Ineinander von «Privilegrecht» und «Zivilrecht», wie es für das vorliegende dtn Gesetzeskorpus charakteristisch ist.

4. Der jüngste Überblick von H. D. Preuss[7] über die Dtn-Forschung beweist, mit wie vielen Problemen alle bisher vorgelegten Versuche belastet sind, die Strukturprinzipien für Dtn 12-26 erarbeitet haben. Offenbar ist man über die — ebenfalls unbefriedigende — Gliederung durch J. Wellhausen[8] bisher nur wenig hinausgekommen[9]. So ist nach

6. *Das Privilegrecht Jahwes (Rechtsgeschichtliche Untersuchungen zum Deuteronomium)* (FRLANT, 45), Göttingen, 1930, pp. 120-123 (= *Gottes Recht. Gesammelte Studien zum Recht im Alten Testament* [Theologische Bücherei, 12], München 1961, 17-154, pp. 150-154).

7. *Deuteronomium* (Erträge der Forschung, 164), Darmstadt, 1982, pp. 108-112. Eine Synopse der wichtigsten Gliederungsversuche bietet G. SEITZ, *Redaktionsgeschichtliche Studien zum Deuteronomium* (BWANT, 93), Stuttgart, 1971, pp. 92-93. Die Untersuchungen der Systematik von Dtn 12-26 werden am umfangreichsten dargestellt und kritisch besprochen in der noch unpublizierten Dissertation von C. LOCHER, *Die Ehre einer Frau in Israel*.

8. *Die Composition des Hexateuchs und der historischen Bücher des Alten Testaments*, Berlin, 1963, pp. 353-363. Seitz (*Studien* vgl. Anm. 7) erwähnt Wellhausen überhaupt nicht, Preuss (*Deuteronomium* [vgl. Anm. 7], p. 108) zitiert nur die alte Disposition von *Composition*, p. 203ff., die Wellhausen später selbst als ungenügend empfunden und in Nachträgen am Ende der 3. Auflage durch eine «ausführliche Inhaltsangabe des eigentlichen deuteronomischen Gesetzes» ergänzt hat (l.c.).

9. Preuss, *Deuteronomium* (vgl. Anm. 7), p. 108. Ein kurzer Artikel, den Preuss nicht

Preuss «eine einleuchtende Erklärung der Gesamtabfolge der Texte und Textgruppen in Dtn 12-25 voll noch nicht gefunden» [10]. Einen möglichen Weg sieht er aber in dem Nachweis, die Gesetze seien in ihrer Abfolge am Dekalog ausgerichtet worden, wobei es dem Dtn vielleicht um gar nicht mehr als bloß um eine Grobgliederung gegangen sein könnte [11]. «Denn daß Dtn 12-25 zumindest in manchen ihrer Teile und wenigstens grob ... sich an der Gebotsabfolge des Dekalogs orientieren, scheint ein wesentliches Ergebnis neuerer Forschung zu sein, das der weiteren Überprüfung und Bewährung harrt» [12].

5. Das zitierte Fazit könnte den Eindruck erwecken, es stütze sich auf eine Reihe von Untersuchungen zu dieser Thematik. Es gibt dazu jedoch — von ganz wenigen, dazu divergierenden Publikationen abgesehen — nur thesenhafte Behauptungen ohne ausreichende Argumentationen [13].

Erstmals umfassend ist die Funktion des Dekalogs als Aufbauprinzip im Dtn 1895 von Fr. W. Schultz dargestellt worden. Im Vorwort zu seinem Dtn-Kommentar schreibt er: «Im Deuteronomium ... wird das Gesetz ... gewissermassen selber Commentar», weil Mose darin «nämlich jeden Thoraabschnitt durch die Reihenfolge, in welcher er ihn behandelt, zu irgend einem der Decaloggebote in nähere Beziehung gesetzt hat. Er hat dadurch ebensowohl wie den Decalog zum Schlüssel für das übrige Gesetz, das übrige Gesetz auch zur erklärenden Aus-

erwähnt, und eine Monographie verdienen jedoch, besonders hervorgehoben zu werden. H. M. WIENER (*The Arrangement of Deuteronomy 12-26*, in *Journal of the Palestine Oriental Society* 6 [1926] 185-195) hat die gegenwärtige Gesetzesanordnung durch zwei Prinzipien bestimmt gesehen: durch das religiöse Interesse des Verfassers und durch Assoziationen, die sich für ihn nicht aus einer rechtswissenschaftlichen Theorie, sondern durch Zeitumstände und aktuelle Erfahrungen damals als notwendig bzw. natürlich ergeben haben. Einen völlig neuen Ansatz aber hat C. M. CARMICHAEL (*The Laws of Deuteronomy*, Ithaca-London, 1974) gewagt: Das Gesetzesmaterial sei u.a. nach assoziativen Bezügen zu Erzählabfolgen in Genesis und Numeri organisiert worden. Diese umfassende Studie ist freilich «traditions- wie redaktionsgeschichtlich (und oft auch literarkritisch) so abenteuerlich wie unkritisch und wird als Lösungsvorschlag sicherlich nicht weiterführend wirken» (Preuss, *Deuteronomium* l.c., pp. 109-110). Eine umfassende Auseinandersetzung mit diesem und den übrigen Beiträgen Carmichaels zur Diskussion der Anordnung des dtn Kodex enthält jetzt Locher, *Ehre* (vgl. Anm. 7).

10. *Deuteronomium* (vgl. Anm. 7), p. 112.

11. Wie Anm. 10.

12. Preuss, *Deuteronomium* (vgl. Anm. 7), pp. 111-112.

13. So ist z.B. H. BREIT (*Die Predigt des Deuteronomisten*, München, 1933, esp. pp. 31-34) im Anschluß an Calvin und vor allem Luther davon überzeugt, daß der Dekalog der Verkündigung des Dtn zugrunde liege (l.c., p. 33). M. NOTH (*Überlieferungsgeschichtliche Studien. Die sammelnden und bearbeitenden Geschichtswerke im Alten Testament*, Tübingen, [3]1967, p. 101) hat es bei der gewiß wichtigen Feststellung belassen, dem Deuteronomisten erscheine «das spezielle Verhältnis zwischen Gott und Volk», der Bund nämlich, «begründet durch die Mitteilung des Dekalogs, zu dem das deuteronomische Gesetz nach 5,28ff. die authentische göttliche Auslegung bildet». Nach A. PHILLIPS (*Ancient Israel's Criminal Law. A New Approach to The Decalogue*, Oxford, 1970, p. 182) «the Deuteronomic law ... in main constitutes an expansion of the criminal law of the Decalogue».

führung für den Decalog gemacht»[14]. Diese Kommentierung beginnt für Schultz jedoch nicht erst im dtn Kodex, sondern bereits nach dem Dekalogtext in den Kap. 6-11[15]. Wegen der zu gekünstelten[16] Textbezüge, freilich auch wegen seiner Verteidigung mosaischer Verfasserschaft hat Schultz nur wenig Aufmerksamkeit und praktisch keine Zustimmung gefunden. Er wurde erst 1979 wieder von St. A. Kaufman kritisch in Erinnerung gerufen.

In einem kurzen, sogar von Kaufman übersehenen Artikel hat A.E. Guilding nicht nur für Dtn 13-25 (sic!), sondern auch für das Bundesbuch (Ex 20,22-23,17) und die Sammlung Lev 10-23 behauptet, sie wären «an orderly exposition of the decalogue, which is the basis of the whole legal system»[17]. Originell ist dabei, daß Guilding die Dekaloggebote vom 5., dem Elterngebot, an jeweils paarweise zusammenfaßt und einer Gesetzesgruppe in den entsprechenden Ex- bzw. Dtn-Kapitel zuordnet[18].

Ungedruckt und praktisch unzugänglich blieb ein Dissertationsexkurs von H. Schulz[19], in dem er seine Auffassung von Einfluß des Dekalogs auf die dtn Gesetzesabfolge begründet. Nach Schulz «baut das gesamte deuteronomische Gesetzesmaterial von Kap. 12-25 auf dem dekalogischen Anordnungsschema auf. Trotz verschiedenartiger Anreicherungen ... bleibt die grundlegende Dreiteilung in die Bereiche Jahwes und des Kultes, der Eltern und Familie, des Sozialen und Sittlichen noch nachweisbar, ob auch im letzteren nicht mehr so streng geschieden wird»[20].

14. *Das Deuteronomium*, Berlin, 1895, p. III. Der Kommentar wird von Preuss, *Deuteronomium* (vgl. Anm. 7) nicht verzeichnet.

15. Schultz (*Deuteronomium* l.c., pp. 13-24) entwickelt folgende Anordnung: Gebote I-II (Fremdgötter- und Bilderverbot) = Dtn 6-11; III = 12-14; IV = 15-16,17; V = 16,18-18,22; VI = 19-21,9; VII = 21,10-23; VIII = 22; IX-X = 23-25. Innerhalb dieser Entsprechungen meint Schultz außerdem noch zu erkennen, daß ab Kap. 12 Moses «in einer merkwürdigen Regelmäßigkeit» so verfährt, «daß er immer gerade drei Stücke als zu einem Gebote gehörig heranzieht, und daß er, so er eins von den dreien weiter auszuführen hat, dann drei Unterabtheilungen macht» (*Deuteronomium* l.c., p. 16).

16. Vgl. das Urteil von C. STEUERNAGEL, *Die Entstehung des deuteronomischen Gesetzes*, Halle, 1896, p. 10.

17. *Notes on the Hebrew Law Codes*, in *JTS* 49 (1948) 43-52, p. 43.

18. Für das dtn Gesetz ergibt sich folgende Einteilung (l.c., pp. 47-49 und 52):
Honour to parents, no murder: 16,18-22,8 (sic)
no adultery, no stealing: 22,13 (sic)-24,7 (sic)
no false witness, no coveting: 24,10 (sic)-25,16.

19. *Das Todesrecht im Alten Testament*, Diss. Marburg, 1966, pp. 151-157 (Mschr.). Ein kurzer Hinweis findet sich in der gleichbetitelten Publikation in BZAW 114, Berlin, 1969, p. 65; ferner bei O. KAISER, *Einleitung in das Alte Testament. Eine Einführung in ihre Ergebnisse und Probleme*, Gütersloh, [4]1978, p. 118.

20. *Todesrecht* (BZAW) l.c., pp. 66-67. Darüber hinaus wird das dtn Gesetz vom Dekalog, dessen Programm es paradigmatisch darstellen will, und der dekalogisch komponierten Fluchreihe 27,15-26 gerahmt (l.c., pp. 67-68). Letztere wurde program-

Dieser Ansatz wurde 1979 von St. A. Kaufman in dem bisher umfangreichsten Beitrag zu unserem Thema weiterentwickelt [21]. Während freilich Schulz das «decalogue-pattern» nur in seinem großen Umriß als prägend annimmt und mit späteren Eingriffen sowie Ergänzungen rechnet, vertritt Kaufman die These: Das dtn Gesetz stammt von einem einzigen Redaktor. Er hat seine Gesetzessammlung bis ins Detail nach dem Modell des vollständigen Dekalogs strukturiert [22]. Kaufman verzichtet auf literarkritische und redaktionsgeschichtliche Differenzierungen innerhalb des dtn Gesetzes. Abgrenzung und Interpretation der einzelnen Gesetze werden nicht aus dem Text begründet. Textunterschiede werden vorschnell nivelliert und bleiben unausgewertet. Trotz methodischer und exegetischer Mängel bildet aber der vorgelegte Erklärungsversuch der Gesetzesabfolge im dtn Kodex, d.h. genauer in Dtn 12-25,16, und ihres Bezugs zum Dekalog als Aufbaumuster eine Herausforderung für die Deuteronomiumsforschung. Eine Auseinandersetzung erscheint schließlich auch deshalb als vordringlich, weil in anderen altorientalischen Rechtskorpora bereits eine Systematik nachgewiesen werden konnte.

6. Nach den Untersuchungen vor allem von H. Petschow zur Gesetzessystematik des Codex Hammurabi und der Gesetze von Eschnunna [23] kennen wir die wichtigsten Techniken altorientalischer Rechtskodifikation. Diese Ordnungsprinzipien stimmen zwar nicht mit den Gesichtspunkten römischer oder moderner europäischer Gesetzesdisposition überein. Sie konnten aber bereits in Teilen des dtn Gesetzes verifiziert werden [24]. Kaufman weiß sich ihnen verpflichtet [25], und sie

matisch zu liturgischem Zweck als Abschluß der ganzen Rechtsbelehrung des Dtn komponiert und bewußt auf 5,6ff. zurückbezogen (l.c., p. 70).

21. *The Structure of the Deuteronomic Law*, in *Maarav* 1/2 (1978/79) 105-158; s. esp. p. 112 und Anm. 43.

22. *Structure* l.c., p. 112. Zu den Korrespondenzen zwischen der Abfolge einzelner Gesetzespartien und den Dekaloggeboten s. die Übersicht l.c., pp. 113-114. Von diesen Fixpunkten aus untersucht Kaufman die Zwischen- und Randzonen und teilt im Endeffekt das ganze Gesetzesmaterial ohne Restbestand in einer den Dekaloggeboten entsprechenden Reihenfolge auf.

23. *Zur Systematik und Gesetzestechnik im Codex Hammurabi*, in *Zeitschrift für Assyriologie* 57 (1965) 146-172; *Zur «Systematik» in den Gesetzen von Eschnunna*, in *Symbolae juridicae et historicae M. David dedicatae. Bd. 2 = Iura Orientis Antiqui*, Leiden, 1968, 131-143.

24. N. LOHFINK, *Die Sicherung der Wirksamkeit des Gotteswortes durch das Prinzip der Schriftlichkeit der Tora und durch das Prinzip der Gewaltenteilung nach den Ämtergesetzen des Buches Deuteronomium (Dt 16,18-18,22)*, in H. WOLTER (ed.), *Testimonium Veritati. Fs. W. Kempf*, Frankfurt/M. 1971, 143-155, esp. pp. 147-148; V. WAGNER, *Der bisher unbeachtete Rest eines hebräischen Rechtskodex*, in *BZ* 19 (1975) 234-240 (fehlt bei Preuss, *Deuteronomium* [vgl. Anm. 7], und wird auch von Kaufman, *Structure* [vgl. Anm. 21] nicht erwähnt).

25. *Structure* (vgl. Anm. 21), pp. 115-118, esp. pp. 117-118.

stehen auch im Hintergrund meiner eigenen Analyse. Charakteristisch ist erstens die Gliederung des Rechtsstoffes nach Sachgebieten, die sich etwa an Lebensbereichen, Objekten oder Sachverhalten orientieren; zweitens, daß innerhalb der Hauptthemen die Gesetze nach fünf Abfolgeprinzipien gruppiert werden[26]. Besondere Bedeutung kommt zusätzlich dem Phänomen der Attraktion zu, einer durch Stichworte oder Gedankenassoziationen ausgelösten Einfügung von Gesetzesmaterial. Diese Ordnungsgrundsätze trennen freilich teilweise juristisch zusammengehörende Gesetze und weisen sie verschiedenen Sachgruppen zu. Dadurch entsteht dann für uns der Eindruck eines unsystematischen Rechtsbuches.

Im israelitischen Recht dürfte aber jenseits der Einzelparagraphen und ihrer Reihung noch mehr als sonst im Alten Orient ein Gefühl für stilistische Gesamtgestaltung ganzer Gesetzesgruppen bestanden haben. Das wird im folgenden innerhalb der Kap. 12-16 mehrmals deutlich werden. Vielleicht hängt die stärkere rhetorische Formung damit zusammen, daß diese Texte als «Bundesrecht» angesehen worden sind und in öffentlichen, ja kultischen Versammlungen zur Verlesung kommen sollten.

7. Im folgenden setze ich die Gesetzesabgrenzung voraus, die N. Lohfink in der «Einheitsübersetzung» vorgenommen hat. Sie ist für die praktischen Bedürfnisse einer Bibelausgabe angefertigt worden. Sicher aber gelten dabei auch die folgenden Kriterien: neues Thema; Neueinsatz eines kasuistischen Gesetzes (durch *kî* im Hauptfall und *'im* für den Unterfall); Formwechsel (z.B. zwischen kasuistisch, scheinkasuistisch, apodiktisch); Abschlußformeln (etwa die sogenannte *bi'arta*-Formel); Rahmung. Diese Abgrenzung unterscheidet sich teilweise von dem Gesetzesumfang, den Kaufman bestimmt und seiner Studie zugrunde gelegt hat.

Mein Beitrag basiert auf Untersuchungen, mit denen N. Lohfink und ich einen gemeinsamen Kommentar für die Serie «Hermeneia» vorbereiten[27]. Die Frage nach dem Verhältnis von Dekalog und Gesetzeskodex wird, wie die einleitenden Beobachtungen gezeigt haben, nicht von außen an den Text herangetragen, sondern vom Dtn selbst durch

26. Systematisiert wird nach Petschow (*Gesetzestechnik* [vgl. Anm. 23], pp. 170-171):
1. «chronologisch», d.h. «nach der tatsächlichen oder möglichen Abfolge der Ereignisse»;
2. «nach der sachlichen Bedeutung der geregelten Materie oder nach der sozialen Stellung der betroffenen Personen oder der Wertigkeit der Gegenstände»;
3. «nach der Häufigkeit der Fälle»;
4. «als Gegenüberstellung von Fall und Gegenfall»;
5. «in möglichst einheitlicher Reihenfolge bei sachlich und rechtlich gleichartigen Tatbeständen».

27. Vgl. auch das Vorlesungsskript von N. Lohfink: *Das Privilegrecht Jahwes im Buch Deuteronomium. Vorlesungen über Dtn 12-16 und 26*, gehalten an der Philosophisch-Theologischen Hochschule St. Georgen, Frankfurt a.M. 1983.

den spezifischen Gebrauch des Doppelausdrucks *ḥuqqîm ûmišpāṭîm* provoziert. Die folgenden Überlegungen setzen die von Petschow erkannten Systematisierungsprinzipien altorientalischen Rechts voraus. Sie knüpfen ferner kritisch an die Hauptthese von Kaufman über die Dekaloggebote als Strukturmuster der dtn Gesetzessammlung an, ohne jedoch in eine Diskussion aller einzelnen Argumente einzutreten. Ziel dieses Artikels ist es vielmehr, die Disposition des dtn Gesetzeskorpus und den Einfluß des Dekalogs auf die Anordnung seiner Einzelgesetze bzw. Teilsammlungen zu skizzieren. Es geht dabei um die Systematisierung auf der Ebene der Endredaktion. Damit werden weder eine ursprünglich selbständige Existenz einzelner Gesetze noch vorausgehende Redigierungen mit unterschiedlicher Zielsetzung ausgeschlossen. Ferner bestand immer die Möglichkeit, innerhalb eines nach altorientalischen Systematisierungsprinzipien oder auch nach der Dekalogsstruktur aufgebauten Gesetzeskorpus zusätzliches Material über den Weg von Digressionen einzubringen. Im übrigen lassen sich eine Reihe von Unstimmigkeiten im dtn Gesetz wahrscheinlich nur auf der diachronen Ebene erklären, während sie auf der synchronen Ebene bestehen bleiben und die Logik der Aufbaues stören. Sie müssen somit als entstehungsbedingte Spannungen toleriert werden. Trotzdem möchte diese Untersuchung die Struktur des vorliegenden Textes der Kap. 12-26 verdeutlichen und darin den Dekalog als eine Art Groß- bzw. Grobraster für seine Komposition und Disposition erkennbar machen.

Die Ergebnisse lassen sich so zusammenfassen: Zwischen den Kap. 12-18 und dem Dekalog bestehen nur vage und globale Korrespondenzen:

1. Gebot

12,2-13,19: Das einzige Heiligtum und der einzige Gott Israels.

2. Gebot («Namensmißbrauch»)

14,1-21: Jahwes heiliges Volk in Ritualdifferenz zu den Völkern anderer Götter[28].

3. Gebot («Sabbatheiligung»)

14,22-16,17: Kult und Bruderschaft in heiligem Rhythmus — Israels Zusammenkunft auf den drei Wallfahrtsfesten.

4. Gebot («Elternehrung»)

16,18-18,22: Ämter in Israel.

Erst von Kap. 19 an lassen sich genauere Entsprechungen zum 5. bis 10. Dekalogsgebot feststellen. Kaufman hat dies durch mehrere treffende Beobachtungen belegt, die hier nicht resümiert zu werden brauchen. Im

28. Dagegen ordnet Kaufman, *Structure* (vgl. Anm. 21), pp. 122-129, Dtn 13,1-14,27 dem zweiten Dekaloggebot (katholischer Zählung) zu. Dieser Bezug — «a cornerstone of the entire structure» (p. 124) — ist jedoch viel zu weit hergeholt. Das zweite Dekaloggebot wird dabei als Verbot, einen falschen Eid im Namens Jahwes zu schwören, interpretiert. Unberücksichtigt bleibt ferner, daß Kap. 13 ganz enge Verbindungen mit dem ersten Dekaloggebot aufweist und daß 14,22-27 dem folgenden Gesetzesblock zugerechnet werden muß (s. dazu unten).

Unterschied zu den Kap. 12-18 sind jedoch in den Kap. 19-25 zweimal Gebotsblöcke miteinander thematisch verzahnt. Die beiden Übergangsbereiche finden sich in den Grenzzonen zwischen den Gesetzesblöcken, die dem 5. und 6. Dekalogsgebot zugeordnet sind (22,1-12), und zwischen jenen, die dem 6. und 7. Dekalogsgebot zugerechnet werden (23,16-24,5). Solche Übergangsbereiche zwischen Gesetzesblöcken dürften grundsätzlich möglich gewesen sein, da auch der Codex Hammurabi dafür zumindest ein Beispiel bietet [29].

5. Gebot «Leben bewahren»

19,1-21,23: intentionale Tötung (mit Digressionen).

22,1-12: Übergangsbereich vom Thema «Leben bewahren» zum Thema «Sextum». Das Thema «Sextum» klingt erstmals in 22,5 mit dem Motiv der Vermischung an, das Thema «Tötung» ist zum letzten Mal deutlich in 22,8 da.

6. Gebot «Vergewaltigung» und «Familie»

22,13-23,15: ganz auf den Sexualbereich konzentriert.

23,16-24,5: Übergangsbereich vom Thema «Sextum» zum Thema «Eigentum». Das Thema «Eigentum» erscheint zum ersten Mal in 23,16-17 (geflüchteter Sklave), das Thema «Sextum» zum letzten Mal in 24,5 (Befreiung Neuvermählter vom Kriegsdienst).

7. Gebot «Eigentum»

(23,16-26) 24,6-7: Eigentum. Die Thematik wird noch einmal in 24,19-22 und 25,4 aufgegriffen. Doch setzt mit 24,8 schon die nächste Thematik «Gericht» ein.

8. Gebot «(Wahrheit vor) Gericht»

24,8-25,4.

9./10. Gebot «Begehren»

25,5-16. Mit 25,17 beginnt schon die Rahmung des Gesetzeskorpus, die auf Themen aus Dtn 12 zurückgreift, wobei die zwei Rituale in 26,1-15 bewußt als Abschluß des Gesetzeskorpus gedacht sind.

Diese Thesen sollen im folgenden nur an 12,2-18,22, also dem Bereich, wo nur vage Korrespondenz zum Dekalog vorliegt, und an einem der beiden Übergangstexte, nämlich 22,1-12, illustriert werden.

8. Die Überschrift in 12,1 macht zwei entscheidende juristische Aussagen: über den Geltungsbereich (das von Jahwe «gegebene» Land) und über die Geltungsdauer (solange Israel in diesem Land lebt). Damit werden wahrscheinlich auch die beiden Ordnungsprinzipien des folgenden Gesetzesteiles 12,2-16,17 angedeutet. Innerhalb dieses Privilegrechtes Jahwes gehen nämlich die Bestimmungen über die Jahwe-allein-Verehrung in 12,2-14,21 vom Ort des einzigen Heiligtums aus. Es dominiert also die lokale Dimension. Die Kult- und Sozialverpflichtungen in 14,22-15,23 aber gelten für periodisch wiederkehrende Zeiten und

29. Petschow, *Gesetzestechnik* (vgl. Anm. 23), p. 164 Anm. 107.

gipfeln in 16,1-17 in den drei jährlichen Wallfahrtsfesten am Zentralheiligtum. Es dominiert also die temporale Dimension.

Im einzelnen bildet 12,2-31 vom Aufbau her die erste klare Einheit. Israel steht unmittelbar vor dem Einzug in sein Land. Es wird sein Zentrum in einem einzigen Heiligtum haben. Das Gebot der Vernichtung fremder Kultstätten (V. 2-3) und das Verbot kanaanäischer Kultbräuche (V. 29-31) rahmen vier Gesetze, die vom Opferkult an dem einzigen Heiligtum Israels handeln. Die Paragraphen dieses Mittelteiles sind thematisch und sprachlich parallel gestaltet; die aufeinander folgenden Gesetze werden auch speziell miteinander verbunden und konkurrieren nicht miteinander. Die mit «denn» (*kî*) bzw. «jedoch» (*raq*) eingeleiteten, von einander divergierenden Passagen innerhalb einzelner Gesetze entwickeln jeweils die juristischen Konkretisierungen. So gebieten die VV. 4-7 eine einzige Kultstätte für Jahwe. Die VV. 8-12 fixieren zusätzlich den Zeitpunkt für das Inkrafttreten dieses Gebotes. Die VV. 13-19 unterscheiden als Folge der Kultzentralisation zwischen Opfer und profaner Schlachtung. Die VV. 20-28 enthalten dazu eine Legalinterpretation: Sie grenzen die Möglichkeit der Profanschlachtung ein und regeln den Umgang mit Blut bei profaner Schlachtung wie bei Opfern im Zentralheiligtum. Alle diese Gesetze sind thematisch an den einen Ort gebunden, bestimmend ist also der lokale Aspekt. Ehe der ihm entsprechende temporale Aspekt in 14,22 aufgegriffen wird, bietet sich ein anderes Motiv, das das Kap. 12 beherrscht, zur Weiterführung an: das Motiv der Einzigkeit. Die Kanaanäer haben viele Götter, die an vielen Kultstätten verehrt werden. Israel wird nur ein einziges Heiligtum haben, und dort wird es einen einzigen, seinen Gott Jahwe, verehren. So folgen in Kap. 13 nun sinnvollerweise jene Gesetze, die eine ausschließliche Jahweverehrung sichern.

12,29-31 fungiert dabei als strukturelle Schaltstelle. Dieser Paragraph klammert vor allem an die VV. 2-3 zurück, beschließt also rahmend die Thematik eines einzigen Heiligtums. Zugleich aber schlägt dieses Verbot kanaanäischer Kultbräuche mehrere Themen an, die dann in 13,2-19 und 14,1-21 behandelt werden. So wird das Motiv der «Nachfolge anderer Götter» von 12,30 im ersten Gesetz von Kap. 13 (s. V. 3) entfaltet, das Motiv des Götterkultes in allen drei Gesetzen des Kap. 13 (s. VV. 3.7.14). 12,31 liefert mit den Ausdrücken «Greuel», «Söhne», «im Feuer verbrennen» die Stichwörter für das letzte Gesetz in Kap. 13 (s. VV. 13.15.17) und für die beiden ersten von Kap. 14 (s. VV. 1.3). Die Motive und Formulierungen von 12,30-31 werden also ihrer Reihenfolge nach aufgegriffen und in eigenen Gesetzen konkretisiert. Allerdings geht es in Kap. 13 nicht mehr um die Übernahme von Kultformen, sondern um die Götter selber, freilich nicht um die Götter der vernichteten Völker Kanaans, sondern die Götter der Völker ringsum, d.h. alle «anderen Götter» schlechthin. 14,1-21 nimmt das Motiv «Riten anderer Völker» auf und behandelt ihre Ablehnung durch Israel, also eine Ritualdifferenz, die Israel zu einer Kontrastgesellschaft macht.

Die drei «kasuistischen» Gesetze von 13,2-19 sind unter dem Gesichtspunkt der ausschließlichen Loyalität Israels zu Jahwe zusammengestellt. Besonders gattungsmäßig besitzen sie ihre größte formale und inhaltliche Analogie in den «hethitischen Dienstanweisungen», die ebenfalls der ausschließlichen Treue und dem Dienstverhältnis zu einem Oberherrn gelten. In Kap. 13 wird das gemeinsame Anliegen des Alleinverehrungsanspruches Jahwes von drei gesellschaftlichen Grenzsituationen her dargestellt: In den VV. 2-6 die Verführung zum Abfall durch Propheten, die in diesem Sachbereich höchste Kompetenz besitzen und über charismatische Autorität, ja sogar über Wunderzeichen verfügen; in den VV. 7-12 die Verführung zum Abfall durch Familienmitglieder und Freunde, also im Bereich der ersten und stärksten religiösen Erfahrungen und der Intimität; in den VV. 13-19 der Abfall einer großen Gruppe («Stadt») aus dem sozial-religiösen Konsens Israels. Die drei Extremfälle erhellen sich gegenseitig, sind sachlich zu einer Einheit geformt und deshalb auch sprachlich aufeinander abgestimmt. Im übrigen paraphrasieren ganze Passagen in 13,2-19 den Dekaloganfang.

Dem einzigen Gott für Israel entspricht das einzigartige Verhältnis dieses Volkes zu Jahwe. Es hebt Israel als «Kinder Jahwes» und «heiliges Volk» von allen anderen Völkern ab. Dieser Thematik ist die nächste Gesetzeseinheit in 14,1-21 gewidmet. Wie 13,2-19 hängt auch 14,1-21 an 12,31. Die Wortklammern zwischen beiden Stellen verdeutlichen das eigentliche Anliegen der Gesetzesgruppe. 14,1-21 expliziert Israels Besonderheit in drei Paragraphen als Enthaltung von bestimmten Bräuchen und bestimmten Speisen. Die VV. 1-2 verbieten Trauerriten, die VV. 3-21a bestimmte Speisen, V. 21b eine bestimmte Speisenzubereitung. Trotz unterschiedlicher Länge stellen sie eine Einheit dar. Das ergibt sich besonders klar aus der formalen Gestaltung. Die VV. 2 und 21 rahmen die Speiseverbote. In den VV. 1 und 21 liegt dann zusätzlich eine doppelte motivliche Rahmung vor, die in die Sphäre von Leben und Tod führt, den Raum altorientalischen Fruchtbarkeitskultes und altorientalischer Jenseitsreligion. Dem Motiv der «Kinder Jahwes» entsprechen das Zicklein und seine Mutter, dem Verbot von Trauerritualen das Verbot, Aas zu essen. Als Kinder Jahwes aber sind die Israeliten Jahwes Volk, *ʿam*, das heißt eigentlich, seine Familie. Wiederum handelt es sich um eine geschlossene Gesetzesgruppe.

Damit ist eine in Kap. 12 begonnene Assoziationskette zu Ende geführt. Die Disposition kann daher die andere dort angelegte Themenspannung aufgreifen, nämlich jene von Raum und Zeit. Kap. 12 faßt Zentralisationsgesetze unter dem Aspekt des Raumes zusammen, nämlich des einen Ortes, den Jahwe erwählt hat. 13,2-14,21 bilden dazu eine Art assoziativer Digression. Nun setzt 14,22-16,17 wieder beim Zentralheiligtum ein und entfaltet durch die Anordnung seiner Gesetze den Aspekt der Zeit. Im Unterschied freilich zu Kap. 12, wo die Gesetze wegen der einzigen legitimen Kultstätte nicht mehrere Ortsangaben machen können, dienen in 14,22-16,17 verschiedene Zeitangaben direkt als Verknüpfungsprinzip. Die Brücke zwischen diesem Block und den unmittelbar vorausgegangenen Gesetzen schlägt das Stichwort «essen» (*'kl*). Es verknüpft die beiden letzten Gesetze des ersten privilegrechtlichen Gesetzesblockes (12,2-14,21), nämlich die Speiseverbote in 14,3-21, mit den beiden ersten Gesetzen des zweiten privilegrechtlichen Gesetzesblockes (14,22-16,17), nämlich den Geboten des Zehnten in 14,22-29. Die sachliche Nähe wird besonders deutlich, wenn man den Zehnten als «Auftischung» versteht [30].

Eine erste Einheit ist mit der Gesetzesgruppe von 14,22-15,23 gegeben. Ihren Gesetzen ist gemeinsam, daß es darin im Zusammenhang mit heiligen Rhythmen stets um die Aufhebung der in Israel entstehenden Klassenunterschiede geht. Das trifft schon für das erste Gesetz zu, den Zehnten am Zentralheiligtum zu essen, bei dem verfügt wird, daß auch die Leviten einzuladen sind. Der Zehnte wird zwar schon in Kap. 12 erwähnt. Doch werden erst jetzt seine Modalitäten geregelt. Dabei zeigt sich, daß er gar nicht jedes Jahr ins Zentralheiligtum gebracht werden soll. Denn nach 14,28-29 ist er jedes dritte und sechste Jahr innerhalb des Sieben-Jahre-Zyklus am Wohnort für die Armen abzuliefern. Damit ist aber die Ortsfrage sekundär geworden, die Anordnung nach dem Zeitgesichtspunkt tritt in den Vordergrund. Es liegt nahe, nach dem Stichwort «jährlich» und dem Stichwort «alle drei Jahre» nun den Blick auf das Abschlußjahr des Gesamtzyklus zu richten und das zu behandeln, was «alle sieben Jahre» zu geschehen hat. 15,1-6 spricht daher von dem in jedem siebten Jahr fälligen Schuldenerlaß, und die VV. 7-11 schließen logisch für die Zwischenzeit an, daß man trotz dieses im siebten Jahr fälligen Schuldenerlasses dem armen Israeliten Kredit geben soll. Ebenfalls von der Zahl sieben her wird nun noch das Gesetz über die Freilassung von Schuldknechten nach sechs Jahren Sklavenschaft, also im siebten Jahr, angereiht. Wahrscheinlich ist das nicht das festliegende siebte Jahr des Siebenerzyklus, sondern das siebte Jahr nach der jeweils individuellen Versklavung. Solche Sklavenfreilassungen konnten also faktisch in jedem Jahr stattfinden. Es ist naheliegend, nach dieser von Zeitspannen geprägten Digression zu jenen Bestimmungen zurückzukehren, die jährlich aktuell sind. Dies geschieht im Gesetz über das Erstgeburtsopfer. Es ist jährlich, und zwar im Zentralheiligtum, darzubringen. Damit ist aber auch der Ausgangspunkt von 14,22 wieder erreicht.

Die Gesetze in 14,22-15,23 bilden zugleich ein Beispiel für eine

30. N. AIROLDI, *La cosidetta «decima» israelitica antica*, in *Bib* 55 (1974) 179-210.

Gruppierung nach dem Sozialstatus der betroffenen Subjekte. So sollen nach 14,22-27 bei den jährlichen Abgaben am Heiligtum «du und deine Familie» Mahl halten und fröhlich sein; dabei darf der «Levit» nicht im Stich gelassen werden (V. 27). 14,28-29 bestimmt dann, daß in jedem dritten Jahr der Zehnte für die «Leviten, Fremden, Waisen und Witwen» in den einzelnen Stadtbereichen abzuliefern ist. Der in jedem siebten fällige Schuldenerlaß ist 15,1-6 zufolge jedem «armen Bruder» zu gewähren. Nach 15,7-11 ist ihm auch jederzeit Kredithilfe zu gewähren. 15,12-18 fordert für den «versklavten Bruder» die Freilassung im siebten Jahr seiner Schuldknechtschaft. 15,19-23 schließlich bestimmt, daß «du und deine Familie» (V. 20) jedes Jahr die Erstgeburt des Viehs am Heiligtum verzehren sollen. Damit aber ist dieses Sozialgefälle wieder an seinen Ausgangspunkt zurückgebunden. Denn von den Erstlingen der Rinder, Schafe und Ziegen wurde schon 14,23 gesprochen, ebenso vom Familienmahl an der erwählten Stätte.

Wurde der Zehnte am Laubhüttenfest zum Zentralheiligtum gebracht, so dürfte auch das Erstgeburtsopfer von 15,19-23 mit der Wallfahrt zum Herbstfest verbunden gewesen sein (s. die Verknüpfung in 14,23). Damit aber ist die Gesetzesabfolge beim abschließenden Wallfahrtsfest angelangt. In 16,1-17 kann daher eine neue, vom Zeitlauf bestimmte Gesetzesgruppe mit dem Frühlingsfest einsetzen und Pesach-Mazzot, Wochen- wie Laubhüttenfest regeln. Die VV. 16-17 bilden als Zusammenfassung auch eine Art Abschluß. Das Thema «Privilegrecht Jahwes» ist in räumlicher und zeitlicher Dimension durchlaufen. Die eigentlichen Angelpunkte der Gesetzesdisposition sind dabei die Gesetze, die vom Zentralheiligtum handeln: Zunächst die Gruppe in Kap. 12, dann — nach der ersten Digression — in 14,22-27 die Gesetze über den jährlichen Zehnten, dann — nach der zweiten Digression — in 15,19-23 die Gesetze über die Ablieferung der Erstlinge, und schließlich die Gesetzesgruppe in Kap. 16. Die sogenannten «Zentralisationsgesetze» sind also nicht willkürlich eingebaut, sondern strategisch verteilt. Die Zentralisationsthematik findet sich später nur noch in zwei der Ämtergesetze: in 17,7-13, der Bestimmung über das sakrale Gericht am Zentralheiligtum, und in 18,1-8, wo die Rechte der Leviten vom Land am Zentralheiligtum geregelt werden. Beide Gesetze sind jetzt freilich in neue Dispositionsstrukturen eingebettet, in den dtn Verfassungsentwurf.

Läßt sich 12,2-16,17 aufbau- und stoffmäßig dem 1. bis 3. Dekaloggebot zuordnen? Wie die eben nachgezeichnete Anordnung der Gesetze dieses Privilegrechtes zeigt, folgt die Redigierung samt Digressionen offenbar anderen Systematisierungsprinzipien. Darüber hinaus kann vor allem 14,1-21 nur über einige Denkumwege zum Namensgebot in Beziehung gesetzt werden. Redaktionsgeschichtlich dürfte somit kein ursprünglicher Zusammenhang der Kap. 12-16 mit den ersten drei Dekalogsgeboten intendiert gewesen sein. Damit ist freilich nicht ausgeschlossen, daß eine spätere relecture diesen Text in jenes Konzept integrierte, das den Aufbau des ganzen Kodex vom Dekalog her organisiert hat. Nur in diesem Sinn kann gelten, was oben unter Punkt 7 gesagt wurde.

9. Die Disposition von 16,18-18,22 hat N. Lohfink [31] bereits ausführlich analysiert. Wie seine Untersuchung ergibt, wurden die Einzelgesetze vor allem durch assoziative Attraktion zu einem einheitlichen Verfassungsentwurf redigiert.

Die Zuordnung dieses Gesetzesteiles zum 4. Dekalogsgebot erscheint nicht zuletzt aufgrund der modernen Exegese des Gebotes der Elternehrung [32] als problematisch. Trotzdem hat bereits Philo von Alexandrien (De Decalogo XXXI, 165) gemeint, das Gebot «von der Ehrfurcht gegen Eltern deute(t) zugleich auf viele wichtige Gesetze hin, wie die ... über Herrschende und Untergebene» [33]. So dürfte auch eine redaktionelle Reinterpretation der Ämtergesetze 16,18-18,22 von der Dekalogstruktur des gesamten Gesetzeskodex her möglich gewesen sein [34].

10. Als Beispiel für die Strukturierung eines Übergangsbereiches zwischen zwei Gesetzesblöcken soll im folgenden 22,1-12 genauer analysiert werden. Der Text gilt, wo er als ganzer in den Blick genommen wird, bis heute zumeist als unsystematische Sammlung verschiedenster Bestimmungen [35]. Diese werden gewöhnlich als Humanitätsgesetze und alte Tabus zur Abwehr fremdreligiöser Praktiken interpretiert [36]. Wie aber wollte sie der Redaktor verstanden wissen, der sie an dieser Stelle des Kodex und in der vorliegenden Reihung angeordnet hat?

21,1-23 faßt inhaltlich unterschiedliche Gesetze unter dem Gesichtspunkt des Todes mitten im Leben zusammen [37]; in 22,13-29 betreffen alle Gesetze verbotenen Beziehungen zwischen Mann und Frau. Die beiden redaktionellen Einheiten sind chiastisch aufgebaut [38]. Sie sind darüber hinaus auch durch mehrere sprachliche Gemeinsamkeiten mit-

31. *Sicherung* (vgl. Anm. 24), esp. pp. 147-148.

32. S. dazu R. ALBERTZ, *Hintergrund und Bedeutung des Elterngebots im Dekalog*, in *ZAW* 90 (1978) 348-374.

33. Zitiert nach Philo von Alexandrien, *Die Werke in deutscher Übersetzung*. Hrsg. v. L. Cohn u.a., Bd. 1, Berlin, ²1962, 371-409, p. 406.

34. SCHULTZ, *Deuteronomium* (vgl. Anm. 14), pp. 19-21, sieht in 16,18-18,22 Erweiterungen des Elterngebotes; GUILDING, *Notes* (vgl. Anm. 17), p. 52, zitiert Philo. KAUFMAN, *Structure* (vgl. Anm. 21), p. 133, konstatiert bezüglich der Ämtergesetze ohne weitere Ausführungen: «These rules proclaim the authority figures just as the Fifth Commandment proclaims the authority of the parents within the family».

35. S. z. B. A. PHILLIPS, *Deuteronomy* (The Cambridge Bibel), Cambridge, 1973, p. 146; J. A. THOMPSON, *Deuteronomy. An Introduction and Commentary*, London, 1974, p. 233.

36. So z. B. PHILLIPS, *Deuteronomy* (vgl. Anm. 35), p. 146.

37. C. M. CARMICHAEL, *A Common Element in five Supposedly Disparate Laws*, in *VT* 29 (1979) 129-142.

38. G. J. WENHAM/J. G. MCCONVILLE, *Drafting Techniques in Some Deuteronomic Laws*, in *VT* 30 (1980) 248-252.

einander verbunden[39]. All diese Systematisierungen grenzen 22,1-12 indirekt als kompositorisch eigenständigen Zwischentext aus. Denn er vereinigt inhaltlich unterschiedliche Bestimmungen und ist nicht chiastisch strukturiert. Auffällig ist schließlich, daß die Gesetzmäßigkeiten altorientalischer Kodifikation, wie sie Petschow in seinen fünf Anordnungsprinzipien erfaßt hat, zwar in 21,15-21 und 22,13-29 gelten, nicht jedoch in 22,1-12[40].

Während in den kasuistischen Regelungen des Kap. 21 und in 22,13-29 fast ausschließlich die 3. Person dominiert, sind die apodiktischen wie kasuistischen Rechtssätze in 22,1-12 mit Ausnahme von V. 5 stets an die 2. Person adressiert. Trotzdem ist das heterogene Material auch in der vorliegenden Sammlung nicht unter einem einzigen Gesichtspunkt zusammengestellt worden[41]. Sie verbindet vielmehr zwei Gruppen von Gesetzen. So geht es in den VV. 1-3.4.6-7.8 um vier Paragraphen, durch die tierisches wie menschliches Leben bewahrt werden soll. Sie gehören noch in den Bereich des 5. Dekaloggebotes. Dagegen handelt es sich in den VV. 5.9-11.12 um drei (bzw. fünf) Paragraphen, die bestimmte Vermischungen verbieten. Mit ihnen beginnt schon der Bereich des 6. Dekaloggebotes. Diese Auslegung wird später noch verdeutlicht werden. Jedenfalls läßt sich der Zwischentext 22,1-12 nicht in durchgehend geschlossene und unmittelbar aufeinander folgende Abschnitte aufteilen, die dann dem vorausgehenden bzw. anschließenden Gesetzesblock zugeordnet werden könnten[42]. Für ihn ist vielmehr charakteristisch, daß seine beiden Gesetzesgruppen ineinander geschoben werden. Die Geschlechtermischung durch Kleidertausch in V. 5 ist bereits im Sachbereich «Leben bewahren» eingehängt, zu dem dann noch die VV. 6-7.8 gehören. Von der anderen Seite her gesehen: das Lebenlassen der Vogelmutter in den VV.6-7 sowie die Vorkehrung vor einem tödlichen Unfall in V. 8 ragen noch in den Sachbereich «Vermischungen vermeiden» hinein, der bereits mit V. 5 eingesetzt hat. Läge nur eine

39. WENHAM/MCCONVILLE, *Drafting Techniques* (vgl. Anm. 38), p. 252 Anm. 9.

40. Vgl. WAGNER, *Rest* (vgl. Anm. 24), pp. 236-237.

41. Selbst A.D.H. MAYES, (*Deuteronomy* [The New Century Bible Commentary], Grand Rapids/Mich., 1981), der 22,1-12 unter einen gemeinsamen Titel stellt (p. 305), muß für die Redigierung schließlich doch zwei verschiedene Aspekte angeben, um die Verbote der VV. 5.9-11 thematisch einordnen zu können. Die Gesetze seien aneinander gereiht worden «out of a concern for the integrity of all forms of life and the preservation of the distinction of the created order» (p. 306). V. 12 wäre nur wegen des vorhergehenden Gesetzes hier angehängt worden (p. 309).

42. Letzteres gegen KAUFMAN, *Structure* (vgl. Anm. 21), der 19,1-22,8 dem 5. Dekaloggebot (katholischer Zählung) zuordnet (pp. 134-137), 22,9-23,19 aber dem 6. Dekaloggebot (pp. 137-139). 22,5 «seems intrusive and may well be displaced from its original position among other laws of forbidden mixtures in vv 9-10» (p. 136). Doch bildet das Kleidermotiv des V. 5 ein Element in der chiastischen Struktur, die die VV. 5-12 auf Inhaltsebene überspannt, und so einen Übergang zwischen den Gesetzesblöcken schafft (p. 136; s. dazu u. Anm. 46).

Attraktion assoziierter Stoffe vor, hätte man thematisch Zusammengehörendes auch unmittelbar aneinander gereiht. Die beiden Gesetzesgruppen wurden jedoch offenbar redaktionell ineinander verklammert, um so Eigenständigkeit wie Übergang von einem Sachbereich zum anderen stärker zu profilieren. Die gleiche Technik läßt sich übrigens dann auch in 23,16-24,5 für den Übergangsbereich von Thema «Sextum» zum Thema «Eigentum» beobachten.

Erzeugt diese Technik also in 22,1-12 die Verzahnung zweier inhaltlich unterschiedlicher Gesetzesgruppen, so werden diese durch eine subtile Stichwortverknüpfung doch zugleich zu einem selbständigen Zwischentext geformt[43]. Im einzelnen geschieht dies auf folgende Weise. Das Gesetz über die Nachbarschaftshilfe in V. 4 ist syntaktisch wie formulierungsmäßig weitgehend parallel zu V. 1 gestaltet, dem Anfang des Gesetzes über verlaufenes Vieh und verlorenes Gut. Während jedoch V. 1 von Rind und Lamm spricht, nennt V. 4 Esel und Rind. Mit dem Esel aber, der in V. 4 als Lasttier an die Stelle des Lammes von V. 1 tritt, beginnt in V. 3 die Aufzählung weiteren verlorenen Besitzes, demgegenüber man sich ebenso wenig gleichgültig verhalten kann wie dem verlaufenen Rind oder Lamm des V. 1 gegenüber. V. 4 ist also mit V. 1 wie mit V. 3 verklammert, weicht aber von ihnen auch in zwei Punkten ab: Erstens dreht er die Abfolge der Tiere um, führt also zunächst den Esel (*ḥ*^{a}*môr*) aus V. 3 und danach erst das Rind (*šôr*) aus V. 1 an. Zweitens gebraucht er die Wendung «fallen auf dem Weg» (*npl* q. *badderek*), der dann das Aufrichten der Tiere als Hilfeleistung entspricht[44]. Beide Handlungen werden syntaktisch jedoch parallel zu V. 1 formuliert. Durch diese Gemeinsamkeiten wie Unterschiede entfernt sich V. 4 zwar von seiner Vorlage in Ex 23,5, wird aber zum Bindeglied zwischen den VV. 1-3 einerseits und den VV. 6-10 andererseits. Denn die Ausdrücke *ḥ*^{a}*môr* - *šôr* - *npl* q. *badderek* dienen als Stichwörter einer (ornamentalen) chiastischen Struktur und werden in einer zu V. 4 rückläufigen Abfolge in den VV. 6.8.10 wiederholt[45]. V. 4 dürfte somit erst vom Redaktor des vorliegenden Übergangstextes konkret gestaltet worden sein. Die Kleidervorschriften der VV. 5 und 11 werden durch das negierte Verb *lbš* q. miteinander verbunden, das im Dtn nur an diesen beiden Stellen verwendet wird[46]. Schließlich erzeugen auch die gesetzesübergreifenden Wortwiederholungen von *bajit* (V. 2), bzw. *bajit ḥādāš* (V. 8), *śimlâ* (V. 3) bzw. *śimlat ʾiššâ* (V. 5) ein Einheitsgefühl. Da diese

43. Zu manchen der folgenden Bezüge vgl. Seitz, *Redaktionsgeschichtliche Studien* (vgl. Anm. 7), pp. 166, 174-175, 250-251.

44. Die Opposition *npl* q. und *qwm* hi. absoluter Infinitiv mit finiter Verbalform findet sich im AT nur hier.

45. LOCHER, *Ehre* (vgl. Anm. 7).

46. Dagegen bleibt der von KAUFMAN, *Structure* (vgl. Anm. 21), p. 136, für die VV. 5-12 festgestellte Chiasmus undifferenziert: Kleidung (V. 5) — Tiere (VV. 6-7) — Haus (V. 8) — Feld (V. 9) — Tiere (V. 10) — Kleidung (VV. 11-12).

beiden Ausdrücke jedoch nur in Variation aufgegriffen werden, ist ihre Wiederholung von den zuvor genannten Repetitionen innerhalb einer Struktur abgehoben. Trotz ihres divergierenden Inhalts fügen sich die VV. 8 und 9 aufgrund der Topik «Neubau eines Hauses und Anlegen eines Weinberges» (vgl. Dtn 20,5-7) gut aneinander[47]. Formal gehört V. 9 jedoch mit den VV. 10-11 zusammen[48]. V. 12 wurde vom Thema «Kleidung» des V. 11 attrahiert[49].

Trotz alles Gesagten steht 22,1-12 nicht als selbständiger Textblock zwischen anderen, sondern hängt als Brückentext aussage- und formulierungsmäßig auch an den vorausgehenden wie nachfolgenden Gesetzen. So wird *npl* q. im Dtn außer 22,4 und 8 nur noch in 21,1 von einem auf freiem Feld «Gefallenen», nämlich Ermordeten gebraucht. Wenn 22,4 das Aufrichten eines zusammengebrochenen Tieres verlangt, sollte offenbar vom Kontext her mitgedacht werden: Bewahre es dadurch am Leben. Jedenfalls aber bedeutete das Herabfallen von der ungesicherten Dachterasse in V. 8 eine Blutschuld. Sie wird hier und sonst im Dtn nur noch in 19,10 mit *dāmîm* bezeichnet[50]. *npl* q. und *dāmîm* verklammern somit die Gesetze in 22,4 und 8 mit dem Bereich des 5. Dekaloggebotes[51]. Was das Gesetz der Nachbarschaftshilfe in den VV. 1-3 betrifft, so lag beim «verlorenen Gut» (*'ᵃbēdâ*), das «verloren gegangen ist» (*'bd*), die Assoziation des Umkommens bzw. Zugrundegehens nahe. Schließlich besteht noch eine Verbindung zwischen V. 2 und 21,12: das verlaufene Tier und die geliebte Kriegsgefangene sollen in den Innenraum des Hauses (*'el tôk bêtekā*) gebracht werden. Dieser Präpositionalausdruck findet sich im Alten Testament nur an den genannten zwei Stellen.

Eine Schlüsselfunktion für die Diskussion redaktioneller Zuordnung von Einzelgesetzen zu bestimmen Dekaloggeboten kommt den VV. 6-7 zu. Sie untersagen beim Ausheben eines Vogelnestes, die «Mutter über» — d.h. zusammen mit — «ihren Jungen» (*'ēm ʿal bānîm*) «zu nehmen», d.h. zur eigenen Nahrung zu töten. Die Wendung ist nach Gen 32,12 und Hos 10,10 Ausdruck völliger Vernichtung. Dieses Verbot gehört somit zur «Kommentierung» des 5. Dekaloggebotes. Dagegen bringen freilich

47. Vielleicht wurde deshalb das besser zum «Säen» passende «Feld», wie es das parallele Gesetz in Lev 19,19 noch von der alten Vorlage her bewahrt haben dürfte, in Dtn 22,9 durch «Weinberg» ersetzt — so SEITZ, *Redaktionsgeschichtliche Studien* (vgl. Anm. 7), pp. 250-251.

48. Sie könnten auf der Sachebene chiastisch angeordnet sein: Vermischung von Pflanzen (V. 9) — Vermischung von Tieren (V. 10) — Vermischung von (tierischer) Wolle und (pflanzlichem) Flachs (V. 11).

49. KAUFMAN, *Structure* (vgl. Anm. 21), p. 136, sieht eine mögliche Verbindung zwischen den Dachrändern, an denen eine Brüstung zu ziehen ist (V. 8), und den Gewandrändern, an deren Ecken Quasten anzubringen sind (V. 12).

50. Beachtenswert ist überhaupt der häufige Gebrauch von *dām* in Kap. 19 und 21,1-9.

51. Zu Dtn 22,8 vgl. die Bestimmung über fahrlässige Tötung in Ex 21,33-34 im Kontext von Gesetzen über Tötung und Körperverletzung in 21,12-36.

fast alle Ausleger [52] bis in die jüngste Zeit [53] den Schutz der Vogelmutter mit dem Elterngebot, also dem 4. Dekaloggebot, in Verbindung. Sie verweisen dazu auf die Verheißung in Dtn 22,7: «damit es dir gut geht und du lange lebst», die in 5,16 dem Ehren menschlicher Eltern zugesprochen werde. Dieselbe Zusage mit den beiden Verben *jṭb* und *'rk* hi. findet sich sonst nur noch in 4,40. Zwar wird sie hier in zerdehnter Form gebraucht, bildet jedoch die einzige echte Parallele zu 22,7. Denn nur in 4,40 und 22,7 ist das angeredete Israel das Subjekt von *'rk* hi., während es in 5,16 die «Tage» sind. Außerdem kehrt die Motivation des Elterngebotes in 5,16 die Abfolge der Verben gegenüber 4,40 und 22,7 um, führt also zuerst das Langwerden der Lebenstage und dann erst das Wohlergehen an. Im übrigen gilt: Wird die Wendung — mit beiden Verben wie in 22,7 oder auch nur mit einem der zwei Verben wie an anderen Stellen — an Einzelgesetze angehängt, dann handelt es sich dabei stets um die Forderung, «das Leben bzw. die Träger des Lebens zu respektieren» [54]. Das Gesetz, das in 22,6-7 das Ausheben eines Vogelnestes regelt, ist also nur dem 5. Dekaloggebot zuzuordnen [55]. Damit hat aber Guildings These, kommentiert würden stets Gebotspaare des Dekalogs — in diesem Fall das 4. und 5. Dekaloggebot — ihren einzigen Anhaltspunkt in 22,1-12 verloren [56]. Die Gesetze der VV. 1-3.4.6-7.8 gehören zum Sachbereich des Tötungsverbotes.

Dagegen zählen die Gesetze in 22,5.9-11.12 zum folgenden Sachbereich des 6. Dekaloggebotes. Möglicherweise handelt es sich bei ihnen um altes Sakralrecht [57]. Dann könnte der Redaktor sie deshalb den übrigen Sexualbestimmungen vorausgestellt haben. Sie bilden jedenfalls

52. Eine Ausnahme bildet z.B. P.C. CRAIGIE, *The Book of Deuteronomy* (The New International Commentary on the Old Testament), Grand Rapids/Mich., 1976, pp. 288-289. Er äußert sich freilich nicht zu V. 7b.

53. Zuletzt O. KEEL, *Das Böcklein in der Milch seiner Mutter und Verwandtes. Im Lichte eines altorientalischen Bildmotivs* (Orbis Biblicus et Orientalis, 33), Freiburg/Schweiz, 1980, p. 44.

54. R.P. MERENDINO, *Das deuteronomische Gesetz. Eine literarkritische, gattungs- und überlieferungsgeschichtliche Untersuchung zu Dt 12-26* (Bonner Biblische Beiträge, 31), Bonn, 1969, p. 256.

55. Zum Zweck dieser Bestimmung s. CRAIGIE, *Deuteronomy* (vgl. Anm. 52), pp. 288-289.

56. Gegen GUILDING, *Notes* (vgl. Anm. 17), pp. 47-48, esp. p. 48. Eigenartigerweise grenzt er den Textblock, der dem Elterngebot und Tötungsverbot entsprechen soll, mit 16,18-22,8 ab, während der nächste Block erst mit 22,13 beginnt. Die VV. 9-12 bleiben somit ohne weitere Begründung unberücksichtigt.

57. So viele Erklärungen dieser Verse. Der Text selbst bezeichnet die Travestie in V. 5 ausdrücklich als «Greuel für Jahwe» (*tô'ēbâ*); s. dazu W.H.Ph. RÖMER, Randbemerkungen zur Travestie von Deut. 22,5, in M.S.H.G. HEERMA VAN VOSS u.a. (ed.), *Travels in the World of the Old Testament. Fs M.A. Beek* (Studia Semitica Neerlandica, 16), Assen, 1974, pp. 217-222. Die gemeinsame Aussaat und Ernte «wird heilig», d.h. ist dem gewöhnlichen Gebrauch entzogen und verfällt dem Heiligtum. Das Quastentragen, das V. 12 fordert, wird in Num 15,37-41 vom Jahweglauben her (re)interpretiert.

mit den kultisch-sexuellen Bestimmungen über die Aufnahme in die Jahweversammlung (23,2-9), die Reinheit des Heerlagers (23,10-15) und mit dem Verbot sakraler Prostitution (23,18-19) einen redaktionellen Rahmen um das Ehe- und Familienrecht (22,13-23,1). Die Zugehörigkeit zum Bereich des 6. Dekaloggebotes signalisiert im einzelnen für das Travestieverbot der Ausdruck *śimlat 'iššâ*. *śimlâ* spezifisch für Frauenkleidung wird nämlich nur noch in 22,17 verwendet (beachte *'iššâ* in V. 16) [58], der gesetzlichen Vorkehrung bei Beschuldigung der Ehefrau wegen vorehelichen Geschlechtsverkehrs. Die Tabus bestimmter Kombinationen in den VV. 9-11 lassen einen konnotativen Bezug «zu religiösen und speziell sexuellen Vermischungen» erkennen [59]. So ist der «Weinberg», von dem V. 9 spricht, auch ein Topos der Liebessprache. Die untersagte Einsaat dürfte daher vom Redaktor unter sexuellem Aspekt (vgl. Sir 26,20) aufgefaßt worden sein. Nach Dtn 22,10 sollen Rind und Esel nicht zu gemeinsamer Arbeit zusammengebracht werden, die Parallele in Lev 19,19 aber verbietet das Begatten zweier Tiere verschiedener Art. Auffallend ist, daß dieses Verbot von Bastardisierung von Tieren und von anderen Vermengungen in Lev dem Gesetz über die Unzucht der Nebenfrau eines anderen vorausgeht (19,20-21). In Dtn 22,12 könnten die Wörter *k^{e}sût* «Bedeckung» und *ksh* pi. «bedecken», die in der Parallele Num 15,37-41 fehlen, die Intention des Redaktors verraten: das Verdecken der Blöße. Denn *k^{e}sut*, das im Dtn nur hier begegnet, bezeichnet wie in Ex 22,26 die Decke, die vom Armen als Mantel (*śimlâ* - vgl. Dtn 24,13) über den bloßen Leib getragen wird, ebenso in Ijob 24,7; 31,19 und metaphorisch in 26,6. *ksh* pi. aber wird im Dtn nur mehr in 23,14 für das Bedecken der Notdurft verwendet. So dürften die Quasten einfach die Zipfel des viereckigen Gewandfleckens beschwert und herabgezogen haben, um «den Leib also, und besonders die Scham vor Entblössung zu schützen» [60]. Eine Rationalisierung wie in Num 15,38-40 erschien daher unnötig.

11. Die vorausgegangenen Dispositionsanalysen lassen deutliche Unterschiede zwischen der Systematisierung des «Privilegrechts» (12,2-16,17) sowie des «Verfassungsentwurfes» (16,18-18,22) einerseits und jenem Aufbau erkennen, der den Übergangsbereich in 22,1-12 prägt.

58. Im engeren Kontext sprechen 21,13 ausdrücklich von *śimlat šibjāh*, 22,3, und 24,13 von *śimlātô*.

59. C. STEUERNAGEL, *Das Deuteronomium* (HAT, I/3,1), Göttingen, ²1923, p. 132. Auch C.M. CARMICHAEL, *Forbidden mixtures*, in *VT* 32 (1982) 394-415, rechnet mit einer sexuellen Bedeutung. Ihre Entstehung begründet er freilich mit «kryptischen Bemerkungen Jakobs über die Handlungen seiner Söhne» (p. 411). Das sind phantasievolle Vermutungen, denen man exegetisch kaum folgen kann.

60. So schon SCHULTZ, *Deuteronomium* (vgl. Anm. 14), p. 559 (s. auch pp. 559-560 zu entsprechenden jüdischen Anschauungen und Sitten); neuestens PHILLIPS, *Deuteronomy* (vgl. Anm. 35), p. 147.

Darüber hinaus divergiert die Anordnung der Bestimmungen des «Straf- und Zivilrechts» (Kap. 19-25) von den vorausgegangenen Teilen des Kodex auch durch die Weise, in der Gesetzespartien in Verbindung zu einzelnen Dekalogsgeboten gebracht werden. Dazu kommt ferner: Die Gesetze von etwa Kap. 21 bis Kap. 25 sind am wenigsten von dtn Sprache geprägt. Hinter ihnen steht eine Intention, die nicht primär bundestheologisch oder paränetisch, sondern ausgesprochen juristisch interessiert ist. Auch wird hier am häufigsten innerhalb des Gesetzeskorpus auf das Material des Bundesbuches (Ex 21-23) Bezug genommen. Nur innerhalb der Kap. 19-25 sind die sogenannten *bi'arta*-Gesetze [61] jeweils dem richtigen Dekaloggebot zugeordnet [62]. Schon aus diesen Beobachtungen läßt sich für die Entwicklungsgeschichte des dtn Gesetzeskorpus folgern: Wahrscheinlich waren die Kap. 12-18 bereits jener Redaktion vorgegeben, die den dtn Kodex nach dem Dekalog verstehen und dann das als unvollständig empfundene Gesetzbuch im Sinn des Dekalogs juristisch ergänzen wollte. Sie wurden also nur sekundär in dieses Konzept einbezogen und lassen sich daher nur mit Schwierigkeiten vom Dekalogmodell her deuten. Nun dürften die Ämtergesetze erst während des Exils zu einem einheitlichen Gesetzesteil redigiert worden sein [63]. Die dtn Gesetzessammlung kann somit erst in der Exils- oder Nachexilszeit in Anlehnung an den Dekalog erweitert und strukturiert worden sein. Damit ist nichts über das Alter der dort aufgenommenen Gesetze gesagt. Doch dürften die Gesetze der Kap. 21-25 redaktionsgeschichtlich wohl den jüngsten Abschnitt des dtn Kodex bilden.

Die älteren Gesetze waren also vor allem kultisch und sozial interessiert, in der Exilszeit kam dann eine gewaltenteilige (und damit staatskritische) Ämterordnung dazu, danach wurde noch mehr detailliertes Recht eingebracht. Das «Privilegrecht Jahwes» in den Kap. 12-16 und 26, historisch und theologisch somit der Kern der dtn Gesetzessammlung, bildet jetzt um sie eine Art «Rahmen». Nach der Intention der Endredaktion soll man die Systematik des Gesetzeskorpus von der Anordnung der Dekaloggebote her interpretieren. Die Einzelgesetze erscheinen dadurch als Konkretisierung des Dekalogs. Sie braucht mit einer modernen historisch-kritischen Dekalogexegese nicht unbedingt übereinzustimmen. Der Doppelausdruck «Gesetze und Rechtsvorschriften» (*ḥuqqîm ûmišpāṭîm*) signalisiert tatsächlich eine Kommentierung des Dekalogs durch das dtn Gesetzeskorpus, weil sich seine Struktur nämlich auf der Ebene der Endredaktion an der Abfolge der Dekaloggebote orientiert.

61. Gegen F.-L. HOSSFELD, *Der Dekalog. Seine späten Fassungen, die originale Komposition und seine Vorstufen* (Orbis Biblicus et Orientalis, 45), Freiburg/Schweiz, 1982, pp. 279-280, esp. Anm. 247.

62. So sind die Gesetze 19,11-13.16-21; 21,1-9.18-21 dem 5., 22,13-21.22.23-27 dem 6. und 24,7 dem 7. Dekaloggebot zugeordnet.

63. LOHFINK, *Sicherung*, (vgl. Anm. 24), p. 149.

Zweifellos bedarf vieles von dem, was im Vorausgehenden eher thesenhaft skizziert worden ist, noch weiterer Detailuntersuchungen. Sind aber die vorgetragenen Ergebnisse richtig, dann ergibt sich daraus u.a. die folgende theologisch wichtige Konsequenz. Dekalog und Gesetzeskodex sind im Dtn vom Bund Jahwes mit Israel umfaßt. Der Dekalog wurde daher von Israel «niemals als ein absolutes moralisches Sittengesetz verstanden»[64]. Nach dtn Redaktionsentscheid darf aber der Dekalog nicht vom Gesetz gelöst werden, das ihn auslegt. Dieser Bezug des Dekalogs auf die Einzelgesetze als seinen Kontext ist zwar — wie schon seine Parallele in Ex 20 beweist — zeitgebunden. Doch gibt es seither hermeneutisch kein Zurück mehr hinter das Prinzip einer solchen Verbindung von Dekalog und Einzelgesetzen als seinen Durchführungsbestimmungen. Im Gesetz erhält der Dekalog seine «positive Füllung» und vermag so «das Leben positiv inhaltlich zu normieren»[65]. Umgekehrt kann die vom Dekalog her systematisierte dtn Gesetzessammlung nach dem Dekalogprolog (5,6) nur unter der Voraus-setzung jener Freiheit verwirklicht werden, zu der Jahwe sein Volk erlöst hat[66].

Freyung 6 (Schottenabtei) Georg BRAULIK
A-1010 Wien

64. G. v. RAD, *Theologie des Alten Testaments. Bd. 1: Die Theologie der geschichtlichen Überlieferungen Israels*, München, 61968, p. 207.

65. Gegen v. RAD, *Theologie* (vgl. Anm. 64), p. 208, der dem Dekalog mit diesen Wendungen abspricht, «Anweisung zum moralischen Leben» sein zu können (l. c.). Ebenso urteilt zuletzt F. CRÜSEMANN, *Bewahrung der Freiheit. Das Thema des Dekalogs in sozialgeschichtlicher Perspektive*, München 1983, pp. 8-13, 81-82.

66. Diesen Beitrag widme ich in Dankbarkeit Jacob Kremer zu seinem 60. Geburtstag.

DEUTERONOMY 15
AND RECENT RESEARCH ON THE DATING OF P

The Book of Deuteronomy plays a distinctive role in the higher criticism of the Pentateuch. On the one hand, since it is essentially a «source» in and of itself, it takes no part in the skirmishes surrounding the «documentary» composition of the other books. However much the form and redaction critics may care to reconstruct the «literary history» of Deuteronomy, it remains for nearly all critics the very separate thing called «D». On the other hand, the dating of and determination of the relationships among the various other books, sources, documents, codes, etc. of the Pentateuch revolve around D, primarily due to the nearly universal assumption of the direct relationship between Deuteronomy and the reforms of Josiah. Deuteronomy is the chronological peg upon which all theories of Pentateuchal dating ultimately rely.

Accordingly, the precise nature of the relationship between Deuteronomy and the «book of the law» found in the temple in Josiah's time remains a continuing source of scholarly speculation as does the ultimate origin of Deuteronomy itself. Many have long pointed to supposedly Israelite (as opposed to Judean) features within Deuteronomy, usually arguing for some kind of a chain of tradition stemming from northern wisdom teachers having moved to the South after the destruction of the North. In a recent monograph, H. L. Ginsberg has gone even further, arguing that almost in its entirety, Deuteronomy is an Eighth Century «Israelian» composition, profoundly dependent on the prophecies found in the book of Hosea [1]. Unlike many other modern Jewish Bible scholars, Ginsberg has never been convinced by the arguments of Yehezkel Kaufmann and his disciples as to the chronological priority of P as regards D, so that his early dating of D presents no problem for his relative dating of P. Indeed, Ginsberg argues that both P in general and the Holiness code in particular postdate D.

Like Ginsberg, I, Kaufman, have never been convinced by the arguments of Kaufmann, at least as regards the final shape of P. Unlike Ginsberg, I am also not convinced by the arguments of Ginsberg as to the origin of Deuteronomy. For me, the key element in reconstructing the relationship of the literary sources of the Pentateuch has always been what it was for Wellhausen: the development of the religious and social institutions of ancient Israel as reflected in the Pentateuch

1. H. L. GINSBERG, *The Israelian Heritage of Judaism* (Texts and Studies of the Jewish Theological Seminary of America, vol. XXIV), New York, 1982.

vis-à-vis their reflection in the extra-Pentateuchal literature; and one of the key pericopes informing my overall picture of the relationship of the Pentateuchal texts has long been the social welfare legislation in Chapter XV of Deuteronomy. In an article currently in press and in previous papers, I have tried to reconstruct the history of the social welfare legislation of ancient Israel, finding that my reconstruction required the chronological sequence — Covenant Code, Deuteronomy XV, Leviticus 25 [2]. Imagine my surprise, then, to discover that H. L. Ginsberg, my fellow champion for the general priority of D to P, specifically declares himself to have been convinced by the arguments of Sarah Japhet that in fact Deuteronomy XV is dependent on what he calls the «Mount Sinai Covenant», Lev. 25-26 [3].

Now Japhet's article, in the Hebrew volume of the 1978 Festschrift in honor of S. Loewenstamm, is one that I had read but, frankly, dismissed [4]. When Ginsberg is convinced, however, one should certainly reconsider. Let us do so.

All are agreed (except perhaps for Kaufmann himself) that the legislation in Deut XV regarding the manumission of slaves is strongly dependent upon the important paragraph on the «Hebrew slave» at the beginning of the Covenant Code in Exodus 21 [5]. Japhet is struck by the fact, however, that while the Covenant Code begins *ky tqnh ʿbd ʿbry*, itself a highly unusual formulation for the Exodus law code, in Deuteronomy the phrasing is *ky ymkr lk ʾḥyk hʿbry* (*ʾw hʿbryh*) [6].

She properly notes, then, that a strikingly similar protasis is found in the corresponding legislation in Lev 25: *wky ymwk ʾḥyk ʿmk wnmkr lk*, wherein, just as in Deut, one finds the second person addressee, the passive of *mkr* and the key word *ʾḥyk*. One text has obviously borrowed from the other, but which was is the direction of the borrowing? So far, none of this is really new. Others have seen these things and supposed that Deut was primary, most recently Cholewiński and Cardellini [7]. But

2. Stephen A. KAUFMAN, *A Reconstruction of the Social Welfare Systems of Ancient Israel*, in W. B. BARRICK, J. SPENCER, eds., *In the Shelter of Elyon* (G. W. Ahlstrom Festschrift), 1984.

3. GINSBERG, *Heritage*, p. 100.

4. Sarah JAPHET, *The laws of manumission of slaves and the question of the relationship between the laws in the Pentateuch*, in *Studies in Bible and the Ancient Near East Presented to Samuel E. Loewenstamm on his Seventieth Birthday*, Jerusalem, 1978, Hebrew volume pp. 231-249; English volume (abstract), pp. 199-200.

5. For a more elaborate discussion of intra-Pentateuchal dependance see my study *The Temple Scroll and Higher Criticism*, in *HUCA* 53 (1982), 29-43.

6. We must ignore Japhet's explicit agreement with those who deem the formulation of the Covenant Code secondary — those who confidently proceed to reconstruct the text on the basis of subsequent laws. Such groundless and presumtuous emendation is the epitome of much that is wrong with biblical studies today.

7. Alfred CHOLEWIŃSKI, *Heiligkeitsgesetz und Deuteronomium* (Analecta Biblica 66), Rome, 1976, pp. 100ff.; Innocenzo CARDELLINI, *Die biblischen «Sklaven»-Gesetze im*

Japhet, of course, finds the situation reversed. The key, for her, is the term *'ḥyk*. For her, the emphasis on different treatment of the fellow Israelite as opposed to the foreigner is pervasive in the Levitical legislation. Moreover, the entire pericope belongs to a time of movement from tribal to national social structures, hence the use of the term *'ḥ*, all Israel is to be now «your brother». In Lev, *'ḥ* is essential; in Deut it is peripheral. In Lev the relevant law is but one of a series of situations describing the various levels of penury into which one might fall and how they are to be treated. In Deut we have only one sketchy law. Again, she argues, this must mean Lev is primary.

In the compass of what I would call not «short papers» but rather «very short papers» there is not time to detail my responses to all of her points. Suffice it to summarize by saying that each element that for Japhet is indicative of a Levitical primacy is for me indicative of a Deuteronomic one: the passive structure of the protasis is paralleled many times in Deuteronomy [8]; it is unique in Leviticus. The word *'ḥ* in the meaning «fellow Israelite» is ubiquitous in Deuteronomy but extremely rare in Leviticus where the preferred word is *'amit*. And the attempt of the Levitical formulation to cover all possible cases can only be viewed as primary by someone unaware of the general practice in Ancient Near Eastern legislative codifications. These points, too, have all been made before, but have been ignored by Japhet and by Ginsberg. The most important consideration of all, however, is how the social welfare institutions in Deuteronomy and Leviticus relate to one another, to the provisions of the Covenant Code, and to historical evidence. Again here — unless one adopts the principal of the crypto-P espoused by Haran [9] — in this area D is unquestionably earlier than P, as I have tried to demonstrate elsewhere [10]. Those who would totally eschew any recognition of institutional development in the monarchic period are simply blind to religio-historical processes.

Nevertheless, one cannot ignore in their totality the impressive arguments mustered in recent years — mostly by Israeli scholars — for the relative antiquity of much of the language of P and the cultic institutions and regulations prescribed therein [11]. Nor can we ignore the

Lichte des keilschriftlichen Sklavenrechts: Ein Beitrag zur Tradition, Überlieferung und Redaktion der alttestamentlichen Rechtstexte (BBB 55), Bonn, 1981, pp. 269ff.

8. E.g. 15:19, 17:2, 17:8, 21:1, 22:6, 22:22, 24:7.

9. Cf. M. HARAN, *Temples and Temple Service in Ancient Israel*, Oxford, 1978; iem., *Behind the Scenes of History: Determining the Date of the Priestly Source*, in *JBL* 100 (1981), 321-333.

10. KAUFMAN, *Reconstruction*, passim.

11. I am thinking primarily of the works of M. WEINFELD, J. MILGROM and Avi HURVITZ. See especially WEINFELD's *Getting at the Roots of Wellhausen's Understanding of the Law of Israel on the 100th Anniversary of the Prolegomenon*, Jerusalem, Institute

clear evidence offered by recent computer studies of their language that the narrative texts traditionally assigned to P are of a totally different cloth than that of JE, even if those who produced the study choose to ignore it [12]. The implications of all of this are so obvious that one wonders why it is not common knowledge: In its final shape, the Pentateuch is the result of a relatively late, perhaps post-Exilic, reworking of ancient material — some have called this R, but P and R are, by and large, the same — and some of the final Levitical material clearly postdates D (among it Lev. 25). Yet much of the so-called P material (including some, but certainly not all, of the «Holiness Code») is ancient Priestly lore — lore that was given a Mosaic garb probably only in its latest stages, perhaps as a reaction to D.

This is as far as we can go. As I have shown in my study of the Temple Scroll, to go further — to attempt to do «redaction history» of the bits and pieces — is so much wasted effort, wasted effort that, unfortunately, many of my European friends seem to relish. I lament that waste.

3101 Clifton Ave.
Cincinnati, Ohio 45220, U.S.A.

Stephen A. KAUFMAN

for Advanced Studies, Hebrew Univ., 1979; idem., *Julius Wellhausen's Understanding of the Law of Ancient Israel and its Fallacies*, in *Shnaton* IV (1980), 62-93 (Hebrew), and Avi HURVITZ, *A Linguistic Study of the Relationship beween the Priestly Source and the Book of Ezekiel* (Cahiers de la Revue Biblique 20), Paris, 1982.

12. Of course we have in mind Y. RADDAY, *et. al.*, *Genesis, Wellhausen and the Computer*, in *ZAW* 94 (1982), 467-481.

LE ROI D'ISRAËL: Dt 17,14-20

Dt 17,14-20 a été et continue à être l'objet de nombreuses polémiques. Selon Hempel, on trouve difficilement dans le Deutéronome — à l'exception de la loi sur la Pâque — un texte aussi controversé que celui-ci [1]. Notre but n'est pas de passer en revue toutes les opinions, mais nous voudrions, avant d'aborder directement l'analyse du texte, présenter les principaux points autour desquels ont tourné les discussions.

1. Histoire de la Recherche

1. *Homogénéité et datation*

Plusieurs auteurs ont cru trouver en Dt 17,14-20 un point d'appui solide pour la datation du Deutéronome [2]. Il faut cependant reconnaître que les opinions à ce sujet sont très diverses: de la défense de l'authenticité mosaïque de la péricope à l'affirmation de son origine exilique ou postexilique s'ouvre un large éventail d'hypothèses, qui envisagent à peu près toutes les périodes de l'époque monarchique [3]. Pour Wellhausen, Dt 17,14-20 est un texte rédactionnel ajouté tardivement au Deutéronome primitif [4]. Steuernagel et Hölscher, en revanche, distinguent en Dt 17,14ss un texte original, partie intégrante du Deutéronome primitif, et quelques additions postérieures [5]. Dans les études critiques les plus récentes, on distingue également un texte primitif et quelques additions

1. *Die Schichten des Deuteronomiums. Ein Beitrag zur israelitischen Literatur- und Rechtsgeschichte*, Leipzig, 1914, p. 237.

2. Cf. G. Seitz, *Redaktionsgeschichtliche Studien zum Deuteronomium*, (BWANT, 93), Stuttgart, Berlin, Köln, Mainz, 1971, p. 231.

3. Cf. J. de Fraine, *L'aspect religieux de la royauté israélite. L'institution monarchique dans l'Ancien Testament et dans les textes mésopotamiens* (AnBib, 3), Roma, 1954, pp. 142ss; A. Caquot, *Remarques sur la «loi royale» du Deutéronome (17/14-20)*, in *Sem* 9, 1959, pp. 21ss; P.C. Craigie, *The Book of Deuteronomy* (ICOT), Grand Rapids (Mich.), 1976, pp. 253ss.

4. *Die Composition des Hexateuchs und der historischen Bücher des Alten Testaments*, Berlin, 1899³, pp. 191s.; cf. C.H. Cornill, *Einleitung in die kanonischen Bücher des Alten Testaments*, Tübingen, 1908⁶, pp. 33s.; A.F. Puukko, *Das Deuteronomium. Eine literarkritische Untersuchung* (BWAT, 5), Leipzig, 1910, p. 255.

5. Cf. C. Steuernagel, *Deuteronomium und Josua*, Göttingen, 1900, p. 66; 1923², p. 118; G. Hölscher, *Komposition und Ursprung des Deuteronomiums*, in *ZAW* 40, 1922, p. 199; voir aussi F. Horst, *Das Privilegrecht Jahwes. Rechtsgeschichtliche Untersuchungen zum Deuteronomium* (FRLANT, 45), Göttingen, 1930, pp. 107s. = *Gottes Recht. Gesammelte Studien zum Recht im Alten Testament* (ThB, 12), München, 1961, pp. 136s; K. Galling, *Das Königsgesetz im Deuteronomium*, in *ThLZ* 76, 1951, c. 136, n. 1.6.

secondaires, ces dernières étant tributaires de deux rédactions (deutéronomique et deutéronomiste)[6].

Sans arriver à un accord total, on observe aujourd'hui une certaine convergence sur deux points: premièrement, on admet un noyau primitif, qui comprend au moins les v. 16a.17[7]; deuxièmement, on soustrait de la strate originale les v. 18-19[8].

2. *Forme, genre littéraire et Sitz im Leben*

Dans l'histoire de la recherche, on a prêté peu d'attention à la forme ou au genre de Dt 17,14-20. Les exégètes caractérisent généralement ce passage comme «loi royale»[9], désignation qui ne lui convient qu'en partie. De là les précisions de quelques auteurs: selon Horst, «was hier in der Form eines Königsgesetzes formuliert worden ist, sind politische Leitsätze, wie sie sich aus einer theologisch-politischen Grundposition ergeben müssen»[10]. Pour Lods, au contraire, «la 'loi royale' ... est moins une charte politique qu'une exhortation morale et religieuse»[11]. Dans leurs études sur le droit apodictique, Rabast qualifie Dt 17,16-17 de «Königsspiegel», «ein Stück Königsinvestitur» et Gerstenberger de «Amtsspiegel», «ein fünf-(vier)gliedriger Katalog»[12].

6. Cf. R.P. MERENDINO, *Das deuteronomische Gesetz. Eine literarkritische, gattungs- und überlieferungsgeschichtliche Untersuchung zu Dt 12-26* (BBB, 31), 1969, p. 185; G. SEITZ, *Redaktionsg. Studien* (n. 2), pp. 233.242s.

7. Cf. C. STEUERNAGEL, G. HÖLSCHER, F. HORST, K. GALLING, R.P. MERENDINO, G. SEITZ (n. 5-6); K. RABAST, *Das apodiktische Recht im Deuteronomium und im Heiligkeitsgesetz*, Berlin-Hermsdorf, 1948, pp. 10s.; E. GERSTENBERGER, *Wesen und Herkunft des «Apodiktischen Rechts»* (WMANT, 20), Neukirchen-Vluyn, 1965, pp. 67s.

8. Cf. C. STEUERNAGEL, G. HÖLSCHER, K. GALLING, G. SEITZ (n. 5-6); A. ALT, *Die Heimat des Deuteronomiums, KlSchr* II, München, 1953, p. 264, n. 3; G. VON RAD, *Das fünfte Buch Mose. Deuteronomium* (ATD, 8), Göttingen, 1964, p. 85; E.W. NICHOLSON, *Deuteronomy and Tradition*, Oxford, 1967, pp. 93.111; M. WEINFELD, *Deuteronomy and the Deuteronomic School*, Oxford, 1972, p. 5, n. 1; T. VEIJOLA, *Die ewige Dynastie. David und die Entstehung seiner Dynastie nach der deuteronomistischen Darstellung*, Helsinki, 1975, p. 141; T.N.D. METTINGER, *King and Messiah. The Civil and Sacral Legitimation of the Israelite Kings* (CB.OTS, 8), Lund, 1976, p. 290.

9. Cf. F. HORST, *Das Privilegrecht Jahwes* (n. 5), pp. 107ss = *Gottes Recht*, pp. 136ss; A. LODS, *Israël. Des origines au milieu du VIIIe siècle*, Paris, 1930, p. 459; M. NOTH, *Die Gesetze im Pentateuch. Ihre Voraussetzungen und ihr Sinn, Schriften der Königsberger Gelehrten Gesellschaft. Geisteswissenschaftliche Klasse* 17,2 Halle (Saale), 1940, pp. 14.29 = *Gesammelte Studien zum A.T.* (ThB, 6), München, 1957, pp. 30.52; K. GALLING, *Das Königsgesetz* (n. 5), c. 133ss; A. CAQUOT, *Remarques sur la «loi royale»* (n. 3), pp. 21ss; Z. BEN-BARAK, *The Religious-Prophetic Background of the «Law of the King» in Deuteronomy*, in *Shnaton* 1, 1975, pp. 33ss.viii (hébreu; résumé en anglais).

10. *Das Privilegrecht Jahwes* (n. 5), p. 111 = *Gottes Recht*, p. 140; cf. K. GALLING, *Das Königsgesetz* (n. 5), c. 138.

11. *Israël* (n. 9); pp. 458s.; cf. J.A. SOGGIN, *Problemi di storia e di storiografia nell'antico Israele*, in *Henoch* 4, 1982, pp. 1ss.

12. Cf. K. RABAST, *Das apodiktische Recht* (n. 7), p. 11; E. GERSTENBERGER, *Wesen und Herkunft* (n. 7), p. 68; voir aussi N. LOHFINK, *Die Sicherung der Wirksamkeit des*

Selon l'opinion de Carmichael, la «loi royale» utilise la forme «request-permission». De la forme et du genre littéraire, l'auteur passe au *Sitz im Leben*[13]. Chez d'autres auteurs, ce passage n'apparaît pas si évident, même s'il faut reconnaître que nombreux sont ceux qui ont essayé d'éclaircir le fond sociologique et idéologique de Dt 17,14ss, et cela sous deux angles différents: 1) Dt 17,14-20 constitue-t-il une loi purement théorique et idéale, ou s'agit-il d'une législation pratique? Le texte se fonde-t-il sur une expérience et sur une situation historico-politique concrète, ou est-il anhistorique et d'ordre strictement moral et religieux? 2) Quel modèle de monarchie présuppose-t-on dans la «loi royale»: une monarchie charismatique ou dynastique?

La première question implique le facteur temps. Hölscher pense que cette loi ne peut se comprendre que «als die ideale Forderung eines Theoretikers jüngerer Zeit»[14]. Plusieurs auteurs coupent court à cette opinion et défendent au contraire la portée pratique et la base historique de la «loi royale». Selon Gressmann, Dt 17,14ss n'est compréhensible que si «das Königtum mit seiner Erbfolge noch besteht»[15]. Nyström voit dans 17,14ss «eine Streitschrift mit einem ganz bestimmten 'Sitz im Leben'», antérieur à l'exil[16]. Pour Bächli, les interdits de Dt 17,14-20 peuvent être compris à partir du développement historique de la royauté en Israël et dans les royaumes voisins[17].

La deuxième question a rapport avec l'origine géographique de la péricope. Galling soutient que derrrière la «loi royale» se trouve l'idéologie charismatique propre au royaume du Nord[18]. Pour Caquot, au contraire, «la 'loi royale' se comprend plus aisément comme un élément du programme du règne de Josias, conçu en Juda»[19]. Von Rad croit que l'idée selon laquelle la monarchie remonte à un désir du peuple et non à l'initiative de Yahvé contredit autant la conception nord-

Gotteswortes durch das Prinzip der Schriftlichkeit der Tora und durch das Prinzip der Gewaltenteilung nach den Ämtergesetzen des Buches Deuteronomium (Dt 16,18-18,22), in *Testimonium Veritatis* (Fs. W. Kempf), éd. par H. Wolter, Frankfurt, 1971, p. 145.

13. *The Laws of Deuteronomy*, Ithaca and London, 1974, pp. 140ss; cf. P.C. CRAIGIE, *The Book of Deuteronomy* (n. 3), p. 253.

14. *Komposition* (n. 5), p. 200.

15. *Josia und das Deuteronomium. Ein kritisches Referat*, in *ZAW* 42, 1924, p. 333; cf. A.C. WELCH, *The Code of Deuteronomy. A New Theory of its Origin*, London, 1924, pp. 118ss; E.W. NICHOLSON, *Deuteronomy and Tradition* (n. 8), p. 80.

16. *Beduinentum und Jahwismus. Eine soziologisch-religionsgeschichtliche Untersuchung zum Alten Testament*, Lund, 1946, pp. 165; cf. K. GALLING, *Das Königsgesetz* (n. 5), c. 133.

17. *Israel und die Völker. Eine Studie zum Deuteronomium* (AThANT, 41), Zürich, Stuttgart 1962, p. 89.

18. *Das Königsgesetz* (n. 5), c. 134ss; cf. F.R. MCCURLEY (Jr.), *The Home of Deuteronomy Revisited: A Methodological Analysis of the Northern Theory*, in *A Light Unto My Path. Old Testament Studies in Honor of Jacob M. Myers*, éd. par H.N. Bream, R.D. Heim, C.A. Moore, Philadelphia, 1974, pp. 297ss.

19. *Remarques sur la «loi royale»* (n. 3), p. 33.

israélite que celle de Juda[20]. Clements parcourt d'autres chemins: Dt 17,14ss n'oppose pas un principe charismatique personnel à un autre qui serait dynastique, mais «a simple contrast between kings who were divinely chosen and kings who were not»[21].

3. *Textes apparentés*

Comme parallèles à Dt 17,14-20, les exégètes allèguent généralement quelques textes de 1 Sam 8-12 et d'Osée. Plusieurs auteurs se contentent de signaler les points de contact entre ces textes; d'autres essayent de déterminer dans quel sens va la dépendance. Wellhausen se demande si c'est Dt 17,14ss qui dépend de 1 Sam 8 ou si c'est l'inverse; plus sûre, selon lui, est la référence de Dt 17,16 à Osée[22]. Budde, qui juge décisive la relation entre 1 Sam 8,5b.19s; 10,19a.24a et Dt 17,14ss, pense qu'il existe dans les textes de 1 Samuel une base Elohiste, postérieure à Osée, mais antérieure au Deutéronome[23]. Welch reconnaît aussi la connexion entre Dt 17; 1 Samuel et Osée, mais soutient que le Deutéronome est antérieur à Osée[24]. Selon Buis et Leclercq, il existe une relation, mais non une dépendance réciproque, entre Dt 17,14ss et quelques textes de 1 Samuel et Osée[25].

Outre la question de l'interrelation entre 1 Samuel, Osée et Dt 17, on discute la *tendance* plus ou moins *antimonarchique* de la péricope. Selon l'opinion de Wolff, Osée s'oppose radicalement à la monarchie et le Deutéronome comme le Dtr reflètent son idéologie[26]. Weinfeld, au contraire, estime que le rapprochement entre le Deutéronome et Osée en ce qui concerne leur attitude négative envers la monarchie manque de fondement[27]. La section communément dénommée «droit du roi»

20. *Das fünfte Buch Mose* (n. 8), p. 85.

21. *The Deuteronomistic Interpretation of the Founding of the Monarchy in I Sam. VIII*, in *VT* 24, 1974, pp. 398-410.

22. *Die Composition des Hexateuchs* (n. 4), p. 358. Voir, cependant, la seconde édition (1889, pp. 242.246) dans laquelle Wellhausen estime que I Sam 8 est un texte dtr, dépendant du Deutéronome. Pour plus de détails, cf. F. LANGLAMET, *Les récits de l'institution de la royauté (I Sam., VII-XII). De Wellhausen aux travaux récents*, in *RB* 77, 1970, pp. 163s. Récemment, T. VEIJOLA a défendu que 1 Sam 8,1-5.22b dépend de Dt 17,14ss (*Das Königtum in der Beurteilung der deuteronomistischen Historiographie. Eine redaktionsgeschichtliche Untersuchung*, Helsinki, 1977, p. 68).

23. *Saul's Königswahl und Verwerfung*, in *ZAW* 8, 1888, pp. 234-36; cf. H. J. STOEBE, *Das erste Buch Samuelis* (KAT, 8/1), Gütersloh, 1973, p. 217, n. 32.

24. *The Code of Deuteronomy* (n. 15), pp. 128-132.

25. *Le Deutéronome*, Paris, 1963, p. 133; voir aussi J. DE FRAINE, *L'aspect religieux de la royauté israélite* (n. 3), p. 147; K.-H. BERNHARDT, *Das Problem der altorientalischen Königsideologie im Alten Testament* (VTS, 8), Leiden, 1961, p. 137.

26. *Hoseas geistige Heimat*, in *ThLZ* 81, 156, c. 83ss = *Gesammelte Studien zum Alten Testament* (ThB, 22), München, 1973², pp. 232ss.

27. *Deuteronomy* (n. 8), pp. 369s.168; cf. J. R. PORTER, *Moses and Monarchy. A Study in the Biblical Tradition of Moses*, Oxford 1963, p. 25. Mais, voir aussi, W.H. SCHMIDT, *Kritik am Königtum*, in *Probleme biblischer Theologie (Fs. G. von Rad)*, éd. par H.W. Wolff,

(1 Sam 8,11-17) si distingue, selon Nyström, par son hostilité à la monarchie[28]. Certains auteurs ont voulu y voir un parallèle à Dt 17,14ss[29]. Boecker, cependant, pense qu'il n'est pas possible d'établir une dépendance directe entre les deux passages[30]. Birch et Mettinger ont souligné récemment les affinités entre ces textes[31].

En guise de conclusion à ce paragraphe, il convient de rappeler les opinions de Seitz et de Mayes. Tous deux font ressortir les similitudes entre Dt 17,14ss; Is 2,7-9 et Mi 5,9-14, mais Seitz précise que, malgré leurs convergence, on ne peut parler de dépendance entre les trois péricopes[32].

4. *Composition-rédaction*

Dans leurs efforts pour découvrir l'articulation de Dt 12-26, les exégètes sont arrivés à des résultats très divers. Ils sont cependant presque tous d'accord sur un point: Dt 16,17 marque une césure dans le Code[33]. Certains auteurs reconnaissent dans Dt 16,18-18,22 un petit recueil de lois sur les autorités[34], mais le critère d'assemblage des éléments, autant à l'intérieur de ce petit corpus qu'à l'intérieur de l'ensemble du Code[35] reste discuté. Négativement, on peut dire que ni l'homogénéité ni la datation n'ont joué un rôle déterminant dans l'assemblage des éléments de Dt 16,18-18,22, puisqu'il s'agit d'un texte

München, 1971, pp. 450s.; A. GESTON, *Kingship in the Book of Hosea*, in *Language and Meaning. Studies in Hebrew Language and Biblical Exegesis* (OTS, 19), Leiden 1974, p. 71; A.W. JENKS, *The Elohist and North Israelite Traditions* (SBL.MS, 22), Missoula, Montana, 1977, p. 116.

28. *Beduinentum und Jahwismus* (n. 16), p. 80.

29. Cf. J. DE FRAINE, *L'aspect religieux de la royauté israélite* (n. 3), p. 143.

30. *Die Beurteilung der Anfänge des Königtums in den deuteronomistischen Abschnitten des I. Samuelbuches. Ein Beitrag zum Problem des «Deuteronomistischen Geschichtswerks»* (WMANT, 31), Neukirchen-Vluyn, 1969, p. 30; cf. F. HORST, *Das Privilegrecht Jahwes* (n. 5), pp. 110s.= *Gottes Recht*, pp. 139s.

31. Cf. B.C. BIRCH, *The Rise of the Israelite Monarchy: The Growth and Development of I Samuel 7-15* (SBL.DS, 27), Missoula, Montana, 1976, pp. 28s.; T.N.D. METTINGER, *King and Messiah* (n. 8), p. 81. Pour CLEMENTS, Jer 22,13-17 offre le parallèle le plus proche de 1 Sam 8, 11ss (*The Deuteronomistic Interpretation* [n. 21], p. 399); tandis que BEN-BARAK découvre un parallélisme étroit entre Dt 17,14ss et Jer 22,13-17 (*The Religious-Prophetic Background* [n. 9], pp. 33ss).

32. Cf. G. SEITZ, *Redaktionsg. Studien* (n. 2), pp. 234s.; A.D.H. MAYES, *Deuteronomy* (NCB), Grand Rapids, London, 1981, pp. 270ss.

33. Cf. G. SEITZ, *Redaktionsg. Studien* (n. 2), p. 92.

34. Cf. S.R. DRIVER, *A Critical and Exegetical Commentary on Deuteronomy* (ICC), Edinburgh, 1896, p. 135; A. KLOSTERMANN, *Der Pentateuch. Beiträge zu seinem Verständnis und seiner Entstehungsgeschichte. Neu Folge*, Leipzig, 1907, p. 296; S.G.E. WRIGHT, *The Book of Deuteronomy* (IB, 2), New York, Nashville, 1953, p. 315; W.L. MORAN, *Deuteronomy*, in *A New Catholic Commentary on Holy Scripture*, London, 1969, p. 269; W.H. SCHMIDT, *Einführung in das Alte Testament*, Berlin, New York 1969, p. 121.

35. Cf. S.A. KAUFMAN, *The Structure of the Deuteronomic Law*, *Maarav* 1, 1978/79, pp. 105ss.

composé. Lohfink se demande si, à partir d'une période déterminée de leur histoire, les lois sur les autorités n'appartiennent pas à un même recueil et si, à partir de ce moment là, elles ne forment pas alors un unique «Aussagensystem» pour ses lecteurs. Il en conclut que le projet du rédacteur deutéronomiste consiste à «distinguer et équilibrer les différentes fonctions d'Israël» — dans le sens d'une séparation des pouvoirs — et «à ordonner toutes les fonctions autour d'une même réalité, la torah écrite»[36]. Ces observations laissent entrevoir qu'il s'agit du dernier stade de la rédaction de Dt 17,14ss, mais une question reste ouverte, à laquelle on n'a pas prêté une attention suffisante au cours de l'histoire de la recherche: si Dt 17,14-20 est un texte composé, rédigé et élaboré à différentes époques, quel rôle ont joué chacun de ses rédactions et élaborations dans le Code deutéronomique, ainsi que dans l'ensemble du Deutéronome et dans l'histoire deutéronomiste?

2. Critique Littéraire

1. *Dt 17,14-15a*

La formule d'introduction *ky-tb' 'l-h'rṣ* (v. 14a) dispose d'un parallèle strict en Dt 26,1aα. Cette même formule, mais au pluriel, apparaît en Ex 12,25a, d'aspect deutéronomique, et dans Lv 19,23a; 23,10a; 25,2a[37]. Dans tous ces textes, sauf dans Lv 19,23, *ky-tb'(-) 'l-h'rṣ* se continue par une proposition relative, qui fait référence à la donation de la terre; en Dt 17,14a sa formulation est nettement deutéronomique[38]. Un double w-qatal (*wyršth wyšbth bh*: v. 14aβ) termine le v. 14a, comme en Dt 26,1[39].

L'encadrement générique du v. 14a se concrétise dans le v. 14b. Ici, un w-qatal (*w'mrt*) introduit le cohortatif *'śymh*, qui possède clairement une nuance volitive: un désir qui implique une permission[40]. Dans 1 Sam 8,5 se manifeste un désir similaire, mais la formulation change. Du point de

36. Cf. N. Lohfink, *Die Sicherung* (n. 12), pp. 147.154.

37. Ex 12,25a: «typiquement D»: C.H.W. Brekelmans, *Éléments deutéronomiques dans le Pentateuque*, in *Aux grands carrefours de la révélation et de l'exégèse de l'Ancien Testament*, éd. par Ch. Hauret (Recherches Bibl., 8), Louvain, 1966, p. 81; Lv 19,23a: dépendant de Dt 26,1a: A. Cholewiński, *Heiligkeitsgesetz und Deuteronomium. Eine vergleichende Studie* (AnBib, 66), Rome, 1976, p. 273. Autres parallèles dans le Pentateuque, cf. N. Lohfink, *Das Hauptgebot. Eine Untersuchung literarischer Einleitungsfragen zu Dtn 5-11* (AnBib, 20), Romae, 1963, pp. 113s.

38. *'šr yhwh 'lhyk ntn lak/l^eka*: Ex 20,12; Dt 4,40; 5,16; 7,16; 12,9; 13,13; 15,7; 16,5.18.20; 17,2(14); 18,9; (19,1); 25,15; 26,2; 27,2.3; 28,8; Cf. Dt 4,21; 15,4; 19,10; 20,16; 21,23; 24,4; 25,19; (26,1) (*nḥlh*); Dt 19,2.14; 21,1 (*lršth*). En pl. cf. Dt 1,20,.25; 2,29; 3,20 (4,1; 5,31); 11, (17).31; (12,1); Jos 1,11.15.

39. Cf. Dt 6,18; 12,29; 16,20; (17,14; 26,1); 30,5 (*wyršt[h]*); cf. Dt 4,1; 8,1; 11,8.31; 19,1; 31,3 (*wyrštm*); Gen 27,44; 45,10; Dt 8,12; 12,29; 19,1; 26,1 (*wyšbt[h]*).

40. Cf. P. Joüon, *Grammaire de l'hébreu biblique*, Rome, 1923, §114c.

vue syntactico-stylistique, le v. 14b se trouve plus proche de Dt 12,20 [41] que de 1 Sam 8,5. Cette plus grande proximité avec un texte du Code deutéronomique invite non seulement à penser à la tonalité deutéronomique de 17,14bα, mais aussi à son étroite connexion avec le v. 14a, dont nous avons déjà souligné la tendance deutéronomique. Dans la formule du v. 14bβ, au contraire, les caractères deutéronomiques se trouvent beaucoup moins marqués. Il suffit de constater que l'expression *'šr sbybty*, dépendant de *hgwym*, n'apparaît que dans la littérature de l'exil et de la période postexilique [42] (en dépendance de *h'mym*, elle paraît trois autres fois, toujours dans des textes tardifs) [43]. Il faut remarquer, en outre, que le roi d'Israël tel qu'il est souhaité par le peuple n'est pas, en réalité, «comme celui des autres nations avoisinantes», car aux v. 15ss quelques limitations inconcevables chez les autres rois de l'ancien Orient [44] sont imposées au roi d'Israel. Ces données font douter sérieusement de l'authenticité du v. 14bβ car, s'il diffère du restant du verset par son langage et sa formulation, il s'écarte aussi du contexte par sa thématique [45].

Le v. 15aα reprend certains termes du v. 14bα (cf. Dt 12,20b/20aβγ). Le verbe *śwm*, accompagné de *mlk* comme objet direct, réapparaît en 1 Sam 8,5; 10,19; 1 Rois 10,9. En Dt 17,14s et 1 Sam 10,19, il se construit avec *'l*, tandis que les deux autres textes proposent une construction en *l-* [46]. Du point de vue syntactico-stylistique, Dt 17,15a se différencie des textes de 1 Sam et 1 Rois; il est à remarquer, en outre, que sa construction (inf. abs. + yiqtol du même verbe) est fréquente dans le Deutéronome, spécialement dans le Code [47].

41. Cf. C.M. CARMICHAEL, *The Laws of Deuteronomy* (n. 13), pp. 104ss.

42. Cf. Lv 25,44; 2 Re 17,15 (= *dtr*: M. NOTH, *Überlieferungsgeschichtliche Studien. I, Die sammelnden und bearbeitenden Geschichtswerke im Alten Testament*, Halle [Saale], 1943, pp. 6.85.108; *DtrN*: W. DIETRICH, *Prophetie und Geschichte. Eine redaktionsgeschichtliche Untersuchung zum deuteronomistischen Geschichtswerk* [FRLANT, 108], Göttingen, 1972, pp. 42ss.76); Ez 5,7.7.14.15; 11,12; (36,36); Neh 5,17; 6,16.

43. Cf. Dt 6,14 (*dtr*: G. MINETTE DE TILLESSE, *Sections «tu» et sections «vous» dans le Deutéronome*, in *VT* 12, 1962, pp. 69s; tardif: F. GARCÍA LÓPEZ, *Deut., VI et la tradition-rédaction du Deutéronome*, in *RB* 85, 1978, pp. 168ss); Dt 13,8aα (*dtr*: R.P. MERENDINO, *Das deuteronomische Gesetz* [n. 6], p. 67); Jug 2,12 (*dtr*: M. NOTH, *Überlieferungsg. Studien* [n. 42], pp. 53.91; *DtrG*: W. DIETRICH, *Prophetie und Geschichte* [n. 42], pp. 89ss; T. VEIJOLA, *Das Königtum* [n. 22], p. 47).

44. Cf. M. NOTH, *Die Gesetze im Pentateuch* (n. 9), p. 30.

45. Cf. F.R. MCCURLEY (Jr.), *The Home of Deuteronomy* (n. 18), p. 300. L'expression *kl-hgwym* s'emploie dans 1 Sam 8,5.20; Ez 25,8. Selon H.J. STOEBE cette expression serait additionnelle dans 1 Sam 8,5 (*Das erste Buch Samuelis* (n. 23), p. 184, n. 13. Voir, cependant, T. VEIJOLA, *Das Königtum* (n. 22), p. 68. Nous jugeons insuffisante l'analyse que fait Veijola des termes *gwym/'mym* dans le Deutéronome; l'étude de l'expression *'šr sbybty(-)* en connexion avec *hgwym/h'mym* nous semble plus significative.

46. La construction *śwm l-* apparaît déjà dans les lois primitives du Code de l'Alliance: cf. Ex 22,24.

47. Cf. Dt 7,2; 12,2; 13,10.16; 15,8.14; 21,23; 22,1.7; 24,13.

La proposition relative (v. 15aβ) crée une tension avec le restant du verset. Le verbe *bḥr*, en référence avec le roi, s'emploie aussi dans des textes des livres de Samuel et Rois [48], mais il ne semble pas que Dt 17,15 dépende d'eux. Boecker pense que Dt 17,15aβ est une addition dtr [49], tandis que Seebass découvre dans ce texte les traces d'une tradition très ancienne et exclut la possibilité qu'il s'agisse d'un deutéronomisme [50]. En ce qui concerne sa formulation, 17,15aβ répète la formule communément employée dans le Code deutéronomique pour l'élection du sanctuaire [51], tout en se différenciant des formules utilisées dans les livres de Samuel et des Rois. Il est possible de percevoir encore au v. 15aβ l'écho d'une tradition ancienne portant sur l'élection du roi, mais sa formulation est relativement récente, car elle dépend des textes du Deutéronome signalés plus haut.

En résumé, les v. 14-15a (sauf 14bβ.15aβ) sont homogènes et — malgré les points de contact avec Samuel et Rois — constituent un témoignage clair de la tradition littéraire et du style propres au Deutéronome.

2. *Dt 17,15b*

Dt 17,15b a été l'un des passages les plus controversés, donnant lieu aux hypothèses les plus variées quant à la datation ou quant à l'identification des rois étrangers auxquels il est fait implicitement allusion dans ce verset [52]. On a souvent voulu résoudre ces questions en ayant directement recours à l'histoire, en brûlant une étape — celle de l'analyse de la critique littéraire — qui peut aider à mieux orienter la discussion.

Il existe un parallélisme clair entre le v. 15bα et le v. 15bβ: le v. 15bβ dit sous forme négative ce que le v. 15bα exprime affirmativement. Le v. 15b est délimité par les expressions *mqrb 'ḥyk ... 'ḥyk hw'*, qui l'ouvrent et le ferment par mode d'inclusion. La première expression trouve ses parallèles les plus proches dans deux textes tardifs du Deutéronome: 18,2.18a, tous deux appartenant au même groupe de lois sur les autorités [53]. L'expression *bqrb 'ḥyw* apparaît une autre fois dans l'AT,

48. Cf. 1 Sam 10,24; 16,8.9.10; 2 Sam 6,21; 16,18; 1 Re 8,16; 11,34.

49. *Die Beurteilung* (n. 30), p. 49, n. 1.

50. *bāḥar*, *ThWAT*, I, Stuttgart, 1973, c. 603.

51. Cf. Dt 12,18; 14,25; 16,7; 17,8.

52. Cf. A. DILLMANN, *Numeri, Deuteronomium und Josua*, Leipzig, 1886², p. 322; S. R. DRIVER, *Deuteronomy* (n. 34), p. 210; K. BUDDE, *Das Deuteronomium und die Reform König Josias. Ein Vortragsentwurf*, in *ZAW* 44, 1926, pp. 211ss; K.-H. BERNHARDT, *Das Problem der altorientalischen Königsideologie* (n. 25), p. 137; etc.

53. Dt 18,16-18 connaît Dt 5; 9,7ss (cf. H. JUNKER, *Deuteronomium*, Würzburg, 1952, p. 84). Sur le caractère rédactionnel, tardif, de Dt 5; 9,7ss, cf. F. GARCÍA LÓPEZ, *Analyse littéraire de Deutéronome, V-XI*, in *RB* 85, 1978, pp. 5-49. Voir aussi notre article, *Un profeta como Moisés. Estudio crítico de Dt 18,9-22*, in *Simposio Bíblico Nacional Español*, Madrid, 1984, pp. 289-308. Dt 18,2 est secondaire (df. A. BERTHOLET, *Deuteronomium*, Freiburg i.B., Leipzig und Tübingen, 1899, p. 57). Sur *m/bqrb*, cf. F. BROWN, S. R. DRIVER, C. A. BRIGGS, *A Hebrew and English Lexicon of the Old Testament*, Oxford, 1906, p. 899.

précisément dans un texte dtr, concernant l'élection du roi (cf. 1 Sam 16, 1-13)[54]. Quant à la formule *nqry 'šr l' 'ḥyk hw'* (v. 15dβ), son meilleur parallèle formel se trouve dans 1 Rois 8,41, texte tardif[55]. Finalement, l'expression *ltt 'lyk* x, d'un côté, introduit un changement par rapport aux formules précédentes (*śwm/ntn*) et, d'un autre, ressemle de près à une autre formule dtr de 1 Rois 10,9[56]. Ces observations sur le vocabulaire et les formules du v. 15b convergent vers un même point: le caractère tardif de ce demi-verset. Que le v. 15b soit une interpolation maladroitement introduite, entre les v. 15a et 16, la syntaxe même du texte le confirme. La particule *rq*, en tête d'une phrase, «add a limitation on sthg. previously expressed»[57]. Cela dit, le v. 15b suppose déjà une limitation (formulée affirmativement et négativement), ce qui donne à croire que *rq* se rattache directement à l'affirmation expresse et absolue du v. 15a et non au v. 15b, car cela reviendrait à ajouter une limitation à une autre, à limiter ce qui est limité. Un autre trait syntactico-stilistique renforce encore l'impression de se trouver en présence d'un élément ajouté: une construction comme celle du v. 15bβ (*l'* + yiqtol + *l*-inf. + x) dans 17,14-20 ne réapparaît que dans le v. 16b (pl.), dont nous allons montrer le caractère secondaire[58].

3. *Dt 17,16-20*

Il existe un certain consensus, comme nous l'avons indiqué, tant sur l'authenticité des v. 16a.17, que sur la caractère secondaire des v. 18-19[59]. Cependant, les interprétations concrètes des v. 16-17 divergent considérablement, aussi bien en ce qui concerne l'origine ou la portée du texte qu'en ce qui concerne les parallèles vétérotestamentaires auxquels on a recours.

De la série de lois apodictiques négatives qui forment l'armature de ces versets, celles de 16aα.17aα.17b se ressemblent considérablement entre elles en même temps qu'elles se différencient des autres. Rabast et Gerstenberger y ont vu le noyau primitif de la «loi royale»[60]. Quant au v. 17aβ, Gerstenberger a remarqué qu'il lui manque l'objet direct et

54. 1 Sam 16,1-13 est un passage récent (cf. H. J. STOEBE, *Das erste Buch Samuelis* [n. 23], pp. 302s.), postérieur à DtrG, peut-être DtrP (cf. T. VEIJOLA, *Das ewige Dynastie* [n. 8], p. 102, n. 156).

55. Cf. M. NOTH, *Überlieferungsg. Studien* (n. 42), pp. 102s.109; W. DIETRICH, *Prophetie und Geschichte* (n. 42), p. 74, n. 39; T. VEIJOLA, *Das Königtum* (n. 22), p. 89; E. WÜRTHWEIN, *Die Bücher der Könige, 1. Könige 1-16* (ATD, 11,1), Göttingen, 1977, pp. 95-99.

56. Cf. M. NOTH, *Könige* (BK, 9,1), Neukirchen-Vluyn, 1968, p. 226; T. VEIJOLA, *Die ewige Dynastie* (n. 8), pp. 53.131; E. WÜRTHWEIN, *Die Bücher der Könige* (n. 55), pp. 120.122.

57. Cf. F. BROWN, S. R. DRIVER, C. A. BRIGGS, *Lexicon* (n. 53), p. 956.

58. Cf. *supra*, n. 5-6.

59. Cf. *supra*, §1.1.

60. Cf. *supra*, n. 7.12.

qu'il interprète le v. 17aα[61]. Pour Horst le v. 16aβ expose la finalité du v. 16aα, de même que le v. 17aβ expose celle du v. 17aα[62]. En réalité, la finalité du v. 16aβ par rapport au v. 16aα se déduit du v. 16aγ[63]. Le v. 20aα aurait une fonction similaire par rapport au v. 17b. Par conséquent, le caractère secondaire et interprétatif des v16aβ.17aβ semble difficile à démontrer, de même que semble problématique la limitation du noyau primitif aux v. 16aα.17aα.17b.

Quant à leur référence aux parallèles de Dt 17,16a.17*, aucun n'est aussi proche que Dt 8,13. Dans ce texte, comme en 17,16-17*, le yiqtol du verbe *rbh* est répété trois fois; en outre, dans 8,13a l'objet direct coïncide avec celui de 17,17b: *ksp wzhb*[64]. À la lumière de Dt 8,13 la connexion de Dt 17,16aβγb avec le v. 16aα se révèle secondaire. Cette même impression est obtenue à partir d'autres angles. Ainsi, dans le v. 16aγ on passe du pluriel (*swsym*) au singulier (*sws*)[65]; dans le v. 16b, au contraire, on passe du singulier au pluriel. Du point de vue syntactico-stylistique, le v. 16b ressemble, d'un côté, au v. 15b (secondaire) et, d'un autre, à Dt 18,18, dont nous avons déjà signalé le caractère rédactionnel et tardif[66]. Le v. 16b est présenté comme une citation explicite, qui vient renforcer le v. 16aβγ, mais il faut remarquer que cette citation n'est pas conservée ailleurs dans l'Ancien Testament. Dans le Deutéronome, ce genre de citations apparaît généralement dans des textes secondaires[67]. La suite immédiate du v. 17b dans le texte primitif se trouve au v. 20aα[68]. La séquence des vv. 17b + 20aα coïncide en substance avec celle de Dt 8,13-14a; la seule différence significative est la présence de l'expression *m'ḥyw* (17,20aα), probablement due à l'auteur qui ajouta le v. 15b, dans le but de souligner la théologie du frère. De fait, la formule *rwm lbb* dans l'AT fait toujours référence à Yahvé[69]. Le v. 20aβ est secondaire par

61. *Wesen und Herkunft* (n. 5), p. 67, n. 2.

62. *Das Privilegrecht Jahwes* (n. 5), p. 137.

63. F. HORST exclut le v. 16aγ comme secondaire, considérant que la finalité du v. 16aα est déjà exprimée au v. 16aβ (*Das Privilegrecht Jahwes* [n. 5], p. 137).

64. Cf. F. GARCÍA LÓPEZ, *Del «Yahvista» al «Deuteronomista». Estudio crítico de Génesis 24*, in *RB* 87, 1980, p. 390, n. 118.

65. Cf. R.P. MERENDINO, *Das deuteronomische Gesetz* (n. 6), p. 180.

66. CF. F. GARCÍA LÓPEZ, *Un profeta como Moisés* (n. 53), pp. 289ss.

67. Cf. D.E. SKWERES, *Die Rückverweise im Buch Deuteronomium* (AnBib, 79) Rome, 1979, pp. 193s. Pour SEITZ (*Redaktionsg. Studien* (n. 2), p. 233), ce genre de citations est postérieur à la Collection deutéronomique, mais antérieur au deutéronomiste. Mais les textes cités par Seitz ne sont pas de la même catégorie que Dt 17,16b. N. LOHFINK voit dans ce verset une référence à Os 11,5 (*Hos. XI 5 als Bezugstext von Dtn XVII 16*, in *VT* 31, 1981, pp. 226-28).

68. Cf. *supra*, §1.1, n. 8

69. «*lblty rwm lbbw m'ḥyw* verstehen alle Ausleger vom Stolze des Königs gegen das Volk. Aber diese Fassung ist sprachlich und sachlich unrichtig. Denn dafür müsste es *lblty htnś' 'l 'ḥyw* heissen; vgl. Num. 16,3 und Ez. 29,15, da unser Ausdruck gut klassisch nur vom Verhalten eines Menschen JHWH gegenüber gebraucht ist; vgl. 8,14. Ez 31,10. Hos. 13,6. Ausserdem wäre es absurd, von einem König zu erwarten, dass er nicht durch einen

rapport au v. 20aα. La répétition de *lblty* n'est pas nécessaire et rend la phrase un peu lourde [70]; de plus, le v. 20aβ introduit un thème étranger à celui des v. 14-17.20aα. Galling a justement remarqué que le v. 20aβ est postérieur au texte primitif des v. 14-17, mais antérieur aux v. 18-19 [71]. Finalement, le v. 20b emploie une formule de bénédiction qui rappelle l'élaboration deutéronomique des chap. 4-11 [72].

4. *En résumé* de notre analyse de critique littéraire, il s'ensuit que Dt 17,14-20 a été composé par plusieurs auteurs ou rédacteurs. Au premier d'entre eux on devrait les v. 14abα.15aα.16aα.17.20aα (sans *m'ḥyw*). Etant donné leur parenté avec les textes protodeutéronomiques des chap. 6-11, nous pourrions qualifier ces versets de proto-deutéronomiques. Les v. 20aβ, d'un côté, et 15aβ.20b, de l'autre, conserveraient les traces d'une rédaction et d'une élaboration deutéronomiques postérieures. Enfin, les v. 14bβ.15b.16aβγ.18-19.20aα* (seulement *m'ḥyw*) appartiendraient à des rédactions plus tardives, particulièrement proches — si non identiques — de la littérature deutéronomiste.

3. Analyse de la Forme et du Genre

Dans ce paragraphe, nous porterons notre attention sur la forme et le genre du texte protodeutéronomique. Nous faisons abstraction des additions postérieures, puisqu'elles ne possèdent pas d'unité propre et qu'elles n'apportent pas de changement formel qualitatif au texte protodeutéronomique. Elle ajoutent uniquement quelques nuances, destinées à mettre en relief ou à compléter certaines idées, ainsi qu'à établir quelques principes généraux, auxquels le rédacteur deutéronomiste renverra postérieurement.

1. *Formules, formes et genre littéraire*

Dans l'analyse de critique littéraire nous avons signalé comment les lois apodictiques des v. 16aα.17aαb présentent quelques traits particuliers qui non seulement les rendent semblables entre elles, mais les distinguent aussi des autres formules de l'unité. Ces formules se composent de la particule négative *l'*, du yiqtol du verbe *rbh* à la troisième personne du

gewissen Stolz seine Würde gegen das von ihm beherrschte Volk zu behaupten suche» (A. B. Ehrlich, *Randglossen zur hebräischen Bibel. II. Leviticus, Numeri, Deuteronomium*, Leipzig, 1909, pp. 303s.).

70. Cf. G. Seitz, *Redaktionsg. Studien* (n. 2) p. 233.

71. Cf. *Das Königsgesetz* (n. 5), c. 136, n. 6.

72. Cf. F. García López, *Analyse littéraire de Deutéronome, V-XI*, in *RB* 84, 1977, pp. 514ss. *'rk + ymy(-)*, cf. Ex 20,12; Dt 4,26.40; 5,16.33; 6,2; 11,9; 22,7; 25,15; 30,18; 32,47; Jos 24,31; Jug 2,7; 1 Rois 3,14; Is 53,10; Prov 28,16; Qoh 8,13.

singulier, l'objet indirect de personne (= *lw*) plus le complément d'objet direct (différent dans les trois cas) [73]. L'objet indirect de la personne, qui fait référence au roi, donne à ces formules une teneur différente de celle des autres formules plus proches. Mais la présence de cet objet dans les v. 16aα.17aα.17b exige une formule préalable, autrement dit, une référence explicite au roi. Dans notre texte actuel, cette formule se rencontre dans le v. 15aα: *śwm tśym ʿlyk mlk*. Il faut donc se demander maintenant si les lois apodictiques des v. 16-17 ont existé indépendamment du contexte actuel, formant une espèce de «Königs-/Amtsspiegel» [74] ou si, au contraire, elles n'ont pas eu d'identité propre, au moins en référence directe au roi. Du point de vue formel, il serait parfaitement normal qu'une loi commençât par une formulation comme celle du v. 15aα. De fait, dans le Code deutéronomique, la loi sur la dîme a un incipit syntactico-stylistique identique: inf. abs. + futur du même verbe + complément direct (cf. 14,22ss). Il faut remarquer, cependant, que la «loi royale» du v. 15aα ne suppose pas un commencement absolu, comme celle de la dîme. Dt 17,15aα nous renvoie au v. 14bα. On pourrait penser que le v. 14 forme un cadre postérieur, mais — à en juger par Dt 12,20 et par d'autres formes de monologue que nous allons analyser par la suite — il est plus normal de considerer les v. 14bα et 15aα comme partie intégrante d'une même unité. Le v. 14bα, à son tour, présuppose le v. 14a. Par conséquent il semble difficile — pour ne pas dire impossible — de démontrer à partir de notre texte l'existence d'un «Königsspiegel» indépendant de son cadre actuel. Cette conclusion, cependant, ne signifie pas que l'auteur de 17,14ss n'ait pu se servir de matériaux préalables, qu'il aurait adapté à son propre texte. Les traits particuliers entrevus à propos des v. 16aα.17aαb inviteraient à croire qu'il en est ainsi. A l'appui de cette interprétation, on peut alléguer les trois formules de Dt 8,13; elles utilisent toutes le verbe *rbh*, au futur, comme 17,16-17*. Ce qui est dit du roi en particulier en 17,16-17* est appliqué au peuple, en général en 8,13. Étant donné que la personne du roi et son rang social sont particuliers, il est nécessaire d'adapter aussi bien quelques motifs généraux que des traits stylistiques déterminés. Quant à l'aspect formel, deux formes littéraires différentes sont combinées en Dt 17,14ss: celle de l'encadrement historique d'une loi et celle du monologue. Des diverses formules employées dans le Deutéronome pour encadrer un précepte [75], les plus proches de 17,14aα sont celles de 6,10; 7,1; 8,7; 11,29; 18,9; 26,1. Dans toutes ces formules — et seulement dans ces formules — on trouve la particule *ky* + le verbe *bwʾ* + *ʾrṣ* comme complément direct.

73. Le v. 17b place le complément d'objet direct avant la négation et le verbe.

74. Cf. K. RABAST, *Das apodiktische Recht* (n. 7), p. 11; E. GERSTENBERGER, *Wesen und Herkunft* (n. 7), p. 68, Les corrections proposées par Rabast aux formules des v. 16-17 ne sont pas admissibles (cf. K. GALLING, *Das Königsgesetz* [n. 5], p. 135, n. 5).

75. Cf. *supra*, §2.1, n. 37.

Du point de vue syntactique, ces formules — auxquelles d'autres formules s'enchaînent fréquemment — constituent la protase. Sa fonction consiste à introduire et à situer la loi (apodose) dans la perspective de l'entrée dans la terre [76]. Une vue d'ensemble de la protase et de l'apodose de ces textes nous permettra de mieux apprécier quelques points d'intérêt communs. Si nous considérons la séquence syntactico-stylistique des différents textes, aucun texte n'est aussi proche de 17,14ss que 7,1ss. Dans ces deux textes interviennent les éléments suivants:
1. formule d'entête avec *ky* + *bw'* + *'rṣ* (7,1aα; 17,14aα*);
2. proposition relative subordonnée avec *'šr* (7,1aβ; 17,14aα*);
3. série de x-qatal (7,1b-2a; 17,14aβb);
4. loi apodictique affirmative avec inf. abs. + futur du même verbe (7,2bα; 17,15aα);
5. série de lois apodoctiques négatives avec *l'*. . .*wl'* (7,2bβ-3; 17,16-17).
Si nous considérons, en revanche, la série de verbes qui se trouvent dans les textes antérieurement cités, aucun texte n'est aussi proche de 17,14ss: 1) *bw'* (8,7; 17,14); 2) *ntn* (8,10; 17,14); 3) *yšb* (8,12; 17,14); 4) *rbh* (8,13; 17,16); 5) *rbh* (8,13; 17,17); 6) *rbh* (8,13; 17,17); 7) *rwm* (8,14; 17,20). Ceci dit pour tout ce qui se réfère à la séquence dans ses grandes lignes. Mais nous ne pouvons pas laisser de côté quelques détails significatifs. Dans 17,14ss, entre la série de w-qatal et la série de lois apodictiques s'interpose un monologue, qui manque dans 7,1ss [77]. Ce changement est si significatif que quelques auteurs se sont demandé si dans 17,14ss nous avions un précepte de la loi ou seulement une permission [78]. En Dt 12,20 se présente un cas analogue. Dans les couches protodeutéronomiques de Dt 7-8 apparaît également la forme du monologue, mais comme une forme différente et indépendante de la protase ou de l'encadrement de la loi. Le schéma de base du monologue est pratiquement le même dans ces textes et dans 17,14-15a:

1. introduction au monologue au moyen du verbe *'mr* à la 2ᵉ personne du singulier: *w'mrt* (8,18; 17,14); *t'mr* (7,17);

2. le monologue proprement dit à la 1ᵉ personne du singulier (7,17aβb; 8,17b; 17,14bα);

3. réponse au monologue à la 2ᵉ personne du singulier, renvoyant directement à l'un ou l'autre des termes ou expressions du monologue (7,18ss; 8,19; 17,15a).

76. Cf. G. SEITZ, *Redaktionsg. Studien* (n. 2), pp. 95ss.

77. En outre, ce monologue a occasionné la formule du v. 15aα (point 4 du schéma), que en Dt 7,2aα est additionnel (cf. F. GARCÍA LÓPEZ, *«Un peuple consacré». Analyse critique de Deutéronome VII*, in *VT* 32, 1982, pp. 439ss).

78. N. LEIBOWITZ, s'appuyant sur les commentaires juifs classiques, en arrive à la conclusion que Dt 17,14ss est une «permission» et non une «loi». Si c'était une loi de la Torah — dit-elle — 17,15a se rattacherait directement à 17,14a (*Studies in Devarim* [*Deuteronomy*], Jerusalem, 1980, pp. 175-79).

Le contenu du monologue est différent dans chaque cas, bien qu'il s'agisse toujours d'un désir intime qui affleure dans le monologue. Dans 8,17 il s'agit du sentiment d'orgueil. Etroitement associé à ce dernier apparaît la formule *wrm lbbk* (8,14a), par laquelle est mise en relief la suffisance du peuple. En 17,20a réapparaît cette même formule, bien que sa relation avec le monologue ne soit pas aussi directe ni immédiate. Tandis que dans 8,14ss aussi bien la formule signalée que le monologue se réfèrent directement au peuple, en 17,14ss le monologue est placée dans la bouche du peuple et la formule *rwm lbbw* dans celle du roi. Il est curieux de remarquer comment en Os 13,6 cette même formule se trouve dans un contexte qui coïncide, en partie, avec celui de Dt 8 et, en partie, est identique à celui de Dt 17. En Os 13,1-11 le peuple et le roi se donnent rendez-vous, spécialement dans le monologue par lequel le peuple exprime son désir d'avoir un roi.

Si les ressemblances stylistiques et formelles entre Dt 17,14-20 et 7,1-6*.17-21; 8,7-18* invitent à penser à un même auteur pour tous ces textes, les différences signalées exigent quelques précisions. Dans les textes de Dt 7-8, cités plus haut, il faut distinguer un texte primitif et une élaboration protodeutéronomique [79]. Le texte primitif à l'origine eut une existence propre, indépendante de l'élaboration ultérieure. En Dt 17,14-20* il n'est pas possible de séparer un texte primitif d'une élaboration postérieure, sans mutiler gravement le premier. Si les formules des v. 16aα.17aαb invitent à penser à un texte primitif probablement indépendant pendant quelques temps, ces mêmes formules ne peuvent être séparées de leur contexte immédiat, comme nous l'avons vu au début de cette même section. Par conséquent, il n'est guère possible de distinguer en Dt 17,14-20* une couche primitive et une relecture postérieure: on y trouve une seule couche primitive, œuvre d'un auteur qui a pu se servir de quelques matériaux antérieurs. Ce dernier, à en juger par les données que nous possédons, serait à identifier avec l'auteur qui a élaboré les unités primites de Dt 6-11 [80]. Ces unités, bien que primitivement indépendantes, ont toutes reçu ultérieurement la forme d'une loi prêchée. Klostermann a fait remarquer avec justesse que le Deutéronome en même temps que «loi», est «commentaire» de lois antérieures qui sont présentées comme des enseignements oraux [81]. Von Rad, pour qui le Deutéronome plus qu'une loi divine, est une prédication adressée au peuple sur la loi divine, s'est prononcé dans le même sens [82].

79. Cf. F. GARCÍA LÓPEZ, *Deut., VI et la tradition-rédaction du Deutéronome*, in *RB* 85, 1978, pp. 163ss; Id., *Yahwé, fuente última de vida: análisis de Dt 8*, in *Bib* 62, 1981, pp. 30ss.

80. Cf. F. GARCÍA LÓPEZ, *loc. cit.*, n. 79; voir aussi, *En los umbrales de la tierra prometida. Análisis de Dt 9.1-7; 10.12-11.17*, in *Escritos de Biblia y Oriente*, éd. par R. Aguirre y F. García López, Salamanca 1981, pp. 38ss.

81. Cf. A. KLOSTERMANN, *Der Pentateuch* (n. 34), p. 347.

82. Cf. G. VON RAD, *Deuteronomium-Studien* (FRLANT, N. F., 40 = 58), Göttingen, 1947 = *Gesammelte Studien zum Alten Testament II* (ThB, 48), München, 1973, pp. 111s.

Les données signalées à propos de Dt 17,14-20 plaident en faveur de ce double caractère, à la fois oral et rédactionnel, de la «loi royale».

2. *Situation socio-religieuse, horizon et contenu*

Pour cerner la situation socio-religieuse du texte primitif de Dt 17,14-20, il faut le replacer dans le contexte des strates protodeutéronomiques des chap. 6-11. Les observations du paragraphe antérieur ont permis d'établir une plate-forme plus ample sur laquelle s'appuiera par la suite l'analyse de Dt 17,14ss; les chap. 6-11 nous aideront, sans aucun doute, à situer la «loi royale» et à mieux en comprendre la portée.

Dans notre étude des couches protodeutéronomiques des chap. 6-11, nous sommes arrivés à la conclusion que l'auteur de l'élaboration, le prédicateur, ne fait pas de la rhétorique pure, mais qu'il tient compte d'une situation de fond réelle, d'un *Sitz im Leben* précis. Cela ne signifie pas qu'il n'a pas le regard tendu vers un idéal, mais qu'il veut y pervenir à partir de la situation concrète que vit le peuple auquel sa parole s'adresse. Dans ce passage, nous avons qualifié ce peuple de «communauté bien installée» dans la terre de Canaan [83]. Dt 17,14-20 correspond également à une situation de richesse et de bien-être. Le verbe *rbh*, répété trois fois, dans la couche protodeutéronomique de 17,14-20, indique l'abondance. Si l'on met en garde contre cette dernière, c'est parce qu'elle est un fait et qu'elle est conçue comme un danger du point de vue religieux. Les exhortations pressantes doivent être comprises dans ce sens; dans le cas contraire, nous aurions ici de la rhétorique pure. Mais Dt 17,14ss se comprendrait mal s'il n'était précédé d'une pratique. L'écho de cette pratique, qui a été en vigueur dans le royaume du Nord, dont notre texte est originaire, est conservée, en partie, dans Osée et dans 1 Sam 8-12. L'abondance de l'or et de l'argent, à laquelle se réfère 17,17, est signe de prospérité économique; elle correspond à une époque économiquement florissante. Le règne de Jéroboam II est une de ces périodes économiquement prospères. Pendant ce règne ont été écrits quelques-uns des textes d'Amos et d'Osée, proches du Dt 17,14ss (cf. Am 8,4ss; 6,4ss; Os 2,10). Dans Os 2,10 le verbe *rbh* est employé avec *ksp* et *zhb*, comme dans Dt 17,17. Ce sont les seuls textes de l'AT, avec Dt 8,13, dans lesquels l'abondance de l'or et de l'argent est exprimée de cette façon. Ces observations à propos de Dt 17,14ss coïncident avec celles que nous avons exposées sur les textes protodeutéronomiques des chap. 6-11 du Deutéronome [84]. De même que ces textes, Dt 17,14-20 reflète une

83. Cf. F. GARCÍA LÓPEZ, *Deut., VI et la tradition-rédaction du Deutéronome*, in *RB* 86, 1979, pp. 76ss.

84. Cf.F. GARCÍA LÓPEZ, *loc. cit.* (n. 83), pp. 60ss.76-80; J.L. MAYS (*Hosea. A Commentary*, London, 1978, p. 41) et F.I. ANDERSEN, D.N. FREEDMAN, (*Hosea* [AB.24], Garden City, New York, 1980, pp. 242s.) datent Os 2,10 au temps de Jéroboám II. Tous deux soulignent la connexion de ce texte avec la littérature deutéronomique.

expérience particulière du peuple et du roi, sans que pour cela elle ne se réduise exclusivement à un seul moment historique. Dans un cas comme dans l'autre, l'auteur des textes protodeutéronomiques s'élève au-dessus des cas particuliers pour passer au plan des principes plus généraux, valables pour d'autres situations. En ne précisant pas la situation dans laquelle se trouvent le peuple et le roi, il est sous-entendu que le prédicateur donne à ses exhortations pressantes un caractère général, qu'elles sont applicables non seulement à un roi mais à plusieurs. D'un autre côté, il faut tenir compte du fait que les restrictions sur la richesse ou l'abondance de biens matériels sont en lien avec d'autres richesses, les richesses spirituelles. On peut ainsi discerner le but de l'exhortation à ne pas accroître les quantités d'or et d'argent: que le roi ne se révolte pas contre Dieu (cf. 17,17b.20a*). Dans les strates protodeutéronomiques, les biens matériels sont présentés comme un don de Dieu (cf. 8,10; 17,14; voir aussi Os 2,8), mais qui comporte un danger: en oublier le donateur, Yahvé [85]. Une fois admise cette explication pour les v. 17b et 20aα*, nous aurions une clé d'interprétation pour le v. 17a. Il importe de signaler qu'entre les v. 17aβ et 20aα* il existe une relation formelle incontestable: *śwr lbbw* // *rwm lbbw*. On peut même pousser le parallélisme de 17b + 20aα avec celui de 17aα + 17aβ: ne pas augmenter les quantités d'or et d'argent, pour que le cœur du roi ne se soulève pas contre Yahvé, et ne pas accroître le nombre de femmes, pour que son cœur ne s'écarte pas de Yahvé [86]. C'est dans ce sens qu'est utilisé l'expression *śwr lbb(-)* dans Jer 17,5 et dans Ez 6,9. Au fond, c'est la même idée que celle de Dt 8,14ss et d'Os 13,6. Dans ce texte d'Osée on parle, en outre, de suivre les baals; c'est une façon claire d'exprimer l'éloignement du cœur. Plus encore, dans Os 4,18 et 7,14 cet éloignement est exprimé au moyen du même verbe *śwr*. Le v. 16a pourrait s'expliquer de cette même façon. Dans Os 14,4 [87] est établie une relation entre les chevaux et les faux dieux. La puissance militaire, que vise en dernier ressort tant Os 14 que Dt 17,16a, suppose un risque pour la foi yahviste [88]. De même que l'or, l'argent et les femmes peuvent éloigner le cœur du roi de Yahvé, de même la confiance et l'assurance dans ces propres forces militaires (dans ses chars et ses chevaux) peuvent le porter à oublier Yahvé [89]. C'est le même danger contre lequel on veut prévenir Israël dans Dt 8,17-18 (cf. Am 6,13). Par conséquent, la série de mises en garde humaines, sociales, politiques, etc., du Deutéronome à propos du roi visent un but religieux

85. Cf. *supra*, §2.3., n. 72.

86. Cf. M. DELCOR, *Le statut du roi d'après le Rouleau du Temple*, in *Henoch* 3, 1981, p. 50; voir 1 Re 11,2-4.

87. Cf. Is 2,6-8; Miq 5,9-13; *supra*, §1.3.3.

88. Cf. A BERTHOLET, *Deuteronomium* (n. 53), pp. 55s; A. DILLMANN, *Deuteronomium* (n. 52), p. 323; A. CAQUOT, *Remarques sur la «loi royale»* (n. 3), pp. 27s.; G. SEITZ, *Redaktionsg. Studien* (n. 2), pp. 234s.

89. Cf. W. BRUEGGEMANN, *The Land*, Philadelphia, 1977, p. 76.

supérieur. Ceci est une constante dans la parénèse primitive des chap. 6-11 du Deutéronome. En se fondant sur l'histoire et sur la situation sociale d'Israël, l'auteur des textes protodeutéronomiques signale quelques dangers (en Dt 17,14ss, Yahvé ne s'oppose pas à l'institution de la monarchie, comme en 1 Sam 8) et donne quelques normes. En définitive, c'est un programme de vie qui est en train de s'élaborer, en partie idéal — comme tout bon programme — mais bien fondé sur l'expérience concrète et réelle que le peuple a de la monarchie.

4. Composition et Rédaction

1. *Texte protodeutéronomique*

L'un des problèmes majeurs majeurs qui se pose lors de l'étude de la loi vétérotestamentaire est celui de la structuration des Codes[90]. Au sujet deutéronomique, les exégètes ont proposé diverses solutions. Horst le divise en deux parties: «Privilegrecht Jahwes» (c. 12-18) et «Zivilrecht» (c. 19-25)[91]. Cette division, reprise par d'autres spécialistes en la matière[92], gagne en précision si l'on reconnaît dans 16,18-18,22 une petite collection intermédiaire sur les autorités, partiellement indépendante des collections antérieures[93]. En vertu de cela, Dt 17,14-20 ferait partie de cette collection, placée justement au milieu des lois qui règlent les relations de l'homme avec Dieu (c. 12-16) et celles qui régissent les relations humaines et sociales (c. 19-25).

Le Deutéronome ébauche une constitution pour Israël, dans laquelle il assigne aux autorités (juges, rois, prêtres et prophètes) un lieu et une fonction déterminés[94]. L'auteur de la première édition du Deutéronome, auquel on doit l'élaboration protodeutéronomique de 17,14-20[95], fait preuve d'un grand intérêt pour les autorités, à en juger par la place qu'il leur accorde dans le Code — place beaucoup plus grande que celle qui leur est faite dans les autres Codes de l'AT —, et d'une façon spéciale pour le roi et pour le prophète, vu le soin avec lequel il élabore ces lois[96]. A cet auteur l'on doit beaucoup d'autres textes, sutout celui de l'introduction primitive et de la conclusion du recueil législatif (chap. 6-11 et 26). Ceci met en relief une donnée importante pour l'analyse de la composition-rédaction: l'auteur de l'élaboration protodeutéronomique n'a pas seulement recueilli et agencé avec soin les matériaux qui allaient composer son édition, mais il les a

90. Cf. S.A. Kaufman, *The Structure of the Deuteronomic Law* (n. 35), p. 105.
91. *Das Privilegrecht Jahwes* (n. 5), p. 3 = *Gottes Recht*, pp. 20s.
92. Cf. R.P. Merendino, *Das deuteronomistische Gesetz*, (n. 6), pp. 404s.
83. Cf. *supra*, §1.4, n. 33.
94. Cf. G. von Rad, *Theologie des Alten Testaments*, I, München 1969, p. 112.
95. Cf. *supra*, §3.1.
96. Sur Dt 18,9-22, cf. *loc. cit. supra*, n. 53.

aussi retouchés et élaborés, en y ajoutant un certain nombre d'éléments personnels, particulièrement au début, au milieu et à la fin du Code (c. 6-11; 17-18; 26).

Lors de l'analyse de Dt 6-11, nous avons vu comment l'élaboration protodeutéronomique de ces chapitres s'est servie du monologue comme forme préférée et de la terre comme thème favori[97]. La forme du monologue, comme nous l'avons déjà vu, réapparaît avec des caractéristiques similaires dans le texte protodeutéronomique des chap. 17 et 18[98]. Quant au thème de la terre, on doit admettre qu'il est très fréquent dans la Deutéronome, mais il faut reconnaître aussi que dans leur formulation, les textes de l'élaboration protodeutéronomique présentent quelques traits particuliers par rapport à tous les autres textes du Deutéronome. En effet, les formules avec *ky* + *bw'* + *'rṣ*, qui introduisent le thème de la terre en même temps qu'elles encadrent un précepte, n'apparaissent que dans les textes protodeutéronomiques. Moyennant ce genre de formules un lien solide s'établit entre deux piliers fondamentaux du livre du Deutéronome: la loi et la terre[99]. L'importance de ce lien est accentuée par la disposition structurelle même de ces formules, puisqu'elles ont été placées dans l'introduction primitive (cf. 6,10; 7,1; 8,7), au centre (17,14; 18,9) et dans la conclusion (26,1) du Code[100]. De cette façon, elles servent d'armature non seulement aux textes de l'élaboration protodeutéronomique, mais aussi à tout le Code, à la première édition du Deutéronome. Les textes protodeutéronomiques de l'introduction nous laissent au seuil de la terre (cf. 11,10-12), qui est la plate-forme à partir de laquelle doit s'accomplir la loi (c. 12ss). Placées au centre du Code deutéronomique, les formules de 17,14 et de 18,9 servent de pont entre l'introduction et la conclusion, de même qu'elles unissent — dans la perspective de la terre — les lois de la première et de la seconde partie du Code. Ainsi, la terre devient l'espace vital pour l'accomplissement de la loi[101]. Ces formules ont la fonction de points de suture; grace à elles la relation des éléments qui composent l'édition protodeutéronomique ressort davantage, de même qu'est obtenue une certaine homogénéité de l'ensemble. L'édition primitive du Code deutéronomique a été préparée pour des destinataires particuliers: pour une communauté bien installée dans la terre de Canaan, à une époque de richesse et de prospérité, ce qui comportait quelques dangers d'ordre religieux. Parce qu'elle est la terre dans laquelle le peuple doit garder les lois et compte

97. Cf. F. GARCÍA LÓPEZ, *Deut., VI et la tradition-rédaction du Deutéronome* (n. 83), pp. 59ss.

98. Cf. *supra*, §3.

99. Cf. *supra*, §3.2.

100. Voir aussi Dt 11,29, addition tardive, qui dépend des textes protodeutéronomiques; cf. *supra*, §3.1.

101. Cf. J.G. PLÖGER, *Literarkritische, formgeschichtliche und stilkritische Untersuchungen zum Deuteronomium* (BBB, 26), Bonn, 1967, p. 91.

tenu des dangers signalés, l'accent est mis tout particulièrement sur l'accomplissement de ces lois. De là le ton d'exhortation et le cachet parénétique de cette première édition, ton et cachet auxquels l'élaboration protodeutéronomique a contribué de façon décisive, spécialement dans les textes de l'introduction, du centre — parmi eux 17,14-20* — et de la conclusion.

2. *Textes tardifs*

Après la chute de Samarie, les textes protodeutéronomiques du royaume du Nord passèrent au royaume du Sud. À Jérusalem on procéda à une nouvelle rédaction du Code deutéronomique, probablement à l'époque d'Ezéchias. Quelques textes et formules sur les commandements en général sont caractéristiques de cette réédition [102]. On conserve un reflet de cette rédaction vraisemblablement dans 17,20aβ: *lblty św̌r mn-hmṣwh ymym wśm'wl* [103]. Cette édition a reçu une élaboration postérieure au temps de Josias. Les bénédictions et malédictions relatives à l'accomplissement des commandements en seraient spécifiques. La renaissance religieuse nationale du royaume de Juda et l'approfondissement de l'idée de l'élection divine contribuèrent à un certain optimisme, qui se reflète en partie dans ces mêmes bénédictions [104]. En Dt 17,15aβ. 20b, textes relatifs à l'élection divine du roi et à la bénédiction-perpétuation pendant son règne, on peut encore percevoir l'écho de cette élaboration.

Les dernières retouches de 17,14-20 se firent après la destruction de Jérusalem, le regard tourné vers la communauté qui avait enduré l'exil. La nouvelle situation dans laquelle vivait la communauté juive après la chute de Jérusalem réclamait une adaptation des textes sacrés; ce fut concrètement celle de l'édition deutéronomique. Quelque retouches de la «loi royale» se comprennent certainement mieux dans la perspective de l'exil. Ainsi, l'idée que le roi doit être «un frère et non étranger» (cf. 17,15b) se comprend difficilement à l'époque monarchique [104]. Pedersen trouve «absurde» une telle idée pendant la monarchie [106]. A partir de l'exil, par contre, les étrangers ont joué un rôle plus important et décisif

102. Cf. F. GARCÍA LÓPEZ, *Deut., VI et la tradition-rédaction du Deutéronome* (n. 83), pp. 81-86.

103. Cf. *supra*, §2.3 + n. 71.

104. Cf. F. GARCÍA LÓPEZ, *Analyse littéraire de Deutéronome, V-XI* (n. 72), pp. 513-521; ID., *«Un peuple consacré»* (n. 77), pp. 461-62.

105. A. DILLMANN pense que cette exigence était «fast selbstverständlich, u. Verfehlungen dagegen sind nicht berichtet» (*Deuteronomium* [n. 52], p. 322); P. BUIS écrit à ce propos: «Cette exigence va de soi dans une monarchie du type national et elle fut toujours observée en Israël» (*Le Deutéronome*, Paris, 1969, p. 278).

106. *Israel. Its Life and Culture, III-IV*, London, Copenhagen, 1940, pp. 96.586.

dans la vie d'Israël[107]. De là l'intérêt d'éclaircir les relations religieuses et sociales avec eux. Ainsi, dans 1 Rois 8,41-43, formellement apparenté à Dt 17,15b[108], on constate la préoccupation de déterminer les règles à observer lorsque des étrangers désirent rendre un culte au temple de Jérusalem. D'un autre côté, en adaptant l'ancienne loi sur le roi à la nouvelle situation créée avec l'exil on tient compte des autres nations (cf. 17,14bβ). Le problème du roi était une préoccupation certaine, à l'époque exilique et postexilique. Plus encore, dans quelques textes exiliques du livre de Jérémie apparaissent les mêmes préoccupations qu'en Dt 17,15b; concrètement on laisse entendre en Jer 30,21 que le roi doit être un Israélite, signe évident qu'il s'agissait d'un problème qui inquiétait le peuple pendant l'exil[109]. En cette période de l'histoire d'Israël, les espérances du peuple quant à son avenir essayent de trouver des points de référence dans les institutions du passé. Pour cette raison même, se développe l'idéologie royale, qui au fur et à mesure que le temps passe tend à se spiritualiser de plus en plus. Après la chute de Jérusalem, la fonction royale est idéalisée[110]. Dt 17,18s doit être interprété en ce sens: la tâche fondamentale du roi sonsistera à copier la torah et à la mettre en pratique. La conception d'un ri familier de la torah coïncide avec l'exigence selon laquelle le roi ne sera pas un étranger[111]. La torah joue un rôle clé dans la théologie deutéronomiste. C'est sur leur fidélité à la torah de Moïse que les rois sont jugés (cf. 1 Rois 2,3; 2 Rois 10,31; 14,6; 21,8; 23,24s.)[112]. Ces observations nous mènent à une conclusion au niveau rédactionnel: si le texte protodeutéronomique de 17,14-20 joué un rôle important dans la première édition du code du Deutéronome, ce même texte, retouché, tient aussi une place décisive dans l'œuvre de l'«historien deutéronomiste». Le «Königsspiegel» de la première édition, complété et adapté, se présente comme un nouveau modèle vers lequel on tourne son regard à l'heure de juger les rois d'Israël et de Juda.

107. La théologie sur le «frère-étranger» appartient, certainement, à cette époque (cf. L. PERLITT, *«Ein einzig Volk von Brüdern». Zur deuteronomischen Herkunft der biblischen Bezeichnung «Bruder»*, in *Kirche. Fs für G. Bornkamm*, éd. par D. Lührmann, G. Strecker, Tübingen, 1980, pp. 40s. R. MARTIN-ACHARD, écrit sur les étrangers: «Sowohl *nēkār* als auch *nokrī* scheinen, obwohl schon vorexilisch belegt, erst in nachexilischer Zeit eine grössere Bedeutung bekommen zu haben...» (*nēkār*, in *Theologisches Handwörterbuch zum Alten Textament*, II, éd. par E. Jenni, C. Westermann, München, Zürich, 1976, c. 67,

108. Cf. *supra*, S2.2.

109. Cf. R.P. CARROLL, *From Chaos to Covenant. Uses of Prophecy in the Book of Jeremiah*, London 1981, pp. 207s.; E.W. NICHOLSON, *Preaching to the Exiles. A Study of the Prose Tradition in the Book of Jeremiah*, Oxford, 1970, pp. 87ss; B. ODED, *Judah and the Exile*, in *Israelite and Judaean History*, éd. par J.H. Hayes, J.M. Miller, London, 1977, pp. 481ss; voir aussi Jer 30,8s.; Os 3,5; Ez 34,23s.; 37,24s.

110. Cf. J. PEDERSEN, *Israel. Its Life and Culture*, *loc. cit.* n. 106.

111. Cf. A. PHILLIPS, *Deuteronomy* (CBC), Cambridge, 1973, p. 121; W. BRUEGGEMANN, *The Land* (n. 89), p. 76.

112. Cf. G. LIEDKE/C. PETERSEN, *tōrā*, in *THAT*, II (n. 107), c. 1041.

5. Récapitulation et Conclusion

L'analyse de la *critique littéraire* (§2) nous a conduit à distinguuer en Dt 17,14-20, un texte primitif et quelques additions tardives. Comme le montre sa *forme littéraire* (§3), le texte primitif est dû à l'auteur de l'élaboration protodeutéronomique des chap. 6-11. Une fois cette donnée admise, nous disposons déjà d'un point d'appui précieux — plus ample et solide que celui de beaucoup d'autres *recherches* (§1) — pour déterminer le *Sitz im Leben* et la datation de la «loi royale». Le texte proto-deutéronomique de 17,14-20, de même que celui des chap. 6-11, a vu le jour dans le royaume du Nord, avant la chute de Samarie, et s'inscrit dans le même courant/tradition que le prophète Osée. Les additions tardives, en majorité postérieures à la chute de Jérusalem, ont beaucoup de points de contact avec d'autres textes de la littérature exilique et postexilique, spécialement de l'œuvre deutéronomiste. L'étude de la *composition et de la rédaction (*§4) a mis en relief l'importance de 17,14-20 non seulement dans la première édition du code deutéronomique (§4.1.5), mais aussi dans l'œuvre rédactionnelle deutéronomiste (4.2.). En conclusion, Dt 17,14-20 conserve les lignes maîtresses de deux programmes ou modèles de rois: le premier, composé pendant la monarchie, s'appuie sur l'expérience concrète et tend à s'élever au-dessus d'elle pour proposer un idéal; le second, postérieur à la monarchie, provient d'une conception idéale de la royauté, à la lumière de laquelle sont jugés certains rois du passé.

Universidad Pontificia
Compañía, 1
Salamanca, España

Félix García López

DEUTERONOMIUM 22,13-21

VOM PROZESSPROTOKOLL ZUM KASUISTISCHEN GESETZ

A. Die Kriterien, deren sich die atl. Literarkritik bedient — z.B. «Doppelungen und Wiederholungen», «Spannungen und Widersprüche», stilistische Unähnlichkeit von Textbestandteilen [1] —, sind weitgehend bei der Arbeit an *erzählerischen* Texten gewonnen und entwickelt worden. Das gilt sowohl für die klassische Pentateuchkritik als auch für jüngere literarkritische Versuche im Bereich des dt Gesetzbuchs (hauptsächlich in den Arbeiten von H. Peucker, R. P. Merendino, G. Nebeling, G. Seitz, H. D. Preuß) [2]. Gerade deren stark divergierende Ergebnisse bestätigen, daß vorgängig zu literarkritischer Arbeit eine von N. Lohfink formulierte Frage unverzichtbar ist: «Was fordert die 'Einheit' eines Textes? Gibt es vielleicht je nach Gattung und Sitz im Leben eines Textes verschiedene Maße der geforderten Einheit?» [3] Falls dies zutrifft, wäre damit auch die Reihenfolge der Methodenschritte in Frage gestellt, die W. Richter als für die Arbeit am Einzeltext obligatorisch erklärt hat [4]. Denn damit müßte, gegen Richter, eine gattungskritische Frage bereits *vor* der Literarkritik entschieden werden.

Im folgenden werden solche Fragen nicht methodentheoretisch, sondern anhand eines Einzeltextes erörtert: *Dtn 22,13-21*. Mit welchen Inkonsistenzen ist in einem solchen Gesetzestext zu rechnen? Was folgt daraus für die Kriteriologie einer Literarkritik im Bereich von atl. Gesetzestexten? Einer Antwort auf diese Fragen kommt man ein Stück näher, wenn man unseren Text mit außerbiblischen, konkret mit altmesopotamischen 'Parallelen' vergleicht.

B. Welche Probleme hatten die Literarkritiker der letzten 25 Jahre mit unserem Text? Ganz kurz seien die Argumente zusammengestellt, die *zugunsten der Nicht-Einheitlichkeit* des Textes 22,13-21 vorgebracht wurden [5]:

1. Vgl. W. RICHTER, *Exegese als Literaturwissenschaft*, Göttingen, 1971, bes. S. 49-62.

2. H. PEUCKER, *Deuteronomium Kapitel 12-26, form- und rechtsgeschichtlich untersucht*, Diss. theol. (unveröffentlicht), Greifswald, 1962; R. P. MERENDINO, *Das deuteronomische Gesetz* (*BBB*, 31), Bonn, 1969; G. NEBELING, *Die Schichten des deuteronomischen Gesetzeskorpus*, Diss. theol. (unveröffentlicht), Münster i.W., 1970; G. SEITZ, *Redaktionsgeschichtliche Studien zum Deuteronomium* (*BWANT*, 93), Stuttgart-Berlin-Köln-Mainz, 1971; H.D. PREUSS, *Deuteronomium* (*EdF*, 164), Darmstadt, 1982, bes. S. 44-61 (eher programmatisch).

3. So N. LOHFINK, *Die Landverheißung als Eid* (*SBS*, 28), Stuttgart, 1967, S. 29; als «wichtig» zitiert von W. RICHTER, *Exegese* (oben Anm. 1), S. 45 Anm. 48.

4. Vgl. W. RICHTER, *Exegese* (oben Anm. 1), bes. S. 33.44-46.72.131.177.

5. Im folgenden werden die wichtigsten Argumente folgender Autoren kurz zusammengefaßt: H. PEUCKER, *Deuteronomium* (oben Anm. 2), S. 107; R.P. MERENDINO,

1. *Anschaulichkeit und direkte Rede*, wie in 22,13-19 (bes. 22,14b.16b-17a) gegeben, gehören nicht in ein kasuistisches Gesetz, sind also Zeichen von nachträglicher Überarbeitung.
2. Am Anfang stand die «einfache Form»; *Wiederholungen* (vor allem zwischen v. 13f. und v. 16f.) deuten auf Überarbeitung hin.
3. *Motivsätze*, zumal solche mit Nennung von «Israel» (in unserem Text die vv. 19aβγ und 21aβγ), sind überlieferungsgeschichtlich jünger, also auch textgeschichtlich sekundär.
4. *Zwischen 22,13-19 und 22,20f.* bestehen formale und inhaltliche *Spannungen*:
   — *Formal*: 22,13-19 (lebendig-anschaulich) und 22,20f. (juristisch knapp) sind stilistisch heterogen.
   — *Inhaltlich*:
   Die 'Einleitung' der Tatbestandsdefinition (vv. 13-14a) ist nicht 'neutral' für beide Fälle, sondern nur für den 'Fall' 22,13-19 formuliert. Das erkennt man am besten daran, daß der Gesetzgeber ('Einleitung' vv. 13-14a) und die eine Partei, der Vater der verleumdeten Ehefrau (vv. 16b-17a), die gleiche Sprache sprechen. Die in den beiden Fällen vorgesehenen Sanktionen können nicht gleichzeitig geltendes Recht gewesen sein, da dies dem in Dtn 19,19 feierlich proklamierten *Talionsprinzip für falsche Anschuldigung* widersprechen würde.
5. Ein weiteres Anzeichen für Zusammengesetztheit des Textes (auf das in der Literatur aber kaum hingewiesen wurde) ist das Problem des *Beginns der Rechtsfolgebestimmung*: mit v. 15 oder mit v. 18? Oder liegt eine 'doppelte Rechtsfolgebestimmung' vor? Eindeutige syntaktische Kriterien fehlen.

Bereits von diesen Argumenten her scheint mir einiges dafür zu sprechen, daß 22,13-19 und 22,20f. mindestens nicht im gleichen Arbeitsgang entstanden sind. Die Frage bleibt zunächst noch offen — ebenso die Entscheidung bezüglich der anderen soeben aufgezählten Kriterien.

C. Dtn 22,13-21 ist ein 'Doppelgesetz', also eine Kombination von 'Fall' und 'Gegenfall'. Lassen sich Inkonsistenzen, wie sie dieser Text aufweist, vielleicht auch in anderen 'Doppelgesetzen' beobachten? Zum Vergleich ziehe ich zwei altmesopotamische, inhaltlich und formal verwandte Gesetzestexte — Codex Hammurapi (CH) §142/43 und

Gesetz (oben Anm. 2), S. 257-260; G. NEBELING, *Schichten* (oben Anm. 2), S. 189-194; G. SEITZ, *Studien* (oben Anm. 2), S. 119.131f.136f.; H.D. PREUSS, *Deuteronomium* (oben Anm. 2), S. 56f.; A. PHILLIPS, *Deuteronomy* (*The Cambridge Bible Commentary on the New English Bible*), Cambridge, 1973, S. 148; A. ROFÉ, *Family and Sex Laws in Deuteronomy and the Book of the Covenant*, in *BetM* 22(68) (1976/77), S. 19-36 (*hebr.*).155f. (english summary), bes. S. 23-29.155; A.D.H. MAYES, *Deuteronomy* (*New Century Bible Commentary*), London, [2]1981, S. 309-311.

Mittelassyrische Gesetze (MAG) A §55/56 — heran. Die Texte lauten in Übersetzung[6]:

— *CH § 142/43*:

§142: Wenn eine Frau gegen ihren Ehemann Abneigung bekommt und sagt: «Du sollst nicht mit mir verkehren», so soll ihre Angelegenheit von ihrer Behörde überprüft werden; wenn sie unbescholten ist und keine Schuld trägt, ihr Ehemann dagegen aushäusig ist und sie schwer vernachlässigt, so ist diese Frau schuldlos, sie darf ihre Mitgift nehmen und weggehen zum Hause ihres Vaters.

§143: Wenn sie nicht unbescholten ist, aushäusig ist, ihren Haushalt verschlampt und ihren Ehemann vernachlässigt, so soll man diese Frau ins Wasser werfen.

— *MAG A § 55/56*:

§55: [Wenn ein Bürger] die junge [Tochter] eines (anderen) Bürgers, [die im Haus] ihres Vaters wohnt, deren [...] nicht *beschmutzt ist*, die nicht mit Gewalt entjungfert ist, die nicht verheiratet ist, und gegen deren Vaterhaus er keinen Klageanspruch hat — (wenn) dieser Bürger inmitten der Stadt oder auf dem Felde, in der Nacht auf einem Platze, in einem Festhause oder bei einem Stadtfest, (wenn) dieser Bürger mit Gewalt die junge Frau ergreift und sie vergewaltigt, so darf der Vater der jungen Frau die Gattin des Beischläfers der jungen Frau nehmen und sie der Notzucht preisgeben; er braucht sie ihrem Gatten nicht zurückzugeben, er darf sie behalten. Der Vater darf seine beschlafene Tochter ihrem Beischläfer *zur* Ehe geben. Wenn er keine Gattin hat, so soll der Beischläfer das Dreifache des Kaufpreises für eine junge Frau geben. Ihr Beischläfer soll sie heiraten und darf sie nicht ... Wenn der Vater das nicht will, so kann er den dreifachen Geldwert für eine junge Frau annehmen und seine Tochter, wem er will, geben.

§56: Wenn eine junge Frau sich aus eigenem Antrieb einem Bürger hingibt, so soll der Bürger schwören, und man darf seiner Gattin nicht nahetreten. Das Dreifache des Kaufpreises für eine junge Frau soll der Beischläfer geben. Der Vater kann seine Tochter, wie er will, behandeln.

Ein Vergleich von Dtn 22,13-21 mit den beiden Texten ergibt folgendes:

— Nur in CH ist das 'Doppelgesetz' kompositionell konsequent und (im Sinne moderner Gesetzesformulierungstechnik) logisch stringent gestaltet: Auf die für beide Fälle geltende Tatbestandsdefinition (§142: «Wenn eine Frau ... — überprüft werden») folgt zuerst der 'Fall' (§142: «Wenn sie unbescholten ist» usw.), dann — streng parallel aufgebaut — der 'Gegenfall' (§143).

— Dagegen liegen in MAG A §55/56 Inkonsistenzen von gleicher Art wie im dt Text vor:

6. Übersetzung von R. BORGER, in O. KAISER (Hrsg.), *Texte aus der Umwelt des Alten Testaments*, I/1, Gütersloh, 1982, S. 60 bzw. 91f. Vgl. die englische Übersetzung von Th. J. MEEK, in J. B. PRITCHARD (Hrsg.), *ANET*³, S. 172 bzw. 185. Vgl. ferner die Standardausgaben und -kommentare von G. R. DRIVER/J. C. MILES: *The Babylonian Laws*, Bd. 1, Oxford, 1952; Bd. 2, Oxford, 1955; *The Assyrian Laws*, Oxford, 1935. Zu MAG vgl. außerdem Übersetzung und Kommentar von G. CARDASCIA, *Les lois assyriennes* (*LAPO*, 2), Paris, 1969.

Die Tatbestandsdefinition von §55 ist nur für diesen Text, nicht aber auch für §56 konstruiert. In §56 wechselt jedenfalls das Subjekt; ob die Beschreibung der 'Eigenschaften' der «Jungfrau» (*batultu*), mit der die Tatbestandsdefinition von §55 eingeleitet wird, auch in §56 noch gilt, ist unklar. §55 ist eindeutig nur auf die Schuld des Mannes, §56 nur auf die Schuld der «Jungfrau» angelegt — mit der für die altorientalischen Gesetze laut J.J. Finkelstein typischen Schwarz-Weiß-Malerei [7].

Auch stilistisch ist §56 sehr viel knapper als der umständlich wirkende §55.

Von der Redaktionstechnik bei altorientalischen Doppelgesetzen her sind also manche Inkonsistenzen in Dtn 22,13-21 mindestens nicht ausgeschlossen. Auch inhaltlich spannungsreiche und stilistisch unausgeglichene Texte konnten damals geltendes Recht sein.

D. Die Gestalt von Texten wie Dtn 22,13-21 und MAG A §55/56 läßt sich möglicherweise von ihrer Entstehung her erklären. G. Liedke und A. Rofé nehmen an, daß die kasuistischen Gesetze der atl. Rechtskorpora ganz oder teilweise auf *gerichtliche Aufzeichnungen* zurückgehen; nach A. Rofé ist dies auch bei Dtn 22,13-19 der Fall [8]. Diese Hypothese scheint mir hier in der Tat angebracht. Sie wird vor allem durch einen Vergleich mit dem sumerischsprachigen Prozeßprotokoll *3 N-T 403+340* bestätigt. Der Text lautet übersetzt [9]:

2' L., Sohn des N.,
hat die K.(?), Sklavin des K.,
gepackt,
5' in den {Kaufladen (Vorbau des Hauses)} gebracht
und sie entjungfert. Nachdem er sie entjungfert hatte,
ist K., ihr Eigentümer,
die Ratsversammlung von Nippur
angegangen, ist (vor ihr) erschienen und
10' «L. hat meine Sklavin gepackt,
sie in den {Kaufladen} gebracht
und sie entjungfert», hat er erklärt.
L. ist erschienen und

7. Vgl. J.J. FINKELSTEIN, *Sex Offenses in Sumerian Laws*, in *JAOS* 86 (1966), S. 355-372, hier S. 364 (mit Anm. 33) und 367f.; W.W. HALLO, *The Slandered Bride*, in R.D. BIGGS, J.A. BRINKMAN (Hrsg.), *Studies presented to A.L. Oppenheim*, Chicago, 1964, S. 95-105, hier S. 99 Anm. 35.

8. G. LIEDKE, *Gestalt und Bezeichnung alttestamentlicher Rechtssätze* (*WMANT*, 39), Neukirchen-Vluyn, 1971, S. 53-59; A. ROFÉ, *Family and Sex Laws* (oben Anm. 5), S. 31f., vgl. S. 155.

9. Die Übersetzung lehnt sich an diejenige der neuesten Textbearbeitungen an: J.J. FINKELSTEIN, *Sex Offenses* (oben Anm. 7), S. 359f.; vgl. DERS., in *JAOS* 90 (1970), S. 245f.; B. LANDSBERGER, *Jungfräulichkeit: Ein Beitrag zum Thema 'Beilager und Eheschließung'*, in J.A. ANKUM u.a. (Hrsg.), *Symbolae iuridicae et historicae Martino David dedicatae*, Leiden, 1968, Bd. 2, S. 41-105, hier S. 47-49.

«Seine Sklavin kenne ich nicht,
15' ich habe sie nicht entjungfert»,
hat er erklärt.
Seine (des K.) Zeugen
sind aufgetreten
und haben es [sc. die Klage des K.] bewiesen.
20' Die Ratsversammlung von Nippur
ist erschienen und
«Weil er die Sklavin ohne (Kenntnis/Einverständnis) (ihres) Eigentümers
entjungfert hat» — so erklärten sie —,
«muß L. 1/2 Mine Silber
25' dem K., ihrem Eigentümer, darwägen.»
Die Ratsversammlung
hat dieses Urteil gefällt.

Diese aus Nippur stammende altbabylonische Urkunde (ca. 19. Jh. v. Chr.) gehört zu einer Gattung, die man als «'literary' legal decisions» bzw. als «model court records» bezeichnet hat [10]. Der Text hat mit Dtn 22,13-19 die äußeren Merkmale der 'Ausführlichkeit' und des Gebrauchs der direkten Rede gemeinsam. Dtn 22,13-19 läßt sich zu einem mit dem sumerischen Text strukturähnlichen Prozeßprotokoll 'zurücktransformieren'. Ich nehme daher an, daß ein solches altisraelitisches Dokument die Vorlage des dt Textes gebildet hat.

Ein Vergleich der beiden Texte ergibt im Hinblick auf die oben (unter B) zusammengestellten Kriterien für eine literarkritische Scheidung:

1. Anschauliche Schilderung und direkte Rede sind von einer solchen Vorlage her erklärbar, zumal der 'gesprochene Stil' und die hochemotionale rhetorische Sprache der beiden Redestücke in 22,13-19 [11].
2. In beiden Texten wird der Tatbestand *dreimal* (und zwar variierend) *wiederholt*:
   — gleich zu Beginn aus der Sicht des Gerichts (3 N-T 403+340 Z. 2'-6') bzw. des Gesetzgebers (Dtn 22,13-14a): beide Texte setzen also mit dem *Ergebnis* der gerichtlichen Untersuchung ein;
   — aus der Sicht einer der beiden Parteien in direkter Rede (Z. 10'-12' // 22,16b-17a);
   — erweitert (im sum. Text) oder verallgemeinert (im Dtn) in der Urteilsbegründung (Z. 22'-23' // 22,19aβγ).

   Daraus ergibt sich, daß Wiederholungen wie in unserem dt Text nicht einfach deshalb, weil es sich um Wiederholungen handelt, literarkritisch beseitigt werden dürfen.

10. «'literary' legal decisions»: so S. GREENGUS, *A Textbook Case of Adultery in Ancient Mesopotamia*, in *HUCA* 40/41 (1969/70), S. 33-44; «model court records»: so M. T. ROTH, *The Slave and the Scoundrel*, in *JAOS* 103 (1983), S. 275-282, bes. S. 279 und 282 unter (3).

11. Direkte Rede kommt auch sonst in altorientalischen Gesetzen vor: Listen von Belegen bei A. ROFÉ, *Family and Sex Laws* (oben Anm. 5), S. 20 Anm. 2; F. LANGLAMET, in *RB* 77 (1970), S. 589.

3. Die Urteilsbegründung im sum. Text (Z. 22'-23') zeigt, daß der *Motivsatz* 22,19aβγ bereits zur Vorlage von 22,13-19, also zum Prozeßprotokoll, gehört haben kann. In einer solchen Begründung konnte durchaus von einer «Jungfrau *Israels*» die Rede sein.
4. Aus einer dem sum. Modell entsprechenden Vorlage ergibt sich, daß die 'Einleitung' vv. 13-14a nur im Hinblick auf den bis v. 19 reichenden 'Fall' formuliert ist, nicht für einen alternativen Prozeßausgang. Die Spannungen zwischen 22,13-19 und 22,20f. erklären sich ohne weiteres, wenn der erste Teil von einer solchen Vorlage abhängig, der zweite Teil dagegen nachträglicher Zusatz des 'Gesetzgebers' ist, der das Prozeßprotokoll zu einem kasuistischen Gesetz umformte. Er fügte vermutlich auch die seiner Meinung nach bei einem Kapitaldeliktsfall notwendige *bi'arta*-Formel an (v. 21b, ebenso vv. 22b.24b) [12].
5. Das Problem des nicht klaren *Beginns der Rechtsfolgebestimmung* beantwortet sich ebenfalls aus der angenommen Vorlage: vv. 15-17 (Handeln und Reden der Eltern) stammen aus der Schilderung des Verfahrenshergangs im Protokoll, vv. 18-19 aus der Urteilsformulierung.

E. Die hier vorgelegten Ergebnisse [13] hätten nicht nur aufgrund des Vergleichs mit altorientalischen Rechtstexten erzielt werden können. Manches, vielleicht das meiste, setzt einfach eine genauere, vor allem 'stilbewußtere' Analyse der Texte voraus, als sie von manchen Literarkritikern praktiziert worden ist. Sie dürften gelegentlich der Versuchung erlegen sein, den Gegenstand ihrer Forschungen selbst herzustellen, wie F. Langlamet zu Recht bemerkt hat: «Le critique littéraire ne risque-t-il pas plus d'une fois de créer son objet ...?» [14] Wenn der rechtshistorische Vergleich eine gattungs- und stilbewußte Analyse der atl. Texte bestätigt, hat er seinen Zweck erfüllt [15].

Scheideggstraße 45
CH-8002 Zürich

Clemens LOCHER

12. Das oben signalisierte Problem der Nicht-Anwendung des Talionsprinzips löst sich, wenn man die altorientalischen Gesetze über falsche Anschuldigung miteinander vergleicht; darauf ist hier nicht näher einzugehen.

13. Ausführlichere Begründung in meiner demnächst erscheinenden Monographie: *Die Ehre einer Frau in Israel* (*OBO*; Freiburg/Schweiz-Göttingen, 1985).

14. F. LANGLAMET, in *RB* 77 (1970), S. 587.

15. Ich danke N. Lohfink für seine weiterführende Kritik an einer ersten Fassung dieses Beitrags.

THE STORY ABOUT THE BUILDING OF AN ALTAR ON MOUNT EBAL

The History of its Composition and the Question of the Centralization of the Cult

My subject is the clarification of the stages of the composition of two Deuteronomic passages: Deut 27,2-8 and Josh 8,30-32. The discussion of tis question touches upon the basic Deuteronomic ideology — the centralization of the cult.

Let us begin the discussion with Josh 8 after the Israelites cross the Jordan they encamp at Gilgal (Josh 4,20), and from there they set out to battle against Jericho and Ai. The victory over Ai is followed abruptly with 'az «At that time» (8,30) by the account of the building of an altar on Mount Ebal and the ceremony of the blessing and curse between Mount Gerezim and Mount Ebal in the presence of «the whole congregation of Israel» (8,35). However, further on, in the account of the covenant with the Gibeonites, we learn that, in effect, the Israelites are still at Gilgal (9,6). It is thus clear that the ceremony described in Josh. 8,30-35 is out of context and was interpolated into its present place artifically[1]. Moreover, it is not conceivable that after the conquest of Ai all the people would have assembled in the heart of the enemy territory, 30 km north of Ai, in order to hold a solemn ceremony. If we remove the passage 8,30-9,2[2] we are left with a smooth continuous narrative: the conquest of Jericho and Ai immediately followed by: «And when the inhabitants of Gibeon heard what Joshua had done to Jericho and Ai» (9,3). It seems that the author of our passage looked for a suitable place to include it in the text by using the neutral conjunction *'az* (8,30)[3].

Let us now turn to the building of the altar by Joshua, Josh 8,30-32. Whoever reads the passage cannot fail to understand that Joshua wrote «a copy of the law of Moses» (v. 32) on the stones of the altar[4]. This is written explicitly in the Peshitta: «And he wrote there on these stones of the altar»[5]. However, was the original intention that «a copy of the

1. A. DILLMANN, *Die Bücher Numeri, Deuteronomium und Joshua*, Leipzig, 1886, p. 477-478; C. STEUERNAGEL, *Deuteronomium und Joshua*, Göttingen, 1900, p. 147.

2. In the codex Vaticanus of the Septuagint, our passage follows chap. 9,1-2, a short passage which is also out of context.

3. Cf. the use of *'az* in 1 Chr 15,2; 16,7, and also Josh 22,1 and 1 Kgs 8,1,12.

4. STEUERNAGEL, p. 97, 184; M. NOTH, *Das Buch Joshua*, ²Tübingen, 1953, p. 52; M. WEINFELD, *Deuteronomy and the Deuteronomic School*, Oxford, 1972, p. 166; A. ROFÉ, *Introduction to Deuteronomy*, Jerusalem, 1977, p. 23 (Hebrew).

5. In the *Jerusalem Talmud*, Soṭa 7,5, Rabbi Jose says: «On the stones of the altar they were inscribed».

law of Moses» was written on the stones from which the altar was constructed? In order to answer this question we must turn to the source on which this passage is based. This source is Deut 27,4-8:

Joshua 8	*Deuteronomy 27*
אז .30	והיה בעברכם את־הירדן .4
	תקימי את־האבנים האלה
	אשר אנכי מצוה אתכם היום
	בהר עיבל
	ושדת אותם בשידד
יבנה יהושע מזבח לה' אלהי ישראל	ובנית שם מזבח לה' אלהיך .5
בהר עיבל	
כאשר צוה משה עבד־ה' את־בני ישראל .31	
ככתוב בספר תורת משה	
מזבח אבנים שלמות	מזבח אבנים
אשר־·לא־הניף עליהן ברזל	לא־תניף עליהם ברזל
	אבנים שלמות .6
	תבנה את־מזבח ה' אלהיך
ויעלו עליו עלות לה'	והעלית עליו עולת לה' אלהיך
ויזבחו שלמים	וזבחת שלמים .7
	ואכלת שם
	ושמחת לפני ה' אלהיך
ויכתב־שם על־האבנים .32	וכתבת על־האבנים .8
את משנה תות משה	את־כל־דברי התורה הזאת
	באר היטב
אשר כתב לפני בני ישראל	

Chapter 27 in Deuteronomy, like our passage in Joshua, is out of place and separates the connected passages: 26,16-19 and 28,1 [6]. This chapter itself is not of one piece [7], but here we will only discuss the passage relevant to our subject, 27,2-8. The first thing that strikes one in our passage is the existence of two commands to set up great stones, plaster them over and inscribe on them: [8]

	Deuteronomy 27
והיה בעברכם את־הירדן .4	והיה ביום אשר תעברו את־הירדן .2
	אל־הארץ אשר־ה׳ אלהיך נתן לך
תקימו את־האבנים האלה	והקמת לך אבנים גדלות
אשר אנכי מצוה אתכם היום	
בהר עיבל	
ושדת אותם בשיד	ושדת אתם בשיד

6. S. R. DRIVER, *Deuteronomy*, Edinburgh, 1902, ³1960, p. 294-295. It is probable that 27,9-10 were also included in the original context: M. NOTH, *Das System der Zwölf Stämme Israels*, Darmstadt, (1930) 1966, p. 144; DRIVER, p. 297-298.

7. DILLMANN, p. 364; DRIVER, p. 294-295, 297-300; STEUERNAGEL, p. 96-99. It appears to us that the original nucleus of the chapter included vv. 4.8.11-13. The other components of this chapter were added later.

8. Examples of writing on plaster have been found at Deir Alla and Kuntillet Ajrud, both inside buildings. Writing on plaster in the open would not survive due to weathering.

8. וכתבת על־האבנים	3. וכתבת עליהן
את־כל־דברי התורה הזאת באר היטב	את־כל־דברי התורה הזאת
	בעברך
	למען אשר תבא אל־הארץ
	אשר־ה' אלהיך נתן לך
	ארץ זבת חלב ודבש
	כאשר דבר ה' אלהי־אבתיך לך

A comparison of the two versions clarifies the construction of the second version: between the command to set up the stones and the command, to plaster them over and inscribe on them, is interpolated the law of the altar [9] which is a Deuteronomic adaptation of the law of the altar in Ex 20,24-25 [10]:

Exodus 20	*Deuteronomy 27*
25. ואם־מזבח אבנים תעשה־לי	5. ובנית שם מזבח לה' אלהיך
	מזבח אבנים
לא־תבנה אתהן גזית	
פי חרבך הנפת עליה ותחללה	לא־תניף עליהם ברזל
	6. אבנים שלמות תבנה את־מזבח ה' אלהיך
24. ... וזבחת עליו את־עלתיך	והעלית עליו עולת לה' אלהיך
ואת־שלמיך ...	7. וזבחת שלמים
	ואכלת שם
	ושמחת לפני ה' אלהיך

The purpose of interpolating a new passage within an existing passage is to «defend» the new material [11]. The aim of this interpolation was to compare the ceremony of Mount Sinai (Ex 24,4-5) with that of Mount Ebal, as the covenant of Sinai (Ex 19-24) is parallel to the covenant of Shechem (Josh. 24). The interpolation of the altar law led to the separation of the command to set up the stones (v. 4) from the command to inscribe on them (v. 8). Thus the composite text was formed, beginning with the command to set up stones, followed by the command to build an altar, offer whole-offerings and slaughter shared-offerings, and concluding by going back to the stones with the command to inscribe

9. DILLMANN, p. 364; DRIVER, p. 295; STEUERNAGEL, p. 96, 184.

10. G. HÖLSCHER, in *ZAW* XL (1922), p. 218. As for single points:
v. 5 YHWH ʾlhyk — it appear tens of times in deuteronomy, but is also found in other books of the Bible.
v. 6 — brzl — the name of the material rather than the tool, cf. Deut. 19,5; 2 Kgs 6,5-6.
ʾbnym šlmwt — cf. Deut. 25,15; 1 Kgs 6,7; Prof 11,1, and see WEINFELD, p. 363, no. 21a.
mzbḥ Y. ʾ. — cf. Deut. 12,27 (twice).
whʿlyt ʿlyw ʿwlt — cf. Deut. 12,13-14.
v. 7 — wʾklt šm — cf. Deut 12,7; 14,23,26; 16,7.
wśmḥt lpny Y. ʾ. — cf. Deut 12,18; 16,11; 27,7.
The scribe apparently unwillingly retained the term *šlmym*, a term which is alien to Deuteronomic language which employs the word *zbḥ*, *zbḥym*, cf. DILLMANN, p. 366; DRIVER, p. 297.

11. Another example of this kind of addition in the book of Deuteronomy is to be found in Deut. 17,18-19, which separates v. 17 from v. 20. The original connection of these two verses is evident by comparison with Deut. 8,13-14, cf. STEUERNAGEL, 67.

on them all the words of the Law. It was this new version that lay in front of the Deuteronomic scribe who wrote the passage in the book of Joshua describing how Joshua fulfilled the command of the Torah (Josh 8,30-32) [12]. However, how did it come about that instead of the command instructing the inscribing of the Law on plastered stones specially for this purpose, according to the scribe of the Joshua passage, Joshua wrote the Law on the stones of the altar? The scribe who adopted the Deuteronomy command did not report the setting up of the stones because in the book of Joshua which lay in front of him, the setting up of the stones by Joshua (although not the inscribing on them) was already accounted, at Gilgal (4,20)! [13] The scribe of Josh 8,30-35 intended only to relate the story of the building of the altar and the holding of the ceremony, but in adapting the material of the book of Deuteronomy, he did not realize that v. 8 does not relate to v. 5-7 but goes back to v. 4. He therefore also included this verse, thinking that it was the continuation of v. 7[14], as was understood by the translator of the Peshitta too[15]. Hence the inscribing on the stones of the altar[16].

Now we come to discuss the first command to set up the stones, plaster them and inscribe on them: *Deut 27,2-3//4.8*.

This is a more developed text than the other one[17], with more characteristic Deuteronomic phraseology and has uses of language indicating its late date [18]. Why was this version written? The comparison

12. B. W. BACON, *The Triple Tradition of the Exodus*, Hartford, 1894, p. 263; NOTH, p. 51.

13. Cf. STEUERNAGEL, p. 96-97; HÖLSCHER, p. 218; NOTH, *System*, p. 148; E. NIELSEN, *Shechem*, Copenhagen, 1955, p. 52-53; WEINFELD, p. 164-165. In a discussion with Rabbi Yose, Rabbi Yudah claims the identity of these two sets of stones: Soṭa 7,5. And in the *Mishnah* (Soṭa 7,5), we read: «And afterwords they brought the stones, built the altar, plastered it with plaster and inscribed upon it all the words of the Law ..., and they took the stones and came and lodged in their place (Gilgal)».

14. NIELSEN, p. 78.

15. As the author of the addition in 1 Kgs 18,31-32a understood Ex 24,4.

16. It is of interest to note that the Samaritan scribe who brought Deut 27,2-7 after the Ten Commandments of the Massoretic version, Ex 20, overcame the strange construction of Deut 27,4-8 by the omission of v. 8 and of «and you shall plaster them with plaster» in v. 4. He thus separated the command to set up the stones from that to build the altar.

17. DILLMANN, p. 364; BACON, p. 263; NIELSEN, p. 63; J. L'HOUR, in *RB* 69 (1962), p. 176; ROFÉ, p. 24-25. It would apparently be possible to think that the sentence: «These stones which I command you this day» (v. 4) must relate to the stones mentioned in vv. 2-3, but the following examples show that both the demonstrative pronoun and the subordinate sentence can relate to what follows them: Deut 4,2; 8,1; 11,22b; 28,2,15; 31,1.

18. STEUERNAGEL, p. 97; HÖLSCHER, p. 218, n. 2; ROFÉ, 24.
vv.2-3 — *h'rṣ 'šr Y. '. ntn lk* — (3aβ.3b are missing in Codex Lucianus) cf. Deut 4,1.40; 9,23; 11,17,31; 12,9; 15,4,7; 16,20; 17,14; 18,9; 19,10,14; 21,1,23; 26,1; 28,8,11.
v. 3 — *'rṣ zbt ḥlb wdbš* — cf. Deut 6,3; 11,9; 26,9,15; 31,20. *k'šr dbr Y.'.'btyk lk* — cf. Deut. 1,21; 6,3.
The conjunction *lm'n 'šr*, v. 3, instead of *lm'n* is uncommon and apparently late. In the

between the two versions shows that there are two striking differences between the earlier and later versions. Firstly, in the late version the stones are to be set up on the day of the crossing of the Jordan prior to entering into the land (vv. 2a,3b) [19].

Secondly, the geographical designation «on Mount Ebal» is omitted, and thus a new command was created instructing the setting up of stones next to the Jordan. The scribe who wrote this version wanted to remove the command to set up the stones on Mount Ebal [20], and he therefore relied on the story about the setting up of the stones by Joshua after crossing the Jordan by anticipating the command to the event [21]. He placed his new version, as was sometimes done, before the old version [22].

According to the above description the following order ensues in the literary development of our passage:

1. Deut 27,*4.8*
2. Deut 27,4.*5-7*.8
3. Josh 8,*30-32*
4. Deut 27,*2-3*.4-8

This solution, however, leaves us with two difficulties: 1. Why did not the scribe adapt also the command to build an altar? 2. According to this reconstruction one must assume that the later scribe was a better philologist than his colleaque who wrote the passage in Josh 8, because he realized that v. 8 was the continuation of v. 4. It is possible to suggest another order, whereby the adaptation preceded the interpolation of the command to build the altar:

1. Deut 27,*4.8*
2. Deut 27,*2-3*.4.8
3. Deut 27,4.*5-7*.8
4. Josh 8,*30-32*

However, this assumption is also problematic. If the scribe of the Joshua passage had in front of him also the text of Deut 27,2-3, would he have made the mistake of connecting v. 8 to v. 7 and not v. 4? There is an even stronger argument against this order: is it likely that after a scribe from the Deuteronomic school wrote a new version in order to replace the older version of the carrying out of the ceremony on mount Ebal, a

Pentateuch it is found in Gen 18,19 (in a Deuteronomic addition); Deut 20,18 (also in an addition); Lev. 17,5; Num 17,5. Its late date is apparent from the comparison of Jer. 42,6: *lm'n 'šr yyṭb lnw* with Gen 12,13: *lm'n yyṭb ly*. It is noteworthy that the time designation *whyh bywm 'šr*, v. 2, is a hapaxlegomenon.

19. L'HOUR, p. 174; DRIVER, p. 295-296.

20. ROFÉ, p. 24.

21. STEUERNAGEL, p. 96-97. *'bnym gdlwt* can also relate to stones which can be carried, as can be learnt from Jer. 43,9.

22. ROFÉ, p. 16-17.

scribe from the same school would write that Joshua held the ceremony in that very place?

It is possible to propose a third order and to understand the two versions in Deut 27,2-3 and 4.8 as two parallel texts[23], which were combined at a later stage after vv. 4-8 were adapted by the scribe of the Joshua passage:

1. Deut 27,*4.8* 1. Deut 27,*2-3*
2. Deut 27,4.*5-7*.8
(3. Josh 8,30-32)
4. Deut. 27,*2-8*

However, does the textual similarity between the two commands permit us to assume that there were two independent commands? I do not know which is the most convincing order. However, whatever the order of the phases in the composition of the passages under discussion is, one thing appears clear to me, namely that our study has shown that Josh 8,30-32 (and indeed all the passage vv. 30-35) reflects a *late* stage in the Deuteronomic work. This raises the central issue — why was the need felt to compose such a late composition accounting the building of the altar on Mount Ebal when at the very heart of the Deuteronomic ideology lay the idea of the centralization of the cult in Jerusalem: «In Jerusalem, which I have chosen out of all the tribes of Israel will I put my name for ever» (2 Kgs 21,7)?[24] Is the explanation that we are dealing with pre-Deuteronomic material[25], or with a reflection of the period prior to the conquest of Jerusalem by David[26] sufficient to explain this phenomenon?[27]

11, Arnon St.
63455 Tel-Aviv
Israel

Moshe ANBAR

23. ROFÉ, p. 24.

24. Deut 12,4,11,14,18,21,26 etc. and cf. DRIVER, p. 297-298; NOTH, *System*, pp. 71, 141-143, 149.

25. F. M. CROSS, *Canaanite Myth and Hebrew Epic*, Cambridge, Massachusetts, 1973, p. 84, n. 15; ROFÉ, p. 28-29.

26. NOTH, *System*, p. 141-142.

27. Further investigation (cf. *Beth Miqra* 100, in press) has led me to the conclusion that Josh 8,30-35 was composed in a late period, when striving for the centralization of the cult was already superfluous, and the central issue in community life was the demand to fulfill *all* the words of the Torah.

THE COVENANT IN THE LAND OF MOAB (DT 28,69-30,20)

HISTORICO-LITERARY, COMPARATIVE, AND FORMCRITICAL CONSIDERATIONS

In choosing «The Covenant in the Land of Moab» as the subject of my address to the Louvain Colloquium, I wanted to pay a tribute to the Catholic scholars, whose contributions to the study of this pericope, and to the study of the Covenant-idea as well, have been paramount, and yet not always recognized as it deserved; I have in mind the names of Paul Karge (in spite of his apologetics), Hubert Junker, Paul Van Imschoot, D. J. McCarthy and Norbert Lohfink.

It is my opinion that the text of «The Covenant in the Land of Moab» begins in Dt 28,69 with the inscription «These are the Words of the Covenant which the Lord commanded Moses to make with the Israelites, in addition to the Covenant which He made with them at Horeb» [1], and the conclusion is to be found in Dt 30,20. Let me just recall a few points that substantiate this view: (a) The other covenant, the covenant at Horeb, is the one that starts in Dt 4,44 and goes on until 28,68; it consists of the Ten Commandments, *ʿăšeret haddĕḇārīm*, which all the people heard at Horeb (5,2-4.6-19), and the Precept, *hammiṣwāh*, the Laws and the Judgements, *haḥuqqīm wĕhammišpāṭīm*, which Moses alone heard at Horeb and later reported to Israel (5,27-28; 6,1.4ff.) [2]. This all extends as far as the end of Dt 26, and is then concluded by the Blessing and the Curse of Dt 28. (b) The reading of the Samaritan Pentateuch at 28,69, sustained by one Greek manuscript and the Ethiopic translation as well, «*And* these are the words of the Covenant etc.», *wĕʾēlleh diḇrēy habbĕrīt*..., favors with its diction the opinion that this verse is not the conclusion to what came before, but an inscription to what follows. (c) And dealing with introductory formulae, let us recall that the same form of inscription and then an opening running: «And Moses called all Israel saying to them» occurs in 4,44-5,1 and in 28,69-29,1. In both cases the inscription and the opening have been obliterated by the Massorah as well as by the Christian division into chapters. (d) Indeed, a covenant is made in our pericope. 29,8 runs: «Observe faithfully all the terms of this

1. To my knowledge, the first to have clearly stated this view was Don YIṢḤĀQ ABRAVANEL, in the introduction to his *Commentary on Deuteronomy* (Hebrew), Reprinted: Jerusalem, 1964, p. vii.

2. The last two verses of Dt 5, namely vv. 29-30 in Letteris edition, appear to be a late homiletic expansion; cf. A. ROFÉ, *Deuteronomy 5:28-6:1 — Composition and Text in the Light of Deuteronomic Style and Three* Tefillin *from Qumran (4 Q 128,129,137)*, in *Tarbiz* 51 (1981/2), 177-184 (Hebrew); Reprinted in: *Introduction to Deuteronomy — Further Chapters*, Jerusalem, 1982.

covenant etc.», and vv. 11-12 run: «to enter into the covenant of the Lord your God etc.». (e) And this covenant — I believe — ends with the end of ch. 30 where one finds, as usual in treaties and covenants, blessings and curses and witnesses to all. Yet, not everything in Dt 29-30 belongs to the Covenant of the Land of Moab; our task, in the first place, is to identify and detach the extraneous sections.

Let us start with Dt 30,1-10. I would describe this remarkable passage as a majestic fugue on the theme of *šūḇ*. Seven times does this verb appear here (vv. 1.2.3.3.8.9.10), and with *šĕḇūt* (restoration) at v. 3 it makes eight. Different meanings are alternating each other: revolve in the heart (*wahăšēḇōtā 'el lĕḇāḇekā*), return to God, which is repent (*wĕšāḇtā 'ad YHWH 'ĕlōheykā*), the restoration of Israel by the Lord (*wĕšāb YHWH 'ĕlōheykā 'et šĕḇūtĕkā*) and the reversal of previous actions: *wĕšāḇ wĕqibbeṣkā* — God who scattered Israel reverses His action and gathers them; *wĕ'attāh tāšūḇ wĕšāma'tā* — Israel who disobeyed God reverses to obedience [3]. God returns to delight in Israel (*yāšūḇ YHWH lāśūś 'ăleykā*), Israel returns to the obedience of God (*kī tāšūḇ 'el YHWH 'elōheykā*). All is change, inversion of the course of history and restoration of the happy past. The passage does not merely tell it; it expresses it with its special choice of words.

I will not try to tell how my forefathers, men of faith, who day per day expected redemption and the return to Sion, read this passage; what must they have felt every year when they chanted it from the Torah, during the days of repentence, on the eve of the New Year! What I can tell is the feeling of a great Jewish interpreter, Don Yiṣḥāq Abravanel, who knew very well, by personal experience, what uprooting, exile and dispersion meant. This is the comment of Abravanel [4]:

> This passage is still due to happen, because its promises were not yet fulfilled, neither in the first nor in the second Temple; this one is our consolation and hope, this is the overall healing to all our miseries.

Thus far, if we consider the meaning of the passage to its first audience of exiles and to further generations of later exiles. But what about the relation of this passage to its context? Here we have a problem. Indeed, Dt 29,27 speaks about uprooting and dispersion and Dt 30,1-10 — about gathering and return, but the diction of this passage clearly demonstrates that it is not a following to Dt 29, but to Dt 28. First hints to this effect were already made by August Dillmann and Alfred Bertholet in their commentaries to Deuteronomy [5]. Here is some evidence:

3. This meaning of reversing an action, doing the opposite of before — as in II Kings 24,11 — was rightly recognized by Prof. Holladay in his dissertation 25 years ago; cf. W. L. HOLLADAY, *The Root Šubh in the Old Testament*, Leiden, 1958, pp. 68-70.

4. Cf. Supra, note 1, ad locum.

5. A. DILLMANN, *Numeri, Deuteronomium und Josua* (KEHAT[2]), Leipzig, 1886; A. BERTHOLET, *Deuteronomium, erklärt* (KHAT), Leipzig etc., 1899.

(a) blessing and curse are not mentioned in ch. 29, which mentions only a curse, but in ch. 28 where we have blessings and curses;

(b) «to obey the Lord» (30,2.8.10), literally «to hearken to the voice of the Lord» — it obtains in 28,1.15.45. As against it ch. 29 has a distinct expression: «whose heart turns aside from the Lord» (v. 17);

(c) 30,3: «He will gather you from all the peoples where the Lord your God has scattered you there» corresponds to 28,64: «the Lord will scatter you in all the people». As against it 29,27 speaks differently about uprooting from the soil and throwing away to another land.

(d) 30,9 «The Lord your God will grant you abundance in all your undertakings, in the issue of your womb, the offspring of your cattle, and the produce of your soil» — this catches on 28,11 which has a very similar diction.

(e) Again in 30,9: «The Lord your God will return to delight in your well-being» — this corresponds to 28,63: «As the Lord delighted etc., so He will delight etc.»

Only 30,7: «The Lord your God will inflict all those curses upon your enemies and foes who persecuted you» — connects with ch. 29, specifically with v. 20 which mentions the curse of the covenant (*'ālōt habbĕrīt*). This, however, strengthens our case, because already August Dillmann, followed by Carl Steuernagel, Alfred Bertholet and George Adam Smith, in their commentaries a.l. [6], noted that v. 7 interrupts the sequence between v. 6 and v. 8: «The Lord will circumcise your heart... and you will reverse and obey...». I have no doubt that 30,7 should be considered a late interpolation into this passage.

Thus, in my opinion, it becomes evident that 30,1-10 are the continuation of ch. 28, or in other words this majestic fugue of repentence, restoration and return is the conclusion of the blessings and the curses. What is more: it is the conclusion of the great covenant of Horeb which constitutes the main body of the Book of Deuteronomy. This passage does not belong to the «Covenant of the Land of Moab»; it was transferred here by a scribe who wanted the consolation to follow all punishment, even the one mentioned in 29,21-27.

Turning now to ch. 29, we realize at once that the coherence of this chapter is even more troubled. Let us start with v. 13 where it is said that a covenant has been made and it includes those present as well as the absentees. The latter should not be understood as future generations, but as members of the community who, for some reason, did not participate in the ceremony [7]. Then, at v. 17, the possibility is mentioned that somebody is there, a single *'īš* at first, whose heart turn away from the

6. Cf. supra, n. 5, and further: C. STEUERNAGEL, *Das Deuteronomium, übersetzt und erklärt*² (GHAT), Göttingen, 1923; G.A. SMITH, *The Book of Deuteronomy* (CB), Cambridge, 1918.

7. S.D. LUZZATTO, *Il Deuteronomio*, Padova, 1876 (op. post.).

Lord — such a person is defined as a poisonous root: *šōreš pōreh rō'š wĕla'anāh.*

Now, this individual has some inner thoughts (v. 18: *bilbābō* — which proves all the more that he is a single person), and the thought is: «I will be safe, even though I follow my wilful heart» (*šālōm yihyeh lī kī bišrīrūt libbī 'ēlek*). Here comes a very difficult expression — *lĕma'an sĕpōt hārāwāh 'et haṣṣĕmē'āh* — a real crux for interpreters! Its meaning should be construed in accordance with the next verses: at v. 19 — «The Lord will not forgive him»; at v. 20: «The Lord will single him out». So, that individual expected to be forgiven and saved by the covering of the whole people, and this expectation was expressed with the words «*lĕma'an sĕpōt hārāwāh 'et haṣṣĕmē'āh.* Clearly we have here a simile, but what does it mean? I would suggest that *sĕpōt* should be derived from *s.p.'.* [8], which appears in Ugaritic with the meaning 'to eat' and obtains in Biblical Hebrew as *mispō'* = 'fodder' and in Rabbinic Hebrew as *s.p.y.* = 'feed'. We have a simile here from cases of drought and hunger: the sated, irrigated land will feed the thirsty, dry-land [9]. That individual expected to escape punishment hiding amidst the righteous community, but the Lord will not forgive him, the Lord will single him out and punish him.

Up to here, and down to v. 20, it is all about an individual; suddenly at v. 21 everything becomes plural and collective: all the land is devastated (21-23, 26) and the whole people is charged with idolatry (vv 24-25), uprooted and thrown out to another country (v. 27). Then, abruptly again, at v. 28 the content of v. 19-20 is resumed. «Concealed acts — i.e. the hidden sins of the individual — concern the Lord our God (meaning: the Lord will single out the sinner and punish him etc.), but with overt acts, it is for us and our children to apply all the provisions of this Torah». The connection of v. 28 with v. 20 was realized by the Talmud teachers (Sanhedrin 43b) who passed it over to all Jewish medieval commentators. It seems to me that Dillmann, who did not perceive it, led astray three following generations of critics.

Clearly, then, what comes in between, vv. 21-27 is interpolated. But for what purpose? Apparently a late scribe wanted to update the terms of a covenant of old. He needed to read the reality of his own times in the old scroll which he inherited from his forefathers.

It is interesting for the history of biblical research that this interpolation has been noted by rather conservative scholars only: Paul Kleinert, Hubert Junker and Norbert Lohfink [10]. Classical critics did

8. With a different interpretation this has been already conjectured by N. H. TUR-SINAI, in his *Pĕšūṭō šel Miqrā'*, Vol. I, Jerusalem, 1962, a.l.

9. The root *r.w.h.* about irrigating or irrigated land occurs in Is 55,10; 58,11; Jer 31,11; Ps 65,11. For *ṣ.m.'.* about dry land see Dt 8,5; Is 35,7; Jer 48,18; Ez 19,13; Ps 107,33.

10. P. KLEINERT, *Das Deuteronomium und der Deuteronomiker*, Bielefeld und Leipzig, 1872, pp. 204-5; H. JUNKER, *Das Buch Deuteronomium*, in *Die Heilige Schrift in deutscher*

not recognize it, and the reason becomes clear reading in Steuernagel's commentary: they could not admit that individual retribution came first, and collective retribution was later interpolated. Indeed, the history of ideas of Ancient Israel was much more complex than it is sometimes assumed to be. In our particular case, it was not the theological interest in collective retribution that prompted the interpolator, but rather his desire to see the events of his own times foretold in his sacred scroll!

The situation just observed, that what we view as a patent interpolation was not recognized as such by the most audacious critics, stands to indicate on what unfirm, slippery ground we are stepping here. Indeed, interpolations have been, and are being, detected in a rather cavalier, or arbitrary way, in order to make the text adhere to the critics' own preconceptions about its original form, contents and message. However, if one does not want this area of our discipline fall under utter discredit, he better try and lay down some rules about the legitimate detection of interpolations. To my mind, the presence of an interpolation, or secondary accretion, is made plausible only when three different types of evidence can be adduced: (a) a discrepancy (contradiction or fraction) in the textual sequence; (b) external signs, such as the resumptive repetition (*Wiederaufnahme*)[11], or a clear change of style; (c) a detectable intention on the side of the interpolator which can be shown to befit the purpose of late scribes. All three types of arguments can be summoned here: the break of sequence is patent, the interpolator's intention of justifying the Destruction and the Exile corresponds to similar editorial passages in I Kings 9,6-9; Jer 22,8-9. As for the Wiederaufnahme — it is extant twice: the ending of v. 19a reoccurs at the end of v. 20 and of v. 26 (not 27!). This strange phenomenon will itself need some explanation.

Let us try to understand first the cause of the first resumption, at the end of v. 20. If it is true that a Wiederaufnahme may delimit a secondary insertion, then one should start by asking what could be the purpose of the alleged insertion of vv. 19b-20. One can indeed sense the difference of religious concepts vis-à-vis the preceding half verse (19a). While there one read about «the curse written in this book», here one finds an obvious restatement: «the curses of the covenant written in this book of Torah». What once was just a document, stating the terms of the covenant between the Lord and Israel, has become in v. 20 the

Übersetzung (Echter Bibel), Band I, Würzburg 1955, p. 529; N. LOHFINK, in *Der Bundesschluss im Land Moab. Redaktionsgeschichtliches zu Dt 28,69-32,47*, in *BZ* (N.F.) 6 (1962), pp. 32-56.

11. Cf. H. M. WIENER, *The Composition of Judges II,11 to I Kings II, 46*, Leipzig, 1929, p. 2; C. KUHL, *Die 'Wiederaufnahme' — ein literarkritisches Prinzip?*, in *ZAW* 64 (1952), pp. 1-11; I. L. SEELIGMANN, *Hebräische Erzählung und biblische Geschichtsschreibung*, in *ThZ* (Basel) 18 (1962), pp. 305-325, ad pp. 314-324; S. TALMON-M. FISHBANE, in *Tarbiz* 42 (1972/3), pp. 27-41, esp. pp. 35ff. (Hebrew).

comprehensive book of Torah in which the covenant is included. Secondly, there is a shift in the character of the punishment: while in v. 19a it is the curse, as a semi-magical entity, that lies on, or cleaves to [12], the sinner, in vv. 19b-20 the action is attributed to the Lord alone: He blots out the name of the sinner from under heaven, He singles the sinner out of all the tribes of Israel for misfortune. The interpolation appears to have rectified the notions of divine retribution. But the central point of the interpolation seems to lie in another direction. Already at v. 17, in the words «or a woman, or a family, or a tribe», one can sense the tentative to bridge up the individual sin and punishment of vv. 17-19a.28 with the collective ones of vv. 21-27. It goes to the credit of Nachmanides to have first related vv. 19-20 to the different subjects of v. 17:

The Lord's anger and passion rage against that man — curse of the single, man or woman; *and the Lord blots out his name* — curse of the family, because every clan has a single name [13]; *and the Lord singles him out for misfortune* — to the tribe; *from all the tribes of Israel* — the rest of them [14].

Thus, the passage enclosed by the Wiederaufnahme, vv. 19b-20, appears to be a secondary interpolation which tried to reconcile the original act of covenant with the first expansion in vv. 21-27. The lack of a clear discrepancy between vv. 19b-20 and the preceding verses finds its explanation in the special character of this insertion, i.e. its function as a harmonizing bridge between two contrasting passages.

To the history of the covenant concept it is relevant to determine when the main interpolation, that of vv. 21-27, was done. Two data can help in this matter: (a) Question and answer schemata of this kind seem to appear in Assyrian vassal treaties as early as the mid-eighth century, namely in the treaty of Aššurnirari the vith with Mati'ilu of Bit-Aguši [15]. And one should recall here that between 841 and 738 at least three Israelite kings sent tribute to the Assyrian emperors: Jehu in 841, Joash around the year 800, and Menahem in the year 738. Thus, the question

12. Cf. LXX a.l. Its Hebrew Vorlage was extant at Qumran; cf. 1QS II:12-17; CD I:16-17 where Dt 29,18-20 is quoted. But read MT: the same gross image is used in Zech 5,3-4.

13. About the relation between name and family, cf. e.g. Dt 25,6; Ps 109,13.

14. Cf. NACHMANIDES' Hebrew Commentary in: *Miqrā'ōt Gĕdōlōt*, Wien, 1859. First hints were already made by ABEN-EZRA (cf. *ibidem*). The point did not escape DILLMANN (supra n. 5).

15. E. F. WEIDNER, *Der Staatsvertrag Aššurniraris vi von Assyrien mit Mati'ilu von Bit Aguši*, in *AfO* 8 (1932) pp. 17-34; English Translation by E. REINER, apud: J. B. PRITCHARD (ed.), *ANET*^{3}, Princeton, 1969, pp. 532-3. The first to note the relevance of this treaty for biblical studies was P. KARGE in his monograph: *Geschichte des Bundesgedankens im Alten Testament* (Alttestament. Abhandl., II), Münster i. W., 1910. The presence of the question and answer in that treaty was pointed out by Long and Weinfeld; cf. B. O. LONG, *Two Question and Answer Schemata in the Prophets*, in *JBL* 90 (1971), pp. 129-139; M. WEINFELD, *Deuteronomy and the Deuteronomic School*, Oxford, 1972.

and answer scheme about the desolation of the land, following a breach of treaty, may have entered Israelite history-writing as early as the beginning of the eighth century. (b) Yet, a better clue for its dating will be obtained by the inner analysis of the interpolated passage; let us take a look into it and see.

One can easily realize that two punishments follow one another [16]: in vv. 21-26 — the land; it is devastated by sulfur and salt, like Sodom, Gomorrah etc. If anything can be construed out of this description it is the impression of a nature-calamity — an earthquake, which at one recalls the earthquake of the times of Uzziah, in the mid-eighth century, which was mentioned, or hinted to, by Amos (5,11), Isaiah (5,25) and Deutero-Zacharaiah (14,5). This section ends in v. 26 with a Wiederaufnahme of vv. 19a and 20: «all the curse written in this book» — a clear sign that the first interpolation did *not* include v. 27. As for v. 27, here only the people and its exile are mentioned. This verse must be considered, therefore, as a second expansion, aiming at introducing a mention of the exile into a text that did not contain it at first; this was certainly added after the destruction of Samaria in 722/1. That only a partial exile, not of the whole people, is contemplated is made clear by the harmonization at v. 17 «or a woman, or a family, or a tribe»: the collectivity is still limited to a fraction of Israel; that only has gone into exile.

All in all, we have to reckon here with a fairly old act of covenant which was updated twice at least. By the eighth century the old act of covenant was already dated and needed to be revised. The original text of 29,15-28 only contained a warning to the individual not to try hiding himself behind the back of the community, as well as an injunction to the community to exterminate such an individual should his actions become known.

This latter point needs emphasizing, because of its importance to what will follow — the question of the original structure of our pericope. What is extant now in the second half of ch. 29 looks like one big curse of the covenant. Originally it was not; it was mainly one stipulation of the covenant: if an individual break the covenant and his act become known (*hanniglōt*), all the congregation is supposed to punish him. As usual, the expansion of the text has also affected its literary type.

Turning now to the structure of the vassal treaties of the Second Millenium, I have little to add to what was pointed out by Korošec, some 52 years ago [17], namely that in many of these treaties — at that time only Hittite ones were known — one finds the following typical pattern: (a) inscription, (b) historical prologue, (c) a solemn declaration

16. As already noted by LOHFINK (supra n. 10).

17. V. KOROŠEC, *Hethitische Staatsverträge* (Leipziger Rechtswissenschaftliche Studien 60), Leipzig, 1931.

of bond, (d) various stipulations, (e) witnesses (various gods and deified nature-elements, heaven and earth inclusive), (f) curse and blessing (short and nearly symmetrical) [18]. Let me emphasize that Aramaic and Assyrian treaties of the First Millennium are quite dissimilar in their structure.

Since the early fifties, when Mendenhall first attempted to identify the structure of the Hittite Vassal treaties in the Biblical covenant [19], not a few tentatives have been made to draw out lines of correspondence between the two institutions. G. von Rad, D.J. McCarthy, K. Baltzer and others have tried to identify the treaty structure in the Covenant of the Land of Moab [20]. A.D.H. Mayes has recently contested this parallelism pointing out inter alia that «the only really essential element of such a ceremony (and so also of the form), the stipulations, is missing; furthermore, the chapter in fact fall into almost self-contained units» [21]. Mayes is certainly right about the text in its present form. It is my contention, however, that once we identify the secondary passages, 29,21-27 and 30,1-10, the true character of our pericope and its correspondence to the Hittite vassal treaties come to light. Nearly all the elements of the Hittite treaties show here, and in the very same order: (a) the inscription — in 28,69; (b) the historical prologue — in 29,1-9; (c) the statement of bond — in 29,10-14, centering on v. 13: «to the effect that He establish you this day as His people and He be your God as He promised you»; stipulations — indeed, only one stipulation obtains here: the punishment of individual transgressors (29,15-19a.28); I suspect that further paragraphs followed, but they were later transferred from here to the main body of Deuteronomy with the intention of forming a continuous book of law; (e & f) Witnesses and concised curse and blessing — these show together at the end of our pericope (vv. 15-20); the deities heaven and earth have been transformed, as we could have expected, into passive nature-elements.

18. E.F. WEIDNER, *Politische Dokumente aus Kleinasien* (Boghazkoei-Studien 8-9), Leipzig, 1923 (Reprinted: Hildesheim-New York 1970), pp. 30-31, 50-51, 68-69, 74-75; J. FRIEDRICH, *Staatsverträge des Hatti-Reiches in hethitischer Sprache* (MVAG 31), Leipzig, 1923, pp. 24-25; idem, MVAG 34), Leipzig, 1930, pp. 16-19, 80-83, 134-136; J. NOUGAYROL, *Le palais royal d'Ugarit* IV (MRS IX), Paris, 1956, pp. 84-101.

19. G.E. MENDENHALL, *Covenant Forms in Israelite Tradition*, in *BA* 17 (1954), pp. 50-76 = *The Biblical Archaeologist Reader*, Vol. III, New York 1970, pp. 25-53. I hope the present article answers the stricture of E. BICKERMAN (*Couper une alliance*, in *Studies in Jewish and Christian History*, Part I, Leiden, 1976, pp. 1-32) who maintains (ad p. 26) «qu'aucun texte de la *berith* hébreu n'est arrivé jusqu'à nous».

20. G. VON RAD, *Deuteronomy, A Commentary* (English Translation), London, 1966; D.J. MCCARTHY, *Treaty and Covenant*[2] (AnBib, 21A), Rome, 1978; K. BALTZER, *The Covenant Formulary* (English Translation), Oxford, 1971.

21. A.D.H. MAYES, *Deuteronomy* (The New Century Bible Commentary), Grand Rapids, Michigan/London, 1981, a.l.

Let us now attempt some conclusions from what we have seen. In the first place one can only express his satisfaction at the fact that the results of historico-literary criticism are confirmed by formcriticism applied to extra-biblical sources. To state it again: the structure of old treaties as analyzed by Korošec corresponds to that of the Covenant in the Land of Moab, *minus* those elements that our historico-literary criticism revealed to be interpolated, as 29,21-27, or just transposed from another context, as 30,1-10 [22]. Both methods appear to sustain each other which seems to submit the essential validity of these two directions of research.

The Covenant in the Land of Moab, therefore, reflects an ancient pattern of covenant between the Lord and Israel. That is not to say that all its very text is old. Some elements might be so, especially the primary verses in 29,9-28. But otherwise it is very likely that original sections were substituted by more recent compositions. To be more explicit: the inscription itself — the present one befits the literary framework, namely the Deuteronomic fiction of Moses addressing Israel before their crossing over into the Land. But if it has become plausible that the origin of this pericope was in a ritual act-of-covenant between God and Israel in one of the Israelite sanctuaries of historical times, then the original inscription told us right about that and therefore it had to be substituted. The same about the historical prologue. The present one repeats the usual scheme of Deuteronomic history. A covenant act at one of the Israelite sanctuaries could have told a different history (let us recall the peculiar history told in Joshua 24!) and one that reached a later date for that. Therefore it could not survive its inclusion in the Fifth Book of Moses. The pattern, however, has been kept, along with some old elements.

How is one to account for the fact that the old structure of the treaties has been detected right here? The answer, in my opinion, lies at hand. Since the covenant was a central issue in the religion of Israel, it was reworked in the course of time again and again by generations of scribes. We cannot expect to find the old material and structure neither in Ex 19-24, nor in Ex 34, nor in Dt 5-28, and certainly not in the late Priestly Code. Just as old pieces of furniture are likely to be found in basements and attics, so the old treaty-pattern does not show in the main body of Deuteronomy, but appears where one should expect to find it — in the appendix to Deuteronomy, ch. 29 and 30. The phenomenon is well known. The appendix to the Book of Joshua, in Jdg 1,1-2,5, contains remnants of ancient pre-Deuteronomic accounts about the conquest. The appendix to the Book of Samuel, in II Sam 21-24, also preserves some ancient documents. The appendix to the Book of Judges, in Jdg 17-21, was indeed compiled by a rather late redactor, but some of its

22. The passage 30,11-14 needs a detailed examination (cf. *infra*, n. 25). In any case its diction and contents make it clear that the passage is extraneous to its present context.

material, like the story of the idol of Micah, is relatively old. These appendices were the deposits of old, partially superseded, material.

Our conclusion is that the origins of the Covenant of the Land of Moab go back to an ancient ritual, moulded by the Israelites after the pattern of political vassal treaties of the Second Millennium. This conclusion runs against that of many distinguished scholars, in our times e.g. Lothar Perlitt and Rudolf Smend [23], who maintain the late, seventh century or exilic origin of the covenant-concept. I would like, therefore to add a few words of a more general character about the theological meaning of the covenant-idea and its historical framework.

From a theological point of view the covenant-concept does not fit in with the basic tenets of Deuteronomy. And the reason lies at hand. Deuteronomy is a monotheistic work; the covenant-concept is not necessarily monotheistic. In the same way as a vassal-king who accepts the treaty of a great king (šarru rabû) does not have to deny the mere existence of other great kings, but is only forbidden to serve them, so here: Israel, by committing himself in the covenant to serve the Lord alone, does not implicitly deny the existence of other gods. In other words: the covenant-idea is not inherently monotheistic, although there is no doubt that it can be also fitted into a monotheistic faith, as proved by both Judaism and Christianity.

This situation is confirmed by the examination of the covenant-formula. The original formula is similar to what we found in Dt 29,12: «You will be for Him a people and He will be for you a God». But the Deuteronomic authors were dissatisfied with this formula. They felt the need of modifying it according to their monotheistic creed, indeed — the need of expressing through it their monotheistic creed. Therefore they modified the usual formula as follows: «You will be to Him as people of treasure-trove (*ʿam sĕgullāh*) [24]; you will be supreme above all peoples that He made (*ʿelyon ʿal kol haggōyīm ʾăšer ʿāśāh*); you will become a sacred people (*ʿam qādōš*) — which means: nearer to Him, consecrated like priests to His worship. These are the expressions of Dt 26,17-19, in the solemn conclusion of the main Deuteronomic covenant and law-book; some of them re-occur in Ex 19 and Dt 7 and 14. Thus it becomes clear, in my view, that for the Deuteronomic writers the proper way of describing the relation of Israel to the Lord is in terms expressing election, either directly by *b.ḥ.r.* or indirectly by *ʿam sĕgullāh*, *ʿam qādōš*, *ʿam ʿelyōn*, because with these terms the Lord's dominion over the whole world is reaffirmed. The term of covenant, which they inherited from

23. R. SMEND, *Die Bundesformel* (ThSt 68), Zürich, 1963; L. PERLITT, *Bundestheologie im Alten Testament* (WMANT 36), Neukirchen-Vluyn, 1969. Older critics were answered by P. VAN IMSCHOOT in his sober treatment: *L'alliance dans l'Ancien Testament*, in *Nouvelle Revue Théologique* 84 (1952), pp. 785-805, and again in his book: *Théologie de l'Ancien Testament*, T. 1, Tournai, 1954.

24. M. GREENBERG, *Hebrew* segulla*: Akkadian* sikiltu, in *JAOS* 71 (1951), pp. 172-174.

preceding writers, was for them inadequate; yet it was already so central a term in the religious conscience of Israel that it continued to express the solemn obligation of Israel to the Lord his God.

This, I believe, proves the relative antiquity of the covenant-concept (and covenant ritual) in Israel. A plausible conjecture is dating it to late pre-monarchical times. Much is to be said about this inherently non-monotheistic concept, nevertheless so important in shaping the faith of Israel. But this already belongs to a distinct paper[25].

6, Magnes Circle
Rehaviah
92304 Jerusalem, Israel

Alexander Rofé

25. A more detailed version of this paper will appear in Hebrew in *Beer-Sheva*, Vol. 2 (= *Fs. Sh. Abramsky*), in preparation. For translation of biblical passages in the present essay I have generally followed the NJPS.

DEUTERONOMY 29, JOSHUA 9, AND THE PLACE OF THE GIBEONITES IN ISRAEL [1]

Within Josh 9 there is clear indication of a process of interpretation at work on the earlier tradition: vv. (17)18-21 bear all the marks of a priestly addition, in which it is the «leaders of the congregation» who swear an oath to the Gibeonites and these Canaanites become «hewers of wood and drawers of water for all the congregation» rather than «for the altar of the Lord» [2]. The intention of the supplement is clear: responsibility for making a treaty with the Gibeonites, and so for failing to fulfil a provision of the deuteronomic law (Deut 20,10-18), is to be transferred from Joshua to the leaders, and the connection of these Canaanites with Israelite worship at the central sanctuary is to be broken.

Probably a comparable concern lies behind a relationship which may be established between Josh 9 and Deut 29, so that one element basic to Deut 29 is the need to cope with the anomaly which the presence of Canaanites in a functional capacity in the Israelite sanctuary constituted.

The most striking links between the two chapters are these: firstly, the common use of the phrase «hewers of wood and drawers of water», which, in its full form, is found only in Deut 29,10 of the *gēr*, or sojourner, in the Israelite camp, and in Josh 9,21.23.27 of the service of the Gibeonites at the sanctuary or for the congregation; secondly, the declaration of Deut 29,4 that «your clothes have not worn out upon you, and your sandals have not worn off your feet», and the record of Josh 9,5(13) that the Gibeonites put on «worn out, patched sandals on their feet, and worn out clothes» [3]; thirdly, the references in Deut 29,5 and Josh 9,12-14 to bread and wine in order to establish the truth of a claim, on the one hand that Yahweh is Israel's God and on the other that the Gibeonites come from a distant land [4].

1. This paper was written during a period of research in Tübingen generously supported by the *Alexander von Humboldt Stiftung*.

2. For details cf. J. HALBE, *Gibeon und Israel*, in *VT* 25 (1975) 613-641, pp. 613-619, where the possibility of pre-priestly interpretation is also discussed.

3. Only in these two passages is the verb *bālāh*, «wear out», used of clothes and sandals.

4. Bread and wine are a common combination, but only here in this confirmatory role. On these and other contacts cf. also J. BLENKINSOPP, *Are there Traces of the Gibeonite Covenant in Deuteronomy?*, in *CBQ* 28 (1966) 207-219, pp. 208-209; P. J. KEARNY, *The Role of the Gibeonites in the Deuteronomic History*, in *CBQ* 35 (1973) 1-19, pp. 1-2. One might point also to the use of the phrase «all the men of Israel» (*kōl 'îš yiśrā'ēl*) in Deut 29,9 and Josh 10,24 (cf. also *'îš yiśrā'ēl* in Josh 9,6.7), and to the common reference to the miraculous events in Egypt and Israel's defeat of Sihon and Og in Deut 29,1-7 and Josh 9,9b-10, and to the general parallel that in neither Deut 29 nor Josh 9 is the covenant referred to; cf. also R. POLZIN, *Moses and the Deuteronomist*, New York, 1980, pp. 117ff.

The nature of the connection between the two chapters is undoubtedly that Deut 29 is dependent on and alludes to Josh 9. This is indicated by a variety of internal considerations, such as the absence of the term *gērîm* in Josh 9, and the use of the quite anomalous phrase «your sojourner who is in the midst of your camp» in Deut 29,10 [5] which takes up the reference to camp in Josh 9,6 and the preposition *b^{e}qereb* in the same story (Josh 9,7.16.22; 10,1). This is confirmed by other observations relating to the times of origin of Deut 29 and Josh 9, for while the former gives every indication of belonging to a late deuteronomistic stage in the development of Deuteronomy [6], the latter is to be traced back at least to an early stage of the deuteronomistic movement, as is shown by the appearance of some quite distinctive deuteronomistic additions in that chapter [7].

If it is true that Deut 29 may in part at least be read as a comment on the tradition of the covenant between Israel and the Gibeonites, it is likely that one purpose in making this allusion was to identify the Gibeonites as *gērîm*, «sojourners», and also to relate them to Israel as a whole rather than particularly to the sanctuary. They are identified as sojourners through the phrase «hewers of wood and drawers of water» being set in apposition to «your sojourner who is in the midst of your camp» without the use of the conjunction; they are identified as servants to Israel as a whole through the use of the possessive pronoun «your» with «wood» and «water». The deuteronomist has thus anticipated the work of the priestly editor in Josh 9 by breaking the direct connection between the Gibeonites and the sanctuary.

The motive behind this was probably to a large extent the same with deuteronomist and priestly writer; both were concerned with the problem of the presence of foreigners in the sanctuary, a problem which, as Ezek 44 indicates, was of some general concern. However,

5. Elsewhere Deuteronomy refers to the *gēr* either «in your midst» (*b^{e}qirb^{e}kā*, 26,11; 28,43), or «in your towns» (*biš'ārekā*, 5,14; 14,21.29; 24,14; 31,12).

6. On the formal structure of Deut 29-30 see especially D.J. McCarthy, *Treaty and Covenant*^{2} (AB 21A), Rome, 1978, pp. 199ff. On the question of its unity, the strongest case for a later addition relates to 29,21-30,10, where destruction is no longer a threat for the future but a present reality; cf. N. Lohfink, *Der Bundesschluss im Land Moab*, in *BZ* 6 (1962) 32-56, esp. p. 44. But even here caution is necessary in view of the character of the whole section as a series of fairly loosely strung together sections. On the phenomenon of change of address between singular and plural, which features in these chapters as elsewhere in Deuteronomy, see the discussion, with bibliography, in my *Deuteronomy 4 and the Literary Criticism of Deuteronomy*, in *JBL* 100 (1981) 23-51, pp. 27-30. Here also (esp. pp. 50-51) the late time of origin of the deuteronomistic editing to which Deut 29 belongs is indicated.

7. The clearest example of a deuteronomistic addition is the centralization formula in v. 27, a verse which has its aetiological conclusion at an earlier stage. For a noteworthy attempt to reconstruct the pre-deuteronomistic tradition in the chapter, cf. Halbe, *op. cit.*, esp. 616-630.

the deuteronomic concern was even wider: the deuteronomist wished to define the place of the Gibeonites now that the covenant with Israel had been made. So the Gibeonites are classified as *gērîm*, «sojourners».

In using this term for the Gibeonites the deuteronomist was effectively incorporating them into the community of Israel. By this time the term *gēr*, though still as always carrying the sense of «stranger», had undergone a change of significance which made necessary the definition of the rights and responsibilities associated with that status. Apparently, it could originally be used of an Israelite living in the territory of a tribe to which he did not belong [8], but by the time of Deuteronomy it has come to be reserved for a foreigner, a non-Israelite living within Israel [9]. It seems always to have been the case that the *gēr* could expect not to be made a slave, and this in itself is of considerable significance in the context of its application to the Gibeonites: for the deuteronomist they were not slaves, whatever may have originally been the significance of «hewers of wood and drawers of water» [10]. However, the economically weak and vulnerable position of the *gēr* in society is constantly recognized: in the early narratives, for example, Abraham's descendents will be enslaved *gērîm* (Gen 15,13) [11], and in the early law the Israelite is constantly exhorted not to oppress the *gēr* (Ex 22,20; 23,9); in the deuteronomic and priestly law too the *gēr* is commended to the charitable concern of the Israelite (Deut 14,29; 24,14; Lev 19,33f. etc.). The possibility of his holding land may always have existed [12], even though it is only in Ezekiel (47,22f.) that it is explicitly commanded that the *gēr* is to be given his land allotment; yet, while the possibility that the *gēr* might become wealthy existed (Lev 25,47), the actual inferior

8. So the Levite in Judg 17,7f.; 19,1.

9. Cf. G. VON RAD, *Das Gottesvolk im Deuteronomium* (BWANT III,11), 1929, p. 45. So Deut 14,21 presupposes a distinction between Israelite and *gēr*, and the Levite in Deuteronomy is no longer a *gēr*. On the subject cf. also A. CODY, *A History of Old Testament Priesthood* (AB 35), Rome, 1969, pp. 54ff.; O. BÄCHLI, *Israel und die Völker* (ATANT 41), Zürich, 1962, pp. 127f.; S. R. DRIVER, *Deuteronomy*³ (International Critical Commentary), Edinburgh, 1902, pp. 126, 165.

10. That the formula may originally have implied slavery in particular rather than menial service in general is not here disputed (on this cf. J. M. GRINTZ, *The Treaty of Joshua with the Gibeonites*, in *JAOS* 86 (1966) 113-126, pp. 120-121).

11. The passage goes on to declare that punishment will follow this affliction of the *gēr*; so the exodus to which reference is being made thus appears as God's rescue of Israel and punishment of Egypt for illegal action towards those living in their midst with the status of *gēr*. Lev 25,45 provides that Israel may get slaves from among the strangers (*tôšābîm*) who sojourn with them. The terms *tôšāb* and *gēr* are paired on several occasions (cf. Lev 25,23.35; Ps 39,13; 1 Chr 29,15), and the difference between them is not always clear. However, Ex 12,45 excludes the *tôšāb* from the Passover, while the *gēr*, provided he is circumcised, may participate (Ex 12,48); the former thus appears to be a temporary resident without the privileges (including freedom from slavery) extended to the *gēr*. For Deuteronomy (24,14) the *gēr* may be a hired servant (*śākîr*).

12. So Abraham, though a *gēr*, could buy land (Gen 23, cf. v. 4).

position which probably invariably characterized his status is clearly indicated by his regular appearance along with other socially deprived elements of society in Deuteronomy (14,29; 16,11.14; 24,20f.; 26,12f. etc. [13]) and P (Lev 19,10; 23,12), and by the curse in Deut 28,43 that the position of the *gēr* and the Israelite will be reversed in the case of Israel's disobedience to the law.

It is of particular interest in this context, however, that despite the socially inferior position of the *gēr*, there is a tendency discernible through the law to make the *gēr* more and more a member of the Yahwistic community through subjecting him to the law. So, while the book of the covenant (Ex 22,20; 23,9.12) is content with ensuring that the *gēr* is not economically oppressed, the deuteronomic law, and even more so that of P, wish to set Israelite and *gēr* on the same level as members of the cult community. The deuteronomic law does to a certain extent distinguish Israelite and *gēr* in that it prohibits the Israelite from eating what dies of itself but allows this to be given to the *gēr* for food (14,21), but the deuteronomist has gone far forwards undermining this position by including the *gēr* among those summoned to listen to and to obey the whole law (Deut 29,10; 31,12). The priestly writer then has continued this tendency by giving expression to a wide variety of laws to which the *gēr*, like the Israelite, is explicitly subjected (Lev 16,29; 17,8.10.12.13.15; 20,2; 22,18; 24,16; Nu 9,14; 15,14ff.26.29.30; 19,10; 35,15), to the extent of saying that there shall be one law for the *gēr* and for the native (Lev 24,22) [14].

By applying the term *gēr* to the Gibeonites the deuteronomist has removed them from the position of being Canaanites in cultic service to that of sojourners, subject, like all Israelites, to the requirements of the divine law. This seems to be understood by the deuteronomist as the implication of the covenant between Israel and the Gibeonites, and also as the best way to cope with the problem posed by the traditional representation of foreigners with a role in the Israelite sanctuary.

That this is the way to view the relationship between Deut 29 and Josh 9, and to describe one aim of the deuteronomist in Deut 29, seems to be corroborated by two points.

In the first place, the work of the deuteronomistic editor in Deut 29 and elsewhere seems to be characterized by a desire to allude to and sometimes to interpret existing texts in a particular way. So a connection may be established between Deut 29,15-27 and the story of Achan in Josh 7 [15], a connection which may be explained as arising from the

13. See also Deut 24,17; 27,19, which prohibit the perversion of the justice (*mišpāt*) due to the *gēr*, the orphan (and the widow).

14. In Lev 17,15 the priestly writer implicitly corrects the distinction made by the deuteronomic law in Deut 14,21.

15. Cf. KEARNEY, *op. cit.*, p. 8. The reference in Deut 29,17 to man, woman, family and tribe is reminiscent of the process by which Achan was singled out (cf. Deut 29,20) for

intention to interpret the sin of Achan as idolatry, while Deut 4,1-40, which very probably derives from the same hand as Deut 29, is an extended commentary on the decalogue, highlighting the prohibition of the making of images and understanding it as a prohibition of the worship of other gods. Thus, the possibility that Deut 29 should also comment on Josh 9 is not to be ruled out as unlikely.

Secondly, there is some indication that the Gibeonite question was one which exercised other than deuteronomistic minds, that it was a problem fairly widely felt to require comment and correct understanding. Both the deuteronomist and the priestly writer in Josh 9 resolved it by removing the Gibeonites from their immediate attachment to the sanctuary. In 1 Chr 22,2 David is said to have «commanded to gather together the *gērîm* who were in the land of Israel, and he set stone cutters to prepare dressed stones for building the house of God», and in 2 Chr 2,16f. «Solomon took a census of all the *gērîm*... and there were found a hundred and fifty three thousand six hundred. Seventy thousand of them he assigned to bear burdens, eighty thousand to quarry in the hill country, and three thousand six hundred as overseers to make the people work». That the Chronicler should have used the term *gērîm* in this connection, rather that follow 1 Kings 9,20 in referring to «all the people who were left of the Amorites, the Hittites, the Perizzites, the Hivites and the Jebusites, who were not of the people of Israel», may well be the result of a reading of Deut 29 and Josh 9, and an interpretation of what Josh 9 meant by describing the Gibeonites as «hewers of wood and drawers of water for the house of God». The cultic connection is preserved, but only in the sense that the Gibeonite *gērîm* laboured at the building of the temple. That they were regular ministrants in the temple, in whatever capacity, was, for the Chronicler just as for the deuteronomist and the priestly writer, an unacceptable idea.

Trinity College
Dublin, Ireland

A. D. H. MAYES

punishment in Josh 7,14ff. In both chapters (Deut 29,16; Josh 7,21) gold and silver are involved. Josh 7 also describes the process of seeking the reason for punishment, to which there is a literary allusion in Deut 29,21-27 and other passages (cf. D. E. SKWERES, *Das Motiv der Strafgrunderfragung in biblischen und neuassyrischen Texten*, in *BZ* 14 [1970] 181-197).

A PROPOSAL FOR REFLECTIONS IN THE BOOK OF JEREMIAH OF THE SEVEN-YEAR RECITATION OF THE LAW IN DEUTERONOMY (DEUT 31,10-13)

The emphasis in modern study of Deuteronomy has rightly stressed its programmatic nature, as the basis for the reform under Josiah; it is accepted that much of the book is parenesis. Given the idealistic thrust of the book, our concern for the extent to which the stipulations of Deuteronomy were obeyed has sometimes receded into the background. I should like to propose that there is evidence within the book of Jeremiah for the practice of reciting the law of Deuteronomy every seven years at the time of the feast of booths, as prescribed in Deut 31,10-13, evidence, that is, during the period 615-587 [1].

This proposal grows out of my attempt to locate settings for various pericopes in the book of Jeremiah: it has occurred to me that if the law of Deuteronomy was recited every seven years in the celebration of the feast of booths in Jerusalem, those occasions would have offered Jeremiah an ample audience. If the reform of Josiah is to be dated in 622, then the recitations of Deuteronomy would have taken place in the autumn of 615, 608, 601, 594 and 587.

The evidence is strongest for 594. In December 595 or January 594 there was an attempt in Babylon by elements in the Babylonian army to overthrow Nebuchadrezzar, an attempt which of course failed. But the excitement generated by this attempted *coup d'état* obviously infected the Jewish exiles in Babylon and thereafter the inhabitants of Jerusalem; the result was a conference in Jerusalem called by King Zedekiah in the spring or early summer of 594, to which ambassadors from Edom, Moab, Ammon, Tyre and Sidon came (Jer 27); the prophet Jeremiah insisted that revolt against Nebuchadrezzar was doomed. I would date Jer 11,1-17 in the autumn of 594. This passage is notoriously «Deuteronomistic»: in v. 3 we have the formula *'ārûr hā'îš*, «cursed be the man», and in v. 5, *'āmēn yhwh*, «so be it, Yahweh», which correspond to the formulas in Deut 27,15-27, and in general the references to «this covenant» in vv. 3, 6 and 8. But the clue is the striking word *qešer*, «revolt, conspiracy» in v. 9. This word appears nowhere else in the book of Jer, and nowhere in the book of Deut; the word is specific to the historical context of the passage. It is typically used of rebellion of

1. W. L. HOLLADAY, *The Years of Jeremiah's Preaching*, in *Interpretation* 37 (1983), 146-159.

a vassal against a suzerain: note its occurrence in 2 Kgs 17,4 of Hoshea's plot against the king of Assyria. Jeremiah's point here is that the attempt of Zedekiah and his fellow-kings to plot a revolt against Nebuchadrezzar is really a plot to rebel against Yahweh. Jeremiah uses Deuteronomistic language here because his words are a counter-proclamation to the recitation of Deuteronomy.

Seven years earlier, in 601, there would have been a recitation of Deuteronomy. I follow Norbert Lohfink in dating the fast called by King Jehoiakim to November/December, 601 rather than 604 (that is, in following the LXX of Jer 36,9 rather than the MT, reading «in the eighth year» rather than «in the fifth year»)[2], and I follow Wilhelm Rudolph in proposing that the motive for the fast was the great drought described in Jer 14 (compare 14,12)[3]. If Deuteronomy was recited in September/October, 601, the drought must already have been underway. I point to Jer 8,8-13 as Jeremiah's word on that occasion: 8,8 refers to the «word of the law» being perverted by the «false pen of the scribes», and v. 13 describes a drought: «no grapes on the vine, nor figs on the fig tree; even the leaves are withered».

Seven years earlier, in 608, there would have been a recitation of Deuteronomy. Jehoiakim had been on the throne only a year. I propose that an early form of Jer 2-3 was proclaimed by the prophet on that occasion: I point to the opening words of chapter 2, «Go and proclaim in the hearing of Jerusalem» (v. 2), words which suggest the same setting of a convocation presupposed by Deut 31,11; and I point, too, to the diction of the little poem in Jer 2,2-3. Both Deut 16,13-15 and Lev 23,39, which make provision for the feast of booths, use *t^{e}bû'â* «harvest», which occurs in Jer 2,3, and since the feast of booths was associated both with the vintage (Deut 16,13) and with the exodus from Egypt (Lev 23,24), it is altogether likely that that occasion in 608 formed the setting for this material in Jer 2-3: one notes that that collection is rounded off by a closing appeal (Jer 4,3-4) which is likewise specifically addressed to Jerusalem (4,3) and uses the phraseology of the «circumcision of the heart» (4,4) found also in Deut 10,16.

If one moves back to 615, one is in very uncertain territory; I will simply state a suggestion, very tentatively, without attempting to press it too far. My own chronology of Jeremiah's career is the so-called lower one, by which the date in Jer 1,1, 627 B.C.E., is the date of the prophet's birth (compare 1,5) rather than the beginning of his active career as a prophet[4]. If one assumes for the sake of my proposal the validity of that

2. N. LOHFINK, *Die Gattung der «Historischen Kurzgeschichte» in den letzten Jahren von Juda und in der Zeit des Babylonischen Exils*, in *ZAW* 90 (1978) 324-328.

3. W. RUDOLPH, *Jeremia* (HAT, 12), Tübingen, 1968, p. 233.

4. W. L. HOLLADAY, *A Coherent Chronology of Jeremiah's Early Career*, in *Le Livre de Jérémie* (BETL, 54), Leuven, 1981, pp. 58-73.

dating, then clearly Jeremiah is only five years old at the time of Josiah's reform in 622; thus, I submit, his silence on the reform itself. But in 615, seven years later, Jeremiah is twelve years old, old enough to join the congregation in Jerusalem at the time of the recitation of Deuteronomy. Now it has long been noticed that there are resemblances between the diction of Jeremiah's call and that of Deuteronomy, particularly to the matter of the «prophet like Moses» in Deut 18,18. It is possible, then, that a very young Jeremiah, «only a youth» (1,6) of twelve years, heard the call of Yahweh on that occasion. Whether that is the case or not, Lohfink has proposed the core of Jer 30-31 as material proclaimed by the youthful Jeremiah before the death of Josiah [5], and I have proposed some verses of Jer 2-3 to have their original setting in that early period [6], so that a call in 615 is not implausible.

Finally, what of 587? The city fell to Nebuchadrezzar's army in July of that year, and in August the temple and palace were burned and the city walls destroyed. Jeremiah had drafted a scroll of hope (30,1-3), the closing of which, I propose, is 31,27-28. Given the circumstances, can one imagine a recitation of Deuteronomy in the autumn of that year? My answer is yes; I believe that that was the destination of the pilgrims from the north mentioned in 41,5 (the year is not given, but the month is correct [41,1], and it is not unlikely that the events described followed immediately on the fall of Jerusalem). My proposal for Jeremiah's word on that occasion is the «new covenant» passage, 31,31-34. It stands outside the «scroll of hope», or rather serves as an appendix to that scroll; its diction is again somewhat Deuteronomistic, though it insists that the old covenant is a dead letter, and altogether serves as an admirable counterpoint to the Deuteronomic law which, I propose, was recited on that occasion.

If this proposal is correct, it not only gives more chronological structure to the career of Jeremiah but offers evidence for obedience to the instructions for the seven-yearly recitation of the law of Deuteronomy for the first 35 years after Josiah's reform.

210 Herrick Road
Newton Centre, MA 02159
U.S.A.

William L. HOLLADAY

5. N. LOHFINK, *Der junge Jeremia als Propagandist und Poet, Zum Grundstock von Jer 30-31*, in *Le Livre de Jérémie* (BETL, 54), Leuven, 1981, pp. 351-368.

6. HOLLADAY, *The Years of Jeremiah's Preaching*, p. 148.

LES TROIS RÉDACTIONS CONSERVÉES ET LA FORME ORIGINALE DE L'ENVOI DU CANTIQUE DE MOÏSE (DT 32,43)

Le dernier verset, en forme d'envoi, du Cantique de Moïse (Dt 32,1-43) a fait l'objet d'études importantes depuis 1954, date de la publication de 4QDt^{q} (dorénavant: Q) par Mgr Patrick W. Skehan [1]. Rudolf Meyer, en particulier, a montré en 1961 le lien étroit entre les formes des vv. 8-9 et celles du v. 43 dans le texte massorétique (dorénavant H) d'un côté, dans le grec et à Qumran de l'autre [2]. Ici, comme souvent, la critique textuelle fournit un point de départ solide pour la critique littéraire. L'hébreu H a démythologisé la forme originale du Cantique.

Pour R. Meyer [3], les huit stiques du texte de la Septante (dorénavant: G) [4] résultent d'une contamination d'un texte en six stiques correspondant au fragment de la grotte 4 de Qumran par le texte hébreu standard en quatre stiques (H), confirmé sur plusieurs points par Aquila et connu de Jérôme. Je me rallie pleinement à cette observation fondamentale.

R. Meyer va jusqu'à laisser entendre que la contamination a eu lieu à l'intérieur de la tradition du grec. La *Vorlage* de la Septante correspondrait exactement à Q et n'aurait eu que six stiques [5]. Sur ce point, à certains égards secondaire, je ne le suivrai pas.

De plus, pour R. Meyer, le texte en quatre stiques de l'hébreu standard (H) est un état modifié, théologiquement actualisé, du texte original en six stiques (Q) [6]. Il propose donc la succession chronologique suivante:

1. P.W. Skehan, *A Fragment of the «Song of Moses» (Deut. 32) from Qumran*, dans *BASOR* 136 (1954) 12-15. Mgr Skehan a apporté quelques observations complémentaires: *The Qumran Manuscripts and Textual Criticism*, dans *Volume du Congrès. Strasbourg 1956* (Suppl. to VT, 4), Leiden, 1957, pp. 148-160, 1 pl; voir p. 150, n. 1, et *Qumran and the Present State of Old Testament Text Studies: The Masoretic Text*, dans *JBL* 78 (1959) 21-25, pp. 21-22. — Je retiens le sigle 4QDt^{q} (J. A. Fitzmyer, *The Dead Sea Scrolls Major Publications and Tools for Study*, Missoula [Montana], 1975, p. 23). Sur le phylactère N (Dt 32,14-20.32-33), lire J.T. Milik, dans *Qumran Grotte 4*. Tome II (Discoveries in the Judaean Desert, 6), Oxford, 1977, pp. 72-74.

2. R. Meyer, *Die Bedeutung von Deuteronomium 32,8f.43(4Q) für die Auslegung des Mosesliedes*, dans A. Kuschke (éd.), *Verbannung und Heimkehr. Beiträge zur Geschichte und Theologie Israels im 6. und 5. Jahrhundert v. Chr. W. Rudolph zu 70. Geburtstage*, Tübingen, 1961, pp. 197-209; voir aussi O. Loretz, *Die Vorgeschichte von Deuteronomium 32,8f.43*, dans *Ugarit-Forschungen* 9 (1977) 355-357.

3. R. Meyer, *Die Bedeutung*, pp. 200-201.

4. J.W. Wevers et U. Quast, *Deuteronomium* (Septuaginta. Vetus Testamentum Graecum auctoritate Academiae Sc. Gottingensis editum, III,2), Göttingen, 1977, p. 359.

5. R. Meyer, *Die Bedeutung*, p. 200 fin.

6. R. Meyer, *Die Bedeutung*, p. 205 fin.

Q (six stiques), H (quatre stiques), G (huit stiques)[7]. Tout en acceptant que Q soit antérieur à H, je ne pense pas que le texte en six stiques soit original.

Voici synoptiquement les données du problème[8].

	H(TM)	Q (4QDt^{q})	G (LXX)
a		*hrnynw šmym ʿmw*	εὐφράνθητε, οὐρανοί, ἅμα αὐτῷ,
b		*whšthww lw kl ʾlhym*	καὶ προσκυνησάτωσαν αὐτῷ πάντες υἱοὶ θεοῦ·
a'	*harnînû gôyîm ʿammô*		εὐφράνθητε, ἔθνη, μετὰ τοῦ λαοῦ αὐτοῦ,
b'			καὶ ἐνισχυσάτωσαν αὐτῷ πάντες ἄγγελοι θεοῦ·
c	*kî dam-ʿabādāyw yiqqôm*	*ky dm bnyw yqwm*	ὅτι τὸ αἷμα τῶν υἱῶν αὐτοῦ ἐκδικεῖται,
d	*wĕ-nāqām yāšîb lĕ-ṣārāyw*	*wnqm yšyb lṣryw*	καὶ ἐκδικήσει καὶ ἀνταποδώσει δίκην τοῖς ἐχθροῖς
e		*wlmśnʾyw yšlm*	καὶ τοῖς μισοῦσιν ἀνταποδώσει,
f	*wĕ-kippèr ʾadmātô ʿammô*	*wykpr ʾdmt ʿmw*	καὶ ἐκκαθαριεῖ κύριος τὴν γῆν τοῦ λαοῦ αὐτοῦ.

S'il y a quelque utilité à reprendre cette question, c'est que des difficultés demeurent sans solution dans l'argumentation de R. Meyer.

La première, et la plus importante, est que, si les quatre stiques de H s'expliquent à partir des six stiques de Q, il faut supposer que le rédacteur de H a supprimé deux stiques. Or l'histoire de la rédaction révèle que, pour un texte aussi anciennement canonique que la Tora, l'addition reste possible alors même que la suppression ne l'est plus. A cela s'ajoute que les stiques *b* et *e* qui disparaissent sont bien innocents; la modification théologique, mise en évidence par R. Meyer, porte sur la transformation de *a* en *a'*; *b* et *e* n'ont rien à y voir. Les tenants de l'originalité du texte reçu (TM = H), rares il est vrai pour le v. 43, supposent cet argument sans l'expliciter[9]. D'autres, tels Mgr Skehan[10] et le Professeur Cross[11],

7. Nous excluons que la forme en six stiques soit originale; et a fortiori la reconstitution en huit stiques, partiellement différente de la Septante, proposée par W. F. ALBRIGHT, *New Light on Early Recensions of the Hebrew Bible*, dans *BASOR* 140 (1955) 27-33, et légèrement modifiée dans *Some Remarks on the Song of Moses in Deuteronomy XXXII*, dans *VT* 9 (1959) 339-345; p. 340:

Harnînû šāmáyim ʿimmô — *w^{e}-hištaḥwû-lô benê ʾElohîm*
Harnînû gôyîm ʾet ʿammô — *w^{e}ḥizqû(?)-lô kol malʾakê ʾEl*
Kî dam bānâw yiqqóm — *w^{e}-nāqām yašîb l^{e}ṣarâw*
. . . . — *w^{e}-kipper ʾadmat ʿammô.*

Albright estime que le septième stique, emprunté au v. 41, ne peut être celui attesté par la Septante. Je réponds que Lv 5,16 met *šlm* et *kpr* en relation. Par ailleurs, ce serait une gageure que de vouloir expliquer Q et H à partir de la reconstruction de Albright.

8. Chaque stique est désigné par une minuscule italique. J'écris *a, b, a', b'* plutôt que *a, b, c, d*, comme le fait Meyer, pour mettre en évidence le parallélisme strict *a-b/a'-b'* et le doublet *a, a'*.

9. Elia S. ARTOM, *Sul testo di Deuteronomio XXXII,37-43*, dans *Rivista degli studi orientali* 32 (1957) = Scritti in onore di Giuseppe Furlani, 285-291.

10. P.W. SKEHAN, *A Fragment*, p. 15, propose la reconstitution suivante:
harnînû šāmayîm ʿimmô
w^{e}hābû ʿoz lô kol b^{e}nê ʾēlîm
kî dam bānā(y)w yiqqōm
w^{e}kippēr ʾad^{e}mat ʿammô.

Le deuxième stique est une rétroversion du stique propre au grec (*b'*) qui me paraît avoir recours à Ps 29(LXX 28),1; 96(LXX 95),7; 1 Ch 16,28. Les êtres divins viennent au secours

ont proposé une reconstitution de l'original en quatre stiques dont le défaut est qu'elle ne rend pas compte des tranformations aboutissant à l'hébreu de Qumran et à l'hébreu reçu.

Si la reconstitution de Mgr Skehan est exacte, G dépend à la fois de Q, de H (pour *a'*) et de sa reconstitution de l'hébreu; ce qui est fort compliqué et improbable. Plus grave, il faut supposer que H et Q *indépendamment* aient eu recours au v. 41 et qu'ils aient omis, de nouveau *indépendamment*, le stique *b'*. Autrement dit, le texte reconstitué par Mgr Skehan ne peut être séparément la source de Q et de H. Si Q et H ne dépendent pas séparément de la reconstitution de Skehan, il faut alors imaginer une autre solution où H dépend de Q par modification et suppression, et l'on retombe dans la difficulté susmentionnée, avec le détour peu vraisemblable d'un texte en quatre stiques donnant naissance à un texte en six stiques, lui-même transformé en un texte en quatre stiques.

Pour F.M. Cross [12], qui entre dans plus de détail que Mgr Skehan, presque toutes les modifications importantes sont dues à des doublets ou à des haplographies; les plus petites à la modernisation de l'expression. Il n'a pas recours à des modifications intentionnelles portant sur le sens. Il reconstruit l'histoire de la manière suivante (que je schématise ici avec ma notation). Le texte original avait quatre stiques (*a b' c f*); par emprunt au v. 41, attiré par le mot *nqm*, et par dédoublement de *a* en *a'*, naît le texte proto-massorétique en sept stiques (*a b' a' c d e f*). Celui-ci est à la source de H (omission de *ab'* et de *e* par haplographie) en quatre stiques de nouveau (*a' c d f*). Le texte proto-massorétique (sept stiques) est aussi à la source du texte proto-4Q par dédoublement de *b'* en *b*, ce qui fait huit stiques (*a b' a' b c d e f*), source de la Septante (*a b a' b' c d e f*). Ni ce cheminement très compliqué, ni le caractère purement mécanique des modifications ne sont vraisemblables.

La seconde difficulté de la proposition de R. Meyer tient à l'origine inconnue du stique *b'* attesté seulement en grec. R. Meyer [13] y voit, sans autre commentaire, un doublet de *b*, ce que suggère le parallélisme. Mais l'explication est courte.

Si donc il est, par hypothèse, difficile d'admettre le passage d'un texte long à un texte court, en l'occurence de Q à H, si par ailleurs l'antériorité de Q par rapport à H est démontrée — et elle l'a été par R. Meyer —, ne

de Yahvé, au lieu que dans le grec ils viennent — et c'est de loin préférable — au secours du peuple.

11. F.M. CROSS, *The Ancient Library of Qumran and Modern Biblical Studies* (The Haskell Lectures 1956-1957), New York, p. 135-136, n. 30; 1961², p. 182-183, n. 30.

12. La reconstitution de Cross est la suivante (*The Ancient Library*, 1961², p. 182):
hrnynw šmym ʿmw *whbw ʿwz(?) lw bny ʾlhym*
ky dm bnyw yqwm *wkpr ʾdmt ʿmw.*

13. R. MEYER, *Die Bedeutung*, p. 200.

peut-on proposer l'existence d'une source commune à quatre stiques, que nous noterons H*? Ce texte H* à l'origine de H et de Q devrait être assez proche de H (quatre stiques), mais il devrait porter en lui les raisons qui l'ont fait modifier, exigence à laquelle ne répondent pas les reconstitutions de P. W. Skehan et de F. M. Cross.

Avant même de faire intervenir des données de fond, il est possible d'arriver à un résultat par la seule comparaison du texte consonantique de H et de Q (G) pour leurs quatre stiques communs:

		H			Q (et G[14])
a'	1	*hrnynw* gwym *ʿmw*	a	1	*hrnynw* šmym *ʿmw*
c	2	*ky dm* ʿbdyw *yqwm*	c	3	*ky dm* bnyw *yqwm*
d	3	*wnqm yšyb lṣryw*	d	4	*wnqm yšyb lṣryw*
f	4	*wkpr ʾdmt*-w *ʿmw*	f	6	*w*-y-*kpr ʾdmt ʿmw*

H et Q ont en commun, presque sans variantes, *d* et *f*. En *a' a* et en *c*, un mot chaque fois est différent; à première vue, seul le sens de *a'* est vraiment différent du stique correspondant *a*.

Si l'on examine le sens, tous les arguments utilisés pour démontrer l'antériorité de Q sont valables: la leçon *šāmayîm* de *a* oriente le regard dans la même direction que *ʾĕlohîm* de *b*, parallèle à *šāmayîm* dans Q, mais absent de H.

En c, il est plus difficile de choisir entre *ʿbdyw* et *bnyw*, apparemment synonymes: «ses serviteurs» ou «ses fils». On trouve *ʿbdyw* au v. 36, pris en bonne part: il s'agit des fidèles du Seigneur; on trouve la mention des fils à plusieurs reprises (vv. 5.8.19.20), mais pris en mauvaise part: il s'agit des fils rebelles dans tous ces cas, sauf au v. 8 (en corrélation avec Dieu Père du v. 6). Dans le contexte du v. 43, ces serviteurs ou fils ne sont pas des êtres célestes (fils de Dieu), puisqu'il est question de leur sang.

Peut-on aller plus loin dans le reconstitution de H*, source de H et de Q?

I. *Le texte reconstitué H* à l'origine de H et de Q*

Pour faire progresser la reconstitution de la source commune H*, deux types de raisonnement sont possibles. L'on peut caractériser H et Q pour en saisir la cohérence interne; il faut aussi qu'à partir du texte reconstruit il soit possible d'expliquer H et Q.

Dans H, les stiques *c* et *d* se présentent en parallélisme antithétique: des deux côtés il s'agit de vengeance, en faveur des serviteurs (*c*), contre les ennemis (*d*). Il est vrai que toutes les traductions récentes qui considèrent que l'original est Q comprennent *ky dm bnyw yqwm* comme l'annonce que Dieu vengera les siens: les fils ne sont pas différents des

14. Les mots consonnantiquement identiques sont en italique. Q et le modèle hébreu de G pour les six stiques qu'ils ont en commun pouvaient être identiques en dépit de petites différences entre Q hébreu et G grec: voir R. MEYER, *Die Bedeutung*, p. 200 et n. 14.

serviteurs; la variante ne comporte pas de changement de sens. Cependant il n'est pas vrai que *nqm* au qal suivi d'un objet direct signifie nécessairement une action favorable, ici «venger le sang de ses fils»[15]. En Josué 10,13, poème sur la victoire de Gabaon, la même tournure désigne une action défavorable. Si l'on se souvient que les fils du Cantique de Moïse sont le plus souvent rebelles, on peut rendre *dm bnyw* par «le crime de ses fils» ou «le sang versé par ses fils» et comprendre le stique: «car il vengera le crime de ses fils». Dans la reconstitution H*, la leçon *bnyw* a le mérite d'être attestée par Q et d'être *difficilior*. On verra l'intérêt qu'il y a à ménager le passage de *bnyw* (H*, Q, G) à *ʿbdyw* (H).

Au stique *a*, au lieu de retenir *šāmayîm* avec presque tous les commentateurs récents (et de rejeter *gôyîm*), j'en appelle à un *tertium quid*, *'ĕlohîm*. Certes, il serait possible de partir de *šāmayîm*, sans que la suite du raisonnement en soit affectée, mais il me paraît plus logique que l'expression mythologique qui faisait le plus difficulté se soit trouvée dès le début dans le texte. Les remaniements ultérieurs, en particulier l'appel à Ps 97(LXX 96),7, s'explique mieux ainsi.

Supposons donc au départ le texte suivant en quatre stiques:

H*	1 Faites réjouissance, *'ĕlohîm** (cieux?), avec Lui (*ʿmw*),	*a*
	2 car Il vengera le crime (sang) de ses fils	*c*
	3 et Il retournera la vengeance contre ses ennemis[16],	*d*
	4 et Il fera l'expiation du sol de son peuple.	*f*

Les dieux auxquels les nations ont été distribuées (vv. 8 et 9 selon la LXX et un autre témoin de Qumran) sont invités à s'associer à la victoire finale de Yahvé[17]. Comme ailleurs dans le cantique, *bānāyw* désigne les Israélites infidèles; par contraste, les *ṣārāyw* pourraient être les nations, mais ce n'est pas sûr. Dans cette perspective, Dieu n'épargne pas son peuple. Seul le dernier stique (*f*), en évoquant l'expiation, rappelle que Dieu se ravisera (voir les vv. 26 et 27).

15. L'examen des usages bibliques de *naqam* au qal avec complément donne les résultats suivants. La personne contre qui se porte la vengeance est introduite par *l-* (Na 1,2; Ez 25,12), par *ʿal* (Ps 99,8), par *mé'ét* (Nb 31,2), par *mîn* (1 Sa 24,13). Elle est introduite aussi par *'èt* (Lv 19,18) et sans préposition (Jos 10,13). Jos 10,13 est par ailleurs très voisin dans sa formulation de Dt 32,43; tous deux sont des textes poétiques. Le seul exemple de *nāqam* au qal avec un complément désignant une personne en faveur de qui se fait la vengeance est en 1 Sa 24,13 déjà cité: «que Yahvé me venge (*ûnqāmanî*) de toi (*mimmèkkā*)».

16. Selon la vocalisation retenue, on peut traduire: «et il retournera la vengeance contre ses ennemis» (TM) ou «et il se vengera et revaudra la châtiment à ses ennemis» (ainsi comprend la Septante). Dans le premier cas, *nāqām* est substantif; dans le second, *nāqām* est verbe.

17. Les observations fondamentales à cet égard ont été faites par R. Meyer. On fera bien de lire aussi sur les vv. 8-9 les excellentes pages de D. BARTHÉLEMY, *Les Tiqquné Sopherim et la critique textuelle de l'Ancien Testament*, dans *Congress Volume, Bonn 1962* (Suppl. to VT, 9), Leiden, 1963, pp. 285-304, spéc. pp. 295-303; réimpr. dans D. BARTHÉLEMY, *Études d'histoire du texte de l'Ancien Testament* (Orbis Biblicus et Orientalis, 21), Fribourg S. et Göttingen, 1978, pp. 91-110.

Comme aux vv. 8-9 de la Septante, il y a dans H* au ciel la cour divine (Dieu et les *benéy-'ĕlohîm*) et sur terre Israël (infidèle) et les nations, si *ṣārāyw* les désigne.

II. *Du texte reconstitué H* au texte hébreu reçu H*

A partir de H*, il est assez facile d'expliquer pourquoi le rédacteur de H a apporté une modification similaire à celle introduite aux vv. 8-9.

H 1 Faites se réjouir, nations, son peuple (*'mw*), *a'*
2 car Il vengera le sang de ses serviteurs, *c*
3 et Il retournera la vengeance contre ses ennemis, *d*
4 et Il fera l'expiation de son sol, (de) son peuple. *f*

Au stique *a'*, l'association nations (*gôyîm*) — peuple (*'am*) remplace l'association des dieux des nations et du Dieu d'Israël. On descend du ciel sur la terre. Comme aux vv. 8-9, le résultat est de subordonner les nations à Israël et d'écarter la mention des *'ĕlohîm*. Il était facile de passer de *'immô* «avec Lui» à *'ammô* «son peuple». Le remplacement de *'ĕlohîm* (ou de *šāmayîm*) par *gôyîm* est plus violent, mais compréhensible si les dieux ou les étoiles des cieux sont précisément les dieux des nations.

La raison principale du changement est probablement la volonté d'éviter, comme au v. 8, d'associer sur un pied de quasi-égalité Dieu et les dieux. Dans les cieux, Dieu règne seul (Dt 4,39). Qui donc pourrait se réjouir avec lui? Aux vv. 12 et 39 du même cantique, l'hébreu affirme clairement qu'il n'y a point avec Dieu d'autres dieux. On peut répéter ici ce que le P. D. Barthélemy a mis en évidence pour les vv. 8-9: il y a *tiqqûn soferîm*[18].

Mais il faut ajouter que le début du v. 43 ainsi modifié donne une signification nouvelle à la fin du cantique: «Nations, faites se réjouir son peuple». Il ne s'agit plus de l'assentiment du ciel à la vengeance divine, mais les félicitations des nations à Israël vengé par Dieu.

Au stique *c*, le changement de «ses fils» en «ses serviteurs» résout l'équivoque: la vengeance est en faveur des bons serviteurs. Simultanément, l'antithèse entre les bons (ses serviteurs) et les mauvais (ses ennemis) se distingue de l'association des nations au peuple élu. La frontière entre le bien et le mal n'est pas celle qui sépare Israël de ses voisins.

Au stique *f*, le suffixe de *'admātô* n'entraîne pas de modification perceptible du sens et est souvent considéré comme fautif.

III. *Du texte reconstitué H* au texte hébreu de Qumran Q*

A partir de ce même texte H*, il est possible de rendre compte de Q.

18. D. BARTHÉLEMY, *Les Tiqquné Sopherim*, p. 302 (réimpr., p. 108).

Q 1 Faites réjouissance, cieux, avec Lui (*ʿmw*) *a*
2 et adorez-le (qu'ils l'adorent), tous les *'ĕlohîm*, *b*
3 car il vengera le crime (sang) de ses fils, *c*
4 et il retournera la vengeance contre ses ennemis, *d*
5 et à ceux qui le haïssent il rendra la pareille, *e*
6 et il fera l'expiation du sol de son peuple. *f*

La perspective générale de Q reste très proche de celle de H*, mais elle évite quelques écueils.

1. Pour le réviseur qui a modifié H* en Q, également, la mention des *'ĕlohîm* à côté de Dieu et sur le même plan a fait difficulté. Mais au lieu de modifier ponctuellement, il a explicité. Il a doublé le stique *a* par un second, *b*, emprunté au Ps 97(LXX 96),7, avec pour résultat de compenser l'affirmation discutée de *a* par une autre exprimant clairement que les dieux doivent adorer Yahvé. Au lieu d'un terme, *'ĕlohîm*, il en a mis deux en parallèle, *šāmayîm* et *'ĕlohîm*, le premier glosant le second. C'est la raison pour laquelle nous préférons supposer *'ĕlohîm* à l'origine dans H*.

D'où vient *šāmayîm*? Le cantique s'ouvre sur une invocation des cieux et de la terre (v. 1); il s'achève désormais sur une invocation des cieux et une mention du sol (*'ădāmāh*). Cette inclusion boiteuse s'explique mieux comme le résultat d'une modification théologique que d'une retouche littéraire.

Le parallélisme *'ĕlohîm* (*b*)//*šāmayîm*(*a*) que je suggère s'explique, lui, par une certaine synonymie des deux termes. Les cieux désignent la cour céleste où résident les dieux, et ils sont parfois personnifiés et invoqués [19]. L'expression «Dieu des cieux» [20] est parallèle à «Dieu des dieux» [21], particulièrement en Dt 10,14 et 17, et en Ps 136,2 et 26 (deuxième et dernière invocation). On sait par ailleurs que Yahvé Sabaôt est le Dieu de «l'armée des cieux» [22].

2. Dès lors que le stique *b* était introduit dans Q, la succession binaire des stiques était rompue. Le stique, emprunté au v. 41b et appelé par la ressemblance entre le stique *d* et 41b, fut alors ajouté pour donner le texte en six stiques attesté à Qumran. Plus long que H*, il en aménage les difficultés par des additions prudentielles.

19. La racine *rnn* avec invocation des cieux (et de la terre) se retrouve en Is 44,23 et 49,13 et en Jer 51,48. Il y avait là aussi une raison pour introduire *šāmayîm*.

20. Gn 24,3.7; Ps 136,26; Dn 2,18.19.37.44; Jon 1,9; Esd 5,11-12; 6,9-10; 7,12.21.23; Ne 1,4-5; 2,4.20; 2 Ch 36,23.

21. *'ĕlohey-ha'ĕlohîm*: Dt 10,17; Ps 136,2; *'él-'ĕlohîm*: Ps 50,1; Jos 22,22; *'él-'élîm*: Dn 11,36.

22. Dt 17,3; 2 R 17,16; 21,3; 23,4-5; Is 34,4; Jer 8,2; 19,13; 33,22; Za 1,5; Dn 8,10; Ne 9,6; 2 Ch 33,3.5, et surtout 1 R 22,19 et 2 Ch 18,18.

IV. *La Septante G et son modèle hébreu*

Avec Elia S. Artom [23] et R. Meyer [24], je tiens pour acquis que le texte en huit stiques de la Septante (G) est issu du texte en six stiques de Qumran, complété par le stique *a'* du texte hébreu reçu (H), le seul a être distinct de Q pour le sens. En revanche, il ne va nullement de soi que cette opération, qui a entraîné l'adjonction d'un stique nouveau *b'* pour les besoins du parallélisme, s'est faite en grec. Voici d'abord une traduction de G.

G 1 Réjouissez-vous, cieux, avec Lui *a*
2 et qu'ils l'adorent, tous les fils de Dieu. *b*
3 Réjouissez-vous, nations, avec son peuple *a'*
4 et qu'ils lui donnent force, tous les anges de Dieu. *b'*
5 Car Il vengera le sang de ses fils *c*
6 et Il retournera la vengeance contre ses ennemis, *d*
7 et à ceux qui Le haïssent Il rendra la pareille, *e*
8 et le Seigneur purifiera la terre de son peuple. *f*

Pour Artom et Meyer, le stique *b'* καὶ ἐνισχυσάτωσαν αὐτῷ πάντες ἄγγελοι αὐτοῦ ne peut avoir été ajouté qu'en grec. Et, puisqu'il l'est pour maintenir le parallélisme et le nombre pair de stiques, c'est aussi en grec que *a'* s'est introduit, emprunté au texte hébreu reçu H. Mais est-ce si sûr? P. W. Skehan et F. M. Cross tiennent pour un original hébreu de *b'*, et ils proposent même une rétroversion [25].

1. Observons d'abord qu'il y a parallélisme strict entre *b* et *b'*. Les expressions ἄγγελοι θεοῦ et υἱοὶ θεοῦ sont synonymes. En dépit d'une hésitation assez marquée de la tradition manuscrite [26], il faut préférer, avec A. Rahlfs et J. W. Wevers, ὑίοὶ θεοῦ en *b* et ἄγγελοι θεοῦ en *b'*. La rétroversion cependant est délicate. Le Ps 97(LXXX 96),7, utilisé en *b* a *'ĕlohîm* en hébreu (et ἄγγελοι θεοῦ en grec), et de même Q. Or je ne connais pas d'exemple où *'ĕlohîm* (sans *benéy*) est traduit par υἱοὶ θεοῦ. En revanche, ἄγγελοι θεοῦ de *b'* pourrait rendre soit *benéy 'ĕlohîm* (*'él*) [27], soit *'ĕlohîm* [28]. Un élément cependant intervient ici de manière

23. Voir ci-dessus n. 9.
24. Voir ci-dessus n. 3.
25. Voir ci-dessus notes 10 et 12.
26. Voir l'édition critique du grec de J. W. Wevers, citée n. 4.
27. *benéy-'ĕlohîm* est rendu ἄγγελοι τοῦ θεοῦ en Jb 1,6; 2,1; 38,7, et en Dn 3,25(92) LXX (trad. de l'araméen); il intervient comme variante en Gn 6,2 (bien attesté) et 4 (peu attesté). En Dt 32,8, une forme similaire attestée seulement à Qumran est rendue par ἀγγέλων θεοῦ que A. Rahlfs a retenue. Quelques témoins, inspirés de l'hébreu standard (106ᶜ Justin) ont υἱῶν Ισραηλ. J.W. Wevers (p. 346-347), influencé par le papyrus pré-chrétien 848 qui lit υἱῶν devant une lacune, propose dans son édition ce que je crois un hybride: υἱῶν θεοῦ. Cette leçon n'a peut-être jamais existé à cette place. Le choix est entre ἀγγέλων θεοῦ et υἱῶν Ισραηλ. Plus généralement, le υἱός du grec correspond toujours à *benéy-* en hébreu (ou araméen), mais l'inverse n'est pas vrai: le ἄγγελος du grec peut rendre soit *benéy-'ĕl(ohîm)*, soit *'ĕlohîm*.
28. *'ĕlohîm* est rendu par ἄγγελοι en Ps 8,6; 97 (96),7; 138 (137),1 et en Dn 2,11 (araméen); *'él* est rendu par ἄγγελος en Jb 20,5.

décisive: le stique *c* (dans Q et dans G) mentionne «le sang de ses fils», et il ne peut s'agir que des Israélites. Dès lors, aussi bien en hébreu qu'en grec, il fallait éviter le contact de deux acceptions distinctes du mot «fils». Comme le grec, le modèle hébreu du grec devait avoir «fils de Dieu» en *b*, ce qui suppose un aménagement de Ps 96(97),7, et *'ĕlohîm*/ἄγγελοι θεοῦ en *b'*[29].

2. Reste à déterminer le sens et l'origine de *b'*. Rien de semblable dans la Bible hébraïque et encore moins dans la Septante. Le sens de *b'* est que les êtres célestes doivent non seulement adorer Dieu (*b*), mais aussi prêter main forte au peuple de Dieu (αὐτῷ doit renvoyer à λαοῦ). Pour l'origine, on peut songer à 1 Chr 16,28; Ps 96(LXX 95),7; Ps 29(LXX 28),1, et surtout à ce dernier qui mentionne les *benéy-'élîm*:

hābû l-YHWH benéy-'élîm
hābû l-YHWH kabôd wa'oz.

Ce qui donne pour *b'* selon Skehan:

wĕhabû 'oz lô kol benéy 'élîm[30].

Il se peut que la formule *habû l-* ait été appelée par le début du cantique (Dt 32,3), mais surtout l'idée exprimée en Ps 29(28),1 est parallèle à celle exprimée en Ps 97(96),7 et reprise en *b*.

Une difficulté toutefois, la suppression de *kabôd*. Venant après le stique *a'* qui ne mentionne ni Dieu ni les dieux, mais les nations et le peuple, l'invitation aux anges à donner vigueur est destinée au peuple. Le mot *kabôd* ne pouvait convenir, il a été remplacé par *'oz* (ou par un synonyme).

Autre ligne de recherche. Certains textes emploient la racine *ḥzq*[31], surtout au hifil et au pièl pour décrire les anges se portant au secours d'Israël, ainsi en Daniel (10,21; 11,1) et dans le Cantique de Débora (Jg 5,20). L'angélologie sous-jacente se retrouve à Qumran et dans le judaïsme rabbinique, mais elle peut être plus ancienne. D'ailleurs, quels que soient les mots employés, c'est ici le sens le plus probable, qui rejoint celui de Dt 32,8-9 selon l'hébreu reçu: non seulement les nations sont soumises à Israël, mais les anges des nations servent Israël. L'addition de *b'* est théologiquement apparentée à l'hébreu reçu du v. 43 (stique *a'*), mais sa mention des anges la rattache à la forme qumranienne.

L'addition *b'* suppose aussi connu le stique *b*, car *b* et *b'* sont étroitement parallèles, mais elle ne se comprend qu'avec le stique *a'* de l'hébreu reçu, puisqu'elle se rapporte au peuple. Dès lors, l'addition est

29. La citation de Hb 1,6 ne dirime pas le débat en faveur d'ἀγγέλων au stique *b*, mais elle atteste que la forme grecque de Dt 32,43 est citée, contaminée soit par le stique *b'*, soit par le Ps 97(96),7 très voisin. Voir cependant J. DE WAARD, *A Comparative Study of the Old Testament Text in the Dead Sea Scrolls and in the New Testament* (Studies on the Texts of Desert of Judah, 4), Leiden, 1966, pp. 13-16.

30. La reconstitution de Skehan met en contact deux sens différents du mot fils, ce qui est peu vraisemblable (voir ci-dessus n. 10).

31. Albright a cherché de ce côté; voir sa reconstruction à la n. 7.

plus vraisemblable en hébreu qu'en grec. Il n'est d'ailleurs guère concevable que le procédé littéraire consistant à créer un répondant au stique *b* pour assurer le parallélisme ait joué à l'intérieur de la tradition du grec. La forme confluente en huit stiques attestée par la Septante a donc toute chance d'avoir déjà existé en hébreu.

Si, au regard de l'histoire du texte, le grec en huit stiques et son modèle hébreu apparaissent comme un hybride, il n'en est pas de même théologiquement. Ce texte long incorpore l'association des nations à la joie du peuple élu, sans contredire, mais en enrichissant la forme première qui visait surtout Israël dans ses rapports avec son Dieu. Simultanément, le stique *c*, bien que non modifié (τῶν υἱῶν αὐτοῦ = *bānāyw*), est tiré dans le sens des stiques *a'b'* qu'il suit et rejoint la signification favorable de l'hébreu reçu («ses serviteurs»).

* * *

Venant à la suite de plusieurs études, dont celles de P. W. Skehan, de W. F. Albright et surtout de R. Meyer, le présent travail a visé à établir une cohérence entre les observations littéraires et les données de sens et de contenu théologique.

1. Au plan de la critique textuelle et de la critique littéraire (le *lower criticism* devient ici tout naturellement *higher criticism*), il met en évidence les mécanismes ayant déterminé les passages successifs du v. 43 de quatre à six et de six à huit stiques: le stique *a* modifié en *a'* dans l'hébreu reçu — c'est le changement le plus drastique —, le stique *a* doublé par *b* en 4QDt^{q} et l'appel de *e* pour garder un nombre pair de stiques, création de *b'* (d'après Ps 29,1) dans le modèle hébreu de la Septante pour assurer le parallélisme *ab/a'b'*. Le postulat de départ selon lequel l'original devait avoir quatre stiques comme l'hébreu reçu (on pouvait ajouter, non retrancher) et comporter les particularités théologiques de 4QDt^{q} (qui pouvaient faire difficulté) se révèle fécond. La reconstitution proposée rend compte de l'histoire ultérieure.

2. Au regard de la théologie impliquée dans le v. 43, le présent travail reconnaît les deux lignes de pensée mises en évidence par R. Meyer, mais il formule la thèse autrement. Il y a d'une part la ligne théologique de 4QDt^{q} qui est une interprétation prudentielle en six stiques de l'original en quatre stiques: la scène est au ciel et elle associe le Dieu d'Israël et les dieux des nations. Il y a d'autre part la ligne de l'hébreu reçu: la scène est sur terre; les nations acclament le peuple d'Israël. Le texte en huit stiques de la Septante combine les deux perspectives, céleste et terrestre. De plus, le stique *c* a eu à l'origine (*ky dm bnyw yqwm*) un sens différent de celui qu'on lui donne habituellement; il faut comprendre: «il vengera le crime de ses fils». A ce stade, la vengeance de Dieu se porte non au secours d'Israël, mais contre lui.

3. Le v. 43 est l'envoi, la finale en panache, du Cantique. Le poète —

ce n'est plus Dieu qui parle en personne — achève le Cantique par un appel aux témoins célestes (les cieux, les *'ĕlohîm*) ou aux nations. R. Meyer a mis en évidence la similitude des préoccupations qui ont entraîné la modification des vv. 8-9 et du v. 43 tels qu'ils sont attestés à Qumran et dans la Septante pour aboutir à l'hébreu reçu. Mais on n'a guère remarqué le supplément de cohérence que la lecture de ces versets selon le texte de Qumran (et de la Septante), comme aussi selon le texte de notre reconstitution en quatre stiques, apportait au Cantique lui-même et aux ch. 31 et 32 dans lesquels il est encadré.

L'introduction au Cantique, spécialement 31,19-22, le donne comme un témoignage contre Israël. Cependant le Cantique lui-même, qui vise surtout Israël jusqu'au v. 25, affirme à partir du v. 26 que la jalousie divine n'ira pas jusqu'à l'extermination des siens; Dieu déchaînera sa colère contre les ennemis qui avaient été chargés des hautes œuvres divines contre Israël (vv. 21-25,27). Ce retournement n'a en soi rien d'unique, mais il est inattendu dans le contexte des ch. 31 et 32 où Israël seul est visé.

Lu à la suite des vv. 40-42 qui décrivent la colère de Yahvé ivre de sang, le v. 43 selon Qumran et notre reconstitution poursuit sur le même ton vengeur. La cour divine est invitée à se réjouir de ce que Dieu punit ses fils infidèles (ce qui rappelle les vv. 21-25) et leurs adversaires (vv. 40-42). L'expiation du sol (dernier stique), pour salvifique qu'elle est, n'en suggère pas moins des images sanglantes de sacrifices. La mention des Israélites (*bānāyw*) et des ennemis (*ṣārāyw*), les uns et les autres poursuivis par la colère divine, correspond au deux grands climats du Cantique, celui qui vise les Israélites (vv. 1-26) et celui qui fait intervenir les nations exécutrices du châtiment (vv. 27-42) [32].

32. Sur le plan du Cantique de Moïse, voir P. W. SKEHAN, *The Structure of the Song of Moses in Deuteronomy (Deut. 32,1-43)*, dans *CBQ* 13 (1951) 153-163 (repris dans P. W. Skehan, *Studies in Israelite Poetry and Wisdom* [The Catholic Biblical Quaterly Monograph Series, 1], Washington, 1971, pp. 67-77; O. EISSFELDT, *Das Lied Moses (Dt 32,1-43) und das Lehrgedicht Asaphs (Ps 78) samt einer Analyse der Umgebung des Mose-Liedes* (Berichte über die Verhandlungen der Sächsischen Akademie der Wissenschaften zu Leipzig, 104,5), Berlin, 1958, 54 p.; *Die Umrahmung des Mose-Liedes Dtn 32,1-43 und des Mose-Gesetzes Dtn 1-30 in Dtn 31,9-32,47*, dans *Wissenschaftliche Zeitschrift der Martin-Luther Universität Halle-Wittenberg*, Gesellschafts- u. Sprachwiss. Reihe, 4 (1954-1955) 411-417 (réimpr.: *Kleine Schriften*, t. 3, Tübingen, 1966, pp. 322-334); P. WINTER, *Der Begriff «Söhne Gottes» im Moselied Dtn 32,1-43*, dans *ZAW* 67 (1955) 40-48; E. BAUMANN, *Das Lied Mose's (Dtn. 32,1-43) auf seine gedankliche Geschlossenheit untersucht*, dans *VT* 6 (1956) 414-424; N. LOHFINK, *Der Bundesschluß im Lande Moab. Redaktionsgeschichtliches zu Dt 28,69-32,47*, dans *BZ* 6 (1962) 32-56; J. HARVEY, *Le «Rîb-Pattern», réquisitoire prophétique sur la rupture de l'alliance*, dans *Biblica* 43 (1962) 172-196; *Le plaidoyer prophétique contre Israël après la rupture de l'alliance. Étude d'une formule littéraire de l'Ancien Testament*, Bruges et Montréal, 1967, 186 p.; C. J. LABUSCHAGNE, *The Song of Moses: Its Framework and Structure*, dans *De Fructu Oris Sui. Essays in honour of Adrianus van Selms* (Pretoria Oriental Studies, 9), Leiden, 1971, pp. 85-98; J. R. LUNDBOM,

Dans le texte hébreu reçu, la réjouissance simultanée des nations et d'Israël parce que les impies sont punis n'est pas préparée. En revanche, dans le texte de Qumran et le texte reconstitué en quatre stiques, les nations ne sont visées qu'accessoirement. S'achevant sur une menace de vengeance et une annonce d'expiation, le Cantique du Deutéronome est bien alors la solennelle mise en garde des Israélites annoncée au ch. 31.

Abbaye de Maredsous
B-5642 Denée

Pierre-Maurice BOGAERT

The Lawbook of the Josianic Reform, dans *CBQ* 38 (1976), 293-302; S. HIDAL, *Some Reflections on Deuteronomy 32*, dans *Annual of the Swedish Theological Institute* 11 (1977, paru en 1978) 15-21.

PRIMEVAL AND ESCHATOLOGICAL OVERTONES IN THE SONG OF MOSES (DT 32,1-43)

The Song of Moses in Dt 32, from a form-critical point of view is a real psalm and, at the same time, canonically, thematically and partly also lexically [1] an integral part of the Book of Dt. What characterizes this «most impressive literary composition» [2] as a psalm and as a part of Dt are its primeval and eschatological elements.

There are in the Hebrew bible some nine psalms which comprise not just references to separate historical events, to «Einzeltraditionen», but «eine Geschichtsreihe», a certain continuous survey of Israel's salvation history [3]. Almost half of them are mere hymns: Ps 114; 135; 136 and Ex 15,1-18. The others are composite poems: hymnic and didactic (Ps 105); hymnic, didactic and admonitory (Ps 78); hymnic, penitential and supplicatory (Ps 106 and Is 63,7-64,11); hymnic, sapiential and prophetical (Dt 32,1-43, the most complex composition of them all) [4].

The dominant or classical scheme of Israel's salvation history, in prose summaries as well as in poetical surveys, extends from the deliverance from Egypt until the gift or conquest of the land. It is especially in more complex and rather late texts that this scheme has been broken, both at the beginning and at the end.

Primeval elements

The upper limit of the classical scheme, the Egyptian stage, is most constant. If we look at the Book of Psalms, there is only one psalm, Ps 105, where the historical survey is preceded by what Kühlewein calls «der Vorbau der Vätertradition», the entrance-hall of the patriarchs [5]. In

1. Cf. the strikingly similar use (in both Dt 32 and the prose texts of Dt) of some terms and phrases, like: *šiḥēt* in 32,5 and 9,12; *hinḥîl* in 32,8 and 4,20; *y^{e}bûl* in 32,22 and 11,17; *killāh* in 32,23 and 28,21; *šillēm* in 32,41 and 7,10; *ʿam (lōʾ) ḥākām* in 32,6 and 4,6; *ʾ^{e}lōhîm (ʾ^{a}šer) lōʾ y^{e}dāʿûm* in 32,17 and 29,25. On the whole, however, the language of Dt 32 is very original, presenting at least fourteen hapax legomena and showing special connections with the vocabulary of Dt 33, Jg 5, Jeremiah, Deutero-Isaiah, Ezechiel, some Psalms, Job, Proverbs, etc.

2. Cf. C. J. LABUSCHAGNE, *The Song of Moses: Its Framework and Structure* (Pretoria Oriental Series XI), pp. 85-98, esp. p. 92.

3. J. KÜHLEWEIN, *Geschichte in den Psalmen* (Calwer Theol. Monogr. 2), 1973, esp. pp. 161-162. It is strange that Kühlewein does not mention Dt 32 in this context.

4. Cf. S. CARRILLO ALDAY, *Género literario del Cántico de Moisés (Dt. 32)*, in *Est. Bibl.* 26 (1967) 69-75, who concludes: «... el Cántico de Moisés, con participar del género hímnico, de las fórmulas deuteronómicas y proféticas, del estilo sapiencial, es sin embargo una sola obra de un único autor».

5. *Op. cit.*, p. 158-161.

the collective lament of Trito-Isaiah, Abraham and Isaac are also mentioned, but only after the retrospect of 63,7-14, in v. 16. In this respect, the Book of Dt presents almost the same picture. More than fifteen times the promise of the land made to the fathers is recalled; seven times the triad Abraham, Isaac and Jacob is mentioned, but only once the remembrance of one of the patriarchs precedes the reference to the Egyptian period in a continuous historical survey (namely, in the so-called Creed of Dt 26,5-9, a combination of old and young material as was shown by L. Rost and other scholars)[6].

Already in the Pss 135 and 136 the praise of Yahweh as the Saviour of Israel from the exodus until the conquest of Canaan is preceded by the praise of Yahweh as the Creator of heaven and earth. Only in Dt 32, however, in the vv. 8 and 9, the history of Israel itself starts in the primeval times, before the patriarches[7]:

b^{e}*hanḥēl ʿelyôn gôyim* *b*^{e}*haprîdô b*^{e}*nê ʾādām,*
yaṣṣēb g^{e}*bulōt ʿammîm* *l*^{e}*mispar b*^{e}*nê ʾ*^{é}*lōhîm* (4Q, LXX)
kî ḥeleq YHWH ʿammô *yaʿ*^{a}*qōb ḥebel naḥ*^{a}*lātô*[8].

In this beautiful stanza of six cola many biblical and extra-biblical motifs have been combined and, eventually, amplified and transposed:
— the motif of a national god who gives his people a land to possess, who forms a unity with his land and his people (cf. Jg 11,24; Num 35,34);
— the motif of the separation of peoples in the beginning of history (cf. Gn 10 and 11, esp. *nipr*^{e}*dû* in 10,32);
— the motif of the upper-god (*ʿelyôn*) presiding the sons of the gods (cf. Ugaritic texts; Pss 29,1; 82,6; Job 1,6; 2,1; 38,7);
— the motif of Yahweh who establishes (*hiṣṣîb*) and, eventually, removes the boundaries of the earth and of the peoples (cf. Ps 74,17; Is 10,13);
— the motif of a fixed number (*mispar*) of members of a heavenly or earthly assembly (cf. the seventy sons of Athirat in U.T.[9]; the seventy peoples of Gn 10; the seventy members of Jacob's family who went to Egypt (Ex 1,5; Dt 10,22); the seventy shepherds of Ap Hen 89,59;
— the motif of the supreme deity who assigns to each god or heavenly guardian his people or country and, vice versa, to each people its

6. Cf. H. D. PREUSS, *Deuteronomium* (Erträge der Forschung, 164), 1982, pp. 144-148. Dt 4,32 has the only allusion to creation in the prose of the book.

7. Cf. S. A. GELLER, *The Dynamics of Parallel Verse. A Poetic Analysis of Deut 32:6-12*, in *HTR* 75 (1982) 35-56, esp. p. 44. Probably to stress this view, the exodus from Egypt which commonly is presented as the birth of the nation, has been left out completely.

8. Or perhaps originally (because of LXX): «But Yahweh took Jacob as his share (*ḥālaq*)/Israel as his allotted possession». Cf. R. MEYER, *Die Bedeutung von Deuteronomium 32,8f.43 (4Q) für die Auslegung des Moseliedes*, in *Fschr. W. Rudolph*, Tübingen, 1961, pp. 197-209, esp. p. 199.

9. Cf. S. CARRILLO ALDAY, *El Cantico de Moisés (Dt. 32). Analisis Exegetico*, in *Est. Bibl.* 26 (1967) 143-185, esp. p. 167f.

god (cf. U.T.; Dt 4,19; 29,25; Dan 10,13; Test Napht and other apocalypses);
— the motif of Israel being the special possession (*naḥ^a^lāh, s^e^gullāh*) of Yahweh (Dt 4,20; 9,26.29; 26,18; Ex 19,5; Jer 10,16; Ps 33,12).

The main theme of the whole passage, however, — Yahweh elected Israel as his people already in primeval times, — is unique, relating both to psalm literature and also to Dt. It re-appears only in Sir 17,17 and 24,7-8, in Qumran (e.g. 1QM 17,5ff.), in Targ Jerusch I and in later apocalypses [10].

That the primeval retrospect of vv. 8-9 is not a *Fremdkörper* in the Song becomes evident from stylistic analysis, as has been done by S. A. Geller [11]. Il also becomes clear from the appearance in the context of the idea of Yahweh as father-creator of Israel:

6cd Is he not your father who created you (*'ābîkā qān^e^kā*)?
Did he not make and establish you (*'āś^e^kā waykōn^e^nekā*)?
15c He abandoned the God who made him (*'^e^lô^a^h 'āśāhû*);
18a You deserted the Rock who begot you (*ṣûr y^e^lād^e^kā*),
you forgot the God who gave you birth (*'ēl m^e^hōl^e^lekā*).

If we also take into account vv. 5a, 19b, 20c and, eventually v. 43 (4Q and LXX), where the Israelites are called the «sons» or the «sons and daughters» of Yahweh, we get eight cola, which together use seven completely different terms to express the notion of Yahweh, the father-creator of Israel. In the whole psalm literature there is no other clear witness to this notion except in Is 63,16 and 64,7 [12]. In the rest of Dt this idea is only expressed in 14,1. Even Deutero-Isaiah needs 16 chapters to express the same idea as many times, and he uses, in addition to the terms «sons» and «daughters» (Is 43,6; 45,11), only three different terms: *bārā'*, *yāṣar*, and *'āśāh* (Is 43,1.21; 44,2.21.24; 45,11; 51,13) [13].

Finally, it must be noticed that the primeval resonance of all these passages in Dt 32 is heightened by the occurrence, excluding the Tetragrammaton (8 times) of four other divine names, — *'elyôn* and *'^e^lōhîm* in v. 8, *'^e^lô^a^h* in v. 15c, *'ēl* in v. 18b. Further, in v. 18a occurs the term *ṣûr*, «Rock», a key word, used seven times as a divine appellative throughout the poem.

10. Cf. R. MEYER, *op. cit.*, p. 203-207; C. ROWLAND, *The Open Heaven. A Study of Apocalyptic in Judaism and Early Christianity*, London, 1982, p. 89ff.

11. According to the analysis of GELLER, *op. cit.*, p. 40ff., v. 9 is not only the culmination of vv. 8-9 but also «the central couplet, the axis of the passage (viz. vv. 6-12) in regard both to its placement and meaning».

12. Although there can be little doubt that also in Ex. 15,16 *qānāh* means «to create» or «to procreate».

13. Cf. B. BYRNE, '*Sons of God*' — '*Seed of Abraham*' (An. Bibl., 83), Rome, 1979, p. 13-16. The idea of the 'Israelite' sonship of God may go back «to the very origins of the nation» (p. 13), but, when Dt 32 «provides perhaps the most extensive employment» of the 'Father-creator' motif (p. 14), it cannot be concluded that we have here a very old text: on the contrary.

Eschatological elements

The gift of the land is commonly the lower limit in the biblical surveys of Israel's salvation history. In the psalm literature two remarkable exceptions emerge: Ps 78 and Dt 32. It was the main merit of Eissfeldt's study of 1958 [14] to draw attention on the striking similarities between these two poetical compositions. Having recalled alternatively the gracious acts of the Lord and Israel's rebellions and incurred punishments in Egypt, in the wilderness, and during the conquest of the «holy land» (v. 54), Ps 78 concludes with some lapidary statements in vv. 67-72 about: the election of Judah instead of Ephraim, the election of Zion for the building of the temple, and the election of David to lead Israel, the people and inheritance of Yahweh.

Dt 32 first remembers, in separate stages, the gracious acts of Yahweh from primeval times until the settlement in the land (vv. 6b-14), the rebellion of Israel (vv. 15-18), and God's anger and punitive purposes (vv. 19-25). Then, in a mixture of reflexion and oracular proclamation, the reasons follow for Yahweh's change of mind, and the announcement of future vindication (vv. 26-43).

The main difference between the two texts is twofold. (1) The outlook of Ps 78 remains limited to the past, although the author certainly intends to actualize the past events for his own, much later days [15]. The finale of Dt 32 is completely future oriented. (2) In Ps 78 only 10 % of the verses deal with the gracious acts of the Lord after the conquest of the land. In Dt 32 30 % of the poem deals explicitly with the future retribution of God's enemies and the future salvation of his people (vv. 34-43).

In the eschatological finale of the vv. 34-43, just as in the primeval passage, many biblical and extra-biblical motifs are combined, amplified and transposed:

1. the motif of a vindication which Yahweh has in reserve, which is hidden (*kāmus*) and sealed up (*ḥātum*) in his storehouses (v. 34). The culmination of this notion appears in Dan 12,9 in «the things that are shut up (*sᵉtumîm*) and sealed (*ḥᵃtumîm*) until the time of the end» (cf. also Jer 50,25; Mal 3,16);

2. the motif of «a day of vengeance and requital» (*yôm nāqām wᵉšillum*, v. 35a LXX; cf. Is 34,8; 59,17; 61,2; 63,4; Jer 46,10):
— a day of final disaster (*yôm 'êdam*, v. 35c; cf. Ob 13; Zeph 1,15),
— when Yahweh will give justice (*yādîn*) to his people and have

14. *Das Lied Moses Deuteronomium 32,1-43 und das Lehrgedicht Asaphs Psalm 78 samt einer Analyse der Umgebung des Mose-Liedes*, Berlin, 1958. The arguments, however, for a date, respectively, in the 11th and 10th cent. B.C. are not convincing.

15. Cf. R. P. CARROLL, *Psalm LXXVIII, Vestiges of a Tribal Polemic*, in *VT*, 21 (1971) 133-150; R. J. CLIFFORD, *In Zion and David a New Beginning: An Interpretation of Psalm 78*, in *Fschr. F. M. CROSS*, Winona Lake, 1981, pp. 121-141.

compassion (*yitneḥam*) on his servants (v. 36a; cf. Ps 135,14; Is 49,13; 57,18),
— when he will set his hand to judgment (*b^e^mišpāṭ*, v. 41b; cf. Is 34,5; Zeph 3,8; Jl 4,2; Ps 149,9),
— when he will take vengeance (*'ašîb nāqām*) on his adversaries (v. 41c and 43c),
— and repay (*'^a^šallēm*) those who hate him (v. 41d and 43 with Q),
— when he will avenge (*yiqqôm*) the blood of his 'sons' (v. 43b with Q and LXX; cf. Ps 79,10),
— and make expiation (*kipper*) for 'his people's land' (v. 43d with Q and LXX; cf. Jl 4,17.19; Zech 13,1-2) [16].

The idea of the day and the execution of a twofold vindication — punishment for the enemies and salvation for Yahweh's people — is expressed in this eschatological finale in some ten cola, in ten different ways. Moreover, the key roots *nqm* and *šlm* with the meaning «to vindicate» or «vindication» are used, respectively, four and three times (if we reckon with the Q. fragment). In no prophetical oracle against the nations is there such a heaping up of synonymous phrases and such an emphasis relating to this very notion of God's vindication [17];

3. the motif: doomsday is near (*qārôb*, v. 35c; cf. Ob 15; Zeph 1,14; Jl 4,14; Is 13,6; Jer 48,16), paralleled in v. 35d by the unique phrasing: *w^e^ḥās '^a^tîdōt lāmô*, «the events to come», the fate prepared for the enemies, «are speeding (cf. Is 60,22) towards them»;

4. the ironical questioning after the power of the other gods, addressed in vv. 37-38 not to Israel, as in Jer 2,28 and 11,12, but to all the enemies of Yahweh and his people;

5. the solemn *Schwurformel*, introduction to a divine oath, *ḥay '^a^nî*, which occurs 23 times in the O.T., 16 times in Ez [18]. In v. 40b, however, the formula is amplified to *ḥay 'ānōkî l^e'^ôlām*, «as surely as I live for ever», and combined with the other oath formula «I lift my hand». This last phrase, typical for Ez 20, is also amplified here to «I lift my hand to heaven» (cf. Dan 12,7);

6. the cluster of motifs in vv. 41-42 around the theme of the divine warrior: who whets his sword, his flashing sword, who makes his sword and arrows drunken of blood, whose sword devours the flesh and blood

16. The cultic term *kipper* is used this way only here. B. JANOWSKI, *Sühne als Heilsgeschehen* (WMANT, 55), 1982, pp. 129-131 relates v. 43 to v. 8f. By vindicating Israel on the enemies «in der künftigen Zeit der Heilsvollendung» God will restore «die — durch das an Israel begangene Unrecht gestörte — kosmische Ordnung».

17. In the whole complex of Is 34-35 and 40-66 the root *nqm* occurs six times and the root *šlm* four times in similar contexts, in six different chapters.

18. Cf. S. KREUZER, *Der lebendige Gott* (BWANT, 116), 1983, who remarks at the end of his dealing with Dt. 32,40 (pp. 230-235): «Dtn 32,40 steht literarisch und formgeschichtlich nicht am Anfang sondern fast am Ende der Belege für die Schwurformel im AT, jedenfalls jene in der 1. Person. Von hier ist unmittelbar hinüberzublicken auf Dan 12,7 ...»

of the ennemies. These motifs, rooted in old mythology and in the theophanies of holy war, are transformed in the prophetical oracles against Israel and, especially, against the nations [19]. As they are used here, they have their closest parallels in the eschatological, «proto-apocalyptic» [20] texts of Is 63 and 34;

7. and right in the center, — especially if we accept six original cola in v. 43 on the basis of Q and LXX, — Yahweh's self-proclamation as the only existing and the only acting God in v. 39. Although it has many parallels, mainly in Is 40-55 [21], this verse — with its seven qualifications of Yahweh, its seven first person initial Alephs, its seven first person concluding Yodhs, and its fourfold repetition of *ʾ^{a}nî*, — is probably the most impressive monotheistic formula of the O.T.:

r^{e}ʾû ʿattāh kî *ʾ^{a}nî ʾ^{a}nî hûʾ* [22]
w^{e}ʾên ʾ^{é}lōhîm ʿimmādî *ʾ^{a}nî ʾāmît waʾ^{a}ḥayyeh*
māḥaṣtî waʾ^{a}nî ʾerpāʾ *w^{e}ʾên miyyādî maṣṣîl.*

The primeval outlook of vv. 8-9 is no foreign matter in the Song; neither is the eschatological finale of vv. 34-43. Eschatological also permeates the preceding verses, for instance:
— vv. 28-29 which insist on the stupidity of the enemies, who are unwise and do not understand what their future fate (*ʾaḥ^{a}rîtām*) will be [23];
— and vv. 32-33 with their combination of the Sodom-Gomorra and the vine imagery [24].

The comparison with the other history oriented psalms suggests that the expansion of an historical retrospect into an eschatological perspective witnesses to the end rather than the beginning of historical references in the psalm literature. The same seems true of the Book of Dt. The theme of the gift of the land, a land that flows with milk and honey, dominates the historical references of Dt. Only in the introductory ch. 4 and the concluding chs. 29-30, which belong to the younger layers of the book, do we find references to Israel in Egypt, in the desert and in the land which, just as in Ez 20, are continued by an evocation of the exile and the return. Only in the Song of Dt 32 is the historical survey sealed by an eschatological unit.

The primeval and eschatological elements of the Song break through

19. Cf. D.L. CHRISTENSEN, *Transformations of the war oracle in the Old Testament Prophecy* (Harv. Diss. in Rel., 3), 1975.

20. Cf. R.E. CLEMENTS, *Isaiah 1-39* (The New Cent. Bible Comm.), Grand Rapids, 1980, pp. 271-277.

21. Cf. A.D.H. MAYES, *Deuteronomy* (The New Cent. Bible Comm.), 1979, *ad loc.*

22. Meaning «See now: I, I (alone) am the (only) one». «Wie bei DtJes geht es in diesem Vers um das Allein-Gott-Sein und das Allein-Handeln JHWHs»: H.-J. FABRY, *art. hûʾ*, TWAT II (1977), col. 363-368, esp. col. 367.

23. Cf. in the context of the eschatological oracles of Jer. 51 «the hymn of praise and folly» of vv. 15-19, esp. v. 18b (D.L. CHRISTENSEN, *Op. cit.*, p. 270).

24. «The whole complex of ideas and images (viz. the vine and the wine, Sodom and Gomorrah, and the poison) serves the purpose of indicating the coming judgment» (C.J. LABUSCHAGNE, *op. cit.*, p. 96f.).

the historical schemes of the Psalms and the prose texts of Dt. At the same time the Song breaks through its actual framework in ch. 31 and 32. There it is emphatically stated that this poem is meant as a witness against Israel (31,19 and 21). In fact, it is not, and such cannot have been the purpose of the author of the Song. The poem stresses much more the Lord's care and affection for the people than his anger and punitive plans. The twenty-two cola of vv. 20-25 wherein Yahweh speaks out his anger and punitive purposes, are neutralized by the twenty-two cola of vv. 26-33 which expose the reasons for his complete change of mind. The panel about the great deeds of Yahweh on behalf of his people in the past (vv. 6b-14) forms a complete diptych with the panel about Yahweh's great deeds in the future (vv. 34-42) and each of them is twice as long as the passage which exposes Israel's unfaithfulness (vv. 15-18).

In the framework, heaven and earth are summoned to witness against Israel (31,28). In the introduction of the Song heaven and earth are asked to listen to the words which will drop from the mouth of the poet as the gentle rain upon the tender grass (vv. 1-2). The fourfold rain image of that most delicate and melodious quatrain of v. 2 certainly does not have the function of announcing the story of Israel's rebelliousness and Yahweh's furious reaction to it. Its purpose must be to announce the story of the divine love which spread its wings over Israel from the beginning of times and which will shield it powerfully in the end of days. Heaven and earth, and all the heavenly beings shall recognize that God's primeval plans have not been changed, that the «new things» (Is 48,6), the salvation to come, will be still more wonderful than the «former things» (Is 48,3), the salvation of the past.

The actual framework of the Song probably belonged originally to a more ancient poem, which was a real law-suit against Israel [25], and which may have been used as building material by the great architect of the final form of the Song [26]. In any case, the great variety of motifs, the richness of vocabulary, the flamboyant style, the broad spectrum of parallels with all kinds of biblical literature strongly suggest that the song of Moses of Dt 32 is the work of someone who was versed in the law and the prophets, in psalm and wisdom literature, of someone who was a forerunner of the apocalypticists, the men especially interested in the beginning and the end, in primeval history and eschatology.

Don Boscolaan 15
B-3031 Oud-Heverlee

JOS LUYTEN

25. Cf. G.E. WRIGHT, *The Lawsuit of God: A Form-Critical Study of Deuteronomy 32*, in B. ANDERSON & W. HARRELSON, *Prophetic Heritage*, London, 1962, pp. 26-27. According to Wright, the original lawsuit was later expanded and became a «broken» *rîb*.

26. « It must suffice to say that it (viz. the Song) must have existed at the time of the Deuteronomist and that it is, like Ps. 78, probably based on a more ancient poem» (C.J. LABUSCHAGNE, *op. cit*., p. 93). We do agree with the second part of the statement, not with the first one. The Song is from a later time than the deuteronomistic history.

VIERTER TEIL

DEUTERONOMISTISCHES GESCHICHTSWERK

SPUREN DES PENTATEUCHREDAKTORS IN JOS 4,21ff.

Anmerkungen zur Deuteronomismus-Rezeption

Die «Kinderfrage» begegnet in AT 5mal (Ex 12,26ff.; 13,14ff.; Deut 6,20ff.; Jos 4,6f.21ff.) und ist Gegenstand zahlreicher Untersuchungen [1]. Gattungskritisch handelt es sich weder um eine «Kinderfrage» noch um eine «kultisch-ätiologische Belehrungsrezitation» [2]; am ehesten könnte es eine «Belehrung des Hausvaters» sein [3], deren geistesgeschichtlicher Ort z.B. in der Kontrastgesellschaft zur Zeit des Deuteronomiums zu bestimmen wäre [4]. In dieser Zeit wurde «zum erstenmal in der Geschichte Israels zugunsten des Jahweglaubens geradezu technokratisch zum 'Lernen' gegriffen» [5]. Spätestens hier muß man das «Glauben lernen» ansetzen, das in der Folgezeit breit rezipiert werden wird. Da zur Gattungsbestimmung notwendig auch die Bestimmung eines «Sitzes im Leben» gehört, letzterer aber im Zusammenhang mit der «Kinderfrage» nicht zu erheben ist, schlage ich vor, in der «Kinderfrage» ein literarisches Schema zu sehen. Es handelt sich also nicht um eine Gattung im üblichen Sinne, sondern um ein literarisches Konstrukt, das — in der vorliegenden Form — eine literarische Fiktion ist [6]. Dies wird besonders deutlich in Jos 4,21ff.

Die «Kinderfragen» in Deut 6 sind dem Deuteronomen, die in Ex 12 und 13 wahrscheinlich dem Deuteronomisten zuzusprechen [7]. Sie wollen im Anschluß an die Gesetzesparänese (Deut 6,20-24) anhand konkreter Festgeheimnisse (Ex 12,26ff. JE-Zusammenhang: Passahfest; Ex 13,14ff. JE+Dtr.-Zusammenhang: Mazzotfest) das Spezifikum der israelitischen Gemeinschaft (in ihrem Kontrast zu den anderen Völkern) lerntechnisch umsetzen. Wie aber sind die beiden(!) Kinderfragen in Jos 4 einzuordnen?

1. Unbedingt zu nennen sind; A. Soggin, *Kultätiologische Sagen und Katechese im Hexateuch*, in *VT* 10 (1960) 341-347; N. Lohfink, *Das Hauptgebot. Eine Untersuchung literarischer Einleitungsfragen zu Dtn 5-11* (AB, 20), Rom, 1963, pp. 113ff.; J. Loza, *Les catéchèses étiologiques dans l'Ancien Testament*, in *RB* 78 (1971) 481-500.

2. E. Otto, *Das Mazzotfest in Gilgal*, (BWANT, 107), Stuttgart, 1975, pp. 131ff.

3. H.-J. Fabry, *Gott im Gespräch zwischen den Generationen. Überlegungen zur «Kinderfrage» im AT*, in *Katechetische Blätter* 107 (1982), 754-760.

4. Vgl. N. Lohfink, *Glauben lernen in Israel*, in *Katechetische Blätter* 108 (1983) 84-99, bes. 93.

5. N. Lohfink, *op. cit.* 91.

6. Das schließt natürlich nicht aus, daß diese literarische Fiktion ein Geschehen widerspiegelt, das so oder ähnlich zu jeder Zeit real ablaufen konnte.

7. Zur literarkritischen Einordnung vgl. meine Argumentation in *Katechetische Blätter* 107; vgl. weiter N. Lohfink, *Das Hauptgebot*, 113ff.; J. Schreiner, *Ex 12,21-23 und das israelitische Pascha*, in: *Studien zum Pentateuch*, W. Kornfeld zum 60. Geburtstag, Hg.: G. Braulik, Freiburg, 1977, pp. 69-90.

1. Jos 4 macht «in seiner vorliegenden Gestalt einen ungewöhnlich komplizierten Eindruck»[8], was durch die auffällige Variationsbreite in der Ladeterminologie verdeutlicht wird. Man wird sogar mit sehr späten literarischen Schichten rechnen müssen[9]. Trotzdem läßt sich die «Kinderfrage» Jos 4,6f. dem Deuteronomisten zusprechen[10]. Dies läßt sich noch näher spezifizieren: Da Jos 4,6f. keine Landnahmereminiszenz aufweist, kann man hier den gleichen Redaktor vermuten, der sich auch in der 1. dtr. Redaktion des JE artikuliert. Er nimmt die Jordan-Durchquerung zum Anlaß, seine Reaktion auf die Zerstörung Jerusalems, auf die Deportierung weiter Bevölkerungskreise und die faktische Beendigung des israelitischen Gemeinwesens zum Ausdruck zu bringen, indem er auf die ständige und aktuelle Notwendigkeit der lerntechnischen Umsetzung zentraler Glaubenswahrheiten gerade im Zusammenhang mit heilsgeschichtlich bedeutsamen Ereignissen hinweist[11].

2. Wenn Jos 4,6f. dem Deuteronomisten zugesprochen werden muß, dann ist dies für Jos 4,21ff. zwar nicht ausgeschlossen[12], muß aber durch literarkritische Untersuchungen erhoben werden. Hier nun zeitigt die Analyse einen merkwürdigen Befund:

V. 21bα

— *'ᵃšær* als Einleitung der Kinderfrage gegenüber dem *kî* (in v. 6) ist auffällig. In dieser Funktion begegnet es in priesterlichen und dtr. Texten[13].

— *bᵉnêkæm ... 'ᵃbôtām*: Die Differenz in der Suffigierung ist syntaktisch schwierig. Entweder ist diese Schwierigkeit textkritischer Art[14], oder

8. M. NOTH, *Josua* (HAT, I, 7, ³1971, 31); «extrêmement difficile» (R. DE VAUX, *Histoire Ancienne d'Israël. Des Origines a l'Institution en Canaan*, Paris, 1971, p. 552); einen instruktiven Überblick zur Problematik bieten R. DE VAUX, *op. cit.*, pp. 552-556, und M. GÖRG, TWAT III, cc. 907f.

9. Dafür sprechen Bezeichnungen für die Lade, die eindeutig kombinatorischen Charakter tragen (z.B. *'arôn habbᵉrît 'ᵃdôn kŏl ha'aræṣ*, Jos 3,11).

10. Argumente: *'arôn habbᵉrît* (v. 7) ist mit H.J. ZOBEL (TWAT I, c. 400) deut und später; *nikrᵉtû mê hajjarden* nach E. OTTO, *op. cit.*, zu Jos. 3,13, dtr; *zikkarôn* (v. 7b) spätdtr. nach F.-L. HOSSFELD, *Der Dekalog* (OBO, 45) Freiburg-Göttingen 1982, p. 42, Anm. 93, dtr. und auch P nach H. EISING (TWAT II, c. 586).

11. Die Wahl ausgerechnet der «Kinderfrage» zu diesem Zweck scheint mir eine gewisse Systemkritik anzudeuten, die den Erziehungsauftrag des Elternhauses gegenüber Schule und Priesterschaft hervorheben will.

12. Vgl. die beiden dtr. «Kinderfragen» in der kurzen Abfolge Ex 12 und 13. E. OTTO, *op. cit.*, hält Jos 4,21ff. für dtr.

13. Vgl. Lev 4,22 P (Aaronidenschicht), als «umständliche Sprache» charakteristisch für P (vgl. R. SMEND, *Die Entstehung des AT* [Theologische Wissenschaft 1], Stuttgart, ² 1981, p. 49); vgl. auch Deut 11, 27, jetzt vorläufig zur 2. dtr. Überarbeitung der sing. Grundschicht in Deut 6,4-11,32 gerechnet (vgl. H.D. PREUSS, *Deuteronomium*, [EdF, 164], Darmstadt, 1982, pp. 51.103). G. BRAULIK, *Die Mittel deuteronomischer Rhetorik* (AB, 68) Rom, 1978, pp. 136-139, hat gezeigt, daß Deut *'ᵃšær* als Relativpartikel, selten dagegen zur Einleitung eines Temporal- oder Finalsatzes verwendet. In dem von ihm analysierten Textbereich begegnet *'ᵃšær* in konditionaler Bedeutung nicht.

14. Vgl. bereits die von LXX vorgenommene Korrektur.

aber sie signalisiert eine Diktion, die eine Verwischung der Generationengrenze beabsichtigt. Das erinnert aber an Ex 20,5 im Vergleich zu Deut 5,9 und ist Gedankengut des Pentateuchredaktors [15].

— *'abôt* begegnet in keiner anderen «Kinderfrage». Da Dtr *'abôt* nur in der Bedeutung «Patriarchen» verwendet [16], ist eine Zuweisung unserer «Kinderfrage» zum Dtr. bereits definitiv ausgeschlossen. Während in den anderen «Kinderfragen» durch die Wahl der Suffixe für «euch» oder «ihr» eine Unmittelbarkeit zum Hörer gestiftet wird, ist diese hier nicht angestrebt.

V. 22a

— *hodi'a* (vgl. *'āmar* v. 7) begegnet im Pentateuch fast ausschließlich in redaktionellen Stellen und gehört am ehesten zum P-Vokabular [17].

V. 22b

— *jabbāšāh* und *hobîš* (v. 23) gehören zum P-Vokabular [18], während Dtr vom «Teilen (*kārat*) des Wassers» (v. 7) spricht.

— Abfolge und Alternierung der Verben *'ābar* und *hobîš* in v. 22 konstituieren eine Sprachfigur, die man als erweiterte «Short-Circuit-Inclusion» bezeichnen kann. In einfacher Form ist diese typisch für P [19], in erweiterter Form begegnet sie bei R^{P} [20].

— *'ābar bajjabbāšāh* ist eine Wendung, die literarkritisch Mischvokabular enthält, das ein Element aus P und vom Dtr enthält [21].

V. 24a

— Die Erkenntnisformel ist in der freien Formulierung *l^ema'an da'at* + Akk. wenig verbreitet und könnte eine nachpriesterliche Diktion vertreten [22].

15. Hierzu verweise ich auf die Analyse von F. L. HOSSFELD, op. cit., pp. 26-32.

16. Vgl. D. W. SKWERES, *Die Rückverweise im Buch Deuteronomium* (AB, 79), Rom, 1979, p. 106.

17. Vgl. Ex 33,12.13; Num 16,5; Deut 4,9; 8,3.

18. Vgl. H. D. PREUSS, in *TWAT* III, c. 403, und J. L. SKA, *Séparation des eaux et de la terre ferme dans le récit sacerdotal*, in *NRT* 113 (1981) 512-532; als Gegenposition zu nennen ist F. LANGLAMET, *Gilgal et les récits de la traversée du Jordain (Jos 3-4)*, Paris, 1969.

19. Vgl. Gen 6,22 und S. E. MCEVENUE, *The Narrative Stile of the Priestly Writer*, (AB, 50), Rom, 1981, pp. 43f.

20. Vgl. Ex 6,26f. und E. ZENGER, *Israel am Sinai. Analysen und Interpretationen zu Exodus 17-34*, Altenberge, 1982, p. 26.

21. P spricht Ex 14,16.22.29 nur vom *bô' bajjabbāšāh*, während Dtr in Jos 4,6ff. von *'ābar* spricht (vgl. auch Ex 15,16). Zur innerdeuteronomischen Sprachentwicklung von *bô'* und *'ābar* im Zusammenhang der Landnahmeformel vgl. G. BRAULIK, op. cit., pp. 93ff.; P. DIEPOLD, *Israels Land* (BWANT, 95), Stuttgart, 1972, p. 29.

22. Die priesterliche Erkenntnisformel im Exodus-Zusammenhang besteht aus verbum finitum + *kî* (z. B. Ex 14,4.18 u. ö.).

— Die Erwähnung der *jad JHWH...ḥazāqāh* weist wiederum in dtr. Sprachgebrauch[23].

V. 24b
— Die finit formulierte Gottesfurchtformel weist in die Zeit des Dtr[24], da Deut sie mit Inf. cstr. formuliert[25].

3. Die literarkritische Analyse weist als Ergebnis klar aus, daß Jos 4,21ff. eine Mixtur priesterlichen und dtr. Vokabulars enthält. Stil und Gesamtduktus weisen auf P[26], doch beobachten wir allenthalben die beginnende Auflösung formelhafter Wortverbindungen. Die sprachliche Mixtur weist in die nachexilische Zeit, zugleich spricht sie gegen einen Autor und für einen Redaktor. Das Fehlen jeglicher Landnahmereminiszenz einerseits und die Situierung der «Kinderfrage» bei Gilgal im Kulturland andererseits läßt auf einen Redaktor schließen, der in einem großen Abstand von der Rückkehr aus dem Exil seine Redaktionsarbeit verrichtete. Damit aber geraten wir in die Zeit des Pentateuchredaktors R^P, der um 400 v. Chr. in einer trostlosen Lage mittels Injektion von Verheißungselementen eine eschatologisch-universalistische Hoffnung artikulierte[27]. Auch R^P bedient sich des katechetischen Stils[28].

4. Von besonderer Bedeutung ist die Frage nach der redaktionellen Absicht des R^P. Diese Frage hat zweierlei zu bedenken: Jos 4,21ff. ist zuerst zusammenzusehen mit den übrigen Versen in Jos, die R^P zuzuschreiben sind. Graduell davon zu differenzieren ist dann die Analyse der redaktionellen Absicht, wenn der vermutete Redaktor R^P zugleich der Schlußredaktor ist. Bei der Suche nach weiteren R^P-Stücken ist zuerst auf das sog. Schlußitinerar von P^G in Jos 4,19 und Jos 5,10-12 zu verweisen[29]. Gegen die Zuteilung dieser vv. zu P^G lassen sich jedoch

23. Vgl. Ex 13,3.9.14.16; Deut 6,21; 7,8; 9,26. Die hier in Jos 4,24 vorliegende Formulierung *jad JHWH kî ḥazāqāh hî'* stellt eine Auflösung der alten Formulierung *jad ḥazāqāh* (vgl. Ex 3,19 [J]; Num 20,20 [JE] u. ö.) dar (vgl. im einzelnen P. ACKROYD, in *TWAT* III, 1982, cc. 446-450).

24. H.F. FUHS, (TWAT III, c. 886) schreibt die Gottesfurchtformel in Deut und DtrGW grundsätzlich späteren Bearbeitern zu.

25. Z. B. Deut 4,10 u. ö.

26. P bedient sich gerne des katechetischen Stiles (vgl. MCEVENUE, *op. cit.*, pp. 12ff. 82ff.).

27. Auch in Ex 15,25f. hat Lohfink mit Recht aus der Symbiose von P- und D-Sprache auf R^P geschlossen; vgl. N. LOHFINK, *«Ich bin Jahwe, dein Arzt» (Ex 15,26). Gott, Gesellschaft und Gesundheit in einer nachexilischen Pentateuchbearbeitung (Ex 15,25b.26)*, (SBS, 100) Stuttgart, 1981, pp. 13-73. Die universalistische Tendenz zeigt sich v. 24 *kŏl-'ammê hā'āraeṣ*; zum Universalismus von R^P vgl. Ex 24,9-11, dazu E. ZENGER, *op. cit.*, p. 29, und P. WEIMAR, *Untersuchungen zur Redaktionsgeschichte des Pentateuch* (BZAW, 146) Berlin, 1977, p. 172.

28. Vgl. Ex 10,2.

29. Die Frage, ob P im Buche Jos überhaupt noch nachzuweisen ist, wird in der Forschung konträr beantwortet, vgl. R. SMEND, *op. cit.*, p. 58f.; N. LOHFINK, *Die*

einige Beobachtungen ins Feld führen: Die Anspielung auf das Mazzotfest Jos 5,11 ist für P^G völlig unüblich, da sie den Ritus des Mazzotessens als eigenständigen Ritus nicht überliefert[30]. Am ehesten käme P^S in Frage[31], aber dies läßt die isolierte Stellung dieser Verse nicht zu. Auch das in Jos 5,11 genannte «Röstkorn» entstammt dem Erstlingsritual, das nicht zur P^G gehört (Lev 2,14; 23,14 P^S). Der Doppelfestcharakter Passah-Mazzot wird schließlich wieder von R^P betont[32].

R^P hat also seine theologische Interpretation durch Einbau der «Kinderfrage» in Jos 4,21ff. mit Hilfe der Festreminiszenz Jos 4,19 und 5,10-12 dem bereits massiv dtr. überarbeiteten Text aufgelegt. Er möchte den Jordandurchzug als Exodus der Nach-Exodus-Generation einerseits, dann durch Öffnen der Generationengrenzen als Exodus aller Nach-Exodus-Generationen herausstellen. Durch die Hinzufügung der «Kinderfrage» (zu der von Jos 4,6f.) und durch Rekonstruktion der Synchronie der Zeitangaben[33] paßt R^P den Jordandurchzug inhaltlich und formal dem Erstexodus (Ex 12-14) an[34]. Für ihn ist also der Exodus bereits zum Typos geworden für das jeder Generation, erst recht der in vieler Hinsicht entmutigten spät-nachexilischen Generation je neu zugesagte Heilshandeln Jahwes[35].

Die Gilgal-Perikope ist damit als eine planvolle literarische Komposition durch R^P aufzufassen, die keine hochgespannten Erwartungen auf etwaige kultische Dramatisierungen[36] des Schilfmeer- und Jordan-Durchzugs befriedigen kann.

Priesterschrift und die Geschichte, in *VTSuppl* 29 (1978) 188-225, bes. 199 rechnet Jos 4,19*; 5,10-12; 14,1.2*; 18,1 und 19,51 noch zum Bestand von P^G.

30. Vgl. F.L. HOSSFELD, *Der Durchgang vom Leiden zum Leben. Alttestamentliche Themen der Osternacht*, in *Lebendige Seelsorge 34* (1983) 1-6, bes. 5: «Es fällt auf, daß die Priestergrundschrift das siebentägige Mazzenessen völlig unterdrückt und aus der Gesetzesüberlieferung nur die Pascha-Anteile auswählt und umformt».

31. Erst P^S schließt das von P^G übergangene Mazzotfest wieder an das Passah an (vgl. Ex 12,1-12 [P^G] mit Ex 12,14-20 [P^S]). Diese Regelung findet sich im Heiligkeitsgesetz wieder (Lev 23,5-8).

32. Vgl. Num 28,16-25, «eines der jüngsten Stücke im Pentateuch» (M. NOTH, ATD 7, [1966], p. 190).

33. Vgl. die Zeitangaben 10.1. (Jos 4,19) und 14.1. (Jos 5,10) mit denen in Ex 12,3.6.18.

34. Zeitliche und örtliche Fixierungen sind bei R^P üblich (vgl. Ex 17,7b), auch durch Reminiszenz geschickt aufgebaute Zyklisierung und Typisierung ist ihm nicht fremd (vgl. die Harmonisierung von Ex 17,1-7 und Num 20,1-13).

35. Es überrascht nicht, daß in Qumran später dieser Jordandurchzug in gleicher Weise verstanden wird; dazu vgl. W. BROWNLEE, *The Ceremony of Crossing the Jordan in the Annual Covenanting at Qumran*, in *Von Kanaan bis Kerala*, Festschr. J.P.M. van der Ploeg (AOAT, 211) Neukirchen-Vluyn, 1982, pp. 295-302. Zur Exodus-Typologie im NT vgl. J.S. CROATTO, *Riletture dell'Esodo nel cap. 6 di San Giovanni*, in *Bibbia e Oriente* 17 (1975) 11-20.

36. Dazu vgl. J.N.M. WIJNGAARDS, *The Dramatization of Salvific History in the Deuteronomic Schools*, in *OTS* 16 (Leiden 1969), pp. 58-63.123ff.; vgl. auch DE VAUX, *op. cit.* pp. 556-559.

5. Die hier vorgelegten Beobachtungen werfen Fragen auf, die Pentateuchkritik und Deuteronomismus-Rezeption in gleichem Maß berühren. Hier wird doch eine Redaktion im Buch Josua sichtbar, die noch später anzusetzen ist als die dtr. Überarbeitungen. Während im Bereich des Pentateuch diese Redaktion als die des R^P (um 400 v. Chr.) bezeichnet wird — sie ist per definitionem auf den Pentateuch beschränkt —, ist sie bisher im Bereich des DtrGW nicht näher beschrieben worden. Es scheint so, daß sich noch weitere Indizien aufweisen lassen [37] für einen Redaktor, der zwar Dtr.-Sprache verwendet, sie aber deutlich unter P-Vorzeichen stellt.

Turmfalkenweg 15 Heinz-Josef FABRY
D-5300 Bonn I

37. So zeigt sich P-Vokabular in der Beschneidungsnotiz Jos 5,2f. (vgl. 12,48f.), in Jos 6,18.22ff.; 8,33 (vgl. bereits P. GRELOT, *La dernière étape de la rédaction sacerdotale*, in *VT* 6 [1956], 174-189) und bes. in Jos. 22 (vgl. J. S. KLOPPENBURG, *Joshua 22: The Priestly Editing of an Ancient Tradition*, in *Bib* 62 [1981] pp. 347-371); ebenfalls wird eine solche Überarbeiterhand sichtbar in 2 Sam 7 (v. 6), und H. P. MÜLLER (*TWAT* IV, sub Artikel *molæk*) macht darauf aufmerksam, daß in 2 Kön 17,31 und 23,10 nachdtr. Texte vorliegen.

BEOBACHTUNGEN
ZUR DEUTERONOMISTISCHEN TERMINOLOGIE
IN 2 KÖN 23,25-25,30

Die Entstehung der Kön-Bücher ist nach wie vor umstritten. Zwei[1] Erklärungsmodelle haben Schule gemacht: 1. die Theorie des Deuteronomistischen Geschichtswerks (DtrG) von M. Noth[2] mit ihren Modifizierungen durch H.W. Wolff[3] und R. Smend[4]; und 2. die Theorie einer bereits vorexilischen deuteronomistischen (dtr) Redaktion mit (nach-)exilischer Erweiterung, die (nach Vorgängern im 19. Jh.[5]) besonders im Gefolge von F.M. Cross Verfechter fand[6]. So verwandt die beiden Ansätze scheinen, so unversöhnt stehen sie nebeneinander[7]. Während nach der Cross'schen Theorie gegen Ende von 2 Kön 23 ein

1. Dazu und zu weiteren Modellen vgl. E. CORTESE, *Problemi attuali circa l'opera deuteronomistica*, in *Rivista Bibl. Ital.* 26 (1978) 341-352; R.D. NELSON, *The Redactional Duality of the Deuteronomistic History*, Diss. Union Theological Seminary, 1973, pp. 1-23 (Überarbeitung: *The Double Redaction of the Deuteronomistic History* [Journal for the Study of the Old Test., Suppl., 18], Sheffield, 1981, pp. 13-22).

2. M. NOTH, *Überlieferungsgeschichtliche Studien*, Darmstadt, 1967[3]. Auf der Einheitlichkeit des DtrG besteht neuerdings H.-D. HOFFMANN, *Reform und Reformen* (ATANT, 66), Zürich, 1980.

3. H.W. WOLFF, *Das Kerygma des deuteronomistischen Geschichtswerks*, in *ZAW* 73 (1961) 171-186 = ders., *Gesammelte Studien zum A. T.* (Theol. Bücherei, 22), München, 1973[2], pp. 308-324. Weiterführend u. a.: N. LOHFINK, *Kerygmata des Deuteronomistischen Geschichtswerks*, in J. JEREMIAS, L. PERLITT, (ed.), *Die Botschaft und die Boten. Fs. H. W. WOLFF*, Neukirchen-Vluyn, 1981, pp. 87-100, und die ebd. p. 88 Anm. 8 genannten Arbeiten von G. BRAULIK.

4. R. SMEND, *Das Gesetz und die Völker*, in H.W. WOLFF (ed.), *Probleme biblischer Theologie. Fs. G. VON RAD*, München, 1971, pp. 494-509. Weiterführend u. a.: W. DIETRICH, *Prophetie und Geschichte* (FRLANT, 108), Göttingen, 1972; T. VEIJOLA, *Die ewige Dynastie* (Annales Academiae Scientiarum Fennicae, B 193), Helsinki, 1975; ders., *Das Königtum in der Beurteilung der deuteronomistischen Historiographie* (Ann. Ac. Sc. Fenn., B 198), Helsinki, 1977; H. SPIECKERMANN, *Juda unter Assur in der Sargonidenzeit* (FRLANT, 129), Göttingen, 1982.

5. Vgl. NELSON a.a.O. (vgl. Anm. 1).

6. F.M. CROSS, *The Structure of the Deuteronomic History*, in *Perspectives in Jewish Learning, Vol. III*, Chicago, 1967, pp. 9-24 = ders., *Canaanite Myth and Hebrew Epic*, Cambridge, Mass., 1973, pp. 274-289 (danach zitiert). Weiterführend u. a.: NELSON, a.a.O. (vgl. Anm. 1); R.E. FRIEDMAN, *The Exile and Biblical Narrative* (Harvard Semitic Monographs, 22), Missoula, Mont., 1981, pp. 1-43; N. LOHFINK a.a.O. (vgl. Anm. 3); ders., *jāraš*, in *Theol. Wörterbuch zum A.T.* 3 (1982) 953-985; ders., *kāʿas*, in *Theol. Wörterb. z. A. T.* 4, Lieferung 3/4 (1982) 297-302; wichtig auch H. WEIPPERT, *Die «deuteronomistischen» Beurteilungen der Könige von Israel und Juda*, in *Bib* 53 (1972) 301-339.

7. Eine Vermittlung zeichnet sich in den Arbeiten von N. LOHFINK ab (vgl. Anm. 3 und 6).

redaktioneller Bruch vorliegt [8], weicht nach der Smend'schen Theorie «die Art der dtr Arbeit in 2 Kön 24f. von der in den vorangehenden Partien» nicht ab [9] und ist die dtr Grundredaktion bis 2 Kön 25 zu verfolgen [10].

Immerhin sind von F.M. Cross, R. Nelson, R.E. Friedman, H. Weippert, N. Lohfink u.a. Beobachtungen zusammengetragen worden [11], die sich in die Smend'sche Theorie nicht leicht integrieren lassen. Im folgenden teile ich weitere Beobachtungen mit, die die Cross'sche Theorie stützen.

1. Ab 2 Kön 23,26 fällt die dtr Phraseologie fast ganz aus. Diese Beobachtung ist um so gravierender, als ich «dtr» zunächst recht weit fasse und beispielsweise auch Wendungen einbeziehe, die innerhalb der Kön-Bücher kurrent sind [12]. Gerade der negative Gesichtspunkt, nämlich das Vermissen einer bestimmten Phraseologie, erfordert diese Großzügigkeit [13]. An die Beobachtung, daß ein Großteil der dtr Wendungen ab 2 Kön 23,26 ausfällt, läßt sich die Frage anschließen, was denn ausfällt und was nicht. Interessanterweise fehlen zwei wichtige Themenkreise der dtr Phraseologie vollständig.

1. Von der bei H.-D. Hoffmann aufgelisteten «speziellen Kultterminologie» [14] findet man in den Kön-Büchern bis 2 Kön 23,24 rund 30 verschiedene Wendungen, nachher keine einzige [15]. Dieser Befund gewinnt an Signifikanz, wenn man Hoffmanns «allgemeine Kultterminologie» [16] in die Betrachtung einbezieht: Davon finden sich in den Kön-Büchern bis 2 Kön 23,24 rund 35 verschiedene Wendungen, nachher nur zwei, auf die ich noch zu sprechen komme [17]. Die Listen bei Hoffmann, die eigentlich die redaktionelle Einheitlichkeit des DtrG beweisen sollen, liefern genau besehen ein Argument für den redaktionellen Bruch am Ende von 2 Kön 23 [18].

8. CROSS a.a.O. (vgl. Anm. 6) p. 287 Anm. 49 («obviously»).

9. R. SMEND, *Die Entstehung des Alten Testaments* (Theol. Wissensch., 1) Stuttgart u. a., 1981², p. 113.

10. DIETRICH a.a.O. (vgl. Anm. 4) p. 143.

11. Vgl. die bibliographischen Angaben in Anm. 6.

12. Benützt wurden die Listen bei M. WEINFELD, *Deuteronomy and the Deuteronomic School*, Oxford, 1972, pp. 320-359; HOFFMANN a.a.O. (vgl. Anm. 2) pp. 323-366. Als Beispiel für eine kurrente Wendung sei genannt *kl hymym* (vgl. WEINFELD p. 358).

13. Der negative Gesichtspunkt hebt zudem die berechtigten Vorbehalte gegenüber dem Kriterium «Sprachbeweis» auf.

14. HOFFMANN a.a.O. (vgl. Anm. 2) pp. 341-366; zur Unterscheidung «speziell» vs. «allgemein» vgl. ebd. p. 53.

15. In dieser Behauptung sind nicht berücksichtigt: uneigentliche Verwendungen (etwa *NTṢ* mit nicht-kultischem Objekt) und *'šr*-Sätze (HOFFMANN: «Verknüpfungsformeln»).

16. HOFFMANN a.a.O. (vgl. Anm. 2) pp. 327-340.

17. *'ŚY hr' b'yny YHWH* und *K'S*-H.

18. Auch R. RENDTORFF, *Das Alte Testament. Eine Einführung*, Neukirchen-Vluyn, 1983, p. 198 (vgl. p. 191), wertet Beobachtungen HOFFMANNs zugunsten der CROSS'schen Theorie aus.

2. Ab 2 Kön 23,26 fehlt vollständig der «nomistische» Themenkreis. Mit «nomistisch» meine ich hier neben den verschiedenen Ausdrücken für «Gesetz» alle Wendungen um Gesetzespromulgation und Gesetzesbeobachtung, wozu auch der Vergleich mit dem vorbildlichen David gehört [19]. Das Fehlen der nomistischen Terminologie ausgerechnet am Ende der Kön-Bücher stellt die Extrapolation des Smend'schen Nomisten in die Kön-Bücher hinein durch W. Dietrich [20] in Frage; mindestens scheint mir die Zurechnung sämtlicher nomistischer Wendungen zu einer sekundären nomistischen Schicht nicht haltbar [21].

2. Bei der dtr Phraseologie, die nach 2 Kön 23,25 nicht ausfällt, ist auf Fügungsart, Aussageziel und Kontext zu achten. Dies führt zu zwei Beobachtungen, die für eine Diskontinuität der Redaktionsarbeit sprechen.

Manche Ausnahmen verraten Nachahmung der ersten Redaktion. Dazu gehören zunächst Elemente des Kön-Rahmens. Nelson hat zwei Merkmale der Nachahmung erkannt: Formstrenge und Knappheit [22]. Neben dieser Schematisierung ist ein Zug zur Verallgemeinerung zu beobachten. Er zeigt sich zum einen in der Vorliebe für Relativsätze mit dem inhaltsleeren Verb *ʿŚY* und dem Allquantor *kl* als Bezugswort [23], zum andern in der Pluralisierung vorgegebener Wendungen, vor allem mit *'b* (und außerhalb des Kön-Rahmens *nby'*) [24]. Die beschriebenen

19. In etwa handelt es sich um die bei N. LOHFINK, *Das Hauptgebot* (AB, 20), Roma, 1963, pp. 295-302, und WEINFELD a.a.O. (vgl. Anm. 12) pp. 332-339 (nr. 6-24) und pp. 354-355 aufgelisteten Wendungen. Schon gar nicht wird die «nomistische» Terminologie in «Tischtuchtechnik» (man zieht an einem Zipfel und hat dann immer mehr in der Hand) ausgeweitet. Dies ist vor allem gegen VEIJOLA und SPIECKERMANN (vgl. Anm. 4) gesagt.

20. DIETRICH a.a.O. (vgl. Anm. 4) passim. Die Schichtenzuweisungen DIETRICHS hat F. LANGLAMET in seiner Rezension (in *RB* 81 [1974] 601-606) pp. 603-604 aufgelistet.

21. Vgl. auch die Vorbehalte bei LOHFINK a.a.O. (vgl. Anm. 3) p. 99. FRIEDMANN a.a.O. (vgl. Anm. 6) pp. 7-10 zieht einige nomistische Wendungen zur vorexilischen Redaktion.

22. Vgl. NELSON a.a.O. (vgl. Anm. 1) p. 59=37 («rigidity») und p. 60=38 («strikingly shorter»; «woodenly imitative work»). P. 56=36 zweifelt NELSON an der Zuverlässigkeit der Zahlen in den Kön-Formeln ab 2 Kön 23,26 und nimmt Extrapolationsarbeit an.

23. Die Vorliebe für *kl 'šr* + *ʿŚY* (Suffixkonjugation) zeigt sich auch numerisch: In 1 Kön 1,1 — 2 Kön 23,25 (circa 96 % der Kön-Bücher) steht die Fügung 26mal (79 % der Vorkommen), ab 2 Kön 23,26 dagegen 7mal (21 % auf 4 % Text). Dabei ist damit zu rechnen, daß ein Teil der Belege vor 2 Kön 23,26 zur Erweiterung zu schlagen ist. Stellen: 1 Kön 11,41; 14,22.29; 15,7.23.31; 16,14; 21,26; 22,39.54; 2 Kön 8,23; 10,34; 12,20; 13,8.12; 14,3.28; 15,3.6.21.26.31.34; 18,3; 21,11.17; 23,28.32.37; 24,3.5.9.19.

24. Mit *'b*: Innerhalb von Kön-Beurteilungen steht der Plural nur 2 Kön 15,9; 23,32.37 (1 Kön 14,22 ist textlich unsicher), der Singular dagegen (abgesehen von den Vergleichen mit David) 1 Kön 15,3.26; 22,43.53.54; 2 Kön 3,2; 14,3; 15,3.34; 21,20.21; 24,9; sonst steht der Plural meist in Todes-/Begräbnisformeln (vgl. 1 Kön 2,10; 15,24), bei Bezug auf die Väter der Vorzeit (vgl. 1 Kön 8,21) oder in nicht-dtr Partien (vgl. 1 Kön 19,4). Die Angaben bei E. CORTESE, *Lo schema deuteronomistico per i re di Giuda e d'Israele*, in *Bib* 56 (1975) 37-52, pp. 48-49 sind ungenau. — Mit *nby'*: Der Plural steht in Erfüllungsformeln nur 2 Kön 17,23 (vgl. unten Anm. 38); 24,2; vgl. 2 Kön 17,13. — Weitere Plurale: *kʿsym* in

Phänomene betreffen hauptsächlich die Sündenformel (*ʿŚY hrʿ bʿyny YHWH*) und die Quellenverweisformel (*wytr dbry XY ..*). Bei den weiteren Wendungen des Kön-Rahmens finden sich ab 2 Kön 23,26 im Vergleich mit den vorangehenden Partien keine neuen Elemente; die Vorlage wird also streng nachgeahmt [25].

Neben der Nachahmung verraten manche Ausnahmen die redaktionelle Technik der Anknüpfung: Ein Stichwort oder eine Fügung der ersten Redaktion wird aufgegriffen, jedoch mit verändertem Aussageziel [26]. Für *KʿS*-H hat Lohfink den Nachweis erbracht [27]. Entsprechendes kann von der Wurzel *ḤṬʾ* gelten: Während sie in 2 Kön 24,3 das Tun Manasses qualifiziert, bezieht sie sich vor 2 Kön 23,26 fast ausschließlich auf das Tun Jerobeams und seiner Nachfolger; bei den Ausnahmen liegt Verdacht auf Erweiterungsarbeit vor [28].

Um Anknüpfungsarbeit handelt es sich eindeutig in 2 Kön 23,26-27. *ŠūB mḥrwn ʾp=* mit göttlichem Subjekt ist innerhalb des DtrG nur noch in Dtn 13,18 und Jos 7,26 belegt, jedoch beidemal mit der Wurzel *ḤRM* im Kontext [29]. V. 26 ist in weiterer Hinsicht einmalig: YHWHs Umkehr vom Zorn wird nur hier verneint; *ḥrwn ʾp YHWH* ist nur hier durch ein Attribut (*gdwl*) erweitert; *ḤRY* mit dem Subjekt *ʾp YHWH* steht nur hier im Relativsatz; die eben genannten Wendungen *ḥrwn ʾp YHWH* und *ḤRY ʾp YHWH* sind nur hier kombiniert; *kʿs* steht nur hier im Plural und ist nur hier mit dem (für den Erweiterer typischen) Allquantor *kl* verbunden. Den originellen Satz versteht man am einfachsten als Neubildung durch den Erweiterer; die Anknüpfung an die Vorgabe geschieht durch das Stichwort *ŠūB* (v. 25). Ähnliches gilt für v. 27. Isoliertes *wyʾmr YHWH* als Einleitung zu einem Selbstgespräch steht innerhalb des DtrG nur hier. Die Antonyme *MʾS* und *BḤR* finden sich mit gleichem Objekt nur hier kombiniert [30]. Ich verstehe das als uminterpretierende Anknüpfung: Das dem Erweiterer vorliegende Aussagensystem mit *BḤR*

2 Kön 23,26 und *ḥṭʾt* in 2 Kön 24,3. — Zur verallgemeinernden Kön-Beurteilung ab 2 Kön 23,26 vgl. auch WEIPPERT a.a.O. (vgl. Anm. 6) p. 334.

25. Vgl. NELSON a.a.O. (vgl. Anm. 1) 56-66 = 36-41.

26. LOHFINK a.a.O. (vgl. Anm. 3), esp. p. 89, spricht von der «Mehrheit der Kerygmata».

27. LOHFINK, *kāʿas* (vgl. Anm. 6), pp. 301-302; er beobachtet, daß die Kombination von *KʿS* und *ḤṬʾ* für die vorexilische Redaktion typisch ist. Vgl. auch NELSON a.a.O. (vgl. Anm. 1) pp. 129-130 = 68.

28. 1 Kön 14,22 (Text?); 2 Kön 21,11.16-17 (vgl. unten mit Anm. 38).

29. Vgl. N. LOHFINK, *ḥāram*, in *Theol. Wörterbuch zum A.T.* 3 (1982) 192-213, pp. 209-211. — Zu wenig auf die Differenz der Ausdrucksformen achtet D.J. MCCARTHY, *The Wrath of Yahweh and the Structural Unity of the Deuteronomistic History*, in J.L. CRENSHAW, J.T. WILLIS, *Essays in Old Testament Ethics. Fs. J.P. HYATT*, New York, 1974, pp. 99-110.

30. Durch die Negation *lʾ* wird die antonyme Bedeutung in Synonimität umgepolt (Jes 41,9; Ps 78,67). Kombination mit unterschiedlichen Objekten: 1 Sam 16,7-8; Jes 7,15.16 (vgl. noch Ijob 34,33).

wird aufgegriffen und durch das Antonym *M'S* revidiert. Natürlich wäre die Kombination zunächst auch innerhalb einer einzigen Redaktion denkbar [31]. Dagegen stehen aber die Stellen innerhalb des DtrG, die von einer Erwählung Jerusalems «für alle Zeit» sprechen [32]. Die Berücksichtigung des Kontextes verbietet es, 2 Kön 23,26-27 mit Hilfe des Sprachbeweises dem «Nomisten» zuzuschreiben [33].

Ein Fall von Anknüpfungsarbeit liegt auch bei *SLḤ* in 2 Kön 24,4 vor. *SLḤ* ist innerhalb des DtrG sonst außer dem quellenhaften 2 Kön 5,18 und dem späten Dtn 29,19 [34] nur fünfmal im Tempelweihgebet (1 Kön 8) belegt. Der letzte Beleg (v. 50) dürfte zu einer sekundären Partie gehören [35]. Die ersten vier Belege (vv. 30.34.36.39) setzen für alle möglichen Bedrohungen und Strafen voraus, daß das Gebet im (vorexilischen) Tempel die Vergebung Gottes bewirkt. Der Autor von 2 Kön 24,4 greift das Verb *SLḤ* auf, negiert aber die theologische Aussage. Solche Negationsarbeit ist uns beim Erweiterer aus 2 Kön 23,26 bekannt [36].

3. Zwei weitere Beobachtungen kann ich hier nur eben stichwortartig nennen. Die erste stützt in der Cross'schen Theorie die Annahme, daß der Erweiterer auch vor 2 Kön 23,26 eingegriffen und seine aus exilischer Sicht gemachten Aussagen vorbereitet hat [37]. Die Horizontuntersuchung der dtr Phraseologie ab 2 Kön 23,26 führt nämlich wiederholt auf ganz bestimmte Textsegmente, vorab auf 1 Kön 8*; 2 Kön 17*; 21* [38].

4. Die letzte Beobachtung erkennt 2 Kön 23,25 als passenden Höhepunkt einer vorexilischen Redaktion und macht so den Bruch nach 2 Kön 23,25 zusätzlich glaubhaft. Es ist die einzige Stelle im DtrG, an der *ŠūB 'l YHWH* in einem positiven perfektiv-konstatierenden Satz steht. Joschija allein wird die religiöse Haltung zuerkannt, die im Tempelweihgebet (1 Kön 8,33.48) [39] als künftige Möglichkeit zur Versöhnung

31. Vgl. den Saul-Komplex (*BḤR*: 1 Sam 10,24; *M'S*: 1 Sam 15,23.26; 16,1.7), dessen Einheitlichkeit jedoch nicht gesichert ist.

32. 1 Kön 9,3; 11,36; 2 Kön 21,7. Vgl. auch die Konnotation [+ bleiben] in der *nyr*-Wendung (1 Kön 11,36; 15,4; 2 Kön 8,19); vgl. dazu G. VANONI, *Literarkritik und Grammatik. Untersuchung der Wiederholungen und Spannungen in 1 Kön 11-12* (Arbeiten zu Text und Sprache im Alten Testament, 21), St. Ottilien, 1984, p. 178-180.

33. Gegen DIETRICH a.a.O. (vgl. Anm. 4) p. 142 und SPIECKERMANN a.a.O. (vgl. Anm. 4) p. 45 Anm. 28.

34. Vgl. G. BRAULIK, *Das Testament des Mose. Das Buch Deuteronomium*, Stuttgart, 1976, p. 8.

35. Vgl. die Argumente bei NELSON a.a.O. (vgl. Anm. 1) pp. 138-141 = 71-72.

36. Die Spannung wird indirekt bezeugt durch die Interpolation von Funktionswörtern in den Übersetzungen (vgl. nur die «Einheitsübersetzung» zu 2 Kön 24,4: «mehr»).

37. Vgl. die Listen bei FRIEDMAN a.a.O. (vgl. Anm. 6) pp. 5 und 25-26.

38. Vgl. über die Konkordanz folgende Wendungen: *ŠūB 'l YHWH*, *K'S 't YHWH*, *SūR*-H *m'l pny YHWH*, *M'S + YHWH*, *BḤR + 'yr*, *byt + šm*, *kdbr YHWH + byd nby'* (*'bd*), *dm nqy + ML'*-D, *SLḤ*, *ŠLK*-H *m'l pny YHWH*, *GLY m'l 'dmh*.

39. Hier und an den restlichen Stellen immer (bedingter) zukünftiger Sachverhalt: Dtn

mit Gott gesehen wird. Joschija kehrt zu Gott zurück und leitet so eine hoffnungsvolle Gegenbewegung zur Abkehr[40] früherer Generationen ein. Die vorexilische Redaktion ist so optimistisch, daß sie die Intensität der joschijanischen Umkehr mit dem dreigliedrigen Umstand *bkl lbbw wbkl npšw wbkl m'dw* beschreibt, der sonst nur noch im Hauptgebot Dtn 6,5 vorkommt.

St. Gabriel
A-2340 Mödling

Gottfried Vanoni

30,10; 1 Sam 7,3; mit *'d*: Dtn 4,30; 30,2; Vgl. *ŠūB* + *mdrk*: 1 Kön 13,33 (negiert); 2 Kön 17,13 (Imperativ).

40. Vgl. nur *SūR* in Dtn 11,16; 1 Sam 12,20; (2 Kön 18,6); *'ZB* in Dtn 28,20; 31,16; Jos 24,16.20; Ri 2,12.13; 10,6,10.13; 1 Sam 8,8; 12,10; 1 Kön (9,3); 11,33; 2 Kön 21,22; 22,17.

APPENDIX

A. VAN HOONACKER BIBLIOGRAPHY

Reproduced from J. COPPENS, *Le Chanoine Albin Van Hoonacker. Son enseignement, son œuvre et sa méthode exégétiques*, Paris-Gembloux, 1935, p. xii-xxii, and augmented with some posthumous publications.

J. LUST

1. *De rerum creatione ex nihilo*, in *Un. Cath. Lov. Diss. ad grad. doct. in Fac. theol.* Ser I, vol. 38. Leuven, 1886. 315 p.
2. *Coup d'œil général sur la critique biblique rationaliste*, in *Le Muséon. Miscellanées* 7 (1888) 2-9.
3. *Observations critiques sur les récits concernant Biléam*, in *Le Muséon* 7 (1888) 61-76.
4. *La critique et l'apologétique*, in *Le Muséon* 8 (1989) 4-12, 17-25, 33-42.
5. *L'origine des quatre premiers chapitres du Deutéronome*, Leuven, 1889. 47 p. — In *Le Muséon* 7 (1888) 464-482; 8 (1889) 67-85; 141-149.
6. *Les prophètes d'Israël*, in *Journal de Bruxelles*, 7, 12, 17, 22 July 1889.
7. *Le nestorianisme sous les Mongols*; notice sur l'histoire de Mar Jabalaha et de Raban Sauma (texte syriaque publié par Bedjan), in *Le Muséon* 8 (1889) 270-272.
8. *Le système de M. Stickel sur le Cantique des cantiques*, in *Le Muséon* 8 (1889) 394-398.
9. *Néhémie et Esdras. Une nouvelle hypothèse sur la chronologie de l'époque de la Restauration*, in *Le Muséon* 9 (1890) 151-184, 317-351, 389-400.
10. *Néhémie et Esdras, nouvelle hypothèse sur la chronologie de l'époque de la Restauration juive*. Leuven, 1890, IV-85 p.
11. *Zorobabel et le second temple*, in *Le Muséon* 10 (1891) 72-96, 232-260, 379-397, 489-515, 634-644.
12. *Genèse XXX*, 40, in *Le Muséon* 11 (1892) 470-472.
13. *Zorobabel et le second temple*. Étude sur la chronologie des six premiers chapitres du livre d'Esdras. Gent-Leipzig, 1892. 118 p.
14. *Néhémie en l'an 20 d'Artaxerxès I, Esdras en l'an 7 d'Artaxerxès II*. Réponse à un mémoire d'A. Kuenen. Gent-Leipzig, 1892. 91 p.
15. *Les prophètes d'Israël*, in *Journal de Bruxelles*, 10 July 1892.
16. *The Name of Sesbassar*, in The Academy, 1892, 114.
17. *Le vœu de Jephté*, in *Le Muséon* 11 (1892) 448-469; 12 (1893) 59-80.
18. *Ézéchiel XX*, 25-26, in *Le Muséon* 12 (1893) 126-154.
19. *Le vœu de Jephté*. Ëtude sur le chapitre XI du livre des Juges, suivie d'une notice sur Ézéchiel XX, 25-26. Leuven, 1983. 73 p.
20. *Le lieu du culte dans la législation rituelle des Hébreux*, in *Le Muséon* 13 (1894) 195-204, 299-320, 403-426, 533-541; 14 (1895) 17-38.
21. *Le lieu du culte dans la législation rituelle des Hébreux*. Gent-Leipzig, 1894. 92 p.
22. *Les prophètes d'Israël*, in *Journal de Bruxelles*, 24-28 February 1894.

23. *Lettre au R.P. Lagrange* (sur la chronologie de l'époque de Néhémie et d'Esdras), in *Revue Biblique Internationale* 4 (1895) 186-192.
24. *Nouvelles études sur la restauration juive après l'exil de Babylone*. Paris, 1896. 313 p.
25. *Note sur les lignes 30seqq. de l'inscription du cylindre de Cyrus*, in *Mélanges Ch. de Harlez*, Leiden, 1896, p. 325-329.
26. *The Return of the Jews under Cyrus*, in *The Expository Times* 8 (1897) 351-354.
27. *Divination by the 'Ob amongst the Ancient Hebrews*, in *The Expository Times* 9 (1898) 157-160.
28. *Les prêtres et les lévites dans le livre du prophète Ézéchiel*, in *Rev. Bibl. Intern.* 8 (1899) 177-205.
29. *Le sacerdoce lévitique dans la loi et dans l'histoire des Hébreux*. London, 1899. 465 p.
30. *L'auteur du quatrième évangile*, in *Rev. Bibl. Intern.* 9 (1900) 226-247.
31. *Richard Simon et la critique biblique au XVIIe siècle*, in *Revue d'Histoire Ecclésiastique* 1 (1900) 127-133.
32. *Venticinque anni di storia del Cristianesimo nascente*, in *Rev. Hist. Eccl.* 1 (1900) 489-494.
33. *Le traité du philosophe syrien Probus sur les premiers Analytiques d'Aristote*, in *Journal asiatique* 16 (1900) 70-166.
34. *Ezekiel's Priests and Levites*, in *The Expository Times* 12 (1901) 383, 494-498.
35. *Notes sur l'histoire de la restauration juive après l'exil de Babylone*, in *Rev. Bibl. Intern.* 10 (1901) 5-26, 175-199.
36. *Le prologue du quatrième évangile*, in *Rev. Hist. Eccl.* 2 (1901) 5-14.
37. *L'hypothèse de M. Wendt sur la composition du quatrième évangile*, in *Rev. Hist. Eccl.* 2 (1901) 747-770.
38. *The Four Empires of the Book Daniel*, in *The Expository Times* 13 (1902) 420-423.
39. *Les chapitres IX-XIV du livre de Zacharie*, in *Rev. Bibl. Intern.* 11 (1902) 161-183, 347-378.
40. *Une question touchant la composition du livre de Job*, in *Rev, Bibl. Intern.* 12 (1903) 161-189.
41. *La prophétie relative à la naissance d'Immanu-El, Is. VII*, 14ss., in *Rev. Bibl. Intern.* n.s., 1 (1904) 213-227.
42. *Le caractère littéraire des deux premiers chapitres de Joël*, in *Rev. Bibl. Intern.* 1 (1904) 356-373.
43. *Joël I, 17*, in *Rev. Bibl. Intern.* 1 (1904) 374-376.
44. *Notes d'exégèse sur quelques passages difficiles d'Amos* (Am. II,7-8; II, 13; III, 3-8; III, 12-13; V, 24-27; VI, 1-2; VI, 9-10), in *Rev. Bibl. Intern.* 2 (1905) 163-187.
45. *Un mot grec (Hadès) dans le livre de Jonas II, 7*, in *Rev. Bibl. Intern.* 2 (1905) 398-399.
46. *Notes d'exégèse sur quelques passages difficiles d'Osée* (Os. IV, 4-5; IV, 18; V, 1-2; V, 11; VI, 8-9; VIII, 6; IX, 13; X, 9-10; XI, 4; XI, 6-7; XII, 4-7; XIII, 1-2), in *Rev. Bibl. Intern.* 4 (1907) 13-33.
47. *Les douze petits prophètes traduits et commentés*, in *Études Bibliques*. Paris, 1908. XXIII-759 p.

48. *De Arameesche papyrus-oorkonden van Elefantine*, in *Dietsche Warande en Belfort* 12 (1908) 1-22, 105-124.
49. *Daniel, IX, 26: ve'ên lô*, in *The Expository Times* 20 (1909) 380-381.
50. *Les troubles d'Éléphantine en 411 avant J.-C., d'après les papyrus Euting et Sachau* in *Zeitschrift für Assyriologie und verwandte Gebiete* 23 (1909) 187-196.
51. *Die rechtliche Stellung des jüdischen Tempels in Elephantine gegenüber den Einrichtungen des Alten Testaments*, in *Theologie und Glaube* 1 (1909) 438-447.
52. *L'Ébed Jahvé et la composition littéraire des chapitres XL ss. d'Isaïe*, in *Rev. Bibl. Intern.* 6 (1909) 487-528.
53. *Annales d'Assourbanipal*, IV, 13-20, in *Zeitschrift für Assyriologie* 24 (1910) 334-337.
54. *Malachias*, in *Catholic Encyclopedia*, vol. 9. New York, The Encyclopedia Press, 1910.
55. *Questions de critique littéraire et d'exégèse touchant les chap. XL ss. d'Isaïe*, in *Rev. Bibl. Intern.* 7 (1910) 557-572.
56. *Questions de critique littéraire et d'exégèse touchant les chap. XLss. d'Isaïe*, in *Rev. Bibl. Intern.* 8 (1911) 107-114, 279-285.
57. *Notes sur quelques passages des Annales d'Assourbanipal* (III, 73; IV, 30; IV, 70 ss; V, 24 ss; VII, 48), in *Zeitschrift für Assyriologie* 25 (1911) 358-364.
58. *Micheas*. — *Nehemias* (The Book of), in *Catholic Encyclopedia*, vol. 10. New York, The Encyclopedia Press, 1911.
59. *De profeten, een maatschappelijke stand in Israël*, in *Dietsche Warande en Belfort* (1912) 1-31.
60. *Le titre primitif du livre d'Ézéchiel* in *Rev. Bibl. Intern.* 9 (1912) 241-253.
61. *Het stilstaan der zon op Jozue's bevel*, in *Ons Geloof* 3 (1913) 10-15.
62. *La description de l'autruche dans Job, XXXIX*, 13, in *Rev. Bibl. Intern.* 10 (1913) 420-422.
63. *Over godsdienstige toestanden onder de Joodsche Kolonisten te Elefantine, in de 6e en 5e eeuw v. C.*, in *Handelingen van het tweede Vl. Philologencongres.* Gent, 1913. — Id.: *met naschrift*, in *Dietsche Warande en Belfort* 9 (1914) 216-230.
64. *Rondom de Koperen Slang van Moyses*, in *Dietsche Warande en Belfort* (1913) 307-336, 389-421.
65. *De eigennaam van God in het Oud Testament*, in *Ons Geloof* 3 (1913) 433-444, 481-488.
66. *Een afdoend pleidooi voor de echtheid van Math., XVI, 17 vv.*, in *Van Onzen Tijd*, 1-8 Nov. 1913.
67. *Das Wunder Josua's*, in *Theologie und Glaube* 5 (1913) 454-461.
68. *Sumerisch-babylonische Hymnen und Gebete an Samas*, in *Bull. Bibl. et Pédag. du Musée belge*, March-April 1913.
69. *La vie religieuse en Belgique*, in *Comment and Criticism*, 1914.
70. *La date de l'introduction de l'encens dans le culte de Jahvé*, in *Rev. Bibl. Intern.* 11 (1914) 161-187.
71. *Éléments sumériens dans le livre d'Ézéchiel*, in *Zeitschrift für Assyriologie* 28 (1914) 333-336.
72. *Bethel-TQM*, in *Zeitschrift für Assyriologie* 29 (1914-1915) 204.

73. *La campagne de Sennachérib en Judée en 701 av. J.-C.*, in *Mélanges d'histoire offerts à Charles Mœller*, vol. 1. 1914, p. 1-10.
74. *The Literary Origin of the Narrative of the Fall*, in *The Expositor* 8 (1914) 481-498.
75. *Une communauté judéo-araméenne à Éléphantine en Égypte aux VIe et Ve siècles av J.-C.*, in *British Academy. The Schweich Lectures*, 1914. London, 1915.
76. *Jérusalem et Éléphantine*, in *Le Muséon* 33 (1915-1916) 40-47.
77. *Zach. I, 8, 10f; VI, 1ff. and the Dul-Azag of the Babylonians*, in *Journal of Theological Studies* 16 (1915) 250-252.
78. *Connexion of Death with Sin according to Genesis II-III*, in *The Expositor* 9 (1915) 131-143.
79. *Expository Notes*: *a*) Gen. IV, 7: «... and if thou doest not well ...». *b*) Gen. XLIV, 5: Divination cup? *c*) I Sam. X, 12: «And who is their father?» or: «his father?», in *The Expositor* 9 (1915) 452-459.
80. *The Servant of the Lord in Isaiah XLff.*, in *The Expositor* 11 (1916) 183-210.
81. «*And the sun stood still ...*» (*Joshua, X, 13*), in *The Expositor* 12 (1916) 321-339.
82. *Van Noppen's Engelse vertaling van «Lucifer»*, in *De Stem uit België*, 6 July 1917.
83. *Is the Narrative of the Fall a Myth?*, in *The Expositor* 16 (1918) 373-400.
84. *De «Muur» van Jericho en het verhaal van het zesde hoofdstuk van het boek Josuë*, in *Dietsche Warande en Belfort* (1919) 587-599.
85. *Kanunnik Coppieters*, in *Ons Volk Ontwaakt*, 31 Jan. 1920.
86. *De maagdelijke ontvangenis en geboorte van den messias bij Isaias VII, 14*, in *Ons Geloof* 7 (1921) 481-494.
87. *De jongste waarnemingen op gebied der geschiedenis van het Semietische alfabet, in Verslagen en Mededeelingen der K. Vl. Academie*, Gent, 1921, 91-112.
88. *Grondbeginselen der moraalfilosofie*. Leuven, 1922. 192 + 2 p.
89. *Hammelsar(?) et Aspenaz(?) dans le premier chapitre du livre de Daniel*, in *Le Muséon* 35 (1922) 145-151.
90. *De maagdelijke ontvangenis en geboorte van den Messias bij Isaias VII, 14*, in *Handelingen van het Vlaamsch Maria-Congres te Brussel, 1921*, vol. 1. Brussel, 1922, p. 148-160.
91. *Grondbeginselen der moraalfilosofie*. Antwerpen-Brussel, [2]1923, 194 p.
92. *De profeet Isaias en het Joodsche gemeenebest in de tweede helft der achtste eeuw vóór Christus, in Dietsche Warande en Belfort*, 1923, p. 253-282.
93. *A propos d'une nouvelle édition des papyrus araméens*, in *Le Muséon* 36 (1923) 67-82.
94. *Une parole d'Isthar dans le récit du déluge*, in *Le Muséon* 36 (1923) 293-295.
95. *La vision de l'Épha dans Zacharie* (V, 5ss.), in *Revue Bénédictine* 35 (1923) 57-61.
96. *La succession chronologique Néhémie-Esdras*, in *Revue Biblique* 32 (1923) 481-494.
97. *De Toren van Babel en de verwarring der talen*, in *Verslagen en Mededeelingen der K. Vl. Academie*, Gent, 1923, p. 128-139.
98. *Deux passages obscurs dans le chapitre 19 d'Isaïe*, in *Revue Bénédictine* 36 (1924) 297-306.

99. *La succession chronologique Néhémie-Esdras*, in *Revue Biblique* 33 (1924) 33-64.
100. *Nehemia en Ezra*, in *Verslagen en Mededeelingen der K. Vl. Academie*, Gent, 1924, p. 552-564.
101. *Grondbeginselen der moraalfilosofie*. Antwerpen-Brussel, [3]1925, 194 p.
102. *Het boek der vertroosting van Israël* (Is. XL vlb.), in *Dietsche Warande en Belfort* 25 (1925) 577-601, 675-701.
103. *Het grafschrift van Koning Achiram te Byblos*, in *Verslagen en Mededeelingen der K. Vl. Academie*, Gent, 1925, p. 800-807.
104. *Over den oorsprong van de zevendaagsche week en den sabbatdag bij de Hebreeuwen*, in *Verslagen en Mededeelingen der K. Vl. Academie*, Gent, 1927, p. 250-265.
105. *Toelichting bij een paar regels uit Vondel's Lucifer*, in *Verslagen en Mededeelingen der K. Vl. Academie*, Gent, 1928, p. 789-793.
106. *Antwoord van kanunnik A. Van Hoonacker*, in *Manifestation-Huldebetoon J. Forget-J. De Becker-A. Van Hoonacker*, Leuven, 1928, p. 58-65.80.
107. *Notes sur le texte de La Bénédiction de Moïse (Deut. XXXIII)*, in *Le Muséon* 42 (1929) 42-60.
108. *L'historiographie du livre de Daniel*, in *Le Muséon* 44 (1931) 169-176.
109. *Een Israëlitisch volksman (Amos) uit de achtste eeuw vóór Christus*, in *Verslagen en Mededeelingen der K. Vl. Academie*, Gent, 1931, p. 159-170.
110. *Was Jozef's beker (Gen. 44) een tooverbeker?*, in *Canisiusblad* 25 (1931) 112-116.
111. *Is Saül ook onder de Profeten?*, in *Canisiusblad* 25 (1931) 267-270.
112. *Was Jozef's beker een tooverbeker?*, in *Isidoor Teirlinck Album*, Leuven, 1931, p. 239-244.
113. *Het Boek Isaias, vertaald uit het Hebreeuwsch en in doorloopende aanteekeningen verklaard*. Brugge, 1932, 311 p.

POSTHUMOUS PUBLICATIONS

114. *Quelques notes sur « Absolute und relative Wahrheit in der heiligen Schrift ». Une contribution inédite du chanoine Albin Van Hoonacker à la Question Biblique* (1909), posth. ed. by J. COPPENS, in *ETL* 18 (1941) 201-336.
115. *De compositione litteraria et de origine Mosaica Hexateuchi disquisitio historico-critica. Een historisch-kritisch onderzoek van professor Van Hoonacker naar het ontstaan van de Hexateuch op grond van verspreide nagelaten aantekeningen samengesteld en ingeleid door Jozef Coppens* (Kon. Acad. Wet. Lett. Sch. Kunsten van België, Verhandelingen XI,11), Brussel, 1949.
116. *Le rapprochement entre le Deutéronome et Malachie. Une notice inédite de A. Van Hoonacker (1908)*, posth. ed. by F. NEIRYNCK, in *ETL* (1983) 86-90.

UNPUBLISHED MANUSCRIPTS

Handwritten texts preserved in the Archives of the Library of the Faculty of Theology in Leuven:

1. *Le Prophétisme dans l'Ancien Testament*, 143 p.

2. *Les Institutions religieuses et liturgiques des Hébreux dans la Loi et dans l'Histoire*, 1891-1892, 394 p.
3. Dutch translation of the Pentateuch.
4. Miscellaneous: letters, ...

VERZEICHNIS DER AUTOREN

Abravanel, Y. 310f
Ackroyd, P. 354
Aharoni, Y. 27
Airoldi, N. 263
Albertz, R. 265
Al-Biruni 147
Albright, W.F. 330, 337f
Alonso Díaz, J. 36
Alt, A. 25, 46, 62, 94, 278
Amiran, R. 28
Amsler, S. 5
Anbar, M. 3f
Andersen, F.I. 291
Andrae, W. 225
Archi, A. 104
Artom, S. 330, 336
Avigad, N. 28, 90

Bacon, B.W. 307
Bächli, O. 36, 279, 323
Baillet, M. 130
Baker, H.W. 130
Bakhtin, M. 153
Balandier, G. 71
Baltzer, K. 36, 317
Bardtke, H. 10
Barkun, M. 66, 68
Barrick, W.B. 34
Barth, H. 26, 28, 46
Barthélemy, D. 134, 333f
Bartlett, J.R. 156
Baumann, E. 339
Baumgartner, W. 24
Becker, J. 34f
Begg, C. 3, 160, 198
Begrich, G. 28
Behrens, H. 224f
Ben-Barak, Z. 278, 281
Benjamin, C. 104
Bernhardt, K.-H. 280, 284
Berry, G.R. 20
Bertholet, A. 164, 284, 292, 311f
Beyerlin, W. 177
Bickerman, E. 317
Bin Gorion, M.J. 78
Biram, A. 88, 91
Birch, B.C. 281
Blenkinsopp, J. 103, 321
Blount, C. 10f
Boecker, H.J. 61, 66f, 281, 284
Böhmer, S. 192
Boer, P. de 103
Bogaert, P.M. 3
Bohannan, L. 68
Bohlen, R. 205
Bolingbroke, H.St.J. 10
Borger, R. 300
Bottéro, J. 104
Bowman, J. 147
Brandes, M. 226
Braulik, G. 2, 4, 36, 42, 152, 157, 159, 252f, 352f, 357, 361
Breasted, A.R. 222
Breit, H. 255
Brekelmans, C. VII, 3, 195, 249, 282
Briggs, R.D. 218, 232, 284f
Broshi, M. 90
Brown, F. 284f
Brownlee, W. 355
Brueggemann, W. 292, 296
Budde, K. 280, 284
Buis, P. 193f, 196, 201, 242, 280, 295
Bulbach, S. 28
Burckhardt, J. 157
Burkitt, F.C. 20
Byrne, B. 343

Calmet, A. 10
Calvin 255
Campbell, A.F. 176
Caplice, R.I. 219
Caquot, A. 212, 277-279, 292
Cardascia, G. 300
Cardellini, I. 274f
Carillo Alday, S. 341f
Carmichael, C.M. 255, 265, 270, 279, 283
Carroll, R.P. 296, 344
Cassuto, U. 64

Cazelles, H. 2, 4, 27f, 90f, 105, 177, 184
Chelhod, J. 66
Chigier, M. 99
Childs, B.S. 64f, 150, 152f
Cholewiński, A. 274, 282
Christensen, D.L. 2, 4, 137f, 140, 346
Claburn, W.E. 36
Clarke, R. 17
Clastres, P. 61
Clements, R.E. 110, 280f, 346
Clifford, R.J. 344
Cody, A. 323
Cogan, M. 26-28, 225f
Cohen, R. 103
Conrad, D. 27
Cooper, J.S. 224, 226
Coppens, J. 13, 17-21, 24, 263, 367
Cornill, C.H. 277
Cortese, E. 34, 357, 359
Craigie, P.C. 112, 202, 209, 269, 277, 279
Crenshaw, J.L. 84
Croatto, J.S. 355
Cross, F.M. 26f, 33-35, 43, 171, 179, 248, 309, 330-332, 336, 357f, 361
Crüsemann, F. 61, 176, 272
Cullen, J. 20

Damdamayev, M.A. 105
Daube, D. 67
Davenport, J.W. 212, 214
D'Eichtal, G. 20
Delcor, M. 36, 292
Del Olmo Lete, G. 211f
Diamond, A.S. 67, 71
Diepold, P. 353
Dietrich, W. 25, 32, 36f, 43, 46, 171, 206, 248f, 283, 357-359, 361
Díez Macho, A. 130, 133f
Dillmann, A. 284, 292, 295, 304-307, 311-313, 315
Driver, G.R. 300
Driver, S.R. 14, 20, 99, 112, 164, 237, 281, 284f, 305-306, 308f, 323
Duhm, B. 239
Dupont-Sommer, A. 147
Dussaud, R. 212, 229
Dux, G. 60

Ebeling, E. 220, 232
Ebeling, G. 58
Eder, K. 60f
Ehrlich, A.B. 77, 93, 286f
Eichhorn, J.G. 11f, 158
Eising, H. 352
Eissfeldt, O. 32, 175, 339, 344
Elat, M. 28
Elitzur, Y. 28
Elwert, G. 71
Ephal, J. 88
Erman, A. 222
Evans-Pritchard, E.. 68
Ewald, H.A. 31

Fabry, A.-H. 4, 346, 351
Farber, W. 220
Fensham, F.C. 212, 214
Finet, A. 104
Finkelstein, J.J. 301
Firth, R. 71f
Fishbane, M. 314
Fitzmyer, J.A. 88, 239
Fleming, D. 17f
Fohrer, G. 32, 194
Fortes, M. 66, 70f
Fraine, J. de 277, 280, 281
Frankena, R. 227
Freed, A. 20
Freedman, D.N. 26, 291
Frei, H. 153
Frey, H. 64
Friedman, M.E. 77
Friedman, R.E. 33, 171, 248, 357, 359, 361
Friedrich, J. 317
Fries, S.A. 20
Fritz, V. 27f
Frost, S.B. 36
Fuhs, H.F. 354

Galling, K. 277-279, 287f
Garbini, G. 103
García López, F. 2f, 168, 174, 189, 191-193, 195, 197f, 200-202, 283f, 286f, 289-291, 294f
Gauthier, L. 99
Gehman, H.S. 32
Geller, S.A. 342f
Gerstenberger, E. 66, 278, 285f, 288

Gese, H. 177
Geston, A. 281
Geus, C.H.J. de 66f
Gilmer, H.W. 65
Ginsberg, H.L. 84, 86, 273-275
Gluckman, M. 68, 71
Görg, M. 352
Goetze, A. 221
Gordis, R. 112
Goshen-Gottstein, M.H. 130
Gottwald, N.K. 66
Goudoever, J. van 3, 145
Gradwohl, R. 245
Graf, K.H. 210
Gramberg, C.P.W. 20
Gray, J. 32, 46
Greenberg, M. 319
Greengus, S. 302
Grelot, P. 356
Gressmann, H. 29, 279
Griffiths, J.G. 216f
Grintz, Y.M. 36, 323
Groß, W. 43
Grothus, J. 60
Güterbock, H.G. 60
Guilding, A.E. 256, 265, 269
Gunneweg, A.H.J. 36, 183

Haas, V. 221
Haase, R. 60
Habermas, J. 72
Haelvoet, M. 184
Hahn, J. 209, 211, 214, 223f, 225, 235, 242
Halbe, J. 2, 4, 57, 62, 64f, 67-69, 71, 73, 321f
Hallo, W.W. 301
Halpern, B. 105
Haran, M. 76, 86, 275
Hardt, H. von der 11
Harvey, J. 339
Healey, J.F. 212
Hempel, J. 9, 129, 277
Henninger, J. 99
Hermann, A. 222
Herrmann, S. 58, 183, 192, 206
Herzog, Z. 27
Hidal, S. 340
Higgs, W. 198
Hobbes, T. 9
Hölscher, G. 20, 25, 31, 34, 277-279, 306f
Hoffmann, D. 242f
Hoffmann, H.-D. 22, 28, 34-43, 236-239, 248-251, 357f
Holladay, W.L. 4, 311, 326-328
Hollenstein 36f, 43
Hoonacker, A. Van VII, 1, 13-23, 24, 363-368
Hoppe, L.J. 2, 33, 35f, 46
Horn, H. 183
Hornung, E. 217, 222
Horst, F. 20, 254, 277f, 281, 286, 293
Horst, L. 20
Hossfeld, F.-L. 53, 154, 164, 166-168, 172, 177f, 184, 188, 191, 193-196, 199-202, 271, 352f, 355
Houtman, C. 11, 17, 20
Hunger, H. 97
Hurvitz, A. 275f
Hvidberg-Hansen, O. 212, 214, 251

Ibn Ezra 80, 151, 315
Imschoot, P. Van 310, 319
Isbell, C.D. 36

Jackson, B.S. 67, 153
Jacobs, P. 164
Janowski, B. 345
Japhet, S. 274f
Jenks, A.W. 281
Jenni, E. 26, 32
Jepsen, A. 26, 33, 39, 46
Jeremias, J. 86
Joüon, P. 282
Jüngling, H.-W. 61, 66
Junker, H. 284, 310, 313

Kaiser, O. 34, 99, 256
Kallai, Z. 95
Karge, P. 10, 315
Karl, Z. 26
Kaufman, S.A. 3, 190, 256-259, 265-268, 274f, 281, 293
Kaufmann, Y. 273f
Kearney, P.J. 321, 324f
Keel, O. 27, 68, 224, 269
Kees, H. 216f
Kennet, R.H. 20
Kenyon, K.M. 28

Kermode, F. 153
Kestemont, G. 100
King, L.W. 223, 230
King, R. 136
Kleinert, P. 11, 135, 313
Klem, H. 136
Klengel, H. 104
Klima, J. 60, 71
Klinkenberg, H.M. 63
Kloppenburg, J.S. 356
Klostermann, A. 281, 290
Knevett, E. De 13
Koch, K. 62
Kochavi, M. 90
Köhler, L. 68
Köppel, U. 156
Korošec, V. 100, 212, 316, 318
Krämer, K.F. 112
Kramer, F. 61, 67
Kraus, H.J. 17
Kreuzer, S. 345
Küchler, M. 27
Kühlewein, J. 341
Kuenen, A. 13, 31, 45
Kuhl, C. 314
Kupper, J.R. 104
Kutsch, E. 30

Laberge, L. 3
Labuschagne, C.J. 2, 4, 111, 115-121, 339, 341, 346f
Lagrange, M.J. 22
Lambert, C. 209
Lance, D. 26
Landsberger, B. 96, 301
Lang, B. 99
Langdon, S. 147
Langlamet, F. 280, 302f, 353, 359
Leclercq, J. 242, 280
Le Déaut, R. 130, 133f, 145
Leibowitz, N. 289
Lemaire, A. 103, 105, 186, 194
Lenski, G. 71
Leslau, W. 147
Lessing, G.E. 9
Lestienne, M. 180
Levenson, J.D. 33
Levin, C. 33, 35f, 154, 238
Lewis, D. 79, 82
L'Hour, J. 181, 307f
Licht, J. 79
Liedke, G. 66f, 296, 301
Limet, H. 104
Lindblom, J. 36
Liverani, M. 104
Locher, C. 3f, 254f, 267, 303
Lods, A. 278
Loersch, S. 25
Loewenstamm, S.E. 202, 212-214, 241f, 251
Lohfink, N. 1, 14, 29f, 34, 36f, 40, 43, 45-47, 57, 61, 77, 107, 118, 135, 149-153, 159-161, 164, 166, 168, 171, 174f, 180, 187f, 194, 198, 201, 253, 257f, 265, 271, 278f, 282, 286, 298, 303, 310, 313, 316, 322, 327f, 339, 351, 354f, 357, 359f
Long, B.O. 315
Loretz, O. 329
Loza, J. 242, 351
Luckenbill, D.D. 222f, 225f, 230
Luhmann, N. 55, 63, 66-68
Lundbom, J.R. 30, 36, 339
Luria, B.Z. 36
Lurje, J.M. 60
Lust, J. VII, 1, 14, 24, 31
Luther, M. 152, 255
Luyten, J. 3f
Luzzatto, S.D. 312

Maag, V. 86
Macholz, G.C. 61
Maier, J. 30, 36
Malamat, A. 26-28
Manus, C.U. 3
Margalit, J.B. 212
Martin-Achard, R. 296
Martiny, G. 225
Mauss, M. 71
Mayes, A.D.H. 3f, 34, 36f, 43, 46, 107, 164f, 168f, 171f, 182, 209, 240, 248, 266, 281, 299, 317, 322, 346
Mays, J.L. 291
Mazar, B. 76, 95
McCarthy, D.J. 30, 164, 182, 310, 317, 322, 360
McConville, J.G. 265f
McCurley, F.R. 279, 283
McEvenue, S.E. 353f

McKane, W. 231
McKay, J.W. 29, 36
Meek, T.J. 300
Meenan, A.J. 209
Meier, G. 218f, 232
Meiggs, R. 79, 82
Mendenhall, G.E. 317
Menochius, J.S. 9
Mercer, S.A.B. 217
Merendino, R.P. 36, 154, 164, 269, 278, 283, 286, 293, 298f
Mettinger, T.N.D. 278, 281
Meyer, R. 26, 329-333, 336, 338f, 342f
Michaelis, J.D. 11f
Mihalik, I. 5
Miles, J.C. 300
Milgrom, J. 275
Milik, J.T. 130, 132, 329
Minette de Tillesse, G. 32, 47, 194, 236, 238, 248, 283
Mittmann, S. 42, 154f, 157, 166, 168, 191, 193-197
Moeller, H. 10
Montgomery, J.A. 32
Moor, J.C. De 213
Moran, W.L. 281
Morenz, S. 61
Morgenstern, J. 242
Moshkovitz, S. 27
Müller, H.P. 356

Nachmanides 315
Nadel, S.F. 68
Naveh, J. 103
Nebeling, G. 298f
Neirynck, F. 13f, 19f, 22, 367
Nelson, R.D. 31, 33f, 36f, 43, 46, 171, 248, 357-361
Nemoy, L. 147
Neufeld, E. 66f, 72
Nicholson, E.W. 36, 43, 110, 182, 194, 278f, 296
Niebur, B.G. 149
Niedner, F. 176
Nielsen, E. 174, 215f, 307
North, R. 176
Noth, M. 4, 31-35, 46f, 62, 64, 95, 152, 155, 158, 171, 174, 177, 183, 236, 248, 255, 278, 283, 285, 304f, 307, 309, 352, 355, 357
Nougayrol, J. 317
Nyström, S. 279, 281

Oberforcher, R. 37
Odasso, G. 36
Oded, B. 296
Östreicher, T. 24f, 30, 46
Öttinger, N. 221, 231
Ogden, G.S. 27
Or, M. 36
Otto, E. 28, 351f
Otzen, B. 28

Panufnik, A. 136, 139
Parke, H.W. 79
Parpola, S. 87
Parvish, S. 11
Paton, L.B. 20
Paul, M.J. 1
Paul, S.M. 89
Pedersen, J. 66, 295f
Penna, A. 209, 246
Perdue, L.G. 213
Perlitt, L. 2f, 30, 36, 59, 65, 75, 89, 149, 151, 165, 168, 177, 180, 184, 193, 296, 319
Petersen, C. 296
Petschow, H. 257-260
Peucker, H. 298
Pfeifer, G. 36
Pfeiffer, R.H. 32
Phillips, A. 255, 265, 270, 296, 299
Philo von Alexandrien 151, 265
Plataroti, D. 36
Plöger, J. 154, 294
Poebel, A. 224
Poels, H. 13, 17
Pohlmann, K.F. 35
Polzin, R. 41, 153, 321
Porter, J.R. 280
Poulssen, N. 36
Preiss, H. 20
Press, R. 231
Preuß, H.D. 24, 36, 99, 149, 159, 164, 166f, 174, 197f, 254-257, 298f, 342, 353
Priest, J. 36, 43
Puukko, A.F. 166, 277

Quast, U. 329

Rabast, K. 278, 285, 288
Rad, G. von 1, 5, 25f, 32f, 59, 99, 101, 103, 107, 135, 272, 278-280, 290, 293, 317, 323
Radday, Y. 276
Radjawane, A.N. 32
Rahlfs, A. 336
Rainey, A.F. 27
Rashbam (Rabbi Samuel b. Meir) 77
Reimarus, H. 20
Reiner, E. 96, 218f, 223, 230, 315
Renauld, B. 179
Rendtorff, R. 32f, 176, 358
Rennes, J. 246
Resenhöfft, W. 250
Reventlow, H. Graf 194
Reviv, H. 36, 104
Richter, W. 34, 64f
Ridderbos, J. 112
Rieder, D. 130
Robinson, D.W.B. 26
Römer, W.H.P. 269
Rössler, O. 43
Rofé, A. 2f, 107, 110, 299, 301f, 304, 308-310, 320
Rose, M. 26, 30, 36f, 43, 156, 176, 247
Rosenthal, F. 218
Rost, L. 36
Roth, M.T. 302
Rowland, C. 343
Rudolph, W. 85, 243, 327
Rüterswörden, U. 209, 215-219, 221

Sachs, A. 217
Salsmans, J. 13
Šanda, A. 21
Sauneron, S. 217
Schäfer-Lichtenberger, C. 61, 66
Scharbert, J. 36
Schedl, C. 119, 121f
Schelsky, H. 63, 68
Schmid, H.H. 62, 176f, 181
Schmidt, L. 176
Schmidt, W.H. 176, 199, 280f
Schmitt, H.-C. 176, 183
Schnuttenhaus, F. 177
Schottroff, W. 61, 66
Schreiner, J. 351
Schultz, F.W. 255f, 265, 270
Schulz, H. 256f
Schwarzbach, B.E. 11
Seebaß, H. 284
Seeligmann, I.L. 314
Seinecke, L. 20
Seitz, G. 164, 168, 191, 195, 199, 202, 254, 267f, 277f, 281, 286f, 289, 292, 298f
Sekine, M. 37
Seters, J. van 99, 156, 247, 249
Seux, M.-J. 220
Siewert, P. 80
Sigrist, C. 61, 66f, 71
Ska, J.L. 353
Skehan, P.W. 329-332, 336-339
Skweres, D.E. 115f, 286, 325, 353
Smend, R. 9, 12, 32, 34f, 37, 43f, 99, 150f, 156, 171, 179, 206, 248, 319, 352, 354, 357-359
Smit, E.J. 37, 239
Smith, G.A. 312
Snycer, M. 212
Soggin, J.A. 278, 351
Speiser, E.A. 60
Sperber, A. 130f
Spieckermann, H. 25-29, 31-33, 35, 37, 42-47, 154, 225f, 236-239, 248-250, 357, 359, 361
Spiegelberg, S. 20
Spinoza, B. 151
Stade, B. 43
Stahl, R. 33, 154, 171, 248
Steck, O.H. 205
Steible, H. 224f
Stern, E. 27
Steuernagel, C. 112, 151, 166f, 256, 270, 277f, 304-308, 314
Stoebe, H.J. 280, 283
Strack, H.L. 229
Streck, B. 71f
Sturtevant, E.H. 221
Suzuki, Y. 160, 198
Szlechter, E. 60

Tal, A. 130
Talmon, S. 314
Théodoridès, A. 60f
Thiel, H.J. 221
Thiel, W. 66, 161, 192
Thompson, J.A. 265

Tostatus, A. 9
Tur-Sinai, N.H. 313

Valentin, H. 188, 214
Vandier, J. 226
Vanoni, G. 4, 45, 361
Vater, J.S. 174
Vatke, W. 20
Vaughan, P.H. 37
Vaux, R. de 130, 176f, 181, 352, 355
Veijola, T. 33, 171, 206, 248, 278, 280, 283, 285, 357, 359
Velde, H. Te 226
Vermeylen, J. 2f, 175f, 179
Vernes, M. 20
Virolleaud, C. 211
Volney, C.F. de 10
Voloshinov, V.N. 153
Voltaire 11
Vosté, J. 22

Waard, E.F. de 242
Waard, J. de 337
Wagner, V. 257, 266
Warner, S.M. 105
Watson, P.L. 212, 215-219
Weidner, E.F. 96, 315, 317
Weimar, P. 354
Weinfeld, M. 2, 30, 37, 76, 78-81, 83f, 86, 88f, 91, 93, 96f, 103, 107, 135, 169, 227, 242, 275, 278, 280, 304, 306f, 315, 358f
Weippert, H. 34, 357, 360
Weise, M. 147
Weiss, M. 111
Welch, A.C. 164, 279f
Wellhausen, J. 13, 25, 30f, 99, 157, 175, 254, 273, 277, 280
Welten, P. 26f, 37
Wenham, G.J. 12, 110, 265
Westermann, C. 169
Westphal, A. 10
Wette, W.M.L. de 9-12, 25, 30, 107, 149
Wevers, J.W. 129f, 133, 329, 336
Whitley, C.F. 4
Wiener, H.M. 255, 314
Wijngaards, J.N.M. 355
Wildberger, H. 228
Williamson, H.G.M. 37
Wilson, J.A. 60, 222
Winter, P. 339
Wiseman, D.J. 30, 37
Wolff, H.W. 35, 37, 47, 162, 237, 280, 357
Worden, T. 213
Wright, S.G.E. 281, 347
Würthwein, E. 26, 35, 37, 43, 45f, 285
Wüst, M. 155

Zenger, E. 176-178, 184, 244, 353f
Zevit, Z. 29
Zimmerli, W. 59, 150
Zitelmann, T. 71f
Zobel, H.J. 352

VERZEICHNIS DER BIBELSTELLEN

Gen
8,5 147
15,18 92f
35,4 215

Ex
12 145
12,26ff 351
13,14ff 351
15,25f 354
18 105f
19-34 174-207
19-24 306
19,2 176
19,3-8 184
19,6ff 78
20,18ff 168f
20,22-23,17 256, 274
20,24ff 16
20,24f 306
21,2 102
22,24-26 72
23,1-9 2, 63-74
23,5 267
23,11f 102
23,20ff 81, 183
23,25f 80
24,3-8 77
24,4f 306
24,4 52
31,18 53
32 3
32,20 208-251
34,8-28 183
34,10f 78

Lev
10-23 256
17-26 19-23
25 274-276
25,10 102

Num
1,1 145
5,11-31 229-233, 243f
9 145
13f 161
20,1 145
20,22-29 145
21 159, 161
21,21-31 155f
33,38 145

Dtn
1-34 137-140f
1-11 3, 14f, 129-134, 135-144
1-4 17
1-3 3, 92f, 115, 130, 138, 149-163, 171f
1,1-5 15, 120
1,2f 113
1,2 170
1,3 3, 145-148
1,5 52, 152, 163
1,6-8 114
1,6 163
1,7 93, 100
1,8 112, 131f
1,13-17 93, 103
1,16 105
1,19-2,1 140
1,19-46 161
1,21 131f, 160
1,27 104
1,31 89, 160
1,34-40 121
1,34-39 183
1,35ff 115
1,36 112
1,37-40 114
1,37f 203
1,40 114
1,41 131
1,42 114
2f 153, 155
2 120, 159

2,2-25 140
2,3-5 114
2,4ff 114
2,7 114, 160
2,8 154
2,9 114
2,10-12 112-114
2,13 114
2,14-16 15, 183
2,16-3,17 161
2,17ff 114
2,20-23 112-114
2,24f 114f, 133
2,24 159
2,26-3,11 140
2,26-37 155f
2,29 15
2,30 131, 160
2,31 114, 159
2,33 159
2,34 195
2,37 133
3,6 156
3,8ff 162
3,9-14 113
3,9 100
3,21f 121
3,21 132
3,23-28 203
3,24 163
3,26-28 114
4-11 140
4,1-40 15, 35, 41f, 140f, 152, 171f, 346
4,1f 130
4,2 122
4,3 131
4,5 15, 131ff, 252
4,6 93, 96, 101, 103
4,7f 169
4,9-31 159
4,9-24 184
4,10 167, 170
4,13 53f, 170f
4,14 197, 252
4,15-20 253
4,15ff 171
4,15 170
4,19 84
4,22 166
4,23 170
4,25ff 15
4,29f 19, 88f
4,32 342
4,35 131
4,36 184
4,37 84
4,39 131
4,40 195
4,41-43 15
4,44-6,3 141
4,44-49 15, 164, 191
5-30 47
5-11 3, 174-207
5 164-173, 186-197
5,1f 164f
5,1 191f, 253
5,2-5 165
5,2f 170, 192f
5,3 75
5,4f 193
5,4 129
5,6-21 193-195, 252-272
5,6-10 186
5,11-21 186f
5,11-16 112
5,12-15 110, 194f
5,14 104, 122
5,16 194f
5,22 54, 165-167, 195
5,23-31 25
5,23-27 195f
5,23-26 168
5,27 104
5,28-33 196f
5,28-31 119
5,28 169
5,31 252
5,32f 164f, 170
5,32 196
6,1-3 164
6,2f 197
6,2 131
6,4-7,11 141
6,4f 57

6,5 362
6,9 53, 96
6,10-15 253
6,10 288
6,12 131
6,18 131
6,20-24 351
7,1-6 290
7,1ff 289
7,2-4 100
7,6 57
7,8-11 253
7,9f 183
7,9 170
7,12-8,20 142
7,12 170
7,13ff 81
7,17-21 290
7,19 118
8,2ff 172
8,2 197
8,3 170
8,7-20 253
8,7-18 290
8,12-14 89
8,13 286, 288, 291
8,17f 292
9f 186-191
9 172
9,1-29 142f
9,1-7 198
9,5 131
9,7-10,11 197-203
9,7-10,5 54
9,7 197f
9,8 171, 198
9,9-11 199
9,10 53, 167
9,12-17 199f
9,18f 200
9,18 131
9,20-29 201
9,20 202
9,21 3, 208-251
9,26-29 119, 189
10,1-9 202
10,4 53f, 167
10,6f 113
10,10f 203
10,12-11,32 190
10,12-11,25 143
10,12f 198
10,13 131
10,15 89
10,16 327
11,6 104, 192
11,14f 132
11,20 53, 96
11,24f 91
11,24 93
11,26-30 76
11,26 132
11,29 18
11,30 113
11,31f 253
12-26 2, 252-272
12-18 259-265
12-16 271
12 39, 181
12,1-3 119
12,1 252f
12,2-31 261f
12,2-8 110
12,2 85
12,6-11 21
12,6 102
12,8-12 190
12,15 86
12,17 104
12,20 289
12,29-31 261f
13,1-14,27 259
13 80
13,1 122
13,2-19 262
13,13 104
13,15 237
13,16 92
14,1-21 262
14,1 343
14,22-16,17 262-265
14,22-15,23 263f
14,22-29 101
14,22-27 21, 259
14,22ff 288
14,29 323f
15 3, 273-276
15,6-10 102

15,6 93
15,12-18 3
15,12 102
15,15 195
15,19 102
16,1-17 264
16,1-8 21
16,7 104
16,13-15 327
16,16-17,11 101
16,17 281
16,18-18,22 265, 281f, 293
16,18-20 63, 103
16,18 104f
17,2 170
17,6f 75
17,8-18,22 105
17,9 106
17,11 106
17,14-20 3, 53, 61, 102, 277-297
17,14f 21, 282-284
17,15 96, 284f, 288
17,16-20 285-287
17,16f 288
17,18f 96
17,18 106
17,19 97
17,20 106
18,1-8 21
18,2 284
18,9 294
18,15f 106
18,16 167
18,18 284, 328
19-25 2, 260
19,1-21,23 260
19,2 21
19,3 106
19,7f 21
19,12 104
19,16-21 63
19,17 106
19,19 299
20,1-18 91f
20,1-9 101
20,3 192
20,10-18 321
20,17 194f
21-25 271
21,1-9 110, 240
21,2 105
21,3 104
21,7-9 87
21,10-14 100
21,19f 104
22,1-12 260, 265-270
22,1-4 63, 65
22,13-23,15 260
22,13-21 3, 298-303
22,16 104
22,20f 299
23,2 21
23,8 100
23,10-15 104
23,16-24,5 260
23,16-26 260
24,6f 260
24,8-25,4 260
24,14 323
24,17f 63
25,5-16 260
25,7 104
25,9 104
25,17 260
26 271
26,1-15 260
26,1-11 148
26,5-10 87
26,5-9 342
26,8 84
26,13-15 87
26,16-19 76-79, 119
26,16 253
26,17-19 319
26,17 117f
26,18f 57
26,19 93
27 3, 79-81
27,1-8 96
27,2-8 52, 304-309
27,4 76
27,5 21
27,6 76
27,9f 76
27,11-26 18
27,14-26 81
27,15-27 326

27,15-26 256
27,15 84
27,16-25 73
28-31 10
28,3-6 79f
28,7-14 81
28,13 93
28,16-19 79f
28,20-68 81
28,29 40
28,36 10
28,43 324
28,58 52
28,61 52
28,68 87
28,69-30,20 310-320
28,69 170
29f 2f, 346
29 3
29,4f 132f
29,5-14 321-325
29,8 170
29,9 104, 192
29,10 324
29,12 319
29,15-28 316
29,15-27 324f
29,17 80, 324
29,18-20 315
29,19f 52
29,20 324
29,21-27 213f
29,24 170
29,25 84
29,26 52
29,28 123
30 41
30,1-10 35, 88, 311f
30,3-4 15
30,7 312
30,10 52
30,11-14 318
31-34 138
31 51
31,7 203
31,9-13 54
31,9 51, 96
31,10-13 4, 97, 326-328
31,11f 192
31,12 324
31,16 170
31,19-22 339
31,19 51, 347
31,21 347
31,22 51
31,24-28 51
31,28 104, 347
32 3, 111, 329, 341-347
32,3 337
32,8f 329, 333, 337, 342f
32,8 101, 336
32,10f 89
32,32-35 111f, 119
32,43 3, 329-340, 343
32,48-52 203
32,48 120, 145
32,50 145
33 18
33,7 90
34,1 93
34,4 120
34,9 103
34,10 165

Jos

1-11 162
1,6 203
1,8 51
3-4 81f
3,11 352
4,1-9 182
4,6f 351f
4,19 354f
4,21ff 4, 351-356
5 145
5,2f 356
5,10-12 354f
6,18 356
6.22ff 356
7 324f
8f 3
8,30-32 304-309
8,31 51
8,32-35 52
8,33 356
9 321-325

12f 155
12,1-6 155
15 94f
18 82f
22 356
24 306
24,4f 306
24,25-27 182
24,25f 78
24,26 52

Ri
1,1-2,5 94
17-21 66-68

1 Sam
8-12 280, 291
8,5 282

2 Sam
5,6-11 108
6,1-15 108f
7,6 356

1 Kön
8,40 197
8,41-43 296
9,6-9 314
12,26ff 241, 247
12,30 237
15,12-14 239
15,13 241
18 205
21,8-14 69

2 Kön
10,28 83
11,17 106
11,18 237f, 241
12,3 106
15,19-20 102
17,31 356
18,4 85, 237, 241
18,13-19,37 109
19,18 227f
21,23f 102
22f 1, 4, 13-23, 24-48, 107-109
22 9-12
22,1f 39
22,3 39f
22,12 39f
22,13 45
23 3, 44
23,1-3 97
23,1 39f
23,2f 146
23,4-20 227
23,4-15 43
23,4-14 38f
23,4ff 238f, 241
23,4 39f, 239
23,5-14 47
23,6 201, 236, 239
23,8f 22
23,8 21
23,10 356
23,12 201, 236, 239
23,13 21
23,15-20 38
23,15 21
23,16-18 44, 46
23,20 40
23,21-23 21, 45
23,21 39f, 44
23,22 146
23,24 45
23,25-25,30 357-362
23,25-30 39
23,25-27 44f
23,26-30 41, 45
23,26f 360f
24,4 361
25,27-30 35

2 Chr
19,5 105
30 89

Esra
4,1-4 184
6,19 146

Ps
29,1 337f
78 344
97,7 333, 335-337

104 146
105 146
106 146
107 146
135 342
136 342

Jes
2,7-9 281
5,24 89
9,5 90
10,20f 90f
11,13 90
30,9 89
44,9-17 245
63,16 342

Jer
1,1 327
2-3 327f
7,21 86
8,8-13 327
8,8 96
8,14 231
9,14 231
11,1-17 326
22,8f 314
22,13-17 281
23,15 231
26 205f
30-31 328
30,1-3 328
30,21 296
31,27f 328
31,31-34 192, 328
34,8 102
34,18-20 182
36,9 327
38,8 146
41,5 328

Ez
20 346
44 322

Hos
4,13 85
5,15-6,1 88f
6,7 89
6,11-7,1 88
8,1 89
8,9-13 87
8,11-13 85
8,12 89
9,3 87
10,1f 85
10,5 83
11,1-8 89
11,5 87
12,6 84
13,1-4 84
13,2 83f
13,6 89
14,2-5 88
14,4 84
14,5 89

Am
2,4 89
4,4f 85
5,26 83

Mi
1,7 237
5,1 90
5,9-14 281

BIBLIOTHECA EPHEMERIDUM THEOLOGICARUM LOVANIENSIUM

LEUVEN UNIVERSITY PRESS / UITGEVERIJ PEETERS LEUVEN

* Out of print

1. *Miscellanea dogmatica in honorem Eximii Domini J. Bittremieux*, 1947. 235 p. FB 450.

*2-3. *Miscellanea moralia in honorem Eximii Domini A. Janssen*, 1948.

*4. G. PHILIPS, *La grâce des justes de l'Ancien Testament*, 1948.

*5. G. PHILIPS, *De ratione instituendi tractatum de gratia nostrae sanctificationis*, 1953.

6-7. *Recueil Lucien Cerfaux*, 1954. 504 et 577 p. FB 800 par tome. Cf. *infra*, n° 18.

8. G. THILS, *Histoire doctrinale du mouvement œcuménique*. Nouvelle édition, 1963. 338 p. FB 135.

*9. J. COPPENS et al. *Études sur l'Immaculée Conception. Sources et sens de la doctrine*, 1955. 110 p.

*10. J.A. O'DONOHOE, *Tridentine Seminary Legislation. Its Sources and its Formation*, 1957.

*11. G. THILS, *Orientations de la théologie*, 1958.

*12-13. J. COPPENS, A. DESCAMPS, É. MASSAUX (éd), *Sacra Pagina, Miscellanea Biblica Congressus Internationalis Catholici de Re Biblica*, 1959.

*14. *Adrien VI, le premier Pape de la contre-réforme. Sa personnalité — sa carrière — son œuvre*, 1959.

*15. F. CLAEYS BOUUAERT, *Les déclarations et serments imposés par la loi civile aux membres du clergé belge sous le Directoire (1795-1801)*, 1960.

*16. G. THILS, *La « Théologie Œcuménique ». Notion-Formes-Démarches*, 1960.

17. G. THILS, *Primauté pontificale et prérogatives épiscopales. « Potestas ordinaria » au Concile du Vatican*, 1961. 104 p. FB 50.

*18. *Recueil Lucien Cerfaux*, t. III, 1961. Cf. *supra*, n°s 6-7.

*19. *Foi et réflexion philosophique. Mélanges F. Grégoire*, 1961.

*20. *Mélanges G. Ryckmans*, 1963.

21. G. THILS, *L'infaillibilité du peuple chrétien « in credendo »*, 1963. 66 p. FB 50.

*22. J. FÉRIN et L. JANSSENS, *Progestogènes et morale conjugale*, 1963.

*23. *Collectanea Moralia in honorem Eximii Domini A. Janssen*, 1964.

24. H. CAZELLES (éd.), *L'Ancien Testament et son milieu d'après les études récentes. De Mari à Qumrân* (Hommage J. Coppens, I), 1969. 158*-370 p. FB 800.

25. I. DE LA POTTERIE (éd.). *De Jésus aux évangiles. Tradition et rédaction dans les évangiles synoptiques* (Hommage J. Coppens, II), 1967. 272 p. FB 600.

26. G. THILS et R.E. BROWN (éd.), *Exégèse et théologie* (Hommage J. Coppens, III), 1968. 328 p. FB 600.
27. J. COPPENS (éd.), *Ecclesia a Spiritu sancto edocta. Hommage à Mgr G. Philips*, 1970. 640 p. FB 580.
28. J. COPPENS (éd.), *Sacerdoce et Célibat. Études historiques et théologiques*, 1971. 740 p. FB 600.
29. M. DIDIER (éd.), *L'évangile selon Matthieu. Rédaction et théologie*, 1971. 432 p. FB 900.
*30. J. KEMPENEERS, *Le Cardinal van Roey en son temps*, 1971.
*31. F. NEIRYNCK, *Duality in Mark. Contributions to the Study of the Markan Redaction*, 1972.
*32. F. NEIRYNCK (éd.), *L'évangile de Luc. Problèmes littéraires et théologiques. Mémorial Lucien Cerfaux*, 1973.
*33. C. BREKELMANS (éd.), *Questions disputées d'Ancien Testament. Méthode et théologie*, 1974.
*34. M. SABBE (éd.), *L'évangile selon Marc. Tradition et rédaction*, 1974.
*35. *Miscellanea Albert Dondeyne. Godsdienstfilosofie. Philosophie de la religion*, 1974.
*36. G. PHILIPS, *L'union personnelle avec le Dieu vivant*, 1974.
37. F. NEIRYNCK, in collaboration with T. HANSEN and F. VAN SEGBROECK, *The Minor Agreements of Matthew and Luke against Mark with a Cumulative List*, 1974. 330 p. FB 800.
*38. J. COPPENS, *Le Messianisme et sa relève prophétique*, 1974.
39. D. SENIOR, *The Passion Narrative according to Matthew. A Redactional Study*, 1975; new impression, 1982. 440 p. FB 1000.
*40. J. DUPONT (éd.), *Jésus aux origines de la christologie*, 1975.
*41. J. COPPENS (éd.), *La notion biblique de Dieu*, 1976.
42. J. LINDEMANS – H. DEMEESTER (éd.), *Liber Amicorum Monseigneur W. Onclin*, 1976. 396 p. FB 900.
43. R.E. HOECKMAN (éd.), *Pluralisme et œcuménisme en recherches théologiques. Mélanges offerts au R.P. Dockx, O.P.*, 1976. 316 p. FB 900.
44. M. DE JONGE (éd.), *L'Évangile de Jean*, 1977. 416 p. FB 950.
45. E.J.M. VAN EIJL (éd.), *Facultas S. Theologiae Lovaniensis 1432-1797. Bijdragen tot haar geschiedenis. Contributions to its History. Contributions à son histoire*, 1977. 570 p. FB 1500.
46. M. DELCOR (éd.), *Qumrân. Sa piété, sa théologie et son milieu*, 1978. 432 p. FB 1550.
47. M. CAUDRON (éd.), *Faith and Society. Foi et Société. Geloof en maatschappij. Acta Congressus Internationalis Theologici Lovaniensis 1976*, 1978. 304 p. FB 1150.
48. J. KREMER (éd.), *Les Actes des Apôtres. Traditions, rédaction, théologie*, 1979. 590 p. FB 1600.
49. F. NEIRYNCK, avec la collaboration de J. DELOBEL, T. SNOY, G. VAN BELLE, F. VAN SEGBROECK, *Jean et les Synoptiques. Examen critique de l'exégèse de M.-É. Boismard*, 1979. XII-428 p. FB 950.
50. J. COPPENS, *La relève apocalyptique du messianisme royal.* I. *La royauté – Le règne – Le royaume de Dieu. Cadre de la relève apocalyptique*, 1979. 325 p. FB 848.

51. M. GILBERT (éd.), *La Sagesse de l'Ancien Testament*, 1979. 420 p. FB 1700.
52. B. DEHANDSCHUTTER, *Martyrium Polycarpi. Een literair-kritische studie*, 1979. 296 p. FB 950.
53. J. LAMBRECHT (éd.), *L'Apocalypse johannique et l'Apocalyptique dans le Nouveau Testament*, 1980. 458 p. FB 1400.
54. P.-M. BOGAERT (éd.), *Le Livre de Jérémie. Le prophète et son milieu. Les oracles et leur transmission*, 1981. 408 p. FB 1500.
55. J. COPPENS, *La relève apocalyptique du messianisme royal.* III. *Le Fils de l'homme néotestamentaire*, 1981. XIV-192 p. FB 800.
56. J. VAN BAVEL & M. SCHRAMA (éd.), *Jansénius et le Jansénisme dans les Pays-Bas. Mélanges Lucien Ceyssens*, 1982. 247 p. FB 1000.
57. J.H. WALGRAVE, *Selected Writings – Thematische geschriften. Thomas Aquinas, J.H. Newman, Theologia Fundamentalis*. Edited by G. DE SCHRIJVER & J.J. KELLY, 1982. XLIII-425 p. FB 1000.
58. F. NEIRYNCK & F. VAN SEGBROECK, avec la collaboration de E. MANNING, *Ephemerides Theologicae Lovanienses 1924-1981. Tables générales. (Bibliotheca Ephemeridum Theologicarum Lovaniensium 1947-1981)*, 1982. 400 p. FB 1600.
59. J. DELOBEL (éd.), *Logia. Les paroles de Jésus – The Sayings of Jesus. Mémorial Joseph Coppens*, 1982. 647 p. FB 2000.
60. F. NEIRYNCK, *Evangelica. Gospel Studies – Études d'évangile. Collected Essays*. Edited by F. VAN SEGBROECK, 1982. XIX-1036 p. FB 2000.
61. J. COPPENS, *La relève apocalyptique du messianisme royal.* II. *Le Fils d'homme vétéro- et intertestamentaire*. Édition posthume par J. LUST, 1983. XVII-272 p. FB 1000.
62. J.J. KELLY, *Baron Friedrich von Hügel's Philosophy of Religion*, 1983. 232 p. FB 1500.
63. G. DE SCHRIJVER, *Le merveilleux accord de l'homme et de Dieu. Étude de l'analogie de l'être chez Hans Urs von Balthasar*, 1983. 344 p. FB 1500.
64. J. GROOTAERS & J.A. SELLING, *The 1980 Synod of Bishops: « On the Role of the Family ». An Exposition of the Event and an Analysis of Its Texts.* Preface by Prof. emeritus L. JANSSENS, 1983. 375 p. FB 1500.
65. F. NEIRYNCK & F. VAN SEGBROECK, *New Testament Vocabulary. A Companion Volume to the Concordance*, 1984. XVI-494 p. FB 2000.
66. R.F. COLLINS, *Studies on the First Letter to the Thessalonians*, 1984. XI-415 p. FB 1500.
67. R. BOUDENS (ed.), *Alfred Plummer, Conversations with Dr. Döllinger 1870-1890.* With the collaboration of L. KENIS, 1985. LIV-372 p. FB 1800.
68. N. LOHFINK (ed.), *Das Deuteronomium. Entstehung, Gestalt und Botschaft / Origin, Form and Message*, 1985. XI-382 p. FB 2000.
69. P.F. FRANSEN, *Hermeneutics of the Councils and Other Studies.* Collected by H.E. MERTENS and F. DE GRAEVE, 1985. 543 p. FB 1800.

In preparation:

70. J. DUPONT, *Études sur les Évangiles synoptiques.*

ORIENTALISTE, P.B. 41, B-3000 Leuven